FREEDOM

ANGELA MERKEL, Chancellor of the Federal Republic of Germany from 2005 to 2021, was the first woman to hold the country's most powerful office. Born in Hamburg in 1954 and raised in the GDR, where she studied physics and earned a doctorate in natural sciences, she was elected to the German Bundestag in 1990. From 1991 to 1994 she served as Federal Minister for Women and Youth; from 1994 to 1998 as Federal Minister for the Environment, Nature Conservation and Nuclear Safety; and from 2000 to 2018 as the leader of the Christian Democratic Union of Germany. In 2021, she ended her active political career.

ABOUT THE TRANSLATORS

ALICE TETLEY-PAUL studied German with Dutch at the University of Sheffield before gaining an MA in Literary Translation from the University of East Anglia. She also leads translation workshops for schools, universities, and book festivals.

JAMIE LEE SEARLE translates German- and Portuguese-language writing for publishing houses in the UK and the US, and works with cultural institutions including the Goethe-Institut and Austrian Cultural Forum. She is a co-founder of the Emerging Translators Network and a Royal Literary Fund Fellow.

JO HEINRICH lives near Bristol with her family and translates from German and French. Her translation of *Marzahn, Mon Amour* by Katja Oskamp was awarded the 2023 Dublin Literary Award.

LUCY JONES is a British translator based in Berlin and the co-founder of the Transfiction collective. She has translated works by Anke Stelling, Theresia Enzensberger, and Brigitte Reimann, among others. In 2023, she was the runner-up in the Translators Association's Schlegel-Tieck Prize.

RUTH MARTIN studied English literature before gaining a PhD in German. She has been translating fiction and non-fiction books since 2010, by authors ranging from Joseph Roth and Hannah Arendt to Nino Haratischwili and Shida Bazyar.

SHARON HOWE is a freelance translator based in Devon, UK. She studied at Oxford and Bradford Universities and has been translating for over thirty years. She is a former winner of the Goethe-Institut Award for New Translation (2021).

SHAUN WHITESIDE is a prize-winning translator of fiction and non-fiction from German, French, Italian, and Dutch. His German translations include works by Freud, Nietzsche, Schnitzler, and Musil, as well as novels by authors including Gert Ledig, Ralf Rothmann, and Marlen Haushofer. His translation of Harald Jähner's historical study *Aftermath* was shortlisted for the 2021 Baillie Gifford Prize and the 2022 British Academy Book Prize for Global Cultural Understanding. He is a former chair of the European Council of Literary Translators' Associations, and lives in London. He was the lead translator for this work.

SIMON PARE is a translator from French and German, who lives near Zurich. His translation of *The Flying Mountain* by Christoph Ransmayr made the Man Booker International 2018 longlist, and he was runner-up for the 2021 Schlegel-Tieck Prize. In 2016, he was part of the team that translated *The Panama Papers* into English.

FREEDOM

Memoirs 1954–2021

ANGELA MERKEL

with

BEATE BAUMANN

ST. MARTIN'S PRESS
NEW YORK

Published in the United States by St. Martin's Press, an imprint of
St. Martin's Publishing Group

FREEDOM: MEMOIRS 1954–2021. Copyright © 2024 by Angela Merkel and Beate Baumann,
Verlag Kiepenheuer & Witsch, Köln. Translation copyright © 2024 by Alice Tetley-Paul,
Jamie Lee Searle, Jo Heinrich, Lucy Jones, Ruth Martin, Sharon Howe,
Shaun Whiteside, and Simon Pare. All rights reserved. Printed in the
United States of America. For information, address St. Martin's Publishing Group,
120 Broadway, New York, NY 10271.

Typeset by Palimpsest Book Production Ltd, Falkirk, Stirlingshire

www.stmartins.com

The Library of Congress Cataloging-in-Publication Data is available upon request.

ISBN 978-1-250-31990-6 (hardcover)

ISBN 978-1-250-31991-3 (ebook)

Our books may be purchased in bulk for promotional, educational, or
business use. Please contact your local bookseller or the Macmillan
Corporate and Premium Sales Department at 1-800-221-7945, extension 5442,
or by email at MacmillanSpecialMarkets@macmillan.com.

First published in Germany by Verlag Kiepenheuer & Witsch
First published in the UK by Macmillan, an imprint of Pan Macmillan
First U.S. Edition: 2024

10 9 8 7 6 5 4 3 2 1

CONTENTS

PART FIVE
SERVING GERMANY (II)
September 5, 2015 to December 8, 2021

PROLOGUE

THIS BOOK TELLS a story that will not happen again, because the state I lived in for thirty-five years ceased to exist in 1990. If it had been offered to a publishing house as a work of fiction, it would have been turned down, someone said to me early in 2022, a few weeks after I stepped down from the office of federal chancellor. He was familiar with such issues, and was glad that I had decided to write this book, precisely because of its story. A story that is as unlikely as it is real. It became clear to me: telling this story, drawing out its lines, finding the thread running through it, identifying leitmotifs, could also be important for the future.

For a long time I couldn't imagine writing such a book. That first changed in 2015, at least a little. Back then, in the night between September 4 and 5, I had decided not to turn away the refugees coming from Hungary at the German–Austrian border. I experienced that decision, and above all its consequences, as a caesura in my chancellorship. There was a before and an after. That was when I undertook to describe, one day when I was no longer chancellor, the sequence of events, the reasons for my decision, my understanding of Europe and globalization bound up with it, in a form that only a book would make possible. I didn't want to leave the further description and interpretation just to other people.

But I was still in office. The 2017 Bundestag election followed, along with my fourth period of office. In its last two years the containment of the COVID-19 pandemic was the predominant theme. The pandemic, as I said publicly on several occasions, made huge demands on democracy, on a national, European, and global level. This also prompted me to broaden my outlook and not only write about refugee policy. If I was going to do it at all, I had to do it properly, I said to myself, and if I was, then I would do it with Beate Baumann. She has been advising me since 1992, and is an eyewitness.

I stepped down from office on December 8, 2021. After sixteen years I left it, as I said at the Bundeswehr's Military Tattoo in my honor a few days before, with joy in my heart. By the end I had in fact longed for that moment. Enough was enough. Now it was time to take a break and rest for a few months, leave the frantic world of politics behind me, to begin a new life in the spring, slowly and tentatively, still a public life, but not an active political one, find the right rhythm for public appearances—and write this book. That was the plan.

Then came February 24, 2022, Russia's attack on Ukraine.

It was immediately clear that writing this book as if nothing had happened was completely out of the question. The war in Yugoslavia at the beginning of the 1990s had already shaken Europe to its core. But the Russian attack on Ukraine was a greater threat. It was a breach of international law that shattered the European peace which had prevailed since the Second World War and was based on the preservation of the territorial integrity and sovereignty of its states. Profound disillusionment followed. I will write about that too. But this is not a book about Russia and Ukraine. That would be a different book.

Instead I would like to write the story of my two lives, the first up to 1990 in a dictatorship and the second since 1990 in a democracy. At the moment when the first readers hold this book in their hands, the two halves are of more or less equal length. But in fact, of course, these are not two lives. In fact they are *one* life, and the second part cannot be understood without the first.

How did it happen that, after spending the first thirty-five years of her life in the GDR, a woman was able to take over the most powerful office that exists in the Federal Republic of Germany and hold it for sixteen years? And that she left it again without having to step down during a period of office or being voted out? What was it like to grow up in East Germany as the child of a pastor, and study and work under the conditions of a dictatorship? What was it like to experience the collapse of a state? And to be suddenly free? That's the story I want to tell.

Of course, my account is deeply subjective. At the same time, I have aimed for honest self-reflection. Today, I will identify my misjudgments and defend the things I think I got right. But this is not a complete account of everything that happened. Not everyone who might have expected, or who might have been expected, to appear in these pages will do so. For that I request understanding. My goal is to establish some points of focus with which I attempt to tame the sheer mass of material, and allow people to understand how politics works, what principles and mechanisms there are—and what guided me.

Politics isn't witchcraft. Politics is made by people, people with their influences, their experiences, vanities, weaknesses, strengths, desires, dreams, convictions, values, and interests. People who need to fight for majorities in a democracy if they want to make things happen.

We can do this—*Wir schaffen das*. Throughout the whole of my political career, no phrase has been thrown back at me with quite such virulence as this one. No phrase has been so polarizing. For me, however, it was quite an ordinary phrase. It expressed an attitude. Call it trust in God, caution, or simply a determination to solve problems, to deal with setbacks, get over the lows and come up with new ideas. "We can do this, and if something stands in our way it has to be overcome, it has to be worked on." That was how I put it in my summer press conference on August 31, 2015. That was how I did politics. It's how I live. It's also how this book came about. With this attitude, which is also something learned, everything is possible, because it isn't only politics that contributes to it—every individual person has a part to play.

Angela Merkel

With Beate Baumann
Berlin, August 2024

PART ONE

"I Wasn't Born Chancellor"

July 17, 1954 to November 9, 1989

HAPPY CHILDHOOD

Quitzow

ON NOVEMBER 10, 1989, a Friday, I left my apartment in the block on 104 Schönhauser Allee in Prenzlauer Berg, Berlin at around 6:30 a.m., as I always did, to travel to work from Schönhauser Allee S-Bahn station to Berlin-Adlershof. The train was full, and it was still dark outside, the same as always at that time of day. But in fact nothing was the same as always. The previous evening, Günter Schabowski, Secretary of the Central Committee for Information and Media Policy within the leadership of the SED (Sozialistische Einheitspartei Deutschlands, Socialist Unity Party of Germany), had declared on GDR television: "Applications for foreign travel by private individuals may now be made without the previously existing requirements (demonstrating a need to travel or proving family relationships)." And in response to a question, he had confirmed that this applied "immediately, without delay." In fact, that Thursday, November 9, 1989, he had announced the fall of the Berlin Wall. A short time later, there was no halting the exodus.

In the course of that evening I had joined the queue of people moving toward the Bornholm Bridge border crossing. West Berliners were calling down from apartment windows in all directions saying we could come up and join them, share a beer, raise a glass to this incredible event. Others were even so overjoyed that they actually came down into the street. Complete strangers hugged, and I was right in the thick of it. I followed a little group of people I didn't know into the first side street on the right after the bridge. A West Berliner invited us into his apartment, and I simply went along. He offered us a beer and we were allowed to make a phone call. My attempt to get through to my aunt in Hamburg was unsuccessful. We said goodbye after half an hour. Most people carried on to Kurfürstendamm, West Berlin's magnificent boulevard. I turned around and went home, however, at about 11:00 p.m., because I was thinking that I had to get up very early to go to Adlershof. I wanted to work on a talk that I was supposed to be giving a few days later in Toruń in Poland, and which was still far from completion. During the night I barely closed my eyes, too excited about everything that I had experienced a few hours before.

In the morning a small group of men in uniform were also sitting in my train to Adlershof, border guards from the Feliks Dzherzhinksky Regiment. They were clearly heading back to barracks—near my institute—from their night shift on the border. The soldiers were talking, so loudly that I couldn't help listening to their words. "Man, what a night," one of them smirked. "How is all of this going to affect our officers?"

"They were absolutely clueless, they had no idea what was coming," a second one said.

"They've lost the justification for their existence. Their lives, their careers—all down the toilet!" a third soldier added.

We got out at Adlershof. Each of us went our own way: the soldiers to their barracks, I to my desk in the Central Institute for Physical Chemistry at the GDR's Academy of Sciences. But work was out of the question. Everything was put off, including of course the lecture that was my reason for coming back early from the West the previous evening. I wasn't the only one—everybody was in the same boat. We talked and talked. That morning my sister called me at the Institute. She was working as an occupational therapist at the Construction Workers' Outpatient Clinic. We arranged to pay a visit late that afternoon to a friend of hers in West Berlin, someone she had met a few years previously through some mutual acquaintances.

All that day, the words of the border guards on the train that morning were ringing in my ears. I thought: At last! At last these soldiers and their officers no longer have any power over you. At last they have no power over your family. For twenty-nine years the Berlin Wall hadn't only divided my family and caused such pain to my parents, it had done the same to the family of my husband, Joachim Sauer. The same applied to countless people in both East and West. At last these soldiers couldn't stop us moving freely anymore. At the same time, however, I realized that one phrase from the soldier on the train resonated with me: justification for their existence. What would my life be like after last night? And the lives of my family, my friends, my colleagues? What value would our experiences, our education, our abilities, achievements, private decisions have in the future? I was thirty-five years old. Only thirty-five? Or already thirty-five? What would we be left with, and what not?

I was born in Hamburg on July 17, 1954, the first child of Herlind and Horst Kasner. My father was born in Berlin in 1926, the son of Ludwig Kaźmierczak, born in Poznań (German: Posen) in Poland, and his wife Margarete. Ludwig was a police officer, Margarete, from Berlin, a seamstress and housewife. In 1930 the family had had their Polish surname changed to the German name Kasner, and from then on my father was called Horst Kasner. My grandfather Ludwig Kasner died in 1959, too soon for me to have any personal recollection of him.

My mother, Herlind, was born in Danzig-Langfuhr in 1928, the first of two daughters of schoolteachers, Willi and Gertrud Jentzsch. Her mother, from the East Prussian town of Elbing, had given up her job after the birth of her first child.

Her father, my grandfather Willi, a science teacher and grammar-school principal in Danzig, had brought the family to a certain affluence. They led what we would call today a comfortably middle-class lifestyle. In 1936 the family would move from Danzig to Hamburg, where my grandfather had been offered a job as principal of a high school. All the preparations had been made, a new apartment rented, and a removal firm booked. Then my grandfather fell ill with septic inflammation of the appendix and gall bladder. He died because penicillin, which would have saved him, did not yet exist.

This left my grandmother and her two daughters alone. Even so, they moved to Hamburg, to the big apartment on Isestrasse, for which they had already paid the rent. They now had money worries for the first time. My grandmother did receive a widow's pension, but the whole of her previous life had collapsed. For a long time she wore only mourning, and was constantly concerned about her daughters. If the children came home a little later than agreed, she dissolved into anxiety and kept watch for them from the balcony.

In the summer of 1943, Hamburg was severely hit by British and American bombing raids, including the house where my family lived. My grandmother left the city with her two daughters. First they moved to the village of Neukirchen in the northern Altmark region, where a sister of my grandmother lived with her family, and then, in the autumn of 1943, to Elbing, her birthplace in East Prussia. But only a few months later, in the summer of 1944, she moved back to Neukirchen. In 1944 my mother was sent from there to Pisek in present-day Czechia, where Berlin's Westendschule had been relocated. After the end of the war she made her way back to her mother and sister under very challenging conditions. Between the end of March 1945 and her arrival in the village in October of the same year, the family received no sign of life from my mother.

She often said that the thing she was most afraid of—she was only seventeen at the time—was being raped by the Soviet soldiers that she encountered along the way.

The experiences of the war had an even more powerful effect on my father's life. Along with his father, Ludwig, my grandfather, he often listened to BBC radio secretly under the bedcovers to follow what was happening at the front. Even during the war, my grandfather was convinced that Germany would lose it—and needed to lose it. In May 1943, my father was recruited as a "Flakhelfer" (a member of the anti-aircraft auxiliary staff). He became a soldier in August 1944 and was buried under rubble in the spring of 1945 after a bombing raid. After the war he spent some time in a British POW camp in Denmark. By the time he got back to Germany in August 1945, the country had already been divided into occupation zones. He went to see a friend in Heidelberg, where he caught up on his Abitur, the school-leaving examination. This allowed him to begin studying theology in 1947, greatly influenced, as he later explained, by his wartime experiences.

The groundwork for this had not been laid in the parental home. His father had been baptized a Catholic, and his mother was a member of the Protestant Church, but my grandparents were not practicing Christians. My father himself had been baptized as a Catholic, but was confirmed into the Protestant Church in 1940. After the end of the war and the horrors of National Socialism he was convinced that a peace ethic was needed if there was to be a new beginning. For him this arose from the Christian faith. So he decided to study theology in the then Western occupation zones. From the beginning he connected his studies with the plan to return eventually to the then Soviet occupation zone. He was convinced that people like him were needed there. I think it might be called a vocation.

In 1949 my father was continuing his studies in Bethel, and he finished them in 1954 with his vicariate in Hamburg. He met my mother in 1950, at an event held by the Protestant student group, in which they were both student leaders. My mother was studying English and Latin in Hamburg, and planned to work as a secondary-school teacher later on. Her friends in the student group jokingly called her "Mercedes" because, like her mother, she dreamed even then of having her own car, and one that was as big and fast as possible.

My parents married on August 6, 1952. By the time of their wedding, it was clear to my mother that she would follow her husband as soon as he implemented his plan to return to the Protestant Church in Berlin-Brandenburg, in the German Democratic Republic, founded three years previously. This decision was anything but easy for her. But she made it out of love, with what would prove to be massive consequences for her.

By 1954, the time had come. For many, if not most of us, that year is associated with the miracle of Bern, the first World Cup victory by the national team of West Germany, the Federal Republic. But in my family it was the year when my parents moved from the Federal Republic to the German Democratic Republic, from Hamburg to Quitzow, a little town in the rural district of Prignitz in Brandenburg, just 150 kilometers northeast of Berlin. There my father took up his first church post as a local pastor. He traveled ahead, and my mother followed a short time later with me in a carry cot. I was six weeks old. Just a year had passed since a popular uprising in the GDR, with strikes and political demonstrations, was brutally suppressed by Soviet tanks. And another blow straight to the heart of millions of Germans, our family included, would follow only a few years later with the construction of the Berlin Wall. For now, however, my parents settled with me in their new surroundings.

We had a housekeeper. Her name was Frau Spiess, and she had come to Quitzow from East Prussia with my father's predecessor. After his retirement she continued working for my parents. She taught them everything you needed to know for a life in the country. My father was made to milk goats, and my mother learned to cook nettles and many other things that she had not known as a city child. The story was often told in our family that she had brought a white carpet to her marriage, and initially, after coming to Quitzow, wanted to hold on to her Hamburg habit of not asking visitors, even the farmers from the village, to take their shoes off if they wanted to talk to my father. And they often came to him with their worries, because the period of forced collectivization had just begun, the reason why many of them later left for the West. If the farmers wanted to take off their shoes, because they knew what trails they would leave on the white carpet, my mother told them not to worry, so they tramped over the white carpet in their filthy work boots. Eventually, my mother abandoned her Hamburg habit and let the visitors take their shoes off. She had arrived in Quitzow.

I have no direct personal memory of the place, and everything I know comes from family stories. Templin is a very different matter. In 1957 my parents moved with me and my brother, Marcus, who was born in the same year, to this small town in the Uckermark district of Brandenburg, about eighty kilometers north of Berlin. My father had been called there by the Protestant Church in Berlin-Brandenburg to run the Ecclesiastical Seminary in Templin, later to become the Pastoral College. This meant that he was no longer a classic local pastor. The move also opened up new possibilities for my mother.

The Waldhof estate

My sister, Irene, was born in 1964. When she was about six years old, we had a favorite place of our own. It was on the tin roof of the dormer window on the attic floor of my parents' house. Irene was nimbler than I was and had discovered that we could easily climb out of the window and make ourselves comfortable on the tin roof. From there we could look down on the fir trees and watch them stirring gently in the wind. Between the trees we saw a path that fell gently toward a meadow with the canal connecting the Templiner See and the Röddelinsee passing through it. Up on the roof in summertime we made plans for the things we wanted to do. Go to the spring in the meadow? Cycle to the Röddelinsee to go swimming? Pick blueberries in the forest around Templin? The possibilities seemed endless. We got on wonderfully well, in spite of our ten-year age difference.

The attic-level dormer window belonged to my room. The actual family apartment was a floor below. Our house was on the Waldhof estate, on the edge of town. The major part of the estate was an institute of the Stephanus Foundation for children and adults with learning difficulties. The concept was in line with that of the Protestant Bethel Foundation psychiatric hospital. Apart from taking care of the residents, value was placed on the therapeutic effect of active and meaningful work. The institution was intended to be as self-sufficient as possible, so apart from a kitchen and a farm there was also a nursery, a laundry, a smithy, a carpentry workshop, a cobbler's, and a tailor's. As children we were allowed to go everywhere and chat with the master craftsmen of the various trades and the residents with learning disabilities.

The Pastoral College run by my father included both a building with rooms for course participants and a few apartments, including our family's official quarters, with seven rooms in all. Five of them were on the first floor, while my room and my father's study were on the attic level. There was also a "school," in which the events and training courses led by my father were held.

My mother was also faced with new tasks at the Waldhof, such as training Church administrators, teaching them German and math, or giving lessons in Greek and Latin to the future students of the "Sprachenkonvikt," a theological educational institution operated by the Protestant Church, to prepare them for their studies. Over the years, the college's work concentrated increasingly on the further training of pastors, however, which meant that my mother's field of activity shrank again. Then for a time she worked as my father's secretary. As a pastor's wife she wasn't allowed to teach in a public school; in every area of education in East Germany, Church influences were to be excluded. The GDR saw itself as an atheist state.

There was basically a classic distribution of roles between my mother and my father in our everyday family life, with my mother at least imagining what it would be like if she taught at a school. At the time I thought this would just have meant a double burden, because she would have had to take care of both teaching and doing the housework. As a child I couldn't see any advantage in that. Since my mother was not officially "actively working," in the GDR phrase, meaning that she was not gain-fully employed, my siblings and I were not allowed to attend kindergarten or, later on, to have school meals. Again, I didn't like that at all. Right at the end, in the last year of school, I did manage to gain access to school meals. The reason I wanted to do so lay not so much in the quality of the food, but in the charm of something that had for a long time been forbidden to me. Not having them, however, meant that for many years my mother had to cook lunch for the whole family every day, and the other meals on top of that, of course, and—let's not forget—do the shopping for them all.

It was about three kilometers from the Waldhof estate to the shops in town. When we children were still too small to help, my mother had to bring all the groceries back home on her bicycle by herself. It was a great physical effort for her. Later, when she had her driving license, her mother, my Hamburg grandmother, gave her a Trabant. She did so via GENEX, a company that allowed West Germans to give East German citizens large gifts that were paid for in Western deutsche marks. Being able to drive her own car, even if it was a size or two smaller than the model that had won her the nickname "Mercedes" when she was a student, was an act of self-liberation for my mother. Now she was mobile. She also used it to give English lessons in the Sprachenkonvikt, which led to friction with my father, who didn't like preparing his own meals. But my mother wouldn't be stopped from going her own way.

Pastors in the GDR didn't earn much, but only had to pay a small rent for their official residence; this was true of us as well. They also received material support from the West, known as "Deutsche Bruderhilfe" (literally: German fraternal aid). For our family that meant around seventy deutsche marks a month. My Hamburg grandmother and—after her death in 1978—my aunt, my mother's sister, used Bruderhilfe and regularly sent us parcels. It was a massive organizational task for our Hamburg relatives, but it was incredibly helpful to us.

And the packages were special in another respect as well; we knew this immediately as we opened them and thought: "This smells of the West." By that we meant the delicate scent of good soap or aromatic coffee. The East, by contrast, smelled severely of scouring products, floor polish, and turpentine. I still have that smell in my nostrils.

As far as I was concerned, the official GDR was the embodiment of tastelessness. Synthetic rather than natural materials, never any joyful colors. My parents tried to find the nooks and crannies where they could escape that tastelessness, for example by buying the beautiful furniture of the Hellerau workshops, for which they sometimes had to wait for ages. Perhaps my present-day preference for colorful blazers could be traced back to the primal experience of missing bright colors in East German everyday life.

My father's Pastoral College was able to take advantage of the infrastructure of the whole of the Waldhof, such as the kitchen and the workshops of the Stephanus Foundation. Residents with learning disabilities also did certain jobs in the college. One of them in particular has stayed in my memory. He helped my mother tirelessly and with the patience of an angel, by fetching wood and coal. It was very hard work, because all the rooms were heated by tiled stoves. He concentrated entirely on the work. Otherwise, he talked constantly, stories about his imaginary life as a railway worker. I became friends with him.

While we children didn't yet have to go to school, we spent most of our days outside, only interrupted by meals. At midday and six in the evening a resident of the Stephanus Foundation would ring the bells in the belfry on the Waldhof estate. Even for the children of the parsonage, that meant going home, because it was mealtime. Otherwise, we could spend all day wandering the estate. It was wonderful.

My special friend was the gardener, Herr Lachmann. He taught me all about pricking out seedlings and greenhouse gardening. I could ask him everything and at the same time help him a little with his gardening work. Otherwise, I was quite a rustic child. In Quitzow I was even said to have drunk water from the chickens' water bowl when I was thirsty. And on the Waldhof estate I thought nothing of eating unwashed carrots in the nursery.

My favorite spot in the autumn was a seat on the potato steamer. This was an enormous vehicle that looked like a truck with a big cooking pot. The pot was filled with potatoes, where they were steamed until they were soft. In that way they could be made edible soon after they had been harvested. When I was a child I was allowed to sit next to the driver when this was being done. There was a wonderful smell of potato fields and potato plants. And it was a real delight to me to taste the soft potatoes.

Other children lived on the Waldhof estate, some older then me, some younger. We got up to all sorts of things—we cycled to the lake and went swimming, we messed about in the straw or played the game of Völkerball, popular in the GDR. There was always someone willing to join in. We never got bored.

On the first Sunday of Advent, the children of the Waldhof sang Advent carols for the residents with learning disabilities. We serenaded them at seven o'clock in the morning, waking them up as they slept in big dormitories. That was what it was like in those days—single or double bedrooms were out of the question. We sang "Es kommt ein Schiff, geladen" (A Ship Is Coming, Laden), "Macht hoch die Tür" (Raise High the Door), and lots of other songs. The residents were delighted, and we children sang our hearts out. Over Christmas I also sang in the choir of the Church of Maria Magdalena in Templin. Overall, Christmas was a great highlight of the year for us children on the Waldhof. However, the course of our Christmas Eve was very different from that of many other families. In the parsonage the private and the professional merged seamlessly, as we noticed particularly at Christmas.

On Christmas Eve my father had to perform two or three services in the villages around Templin, and often he didn't come home until six in the evening, still shivering from the cold village churches. When we were little we were obliged to take a midday nap because it would be a late night. When I grew older I accompanied my father to his services.

Of course, my Berlin grandmother came to visit, but on that special evening we were also supposed to think of people who were on their own. From an early age we children were told that the essential meaning of Christmas lay in thinking about people who didn't have it as good as we did, people who were lonely and abandoned. So every year we invited a fellow Waldhof resident who lived on their own and rarely had company to our house on Christmas Eve. Over dinner, which from my childish perspective already began late enough because of my father's church services, our guest was at last able to chat freely and at length; my parents even encouraged them to do so. But we children were fidgeting in our chairs, since all our attention was focused on our keenly awaited presents, but we were forbidden to say a word. So it was often eight o'clock or even later before we were finally allowed to enter the room with the Christmas tree.

There we had a fixed ritual. Once the wax candles were lit, my brother and sister and I told the Christmas story, dividing up the roles between us. Between the extracts from the Gospel of Luke we played short pieces on the recorder and sang Christmas carols. This little performance was of course designed to please our guests, but it was also intended to remind us that Christmas was not primarily about presents.

I have beautiful memories of Christmas morning, when the presents lay unwrapped in front of us, and we sat together in the living room. My father usually didn't have to lead a church service, because as principal of the Pastoral College he was only employed in the parishes on a temporary basis. While my mother prepared the roast goose in the kitchen, we had the chance to talk to our father about the presents. As we did so, we snacked from the plates of Christmas treats that my mother had made for us, and no one told us to hold back on our consumption of sweets. If the presents from the West included one of the Ravensburger jigsaw puzzles that my brother loved so much, we started assembling it together.

We were an open house, not only at Christmas and other holidays. My parents often had visitors all year round. Often friends came after dinner, and the adults drank tea together, or a glass of wine. It wasn't rare for people to ask my parents for advice about how to respond to the state in certain situations; these also included members of the SED, the Sozialistische Einheitspartei Deutschlands (Socialist Unity Party of Germany). At weekends pastors also liked to visit one another. I loved going to other parsonages within the church circle. After coffee we children were often sent away. If we were told we were allowed to go and play, it actually meant that we were *supposed* to go and play. I often tried to stay with the adults, and developed strategies for shrinking into a corner or hiding undiscovered behind a curtain. I desperately wanted to listen to what the grown-ups were talking about. The conversations were mostly extremely political. I was keenly interested, much more so than when they talked about theological issues or Christ's teaching and church services. Sometimes it was about other pastors who had found themselves in conflict with the state, or who were having difficulties with State Security (Staatssicherheit, the "Stasi"). It was always clear that such discussions and encounters could never be mentioned to anyone else. Even as children, we knew not to say anything.

In a state of pure shock

I associate my first memories with my Hamburg grandmother, although I have no idea how far they are actually my own, or whether they became mine through family stories. The first, at any rate, goes back to 1957, when I was three years old. I lived with my grandmother for three months; my mother was expecting her second child, my brother, Marcus. When I came back from Hamburg to Templin after he was born, I couldn't climb the stairs to our apartment on my own, but I could use the formal "Sie" for "you." My mother was startled when I addressed her in this way, and clearly a certain estrangement had crept in while we had been apart.

The second memory takes me to 1959, and once again to Hamburg, where we were celebrating the wedding of my mother's sister, my aunt Gunhild. On the journey from Templin to Hamburg in our grey Wartburg Kombi station wagon my brother and I were actually supposed to be asleep, because we were traveling in the evening. In our luggage was a big floor vase that my parents had bought as a wedding present for my aunt. At the border, when the police asked them what they had with them, I said from the back seat: "You've forgotten something! We packed the vase as well!" Luckily, my cheekiness didn't cause my parents any major problems at the border. When we drove on, they told me off for not having been asleep. I should at least have pretended, they said. I've never forgotten that event. At the time I was so open that I wanted to tell everybody everything. That changed during the course of my life.

It was wonderful at my aunt's house, it really was. But a bad thing happened on the wedding day. Some relatives had come to the party—this was in November—with older children, boys of about nine or ten who suggested that we go for a walk together. I was proud that they wanted to take me along, since I was only five. But soon they'd had enough of me and sent me back, on my own. But I couldn't find the way. I can't remember how I got there, but eventually I ended up at a police station. The policemen questioned me until they worked out where my parents were staying, so that they could tell them where I was and they could come and pick me up. So my first memories of Hamburg are a bit conflicted.

On July 16, 1961, my Hamburg grandmother turned seventy. For her birthday she had asked for a trip to Bavaria with my family. No one could have guessed that this would be our last trip to West Germany together. My grandmother had never had a license, so she was lucky that her son-in-law Horst, my father, liked to drive. We hired a VW Beetle, and spent three weeks of

the summer driving around Bavaria and Austria. My grandmother wanted it to be an extended trip.

From Templin we first set off for Hamburg, collected my
grandmother from there, and then headed south. We stayed in
a little hotel on the Sagberg mountain, near Frasdorf in the
foothills of the Alps in the Chiemgau. I remember the journey
there involving lots of bends. We saw the mountains, went on
outings to the islands of Herrenchiemsee and Frauenchiemsee,
to Munich, Innsbruck, and Salzburg. In Wasserburg am Inn, I
was impressed by the rushing waters of the swollen river.

After three weeks we drove back home, and by August 7 or
8, 1961 my parents, my brother, and I were back home in
Templin. Later my father would often say that he had seen
bundles of wire lying about in the forests surrounding Berlin,
clearly a sign of drastic measures to come.

On the Thursday or Friday before work started on the Wall, my
father took me to Berlin on some sort of errand. He left me with
his mother, my Berlin grandmother. She lived on the Retz-
bacher Weg in the Eastern Pankow district, in an apartment in
a 1930s-built house. That day she went with me from there
toward Wollankstrasse in the French sector of Berlin to buy
cigarettes—she was a heavy smoker, like my father. I clearly
remember her holding me tightly by the hand and dragging me
along behind her, ignoring the fact that I was only seven and
couldn't keep up. In the shop she spoke in quick, staccato tones.
She wanted to get out again as quickly as possible, because
buying cigarettes in West Berlin and taking them to the East
was forbidden. At the time I had no idea that it would be a very
long time before I would be able to come back to West Berlin.
In the evening my father and I drove back to Templin.

On August 13, a Sunday, work began on the construction of
the wall through the middle of Berlin. My father held a church

service as normal—I was there, and will never forget it. Everyone was in a state of pure shock, and people were crying. My mother was in despair. She didn't know when she would see her mother and sister in Hamburg again, and my father was downcast because part of his hometown was now inaccessible to him. Something had happened that was beyond his imagination. The city of his birth was divided by a wall. And not only Berlin, but the whole country.

Even though the two German states had existed since 1949, it was only the building of the Wall in 1961 that fundamentally changed my family's situation, as it did that of millions of other people. It condemned those of us in the GDR to impotence. I remember, for example, the days of the devastating flooding in Hamburg a few months later, in February 1962, when my mother was terribly worried about her mother and sister—and couldn't do anything about it. Our families had simply been separated from one another. In order to maintain some kind of contact, my grandmother and my mother wrote weekly letters to each other. After my grandmother's death in 1978, my aunt continued the tradition.

Goetheschule

As I was born after June 30, according to the rules at the time I couldn't go to school at the age of six in 1960, but had to wait another year. Now, only a few days after the building of the Wall, which had hit my family so hard, the time had come. Early in September 1961, at the age of seven, I was sent to Grundschule IV, the elementary school closest to the Waldhof. Even so, it was quite a distance away, and took me half an hour on foot. As I couldn't really tell left from right yet, my parents only allowed me to cycle there in traffic after second grade. In fifth grade I switched from Grundschule IV to the nearby Goetheschule, an academic high school.

Lessons began at half past seven. I got up at around 6:15, and breakfast consisted only of a slice of bread and butter and a cup of tea or ersatz coffee. There was no time to sit down. Then I usually picked up the children of the family next door, to walk or cycle to school with them. But often they weren't ready, so my mother watched from the kitchen window of our apartment to see when I would finally set off. Sometimes she accused me of simply accepting the risk of being late.

I came home at midday, since I wasn't allowed to eat at school. After lunch I either did my homework or had some free time. Supper was at six o'clock in the evening, usually sandwiches, but sometimes semolina pudding with cherries or blueberries, and it was our family's main meal. Everyone took part. We children talked about what we'd got up to during the day. Our parents listened attentively and gave us good advice so that we siblings could deal with the adversities of everyday life in East Germany. Very often, however, my father had a limited amount of time if evening events at the Pastoral College began at 7:00 or 7:30. Then, after washing up, which we helped with, I kept my mother company as she knitted, for example. As I grew older we also watched the daily news program together.

Unlike all my fellow pupils, in first grade I wasn't allowed to join the Pioneer Organization, the state youth organization for pupils up to seventh grade. That had consequences. I didn't get rewards for good achievements in my schoolwork, unlike the others who were in the Pioneers. I wasn't allowed to help to prepare for upcoming festivities such as Christmas, all because I wasn't a member of the Pioneers.

This was down to my parents. When I started school they said to me, "You'll have to decide after the end of first grade, but not yet, when you're just starting. School is a duty, but membership of the Pioneers isn't." That was their view. I was to learn that even in the GDR there were opportunities for decision-making. My parents had also planned to talk to me at the end of my first school year about whether I wanted to become a member of the Pioneers or not. They would accept either decision. With this method—I only understood the full breadth of this later on, and it gave me a high opinion of my parents—they wanted to achieve two things: that I should learn to make independent decisions, and also that as a pastor's child who was assumed to come from an oppositional household, I shouldn't be prevented from having an academic education and left only with the option of theological studies at the "Sprachenkonvikt." Because if you didn't join the state youth organizations it was barely possible to do the Abitur school-leaving exam and go on to study. My parents didn't want to put extra obstacles in the way of my choice of profession, or that of my siblings, or—even worse—to ruin our futures.

In second grade I decided to join the Pioneer Organization. I became a Young Pioneer, with a blue neckerchief, and from fourth grade onward a "Thälmann Pioneer" (after the German Communist leader Ernst Thälmann, murdered by the Nazis). From 1962 until 1968 I was a member of the Pioneer Organization, and after that the FDJ (Freie Deutsche Jugend, Free German Youth), the state organization for children and young people from eighth grade upward. Later, I was also able to join the class Pioneer leadership team, but wasn't allowed to become group council chair because I was a pastor's daughter.

My siblings and I learned in many ways what it meant to be a pastor's child in the GDR. A particular source of horror for me in this respect was the class book. In it, the origins of parents were noted—A for Arbeiterklasse (working class), B for Bauern (farmers), I for Intelligenz (intelligentsia), S for Selbständige (self-employed). Often, substitute teachers made pupils stand up and say what their father did for a living. Once I whispered to the boy next to me, "Right, I don't feel like saying 'Pfarrer' [pastor] again today, there will just be a thousand more follow-up questions." He replied, "Then just say 'Fahrer' [driver]." (In spoken German, "Pfarrer" and "Fahrer" sound very similar.) As I waited for my turn to come, I worried myself sick about whether I should actually take my neighbor's well-intentioned advice or tell the truth. When my name was called I said my father's profession in a bit of a mumble, but still making it clear that he was a pastor. Luckily, there were no further questions this time about what it was like to live in a parsonage and whether my parents said critical things about the school. I was afraid of such insistent questions. Then I just wanted to sink into the floor—perhaps not least because my mother always told us that as a pastor's children we had to be better than everyone else and stand out as little as possible. The fact that my parents, particularly my father, had allowed us to become members of the Pioneers and the FDJ, even though we were a pastor's children, was different from other parsonages. Sometimes this situation also put me in a state of conflict, when I found out that children the same age as me were not allowed to switch to the Erweiterte Oberschule (EOS, Extended Secondary School) just because they weren't members of the FDJ. My father was more to the left of the political spectrum in any case. He supported Liberation Theology in Latin America and rejected the idea of church tax in West Germany. He believed that pastors should work for a living in their own communities. Even in the days of the GDR his attitudes won him the nickname "Red Kasner." I didn't find his views particularly practical or definitive, as I had reached the conclusion that if we ourselves had implemented the policies for which my father argued in theory, we wouldn't have been able to afford a lot of things. When I said this to my father, however, it fell on deaf ears. He didn't seem to me to reconcile his theoretical considerations with his practical life.

———

I found school easy from the beginning—it was only in sport that I really had to make an effort. I will never forget my first dive from the three-meter board. One day, it appeared on the timetable. I was a very good swimmer but I was afraid of heights. I stood at the back at the school swimming pool next to the Goetheschule, so as to be last in line. All of my fellow pupils had dived and were already swimming down below. That made little difference to me; my survival instinct outweighed my fear of looking ridiculous in front of everybody. But I didn't just want to go back either, it would have been too great a defeat. So I was standing up there. My sports teacher coaxed me gently; he was patient and could tell that I actually wanted to dare to dive. My fellow pupils didn't make fun of me either, because they knew that I'd often helped them. So it dragged on. Perhaps in the end it didn't last as long as it seemed to me in retrospect, only twenty minutes rather than forty-five. At any rate, at last I heard the ringing of the school bell in the distance, a sign for the end of class. The teacher said, "Now you've got to dive or go back." So I dived and landed in the water with a mixture of pride at having done it, and shame because it hadn't been as bad as I had imagined when I was up on the three-meter board.

But at school I encountered other challenges more serious than a poor performance in sport. Even today I'm grateful to my parents—particularly my mother—for helping us children to cope with them.

For example, I remember a German teacher at elementary school who told us in almost every class about the atrocities that the communists had suffered at the hands of the Nazis. As a communist herself she had been affected by them. But apart from the fact that she never mentioned the persecution and murder of the Jews by the Nazis, as I later realized, she confronted us daily—we were only ten years old at the time—with the most vivid descriptions of terrible brutality. I remember it being strong stuff for my young soul. I needed an outlet and found one in my mother when I came home at midday. While she was heating up my lunch I chattered away and poured my heart out. We called it "debriefing."

My brother had a slightly different approach. The first thing he did after school was lie down on the rug in the sitting room and read the newspaper. Marcus needed a break, and my mother let him have one. My sister, by contrast, needed movement first of all, and liked to go outside immediately to play. By being there for us and dealing with each of us individually, my mother helped us to process things we hadn't understood, vent any built-up aggressions, and gain some distance from the things that troubled us.

We were basically living in two worlds in any case. One was school, the other our private lives before and after. We couldn't speak freely to all of our fellow pupils, but we could to our school friends. We weren't worried that they might betray anything of our private conversations. We had quickly learned what we could say in school and what we couldn't. It was part of life, because it was obvious to us that we would get into big trouble if we openly revealed what we were really thinking. Our parents had also warned us not to talk about Western television. One favorite trick question on the part of some teachers, for example, was: "Does your Sandmann [a character in a German television show] have a watch with dots or lines?" They could tell from the answer whether we had seen the Western Sandmann or the Eastern Sandmann on television at home. So even before we started going to school my parents had told us that if we were asked questions of that kind we should simply say that we couldn't remember. We learned very early on to be careful.

If my mother noticed that I was having long telephone conversations with my school friends, which I enjoyed doing, she came into the room and said that I was talking myself into trouble because the Stasi were bound to be recording the call, and that I should be careful if I said anything about the teachers or even just complained about the situation at school. My parents recommended having conversations like that out in the woods. I can still remember as if it was yesterday that my brother once got into real trouble in first grade over a joke about Walter Ulbricht, the head of state, even though it wasn't so much a real joke as a bit of fun. He had described the man with the striking beard to his classmates as "Old Goatee." One of them reported him to their class teacher. My parents were informed and advised to be cautious about making any political statements. The state had no sense of humor.

So obviously it was also taboo to talk outside of our own four walls about what my mother told me one evening. It was November 22, 1963. She came into my room and said quietly, "Something terrible has happened." I was already in bed, and normally she would just have said "Good night," but instead she whispered, "John F. Kennedy has been assassinated." I could tell immediately how shocked my mother was. It was only a few months since the American president had brought us to tears on his visit to Berlin with the words "Ich bin ein Berliner."

From fifth grade onward we learned Russian. One hurdle I had to jump was the brace on my teeth. I had one that you could take out, and couldn't pronounce the Russian "rrr" properly if the brace was in my mouth. So during Russian class I wrapped it in my sandwich paper and put it under my desk. One day I left it there, and didn't realize until I got home. I immediately raced back to school on my bike to look for it. The cleaner had already thrown the sandwich paper containing the brace in the bin, but it hadn't yet been emptied. I could hardly believe it and was incredibly relieved, because the brace was a valuable object, and I didn't even want to imagine what would have happened at home if I had had to confess to losing it.

In fifth grade I joined the school Russian club, a study group. Our teacher, Frau Benn, a staunch communist, was pedagogically very good. She was skilled at motivating us. This included competitions, "Olympiads," as they were called, a way of encouraging achievements outside of lessons. I took part in several of these during my time at school, with average success in the Math Olympiad and excellent results in the Russian Olympiad.

I was in eighth grade when I had my first Russian Olympiad. It was held over a number of rounds, beginning with the School Olympiad, followed by the Regional Olympiad, the State Olympiad, and finally the National Olympiad. I enjoyed taking part. As a year-eight student I was already starting in the age group of what were known as "preparatory classes." That was the name given in the GDR to ninth and tenth grade of the Extended Secondary School, intended as preparation for the actual school-leaving stage, eleventh and twelfth grades. I won a bronze medal. Sibylle Holzhauer, also from Templin, won a gold. She was two years older than me, the daughter of a doctor and my great role model, because her Russian pronunciation was particularly good. We are still in touch. With the medals that Sibylle and I won, the little town of Templin was able to claim success at a national level. Two years later I even won a gold medal.

The GDR-wide competition was held in the marble hall of the headquarters of the Society for German–Soviet Friendship in Berlin, next to the Maxim Gorki Theater. While writing this book I found an old newspaper cutting, which my mother had kept. It gives a detailed account of the Olympiads in May 1969. Among other things, at the start we had to take a vow, which read as follows: "We [. . .] vow today to fight honorably, with determination and all our strength, for the best results, in honor of our school, our county and district, and for the benefit of our socialist homeland."

The competition was held within a wider framework: we students had to visit four locations, in a so-called field camp for young patriots, and engage singly in different conversational situations with Hungarian pupils and a delegation of Komsomol'tsy. Komsomol'tsy were members of the Komsomol youth organization of the Communist Party of the Soviet Union, and the children in the younger classes were called Lenin Pioneers.

I remember being so excited that I didn't sleep the whole night before. Then I was so tired in the morning that I worried about whether I would be able to solve a single exercise. I was quite surprised by the strength I managed to find in the actual competition; of course, it was pure adrenalin.

As a reward, as well as medals we won a trip on the "friendship train" to Moscow and Yaroslavl. Sibylle and I traveled together. Before the trip, there was a preparatory course of lessons held in a camp belonging to the Pioneer Organization, in the Klim-Voroshilov camp on the Röddelinsee near Templin. I wasn't just filled with eager anticipation of the big trip during those days. I was enthralled by being woken up at dawn, the morning sport, the communal atmosphere during the day's events, and the blazing campfire in the evening. Admittedly, we had to wear very unattractive uniforms—along with the FDJ blouse, we were given a brown anorak and a brown skirt, which we drastically shortened by rolling up, something that would get us into trouble later in the Soviet Union, but that didn't put me off. Maybe the socialist idea isn't so bad after all, I thought.

After the course, we traveled from Templin to Berlin-Treptow for the closing parade at the Soviet monument in honor of the Red Army soldiers who fell in the Second World War. Sibylle and I got there a bit later than the rest of the group. We were given such a severe telling off from a supervisor that the positive feelings I had developed for socialism in the Voroshilov camp evaporated in a flash.

Then we had to walk to the school where we were due to sleep the night before we left. It was near the Ostbahnhof in Berlin. On the way—it was Saturday evening—I peered in through the windows of the houses we were walking past, and thought: Oh my, you're walking around here in the uniform of your unit and being ticked off for doing absolutely nothing, while the people behind the windows are watching quiz shows on Western television, and what are you doing? You're marching along in a crowd like this and tomorrow you're taking a train to the Soviet Union. Everything seemed pitiful; I felt lonely and lost and I'd had enough of it all before the trip even began.

In Moscow we met up with a group of Komsomol'tsy. The first thing they said to us was: "It's completely impossible for Germany to stay divided. It would be completely surreal to build a wall between Leningrad and Moscow or through the two cities. It'll last for a while, but one day Germany will be reunited." I was speechless at the idea that young people from the country supposedly responsible for the division of Germany saw it for what it was: unnatural. That was my first discovery on the trip, in 1969, eight years after the erection of the Berlin Wall. Discovery number two was that, unlike in the GDR, you could get vinyl records of the Beatles, and I immediately bought a copy of the *Yellow Submarine* album.

During our time in the country, we stayed in a Russian school, because everyone was on holiday. We danced to Western music, another experience I hadn't expected. From Moscow we went northeast to the city of Yaroslavl. Throughout the whole trip we were constantly visiting monuments commemorating the Great Patriotic War, as the Red Army's fight against Germany in the Second World War is still known. I remember that in a wreath-laying some elderly women, babushkas to us, grandmothers, walked along behind us and I heard them saying: "Look at that, girls in such short skirts, they have no decency, it's shameful and not a way of paying honor to our soldiers." We were slightly ashamed, but not really.

The Russian Olympiads, however, were only a way of improving my knowledge of Russian. I also used every available opportunity to learn more. In Vogelsang, a town near Templin, there was a big Russian estate. The members of the Russian armed forces there were screened off and had barely any access to public life in the GDR. The officers, however, brought their families to Germany, so from time to time we were able to visit their children, Lenin Pioneers or Komsomol'tsy according to their age. We spent afternoons with them in their canteen and chatted together in Russian.

A rather more unconventional method of polishing up my Russian skills arose on my cycle home from school. On some days Soviet soldiers stood on the corner of Lychener Strasse and Parkstrasse, waiting to give columns of military vehicles directions to their exercise grounds in the forests around Templin. During my school days, we estimated that there were three times as many Soviet soldiers in the thinly populated areas around Templin as there were local residents. The soldiers who gave directions often had to stand there day and night, in wind and rain, until the column finally arrived. I couldn't help feeling sorry for them. While they waited, I used the opportunity to talk to them and test and improve my Russian skills.

In East Germany there was no religious instruction in school. This was done after school, as teaching of Christian doctrine, in my case in the parish rooms in Templin. The teachers knew about it, and at the beginning of each school year they scheduled the rehearsals for the school choir at exactly the same time. Those of us who wanted to sing had to ask the teacher to

rearrange Christian doctrine lessons. So, at the start of every
school year, there was a battle over the allotted time.

Once that had been decided, once a week we studied Bible
stories or learned hymns. From seventh grade onward we went
to confirmation classes. I was confirmed in 1970; we celebrated
it in the Ermelerhaus in Berlin, a patrician town house on the
Spree Canal, so that my godfathers and godmothers from the
West could attend the celebration. Their one-day visa allowed
them to travel to East Berlin, but not to the rest of the territory
of the GDR. My godfather came along, a friend of my mother's
from her student days, and I was able to meet his children.
After the very lavish lunch, the young people were allowed to
walk around alone on the Fischerinsel and chat about our
different lives.

I was only confirmed, while some of my fellow students
took both confirmation and "Jugendweihe" (Youth Consecration)—a state celebration in the GDR that marked entry into
adulthood. This was a concession by the Church to the state,
because it didn't want young people and their parents to face a
choice between two options. The state wanted to use Youth
Consecration to entice young people away from the churches.

After confirmation we became members of the Youth
Community, our church community's youth group. At the time,
Manfred Domrös was the youth pastor in Berlin-Brandenburg.
I met up with him again after German unification, on the island
of Hiddensee, part of my parliamentary election constituency,
where he was a local pastor. In my youth, Domrös participated
in further-education events at my father's Pastoral College. I
liked him a lot, because he was brilliant at playing the guitar and
singing new hymns. I loved going to Protestant National Youth
Days, where you could have relatively open discussions, even
with the bishop of the day. Participation in these Youth Days
didn't cause me any additional problems at school.

Holidays

Once a year our parents took us on vacation, whenever possible to a church vacation home. It was fully catered, so that my mother didn't have to worry about cooking. We did not have access to vacation spots run by the FDGB (Freier Deutscher Gewerkschaftsbund, Free German Trade Union Federation), because my parents weren't members of a trade union. There was a state travel agency through which a limited number of vacation spots could be booked, but there was no free market, and restaurant bookings were also hard to come by. We often drove to the Baltic coast, to Kühlungsborn or Dierhagen, between Rostock and Stralsund. There, near our vacation home, there was a guesthouse of the Ministerial Council of the GDR—the government, in other words. Members of the Politburo of the SED also took their vacations there.

The grounds of the building, now a hotel, were fenced on three sides, but not facing the beach. So sometimes we children had fun creeping along the beach from our own accommodation to this guesthouse. In the evening, when these ladies and gentlemen strolled through the forest from their guesthouse to the beach at Dierhagen, they walked right past our church vacation house. Sometimes its guests included pastors' families whose children were not allowed to sit the Abitur. After dinner we stood outside, waiting for the members of the Politburo of the Central Committee of the SED to pass. We said to each other, "Will you go and tell them that I'm not allowed to go to the EOS? Do they know that? See what happens." In the end, however, none of us went. We were too scared.

Later, between the ages of fourteen and eighteen, picking blueberries in the woods of Templin became my vacation job. I would set off in the morning along with other children from the Waldhof on the train from Templin to Rychen, and get off at

Tangersdorf. It was a request stop, which meant that at the start of the journey you had to tell the driver you wanted to get off there. Then we went into the forest and picked blueberries. The aim was to collect ten liters a day, a big bucketful. We had finished by midday. Now we could either take the blueberries we had picked to the Volkseigener Erfassungs- und Aufkauf- betrieb (VEAB, People's Registration and Purchasing Service) with its attached retail outlet, which bought them from us, or give them to our own mothers to bottle. The opportunity to make a little money with the fruit placed a bit of moral pressure on my mother to give me a little money back in return.

Blueberries were a very lucrative business, because a kilo could bring in four or five ostmarks, I can't remember the exact sum. The retail outlet passed on our blueberries to their customers for one or two ostmarks—if the employees didn't immediately divert the goods for themselves and their friends. So if we had waited until the goods were displayed for sale and one of us had bought them back from the retail outlet to offer them again as newly collected berries, we could have made really good money. We never did that, but this simple procedure demonstrated the sheer nonsense of the GDR economy.

My Hamburg aunt's family also spent about ten days with us every summer. Relatives of GDR citizens and their families were allowed to make such visits for up to thirty days. I always drew up a kind of comparison table between the childhood of my cousins in the West and my own in the East. Of course, I envied them a lot of opportunities that existed in the West. Shopping opportunities were many times better for them than they were for us, and my aunt's children were able to travel freely. We, on the other hand, could only dream of holidays in the West and always had to be on our guard against the state. But I was glad that my Hamburg relatives loved our landscape, especially the swimming spots, and thought our sandwiches and cakes were extraordinarily tasty. So we did have some things that they thought were better than what they had at home. I, in turn, was less keen on their accounts of everyday life at school, because the many political discussions during lessons—this was in the late 1960s—sounded to me like an absolute mess. I took the view that West German students lacked the peace and quiet to study properly. My cousins didn't disagree. So, to my child's eyes, the balance between East and West was even, overall.

Prague Spring

In August 1968, our family went on holiday to Czechoslovakia. We had found a place to stay in Pec pod Sněžkou in the Giant Mountains. Our host's son was about the same age as me, and both he and his father could speak some German. Out in the meadow in front of the house he tried to make it clear to me with a few words and gestures of his hands and feet how proud he was of the changes to his country made by the new Party head Alexander Dubček. When I wrote a postcard to my grandmother, he tore up the stamp that I was about to stick on it because it still showed the old head of the Communist Party, Antonin Novotný. A few months previously, Dubček had won a power struggle against Novotný within the Party, and been elected First Secretary of the Central Committee of the Communist Party of Czechoslovakia (KPČ). Dubček represented "socialism with a human face," as it was called at the time. This made him a leading figure in the Prague Spring, a Communist reform movement in Czechoslovakia. In our conversations, both father and son of our host family proved to be deeply convinced that the development in their country could never be turned back. I was very touched and impressed.

During our holiday, my parents traveled alone to Prague for three days. They had planned to do this from the beginning, so the matron of the Pastoral College had unusually come on holiday with us, to keep an eye particularly on my younger siblings while our parents were away. My mother and father came back from Prague completely inspired. They had experienced an atmosphere of hope, of a new beginning, that would have been unthinkable in the GDR. It was with that feeling that we traveled home.

I spent the rest of my summer holidays at my Berlin grandmother's. When I got up on the morning of August 21, 1968 and went into my grandmother's kitchen for breakfast, her radio was on. She was listening to RIAS, Radio in the American Sector, which always announced itself with the words "A free voice of the free world," and was designed specially for GDR citizens. I heard that during the night tanks from four Warsaw Pact states had entered Czechoslovakia. They had come for the bloody suppression of the Prague Spring; dozens of people died; and the hope of the summer was buried beneath the tracks of the tanks. Even today I can remember where my grandmother's radio stood in her kitchen. I can also still feel the blow to the stomach that the news dealt me. At fourteen I learned that there are few things worse in life than shattered hope.

The new school year began almost two weeks later, on September 2, 1968, with the impression of these events still very present. Our class teacher asked us to give an account of what we had experienced in the holidays. When it was my turn I talked with growing enthusiasm about our holiday in the Giant Mountains. I described the conversations with our host's son and got increasingly carried away with my shock at the end of all those dreams. Suddenly, my teacher interrupted me and said, "If I were you, I'd be a bit careful for now." I stopped talking and sat down. That was all that happened. My teacher had only said that one sentence. Perhaps, it occurred to me later, he had wanted to protect me against myself.

At home, at around the same time, my father talked about students who had come to Templin, as they always did at this time of year, to pick potatoes, and whom he had met because they were also involved in the student communities in the places where they studied, and who had been given his contact details by the student pastors there. They told my father that some of their fellow students—exhausted after a day of potato-picking and clutching beers in their hands—had spoken freely about the events in Czechoslovakia. As there was always someone listening in, they were betrayed and many of them immediately expelled.

All of this meant that the suppression of the Prague Spring represented a profound break in my father's relationship with the state. The GDR was not directly involved in the invasion, since memories of the occupation of Czechoslovakia by the German Wehrmacht in March 1939 were to be avoided. The Soviet Union expected the GDR leadership to ensure that there were no protests against the action of their troops. My father, "Red Kasner," who had always been resolved not to overstate opposition to the GDR, but to confront it honestly, was deeply disappointed. He distanced himself more and more from the system.

Subsequently, he and my mother set about making copies of texts that were seen as subversive in East Germany. These included writings by the author and dissident Alexander Solzhenitzyn. My mother typed out the texts, and my father made copies of them on the Pastoral College's copier. Such devices were rare, because it was not in the state's interest for people to get their hands on certain printed texts. Of course, it was well known that the Pastoral College had a copier for further-education essays, and was therefore also a potential source for the distribution of forbidden texts. It wasn't long before the Stasi found out what my father was doing, and they only waited for a suitable opportunity to confront him with their knowledge.

On one occasion, when my father had broken the speed limit in his official car once again, he was reported to the traffic police. But rather than a traffic policeman, my father found himself sitting opposite a representative of the Stasi, trying to recruit him as an unofficial staff member in order to make use of his contacts. My father rejected the offer, with a strategy as banal as it was effective, and one which our parents had taught us very early on: "If the Stasi ever talk to you," they explained, "all you have to do is say that you wouldn't be able to keep it to yourself." That instruction was extremely helpful, because the Stasi relied on conspiracy. It was a piece of wisdom that would be very useful to me later on.

My father did go on copying other texts but became more careful about distributing them. Nonetheless, my parents, particularly my father, were walking on thin ice. I still wasn't worried about him, but may have put from my mind the risk that he was taking.

Hermann Matern School

In September 1969, when I was fifteen, I moved from the Poly-technic High School to the more academic Erweiterte Oberschule (EOS). I joined the first of two preparatory classes for the Abitur level. The school was not named after the SED Politburo member Hermann Matern until 1971, the year he died. It was the only EOS in Templin, and I had been very much looking forward to moving there; by the previous academic year, if not before, classes at the Polytechnic High School had begun to drag due to the very wide range of abilities and interests among the students. The more academic among us were increasingly under-challenged, although teachers made a real effort to be fair to everyone, and the subject teaching was actually very good, especially in the sciences—that was true of both my schools. The EOS also had well-equipped physics, chemistry, and biology labs.

At the end of my second year at the EOS we had to take the same exams as the students who were finishing at the Polytechnic High School and going on to do vocational training. This was intended to ensure that, if anyone later failed their Abitur exams, they would still have a school-leaving certificate to fall back on. Conversely, it was at least theoretically possible for polytechnic students who did very well in these exams to move to the EOS at that point. The state had an ideological stake in this arrangement, too, as a counter to any accusations of elitism against the Abitur level.

There were three classes in each year group at the Hermann Matern School: a, b, and c. I was in class b. Half of the students came from the town of Templin and lived at home, as I did, while the other half came from the surrounding villages in the district and lived in the boarding house attached to the school. In 1970, half of us also had been confirmed into the Protestant Church, a comparatively high percentage. We were a self-assured class. As it later emerged, some teachers took a critical view of us for that reason.

In any case, what was allowed and what was forbidden always depended on the prevailing political climate. In 1971, when Erich Honecker succeeded Walter Ulbricht as First Secretary of the SED's Central Committee, it seemed at first that we might see a little more openness. But the wind soon changed again, and stricter rules returned. They included a ban on wearing jeans to school, and boys were always being sent to the barber because the teachers thought their hair was too long.

But sometimes we were also disappointed in other ways. From time to time we lent our support to "freedom fighters for the socialist idea," as people called them then, from all over the world. I remember a postcard campaign in early 1970 calling for the Greek composer, writer, and politician Mikis Theodorakis to be released from jail—he had been arrested for joining the resistance against Greece's military dictatorship. My mother could speak Greek, and so she helped me call for his release in Greek letters.

One morning, a friend told me: "Mikis has betrayed us."

"What happened?" I asked.

She replied: "He's free, which is what we wanted, but . . ."

"But?"

"He didn't come to us; he went to the West."

The year I was fifteen, a new subject was added to our timetable: civics. The aim of these lessons was to introduce us to Marxist Philosophy, to the Political Economy of Capitalism and Socialism, and to Scientific Communism. We focused on the life and work of Karl Marx and Friedrich Engels, their relationship with the working class, and their development of dialectical materialism. To this end, we had to answer essay questions such as: "Prove that the scientific insights of Marx and Engels were and remain correct." Of course, these were matters of opinion that couldn't be proved scientifically, but instructions of this kind were to remain a constant at every subsequent stage of my education.

Each school day began with the FDJ greeting: "Friendship." There followed a fifteen-minute review of the newspapers. One student was responsible for this on rotation every week. Given the lack of diversity in the East German press, the term "news-paper review" was a joke. There were two papers from which we had to present the news each day: the SED's central, nationwide publication *Neues Deutschland* (New Germany), and our local paper *Freie Erde* (Free Earth), now the *Nordkurier* (Northern Courier). Now and then there would also be an article from *Junge Welt* (Young World), the FDJ's newspaper.

The boys had to complete various forms of paramilitary training, while we girls did civil defense training, both under the aegis of the Society for Sport and Technology. I was completely inept at the compulsory shooting drills. We were instructed to close our left eye and look at the target through our right. And even though I'm right-handed, I couldn't do it. My shots never hit the target.

At the EOS, we also had theoretical lessons in what was called Introduction to Socialist Production. These alternated on a weekly basis with days of practical work, known as Instruction Days in Socialist Production, and later Productive Work. These practical lessons had also been on the curriculum at the polytechnic for the last two years I was there. Now, at fifteen, my classmates and I were sent off to work at the Götschendorf concrete factory, around fifteen kilometers from Templin. We helped in the production of prestressed concrete, and manufactured manhole covers and lamp-posts. Prestressed concrete is made by pouring concrete into molds containing tensioned steel reinforcements. Once the concrete has hardened, the tension on the steel is released. I found this thoroughly interesting, and enjoyed the practical work. I expect we were no real help in fulfilling the quotas, but the factory workers and foremen were kind to us teenagers.

My final year at school was when the written and oral Abitur exams were held. We had applied for places at university already, at the end of the previous year. We were advised to study as close to home as possible, and in my case that was Greifswald University. But I wanted to go elsewhere, far enough from Templin that I wouldn't have to travel home every weekend. For that reason, Berlin was also out of the question. It was the challenge that attracted me—not only of doing a degree, but also of living somewhere new and having to manage on my own. So I applied to the Karl Marx University in Leipzig. Like

Berlin's Humboldt University, it had a very good reputation, and I was interested in Leipzig itself as well: the exhibition halls, the wonderful covered shopping arcades and courtyards in the center, the historic Auerbachs Keller restaurant, the Gewandhaus concert hall, and the St. Thomas Church. I had heard its famous choir when they came to Templin, and on one of these concert tours the choir members had stayed at the Waldhof. I loved their Bach concerts, and loved the idea of being able to hear even more of them in Leipzig.

I was also looking for a new academic challenge once school was over, and so I decided to apply for a Physics course. I hadn't found it the easiest subject at school, but there was another reason for my choice: it was a science, and even the GDR couldn't twist all the scientific facts. Two plus two was still four. It meant I could talk about the new things I was learning without having to censor myself. Before making my final decision I went to visit a friend, a fellow pastor's daughter from Thuringia who was already studying in Leipzig. She was in her first year and told me how difficult everything was, how hard she had to work. It didn't put me off; in fact, I liked that idea. I thought: You'll have to make an effort, and if she can do it, then somehow you will manage, too. In my youthful naivety, I had some confidence in myself.

But of course, that wasn't the whole truth. Like one of my two best friends, I would have liked to study psychology, a subject I was very interested in—but I wasn't allowed to. Not due to poor grades, but because I had not been assessed as "especially suitable." It was up to the school to determine a student's "suitability" for a particular subject, and this suitability related to your character and personality. Once again, my father's profession was a factor. Unlike the daughter of a worker, a pastor's daughter stood no chance of achieving the highest rating of "especially suitable" for psychology. But with anything lower, I wouldn't have been given a university place; there were already enough interested students with the highest rating for the number of places available, which was centrally determined for each university and each subject. And so the school's assessment was an additional instrument of control beyond a student's average grade.

I was rated "especially suitable" for physics, and there was also a desperate shortage of girls in the natural sciences. On January 3, 1973, a good six months before my Abitur exams, I was sent an offer for the 1973/1974 academic year, for "undergraduate studies in physics," addressed to, "Fräulein Angela Kasner, c/o Headteacher, EOS (Hermann Matern)." The offer was provisional at this stage, and the letter stipulated that it could be withdrawn "if the conditions for admission to the degree course are no longer met." Everyone knew that this caveat did not apply to academic qualifications alone.

In each school year, classes were asked to present a cultural program in front of selected teachers and students. In early summer 1973, my class, 12b, had just a few weeks left at school, and we decided not to contribute to the program this time around. We had no desire to come up with anything, and were in any case busy with exams. What could possibly happen, we thought—another few weeks, and school would be a thing of the past. How wrong we were. At morning break on the day of the scheduled presentation, when all the students were in the schoolyard, a teacher informed everyone over the loudspeaker that 12b were refusing to take part in the cultural program. We realized that the school leadership team was trying to turn the other students against us in an attempt to exert pressure. We were being accused of complacency and laziness. It made us uneasy. And so that breaktime we decided to conjure up a presentation out of thin air and at lightning speed, to be given a few hours later. We had no wish to eat humble pie, however. Class 12b wanted to do something different from what was expected of us, to show what we were made of. Lazy and complacent? Not us! And this was when Christian Morgenstern came into play.

I had an edition of his poetry collection *Alle Galgenlieder* (All Gallows Songs) on the bookshelf in my bedroom. I liked his poems very much. At lunchtime I went home, ran up to my room, grabbed the book, and came back down to the kitchen where my father was waiting for me. He was busy heating up our lunch, because, unusually, my mother was away. But we never got round to having a proper lunch—I was in too much of a rush to tell my father what had happened that morning at school. Then I read Morgenstern's poem "A Pug's Life" to him:

"A Pug's Life"

Upon a wall, a pug will take a seat;
He'll find a spot that juts into the street,

And from this vantage point he will observe
Life passing by in all its vim and verve.

O man, take care, lest you this fate befall
And you become a pug upon a wall.

To this day I have an image of myself standing in the kitchen doorway, telling my father about our plans for the cultural program. We intended to read out the "pug on the wall" as a literary interlude. Then, instead of appealing for money to help with reconstruction in Vietnam, we would call for donations to FRELIMO, Mozambique's liberation movement, and to finish we planned to sing the socialist anthem "The Internationale" in English rather than German. My father listened quietly, and nodded his agreement. He thought it all sounded quite sensible, which encouraged me to go ahead with the plan.

I wolfed down my food and raced back to school with Morgenstern in my bag. We rehearsed our program at top speed—I was one of the organizers. Then it was time for the performance. When we had finished, there was a tentative smattering of applause from a few students, who kept their eyes on the floor. The silence from the teachers was deafening. None of them said a word to us as we walked offstage. I could sense that something was wrong, but the full magnitude of it was not revealed until the following morning.

It began with the chemistry teacher failing to greet our class with the usual "Friendship." He then omitted the morning newspaper review, and when we left the chemistry room after the first lesson—our teacher having suffered in silence with us—and walked to our next classroom, we saw that in the meantime all the other classes had written statements against us, which were already pinned to the news sheet on the wall of the corridor. This was something I had not been expecting. I skimmed the statements. Some classes had condemned us for creating a program contribution that deviated from the norm, while others were smarter, and had set out their ideas of what a good cultural program should look like.

Starting in the second lesson, one student after another was pulled out of class. The ones who came back told us they had been questioned by members of the Stasi about the origins of the presentation. Only the four students who had come up with the presentation—one boy, my two best girlfriends, and I— weren't questioned. That created the maximum degree of uncertainty, as we had to ask our classmates what was going on. After school, I went home and told my father how our performance had gone down the previous day. Now he was alarmed. He began to ask around.

A few days later there was a parents' meeting, at which the school leadership team intended as many parents as possible to distance themselves from the presentation's initiators and their parents. Some parents and teachers did just that: "12b is already a class in which a lot of students wear Western clothes and listen to Western music," said one. "They've always thought they were better than everyone else. It's no wonder things have come to this," others complained. Some people seemed to have been waiting a long time for our class to draw attention to itself. But many other parents stood in solidarity with us, and so the school leadership team didn't achieve their aim.

My most painful memory, however, is of my mother's reaction when she returned from her trip. I'd rarely seen her so upset: "I've got you through twelve years of school without any trouble, and the minute I go away this happens . . ." And then she added something that cut me to the quick: "You'll be gone soon, but I have to stay here, and until now we've always been respected!" All I could do was mutter sheepishly: "But you *are* respected." I felt incredibly sorry for her at that moment.

For some time we remained in the dark about what punishment awaited us. There were various possibilities: expulsion; failing our Abitur; the withdrawal of our university offers. Given the potential repercussions, my father decided not to sit there like a rabbit in the headlights and wait for the verdict, but to go on the offensive. And so he turned to the representative for church matters on the district council. He painted the whole business as a provincial farce designed to unsettle students when they were already worrying about exams. He also asked me to put the incident down on paper in the form of a letter to Manfred Stolpe, the canonist for the Berlin-Brandenburg area, part of whose function was to maintain contact with the Secretariat of the Federation of Protestant Churches. I was to hand him the letter in person. And that was what I did, traveling to Berlin-Weissensee one Saturday afternoon to see Manfred Stolpe and give him my letter.

In the meantime, there had been a full assembly for all students and teachers, during which one short, rather chubby girl stood up and said with great indignation: "Me, a pug? Never!" It took all my self-control not to burst out laughing. But in the written essay for my subsequent German exam, I made every effort not to write a single wrong word. And then, finally, the punishment was announced at a whole-school flag ceremony. Class 12b were told to step forward. We were given a reprimand. That was it. Looking back, the only way I can explain the lack of any further repercussions is to assume that my father's efforts with Manfred Stolpe had not been in vain. Now we could concentrate fully on the rest of our Abitur exams.

My parents and I were still deeply troubled by the school's response to our presentation, however, and so I traveled to Leipzig with my father to explain the incident to the admissions office in person. My father was keen to get ahead of any malicious gossip from Templin, but we quickly realized that people in Leipzig seemed to take a more relaxed view of things than they did in my hometown. In any case, soon afterward I received a firm offer of a place on the physics course at Karl Marx University.

When the school held its Abitur leavers' ball for our year, to which parents were also invited, my closest friends and I attended with our parents—but only for form's sake. We left straight after the dinner. The school administration, which had thought it necessary to put such acute pressure on students who had permitted themselves some essentially harmless deviations from the cultural-program norms, had taken all the pleasure out of the event for us. But I have a much happier memory of the party that my closest friends from 12b and I put on. We went out to a small nearby village called Ahrensdorf, and celebrated at the village pub right on the lakeshore. It was a joyous evening. In the words of Christian Morgenstern:

> Let the molecules cavort,
> No matter how they throw the dice!
> Put down the saw, the plane, the vice;
> Keep sacred this ecstatic sport.

As dawn broke, I was sitting in a rowing boat with a friend, having consumed a substantial quantity of "kirsch whiskey." Suddenly, and without any warning, my friend stood up, the boat began to rock, and I fell into the water. I got out again soon enough, but I still had to go home dripping wet. Despite this mishap, it was very much my kind of party.

And so my schooldays came to an end in the early summer of 1973, and with them my childhood and teenage years in my parents' house. I was almost nineteen years old. My parents had done everything they could to create safe, protected spaces for me and my siblings; at least, that is how it felt to me, and I will always be grateful to them for it. I had a happy childhood.

We were protected by the countryside around the Waldhof. We could play in the woods and meadows without any inhibitions, swim, hike, and have adventures. Another safe space was created by the conversations and the inexhaustible intellectual stimulation that living amid the employees and members of the Pastoral College allowed me to enjoy. We were like an extended family. As a sociable child, I had docking stations everywhere. I pestered visitors with questions, and they taught me a lot. A matron who collected art postcards, for example, introduced me to the painters of the early twentieth century.

Once a year, my family went to the theater in Berlin. I will never forget Hilmar Thate as Richard III at the Deutsches Theater, or the performance of *Fiddler on the Roof* (*Anatevka*) in Walter Felsenstein's production at the Komische Oper.

But it was my mother who offered me the most vital safe space. She was there for me whenever I needed her. Life in East Germany was lived constantly on the edge: you might wake up in the morning without a care in the world, but if you overstepped a political boundary, everything could change in seconds, putting your whole existence at risk. Then the state knew no forgiveness, and when it struck, it was merciless. The real art lay in pinpointing exactly where these boundaries were. I was helped by being something of a natural peacemaker, and taking a pragmatic approach to life, but the crucial factor was that we could "blow off steam" on everything at home, and that, in a gentle way, my parents taught me and my siblings how to make independent decisions in this world. Decisions that made it possible to live within the system, but without passing the point where I would no longer have been able to look myself in the eye. Decisions that prevented us children from becoming bitter and jaded.

The political room for maneuver in the GDR was always in flux. At one point, privately owned farms were collectivized; and at another, "Action Ochsenkopf" was launched to ensure that television aerials on the roofs of buildings were not pointing west. Then there was the bullying of artists, and waves of expropriation that hit medium-sized companies.

The most significant difference from life in a democracy, however, was that individuals had no enforceable legal protections; the state's actions were despotic, and its punishments were meted out not only to the person affected, but usually also to their whole family or group. That is the nature of a dictatorship. The safe spaces that my parents created for my siblings and me were therefore important for our survival.

OFF AND AWAY

The study of physics

IN SEPTEMBER 1973, I left my parents' house and moved from Templin to Leipzig, to start my physics degree at Karl Marx University. Before making a proper start, we had to complete a kind of paramilitary course. It lasted fourteen days and was held in Schwarzenberg, a town in the Erz Mountains near the Czech border, in a camp that was something like a youth hostel with a sports field attached. The rooms we stayed in each had two bunk beds. I was quartered with another student, a girl from near Dresden. She spoke a heavy Saxon dialect that I'd never heard before, and I didn't understand some of what she said. We fell into comparing the different words we used for things. In her part of the world, pound cake was called "Schlagasch," as I learned in the first few minutes we were together. She knew how to make the beds properly, as well. "I can do this," she said. "My boyfriend is an officer cadet." Her use of officer training for the National People's Army as authoritative proof of her bed-making skills was a small culture shock for me.

After those two weeks in Schwarzenberg, the real degree course began. There were five seminar groups in my year, each made up of around fifteen students. I lived in a student dorm on Linnéstrasse, southeast of Leipzig city center. Instead of my attic room with its view of woods and meadows, I now lived in a four-bed dorm room with two bunk beds, where each resident also had a Sprelacart table at which to study. Sprelacart was the brand name of the resin laminate surfaces that were widespread in East Germany. At least I had managed to bag one of the bottom bunks. Today, I can't imagine living and working like this—but at the time, I probably coped with it because my roommates came from nearby towns and went home at the weekends, and from Friday afternoon until Monday morning I had the room to myself.

The physics degree was designed to take five years. There was no division of the time into semesters. In the upper years, you could earn a little money from working as an assistant to the professors to supplement your university stipend. That was what I did later, marking the work of students in the lower years, among other things. It wasn't possible to interrupt the degree in Leipzig with a year abroad, at least not in my subject, though I could certainly have imagined myself studying abroad for six months or a whole year, like students did in the West. But one thing we could do was participate in a student exchange for two weeks, or a maximum of three, with the University of Leningrad. I took up this option along with a few friends from my seminar group.

It was June, just before the start of the wonderful "White Nights" when the sky over Leningrad—now Saint Petersburg—was never completely dark. I stayed in a student dorm, polished up my Russian somewhat, and otherwise had little to do. And so I had time to explore the city and the surrounding area. I visited the Hermitage, the Peterhof Palace, the Catherine Palace, Repino (home of the painter Ilya J. Repin), and plenty of other sights. In the evenings, my friends and I sat in the parks with a bottle of red wine and some cheese, soaking up the atmosphere. We didn't have much contact with the Leningrad students, but via a Russian physics lecturer who was looking after us we did get to meet some Russian artists and intellectuals, who also invited us to their homes. Even during this all-too-brief trip, I could see and feel that Leningrad had an exciting intellectual scene that was not entirely under state control.

My timetable in Leipzig was made up of lectures, seminars, and practicals—experiments using lab equipment. We were expected to participate in everything. To begin with, the emphasis was on mathematics, and later the physics subjects dominated. Assessment came in the form of continual in-class tests and practical exercises. Our seminar group leader made sure no one fell behind. And this seemed to be necessary, because, about six months into the course, she looked at our grades and said to us, "Please don't start thinking of C as the new A! You can do a lot better than this!"

When I think back on my early days at university, I see myself sitting steadfastly at my Sprelacart table in that four-bed dorm, solving problems in analysis, algebra, and theoretical physics. Hour after hour I brooded over these problems, until eventually the spark of an idea would come to me. The feeling of having found the solution was wonderful and liberating. It was then that I learned not to throw in the towel at once; that it paid to keep going, to believe in myself, to battle through on my own. Unlike school, university really took me to the limits of my ability. And that was exactly what I had been looking for.

The physics section—in East Germany, university faculties were known as "sections"—was on Linnéstrasse, the same street as my student dorm. This was where all the central physics and math lectures were held. Our physics lecturers had not got their jobs through connections with the SED and the state, but because they were real experts in their field, with international reputations. One of them in particular has remained in my memory: Professor Harry Pfeifer, a short, wiry, bald-headed man. He taught us electronics, had written several successful textbooks, and was given permission to attend conferences in the West. For some time, I had an eight o'clock lecture with him on a Monday morning. At the start of our course, he had told us in no uncertain terms: "First of all, you need to be punctual. And secondly, I won't accept any more homework after eight o'clock. Don't even try it, there's no point." And it was true: he wouldn't accept any homework that wasn't on his desk by the start of the lecture at eight. This was never a problem for me, since the walk from my dorm room to the lecture theater was just a few minutes. But for many others who, although they lived no great distance away, still came in from outside Leipzig, it was torture getting there before eight on a Monday morning to submit their homework. But Pfeifer made no exceptions, probably because he assumed we would have allowed our fellow students to copy from us if we still had our homework with us during the lecture. In all likelihood his strategy was also intended to make us attend his lectures every week.

The practicals sometimes began even earlier in the morning, at seven o'clock. That was a struggle. I had to leave the dorm at around 6:30, because, unlike the lectures and seminars, these were not held in the Linnéstrasse building, but in the university's tower block, next door to the Gewandhaus in the city center. It had been built following the demolition of the venerable university church in 1968—a unique act of cultural barbarism. In addition to the early start, I found it immensely frustrating that the male students would go straight to the equipment and try everything out, without any plan in mind, while I would first spend time getting the experiments clear in my head. When I then wanted to try something on a piece of equipment, I would find it already occupied. The men didn't achieve their results any faster, however. And so I preferred to do practicals with the other female students.

It probably goes without saying that, alongside these

practicals, it was sport that gave me the most trouble at university, just as it had at school. I can laugh about it now, but at the time it was no trifling matter; sport exams were a compulsory part of the curriculum. My real *bête noire* was the hundred meters. Once, I actually had to retake the sport exam, because I would otherwise have been given the lowest possible grade and risked failing the entire year. In the retake, I think my examiner tempered justice with mercy, because as I was running I didn't feel much faster than I had been the first time around. But he clearly didn't want to let a hundred-meter sprint prevent me from completing the year.

Lighthearted

What had begun with civics at the EOS was continued at university with seminars and lectures in Marxism–Leninism, or "ML" as we called it. ML focused once more on the three categories familiar from civics classes: dialectical materialism, political economics, and—this was the worst of the trio—scientific communism. I lived in the same neighborhood as some ML students, the most intelligent of whom were studying political economics and the least gifted (from my physics perspective) scientific communism. Our assumption was that they would have been admitted to the course even with a D in math, because aside from speculating on when the age of communism would arrive they didn't have a great deal to do. How anyone could spend an entire degree course on that was a mystery to me. I found it ridiculous.

This was something that I couldn't completely hide, and as a result I was once summarily ejected from an ML lecture. I was sitting quite far back in the lecture theater. The rows, as is usual in lecture theaters, were raked from front to back, which put me in one of the higher rows. Bored by the ML lecture, I was doing physics homework. But I had failed to notice the man sitting three rows behind me, observing us from above, who could see exactly what everyone was doing. Suddenly, this man leaped to his feet and yelled down to the ML teaching colleague who was giving the lecture: "Stop for a minute! There's someone up here doing homework and not focusing on Marxism–Leninism!" I knew at once that he was talking about me. The lecturer down below shouted at me to "Get out of here!" And in a state of shock, I packed away my things and got up from my seat. Now the real drama began: there was no rear exit through which I could swiftly have disappeared. The only way out was down at the front, on the other side of the room. I had to walk all the way down the stairs. The theater was deathly silent as everyone watched this scene unfold. At the front, I had to walk past the lecturer to get to the door, and it felt like an eternity before I opened it and left. Once outside, I realized my knees were trembling. It had been so upsetting that all I wanted to do was go back to my dorm room, where I lay down on my bed to compose myself. I was worn out. When the others came back later, they tried to reassure me. There were no repercussions to the incident, but I will never forget that walk. It was humiliating—pure victimization.

Looking back, I find it interesting that this experience actually had the capacity to shock me to that degree. I had been caught in the act, and I really should have known better. It should have come as no surprise. You always had to assume that someone was watching, that there were informants among us who were reporting our innocent meet-ups to the Stasi, and this was far from being something I had only learned in Leipzig. It had been part of life in Templin, too. All the same, the incident affected me deeply. Even writing these lines today, I can feel the acute embarrassment of that scene. But there is another feeling that has lingered, as well. I don't know exactly what to call it, and I'm searching for the right word. Perhaps this is it:

superiority. Superiority in relation to the state's efforts at discipline and intimidation. This was a state that never trusted its citizens, or, most importantly, itself—and as a result it was as petty, narrow-minded, tasteless, and—yes, that too—humorless as it could possibly be.

But why do I now feel something like a sense of superiority? Because, despite it all, this state didn't manage to take from me something that allowed me to live, to sense, to feel: a degree of light-heartedness. It had been with me since I was a little girl. And the fact that the GDR couldn't take it from me is what I feel to be my greatest personal victory over the system. Without this light-heartedness—and in retrospect I am convinced of this—I never would have guilelessly done my homework during that ML lecture. Without this light-heartedness I would have acted in bad faith much more than was good for me. I would eventually have wondered why, throughout my degree, I was hardly ever bothered with FDJ projects, or why I was never impeded in my regular visits to the Protestant student community. In this respect, there would be a rude awakening only after I had finished my degree. Until then, my time as an undergraduate was the academic challenge I had been seeking, and life was essentially untroubled.

My seminar group worked well as a team. A few of us, including me, decided to put on discos in our free time. From then on, once or twice a week, you could dance in the communal areas of the main physics building, from 7:00 p.m. to 11:00 p.m. Admission was open to all students who were interested, as long as we had enough tickets. Other members of my seminar group took care of the music. They had constructed the technical equipment, the amps and loudspeakers, themselves. We played Western and Eastern songs at a ratio of 40:60—it was forbidden to play more than 40 percent Western music. We didn't play the Eastern songs all the way to the end, though, so in practice Western music was playing at least half of the time. I was responsible for selling drinks, which made me a kind of barmaid. It was a lot of fun, and I earned a little extra money from it, as well. We found the practicals that would often begin early the next morning a real challenge, however, as we had to ensure we left the physics building clean and tidy.

I went on annual vacations with friends from the group, sometimes also with my brother, and later with my first husband, Ulrich Merkel. We took our backpacks and traveled to Prague, Budapest, Bucharest, Sofia, to the Pirin Mountains and the Făgăraș Mountains, and to Burgas on the Black Sea coast. We never had anywhere near enough money. We were only permitted to exchange around thirty marks per day; even our socialist "brother states" were frightened that tourists from other so-called "brother countries" within the bloc would buy up scarce consumer goods meant for their own people. But that didn't prevent us from having a good time.

Timbres and gold dust

"Don't read so much *Neues Deutschland*. It spoils the language and people's feeling for language," the writer, literary translator, and dissident Reiner Kunze told us. He was speaking at a weekend convention of the Protestant student community in Klostermansfeld. Instead, he counseled us to "read Goethe, Schiller, and Heine." We may not have gone off and read any Goethe, Schiller, or Heine during this convention, but it was a wonderful experience—particularly as I already liked Kunze's writing. My father had a few of his books that had been banned from publication in the GDR. Some, such as his poetry collection *Brief mit blauem Siegel* (Letter with a Blue Seal) had been published in the East, but many others were banned.

In Klostermansfeld, we focused on the translation of poems

from other languages into German. "The most difficult thing," Kunze explained, "is to translate poems from Hungarian. The language has so many different E and A sounds for which German has no equivalent." Translation, he said, is about much more than transposing individual words and sentences, particularly in poetry. "If you want to get to the core, you have to listen to the timbre of the language," he ended. The idea of language being almost like music touched me deeply.

Unfortunately, I can't remember the exact weekend on which the convention took place, but it must have been in late 1976 or early 1977—the time between the songwriter and lyricist Wolf Biermann being expatriated from the GDR on November 16, 1976, during a concert tour to West Germany, and Reiner Kunze leaving for the West on April 13, 1977. Kunze spoke so quietly, it was as if the State Security were sitting right beside him. It was a time of departures. Biermann's expatriation had shaken East Germany deeply, far beyond artistic circles. Countless other artists left the country after that. My parents had some cassette tapes of Biermann songs, which were circulated privately, and the Pastoral College had a cassette player that we were allowed to use. On some Saturday evenings, the whole family would sit together and listen to his songs.

I can still remember the afternoon when we students were summoned to the lecture theater, and the physics lecturer responsible for our year group stepped up to the podium and told us that Wolf Biermann had been expatriated. He concluded his brief announcement with the words, "Do not speak about this further." He seemed keen not to be dragged into a discussion with us, and I couldn't tell whether that was to spare himself any awkwardness, or to protect us. And so we dispersed, shocked, saddened, and uncertain as to what else was to come.

It was not in my nature, however, to spend day after day, morning till night, contemplating what the next threat might be. I could not have coped with being always on high alert; it would have made me ill. Of course, I knew there were always students whose parents were in the SED, for example, and for that reason you would be well advised not to be too trusting in your dealings with others. But in order to survive, I needed a sense that I didn't have to just stay quiet, despite it all; I still felt I could be unselfconscious with other people, especially my friends. For me, that was as essential as having air to breathe. I have always felt this way, and not just since Wolf Biermann's expatriation. A degree of light-heartedness, then.

And from time to time, every six to eight weeks, I also needed a trip home to my parents' house in the Waldhof estate. The journey from Leipzig was not straightforward. I took the express train part of the way, to Oranienburg. The best thing about this train was that it had a Mitropa buffet car, where I could buy either Czech beer, Original Pilsner Urquell, or German Radeberger Pilsner as a treat for my father, because they were not available in the stores in Templin. I then had to wait in Oranienburg, sometimes for up to two hours, to catch the local train to Templin.

At home, I liked being back in my bedroom, which was kept as mine for a while. Home was home. I was never homesick in Leipzig, but I did sometimes feel that something was missing, particularly in my early days there. I missed the sound of bells. For the first time, I realized how structured my day had been on the Waldhof estate, regulated by the bells ringing at lunchtime and in the evening. In Leipzig, I could eat when I liked, and go to bed when I liked, too. No one was paying attention to when I did things. On the one hand, it was liberating. And on the other, I felt a small pang of sadness at knowing that this was all up to me now. On Saturday afternoons, coming back to my dorm alone from a Bach concert at the St. Thomas Church, I missed the conviviality of the Waldhof, which had been most in evidence at the weekends. I missed my family, especially my sister, and my two best friends from school. I missed the landscape, the woods, the solitude you find in nature, and swimming in the lakes. The bathing lakes around Leipzig—and please forgive me for saying this—were no substitute, from my Uckermark perspective. And the television in the dorm was of no interest to me, either, because of course we weren't allowed to watch Western shows. The TV was therefore only good for football matches and that kind of thing, but even then it was of limited use. This was brought home to me during the 1974 World Cup. West Germany's match against the GDR on Saturday, June 22, in Hamburg—the city of my birth—was one I was desperate to watch, with my fingers crossed for the West German team, the free part of Germany. There was no way I could do that in the dorm, and so I went home to Templin that weekend. There, I could give free rein to my anger at East Germany winning this of all games. My satisfaction was then all the greater when West Germany went on to become world champions.

Overall, I realized that my decision to attend a far-off university—far-off in GDR terms, at least—was having the desired effect: I had hoped that I would enjoy going home if I was studying far enough away from my hometown of Templin. And that afterward, I would also enjoy returning to Leipzig.

It was there, in 1974, one year after starting university, that I met Ulrich Merkel. We were in different seminar groups, but both studying physics. It was a student romance. He also introduced me to a world I had not known before: at home, the focus had always been on intellectual matters, but in his family's house I experienced a more practical, hands-on approach to life. His father had owned a medium-sized textile company, which had been nationalized in 1972. After that, he worked there as general manager. I gained a completely new insight into the textile industry and the entrepreneurship that had previously existed, but I also saw my father-in-law's frustration at the inefficiency of business after nationalization. There was always something to be done around my in-laws' house and garden, and so Ulrich and I went to visit his family in Vogtland on a lot of weekends.

On September 3, 1977, a year before we completed our degrees, we were married. I was twenty-three years old, and he was twenty-five. I have especially good memories of our honeymoon. It took us to the island of Hiddensee. If you have ever been to Hiddensee in September, you will know how beautiful it is at that time of year. We had very little money, but somehow we still managed to find a room. Like gold dust.

Getting married also meant that we were permitted to get jobs in the same place after graduation. At that time, on admission to university you had to give a written promise to go wherever the state saw fit in your first three years after graduation. Had Ulrich and I not been married, we could easily have been given jobs in different parts of the country. And of course, this was something we wanted to avoid. But at that point, we could not have guessed that our first graduate appointments would be complicated all the same.

The diploma

Our fifth and final year of study was devoted to our diploma project, the equivalent of a Master's dissertation. Ulrich was doing his diploma at the university, which was the usual way. But another possibility had opened up for me. Professor Reinhold Haberlandt at the Leipzig Central Institute for Isotope and Radiation Research, part of the East German Academy of Sciences, also gave lectures at Karl Marx University, and he offered to let me write my diploma project at his institute. I didn't need to be asked twice, even if I was the only person in my year to go. My seminar group and the conditions in the physics section were all familiar by now, while the Academy was another opportunity to learn and experience new things. I said yes immediately.

There, I met some interesting people. My diploma supervisor was one of them: Ralf Der was a mountaineer, as well as a very independent and politically critical person. He introduced me to people in Jena, who later all emigrated to West Germany. At the Institute I also met Erika Hoentsch, who became one of my best friends. Erika is a little older than me, and by that point she already had her doctorate. She had an apartment of her own, and moved in Russian artists' circles. Where previously I had known only students in neighboring dorm buildings and the Protestant student community, the Academy brought me into contact with another, critical Leipzig milieu that broadened my horizons quite significantly. Many of my new Academy friends went on to play important roles during the fall of the Berlin Wall, one of them in the St. Nicholas Church—the center of the peaceful Monday Demonstrations against Communist rule—and another on the city council.

The diploma was a challenge for me. The title of my dissertation was "On the influence of spatial correlations on the rate of chemical reactions in dense systems." The topic was the first step on a path that I would continue down after graduation, at the Central Institute for Physical Chemistry at the Academy of Sciences in Berlin. Essentially, I was looking at the use of statistical physics in questions of chemistry—physical chemistry, in other words.

Inevitably, an ML exam was part of the diploma year. There was a rule that the final grade for your diploma project could only be one higher than your ML grade. I had a heart-stopping moment during the ML oral exam. The examiner asked me: "In 'real socialism', what does not yet function as it should in theory?" I have a good answer to that, I thought, and began: "Some things still aren't good: if you want a car, you have to wait seven to ten years; you're allowed to exchange very little money when you travel abroad; our computers aren't the newest and fastest; I have to run around for hours before I can find somewhere selling tissues . . ." I talked and talked, for what must have been seven minutes, until suddenly a thought dawned on me: Careful, this is a trick question! You're talking yourself into a whole world of trouble. And then I backed up and said, "But of course, I would also like to stress that a lot of things do function very well." To which the examiner replied, "Well, it's about time." I was given a B in Marxism–Leninism and finished university on July 18, 1978, the day after my twenty-fourth birthday, with a Master's in physics and a rating of "very good."

Ilmenau

Before we had even submitted our diploma projects, we were expected to have a clear idea of what we wanted to do after university. We could take the summer holiday between completing our studies and starting work if we wanted to, but no longer than that. The GDR was always keen to ensure there was no idling, and that it had complete surveillance of its citizens. Anyone who said they had some money from their parents and didn't want to work for a while would have been regarded as antisocial. Taking time out after university, then, was not an option. But there was never any worry about unemployment in East Germany. On the contrary, there were always too few people and too much work. We were offered jobs at various companies, including the Stassfurt VEB Fernsehgerätewerk, the largest manufacturer of television sets in the country. None of these jobs interested me.

But the state had ways of guiding your decision. Its most significant lever was the distribution of accommodation. A housing shortage meant that the state had a strong interest in students going back to where they had come from once their degrees were finished, back to their hometowns. But the state had other options, too. If, for example, the Piesteritz nitrogen works or the factories in Schkopau and Leuna were to be expanded, and therefore required physicists and chemists, then an employment contract and a nearby apartment would be offered at the same time. The latter was often the most important factor in deciding whether to take a job, because East Germany's housing shortage really did eclipse many other things.

Ulrich was keen to work toward his doctorate at the Technical University in Ilmenau, a town in the far southeast of the country. I thought this was a good idea, and the prospect was also something that interested me. Ilmenau was somewhere I had briefly considered when choosing where to apply for my first degree, because it offered the intriguing subject "bionics," in which you learned about the inventions of nature—how we can take the flexibility of a reed as a model for our own technological developments, to give just one example. On closer inspection I had decided against bionics: my spatial awareness and my ability to calculate and work practically in three dimensions at all times were not sufficiently developed.

As a place for doctoral studies, however, Ilmenau was perfect for both my husband and me. And so we both applied and were invited for interview. The college's head of personnel, something similar to today's HR manager, took me aside for a private conversation. I had a terrible cold and was finding it difficult to concentrate, but before long I was wide awake, because at no point did this conversation turn to my academic performance. This seemed to have been ticked off as good already. Instead, he began to question me in a strident voice: "You attend the Protestant student community. Do you mean to continue this in Ilmenau?" He stared fixedly at me all the time he was speaking. I was flabbergasted. He had gone straight to a topic that had never been any kind of problem in Leipzig. Now I realized how naive I had been. I might have been left alone there, but now my activities in the student community seemed to be an issue. My mind was racing. Alright, I thought, try to answer as honestly as possible; anything else is just going to make it worse. I replied, "Yes, I think so. It's important to me."

"That's not ideal," he shot back. "If you become an academic assistant here, you'll be working with students. Are you going to talk to them about what you do in your free time?"

"I hadn't really thought about it," I said, before adding, "Until this point, I haven't made a distinction between the things I tell different people."

"Well, yes, but here your job would be to perform to the best of your academic abilities, and also do something meaningful for the GDR's economy," he pressed on. "We really can't be doing with so many distractions."

For what felt like another twenty minutes, the conversation circled around and around the question of whether I would keep going to the Protestant student community, and to what extent I would bring this into my work as a teaching assistant. And so, eventually, I asked: "So, what should I take from this? To be honest, I thought you were going to talk to me about my academic qualifications and my expectations of the job."

The head of personnel said, "That's as may be, but I thought it was very important to speak to you about the other matters. Let's leave it there. You'll be hearing from me."

I was about to get up and leave, when he said, "You must get your travel costs reimbursed right away. You can go straight to the travel office and collect the money there."

I can still hear myself replying, "Well, I would like the money back, but it isn't that urgent." And with that, the interview was over. I left the room.

As I was walking down the stairs to the travel office, I

encountered two men in the stairwell who had clearly been waiting for me there. They asked me quite abruptly to come with them, and led me into a nearby room. There, they introduced themselves as Stasi employees; they had a few additional questions for me. And the grilling began again, along the same lines that the head of personnel had taken. "We can only use teaching staff who have a solid socialist worldview. We have questions, but also expectations." My head was spinning. All I heard were fragments of sentences: "still a thoroughly productive individual"; "peak performance"; "information, including about other students."

I told them I had already had a conversation like this, about the student community.

"Oh, no, you're welcome to keep going there, that isn't the point at all," one of them said. "The point is," the second one continued, "that really, we always need an overview of how hardworking and how good the students are."

All I could think was: Where is this going? Then I decided to ask them straight out: "Am I to understand that you want me to spy on them?"

They replied, "Now, don't use words like that. It's just that we require teaching staff to tell us certain things."

"But you aren't from the physics section, you're from the Stasi, and you want me to pass on information to you. That's going to cause me problems," I said.

"You don't need to take it so seriously," they told me. "There are many different ways in which we can exchange views."

As the two men went on trying to convince me, I resolved to put an end to the matter. I remembered the advice my parents had given me in childhood for getting out of such situations, and said: "You know, I have been deeply affected by what we've discussed here. I'll have to tell my husband right away—he's actually here as well. I'm a communicative person, and I always have to tell other people what's on my mind."

That was the end of the conversation. I was given my travel costs, and told, "We'll be in touch."

But no one was in touch, either by phone or in writing. My husband, who had been subjected to no such questioning during his interview, had long since received his acceptance for Ilmenau. I, however, heard nothing. After two weeks I decided to phone the head of personnel and inquire.

"I'm glad you've called," he said. "It doesn't look so good for you at the Technical University of Ilmenau, but I've spared no effort on your behalf. There is a possibility you might get a job with the VEB technical glass factory here in Ilmenau."

I told him I had no interest in that.

"I feel that's rather ungrateful," he said.

We ended the call.

Looking back, I am convinced that, from the outset, I had no chance of getting the position in Ilmenau without signing up as a Stasi informant at the same time. From their perspective, it had been worth a try—I might have made a good informant.

Afterward I was naturally somewhat uneasy, knowing that everything would be reported back to Leipzig. I could no longer predict how anything would go for me professionally. There was no risk of ending up unemployed, but having to start work in some power plant rather than at a research institute would have been a nightmare for me.

In the meantime, Ulrich had succeeded in getting an academic assistant position at the Humboldt University in Berlin as well as his acceptance to Ilmenau. And so I began to look around in Berlin as well.

I told my colleagues in Leipzig what had happened. It now seemed advantageous that I was doing my diploma project at the Academy. The Leipzig institute had a very good relationship with the Central Institute for Physical Chemistry (ZIPC) at the Academy of Sciences in Berlin. One of the scientists there, Hans-Jürgen Czerwon, worked closely with us in Leipzig, but he was about to resign from his institute, and his position would then become vacant. My Leipzig colleagues told him of my difficulties finding a job. The only problem was that the Theoretical Chemistry department at ZIPC, which is where he worked, already had a head of department who was not a member of the SED, Professor Zülicke, and what the whole working group really wanted was a party stalwart, not a rejected church-goer. In East Germany it wasn't entirely helpful to have a boss who was not in the SED; someone above you with a party membership card could wield it like a shield. But if a working group's boss was under pressure himself, then everyone in the group often had to suffer more than their fair share of scrutiny. All the same, Hans-Jürgen Czerwon managed to convince the doubters, which allowed me to interview with Lutz Zülicke and ultimately get the job. Professor Zülicke became my doctoral supervisor. Perhaps it also helped a little that, before my arrival, the working group didn't have any female scientists.

AT THE EAST GERMAN ACADEMY OF SCIENCES

Rate constants

IN THE LATE summer of 1978, Ulrich and I packed our bags and moved from Leipzig to Berlin. He started work as an academic assistant in the physics section at the Humboldt University, and on September 15, 1978, I started at ZIPC. I was glad to have put the stress of the Ilmenau episode behind me, and keen to discover what awaited me at the Academy. At the time, I knew almost no one in Berlin beside my husband and my grandmother in Pankow. In many respects, it soon became clear, student life was over.

But before I turn to this new phase of my life, I would like to take a step back and look at the five years I devoted to my studies from an outside perspective. As I have said, the expatriation of Wolf Biermann at the end of 1976 and the cultural bloodletting that followed shook East Germany to its core. However, these things did not happen in isolation, either within the GDR or beyond its borders.

A few years previously, in June 1973, a treaty had come into force. Its full title was: "Treaty concerning the basic relations between the Federal Republic of Germany and the German Democratic Republic," or the Basic Treaty for short. It was a document via which the West German government led by Willy Brandt, the first Social Democrat to become chancellor since the state was founded, acknowledged the principle of two sovereign

German states. The treaty came out of a belief that the reality of
two German states first had to be recognized if it was one day
to be overcome. The Basic Treaty was part of the new "Ost-
politik" (West Germany's policy on the Soviet-bloc countries)
from the social-liberal coalition that had governed since 1969,
and both were highly controversial in West Germany. The
Christian Social Union (CSU), which was in opposition at the
time, launched an appeal against the treaty at the Federal
Constitutional Court in Karlsruhe, but its objections were not
upheld. In its verdict, the court nevertheless mentioned the
provision for reunifying the two German states contained in the
West German constitution. As a result of the treaty, both East
and West Germany became members of the United Nations.
They exchanged "permanent representatives" rather than
ambassadors, and each country's journalists could now be officially accredited in the other.

Of course, at the time I didn't see any of this from a politician's perspective. The idea that I might one day become a
politician in a reunified Germany lay beyond my powers of
imagination. In 1973, I had just finished school. I came from a
family that had suffered greatly from the consequences of
Germany's division, and after the Wall went up, we were
grateful for any relief, no matter how minor. For us, this first
came with the détente between the USA and the Soviet Union,
and as a result between East and West Germany from the late
1960s onward. That was one side of the coin.

On the other side, I was glad that this Basic Treaty did not
grant all the wishes of the East German government. West
Germany still did not recognize East German citizenship, so we
in the GDR were still Germans in the eyes of the West German
constitution. That was our life insurance. Whenever voices were
raised in West Germany calling on the government to finally
recognize GDR citizenship—and right up until the fall of the
Berlin Wall they continued to grow not only louder but more

numerous—I was afraid. I had the sense that if that happened, our fate would be sealed.

It is pointless to speculate on what my life might have been like without the fall of the Wall and German reunification. No one can know that. But I do know that the fact it was even just theoretically possible to obtain an exit visa, through which an inhabitant of East Germany could leave the country and become a citizen of West Germany, gave me a reassurance that is hard to describe but was still very real. It was like a kind of back door through which I could slip if the worst came to the very worst. It was important to know that the option existed. My parents were aware of my position. They knew that I had great respect for the calling that had taken my father and my mother from Hamburg to the GDR in 1954, but they also knew that I didn't see it as a model for my own life. I had resolved this issue with them.

But I don't wish to give a false impression here: applying for an exit visa was no walk in the park. As a rule, it was a long and humiliating process. But if you managed it, and were given permission to leave, then you were automatically a West German citizen. That was the point for me, no more and no less. It was the same if you failed to return from a trip to the West, or otherwise fled the country. To begin with, pensioners were allowed to travel to West Germany once a year, and later they could go more often. There, they could apply for a passport that in theory would allow them to travel anywhere.

Nineteen seventy-three, the year that the Basic Treaty came into force, was also when the Conference on Security and Co-operation in Europe (CSCE) began. A total of thirty-five countries participated: seven members of the Warsaw Pact, fifteen members of NATO, and thirteen neutral countries. The conference ended in 1975 with the signing of the Helsinki Final Act, which set out common aims for culture, science, the economy, environmental protections, and disarmament, in order to improve security and the enforcement of human rights in Europe during the Cold War. The far-reaching effect of this document, which was felt beyond the end of the Cold War and long into my time as chancellor, will play a role later on. At the time, I could neither anticipate nor recognize its importance.

Eighteen months later, on January 1, 1977, the Charter 77 Declaration was published in Prague, and on January 7 it appeared in numerous European newspapers. This declaration came from the Czech opposition, organized around the dramatist Václav Havel, the philosopher Jan Patočka, and the former foreign minister Jiři Hájek, and it spoke out against human rights violations by the Communist regime. In East Germany, too, this was a period of constant vacillation between hope and disappointment. State-imposed restrictions and moves toward restoring the old order, such as the introduction of military science lessons as pre-military training, were juxtaposed with liberation efforts right across the Soviet bloc. Issues such as environmental pollution, which had been gaining traction in the West following the first report from the Club of Rome in 1972, also influenced discussions in the East. The limits of growth that this report sketched out were also discussed at length in my family home. And there was as yet no way to assess the effects of electing the Krakow cardinal Karol Wojtyła as the first Polish pope in October 1978, in terms of efforts toward freedom and democracy in Poland and beyond. In 1980, the Solidarność union was founded in Poland. The Polish state responded in 1981 by imposing martial law. This, as we know, only succeeded in postponing rather than preventing the victory of freedom against dictatorship and injustice.

My time as an undergraduate and the beginning of my career in Berlin at the Academy of Sciences fell in this rather vague and uncertain political climate. At the Institute for Physical Chemistry, I worked in the theoretical chemistry department. Ten or so scientists worked here, all in the area of quantum chemistry. Apart from the secretary, I was the only woman. Altogether, the Institute had around seven hundred staff. My workplace was in Adlershof, southeast Berlin, in a brick-built barracks opposite the buildings of the Fernsehfunk state television broadcaster. My daily routine was very different from what I had known as a student. I was familiar with academic life from the Institute in Leipzig, but now, in addition to the core research, which I enjoyed, there was now a fixed routine that took place within rigid and compulsory working hours. It felt like being crammed into a corset. The freedoms of student life were gone, which came as a shock to me. And the fact that all this played out more or less directly in view of the Berlin Wall only made it worse. It was frustrating and depressing. More than once, I wondered how I was going to cope with this in the long term.

Work began at 7:15 a.m. I left home at 6:20 a.m. and walked to Friedrichstrasse station to catch the overground S-Bahn train. Ulrich and I lived on Marienstrasse, in the central district of Mitte. There was no free rental market in East Germany, but we needed to prove that we had somewhere to live in order to take up our jobs in Berlin. We were glad, then, when we managed to get an apartment via a doctor in Templin who knew my parents. He had been paying rent on it since his student days, with the intention of holding on to it for when his own children went to university. His children were still very young, and so my husband and I were able to use the apartment in the meantime.

Every day I traveled for forty minutes by S-Bahn from Friedrichstrasse to Adlershof. I found Friedrichstrasse station quite spooky, because tracks led both eastwards and westwards, but only the eastern part was accessible to me. Of course traveling to the West by train was only possible for people with valid papers to leave the GDR. I could hear the guard dogs barking through the partitions. Being reminded of the divisions like that wasn't something I knew from Leipzig. When I boarded the train toward Schönefeld or Königs Wusterhausen, it always took me along the Berlin Wall. When it wasn't pitch dark, as it was on my way there and back in autumn and winter, for the whole journey my gaze roamed over places that were inaccessible to me.

Work finished at 4:30 p.m., and then I got back on the S-Bahn and arrived in Marienstrasse, which was also close to the Berlin Wall, around an hour later. The stores closed soon after, at 6:00 p.m. There was a place to buy necessities in the grounds of the Academy, but that wasn't much help to me, either. As a student in Leipzig, after lunch in the university canteen, friends and I had often strolled around the various stores and bought a few things, though that was always an adventure in view of the shortages in East Germany. There was no more of that now.

Arriving in my new office on my first day at work, I found a book on my desk about calculating the rate constants of simple chemical reactions. This was to be the focus of my future work and my PhD. It was an area that no one in the working group had covered until now. But it had a practical application, to do with the delivery of crude oil through the Druzhba pipeline, which came to East Germany from the Soviet Union, via Poland. The oil was used by the Leuna and Buna chemical works to make Plaste and Elaste, among other things. Plaste was a brand name for thermoplastics, and Elaste for elastomers, hard and soft plastics that had first been developed at the Buna works in the early 1930s. East Germany had barely any oil deposits of its own, but it did have modest deposits of natural gas, and so the state was interested in finding out how this gas could be used to produce longer-chain hydrocarbons, the base material for Plaste and Elaste. The process involves adding energy to the gas, which essentially consists of methane (CH_4), drastically raising the temperature and thereby splitting off a hydrogen atom (H). This produces a highly reactive methyl radical (CH_3), which reacts immediately with a second methyl radical to form ethane (C_2H_6), the starting point for longer-chain hydrocarbons.

My PhD project consisted of using quantum-chemistry calculations to discover how high the temperature had to be for this process to take place. It meant working both at my desk and in the Institute's computing center with quantum-chemistry computer programs that had been developed in Western countries. In the computing center, I put programming commands into a machine that punched holes in a card (called a "punch card") to reflect my input. Feeding all the cards into the computer then told it what it had to calculate. A lot of calculation time was required to achieve a result, and that time was a crucial resource in quantum chemistry. But at our institute, it was also a scarce resource. I had to fight hard for my share of it. A significant part of my working day was spent carrying carboard boxes half a meter in length and filled with punch cards several hundred meters from my desk to the computing center, often only to discover that either the hole-punching machine or the card-reading device was out of action and I was unable to make use of the valuable and painstakingly booked computing time.

We used BESM-6 computers, built in the Soviet Union, which were not of the same quality as Western IBM computers. And since, alongside the availability of computing time, the quality of the computers available to us was crucial to the success of our quantum chemistry work, we were at an obvious disadvantage compared to West Germany from the word go.

I shared my office with Frank Schneider, a slightly older colleague. Our desks were perpendicular to one another, his with a view out of the window, and mine, at right angles to it, with a view of the wall. Silence reigned. This made perfect sense given the nature of our work, but it still took me a long time to get used to it. I was always glad when we met up with our colleagues from the next office, Utz Havemann and Christian Zuhrt, for coffee at around 9:00 a.m. or half past, and again at three in the afternoon. Frank Schneider and I were responsible for preparing the coffee, because our office had a hand basin and a kettle. One spoon of ground coffee in the cup, hot water poured over the top, and what we called our "Turkish coffee" was ready. To this day I still don't own a proper coffee machine, and in any case we drink more tea than coffee at home. We would put the cups on a tray and take it in to our other colleagues. Like Frank, Utz and Christian were older than me and already had children. Our conversations over coffee were not just about work, but the rest of life as well. We talked about recently published books, theater premieres, but also where you might get hold of a drill, or who knew a handyman. Somewhat later, Michael Schindhelm became the fifth member of our group; he was another scientist, but in addition to his scientific acumen he was also a gifted artist and writer, and he enriched our conversations enormously. Sometimes, our coffee group also met for lunch in the Academy's canteen. Apart from the two coffee breaks, it was the only interruption to our silent work.

The FDJ and Marxism–Leninism

When I joined the Institute, I was by far the youngest in the theoretical chemistry department. I wanted to get to know some people my own age there. It wasn't easy; there were rarely any scientific events where we could get together. There were, however, two ways to meet people. One was the FDJ. Many scientists who, like me, were under thirty were still members of it. The FDJ organization in the Institute occasionally met in a room in the basement of the building where I was working. I contacted the organizers to find out what they discussed and whether it might appeal to me. The meetings always followed the same pattern. There were around ten to fifteen of us. To start with, the meeting leader would read out a report sent by the FDJ's Central Council for distribution to its members. Once this obligatory item on the agenda had been ticked off, the discussions I was interested in could begin: what the younger Institute employees were researching in other departments, their working conditions, or cultural events in East Germany. As Institute staff, we were able to order discounted theater tickets. When I was a child, I had always liked organizing group activities. I had taken on this kind of task with the Pioneers at Christmas time or for Carnival, and so now I took charge of theater trips. In 1980 I became "Cultural Functionary" (Kulturfunktionär) within the FDJ management committee at my Institute—in the resumé I submitted on April 8, 1985, for access to my doctoral studies, I used the masculine rather than the feminine form of the word, as was customary in the GDR. A year later, I was elected to the Institute's union leadership; my role focused on young people's work. I took concerns we had discussed in the FDJ committee to the union, and vice versa. I had been a member of the union, the Free German Trade Union Federation, since starting at the Academy in September 1978.

The compulsory courses on Marxism–Leninism were another way to meet younger scientists. No one could complete a doctorate without an ML certificate. Once again, just like at school in our civics lessons and at college, we had to study the three elements: Dialectical Materialism, Political Economy, and Scientific Communism. There were several hours of this every month for three years. As I grew older, it became more and more depressing to keep going over this trio again and again. We all had degrees; we were all meant to be achieving world-class results in our research work; it was a struggle, first to get vital computer time, and then to contend with the computers' shortcomings—and on top of all this, we were supposed to apply ourselves to ML every month too, something alien to our daily working life. It seemed absurd, not only to me but to most of the other students too. During the sessions, we often peevishly made no secret of the gap between theoretical perspectives and our real-life experiences in our scientific work and other areas of our lives.

Shortly after martial law was imposed in Poland at the end of 1981, there was an ML session where the declaration of martial law was discussed openly and heatedly. I only heard about it from my co-workers as I was away from Berlin at the time, at the Czechoslovak Academy of Sciences in Prague. When I got back, I learned that someone I very much liked after meeting him on the ML course had been suspended from his doctorate because of what he had said condemning Polish martial law at the session. He had spent some time researching in the Antarctic, and we had given him the nickname "Antarctic Man." He was a brilliant scientist. Now his path to a doctorate had been blocked. I kept in touch with him.

At the end of the ML course, we had to hand in a written assignment. In mine, I focused on the working class and the farmers in "real socialism." But clearly I had under-appreciated the leading role of the working class and, coming from the countryside, I had portrayed the farmers in too positive a light, or at any rate that was what Professor Dr. Joachim Rittershaus decreed on behalf of the Educational Institution for Marxist–Leninist Further Education at the Academy of Sciences on the ML certificate issued to me: "Frau Angela Merkel [. . .] attended Marxist–Leninist Further Education of Doctoral Students from 1980 to 1983 with the overall result 'satisfactory (rite).'" As with my undergraduate degree, my overall doctorate grade was only allowed to be one grade higher than the one on my ML certificate. In my case, an exception was made later on. When I was defending my doctoral thesis, a research assistant who knew me from the FDJ suggested I should be awarded an additional bonus for good community work. As a result, I was able to complete my doctorate with a "Magna Laude" (excellent) grade overall, and my achievements in physics were not entirely canceled out by my "rite" (satisfactory) grade in Marxism–Leninism.

Marienstrasse

Our apartment in Marienstrasse was on the fourth floor, over-looking the building's courtyard from a side wing. The apartment's front door opened straight into the kitchen; we would walk through it to reach a living room and an adjoining box room. The kitchen had a sink; we had no toilet of our own. The communal toilet for the three side-wing apartments was on the first floor. Ulrich was good at home improvements and, with the help of my parents-in-law, he installed a shower and toilet in our apartment. We had been unable to get hold of the materials we needed on the free market with our modest means, so I contacted the state housing authority to ask for a coupon, as it was known, to help with the cost of the most important things for the construction work.

"Where are you from?" the woman at the housing authority asked me when I went to see her. "Surely you could live with your parents?"

"I'm from Templin," I replied. "I studied physics in Leipzig, but unfortunately there aren't any jobs for physicists in Templin."

In typical Berlin style, the woman then said to me, "You could have thought about that beforehand."

I didn't want to be browbeaten, and in the hope of some sympathy, I looked her in the eye and gave it my best shot: "That's true! When I was looking at courses, I completely forgot to think about the housing issue. But no one at school told me about it either. What am I supposed to do now? I've found a really interesting job and now I've got this problem. We want to renovate the apartment. It's in your interest too, and in the state's."

And it worked: she said nothing more, but just nodded and gave me the coupon I needed.

After about eighteen months, the apartment was completely renovated. Nevertheless, I was unable to take any pleasure in it, or in my research work at the Academy, interesting though it was. I kept asking myself if this was it for life. I was twenty-five years old, and for women in East Germany the retirement age was sixty. Thirty-five years of work lay ahead of me. Some quite fundamental questions were also bothering me deeply: Should I put all my strength and commitment into doing the best work I could in East Germany, even though it would only reinforce the state I was critical of? It was never something I'd questioned about my parents: there was no doubt that their work educating pastors and church employees was worthwhile. For me as a physicist, the answer wasn't so clear. I couldn't rid myself of questions like this. It put a strain on my relationship with my husband.

By chance, some medical students lived in the apartment below ours, and we became friends. We had heated discussions with them about the issues on my mind: "It's obvious that doctors should work hard in any political system because their job's all about people's health," I said. "But what about us physicists? If we do good work, we're sustaining a state like East Germany, which is constantly showing us it's opposed to common sense and individual needs." Our friends argued: "Doctors can't save lives without good medical equipment, and that's exactly what good physicists are for." So it went on, back and forth, for hours. We would lose ourselves in the labyrinth of these thoughts.

At some point, I changed my perspective. Never mind the state, wasn't it about making the most of my life, selfish though that might be? Wasn't it in my own interests to push myself to the limits, even under adverse conditions, and show what I could do? In East Germany there were so many more restrictions than in the West. Nonetheless, I realized, I wanted to do the best work I could in the circumstances, and for my own sake, to avoid becoming apathetic, embittered, or jaded at a young age.

This realization made me want to fundamentally change my life again. I decided to make a new start—a personal one at that. One morning in the spring of 1981, I left the apartment we shared in Marienstrasse, a suitcase in my hand. I temporarily moved in with a co-worker. I relinquished our apartment to my husband; he had put so much work into it. I was once again in search of somewhere to live. Ulrich Merkel and I divorced in 1982; I kept his name.

Templiner Strasse

I was in a difficult situation, as I needed a place to stay. One day, an acquaintance who lived in Zionskirchstrasse in Berlin's Mitte district gave me a tip-off. Looking out over the courtyard from his kitchen window, he had noticed that an apartment in the side wing of a building on Templiner Strasse was empty. Friends persuaded me to squat in that apartment. It was far from an easy decision for me, but I had no choice; I couldn't live with my co-worker indefinitely and I had to do something. A friend who was handy with tools helped me move in, if you can call breaking into an apartment "moving in."

We went there on a Sunday afternoon and simply installed a new lock in the door. The electric drill needed for the job made a terrible din though, seriously disturbing the Sunday afternoon peace and quiet so dear to Germans.

As we were making haste across the courtyard on our way out, a woman leaned out of a window and shouted across to me in a voice loud enough for everyone in the building to hear, "Are you the new girl?" I did my best to reply with a firm "Yes" and we hurried away, even faster.

My new apartment was in a pitiful state, but at least it had its own toilet, built into a corner of the kitchen. Behind the kitchen was a classic dark Berlin-style room, with the customary window overlooking the inner courtyard. Most of my furniture was things that other people had thrown out; I just added a lick of paint. I slept on wooden pallets with a mattress on top. My standard of living was extremely modest, but I was comfortable.

To avoid getting in trouble with the state housing authority, I had to gradually legalize my new living conditions. It helped that the housing managers had great difficulty collecting rent from all the tenants and were always very pleased to receive payments. I asked the neighbors above me how much they paid, and I then transferred precisely that amount to the authority in Schwedter Strasse once a month. No one turned down the money. Unfortunately, though, the caretaker refused to add my name to the obligatory house book: he probably had his son in mind for the apartment I'd moved into. Back then, every apartment building had its own house book, with details of each resident. The caretaker knew something I didn't: the building was due to be renovated at some point, and his plan had been to wait until just before the renovation started to take over the apartment. I had beaten him to it.

So I had to find another way to make it legal, other than getting my name in the house book. My co-worker Utz Havemann gave me some valuable advice: the key was getting the police to add the address to my identity card. It was May 1981. There were elections to the Volkskammer (the East German parliament) on June 14. Utz Havemann said to me, "You know what? Let's go to the police together: just say you want to get your things in order before the elections."

We saw an amenable police officer; I started with a little diversionary tactic.

"Isn't it an amazing coincidence that I grew up in Templin and now I'm living in Templiner Strasse? What a twist of fate!" I said.

The police officer grinned; he didn't hesitate for a second before entering my new address in my identity card. And just like that, my situation became legal.

About two years later, when the building was finally due to be renovated, all the tenants had to move out. In exchange, the state housing authority offered us apartments that were already renovated. I fell on my feet: I was given a perfectly equipped one-bedroom apartment with a kitchen, bathroom, and gas heating in every room at 104 Schönhauser Allee, at the rear of a courtyard.

In the meantime, I was becoming more and more used to the working conditions at the Institute. Having made contact with other young people there helped enormously, but also I had some variety with the trips I occasionally took for the Institute. Once, for example, I spent a winter break at the Academy's vacation center in Juliusruh on the island of Rügen, looking after Institute employees' children, and I took part in a three-week Russian-language course in the Soviet Union. Russian still fascinated me. Working in sciences, however, where English predominated, there was scarcely any opportunity to speak Russian. I can't remember exactly when the language course took place, other than that it was in the early 1980s. But I haven't forgotten that it took place in Donetsk, a city in the center of the Donbass coalfield in eastern Ukraine, which has been occupied by Russia since 2014. I befriended one of the other people on the course. In 1983 I backpacked around Georgia, Armenia, and

Azerbaijan with him and his girlfriend—an unforgettable tour. Back then, I was like a sponge, absorbing anything that could broaden my horizons beyond East Germany, even if this curiosity and thirst for knowledge didn't necessarily help me get my doctorate finished quickly.

International exchanges

I was able to keep up with what was happening internationally in my research area in the Institute's library, as it had copies of all the major English-language journals. However, I came up against a problem that was already familiar to me: we weren't allowed simply to make copies of publications that interested us. Copying texts was a highly political issue in East Germany, as I'd already found out from my parents. The head of the copy office registered every single sheet copied to prevent politically controversial reading matter being reproduced. We had to apply for copying permission from the supervisor, but this was rarely approved. So, if I wanted to have works by American or British authors to hand, I had to take a different approach and use pre-prepared postcards to order offprints—special editions of these texts—directly from them. If they were Israeli authors, which was often the case with my research subject, I had to go down another route, because East Germany and Israel had no diplomatic relations and there was therefore no postal communication with Israel. In this case, too, I turned to American and British co-workers I knew from conferences in our country, who would send me offprints by Israeli researchers. It was a tiresome process, yet it was always a treat to get mail from the West, immediately recognizable from the stamps, at the Institute. This was how I received not only the articles that were vital for my research, but sometimes a handwritten note about the papers as well—greetings from the free world!

To make copies of our own publications available to others, we used blue carbon paper when we typed up our texts on the typewriter. But if I accidentally put it the wrong way up, I had to type everything out again. That was insufferable, and it happened to me more than once, which was why I often dispensed with the carbon copy.

As I wasn't a travel cadre for the Non-Socialist Economic Area, as it was called at the time, and so wasn't allowed to go to Western countries on business, I was only able to communicate with scientists from there who came to quantum chemistry conferences in East Germany—in Kühlungsborn or Heiligendamm—or in Czechoslovakia or Poland. It was a high point in our working lives when eminent international experts took the time to come and visit us. For one thing, they appreciated the quality of our research, and for another, they knew how happy we were to be in contact with them. It was so exciting for me as a young scientist when I had an opportunity—along with many other scientists—to present my research findings on a poster. We would stand in a large room next to the posters we had made and glued onto sheets of cardboard, waiting eagerly for interested people we could engage in conversation about our subject matter. It was even more exciting if I was allowed to present my work in a brief lecture to top researchers from West Germany, Great Britain, or the US. They expected precise answers to their questions; sometimes I had to speak English, which was an added challenge. And I was so relieved if I'd managed to handle the situation reasonably well.

Personal friendships developed from these encounters, for example with Professor Reinhart Ahlrichs from Karlsruhe in West Germany. Ahlrichs was a quantum chemist who had developed highly acclaimed computational programs for molecular structures with his research group. He was tall and self-assured, and he would light-heartedly question scientific claims as well as social issues. Conversations with him were always inspiring. The same was true of Professor Nick Handy from Cambridge in Great Britain. With his British sense of humor, he was able to demonstrate the absurdity of the East German system with his questions. When I was minister for women and youth in the 1990s, he invited me to his college to talk to the students about my life in the GDR and German reunification.

For many years, the quantum chemists at the Institute worked particularly closely with the J. Heyrovský Institute of Physical Chemistry and Electrochemistry at the Czechoslovak Academy of Sciences in Prague. I had several three-month stays there myself during my doctoral studies. The man at the heart of the collaboration between Prague and the Institute was Professor Rudolf Zahradník, an inspirational character whose career, despite his extraordinary scientific talent, had stalled due to his political involvement in the Prague Spring. At least the state let him carry on with his research at the Academy of Sciences.

Rudolf Zahradník often invited his guests into his home, and I spent some unforgettable evenings with him and his wife Milena. She was very good at telling political jokes. Rudolf Zahradník did everything he could to ensure that the next generation of scientists was comprehensively educated in art and culture even under socialist conditions, and not just in their own field. He insisted on his employees—among them Zdeněk Havlas, with whom I worked most closely—learning German as well as English.

Zahradník's view of socialism's future prospects in the real world was very pragmatic. Once, when I was seriously annoyed about arriving in the Czechoslovak capital several hours late on the Vindobona train, which connected East Berlin with Prague and Vienna, he calmly replied, "Why are you upset? We both know we're part of a great experiment that's bound to fail. It's only the others who don't yet know it." It pleases me enormously to know that this extraordinary person and scientist, almost the same age as my mother, both born in 1928, was able to spend thirty years of his life researching and living in freedom after the end of communism, until his death in 2020.

Increasing disengagement

Częstochowa is a large city in southern Poland. It is world famous for an icon of the Black Madonna; people make a pilgrimage to the Pauline monastery there to see it. I went there once myself during a vacation in Poland: although I'm Protestant, I was very interested to learn that tens of thousands of Catholics in the very religious country of Poland use their vacation to go on a pilgrimage to the Black Madonna. That kind of thing was unimaginable in East Germany. The desire for freedom and independence from the socialist system was much more evident in Poland than it was at home. That fascinated me.

I visited Poland again with a co-worker in the summer of 1981—this time Gdansk, my mother's birthplace. It was a private trip rather than one organized for us, and as soon as we arrived in Gdansk on the night train, we spent the morning in a cinema near the station watching Andrzej Wajda's famous movies *Man of Marble*, from 1977, and *Man of Iron*, which had just been released, one after the other. Although they were shown in Polish, which I don't speak, the atmosphere captivated me, both in the movies and in the auditorium. At the end of the screenings, the Polish audience stood up and applauded for a long time, even though none of the actors were present. They were showing their appreciation for the films' content. I had tears in my eyes.

In Poland, I was also impressed by the fact that many

intellectuals systematically carried on with their education and founded underground universities just for this purpose. They developed the curricula themselves, and it was clearly easier to copy documents there than it was in East Germany. I remember one of my Czechoslovak co-workers once comparing all the socialist states to a military base: "You're the happiest barracks," he told our Polish colleagues. By this he meant the bravest and most determined.

In December 1980, the year Solidarity was founded, a monument was erected in memory of the 1970 strikes at the Lenin Shipyard in Gdansk, which were violently quashed by the Polish army, killing forty-five people according to official figures. During the trip I bought a postcard of the monument, which I wanted to take home with me. On my way back to the GDR, however, I was in trouble when the border guard saw the card.

"This is provocation," she said.

I, on the other hand, insisted: "It's a city view from an allied socialist country."

But I couldn't win the argument. The postcard was taken from me. The incident was reported to the Institute's staffing department; even though I didn't see any consequences, it was a frustrating experience.

During that time, I became increasingly disengaged from the Institute's offerings for academy staff, which included Russian courses, vacation support, or discounted theater tickets. I had built up my own network of stimulating friends and acquaintances. In the early 1980s, in a small group of three or sometimes four people, including "Antarctic Man" and his wife, we read and discussed the book *The Alternative in Eastern Europe* by the East German author Rudolf Bahro, which had been published in 1977. Shortly after an excerpt from it was published in the West German news magazine *Der Spiegel*, Bahro was arrested and sentenced to eight years in prison. After a wave of solidarity in West Germany, he was granted amnesty and left the GDR for the West in 1979. I can't remember how we came across the book, but we probably got it from the West somehow. From what I can recall, I found Bahro's analysis of real-world socialist production conditions captivating and brilliant. I couldn't relate at all, on the other hand, to his ideas for the future, or his suggestion that socialism could be reformed, which seemed completely unrealistic to me. Purely intuitively and without an in-depth understanding of the social market economy, I felt that the West German economic system would be the best guarantee of prosperity for as many people as possible.

Beyond this small private group, the most exciting political discussions were held under the auspices of the Church. As I lived in Schönhauser Allee, I was in the Gethsemane Church's parish. I went to what was known as the "family circle" there, together with Helmut Haberlandt—another co-worker from my department and my former lecturer Reinhold Haberlandt's younger brother—and his wife Rosemarie. Unlike me, the two of them had young children, but the discussions in the circle went far beyond parenting issues. From time to time I also went to events such as the Blues Masses with Rainer Eppelmann, a pastor at the Samaritan Church in Friedrichshain whom I knew from my father's Pastoral College. In his services, the focus was mainly on peace and environmental issues. Here, though, I was in the minority, because I personally believed the Soviet Union arming itself with SS-20 missiles should have had a response from the West, and because later I didn't see the Chernobyl reactor accident as a systemic failure of nuclear power, but as simply a result of Soviet sloppiness. When I attended open events, it was because I believed initiatives critical of the state should be supported at all costs. That was why I went to Robert Havemann's funeral in Grünheide near Berlin in 1982. Robert Havemann was my co-worker Utz Havemann's stepfather; he was a chemist, a staunch communist, and in his later life a critic of the East German regime. I didn't share his socio-political view that what was needed was a reformed socialism, but I admired his courage, and wanted to quietly offer some support with my presence.

In my discussions with other people back then, the question of exactly how society should look didn't predominate. It was more primarily about a show of unity against the East German state. The focus was on what we were *against*. What exactly we wanted to stand up *for* would only come into play later. At the time, we had no idea how soon that would become significant.

In the mid-1980s, my life changed profoundly once again. I became closer to Joachim Sauer, now my husband. We had already known each other on a professional basis, but now it was different. We fell in love. Many years later, he told me he had first become aware of me when he saw my name on the list of the Institute's union leadership members. He wasn't particularly interested in the union or in me at that point, but he had noticed the remark after my name: born in Hamburg, in other words in the West. When one day as chancellor I had to deal with an inquiry from a journalist about my time in a trade union and couldn't remember whether I had been in the Free German Trade Union Federation at the Institute, Joachim immediately knew: "Yes, you were; I saw your name on the list. It said you were born in Hamburg."

Joachim is five years older than me. When he was in his final year at school, the students had to learn a profession as well as studying for their exams. He became a chemical laboratory assistant. He then did chemistry at Humboldt University, where he received a doctorate after his research studies. For political reasons, though, he wasn't offered a permanent position at the university, so he went on to the Academy of Sciences. We both worked at the Institute, both in quantum chemistry, but in different departments. He completed his B doctorate there, equivalent to the habilitation degree now offered in some European countries after a doctorate, and he worked on more complex chemical structures than I did—zeolites, in his case. Joachim, father of two sons from his first marriage, was and still is passionate about the sciences. He was in contact with the Heyrovský Institute in Prague and Professor Rudolf Zahradník long before I was. I was impressed by his clear political analysis, and the joy he took in art and culture, especially in music. We both loved and still love nature and travel. It was through him that I really got to know and understand Richard Wagner's music. With him, I found my way back to academic discipline, at long last.

Buying a home

"Examination of the mechanism of decays with singular bond breaking and calculation of their coefficient of reaction rate on the basis of quantum mechanical and statistical methods": that was the title of my doctoral thesis. I submitted it—finally—in 1985. All doctoral students had what was known as a "perspective plan." Mine had specified that my thesis should be written between 1980 and 1984. I had gone over this time by six months, but it didn't make any difference. I was relieved when the oral examination was finally over on January 8, 1986. Afterward, I celebrated with home-made meatballs, beer, and wine in the basement of the building where we worked, with Joachim and my co-workers from the department and the Institute. I was thirty-one years old.

After I had completed my doctorate I moved to another department in the Institute, where I was the only theoretician. Everyone else was working on experiments with EPR (electron paramagnetic resonance) spectroscopy, and NMR (nuclear magnetic resonance) spectroscopy. I was dealing with more complex chemical reactions than before, but I was able to carry on working closely with my Prague co-worker Zdeněk Havlas. In general, I didn't have as clear a goal in mind for my work as I had during my doctorate. For political reasons, I was never going to be a travel cadre and allowed to visit Western countries; that much was clear to me. And a B doctorate didn't feature in my plans either. I think I was a good scientist, but I was never as fascinated by science as people had to be to achieve the very best results in their basic research. So, when something completely different to do—something more personal—opened up, quite by chance, I welcomed it. I bought a home near Templin, where I had grown up.

In fact, it was my sister who was looking for a place of her own in the Uckermark area where she could relax at weekends, and she wanted to place an ad for one in the local newspaper *Freie Erde*. I asked her to do the same for me, and was curious to see what would come of it. It turned out that we needed permission from the county council's Department of Tourism and Recreation—the local authority. I offered to get it for both of us. However, the woman in charge told me, "I can't give you permission to advertise for something like that: no places will be available anyway." I need to point out here that renting rooms or houses privately wasn't allowed in East Germany. As I was about to leave disappointed, she added, "But you could try in the housing department. You'll have to be prepared to change your main place of residence from Berlin to the Uckermark, though. Otherwise, nothing will come of it." I wasn't averse to that idea, and I was keen to see what that department had to offer.

When I got there, the woman had told them I was coming, and amazingly there was something there for me: that very morning, Neubrandenburg District Council had informed the county council that they had received an application for state liability for a "new farmer's house" in Hohenwalde, a village twenty kilometers from Templin. It meant that the state was liable for the house's loss in value.

The story behind it all was that, after the land reform from 1945 onward, some land and woodland for cultivation and the materials to build a house were given to people formerly employed by large landowners, as well as to the many displaced persons from Eastern and Central Europe in the Soviet occupation zone. These people were called "Neubauern": new farmers. The houses all had roughly the same floor plan. As part of the 1950s forced collectivization, all farmers had to make their land available to the local Landwirtschaftliche Produktionsgenossenschaft (LPG, Agricultural Production Cooperative). In the 1980s, the LPGs were split into two: one for plant production, the other for animal production. If the heirs of a new farmer's house didn't want to use it themselves, they couldn't simply sell it, but had to offer it for sale first to the plant and animal production cooperatives, then to the woodland and forestry management collective. Only once all three had confirmed in writing that they didn't want it could the house be used for other purposes.

This process had already taken two years for the house in question. It was in danger of falling badly into disrepair. The heirs had asked a village resident to represent their interests. The only thing he could think of was to threaten the district council with state liability, as he didn't expect any support from his own county.

And this was where I unwittingly came in, just at the right moment. The county council now wanted to get rid of the property as quickly as possible. I said I was interested and agreed to move my main place of residence from Berlin to the Uckermark. It was unheard of; people didn't do it because you never knew what privileges you might lose if you were no longer a resident of the capital of the GDR. But there was an interest-free loan of twenty thousand East German marks available for extending a private home; the redemption installments were 1 percent per month. On top of this, the various trades—carpenters, joiners, roofers, and plumbers, for instance—had to provide a certain share of their services to homeowners every year, at a very low price set by the state. We would never have been able to take advantage of all these benefits, on which Joachim and I depended given our financial situation, if it had only been a second home for weekends.

The house itself was in a beautiful location, but a truly pitiful condition. I don't want to go into the details here, but suffice it to say that Joachim and I decided to take the plunge. It needed a great deal of personal commitment. Once again, I was learning something completely new: how to organize construction work in a scarcity economy—a thoroughly practical task that was a total contrast to my theoretical work at the Academy. The modernization work dragged on until the demise of the GDR, but the timing of the house purchase was perfect, as my doctorate was finished and I had more time on my hands. After German reunification, our house in the countryside became a retreat for us. I can't imagine how I would have managed a thirty-year political career without that little refuge. Plus, I had, at least in part, gone back to my homeland. I was at home in the Uckermark.

Travels to the West

In 1987 the time had come: for the first time since the Wall was built twenty-six years earlier, I was allowed to set foot in Hamburg again. My first trip to the West had been approved. The occasion was my cousin's marriage; the permit to attend the wedding was, from what I can remember, valid for seven days in total. But before I go into more detail, I'll explain a little so it might be easier to understand the times back then. In 1983 and 1984, East Germany received two billion deutsche marks in loans from the Federal Republic, which were managed by West German banking consortia. Franz Josef Strauss, the premier of Bavaria and CSU leader at the time, played a crucial role in the planning of these cash injections. The provision of the loans was very controversial, both in East and West Germany. Did the loans help an economically foundering GDR, as some people thought, thereby indirectly consolidating Germany's division by supporting the state? Or were the trade-offs demanded of East Germany—among other things, dismantling automatic firing systems and easing travel restrictions in both directions—a way of weakening the system from within, as others argued? I tended to favor this second point of view. Until then, only first-degree relatives were able to travel from the GDR to West Germany on certain occasions. Now it also became possible for second- and third-degree relatives to attend family events. The number of people allowed to travel to the West rose sharply after that, and in 1987, I was one of them.

My mother, my sister, and I each received a travel permit, while my brother and father stayed at home. East Germany always took great care to ensure that entire families never went to the West together: the state authorities judged the risk of defection to be too high. But now, at least my mother, my sister, and I were allowed to travel to the same place at the same time.

As well as the trip to Hamburg for my cousin's wedding, I had something else in mind as well. I was only able to put this plan into action once I arrived there, however. I left East Berlin via Friedrichstrasse station toward West Berlin. At last, I didn't just hear the guard dogs; I could go over to the other side of the station myself. I was nervous, curious, and incredibly excited about what was awaiting me. I had arranged to leave for Hamburg from Zoologischer Garten station in such a way that I could spend some time in West Berlin for the first time since I rushed from Pankow to the French sector and back a few days before the Wall was built, holding my grandmother's hand while she bought cigarettes. I traveled to Kottbusser Tor in Kreuzberg, as it was quite close to my daily S-Bahn route, and I wanted to see what it was like. I noticed that the area was very Turkish. But aside from that, I found it striking that the houses and the streetscape were more colorful and there were more cars than back at home, but in other respects there was not the slightest doubt that it was one and the same city, on both sides of the Oberbaum Bridge border crossing.

Armed with this certainty, I went back to Zoologischer Garten station and boarded the train to Hamburg Dammtor. My aunt picked me up from there, and we drove to her house in Blankenese. We celebrated the eve of the wedding in the garden. I met many friends of my aunt's family: friends I only knew from stories. The church wedding and the lunch afterward took place in the city's rural outskirts. The Western guests were quite awed by me and my sister, and we were awed by the elegance of Blankenese, the parks along the Elbchaussee, the stores, and the majestically flowing river Elbe. Strange though the circumstances were to my sister and me, we were familiar with my aunt's clan, thanks to their many visits to us in Templin.

After the wedding, I immediately began to work on the second part of my first trip to the West: I wanted to visit Professor Ahlrichs, whom I had met at conferences in East Germany as I mentioned earlier, at his home in Karlsruhe. I also planned to visit a scientist from my department who had fled to the West and now lived in Konstanz. I was only able to start the concrete planning for this venture now, in Hamburg. If my intentions had been detected beforehand, my time in the West would have been curtailed at the very least, or the entire trip might have been forbidden. My maternal grandmother had died in 1978; my mother was able to access her inheritance from an account in Hamburg, and she supported me financially for the second part of the trip.

It was a little adventure for me. I suddenly realized I had no concept of daily life in the Western part of Germany. My knowledge of the Federal Republic came mainly from West German television. I wasn't even sure if I was safe staying in a hotel as a woman traveling alone—a silly thought, I now know, but at the time I had no idea. I had stayed in Budapest, Bucharest, the Caucasus, and all manner of other places without anything happening to me.

And something else I spotted in passing bothered me a great deal. I took the Intercity train from Hamburg to Karlsruhe—in my eyes, a marvel of technology and design. I was thrilled. To my horror, though, some of the West German students in the carriage simply put their feet up, leaving their dirty shoes on the elegant upholstery. I found it outrageous. I had never seen behavior like that in the GDR.

In Karlsruhe, I had a warm welcome from the Ahlrichs family. They let me stay in their home, we took a trip to the nearby Black Forest, and I visited Ahlrichs's institute at the university.

In Konstanz, I had to go it alone. I stayed in a small hotel and was impressed by the lakeside city's southern charm. I met my old co-worker for lunch and passed on messages from his former fellow campaigners from the Academy. After fleeing East Germany, he had found opportunities to work in sciences in Konstanz, which was a great relief to him.

Impressed and fulfilled, I finally returned home via Hamburg, as I had to exit and re-enter East Germany from the same place. Staying in the Federal Republic was not an option for me. Joachim was in the GDR, as were my family and most of my friends. I also had the feeling it wouldn't be another twenty-six years before I could visit the West again.

And I was right: at the end of October 1989 it was the eighty-fifth birthday of my great-aunt Emmy, the last surviving sister of my Hamburg grandmother. Once again I received a travel permit. A lot had changed in East Germany in the previous three years. Ever since Mikhail Gorbachev had become general secretary of the Communist Party of the Soviet Union in 1985 and the buzzwords "glasnost" and "perestroika" had been on everyone's lips, events were set in motion throughout the Eastern Bloc.

In the GDR, local elections had been held in the spring of 1989. Through the dedication of courageous election observers, it came to light that the state had grossly falsified the election results. In the summer and autumn, thousands and thousands of people left East Germany via Hungary. On September 11, 1989, the Hungary–Austria border was opened—a brave decision by the Hungarian Party leadership. After that, all the events happened in quick succession. On September 30, the West German foreign minister Hans-Dietrich Genscher told GDR citizens seeking asylum on the Federal Republic's embassy premises in Prague that they were allowed to leave for West Germany. Also in September, civil rights movements were founded in East Germany: Neues Forum (New Forum) and Demokratie Jetzt (Democracy Now), followed on October 1 by Demokratischer Aufbruch (DA, Democratic Awakening), and on October 7 the Sozialdemokratische Partei in der DDR (the Social Democratic Party in the GDR, then known as SDP). East Germany's fortieth anniversary on October 7 turned out to be a fiasco for the Party leadership, not least due to the legendary quote attributed to Mikhail Gorbachev, "Life punishes those who come too late," a truly poisoned chalice of a birthday present for Erich Honecker's GDR leadership. In the light of all these events, people gained the courage to show their opposition to the state openly.

When I returned to Schönhauser Allee in Berlin on October

8, 1989, after a weekend visit to Templin, the city was completely changed. There were armored personnel carriers in the deserted streets, the Gethsemane Church was open for prayers, candles were burning in the windows, and tram drivers even lit them in their cabs. They were the lights of the Peaceful Revolution. Images of the scenes were sent around the world, followed by pictures of the largest yet Monday demonstration in Leipzig the next day, October 9, 1989. There was an incredible tension in the air. But the ruling regime did not use violence. Very clearly, there was no order from Moscow, in total contrast to the popular uprising of June 17, 1953, or the ones in 1956 in Hungary, and in Czechoslovakia in 1968, or the enforcement of martial law in Poland in 1981.

Aunt Emmy's birthday was on October 27. I was allowed to stay in West Germany until November 5. After the party in Hamburg I immediately traveled on to Karlsruhe. Unlike the first time I traveled, this time Joachim was staying there too, for a few weeks of research with Professor Ahlrichs. Like an increasing number of co-workers, he had been allowed to travel to the West for professional purposes since the end of 1988, a move by East Germany to prevent more and more scientists leaving. His stay in Karlsruhe was also no longer an obstacle to me receiving my travel permit. Something had dramatically changed.

Apart from Joachim, Professor Gerhard Öhlmann, the director of our institute—and, of course, an SED member—also happened to be a guest there. He didn't object to my surprise appearance in Karlsruhe. We had dinner together with Professor Ahlrichs and all four of us discussed the situation. Even now, I can still hear myself saying, "I don't understand why the local election results were falsified." Professor Öhlmann didn't question this, replying, "I don't understand it either—even a result of 80 percent would be a good outcome." I asked, "And what if it were only 51 percent?" To stay on the safe side, I avoided mentioning a result of less than 50 percent. Öhlmann shot back, "That's not going to happen!" We changed the subject.

I returned home on November 5, 1989. The day before, hundreds of thousands of people had taken part in a demonstration in Berlin. There was a buzz throughout the country, and great changes were on the horizon. It was scarcely possible to concentrate on scientific work anymore.

After a day at work, the first thing I usually did when I got home was listen to the news. That was what I did on Thursday, November 9, 1989. I heard Günter Schabowski's words about travel restrictions being lifted, and couldn't believe my ears. I immediately called my mother in Templin and said, "Have you heard the news? Soon we'll be able to go to West Berlin and eat oysters at the Kempinski." This had long been our standing phrase for a time when the Wall no longer existed. Neither of us expected to bear witness to it soon, though.

"What?! I haven't heard a thing," my mother replied.

"Well, turn on the TV!" I shouted down the phone to her.

After I hung up, I grabbed my sauna bag as I did every Thursday, picked up my friend Rosemarie Haberlandt from Dunckerstrasse as usual, and went to the sauna at the Ernst Thälmann Park swimming pool with her. There, too, Schabowski's words were the hot topic, but not everyone saw the prospect of the Wall opening in as positive a light. Some people, especially in that residential area, had come to terms with life in East Germany and had little desire for change. After the sauna, Rosemarie and I went to a bar nearby, as we did every week, and we drank a beer while the radio reported that people were streaming into the West. The atmosphere was no different from usual; the people who wanted to go to the West simply weren't there. We soon left the bar. My friend went home to her young children, while I made my way to the West.

When I reached the corner of Schönhauser Allee and

Bornholmer Strasse, I saw legions of people walking toward Bösebrücke. I joined the procession, my sauna bag in my hand.

Twenty years later, in the summer of 2009, I was at the Chancellery making a campaign commercial for the Bundestag elections on September 27. I was standing for re-election after being voted in as chancellor of the Federal Republic of Germany for the first time in 2005. At the beginning of the ad, I was looking out of the window from my office toward the Reichstag. The scene was interspersed with stock images of people cheering and standing on the Berlin Wall in 1989, trying to tear it down with picks and chisels. The viewers hear me saying, "I wasn't born chancellor." It was a truly banal opener. Yet, at the same time, I felt it seemed to sum up something incredible. In any case, the sentence didn't flow from my lips nearly as easily as it sounded in the TV commercial. My first attempt was cut. We hired a recording studio. Over and over, I uttered those four words, trying to give them the right emphasis. "I wasn't born CHANCELLOR," "I WASN'T born chancellor," "I wasn't BORN chancellor," until I finally managed it: "I wasn't born chancellor."

What seemed so incredible to me was that there was no equivalent to the word "chancellor" in East Germany. Chancellor: that was the head of government's name in a different nation, the Federal Republic of Germany, whose citizenship I would have been free to acquire at any point had I managed to get there, but which I had been unable to visit for decades.

I had grown up in a country where, on November 9, 1989, its own population, with great help from the people in other socialist Warsaw Pact countries at the time, had brought down the Wall. Here I had grown up; here I had tried to skirt around the obstacles set up everywhere by the state, like a skier on a slalom run. I had tried to make the best of the situation, always to remain curious and enterprising, to do no one any harm, and to push myself to the limits of my capabilities wherever possible.

I knew the parameters inside out. I had been very lucky. When the Wall came down, I was thirty-five years old, still young enough to start afresh. I had no idea exactly how things would unfold. But one thing was beyond doubt for me: East Germany's structure could not be reformed from within. It was like a cardigan: if you fasten the first button incorrectly, you always need to start all over again to be able to do it up properly. And the GDR's first button was fastened incorrectly. That was my firm belief.

PART TWO

A Democratic Awakening

November 10, 1989 to December 2, 1990

UNITY AND JUSTICE
AND FREEDOM

Mixed feelings

BERLIN, A SUNNY day, blue sky, Wednesday, October 3, 1990, around 10:15 in the morning. I still had some time before the German reunification ceremony was due to begin in the Berliner Philharmonie at eleven o'clock. I stood off to one side, about seventy meters from the Philharmonie entrance, watching people arrive. A heady seventy-two hours lay behind me. On Monday, October 1, I not only spoke to Helmut Kohl face-to-face for the first time at the Eastern and Western CDU's unification party conference in Hamburg, but also as a new member of the Eastern CDU, having come from Democratic Awakening and becoming a member of the all-German CDU at that party conference, I gave a short speech to the thousand or so delegates. In it, I outlined the guiding principles of DA, a party that no longer existed, in the following few sentences:

> [. . .] For us, it was crucial to create a socially and ecologically oriented market economy and to complete the reunification of the German nation as quickly as possible. With this ethos, we found friends in the Allianz für Deutschland, and the Volkskammer elections went well for us. Our merger has been an expression of this ethos too: Democratic Awakening's merger with the CDU.
>
> However, we do not want the idea of a new awakening

to be lost in our ongoing political work. And so, we'd like to maintain a Democratic Awakening working group within the all-German CDU. We do not want to isolate ourselves, however; we invite you all to collaborate with us in this working group. I would like to mention two things that will be important to us in what we do.

The first is the reappraisal of our own history: this is the only way we can learn to actively shape democracy.

The second is that we want to maintain contact with our political friends in Eastern Europe. We have learned a lot from them in recent years. They have helped us enormously. Even in a united Germany, we must not forget that Europe does not end at Germany's eastern border. We must not lose sight of other nations' problems.

Dear friends, today we founded the all-German CDU. However, I believe the process of unification is not yet over. We need to share our experiences and our life stories with each other.

The DA working group was set up, but it soon disappeared into oblivion; later on, though, its ideas proved to be important.

After the party conference finished on Tuesday, October 2, I left Hamburg and went back to Berlin, to my workplace in the GDR prime minister's official residence in the Alte Stadthaus on Molkenmarkt. I had been deputy government spokesperson since April. In the late afternoon, I received my letter of dismissal, signed by East Germany's prime minister, Maizière. At 9:00 p.m., I took part in the ceremony our government—a thing of the past three hours later—was hosting at the Schauspielhaus on Gendarmenmarkt. I had a seat off to one side. Beethoven's Ninth Symphony rang out: "Freude, schöner Götterfunken (Joy, beautiful spark of divinity)." Lothar de Maizière stepped up to a lectern and, in a short speech on behalf of all the members of the government, declared our work to be over.

Despite our unbridled joy about German reunification, tears sprang to my eyes at that moment. Valedictory tears, albeit long awaited, and undoubtedly tears of exhaustion too. Gone was the post of deputy government spokesperson, into which I had put my heart and soul. Since our government had come into being, on April 12, 1990, we had worked with great passion for 174 days and nights to make ourselves systematically redundant, paving the way for German reunification. I was relieved when the ceremony was over.

I quickly went home and then set off with Joachim for the high point of the day at the Reichstag. The leading representatives of both German states gathered on the steps of the west wing. Joachim and I were allowed to join them, even as such small fry. My downbeat mood was gone. It was very moving; hundreds of thousands of people had gathered in front of the building. At midnight, the black, red, and gold German flag was raised to mark German unity. From Schöneberg in West Berlin, the peal of the Freedom Bell was broadcast in the square in front of the Reichstag. A replica of the famous Liberty Bell in Philadelphia, financed in large part by donations from Americans, this bell had hung in Schöneberg's town hall since October 1950. To this day, it bears the inscription "That this world under God shall have a new birth of freedom," echoing President Abraham Lincoln's Gettysburg Address in 1863, at the turning point in the American Civil War. The inscription had become reality for us, too. The GDR was history. There was only one German state now. I was a citizen of the Federal Republic. That Tuesday night leading to Wednesday, October 3, was a short one. All trace of melancholy had fled; all that remained was pure joy about what we had achieved and eager anticipation of what the future would bring in a united Germany.

———

Now though, a good forty-five minutes before the ceremony was due to begin, I stood happily to one side of the entrance to the Philharmonie and let my gaze wander. I wanted to savor this moment. Suddenly, I saw a police officer on duty there: a somewhat stocky middle-aged man, probably between fifty and sixty. Our eyes met. It immediately became clear to me that, until barely twelve hours before, this police officer must have been a member of the East German police: a Volkspolizist. It was obvious from his slightly suspicious and maybe even insecure expression, and his stiff, almost military movements. But now he was wearing a West Berlin police uniform. I was taken aback and needed a moment to take it all in: this GDR official had become a police officer for the federal state of Berlin overnight. The infamous Volkspolizei no longer existed. In my mind's eye, I could see images of various encounters with the GDR's armed organs, as they were known—and the Volkspolizei among them. From one day to the next, though, every single Volkspolizist, including the one I could see there outside the Philharmonie, was now responsible for enforcing state power in the constitutional state of the Federal Republic of Germany. What a difference to the police officer's remit in East Germany— and yet still one and the same person. That brief eye contact at that moment suddenly revealed to me the immensity of the task that lay ahead of us: to truly live together as a united Germany.

As I was lost in my thoughts outside, I ran into Peter Klemm, the deputy minister from the Federal Ministry of Finance. "How lovely to see you!" he called out cheerily. We knew each other from the Unification Treaty negotiations. On the spur of the moment, I told him about seeing the former Volkspolizist in Western uniform and ended by saying, "You've probably often thought about how much work we from the East are making for you, but let me tell you: this was just the start, you can be sure of that. Today is just the beginning of German reunification."

"Oh, it'll be fine. Today we're celebrating," Klemm replied.

I wasn't sure he'd understood what had moved me.

For over thirty years, until the very last day I held any political responsibility, I would be haunted by the question of when and how German reunification might actually be complete.

But for now, I went to the ceremony in the Philharmonie, and afterward I wandered through the streets of Berlin with Joachim. The weather was glorious. Hundreds of thousands of people were out in the streets. We were in high spirits, certain that we were witnessing a once-in-a-lifetime experience, just 327 days after the Wall came down on November 9, 1989—not even a year later.

First political steps

On the first weekend after the Wall opened, I was invited to a birthday party in my neighborhood. To my horror, the mood there was gloomy. Most of the guests felt the dream of an autonomous "third way" for East Germany was now dead: "What we ought to do now is seize the opportunity and draft a new constitution," one neighbor said.

"But what will happen instead? The only thing people are going to be interested in is consumption—they'll be happy enough if they get some bananas and jeans," complained another guest.

I couldn't believe it: it couldn't be true. How could they be moping now?

"Oh, come on!" I exclaimed. "It's great that the Wall is open at last. Everything else will become clear, but it's just fabulous right now!" But I couldn't infect anyone with my good cheer.

The next few days were very different. On Monday, November 13, 1989, I went to Poland; for months I'd been planning a lecture I would be giving to some scientists in Toruń that we quantum chemists from the Institute were working with. This was why I'd gone back home to East Berlin before midnight on November 9, against the flow of people. But despite all my good intentions, I could scarcely concentrate on writing my lecture. I didn't want to cancel the trip either, though. So I sat on the train, poorly prepared but looking forward to meeting my Polish colleagues.

One of them picked me up at the station. We spoke English to each other, and he said, "I can tell you're German—what a sense of duty! After events like that, no Pole would have left for another country just four days later."

It was wonderful to be greeted like that. I replied, "I certainly wouldn't have gone just anywhere, but Poland's one place I'd always come to!" We both laughed, and I added, "But I have to warn you, I'm pitifully ill-prepared to give the lecture."

"Oh, that doesn't matter. We're just glad you're here at all. Tell us about Berlin!" the scientist said. "And next time we come to Berlin, Germany will be a united country!"

I couldn't believe what he was saying, just four days after the Wall had come down, but my Polish colleague insisted: "Yes, believe me, the next time we're in Berlin, Germany will be reunified." My look of surprise couldn't sway him from his convictions.

He invited me to his home for dinner with his wife, where we carried on the conversation. I stayed in Toruń for four days, and gave my lecture, but I have no other memories of it— neither of the lecture nor the discussion of it. Science scarcely featured at all during those few days. Politics was all we talked about the whole time.

Once again, Poland itself had been one step ahead of us with its political developments: back in June 1989 the country had held partially free elections to the Sejm, the parliament, and the upper house, the Senate. For the elections to the Sejm, in accordance with an agreement by the Polish Round Table, 65 percent of the seats were reserved for candidates of the Polish United Workers' Party, which had been in power until then, and 35 percent of the seats were open to candidates labeled as "independent." The independent seats were won by candidates from the trade union Solidarność, as were ninety-nine of the hundred seats in the Senate, all of which were included in the free election. Many of my Polish co-workers were overjoyed at these election results. I had experienced that in person, because when the results were announced I was also in Poland, at a quantum chemistry conference in Bachotek, eighty kilometers east of Toruń.

And now, just a few months later, my Polish friends were rejoicing with me about what had happened at home, as if it had been in their country. Even now I still get goosebumps when I think about it and remember how happy I was to have gone there.

Elated, I returned to Berlin on November 16, a Thursday. The next day, I told my co-workers at the Academy about my Polish colleague's prediction. We discussed whether he might be right and whether Germany could be reunified as quickly as he thought. Of course, none of us had any clear idea what was going to happen next, but after in-depth discussion, it became clear to us that the subject of a quick reunification would be on the agenda for the foreseeable future. We had few illusions about East Germany's economic situation. An old East German joke from the 1960s came to mind: The chairman of the State Council, Walter Ulbricht, is sitting in his armchair with his lover on his lap, and asks her if she has a wish. She asks him to open up the Wall, to which Ulbricht gleefully replies, "Oh darling, you want the two of us to be all alone?" This joke had a timeless truth to it, as we had seen so strikingly in the summer and fall of 1989. For this reason alone, it was very likely that a path toward rapid reunification had to be found.

In fact, the changes took place at breathtaking speed: on November 13, 1989, the day I left for Toruń, Hans Modrow, previously First Secretary of the SED Dresden district leadership, succeeded Willi Stoph as chairman of the Council of Ministers, leader of the East German government. Weeks earlier, on October 18, Erich Honecker had been replaced by Egon Krenz, first as the SED's general secretary, and from October 24 also as chairman of the State Council and National Defense Council of the GDR. While still Honecker's deputy, Krenz had previously distinguished himself during a trip to China for the fortieth anniversary of the People's Republic by openly supporting the massacre of the Chinese students protesting in Beijing's Tiananmen Square in June 1989. Because of this, he had heightened our fear of what we called a "Chinese solution" to the Peaceful Revolution. Fortunately, things turned out differently, and fortunately too, Krenz's tenure as chairman of the State Council would be an extremely short episode in the GDR's final phase.

Chancellor Helmut Kohl, on the other hand, had sensed and recognized the zeitgeist with an uncanny certainty. On November 16, 1989, the day I came back from Toruń and exactly one week after the Wall had opened up, he made it clear that the Federal Republic was prepared to provide economic aid, but only if East Germany made changes to its economic system. On November 28, just twelve days later, in a speech delivered during budget debates in the West German Bundestag, he presented a ten-point plan that was downright sensational at the time; in its fifth point he declared his willingness to "develop confederate structures between the two states in Germany with the objective of creating a federation, in other words a federal order in Germany." Kohl then said, though, that this absolutely presupposed "a democratically legitimized government in the

GDR." In the tenth point, the chancellor emphasized that "Reunification—that is, regaining Germany's state unity—remains the political aim of the federal government." As Horst Teltschik, Kohl's foreign and security policy advisor until the end of 1990, describes in his 1991 book *329 Tage. Innenansichten der Einigung* (329 Days. Views of Reunification from the Inside), Helmut Kohl had only involved a very few people when he was developing his plan. He had spoken about it to the CDU Presidium and the Federal Board on the day before the speech, but had neglected to inform his coalition partners, the FDP. Only the White House had received his draft in writing a few hours before he made his speech. My view is that Kohl took this approach as he didn't want to take the slightest risk of skeptics thwarting his vision, or of losing the element of surprise, even in the face of his opponents. To be sure of having an effect, he was prepared to present a fait accompli. To me, what Kohl did is an inspiring example of a chancellor's often-discussed authority to decide policy: following one's own moral compass in certain situations and genuinely assuming ultimate political responsibility.

On December 3, 1989, the entire SED leadership resigned, and then Egon Krenz stood down as chairman of the State Council on December 6, 1989. On the same day, the Volkskammer elected Manfred Gerlach, a member of the Liberal-Demokratische Partei Deutschlands (LDPD, Liberal Democratic Party of Germany), as the new head of state. Less than a month after the Wall came down, the rule of the party of the working class, the SED, was a thing of the past. The system that had been in place quite simply collapsed. In those few days, new parties had already been formed or were coming into being. On December 7, 1989, the Zentrale Runde Tisch (Central Round Table) met for the first time in the Bonhoeffer House in Berlin. It included representatives from the government, from large SED organizations such as the FDJ and the Society for

German–Soviet Friendship, and from bloc parties, opposition groups, and new parties, as well as the churches. From then on, the Central Round Table took all the major political decisions and paved the way for the first free Volkskammer elections.

But that was still a long way off, and I didn't really have a sense of what it would all mean for me personally. There was just one thing I did know for sure: I felt electrified by the developments. I was convinced: something new was emerging here, it was something I wanted to be part of, I was needed now, with my experiences, with my life, with my skills, and with what mattered to me.

On the last weekend in November, I visited Joachim in Karlsruhe. Both while I was there and after he had returned to Berlin in mid-December, we spoke almost non-stop about the future of East Germany. We wanted to play a part in the coming changes and were on the lookout for emerging political forces to support. Joachim was clear that he wanted to use our newfound freedoms and the removal of the old barriers to make progress with his scientific research. He had already flown out from Karlsruhe to the United States to visit a San Diego-based company called BIOSYM Technologies. He was determined to do what he could to eliminate the anti-scientific structures that had held sway in East Germany. My plan was to get involved in politics, and I had Joachim's backing. While he continued to focus on science, I was eager to help some fresh faces to change the political landscape. That took care of the *Do I or don't I?* question, but I still had to decide *how* and *where*. I started investigating.

I wanted to join a party, but it had to be a newly established one. By happy coincidence, Klaus Ulbricht, the head of my team at the Institute, was on the same wavelength. So the two of us went to an event in the Treptow district of Berlin organized by the East German branch of the SPD; this was probably sometime in late November, although I couldn't give a precise date. As far as I remember, the meeting was mainly about reforming local politics, and there was little discussion of German reunification.

Klaus Ulbricht was enthusiastic about the SPD and decided to join. He went on to serve as mayor of Treptow-Köpenick from 1992 to 2006. I told him, "I'm not so sure. They're not the right fit for me. I'd like to look around a bit, find out some more about other parties." He sympathized with my position. "That's what's so new—all this diversity. And it's great if the two of us can set an example by our choices." I took heart from this conversation, which was, remember, a conversation between a boss and his colleague. This was the new era we were entering. I went on with my search.

I can't remember who first told me about Demokratischer Aufbruch (Democratic Awakening, DA). It might have been my brother or maybe his friend Günter Nooke, who served as a member of the Brandenburg state legislature for a period and was also a representative in the Bundestag. What I most definitely recall, though, is that what I heard about DA immediately caught my attention. And so it was that in early December 1989 I arrived at DA's headquarters at 12/13 Marienburger Strasse in the Prenzlauer Berg area of Berlin.

DA had been founded on October 1, 1989, as a coalition of existing political groups. The Stasi were desperate to prevent its establishment so close to the fortieth anniversary of the founding of the East German state. Approximately eighty civil rights activists had initially met at the Samaritan Church in East Berlin and then decided to go to the home of the theologian Ehrhart Neubert, who lived in what was then Wilhelm Pieck Strasse and is now Torstrasse. The Stasi had got wind of this arrangement and surrounded the entrance of the building, so only seventeen actually made it into Neubert's apartment. These seventeen people, including Günter Nooke, founded DA, the aim of which at the time—this was before the Wall came down—was a democratic recasting of socialism.

When I first encountered DA in December 1989, its members were in the midst of final preparations to transform it from a movement into a new party. Its inaugural conference was held on December 16–17 in Leipzig. The party's Berlin headquarters were a hive of activity. It was Günter Nooke himself who recognized me and gave me a friendly welcome. "Is there any way I can help?" I asked.

"If you feel like getting involved politically," he replied, "then come along to the meetings at 47 Christburger Strasse. We meet at the People's Solidarity premises there. You can give us a hand here first, though. See those boxes back there? Those are computers. Donated by the West. Could you unpack them and set them up?"

"Of course, no problem," I said and got straight to work. The Academy was no longer keeping close tabs on our working hours so I had time to spare.

On one of my first days in Marienburger Strasse I got to know Hans-Christian Maass, the then spokesperson of the West German ministry for international development, who was visiting DA's offices with his boss, Jürgen Warnke.

Maass, a man of imposing height, looked around the place and called out to me, "What's this mess? And what are you doing here? Are you part of the team?"

"No, I'm from the Academy," I replied, but obviously so timidly that he didn't hear properly and shouted back, "From *what*?"

"The Academy of Sciences," I answered a little more decisively. "I'm unpacking computers."

"OK, well get on with it!" he cried.

Despite his gruff or even bossy tone, over time I grew confident that his heart was in the right place. He seemed genuinely interested.

"Are you here all the time?" he asked.

"No, I have to go back to work tomorrow," I explained.

It turned out that Hans-Christian Maass, who was born in 1950 and whose father was a pastor like mine, had grown up in East Germany and made a failed escape bid in the 1970s. He was jailed and eventually freed after West Germany paid a ransom. He worked in adult education and other departments at the culture ministry of the state of Lower Saxony before joining the West German civil service.

Back then, in 1989, I occasionally sensed that he would have dearly loved to swap places with me and the others. Very quickly I got the feeling that this was a kind of homecoming for him. He had a flair for detecting historic, unprecedented opportunities in the period after the Wall came down. Maass taught us the basic rules of public relations and communication, as well as explaining the structure of the Federal Republic, its parties, the Bundestag and the Bundesrat, and much more besides. He ran a weekend seminar on these topics at the Hermann Ehlers Akademie in Knesebeckstrasse in West Berlin, and I was one of the few people who attended it. It was a crash course for political novices. Neither of us could have imagined that our paths would cross again later in very different circumstances. Hans-Christian Maass and I remain in touch to this day.

The DA conference in Leipzig elected Wolfgang Schnur from Rostock as party chair, mainly because he wasn't a theologian like most DA members but a lawyer. The conference also approved a manifesto entitled *Democratic Awakening—the Social and Environmental Party for Freedom, Justice, and Solidarity*. Before, during, and after the conference, however, there were discussions about the party's principles and its political direction. Did we want swift German unification and a rapprochement with the policies of the CDU in the West? Or should we take an independent path based on reformed socialism with a longer-term goal of unifying the two German states? These were the two main issues up for debate.

For context, we need to remind ourselves of the general political situation. On December 19, 1989, two days after the DA conference, Chancellor Helmut Kohl went to Dresden to meet the chairman of the East German Council of Ministers, Hans Modrow. Together they signed a memorandum of under-standing for a treaty community between the two German states. Afterward, Helmut Kohl spoke in front of Dresden's ruined Frauenkirche. Thousands had gathered to listen, and I watched the speech on television in Berlin.

"My goal, if this historic hour allows it, remains the unity of our nation," Helmut Kohl declared to the crowd. I was instantly reminded of his words in a public after-dinner speech two years earlier, on September 7, 1987, during Erich Honecker's state visit to Bonn: "The preamble of our constitution is not negotiable because it represents our conviction. With a view to a united Europe, it calls upon the entire German people to achieve in free self-determination the unity and freedom of Germany."

Back in 1987, Kohl had added that this was "not yet on the agenda of world history," but now, a little over two years later, the crowds in Dresden were chanting, "Unity, unity, unity!" They could not have made their point any more powerfully or more resolutely. The unity of Germany *was* on the agenda now; indeed, it had risen to the very top of it. This realization made me shiver.

I celebrated Christmas and New Year's Eve 1989 with Joachim in Hohenwalde and visited my family in Templin. There, too, the question of where East Germany was heading was on every-one's lips. My father had been active locally in the Church's peace initiatives throughout the autumn. He advocated a radical reform of East German society and was also present when the Stasi in Templin was disbanded. Although a member of neither, my father told us that he enthusiastically supported the opposition movements Demokratie Jetzt (Democracy Now) and Neues Forum (New Forum). He disapproved of the idea of speedy German unification. My brother took a similar stance and was briefly a member of Bündnis 90 (Alliance 90). My sister was active in the East German branch of the SPD for a while, and my mother also liked their policies. After German unification, my mother joined the all-German SPD and discovered a passion for local politics. She stood successfully for the local council and was elected chair of the new Templin district council from 1990 to 1994—a belated confirmation of her standing in the community. During that period, my mind would occasionally replay my mother's indignant words shortly before my final school exams in 1973. We were, as ever, a distinctly political and opinionated family.

When I returned from my Christmas holidays, I became engrossed in the battle to determine DA's future direction. I attended the meetings in Christburger Strasse and listened intently to both sides of the debate, which revolved around two fundamental questions. One camp, which included many of DA's founding members, insisted: "We cannot just adopt everything from the Federal Republic or merge with it just like that. We have to take advantage of this historic moment and use it to forge our own path. To do that we need a new constitution." The other argued, "This is no time for hesitation. The East German economy is broken beyond repair, so DA has to campaign for rapid reunification and the adoption of the West German model of social capitalism."

I silently agreed with the second position. I believed that events had now brought matters to a head. The East German state couldn't be reformed: it needed rebuilding from the ground up. It was illusory to believe that a third way was possible, nor did I see any reason why West Germany should have to start afresh.

In early January 1990, the proponents of a rapid process of German unification carried the day and, as a result, the defeated minority left DA and joined other opposition groups. This cleared the way for DA to align its manifesto with that of the West German CDU. On January 23, 1990, I was elected spokesperson for DA's Berlin branch. I had no recollection of the exact date, to be honest, and found it only while studying old newspaper reports for this book. It must be correct, though, because there are photos of me representing the Berlin branch at the subsequent signing of the agreement for the coalition "Allianz für Deutschland" (Alliance for Germany).

Equal opportunities between existing and newly founded parties were a major issue in preparations for the Volkskammer elections. In December 1989, the Central Round Table, which brought together political parties and civil society organizations as a forum for consultation with Hans Modrow's transitional government, had demanded that citizens' movements should receive a minimum level of office space and technical support. As a result, the Council of Ministers had agreed to let these movements work out of the building at 165 Friedrichstrasse previously used by the Berlin-Mitte branch of the SED. This building was renamed Haus der Demokratie (House of Democracy). DA also moved into these premises, which provided a significantly better working environment than our previous headquarters in Marienburger Strasse.

On January 28, it was announced that the first free elections in East Germany's history would be held on March 18, 1990. I took this opportunity to request unpaid leave from the Academy, so I could play a part in the DA campaign, and so on Thursday, February 1, 1990, I officially started working for DA at the House of Democracy. I didn't know it then, but Wednesday, January 31,

1990 was to be my last normal working day at the Central Institute for Physical Chemistry. I would only return there once more to clear my desk.

A special election campaign

The impression I got on my first day at the House of Democracy was that DA was still running a fairly chaotic operation. By now there were, admittedly, somewhere between ten and fifteen full-time employees, galvanized by a great deal of goodwill. Many West Germans had come to lend a hand. The priority was to organize the campaign, but someone also had to respond to inquiries from the national media and the foreign press. I could discern no proper organizational hierarchy, however, and there were only forty-six days remaining until the elections. Most issues were dealt with by shouting across the open-plan office. I found this way of working inefficient.

It was unsurprising, therefore, when a major problem cropped up on only my third day at work. Wolfgang Schnur had agreed to two separate meetings in the same time slot. One was a briefing for a group of Western journalists who wanted to know more about DA; I can't remember the purpose or the subject of the other. All I know is that the two appointments clashed, time was short, and various people were bending Schnur's ear to attend one and not the other. He couldn't make up his mind and instead spent precious minutes trying to figure out who was responsible for the mix-up.

I happened to overhear the drama. Judging that the meeting with the journalists was important, I offered some unsolicited advice. "You ought to meet the journalists or it'll damage DA's reputation."

He replied somewhat curtly, "Well, you do it then."

Staring at him in disbelief, I asked, "How's that going to

work? I can't just walk in there. They're experienced, well-known journalists. If I start making political statements, they're going to feel that we're taking them for fools."

After a second's thought, Schnur said, "I hereby appoint you DA spokesperson."

My jaw almost hit the floor. It was a completely different thing to speak for the national party rather than for the Berlin branch. Yet everyone who had heard Schnur's decision agreed—they were glad the problem had been solved. The actual spokesperson was almost always in Leipzig and seldom came to Berlin where his services were required.

Schnur didn't sound like someone who would take no for an answer. "It's your job now, so go and talk to that group of journalists."

I thought, *You don't get an offer like this every day*, and so I accepted.

The press meeting had been convened at a hotel near Alexanderplatz. The forty or so journalists there looked at me in dismay when I informed them that I'd just been appointed DA spokesperson and would be representing Wolfgang Schnur. The first questions sounded accordingly snippy: Why isn't DA immediately affiliating with the CDU? What does DA think its special point of difference is? What does DA hope to achieve by remaining independent? This back-and-forth went on for a while. I stayed calm and friendly, explaining the issues from my point of view, and felt that the press conference came to a very positive and conciliatory conclusion. My overwhelming impression, though, was: *Now you have a proper job. You can oversee your own area of operations*. It was an exhilarating sensation.

I got to work. Over the following weeks I tried to deal with the flood of requests from inside Germany and beyond to the best of my knowledge and belief. I had a student assistant who drove me to meetings in other parts of Berlin in a VW Polo whenever necessary.

A much more important political decision was reached in those early days. The West German CDU was considering which of the new parties would make for the best ally alongside its natural partner, the East German CDU. The debates within DA about our future orientation had been closely observed by the residents of Konrad Adenauer House, the CDU's national headquarters in Bonn, and especially by the party's then general secretary, Volker Rühe. When the tide within DA turned in favor of CDU policies such as rapid German unification and social capitalism, Konrad Adenauer House made contact with DA and also with the DSU, the Deutsche Soziale Union (German Social Union) under the leadership of Hans-Wilhelm Ebeling. The DSU had a close affinity with the CDU's Bavarian sister party, the Christian Social Union (CSU), with strongholds in the southern German Democratic Republic. The West German CDU came up with the idea of forging a so-called "Alliance for Germany" for the Volkskammer elections. This enterprise sounded entirely logical, but it was fiendishly difficult to put into practice. It was not for nothing that people had set up new parties or joined them, as I had. We had ruled out becoming members of one of the bloc parties allied with the SED and the SED's mass organizations under the banner of the National Front, which had dominated East Germany both ideologically and organizationally. Many of these people may have had sound motives for joining the East German CDU, for example because it enabled them and their families to profess their Christian beliefs, but we didn't believe that the party could be renewed quickly. Apart from the fact that it had exactly the same name as the Western CDU, we saw no role for it in building a nation.

Although we wanted to remain independent, we had to recognize that many people saw Chancellor Kohl as the best champion for rapid German unification. It was likely that the CDU's name on the ballot paper would make them think of

Helmut Kohl more than of the East German CDU. Our reasoning was that some of his appeal might rub off on us if DA was part of the Alliance for Germany. It was also extremely attractive for the Western CDU to pick as its partner a party that had emerged from citizens' movements rather than simply relying on a former bloc party, the Eastern CDU, which might have been changing but was still rooted in the old structures.

Although I wasn't personally involved in the Alliance discussions, I know that it was a laborious process. DA's conditions were that we should be able to stand our own candidates for the Volkskammer elections, count on our own advisors from Bonn, and never be obliged to move from the House of Democracy to the Eastern CDU's offices on Gendarmenmarkt in Berlin. These conditions seemed risible to the Western CDU, but to us they were crucial because they highlighted that we were distinct from their East German sister party. From my perspective as an observer, Helmut Kohl and Volker Rühe deployed all their negotiating skills to seal a coalition deal.

On February 5, 1990 everything was ready. At a meeting with Helmut Kohl, Lothar de Maizière (East German CDU), Hans-Wilhelm Ebeling (DSU, Deutsche Soziale Union, German Social Union) and Wolfgang Schnur (DA), we agreed to present a combined list of candidates for the Volkskammer elections as the Alliance for Germany. This kick-started the campaign and meant that every rally in East Germany featuring Helmut Kohl was a rally for the Alliance for Germany. Each event would draw a crowd of tens of thousands, and something like 100,000 people attended the Erfurt rally alone.

Our task now was to explain what DA would stand for as part of a future East German government. My partner in this assignment was DA's general secretary Oswald Wutzke, a pastor from Gartz, on the Polish border, east of Templin. He had been appointed by Wolfgang Schnur in January, in a spontaneous fashion not unlike my own appointment, after the inaugural party conference in Leipzig had decided not to elect anyone to the post. The two of us worked with the West German publisher and journalist Claus Detjen to produce a newspaper entitled *Der Aufbruch: Zeitung für die demokratische Erneuerung* (*The Awakening: The Newspaper for Democratic Renewal*) as part of our campaign material. It was a time-consuming project. We also designed a series of flyers, including one with the headline "Democratic Awakening demands the de-Stalinization of East Germany."

My first ever article for DA with my name in the byline was published in the *Berliner Zeitung* on February 10, 1990. In it I laid out my arguments in favor of a social capitalist model, citing the importance of competition and the focal points of state involvement, and concluding with the words: "DA will seek to create the conditions in which it will pay for people to invest their skills in society." The editors of the *Berliner Zeitung* did not notice that I'd mangled the names of two founding fathers of social capitalism, transforming Alfred Müller-Armack into Alfred Müller-Arnau and Franz Böhm into Franz Böhlen. More important by far, however, was that for the first time I had publicly articulated my political beliefs. It was an incredible feeling.

One day around the middle of February, Wolfgang Schnur showed a man into my office. He introduced us and briefly explained that this trained journalist would be covering his every step until the Volkskammer elections. I was shocked and worried that our internal discussions would leak straight to the press, my suspicion being that Schnur would do anything to fulfill his avowed ambition of becoming prime minister of East Germany. He agreed to my request for a meeting, just the two of us.

"A party needs privacy for decision-making," I said in a bid to change his mind. "I can't be critical with that man in the room. I won't do it, and I certainly can't imagine he has only your best interests at heart."

"Of course you can carry on telling me important things in private," Schnur said to appease me.

This didn't reassure me, but I didn't press him any further. He was hard enough to talk to as it was. He could never look you straight in the eye, tending to stare diagonally past you instead, a habit of his that I found extremely irritating. Still, at least I had made my point. I could do no more than that.

The campaign was gathering pace. I worked as much and as hard as I could. Rumors that Schnur had been an unofficial Stasi collaborator (Inoffizieller Mitarbeiter, IM) had been swirling around since the start of the year, but they grew louder in early March. He vigorously denied them and proclaimed his innocence. What I didn't know at the time, though, was that members of DA's Rostock branch had already tried to warn Helmut Kohl on March 6, on the margins of a rally in Magdeburg, that Stasi files relating to Schnur had been found in their city. Although they hadn't managed to meet Kohl in person, they had passed on their information to his advisors. The Western CDU didn't really look into these concerns, though, and simply trotted out the same argument every time suspicions were raised about Schnur's Stasi contacts: "Wolfgang Schnur has strongly denied the allegations. We believe him. Who do you believe more, your party chairman or some Stasi documents? Living in East Germany has made you too wary. You can trust us." I found this behavior outrageous and began to suspect that, with only ten days to go until the general election, the Western CDU was observing Christian Morgenstern's line: "For he reasons pointedly, / that which must not, cannot be."

The drama played out to its logical conclusion. Schnur was due to address the accusations against him again at a press conference on March 14. Oswald Wutzke, Rainer Eppelmann, and Fred Ebeling, of whom the latter two were founding members of DA and Eppelmann a minister without portfolio in

Modrow's government, had traveled to Rostock a few days earlier to examine the Stasi files, returning with crushing evidence that the allegations of collaboration were true.

The day before the press conference, a small group of us—Eppelmann, Wutzke, Ebeling, a few DA colleagues, and myself—sat down at the meeting table in our office in the House of Democracy to figure out what to do. We kept that important democratic principle of the assumption of innocence firmly in our minds. The Western CDU representatives in the building were not allowed to sit in on our discussions, as we were being driven mad by their constant accusations that we were too suspicious. We Easterners discussed the matter and reached the conclusion that if Schnur had the brass neck to maintain his claim that he had never worked for the Stasi the next day, we would stand by him. If, on the other hand, he canceled his scheduled press conference, we would know something was up. By the time we made this decision and went our separate ways, midnight had come and gone.

It was a very short night for me because I had invited a dozen journalists to an 8:30 press briefing about DA's vision for the future of the European Community. I laid out my thoughts. Suddenly, someone came into the room and informed the representative of the German news agency dpa that he had an urgent phone call. The reporter left the room. I carried on with my presentation.

The dpa journalist returned a couple of minutes later, sat down, and then interrupted me: "Are you aware that the chairman of the West Berlin CDU, Eberhard Diepgen, and a second representative of the Western CDU are currently at Wolfgang Schnur's bedside in the Hedwigs hospital in Grosse Hamburger Strasse, and that Schnur has made a written confession that he spent decades as an unofficial Stasi collaborator?"

There was more.

"And did you know that Eberhard Diepgen is holding a press conference at eleven o'clock at the offices of West Berlin CDU?"

I knew none of this. I felt as if the ground was giving way beneath my feet. I had been prepared, of course, and the other journalists were all aware of Schnur's rumored past as a Stasi collaborator, but this sensation of facts hardening from theoretical possibility into stone-cold certainty was completely new to me. It was an experience that would be repeated many times in the years to come. Now, though, my task was to convince these journalists that I had not been trying to pull the wool over their eyes and that I was genuinely unaware of that morning's developments.

It was devastating, and embarrassing too. Here I was, lecturing about Democratic Awakening and the European Community at the same moment as Schnur was admitting to representatives of the Western CDU that he had worked for the Stasi. DA and its staff were clearly the least of his concerns. None of us, for all our pride in our independence, counted for anything; indeed, no one from the Western CDU had even felt obliged to let us know. A dpa reporter did the job for them instead.

I couldn't possibly have felt more ashamed, but I had to do something, and fast. I ended the meeting and rushed to my desk. The offices were virtually deserted. All the political leaders were out on the campaign trail—there were only four days left until election day. I decided to go to CDU headquarters in Lietzenburger Strasse, West Berlin. Luckily, I had a driver, so I was able to gather my thoughts on the way there.

When I reached the West Berlin CDU's offices shortly after ten o'clock, I immediately heard a woman's voice shouting into a phone in a far-off office, "I need to get hold of Herr Eppelmann! Now! Eppelmann, Rainer Eppelmann!"

I realized that the Western CDU was desperate to inform him about the situation. Eppelmann was campaigning somewhere out in Thuringia. Neither cell phones nor car phones existed yet, so the CDU had called the local police station and left a message for him to ring back. Shortly afterward, I learned that the police had managed to track down Eppelmann, but he was refusing to talk to the West Berlin CDU. He told them that if they wanted him to comment on Schnur, they needed to get in touch via the House of Democracy. The Westerners were beside themselves, but I thought, He's absolutely right.

I walked into a room where between thirty and forty people were gathered, chattering frantically to one another. They were probably CDU office staff waiting for Eberhard Diepgen to arrive. I didn't know any of them, and no one paid any attention to me, so I sat down inconspicuously in a chair and waited to see what would happen. Everyone was too busy discussing the rumors about Schnur to notice me.

All of a sudden a door opened. A slim man of average height in a suit and tie walked in and shouted in a loud, resonant voice, "Anyone not directly involved in this—out!"

Many of the people there left immediately. Believing that I certainly was *directly involved*, I stayed in my seat. Still no one spoke to me. The man left the room and returned shortly afterward with Eberhard Diepgen.

I whispered to the person next to me, "Who's the man with Diepgen?"

"Thomas de Maizière, Lothar de Maizière's cousin," he answered. "He's the spokesperson for the CDU group in the Berlin parliament."

I couldn't have known it then, obviously, but this was my first sighting of someone who would play a significant role in my life.

Now Diepgen took the floor and told us Schnur had admitted to collaborating with the Stasi and, after suffering a collapse, was now in hospital. Helmut Kohl had given Diepgen the task of announcing this news to the public at eleven o'clock. I noticed how anxious he was and thought: They're no better than the rest of us.

I still felt humiliated. My head was pounding: Schnur, Kohl, Diepgen, West Berlin, CDU, elections . . . Where's Demokratischer Aufbruch in all this? I decided to leave the meeting, head back immediately to my desk in the House of Democracy, and make sure that DA called a press conference as quickly as possible.

Arriving at the Friedrichstrasse office, I learned that Rainer Eppelmann was on his way to Berlin, which reassured me. Somehow or other, he and I agreed on the timing of the press conference. It was to take place early that evening because Eppelmann still had some distance to drive. I invited the press to a large room in the House of Democracy which all the parties and groups that worked there were entitled to use. There was an enormous amount of interest. The media tried to wheedle a comment or two out of me in advance. The building was open to visitors, and I couldn't leave the room without bumping into various inquisitive journalists in the corridors, so I hunkered down. Someone needed to write a statement. As press officer I felt responsible, but I was far too shaken to think clearly. In my distress I phoned Joachim at the Academy and gave him an account of what had happened. He remained utterly calm and dictated a wonderful statement that I was able to hand to Rainer Eppelmann when he reached Berlin. He approved it, and so we had a position for the press conference, at which he and I were accompanied by the deputy chair, Bernd Findeis.

I led proceedings at what would, for many years, be the biggest press conference that I had been actively involved in. Eppelmann seized the opportunity to express our disgust at our chair, Wolfgang Schnur, and to signal that we rejected him. Still, it was a total disaster for all of us who had been working so hard in good faith. The long shadow of the Stasi had caught up with us again in the final days before the first free Volkskammer elections.

On March 18, 1990—election day—Joachim and I met up in the late afternoon with Rainer Eppelmann, Andreas Apelt, another founding member of DA and chair of the party's Berlin branch, and others, either in Christburger Strasse or at a pub called Zur Mühle in Prenzlauer Berg, as far as I remember. The general mood was one of uncertainty as to which party would emerge strongest from the ballot. There was no reliable polling of people's voting intentions because so few people had a phone at home. Another major concern, of course, was how DA would fare in comparison with the CDU and the DSU. It was a good thing we kept ourselves to ourselves, because when the voting stations closed the exit poll gave us a disastrous 0.9 percent of the vote. The disappointment was crushing. We quickly realized that this outcome could not be explained by Schnur's exposure alone: it could only really be attributed to the magnetism of the West German chancellor Helmut Kohl. The final results were 40.8 percent for the CDU, 6.3 percent for the DSU, and 0.9 percent for us—exactly as predicted.

On the one hand, we were delighted that the Alliance for Germany was clearly the largest electoral force. The Social Democrats, now running as the SPD, won just 21.9 percent of the vote; the SED's successor party, the PDS, got 16.4 percent; the Bund Freier Demokraten (BFD, Association of Free Democrats) 5.3 percent; Alliance 90, a coalition of various civil society organizations, 9 percent; the Demokratische Bauernpartei Deutschlands (DBD, German Democratic Farmers' Party) 2.2 percent; and the Greens/Unabhängiger Frauenverband (UFV, Independent Women's Association) 2 percent. Overall, therefore, the election results were an overwhelming mandate for swift German unification.

On the other hand, we judged that our result did not correspond to our significant role in the Alliance for Germany. We
wanted to make sure that the victors knew this, so we went
along to the CDU election party at a restaurant called Ahorn-
blatt at the junction of Gertraudenstrasse and Fischerinsel in
central Berlin. Naturally, the whole place was in a celebratory
mood. The CDU chairman, Lothar de Maizière, was prime
minister-elect and feted accordingly.

I bumped into Thomas de Maizière. "It's great that the Alliance did so well, of course," he said, "but I feel very sorry for you
lot." I was quite composed by this point, so I made sure I sent
him and the CDU a message: "Our share of the vote today may
be dismal, but when it comes to forming the government,
please don't forget that we were a fig leaf for the Eastern CDU."

Then we all moved on to the Palace of the Republic, where
the overall results were reported. Given that these were East
Germany's first free elections, there was an incredible amount
of interest from the national and global media. Lothar de
Maizière couldn't believe his eyes when he entered the palace. I
thought he might be knocked out by a camera or trampled
underfoot at any moment. Thomas de Maizière did his best to
protect him. We would learn to cope with situations like this
later, but this time I just found it all extremely undignified.

There were some absurd scenes too. Günther Maleuda, the
chairman of the DBD, walked past me. I had never seen him
close-up before. Now I noticed that he, like so many GDR officials and bureaucrats, was wearing bright-grey shoes produced
in East Germany for the West German company Salamander.
There they were again: the old days. We called the Farmers'
Party, one of the bloc parties, the "Watermelon Party"—green on
the outside, red on the inside. I wasn't to know that the Farmers'
Party would merge with the CDU only three months later.

It quickly became clear that DA was irrelevant at this event,
and therefore I was too. Joachim and I went home. The Alliance

for Germany had earned the right to form a government led by the CDU. The Alliance had won 192 of the 400 seats in the Volkskammer, with DA bagging four of them, but this still left them in need of a coalition partner.

On the day after the first free Volkskammer elections, the West German SPD had more important matters on its mind than the formation of an East German government. It selected the prime minister of the state of Saarland, Oskar Lafontaine, as its candidate for chancellor of the Federal Republic. For context, we should add that the last regular Bundestag elections had taken place in January 1987, which meant that the four-year legislative term would end in January 1991 at the latest. Although it was not completely nonsensical for a party to choose its candidate for chancellor a year before the next elections, the SPD could easily have waited another couple of weeks. After all, the party's honorary president, the former chancellor Willy Brandt, had displayed his grasp of historic moments when he declared in a radio interview outside Schöneberg town hall the day after the Wall came down: "We are now in a situation in which what belongs together will grow together again."

A short time later, the Eastern SPD suffered the same fate as had befallen DA. Amid accusations that he had worked for the Stasi, its chairman, Ibrahim Böhme, resigned eight days after the elections and vacated his various posts in early April. On April 2, the chair of the Eastern SPD and the leader of the parliamentary party overcame their disappointment at the election results and announced their willingness to start negotiations with the Alliance for Germany to form a governing coalition. The new Volkskammer held its inaugural session on April 5, and Sabine Bergmann-Pohl, a doctor and member of the Eastern CDU, was elected speaker. Coalition negotiations between the Alliance, the SPD, and the Alliance of Free Democrats went smoothly, and were sealed within four weeks of the general election. Matthias Gehler, a theologian and journalist for the *Neue Zeit* newspaper publishing group, was appointed government spokesperson.

At some point I received an offer to work for the new government as its deputy spokesperson. I can't remember the precise day or who offered me the job; I would imagine it was either Matthias Gehler or Thomas de Maizière. There were no particularly strategic reasons behind it. The SPD was actually entitled to the position, but they hadn't nominated anyone and time was running out.

I was overjoyed at the offer but unable to take up the post in time for the swearing-in of Prime Minister Lothar de Maizière's new government on Maundy Thursday, April 12, 1990. That Easter, Joachim was giving a series of lectures in several places, including London. I was determined to go with him, among other reasons to visit my cousin from Hamburg who was working as a doctor there. Throughout the coalition negotiations there was nothing for me to do anyway, and it didn't seem right to abandon my travel plans simply because I had been appointed deputy government spokesperson. I had never been to London and had been looking forward to this journey for such a long time. So I was even more delighted when Matthias Gehler not only offered me the job but also agreed to delay the start date until the Tuesday after Easter.

In London, I did more than just accompany Joachim to his host organization, the Royal Institution of Great Britain, which was founded in 1799 with the purpose of disseminating scientific knowledge and conducting research. We strolled around Hyde Park, went to Speakers' Corner, of course, and were lucky enough to attend the traditional Good Friday performance of Handel's *Messiah* at the Royal Albert Hall. We browsed the amazing variety of international products in a host of small grocery stores, and I felt as if the whole world was at my fingertips. Despite the work to be done in Berlin, I felt vindicated in my decision to go to London.

Friction and conflicts

"If the deutsche mark comes, we'll stay. If it doesn't, we'll go and get it." Crowds had been chanting this repeatedly in the streets of East Germany since early in 1990. It was therefore logical that the first major task undertaken by the federal government and the newly formed GDR administration was to establish a treaty of monetary, economic, and social union between the two states.

Helmut Kohl had announced in early February 1990 that he would offer East Germany a monetary and economic union. The East German side had insisted on a social union too, with the aim of staunching the exodus of its citizens to the Federal Republic—nearly 350,000 had left the GDR in 1989. Together they drew up an ambitious road map. On April 23, the general outline of a monetary, economic, and social union was published; on May 18, the finance minister Theo Waigel signed it for the Federal Republic of Germany and Walter Romberg for the German Democratic Republic; and on June 21 it was approved by the West German Bundestag and the East German Volkskammer. On Sunday, July 1, the deutsche mark became our currency. In my role as deputy government spokesperson, I was involved in managing the historic press conference held jointly by the two finance ministers. It was an uplifting feeling. This treaty not only gave us the deutsche mark as our official currency and with very favorable conditions; it also harmonized the two countries' economic, social, and environmental legislation to the greatest possible extent. Just two weeks earlier, on June 17, it had been decided that all state property in East Germany would be privatized by a government trust agency called the Treuhand Agency. Despite these encouraging developments, Walter Romberg still seemed dissatisfied. He agonized over the consequences of monetary union—a dramatic rise in unemployment, for example. But after weighing up all the advantages and disadvantages, as well as Romberg's legitimate concerns, I could still see no more promising pathway than the swift introduction of the deutsche mark.

We were all working at full tilt, myself included. I had been thrown in at the deep end, so to speak, on April 17, when I took up my post in the Alte Stadthaus, the Old City Hall, where the Council of Ministers met. Matthias Gehler and I worked together without any fuss and we got on well. We had more than enough on our plates, though. Gehler was largely responsible for presenting the government's actions to the outside world— at press conferences, for instance. If he had other matters to attend to, I would stand in for him. In the face of the hundreds of legal regulations passed by the de Maizière government, I was helped by my now famous love of detail when it came to giving accurate answers to factual questions about these many different schemes. Otherwise, I was kept very busy responding to a myriad of requests from the media, and accompanying Prime Minister Lothar de Maizière or Günther Krause to interviews. (Krause was born in 1953 in Halle an der Saale, trained as an engineer before joining the CDU, and was parliamentary secretary to the prime minister of the GDR. He played a key role in the government.)

At the prime minister's office, we cooperated well with the members of staff who had previously worked for the East German Council of Ministers. West German advisors taught us at least the rudiments of how to run a democratic administration.

It was there that I met up with Hans-Christian Maass and Thomas de Maizière again. I can recall as if it was yesterday their reaction to the SPD's decision on August 20, 1990 to quit the Great Coalition formed only four months earlier. This was triggered by fundamental financial and economic differences of opinion between the CDU and the SPD, prompting Prime Minister Lothar de Maizière to sack several ministers on August

16, 1990, including the SPD finance minister Walter Romberg. When the coalition collapsed on August 20, I had to call an early-evening press conference. "It has to make the seven o'clock news," I was told. "*It absolutely has to!*"

"How are we to make that work? We've only got a few minutes," I snapped back.

"Phone around and drum up some journalists," Hans-Christian Maass shouted.

"Are you ready? Have you prepared our official line?" Thomas de Maizière added.

Our advisors were well intentioned, but I could tell that they were also agitated, and pressure from Bonn only made things worse. They had also seen it all before, whereas we knew nothing. It wasn't easy for us to get our own views and reservations across.

We plainly had a Herculean task before us. At the end of a tumultuous all-night session on August 23, the Volkskammer declared with an overwhelming majority "the accession of the German Democratic Republic to the Federal Republic of Germany, and the extension of the field of application of the Federal Republic's Basic Law to the territory of East Germany in line with Article 23 of the Basic Law with effect from 3.10.1990."

As the government, we were responsible from the very beginning for ensuring that, on unification day, laws would be in place which enshrined legal certainty for every individual citizen in every area of life. After forty years of divergence between the two German states, this was a massive undertaking. By July 1, the legislation governing pensions and employment had been almost entirely harmonized, but this undeniably had some negative consequences.

The process always followed the same template. At first, many people were very impatient to follow the West German model, but once it had been introduced the adverse effects on specific sections of the population began to become clear. Then the protests began. One example was the impact of monetary union on those working in the agricultural sector. The introduction of the deutsche mark meant that they were automatically subject to the regulations of the European Economic Community. The European Community did not allow transition periods. Over 10 percent of all employees in East Germany worked in agriculture, while the comparative figure in West Germany was under 4 percent. Unemployment exploded in rural areas. Such effects were inevitable, but many people had been in denial up to this point. It was impossible to introduce the deutsche mark and at the same time take account of everybody's concerns—the government had to choose a course of action. Major demonstrations by farmers were the consequence.

There were many other sectors in which friction and conflict were unavoidable. Completely different supplementary pension and health-care systems, totally divergent property laws, different childcare arrangements, different abortion laws: these were just some of the many issues that Lothar de Maizière's government had to confront from its very first day in office.

A second treaty was needed: the Unification Treaty. The aim was for this agreement to cover every area of domestic policy not encompassed by the first treaty—from allotments to the little green men at pedestrian crossings, you might say. Negotiations began on July 6, and were conducted by the West German interior minister Wolfgang Schäuble, and Günther Krause. I was a member of the East German delegation and in charge of public relations for our side.

This was when I met Willi Hausmann, born in 1942, from Oberhausen in the Ruhr, who was on Schäuble's staff and my counterpart on the West German side. He was one of those who were fascinated by German unification, a good listener, not someone who implicitly believed that he knew better, a man with a calm, caring, and warm approach, not one for airs and graces. He explained many things to me, waiting until I asked a question and answering in detail without lecturing me. It was the beginning of a lifelong friendship.

I will never forget how the negotiations got underway. The delegations of the Federal Republic and the GDR met in the "Bear Hall" in the Old City Hall. Prime Minister Lothar de Maizière was there to open proceedings, and at the end of his welcome speech he sang the lyrics of the East German anthem to the tune of its West German equivalent. For many years we had only ever been permitted to hum the melody of our anthem because the words went thus: "From the ruins risen newly / To the future turned, we stand / Let us serve your good weal truly / Germany, our fatherland. / Triumph over bygone sorrow / Can in unity be won. / For we shall attain a morrow / When over our Germany / Brightly shines the sun."

I saw the West Germans freeze. They couldn't breathe. Was Lothar de Maizière seriously suggesting changing the lyrics of the West German national anthem? I couldn't be sure, but I thought that he was definitely trying to send a message that not everything would necessarily stay the same for West Germany while everything changed for us. I believed this was the right idea, even though I, like most of the other people present, judged it a little tactless to illustrate his point with the national anthem, of all things.

The negotiations proved tricky, and emotions were often high. Some issues could not be conclusively addressed by the time the Unification Treaty was signed on August 31, 1990— different abortion rules, for example, and the matter of how to deal conclusively with the injustices of the SED regime, as well as property-related issues. These sparked incredible levels of controversy and debate. The two German states had already agreed, in a joint declaration on June 15, that unresolved questions concerning assets would be settled according to the principle of restitution before compensation, excluding expropriations that had taken place under the laws of occupation between 1945 and 1949. The West German Free Democratic Party (FDP) disregarded this pact and insisted on raising the subject of these uncompensated expropriations. They affected, amongst others, large landowners with estates of over 100 hectares, and also the proprietors of smaller farms classified by the occupying Soviet administration and the East German state as war criminals or active members of the Nazi Party.

Günther Krause eventually saw no other option than to invite Klaus Kinkel (FDP), a junior minister in the justice department, to accompany him on a visit to an Agricultural Production Cooperative (Landwirtschaftliche Produktionsgenossenschaft, LPG). An LPG was a cooperative of farmers and their equipment for the purposes of joint agricultural production. Krause wanted to show Kinkel the upheaval it would cause if the land reforms were rescinded. I had the impression that this visit significantly influenced Kinkel's opinions. It was hard for me to understand why the majority of expropriation cases should be analyzed in detail and judged in favor of the former owners, when virtually no one showed any willingness to compensate the East German citizens—dissidents, the victims of SED crimes, and many pastors' children, for example—for the lifelong disadvantages they had suffered.

This question of property would preoccupy us all for many years to come, causing much bitterness on both sides. The subject seemed to be taboo. The moment I posed a critical question, I would be bludgeoned with the same old accusations that a citizen of the GDR was incapable of appreciating the value of private property. I was not even arguing on my own behalf, but taking a fundamental stance that justice involved treating all forms of unfairness experienced similarly. My objections were dismissed.

Despite all of these controversies, both the Volkskammer and the Bundestag approved the Unification Treaty on September 20,

1990 with large majorities. The domestic groundwork for unification had been laid.

Diplomacy's finest hour

After the end of the Second World War, Germany had been divided into four occupied zones by the victorious Allies—the United States, the United Kingdom, France, and the Soviet Union. On February 13, 1990, the foreign ministers of these four countries agreed with the foreign ministers of West Germany and East Germany that they would begin negotiations on what was known as a "Two Plus Four Agreement"—a treaty between the Federal Republic of Germany and the German Democratic Republic on one side, and France, the Soviet Union, the UK, and the USA on the other.

The victorious powers and the neighbors of the two German states were concerned about the future role of a united Germany. Could they trust this new country? The UK and France were especially preoccupied by this question, while the US president George Bush campaigned vehemently to overcome their reservations and resolve all outstanding issues as swiftly as possible. These included the territory of the new state, especially its eastern border, the number of troops in its future army, its freedom to enter into alliances, and the withdrawal of Soviet forces that this implied. Negotiations kicked off on May 5, 1990, and the Treaty on the Final Settlement with Respect to Germany was signed in Moscow on September 12, 1990 at the Oktyabrskaya Hotel. Since renamed the President Hotel, it is still run by the office of the Russian president.

I went to Moscow with Lothar de Maizière, who was signing for the East German state. Following the SPD's exit from the Grand Coalition in August, he had also taken on the post of foreign minister. I remember that negotiations continued far into the night before the document was to be signed. On the eve of the signing ceremony, Lothar de Maizière sent me to the embassy of the Federal Republic of Germany, where the West German foreign minister Hans-Dietrich Genscher had invited reporters for a briefing. The official justification for my presence was that the two German states wanted to adopt a common position, making it essential that I attend this meeting. The true reason was that we East Germans were extremely intrigued to find out which arguments the West Germans were going to put forward.

One thing became clear to me during the press briefing on the draft treaty: if I had been in charge of the discussion, I could have explained every provision, right down to details that had not yet been resolved and especially the contentious issue of a united Germany joining NATO. The Soviet Union only agreed to this in principle during a meeting on July 16 in the Caucasus between President Mikhail Gorbachev and Chancellor Kohl, accompanied by the foreign minister Hans-Dietrich Genscher and the finance minister Theo Waigel. My sober take on the individual clauses in the treaty would have been entirely factually accurate, but it would not have done justice to the significance of the agreement.

Hans-Dietrich Genscher's approach in those background discussions was very different. He didn't focus on details, but placed the treaty in its historical context and painted a picture of what it would achieve: a reunited, fully sovereign Germany, firmly embedded in NATO and in a European Community that was destined to become a political union; a Conference on Security and Cooperation in Europe (CSCE) as a nucleus for a comprehensive European security architecture that included the Soviet Union; and the withdrawal of all Soviet troops from the territory of the soon-to-be former East Germany by 1994. He explained that glasnost and perestroika had made such a document possible, but the efforts had been facilitated by the prudent politics and goodwill of all parties—the four victorious powers and many others besides. I felt that I was witnessing one of diplomacy's finest hours and a joyful historical moment. I was very impressed by Genscher, and I learned that what you needed to do was to lay out the objectives and explain the context *before* getting into the details. I took this lesson to heart for my future political career, even if—as many people know—I didn't always heed it.

I returned to our hotel with a skip in my step and reported to my colleagues on the mood in the West German camp. We were all very satisfied.

The final elements were worked out overnight. On Wednesday, September 12, the parties put their signatures to a historic document that drew a line under the post-war era in Germany. Nothing stood in the way of German unification now. Unity and justice and freedom: on October 3, 1990, the country was reunited. In 2011 UNESCO added the Two Plus Four Agreement to its Memory of the World Register, immortalizing the treaty in the documentary legacy of humanity.

STANDING ON MY
OWN TWO FEET

Through gritted teeth

ON JULY 26, 1990, the joint session of the German unification committees of the Volkskammer and the Bundestag set December 2, 1990 as the date for the first Bundestag elections of a reunited Germany. Just prior to this decision, the Volkskammer had announced that state elections in the Eastern federal states, which were due to be established, would be held on October 14. The fourteen districts of the former East Germany would be combined into five new federal states, and East and West Berlin would merge to form the sixth. All I will say here about the bitter debate over the election date and election legislation was that it was a nailbiter. At the end of the day, a judgment of the Federal Constitutional Court declared that separate 5-percent thresholds would apply in the new and old federal states.

Democratic Awakening had been forced to decide what to do after the disappointing Volkskammer election results. Rainer Eppelmann had been elected Wolfgang Schnur's successor as chair back in April. After securing only 0.5 percent of the vote in the May local elections, it was clear that DA had no future under these circumstances. If we wished to safeguard at least some of the objectives of our literal democratic awakening, our only option was to merge with the CDU, which meant relinquishing our independence.

Much to our regret, however, we weren't allowed to join the Western CDU directly. We first had to become members of the Eastern CDU until the Eastern and Western parties could be merged at the party conference in Hamburg on October 1–2, 1990, giving birth to the all-German CDU. I won't speculate here about whether this was the only legally unproblematic option, as was always claimed, or whether the Western CDU simply found it too complicated to incorporate two different parties at once.

The first step in this process was completed in Berlin on August 4, 1990. The mood among us DA members was as bad as might have been expected. Unfortunately, I can't recall where the meeting was held. I do remember, though, that it was a boiling hot day when we administered the last rites to our independence, our sole consolation being that we were allowed to set up a DA working group within the CDU. We had realized that joining the larger party was an unavoidable decision, and yet emotionally we balked at it. It only made matters worse when an excitable Western advisor took to the podium to point out that this resolution required a two-thirds majority of those present, and then thought it necessary to explain to us that two-thirds was a very high threshold. There was a real risk of the whole event going off the rails. We felt as if we were being treated like ignorant children.

I was outraged. How stupid did they think we were? So that the people present could hear, I raged: "There are lots of things we didn't learn in East Germany. But even in the GDR not only did two plus two equal four, but two-thirds was also significantly higher than 50 percent. In fact, we've even known election results touching 99 percent. Everyone is aware that it is perfectly fine that there will be votes against, but that we share responsibility for the overall result. We don't need any lessons about that."

This calmed the atmosphere somewhat, and the requisite majority was achieved, albeit through gritted teeth.

So October 2, 1990 marked the end of DA—and also of my spell as deputy government spokesperson. Amid the daily maelstrom of events, I also had my own future to consider. The Academy of Sciences was now well in the past: I was thoroughly enjoying my new job. Over the summer I had been offered a full-time job at the Federal Press Office in Bonn for the period after October 3, and the time had now come to draw a line under my time at the Academy. I took the U-Bahn one last time to my office in Adlershof, a journey I had made Monday to Friday for eleven years, apart from holidays, research trips, and sick leave. I cleared my desk at the Institute and said goodbye to my colleagues. It had been an inspiring time doing fundamental research, but I felt no nostalgia for it now. I was looking forward instead to facing completely different challenges in a completely different field. I can't remember precisely when I handed in my notice at the ZIPC, but I had been on the payroll of the prime minister's office since April 12.

A public health officer had to issue a certificate before I could take up my new post at the Federal Press Office, so I went to see my assigned doctor in West Berlin in September. I was expecting a routine check-up, and the whole procedure struck me as irritatingly slow in comparison with the pace of my job at the prime minister's office. That probably explains why my blood pressure was so high. The doctor examined me, and everything was fine—apart from my high blood pressure. He told me that this might jeopardize my admission to the civil service. By this point I was getting quite annoyed. Did my future really depend on a public health officer? I got the medical certificate in the end, and permission for the job as well. But what neither the doctor nor I could have suspected at the time was that I might not even need the post at the Federal Press Office.

Your local candidate

During my time working as deputy government spokesperson, I had honed my personal political views. We had worked flat out to bring about German unification in an orderly manner. The first thing that became clear during this process was that the SED had left us in an economic hole, and that, with a populace controlled and spoon-fed by the state for decades, toughening them up to cope with the new freedoms would be a formidable challenge. Second, I'd seen during the Unification Treaty negotiations how much energy it had cost Günther Krause to advocate for East German citizens' legitimate interests, or even innovations for Germany as a whole. After October 3, 1990, there were obviously many issues that still needed to be resolved, and I thought that a seat in the new federal parliament would give me a platform to help tackle those problems. So I decided to stand for the Bundestag rather than go to work at the Federal Press Office.

There was no way I wanted to be a candidate in a Berlin constituency. I hadn't grown up in a city, and my roots were still largely rural. The Uckermark area of Brandenburg would have been a natural political home for me, but I didn't see the regional association of the CDU in Brandenburg as modernized enough. So, in late August or early September, I made contact with Günther Krause, who was the chair of the CDU in the state of Mecklenburg-Western Pomerania. He was willing to help me out and advised me to get in touch with the commissioner for Western Pomerania's Grimmen constituency, Wolfhard Molkentin, who was also chair of the CDU constituency party there. The county of Grimmen had been combined with the

Hanseatic city of Stralsund, outer Stralsund, and the island of Rügen into the new all-German constituency no. 267. The local CDU hadn't selected its candidate yet, although there were already two applicants. The Rügen branch had chosen a West German bank employee from Oldenburg who had helped to build up a savings bank on the island. The party's branches in the city of Stralsund and the surrounding area favored a staff member of the CDU–CSU parliamentary group from Bonn, who was supporting the work of the CDU group on Stralsund council. Only Grimmen, the smallest local party, was still looking for someone. They too wanted to put up their own candidate. Many local people wanted to play a role in their area and had therefore stood in the May local council elections. Bonn and the Bundestag, on the other hand, seemed a very long way away, which is why candidates from other parts of Germany were even being considered.

I phoned Wolfhard Molkentin, as Günther Krause had told him I would. Krause's recommendations carried a lot of weight, and as a favor to him, the party in Grimmen agreed to meet up with me. We arranged an introductory discussion at the council offices there.

My journey there was a disaster. I'd been far too optimistic about how long it would take. Although someone else was driving me, I didn't arrive punctually at 4:00 p.m, as I was supposed to, and didn't get there till around 5:30 p.m. Of course, I didn't have a car phone in those days and there was no mobile network either, so I couldn't inform anyone about the delay.

As we pulled up outside the council offices, some men were locking up and preparing to go home. One of them turned out to be Wolfhard Molkentin, and the others were board members of the CDU in Grimmen. I managed to persuade them to give me a hearing anyway, but there was no doubt that we'd got off on the wrong foot. I hated being late even then and felt very uncomfortable, so I blamed the delay on my duties in Berlin and the bad transport connections. The first point confirmed the men's suspicions that I wasn't really interested in their area and only after a comfortable Bundestag seat. The second was a good icebreaker, though, because they were all convinced that the economy in this part of Western Pomerania would only flourish if it was linked up to the autobahn network. This was the seed of the later A20 autobahn construction project.

In the meantime, Molkentin had unlocked the door again. Once inside, I underwent a thorough vetting. Their skepticism was tangible. They weren't won over by my assurances that I would understand the local problems because my home region of the Uckermark suffered from the same infrastructure deficiencies and faced the same challenges as this part of Western Pomerania. The board members drove it home to me that this was Western Pomerania and, more specifically, Grimmen. It became immediately clear to me that I was dealing with people who knew what they wanted. Most of them had worked in agriculture, and the introduction of the deutsche mark had turned their world upside down. Molkentin used to be the acting chair of the local cooperative and he knew what he was talking about. The men could see that I didn't have much soil under my fingernails. I could tell a fertile field from an infertile one, but I didn't have the faintest idea what made Grimmen tick or what the threat of structural adjustment meant for its oil refinery.

The hour-and-a-half-long meeting earned me some dubious glances and a handful of brochures to signal that I still had a lot to learn before the nomination hustings on September 27, 1990. They were right because I was going to be competing against applicants backed by Stralsund and Rügen. However, I left the meeting with the impression that we had at least one thing in common—we were all determined to beat the other candidates.

———

In the last week of September I traveled to Prora on the island of Rügen. Around lunchtime on decision day, I introduced myself to a section of the CDU branch in Rügen, as I was aware of tensions between long-standing CDU members and people who had only recently joined the party from DA and the Farmers' Party. Keen to cover all possible ground, I courted this latter group, who were delighted to see a former DA member. The other camp wouldn't listen to me, though, and nor would the people from Stralsund. Both were firmly behind their own candidates.

All members of the local CDU branches in the new Bundestag constituency 267 had been invited to the hustings, which were a truly grassroots event. The Rügen branch, who were our hosts by virtue of having the largest number of members, ruthlessly exploited their home advantage. They wouldn't hear of organizing the nomination hustings in Stralsund, which would have made everyone's journey easier.

The only place on the island that could accommodate all the participants was the great hall of the Haus der Armee (Army House), part of the huge and largely abandoned Prora building complex. To make matters worse, the local party had called the nomination hustings for Thursday, September 27, in the middle of the working week, and the event was scheduled to start at 7:30 p.m. The journey from both Stralsund and Grimmen to Prora took between an hour and an hour and a half. The delegates considered this unreasonable, so the Stralsund town, rural Stralsund, and Grimmen branches had decided to bus their members there. This would later prove to be my salvation.

The atmosphere was tense as the meeting began. The whole procedure needed to be precise and by the book. However different their interests might be, no one wanted to carry the blame for an invalid outcome. There were approximately four hundred CDU members present, and the candidates took to the stage in alphabetical order. I was the second to present my plans for the constituency. I stressed: "I'm the only person here who grew up in the GDR. I know the problems first-hand."

After all the candidates had made their pitch, the debate went on for several hours. The people of Rügen wanted to know who would rebuild the piers in the resorts on the Baltic coast, how to protect the area's magnificent tree-lined avenues while also widening the roads, and how the future of Rügen's fishing industry might look. The Stralsund delegates were predominantly interested in the fate of their tradition-steeped shipyard and the reconstruction of the historic old town. More than four hundred buildings in the center of the Hanseatic city were at risk of collapse or at least in desperate need of renovation. The members from Stralsund and Grimmen focused on the future of farming in their rural constituencies. They were all united in their appeals for better transport links.

I realized that all these projects were going to require considerable expenditure, and that the money would have to come from the capital. Like the other candidates, I answered to the best of my knowledge and beliefs. There was mounting suspense as to who the participants thought would best represent their interests in Bonn.

At long last, late in the evening, the time came to vote. The Rügen candidate got the most ballots; I came second; and the Stralsund candidate was eliminated. It would come down to a runoff, and there was a break while new voting papers were prepared.

Two things happened during this interval that were to have a decisive impact on events later that night. The delegates from Stralsund and Grimmen joined forces behind me, but the people from Rügen were so confident of victory that they ignored this development. They didn't have much experience of runoff ballots. As it was already late and they were sure their votes would no longer really count, some of them chose to go home. However, the Grimmen and Stralsund delegates, now steadfast backers of mine, couldn't leave separately because they'd come on coaches.

The second round of voting began shortly before midnight, and the results were announced a little after that. I won by 184 votes to 178, a six-vote margin—it couldn't have been much closer. My supporters were over the moon; the members from Rügen were dismayed; and I was happy. If the results of the imminent Bundestag elections mirrored the recent Volkskammer vote, the CDU and I stood a good chance of winning the constituency.

After the battle was over, I sat with the hardcore Rügen members in the officers' mess until half past two in the morning and gradually came to the conclusion that I should be able to earn their respect if I represented them properly.

Some weeks later, the chair of the CDU parliamentary group on the Mecklenburg-Western Pomeranian state legislature, Eckhardt Rehberg, told me that they had in fact reserved a second potential constituency for me—constituency no. 266, in the area around Rostock. The CDU branches had been informed that there was no need to select their own candidate because Günther Krause had put forward someone from Berlin, the deputy government spokesperson Angela Merkel. Everyone was waiting for me to appear for the requisite official vote, which took place two days after my nomination in Rügen, but I didn't turn up. In the great flurry of activity, no one had thought to let the local party officials know that I had already secured a nomination in constituency 267. I couldn't have informed anyone because I was in the dark about these arrangements.

Such scenes are unimaginable nowadays, as they were only possible in those wild times before a quick cell-phone call could clear up the misunderstanding. The reason behind the whole pantomime was that the Mecklenburg-Western Pomerania CDU had assumed that the islanders would get their way and that I would fail to win in Rügen. This made me all the prouder of triumphing against the odds. The second constituency selected a new candidate who had put her name forward at the last minute.

After October 3, 1990, my workplace moved to the Palais Schaumburg in Bonn, the residence of the Federal Republic's first chancellor, Konrad Adenauer. For the period between the Bundestag elections and the appointment of the new government, the East Germans Lothar de Maizière, Günther Krause, Sabine Bergmann-Pohl, Rainer Ortleb, and Hansjoachim Walther sat in Helmut Kohl's cabinet as ministers with special portfolios. I worked as spokesperson for de Maizière and Krause. There wasn't actually much more for the new ministers to do in that historic palace, so I focused on my constituency campaign almost 450 miles away. There wasn't much time before the Bundestag elections on December 2, and local party officials gave me a lot of help, not only sticking up posters and distributing campaign material, but also drafting my political manifesto. Even the people of Rügen started to get behind me.

Meeting as many people as possible meant a lot of travel, because the constituency was very sparsely populated. A student I knew from my DA days came along to keep me company. I rented a car and bought a trestle table. It was easy to get out and set up, usually in front of the local Konsum (cooperative store) or the Kaufhalle (supermarket), and I would decorate it with campaign material, including my own personal leaflet presenting me as "your local candidate"—"Ihr Direktkandidat." Today, of course, I would use the feminine form of the word, "Ihr Direkt-kandidatin." But in those days, as in the time of the GDR, the masculine form was still used. In response to questions about the profession for which I had studied, after German unification at first I would always say I was a "Physiker," rather than a "Physikerin." Today that is entirely alien to me.

During the campaign I made every attempt to engage

people in conversation—no small task given the taciturn nature of the Western Pomeranians. It's a characteristic I generally like, and I learned to put up with a few seconds of silence, and to be careful not to startle people with a torrent of words.

On November 2, a photographer from Bonn called Michael Ebner came along on my constituency tour. Hans-Christian Maass had asked him because he thought it was important to give West Germans a glimpse of how the campaign in the new Bundesländer was going too.

I was paying a visit to fishermen in Lobbe on the island of Rügen that day, and Michael took a photo of me in a fisherman's hut that has been reproduced countless times since. I'm very fond of that picture because it expresses so many things—the dignity of the fishermen's work and their closeness to nature, the East German ambience with a few indications of the new age that was dawning, and our sociable silence. I can still remember my hesitant conversation with the fishermen. It was the first time I'd ever held a turbot in my hands and felt its distinctive stone-like bumps. There was a lot of uncertainty in the air. What was going to happen to the fishing industry? Their staple catch, herring, no longer guaranteed a decent income. Radical change was underway.

I couldn't promise anything except that I would take on board the fishermen's concerns. Looking back, this was a sad chapter. Despite a great deal of effort, most of the professional fishermen went out of business. European agricultural policy seemed like a monstrous bureaucratic machine impervious to their concerns and unwilling to give them the funding they required. It felt as if I was tilting at windmills when I tried to help. Also, since they were a small group of people and there were always so many other bigger groups with equally legitimate claims, I never had time to pursue their interests as resolutely as I would have liked. Yet even if I'd had the time, it's unlikely that I could have succeeded. Although my visit was a great pleasure at the time, in retrospect that photo in the fisherman's hut is tinged with sadness.

All in all, despite the many problems, I very much enjoyed campaigning. I felt fulfilled by my encounters with so many different types of people. It was up to me to decide how I got to know my constituency, and I grew to love it.

On December 2, 1990, in the first post-reunification elections, I won the seat for the CDU with 48.2 percent of the vote, making me a happy elected member of the first all-German Bundestag. Politically, I was now standing on my own two feet. German unification had ushered in a new stage in my life. I was extremely fortunate. I was thirty-six—young enough for a new challenge but seasoned enough to contribute my drive, experience, and knowledge to this new era of German politics. What's more, in my constituency I found many close friends who supported me until the moment I stepped down in 2021. I had found a political home.

PART THREE

Freedom and Responsibility

December 3, 1990 to November 21, 2005

"AUFBAU OST"

Maundy Thursday

MARCH 28, 1991, just before three in the afternoon: I was being driven from my apartment to Alexanderplatz in central Berlin. My destination was the House of Electrical Industry, the former seat of the GDR's ministry for electro-technology and electronics. After German unification it had been made the home of the Treuhand Agency, the public trust agency tasked with privatizing East German businesses. The agency's final headquarters were on the corner of Leipziger Strasse and Wilhelmstrasse, where the ministry of finance is now based. Today, the building is called Detlev Rohwedder House, named after the third president of the Treuhand Agency. I had arranged to have a meeting with him in his office on Alexanderplatz.

On June 17, 1990, the Volkskammer (the East German parliament) of the GDR had passed the Treuhandgesetz—the Trust Law (officially: Law on the Privatization and Reorganization of the Assets of the People). Its task was defined in an introductory formula: "to restore the state's entrepreneurial activity as quickly and extensively as possible through privatization, to make as many businesses as possible competitive, thus protecting existing jobs and creating new ones, to provide real estate for economic purposes." This was a gigantic and unprecedented task, the privatization of almost the whole of the East German economy. Over eight thousand businesses with around four million employees had been placed under the auspices of the Treuhand Agency on July 1, 1990. It maintained branches in the fifteen former urban districts of the former GDR. All businesses had been transformed into stock corporations. Their competitiveness, already feeble, had been dramatically worsened still further by the 1:1 ostmark to deutsche mark exchange rate. Universal rage, however, was directed not at those who were actually responsible for the plight—the people holding the levers of the GDR state and power apparatus—but at the Treuhand Agency, which now had the task of solving problems arising from years of economic mismanagement.

I had met Detlev Karsten Rohwedder in 1990 in a background discussion that he had had with Prime Minister Lothar de Maizière in the summer of 1990 to inform the press about the political task and methods of the Treuhand Agency, and at the same time to lend political support to their work. I was present as deputy government spokesperson, and watched Rohwedder keenly: a tall man, aged fifty-seven, who emanated an aura of healthy self-confidence. He didn't come out with empty platitudes but listened and spoke quietly, convinced of his own arguments. During his time as chairman of the board of the Dortmund steel and mining company Hoesch AG he had gained practical experience of reorganization. But when answering some of the questions from journalists it was plain that he was unable to see things from the point of view of an East German citizen, so I paid him a visit after the press conference. "That can't have been easy for you. I wish you every success," I said. "This task is a kamikaze mission, I know that. But your work is so important because the lives of so many human beings are affected by it." He seemed to be listening to me, so I bit the bullet and made another observation: "You must have noticed how impatient journalists get when asking questions. I think it would be a good idea if you would put more effort into meeting the questioners where they happen to be emotionally. You could tell them that East German workers really gave their best and continue to do so, but that that's not enough to survive in the market economy. And maybe you could go on to explain that it's not the fault of the East German workers. And that, on the one hand, wages are lower than they are in the Federal Republic, but on the other, competitiveness has been made worse than it was by the 1:1 exchange rate, which means that even more jobs are at risk. You could say that this is all incredibly unjust, but that it's the legacy of 'real socialism.' And also that no amount of economic power and money from the West can undo that."

Rohwedder had listened to my long lecture without interrupting me. And then he had promised to take my advice to heart. "I would be glad if we could carry on our conversation at some point," he said in conclusion. His reaction seemed to indicate very honest interest in what mattered to me.

We met again before the first full federal election of a unified Germany in December 1990. In the meantime, I had already heard a lot about the Treuhand Agency and its work.

When I was a candidate in the Bundestag election campaign, the stories from citizens and managers on the ground had sometimes left me speechless, or puzzled at the very least. In our second meeting I said straight out to Rohwedder, "Do you have any idea of the kind of people who are working for your Treuhand Agency? They're young and smart, you might even say arrogant, twenty-somethings who have probably just finished their legal studies and present themselves as people who have gorged themselves on wisdom. They have everything except an understanding of how people actually work!" He listened to me with interest, as he had done the first time. "And if anyone needs a loan for their privatization idea, they don't help, they just raise the hurdles even higher and reach agreement with young West German bankers who are just like themselves," I went on.

"Can you give me an example?" he broke in.

"During the election campaign I had a conversation with a woman who wanted to open a haberdashery in Rostock," I began. "To do that, she needed a premises and a loan of forty thousand deutsche marks. She hoped to find the premises via the Treuhand Agency real estate office. This woman was neither particularly eloquent nor particularly cunning, but in fact rather shy. She gave an honest and direct reply to every question she was asked, including the question of whether she was sure that she would have enough customers to pay back the loan. She talked about risk and the courage it took to start something new. That was too vague for the young advisors. And what was the result? She didn't get either the shop or the loan," I told him, adding even more furiously, "The people from the SED who learned how to express themselves perfectly and promise the moon, on the other hand, are now being successful all over again! Unscrupulousness is triumphant, as it was under socialism! This isn't how we imagined things were going to be!"

I was done. Rohwedder looked at me thoughtfully and said, "Maybe you're right. Let's stay in touch and talk again, however you do in the Bundestag election."

We said goodbye.

A few months later, on March 1, 1991—by now I wasn't just a Bundestag deputy, but also minister of state for women and youth—I visited two textile works, in Aue and Lengenfeld, small towns in the East of the country. I had been invited by the Cotton Industry Association of Saxony and Thuringia; that branch was in a perilous position. I knew there wasn't much I could do, but as minister for women I still wanted to show that I wasn't going to leave people in the lurch, and that I would answer questions. There was a bit of hope for Curt Bauer GmbH in Aue, a manufacturer of table and bed linen. This family firm, founded in 1882, had been expropriated and nationalized in 1972. Now, the family wanted to keep it going under private ownership. Some employees had been dismissed, but there was a plan for the future. However, as this involved high investment sums and it wasn't clear whether the former owner would be able to raise them, the Treuhand Agency had hesitated about privatizing the business, and the owners had run out of time. On my visit, I had promised to speak to the Treuhand Agency in Berlin about speeding up the process.

The Lengenfeld factory of the Zwickau cotton mill company was a very different story. This case looked simply hopeless: a loss of commissions from the Soviet Union, a temporary layoff for the two hundred or so employees in the mill, most of them women. Temporary layoffs are often an immediate prelude to unemployment. I could give these women, some of whom had passionately opposed the GDR's unfavorable conditions of production, no hope of their business continuing to run: "What am I supposed to do if my husband loses his job as well? We were so pleased about German reunification, and now we're being sidelined, simply thrown away," one of the women said, summing up their situation.

And what about me? I had shown up in a big car, but empty-handed. Then the children from the local kindergarten and their teachers arrived and called out to me, "Give my mom a job!" I had to be careful not to burst into tears. The only option I had was to listen quietly, so that the women could at least tell me about their distress.

I had sworn to myself not to make any promises I couldn't keep. There had already been quite enough disappointment. And I had taken the trouble not to succumb to the temptation to complain about all the people from Bonn who weren't there. My intention was always to say what I meant, always to say the same thing regardless of where I happened to be. So I told the women in Lengenfeld something about outdated production machinery, old markets that were falling away, competition from Asia, and insanely high investment costs. They were at least prepared to let me have my say, even if my words brought them no comfort. On this visit the question of justice had become brutally concrete: How could the bill for decades of economic mismanagement be fairly divided up? I could only offer to argue for state support such as retraining and work creation measures. I didn't believe there was such a thing as a successful privatization of cotton mills in Lengenfeld.

In March 1991, I also visited the training facilities of the Deutsche Reichsbahn (the GDR branch of the German National Railway) in Cottbus. In East Germany everyone leaving high school had had access to an apprenticeship. That was over now, and the dual training system, a success story of the social market economy, which included both in-service and school training, didn't yet exist in the new federal states. Often the idea of apprenticeships didn't feature at all in business privatizations. I was all the more determined, as youth minister, to point this out, not least on the occasion of my visit to Cottbus. Deutsche Reichsbahn had been transferred to a special fund as part of the Unification Treaty, and continued to exist until December 31, 1993, when it was merged with the West German Deutsche Bundesbahn to become Deutsche Bahn AG. At the Reichsbahn, too, the question of places for trainees had been pushed into the background by numerous other problems.

My journey to Cottbus had been a hectic one; transport connections were still poor. I had traveled along with a group of journalists from Berlin, not by car but by bus. We turned up a bit late. I had taken my seat on the podium for the on-site discussion. The first thing I did was light myself a cigarette to relax a little after the journey. I didn't give a thought to the impression that might create, but concentrated immediately afterward on the discussion with the Reichsbahn managers and the trainees. The conversation went back and forth. I quickly had a sense that the railway managers were only trying to stall me when I demanded that, as a large state-owned employer, they had a duty to offer apprenticeships. After a while I couldn't think what to do except to threaten to inform Minister Krause, as I put it. As transport minister he was responsible for the railways, and he was known for his determination. Eventually, they backed down. I added as a parting shot that companies in state ownership like the Reichsbahn needed to be a model for private companies.

On the afternoon of 28 March, 1991, still filled with my impressions of all of these trips to companies in the new federal states, I stepped into Detlev Karsten Rohwedder's office. It was a Thursday, or more precisely it was Maundy Thursday, 1991. I was delighted to see him again. I had experienced a lot in the first three months of the year and was glad that my meeting with him was my last before Easter. I was going to spend the holidays with Joachim in Hohenwalde in the far east of the country. I told Rohwedder about my visits to Aue, Lengenfeld, and Cottbus. As I had promised the family of Curt Bauer GmbH, I advocated for a swift privatization of their business, and I stressed the importance of apprenticeships. I encountered no resistance. He listened attentively when I told him my impressions of the companies I had visited, but at the same time he looked exhausted. That was understandable enough, because even twenty-four hours in the day weren't enough to deal with all the problems that confronted him daily.

We talked together for an hour, then I got to my feet. "And now Easter is just around the corner. You'll be able to have a bit of a rest," I said. He smiled and replied, "Yes, I'm flying back to be with my wife in Düsseldorf today. I can't wait." We said goodbye and went our separate ways.

When I turned on the radio on the morning of the Tuesday after Easter, April 2, 1991, I froze. I couldn't believe my ears: the previous evening, at about 11:30 p.m., Detlev Karsten

Rohwedder, the president of the Treuhand Agency, had been shot through the window of his study on the second floor of his house in Düsseldorf. His wife, Hergard Rohwedder, had also been seriously injured. A letter from the Red Army Faction (Rote Armee Fraktion, RAF) claiming responsibility had been found at the scene. Detlev Karsten Rohwedder had fallen victim to the people who hated our state and the people and institutions that represented that state—and who were now working toward the reconstruction of the East and the success of German unification.

I took part in the state ceremony in honor of Detlev Karsten Rohwedder on April 10, 1991. I stayed in touch with his wife, Hergard Rohwedder, for many years. She wrote back by hand in reply to my letter of condolence: "My husband held you in very high esteem in both human and political terms. I wish you great happiness and success." I was very touched by those lines, and have kept that letter.

I don't know whether Detlev Karsten Rohwedder was able to address the subjects we discussed on Maundy Thursday. At any rate Curt Bauer GmbH is still active today. And I persuaded the labor minister Norbert Blüm to amend the labor laws so that women were reflected in labor market policy measures in line with their high representation in unemployment figures. These included further training, retraining, and work creation measures, as well as the payment of allowances to workers on reduced hours. The Federal Employment Office gave this kind of support to male employees threatened with unemployment more frequently than it did to women in a comparable situation. I had to fight to change this, even with a tried and tested social politician like Norbert Blüm, and over the next few years, after numerous discussions, including one between the federal chancellor and business associations, the training situation in the new federal states also gradually improved.

I should add that an article about my visit to Cottbus was published in the *Frankfurter Allgemeine Zeitung* (*FAZ*) on April 2, 1991, with the headline: "The youngest member of Kohl's Cabinet still smokes in public." So that was the main message of my visit, not my fight for apprenticeships. It was my own fault, and highly embarrassing. There was also the fact that the *FAZ* was the paper that Joachim read every day. Of course, he knew I smoked, but he had never liked it. He thought I shouldn't be surprised about the press report. I had taken up smoking about ten years previously, after moving out of the place I had shared with my first husband. At the time I smoked about a pack a day, filter cigarettes, Club brand. After this event I never smoked in public again, and I gave up shortly afterward. I'd been thinking of doing so for a long time. I had often had colds, which hampered my ability to deliver speeches. I had the feeling that my frequent colds were connected with my smoking.

A broken leg

On Monday, January 6, 1992, I broke my left leg. "It'll take six months," the doctor at the Charité hospital told me as he explained the X-rays. "That's the end of my political career," I lamented. I was completely floored. I'd only been trying to pay a quick visit to the bookshop, which in those days stood at 69 Unter den Linden in Berlin Mitte, two minutes' walk from the new apartment on Wilhelmstrasse, previously Otto Grotewohl Strasse, on the corner with Behrenstrasse, to which Joachim and I had moved in November 1991. I wanted to buy myself a book for the end of the Christmas holidays, I can't remember which one. I was very ashamed of myself in front of the doctors at the hospital because I was lying in front of them in slobby leisure wear leggings and a coat that I had thrown on to go to the bookshop. I'd walked the few meters from my apartment to the bookshop and missed a step when leaving the shop, breaking my leg in two places. The pain was like nothing I had ever felt before. I couldn't take a single step. An ambulance was called, and took me to the Charité. I was given fast-acting pain-killers, but they couldn't do anything about my despair. Where would things go from here? In the afternoon I had planned to take part in an event in Neubrandenburg hosted by the Three Kings Association, and fly back to Bonn on Tuesday. (That was where the Bundestag and the Federal Government were—the move to the new capital of Berlin didn't happen until 1999.) A minister of state out of action for six months? That was impossible, I was convinced of it. Even a Bundestag representative can't stay away for as long as that, I thought. These were the ideas rushing through my head as I lay on the couch in the emergency waiting room. Exactly three weeks before, at the party conference in Dresden in 1991, I had been elected deputy to the head of the CDU, Helmut Kohl. All the plans I had made for the office had come to nothing. Why did I have to have such bad luck?

"That's not the final word. You won't have to lie down for six months, you'll soon be able to walk on crutches," the doctor said, trying to reassure me. I was operated on immediately with that prospect in mind. When I came round from the anesthetic, I was in my hospital bed with an external fixator that held the bones of my broken leg together with a system of screws and bolts. The operation had been successful, which was a relief, but everything else was miserable and depressing. In a situation like that, even small signs can convey big things.

The first sign I had was from Professor Harald Mau, now departed, a former children's surgeon and the dean of the medical faculty of the Charité; Joachim knew him from when the Humboldt University was being restructured after German unification, and I had met him in my political work as a minister. He came to see me on the first weekend after the operation when Joachim was visiting. "You don't leave children lying down for as long as that, and you don't have to do it with adults either," was the first thing he said. Mau fetched a wheelchair, helped me sit down in it, and took the lift with us to the roof terrace of the Charité. Once we were there, he pointed down at the streets of the city and said, "Take a look, you'll soon be walking around with everybody else down there." And sure enough, he managed to cheer me up. The fresh air did the rest. For the first time since the accident, I thought: Maybe you'll do it. Not just get better, but be able to do politics.

The second reassuring sign came from Christian Wulff, a thirty-two-year-old politician from Osnabrück, later to be state premier of Lower Saxony and president of the Federal Republic. Wulff had made a name for himself from the end of the 1970s in the Young Union (Junge Union, the youth organization of the CDU/CSU). He paid me a surprise visit at the Charité—we barely knew each other. I think he also wanted to use the conversation to get to know me better. He asked how I was, and I had a sense that he was interested in other people. I liked that. At the end, when he was leaving, he asked, "Is there anything else you would like?"

I shot back, "Yes, I need someone to work for me in a little office at Konrad Adenauer House in Bonn, during my time as sole deputy chair of the CDU. Do you happen to know anyone?"

"Yes, I think I do. I'll let you know," he replied.

After only a few days he called me and told me he'd spoken to Beate Baumann, twenty-eight years old and also from Osnabrück. She had studied English and German in Münster; he knew her from the Young Union, and she had supported him in the local election campaign in Osnabrück in 1986. He thought she would be interested in the temporary job in my office, and willing to spend a day a week supporting me as a research assistant at Konrad Adenauer House. He gave me her phone number. I was very pleased, and spoke to Beate Baumann on the phone a short time later. I wanted to make her acquaintance as soon as possible. We agreed to see each other the afternoon of the day I was released from the Charité, on Friday, January 31, 1992, at three o'clock in the afternoon, in my apartment on Wilhelmstrasse.

The doorbell rang at exactly three that day. "Press seven in the lift, then you go up half a flight of stairs and you're there," I said over the intercom. I welcomed her inside. "Hello, Frau Baumann, good that you could make it," I said, and tried to give her a friendly smile in spite of my restricted mobility.

I asked her to take a seat at my circular table in the sitting room and rested my iodine-smeared, fixator-trapped leg on a chair. I was aware as I did so that it must have been a terrible sight for my guest. So I got straight to the point. "When I was elected sole deputy chair of the CDU, I said to myself that I didn't just want to be a deputy under Helmut Kohl. I'd like to make something of it, and to do so I need a member of staff for a few hours a week. Christian Wulff suggested you for the post," I said, and asked: "Why are you interested?"

She replied bluntly: "That's exactly why. Because you want to go the extra mile. And I'm also interested in being a West German supporting one from the East." Months later she told me she thought it was interesting that I had started my political career in one of the GDR citizens' movements and not in the East German CDU bloc party. And that while she knew me from television pictures, her personal encounter with me was not what she expected. She had been surprised to discover that I could smile and make eye contact. Until then she had read only that I was a brittle character.

I was relieved that our conversation got going quickly. Unfortunately, with my two crutches I was a complete disaster as a hostess. On my first day after being released from hospital I didn't dare to stand in the kitchen without my crutches and make coffee. So I had to choose an unusual route and asked Beate Baumann, "Do you know how to make Turkish coffee?"

"Of course I can make coffee, but I have no idea what you mean by Turkish coffee," she replied.

I chuckled and said, "I don't know if that's really its name, but it's what we always called it at the Academy. Just boil some water, put a spoonful of coffee powder in each of the cups and pour the hot water over it."

She nodded, went into the kitchen next to the sitting room, and set to work. Once that was done, and found to be satisfactory, I risked broaching another subject: "Everything's in chaos here anyway," I said. "We only moved in here recently, and the new furniture that we ordered finally turned up yesterday. My partner hasn't yet managed to arrange it properly, and he's away on business at the moment. Could you do me one more favor?" I asked.

"Of course," she said.

"Then please go into the next room," I said. "There are drawers lying on the floor and I can't get past them with my crutches. Could you please put them in the chest of drawers by the wall?"

So my guest, whom I was meeting for the first time on what would prove to be a momentous day, put drawers in a cupboard in an apartment that was unfamiliar to her, and made Turkish coffee or what I thought of as Turkish coffee. It was probably a stroke of luck for both of us that in my basic state of crisis I didn't beat around the bush, and Beate Baumann didn't need the job she had come to talk to me about, and was therefore under no pressure. We both said the first thing that came into our heads. Just as I wanted to get to know her to decide if she was right for the job, Beate Baumann had come to find out what I was like, and whether it was going to work for her. We parted after almost two hours, and she immediately set off for home. I had made my mind up, and so had she. When I returned to work in mid-February 1992, we began working together.

Since my election to the German Bundestag and my appointment as minister for women, I had settled down well in Bonn. Parliamentary life was concentrated in the government and parliament quarter, and I could meet colleagues from the Bundestag in the evening in a villa belonging to the German Parliamentary Society, a cross-party association of deputies. At the start of 1991 I had already rented a small apartment in a new building on a hillside in the district of Muffendorf in Bad Godesberg. I loved the historical center of this former wine village, with its typical half-timbered houses. I became very familiar with the city during the years before the government moved to Berlin.

I was very careful with my broken leg. While I was still unable to put weight on my leg, I spent my nights in the Johanniter Hospital in Bonn for safety's sake, on the recommendation of Helmut Kohl's personal physician. Kohl, who had visited me in the Charité in January, wanted me to stay in office in spite of my serious injury.

Over the months that followed, Beate Baumann, along with a secretary from Konrad Adenauer House, supported me in a series of tasks emerging from what I had said at the CDU unification conference in October 1990, in my first brief party conference speech: it was about the reappraisal of injustices suffered in the GDR—for example, we organized an event borrowing the proverbial phrase "They hang the little ones, while the big ones get away with it"; this also dealt with the history of the former Eastern Bloc states, the possibility of making up for missed educational opportunities, and the renewal of the universities. There were specialist discussions with experts on all of these topics. Our work led to a paper entitled "Living Together in a New Country," which dealt with the situation in the new federal states, the content of which fed into the new motions of the CDU party conference in Düsseldorf in October 1992. For me, the party conference ended my interlude as sole deputy leader, the role that had gone first to Lothar de Maizière—until his resignation in 1991 following accusations of being an unofficial member of the Stasi—and then to me. From 1992 onwards I became one of four CDU deputy leaders.

My office on the tenth floor of the CDU's federal head office in Bonn was wound up. But my collaboration with Beate Baumann had only just begun. She became acquainted with my constituency, and in March 1993 I offered her the position of advisor in the ministry for women and youth, meaning that she would be fully professionally involved. I was delighted when Beate Baumann promptly agreed. She enjoyed our political work together, and abandoned her plans for a doctorate and her training to be a teacher that would have followed on from it. We later spoke often about that unexpected turn in her life. I was glad when she told me she had never regretted it.

There's no point in speculating about the course that my political journey might have taken if I had not broken my leg and gone on to meet Beate Baumann. Christian Wulff and I would undoubtedly have held closer discussions, but certainly not so early in 1992. In retrospect, much good did come from my accident.

After the 1994 Bundestag election, Beate Baumann moved with me to the ministry of the environment, and initially went on working as my personal ministerial assistant. From May 1995 she became my head of office, taking over from Peter Rösgen. This excellent legal expert had worked for me since 1991, and now took on new duties in the ministry, and also, from 2006, for many years in the Chancellery. Beate Baumann remained my office manager during our time in opposition at Konrad Adenauer House and in the CDU/CSU faction in the

German Bundestag, and finally for sixteen years in the chancellor's office until I stood down. I have had many very good advisors by my side throughout my life. Without all of them, particularly without Beate Baumann, my political journey would hardly have been possible.

The neighbor

When Joachim and I moved from Schönhauser Allee to Wilhelmstrasse in November 1991, the apartment next door was still vacant. That changed in the spring of 1992, when our new neighbor moved in: Birgit Breuel. On April 13, 1991, three days after the state ceremony for Detlev Karsten Rohwedder, she had been appointed his successor at the head of the Treuhand Agency. Born in Hamburg in 1937 and the mother of three sons, she came from a banking family. She had spent eight years as a member of Hamburg's state parliament. Then, in 1978, Ernst Albrecht, the state premier of Lower Saxony at the time, had appointed her as economics and transport minister, and in 1986 finance minister of the state. She had held that office until the Albrecht government was voted out in 1990. Now we got to know her personally, as neighbors. From time to time we met on Sunday afternoons, usually at her apartment. Because of her enormous workload she was rarely able to go and visit her family in Hamburg at the weekend. We sat in her little kitchen or in the sitting room and drank tea. We had a lot to talk about. Time and again I told her of my experiences as a minister, and as parliamentary representative of my constituency on the coast, and therefore about the fate of the shipyard in Stralsund.

In the 1980s, the shipyard employed over eight thousand people. It was the city's biggest employer and also to some extent its trademark. The citizens identified with it. Like all other businesses in the GDR, since the mid-1990s the shipyard had become the property of the Treuhand Agency. Commissions that had previously come from the Soviet Union had been canceled after monetary union. The shipyard could no longer cover its costs, and since the collapse of the Soviet Union its clients were no longer able to pay. Since my election as Bundestag deputy of the Hanseatic City of Stralsund, many of my conversations with the senior figures in the city, particularly the mayor Harald Lastovka (CDU), had revolved around the shipyard. I had also discussed its future countless times with the economic policymakers in the CDU/CSU Union group. In 1993, the board of the Treuhand Agency had authorized privatization. The new majority owner was now Bremer Vulkan AG, a large shipyard in the Western city of Bremen, run since 1988 by Friedrich Hennemann, the former head of the economic department of the Bremen Senate. The fact that privatization had gone ahead was good news at first. But of the eight thousand employees more than half of them had lost their jobs. And from the start there was a suspicion that funding was going to be diverted to Bremen, because Bremer Vulkan AG was not doing well economically at the time. I discussed this suspicion many times with Hennemenn, but he always vehemently denied the rumors.

Three years later, in February 1996, however, it turned out that millions in funding had in fact been diverted to the Bremen shipyard. The unauthorized use of these funds, meant for the East German shipyards, contributed to the insolvency of Bremer Vulkan AG. Following on from this, the Federal Agency for Unification-Related Special Tasks (Bundesanstalt für vereinigungsbedingte Sonderaufgaben, BvS), which had emerged from the Treuhand Agency in 1995, founded the Baltic Sea Investment Company along with the regional government of Mecklenburg-Western Pomerania. The Stralsund shipyard became a part of that. But the insolvency was a huge disappointment to everyone involved, and grist to the mill of those who were already of the opinion that East German companies were only being bought up by West German competitors to strengthen the West German part of the company in question. I didn't share that general feeling of reproach, but I too was furious, so, on February 23, 1996, I took part in the demonstration by the employees of the shipyard and the IG Metall company to save the shipyard. It was the only time in my life that I have been involved in a trade-union demonstration—I did it because I meant it, and out of concern for the employees.

The shipyard wasn't finished yet. In 1997, a new assembly shop was put into operation, the biggest in the world—300 x 108 x 74 meters—which meant that it was also able to build large container ships. The second privatization followed in January 1998, and this time the shipyard was sold to the Danish company A.P. Møller–Maersk A/S. They would not be the last owners, and it would be far beyond the scope of this book to set out in detail the rest of the shipyard's odyssey. It continues until the present day. It was and remains a sorry tale. The workforce and managers of the city of Stralsund did everything they could to maintain a base for the metalworks industry in the region, as a way of creating extra workplaces. This plan was supported at both state and national level. The works councils in particular rendered outstanding services to the shipyard. They never shirked responsibility when it came to standing up to the owners, but were prepared to sign internal contracts at a wage below the going rate, if that was what was required to secure the continuing existence of the shipyard. They were the epitome of codetermination in the workplace.

I was gathering experiences of the realities of the social market economy. First of all, the collective mentality of the GDR, often with employee numbers in four digits, was a thing of the past. In the mid-1990s, I understood that an economic structure capable of facing the future was inevitably going to be a mosaic of many smaller competitive units. Medium-sized companies were also becoming more and more important in the new federal states.

Secondly, we also became aware that some people tolerate or even encourage serious abuse with their eyes wide open.

Thirdly, I understood that, in times when the economy is weak, owners are interested first and foremost in securing their core possessions. The shipyard suffered from the fact that its new owners never had their headquarters in Stralsund. If the economy was strong, the shipyard did well; if it was weak, the shipyard did not have priority.

Fourthly, I understood that the shipyard in Stralsund was and remains a prime example of the challenges that businesses need to master in a globally contested market such as shipbuilding, which is extremely dependent on the economy as a whole. My idea of the social market economy, in which private initiatives and state framework conditions work together successfully, proved correct while decisions could be made in Germany. If, on the other hand, it was a matter of financial support, meaning grants, the European Commission was responsible. The European Commission, however, concentrated on the working of the European internal market, the equal treatment of all businesses within the member states of the European Union (EU). It did not pay enough attention to the fact that European businesses could be internationally competitive. Higher grants were paid outside the European Union. For that reason, under the investment support regulations of the European Union it is no longer possible to build competitive container ships for the global market in Europe—in spite of the outstanding abilities of European specialist workers. Consequently, jobs are being lost, and Europe is finding itself dependent in ways that it would prefer not to be.

I was able to discuss these matters, which in concrete terms also affected the opportunities for a change in European industrial policy, over tea with Birgit Breuel. She could be very determined, and knew what she wanted. She had learned how to get her arguments across in the male-dominated Hamburg CDU. That and the experience she had gathered in Lower Saxony helped her to deal with constant criticism of the work of the Treuhand Agency. I complained to her about the many shortcomings of the privatization process. She didn't simply accept this as a matter of course. I needed good arguments and solid examples of instances when Treuhand Agency negotiators had failed to advocate on behalf of the East, and of a real gold-digging atmosphere at work in many areas. She didn't immediately seem to believe everything I told her, but she did appear to be interested in my experiences. Her opportunities for action, however, were limited by the fact that the ministry of finance established the frameworks under which privatization could take place. But here again she was clear that profit was now out of the question where privatization was concerned: the closing balance of the Treuhand Agency in 1994 showed a deficit of some 270 billion deutsche marks. The deficit arose from the fact that the Treuhand Agency had already taken over Eastern businesses at a loss and rebuilt them before selling them, or else the purchase sum did not fully cover the companies' debts.

A degree of trust had built up between us—and grown. One Sunday late in 1993, when we once again were having tea in her apartment, Birgit Breuel mentioned that she knew no East Germans whatsoever outside of her professional dealings. I replied that I had only a few West German acquaintances, apart, of course, from my relations in Hamburg and friends from my time in science. Birgit Breuel suggested that we set up a discussion group made up of East and West Germans. I liked the idea. Each of us assumed the task of suggesting some participants— she the West Germans and Joachim and I the Easterners.

A group of some fifteen people from East and West came

together—aside from Birgit Breuel, Joachim, and me, these included the theologian and philosopher Richard Schröder, the pediatric surgeon Harald Mau, the film director Volker Schlöndorff, and the author Helga Schubert. In 1994, we met up every six weeks or so and talked: What is the state of German unity? What are our expectations with regard to the state? Where should individuals do more? What does German unity mean for the European Union? What does it mean for art and culture? What is the state of the renewal of science, using the experience of the Humboldt University? This question touched on Joachim's academic work at the time.

On July 27, 1990, the East German Academy of Sciences had been turned into a public corporation. On July 11, 1990, the Council of Science had introduced a review of the sixty or so institutes within the Academy, including my former institute, the ZIPC. The Council of Science, founded in 1957, is the most important advisory committee on science policy in Germany at both federal and state level. In Article 38 of the Unification Treaty it had been stated that research institutes would continue to exist as federal state institutions until December 31, 1991, if they had not previously been converted or dissolved. Then they were transferred gradually into the existing structure of the West German scientific institutions. This included the attempt to open the way for scientists who had been unable to find a job as professors at universities in the GDR for political reasons, to open up this path to them via the universities, which were also going through a process of renewal. Just such an opportunity arose for Joachim: from 1992 until 1996 he was director of the Max Planck Quantum Chemistry working group at the Humboldt University, and in 1993 he was appointed professor of theoretical chemistry in the Chemistry faculty of the Humboldt University.

Almost twenty years later, in 2011, in his entry for the journal *Nachrichten aus der Chemie* (News from Chemistry), he described his new personal beginning with reference to his faculty, under the heading "The divided East and the successful reunification," and he also said in an interview in the same edition of the journal: "Where conflicts between East and West are evoked, these are in fact conflicts between East and East. Structurally, the reunification has been a great success in science—after twenty years, universities and research facilities in the new and old states are in the same league. Today, more people are working in the scientific site at Adlershof than were working in the academic institutes of the GDR before 1990. It is also clear, however, that not everyone has benefited from, or been able to benefit from, this process." I share this assessment.

Citizens' consultation

Every six to eight weeks I held citizens' consultations in my constituency office in Stralsund, the first on May 2, 1991. I had found a suitable office space on Badenstrasse, directly behind the city hall. I placed an advertisement in the *Ostsee-Zeitung* (Baltic News), inviting people to come and talk. I wanted people to have a direct way of contacting their representative. No one needed to contact me in advance. During these consultations, the chief topics of discussion were the shatteringly high levels of unemployment and questions of private property. In the GDR, house-owners had owned the house but not the plot on which it stood; as a rule there was only a right of use. The same had been true for Joachim and me where our little house in Hohenwalde was concerned. In the days of the GDR this also meant that no one was interested in the price of a square meter of land. That changed suddenly in 1990, with the transition to Federal German law. The Civil Code stated, as it still does, that ownership of a building and the parcel of land on which it stands belong together. In the new federal states, all house-owners were now obliged to buy the parcels of land on which their houses were built. Millions of entries had to be made in the land register. It wasn't until September 1994 that a user's claim to a purchase contract or the order of a hereditary building right could be established in return for compensation from the property owner, which was in many cases the state. The law also covered the extent of the compensation. It was thus clear that charging usual market rates for land in connection with home ownership was out of the question. The purchase of recreational or garage plots proved more difficult. On the one hand, very complicated property relations arose, since many of those who had at some point left the GDR in the forty years of its existence, or had been expropriated, were also able to reassert their claims. Many land registers in the GDR had not been properly kept. By now at least it might have been clear to everyone that it had been a wise and correct decision not to reverse the land reform measures imposed in the Soviet Zone in 1945. And yet this provision, included in the Unification Treaty, was bitterly rejected by many in the Federal Republic.

Usual market rates suddenly applied in the case of private real-estate sales. This had drastic effects in my constituency. People who owned houses on the island of Rügen, right on the Baltic coast, could make a hundred times as much as sellers in the hinterland, in places like the county of Grimmen. All of a sudden my constituency became an area of huge class differences. Many people were left disappointed.

In the mid-1990s, a citizen came to my consultation. He had an urban plot which he did not use himself, and which he had entered in the land registry. He had, he told me, been happy to do so, because by taking that step he thought he had done everything that needed to be done. Far from it, as it turned out. Someone else had registered a claim to the plot, and had brought the case before a court, which had found in their favor.

The entry in the land registry made by the man who came to my consultation had to be canceled. He raged: "The entry in the registry means that the plot belongs to me. I can't be punished for an incorrect entry! This is *my* property! I can't let them take it from me! You've got to do something!" But there was nothing I could do. I had to tell him that Bundestag representatives aren't allowed to give legal advice, and he needed to approach a lawyer. He looked desperately disappointed. Still, I tried to cheer him up a little, and said, "Maybe in spite of everything you can look at it this way: in the days of the GDR you didn't believe for a second that you would get anything for this plot. Even though you're disappointed now, it's true that in the united Germany there are at least a few things we can do that we couldn't have dreamed of doing in the old days. So try not to be too downcast by this bad turn of events, and enjoy the unexpected things. We all have only one life, which we should take care not to spoil." He listened to me carefully. I knew my words couldn't help him in concrete terms, so I would have understood if he had stomped furiously off. Instead he said to me as he left, "It's crap that it went the way it did. But otherwise what you say is true." I couldn't have expected more.

It was also often hard on the farmers who wanted to work independently after the dissolution of the Agricultural Production Cooperatives (Landwirtschaftliche Produktionsgenossenschaften, LPG), and as well as the land that they had brought into the LPG, wanted to buy land from the Treuhand Agency, or the institution that took over from it, the Land Evaluation and Administration Company (Bodenverwertungs- und Verwaltungsgesellschaft GmbH, BVVG). The Treuhand Agency and the BVVG were under the control of the Federal Ministry of Finance, and their legal task was to sell their plots as profitably as possible. If the prices were too high, the local farmers couldn't afford them, and there was a danger that they would be priced out by wealthier Western buyers. That made the locals furious.

As their parliamentary representative I took part in meetings between the farmers affected and the members of the Treuhand Agency, usually along with district administrator Wolfhard Molkentin. As a former deputy LPG chair he was an expert on the subject. Discussions were often heated. Sometimes the situation threatened to get out of control, when the West German Treuhand staff were unfamiliar with the details. I did all that I could to avoid fisticuffs. Somehow, with a lot of time and great attention to detail, we always managed to calm things down. When I had to travel back to Bonn, Wolfhard Molkentin and his people took over.

On the island of Rügen, however, everything revolved around the purchase of properties that were lucrative but in need of renovation. One West German, for example, bought many of the villas along the beach promenade in the resort town of Binz, and also published a free news sheet. No wonder that envy and resentment spread among many of the locals. The buyer renovated the villas according to the rules of cultural heritage protection, in the style of historic seaside architecture. It was utterly beautiful, but the only way of affording it was if the buildings went on to become vacation apartments. Until now the people of Binz had lived in these houses, or else they had been used as old people's homes and kindergartens. New apartments and houses had to be found for many people, with the help of the council—a far from simple matter. Only a very few locals were brave and financially strong enough to participate in the privatizations.

"Blossoming landscapes"?

There was one point on which almost everyone agreed: if the new federal states were to develop economically in any reasonable way, they needed a completely new transport infrastructure.

The transport minister Günther Krause had deemed seventeen transport projects to be absolutely necessary. On April 9, 1991, the cabinet ruled that these so-called "German Unity" transport projects were to be put into effect as quickly as possible. The crucial project for my constituency was number ten, the A20 autobahn. It was to extend from Kreuz Uckermark in Brandenburg, go past Greifswald, Stralsund, and Rostock to Lübeck, and on through Schleswig-Holstein and Lower Saxony to the Dutch–German border. To the representatives of the new federal states, it was clear as day that, with the lengthy planning methods to which we had become accustomed, all seventeen transport projects in the new federal states were in danger of being realized only very slowly or not at all. On October 7, 1991, the cabinet introduced fast-tracked permit procedures.

From now on, local politicians in Western Pomerania, with Wolfhard Molkentin at their head, made it their personal business to achieve visible progress in the form of finished sections of the autobahn. The construction of the A20 kicked off in December 1992, although in Günther Krause's constituency and not in mine. But never again have I worked on a project in which all the levels of decision-making—county, state, and federation—worked as closely together as they did here, to achieve the desired goal as quickly as possible. Even so, it was a long time before the work was completed. It was not until ten years later, in December 2005, as chancellor, that I was able to open the last section of the A20 at Tribsees, thirty-seven kilometers southwest of Stralsund. And in 2007, I was able to officiate at the ceremonial opening of the imposing second bridge of the Strelasund lagoon between Stralsund and Rügen. In 2002, both the Old Town of Stralsund and that of Wismar, 130 kilometers away, became UNESCO World Heritage Sites. Most of the four hundred or so houses in Stralsund that were protected as historic monuments were renovated. The Sea Museum in St. Katharine's Convent and the Ozeaneum on

Stralsund harbor, with my adopted penguin Alexandra, achieved significance beyond the regional borders. These are the "blossoming landscapes" that Helmut Kohl predicted in a speech in 1990. The Old Towns of Stralsund and Greifswald were renovated in line with the latest findings of the department of historic monuments; the old seaside architecture was saved; the piers were rebuilt and biosphere reserves and national parks designated. This was made possible by large amounts of sponsorship money from the German Federation, and hence all German taxpayers—and thanks to the tireless commitment of passionate local, regional, and federal politicians who had dedicated themselves to the success of the reconstruction of the East. Figures like Wolfhard Molkentin and Harald Lastovka stand in for many, many others.

Another part of the picture, however, is that not everyone was able to become involved in the reconstruction of the East as they would have wished. In 1999/2000, some 20 percent of the working-age population were unemployed. Many between the ages of thirty and fifty-five in 1990 were victims of the inevitable changes through no fault of their own. They built their own homes in the GDR; they had worked for industrial concerns; they had been farmers, vets, or craftspeople, and had not simply been able to learn a new profession and move to a new place. Often they spent years commuting long distances, as many dockers did between Stralsund and Hamburg. Their children would later leave their homes in droves. Whole graduation classes at Stralsund technical college went in search of employment opportunities in Munich, Stuttgart, and the surrounding areas. This in turn provoked serious accusations, because the parents of those children didn't see their grandchildren growing up. The children rarely visited with their families, because they had their own professional futures to think about. In many cases their parents, in turn, were not able to spend a long time with them because their apartments were too small and the rents in southern Germany too high for them to move.

The treatment of victims of the SED dictatorship was a particular source of contention. The "Laws Correcting Injustice" had been regularly updated since the early 1990s. In view of this, the Federal Constitutional Court had ruled in 1999 that anyone drawing special and additional pensions from the GDR must also receive them in the unified Federal Republic. These people included, among others, senior civil servants within the state apparatus, employees of the Stasi and the National People's Army, as well as directors of firms and "Kombinate" (combines, integrated industrial groups). Even today, the German government and the new federal states are still paying out sums in the mid-billions. Pensions for victims make up only a tiny fraction of this sum.

The area of my constituency was extended twice, because the number of people living there had dropped since 1990 to such an extent that it was below the figure required for a Bundestag constituency. One county territory reform came hot on the heels of the last. Citizens had to cover ever greater distances: to school, to the hospital, to the land register office, to the law court, to their elected representatives at all levels. Those "blossoming landscapes" do exist, but they do not make up the whole picture, not only because of the shadows of the developmental failures of the GDR, which are longer than we had wished, and which are fading more slowly than we hoped. It is also down to the rancor over the lack of understanding that GDR citizens encountered from the West in 1990 and afterward, and which has dug its way deeply into the souls of many.

My own experience was that it was more difficult than I had expected in 1990 to speak openly to the West German media about one's own life in the GDR. When I said in a podium discussion in Schwerin, on October 3, 1992, that I had got a low mark in my ML work at the Academy of Sciences because I had written too positively about the role of farmers in comparison to the industrial working class, the media launched a hunt for my essay. I would happily have made it publicly available, but I didn't have a copy of it at home, as I had typed it out myself on my typewriter, and had not made a carbon copy. As I've said before, when I tried to use carbon paper I always ended up putting it the wrong way round, so that it printed out on the reverse of the original page. We didn't have access to copying equipment for purposes of this kind. All of a sudden I found myself facing investigative journalists as if I was trying to hush something up—even though I had told them about my essay myself. Later I heard from a Brandenburg colleague in the SPD that journalists had left no stone unturned to find my essay in the archives of the former Academy of Sciences. They couldn't have found it, because even in the days of the GDR, essays were destroyed after only a few years.

On the other hand, I became less self-conscious, and for many years spoke about my life in the GDR, bearing in mind that what I wanted to say might lead to suspicions of some kind. It was not until twenty-nine years later, on October 3, 2021, at my last public speech on the Day of German Unity, that I addressed the issue openly when I asked the question: "Do people of my generation and origin from the GDR need to prove time and again our loyalty to our reunited country, even after three decades of German unity, as if our earlier history, life in the GDR, was some kind of outrage?" I was referring to a volume about my eighteen years as party chair of the CDU, published by the Konrad Adenauer Foundation not shortly after German unification, but in 2020, a passage of which read: "Of course she came to the CDU as a thirty-five-year-old, in the days after the fall of the Berlin Wall, and with her brought the ballast of her life in the GDR; she could not be a dyed-in-the-wool, fully socialized old-Federal-Republic CDU creature." Reading that took my breath away. Even after thirty years, my life in the GDR clearly served at best as a lasting scandal, as in the case of my ML essay. The fact that it was part of our common history and future in reunified Germany seemed to be beyond many people's imagination.

Against aggression and violence

As youth minister, I had to deal with the immaterial conse-quences of forty years of the GDR, and the upheaval that followed German reunification. Unlike the problems of a creaking infra-structure and high unemployment, these were not immediately obvious. As far as I could tell, a majority in the CDU and the CSU saw me as someone who was constantly demanding new jobs and funding for youth work, for which, first of all, the federal states rather than the federation itself were responsible, and for which, in addition, there would have been no need if only parents had accepted their responsibility. Many were convinced that the place would keep running perfectly well on its own if the economy was going well and young people had apprenticeships and jobs. But there was also a minority with a different view, which included, for example, Peter Hintze, born in 1950 in Bad Honnef near Bonn, a theologian and parliamentary secretary of state in my ministry, and Ronald Pofalla, born in 1959 in Kleve on the Lower Rhine, a lawyer and social educator who was a member of the committee for women and youth, both, like myself, members of the German Bundestag since 1990. I would later work closely with both for many years. They shared my opinion that state funding was necessary to support offers from independent sponsors—associations and private initiatives—for children and young people.

This applied particularly to the new federal states, because the former state structures for youth work in the GDR no longer existed, and the offers from independent sponsors had yet to emerge. We were not unaware that the pros and cons of state programs needed to be carefully weighed up. This was especially true of work with young people of far-right and far-left tendencies, and hence also to the action program against aggression and violence, which I had developed after a surge in acts of violence by far-right youths against foreigners in 1991. The miserable climax came in September 1991, with days of racially motivated attacks in the town of Hoyerswerda in Saxony, directed at a hostel for foreign contract workers and refugee accommodation. As youth minister I didn't want to stand aside and watch these acts of brutality. In the action program, twenty million deutsche marks were spent on social work, on 144 projects in thirty main regions across all nine new federal states. They were intended to prevent or at least reduce the readiness of young people to engage in violence. The program was later extended until 1996.

"We have nothing else, no leisure opportunities, nothing at all!" young people told me on February 17, 1993, when I visited a youth club in the Rostock district of Gross Klein. The young people were fifteen, sixteen, seventeen years old. I had previously met up with youth workers from the city. The background to my visit lay in the attacks by several hundred right-wing extremists on the central reception point for asylum seekers in Rostock, and a hostel for former Vietnamese contract workers in the Sunflower House in Rostock-Lichtenhagen, which had left Germany shaken a few months previously, in August 1992; I had also visited the city on that occasion.

My reply to the reproach from the young people was: "OK, my ministry spends money on programs which mean that your club is able to exist. But even so, can't you also try to find places where you can do things yourself?" The young people probably thought I was from another planet. At any rate, I didn't get an answer, just found myself staring into bored faces.

192

FREEDOM AND RESPONSIBILITY

The supervisors I later talked to on their own also looked unsettled. They seemed to be worried that the minister from Bonn would cancel the funding for their project if they had no success stories to report to me. But I wasn't on a tour of inspection, and I didn't want to cancel any funding, but I did want to spend such funding as there was in a sensible way. So I had to be sure that the adults engaging with the young people weren't inclined toward extreme ideologies themselves. That was crucial for the acceptance of the program. From what I could tell at the club in Rostock, that wasn't the case.

Many of the young people I met in Rostock were—sometimes unlike their parents—in work, and had still turned to the far right, even though unemployment never justifies hatred. Xenophobia had already existed in the days of the GDR. Very subtle in its forms of expression, it had been largely directed against Poles, always with an element of envy. People said the Poles were buying up our broom-handles and all kinds of things when they came to our country to shop. And Vietnamese, Mozambican, or Angolan contract workers—in the GDR the term "contract workers" was used, corresponding to the term "Gastarbeiter" (guest workers) in the old Federal Republic— were advised not to make themselves too conspicuous in daily life. They had to live hidden away in hostels. In other cities they were hardly even allowed to meet one another. The notion of integration was an entirely foreign concept.

The authoritarian, dictatorial character of the SED state continued to affect German unification. Admittedly, three-quarters of young people made use of their new opportunities for freedom, but there was also a sense of disorientation, along with feelings of inferiority toward young West Germans and a longing for authority figures. The collapse of the GDR left a roaring void in many people; they lacked the learned and experienced values indispensable for coexistence in a democratic society. Overnight, teachers had to communicate new values and a new vision of history, the state, and society. Many of them struggled, and had little authority over their pupils. In some cases violent perpetrators found open support among the population as a whole, leading them to believe that what they were doing was somehow acceptable.

All of this was happening during a politically charged time for Germany, when many people were fleeing war in the former Yugoslavia, and a debate was raging about the right to asylum enshrined in our Basic Law. In Rostock-Lichtenhagen, but also in two terrible arson attacks in November of the same year on two houses occupied by a Turkish family in the town of Mölln in Schleswig-Holstein, and in May 1993 on a house occupied by a Turkish family in Solingen in the West, a high level of aggression, brutality, and misanthropy began to appear in our society.

Almost twenty years later, in November 2011, the biggest series of far-right murders in the history of the Federal Republic finally came to light. The terrorist group responsible was "National Socialist Underground" (NSU), formed in Thuringia in 1998. Between 2000 and 2007, the NSU had carried out cold-blooded murders of nine people with migrant backgrounds, and from 1999 onward had planted bombs and carried out bank robberies. For over a decade the terrorists, who came from the city of Jena, went undiscovered, and the true background to their actions remained in the dark. The authorities had at first gone looking for clues in Mafia and drug-related circles, or in the family circles of the victims, rather than looking at the possibility of far-right perpetrators. The investigation was a terrible failure. So, in my speech at the memorial event in Berlin, on February 23, 2012, I asked the relatives to forgive the fact that they had been placed under suspicion for years, and also promised them that our constitutional state would do everything in its power to understand the background to the attacks.

In the course of the further investigations by the police and the justice sector, as well as the work by the investigative committees of the regional parliaments of Thuringia and Saxony, it turned out that in 1991 the three main perpetrators of the NSU had attended a recently reopened youth club in Jena-Winzerla, a run-down district of the city, in a building previously used for a similar purpose by the Free German Youth (FDJ). The work of the youth club had—like many other projects of social work with young people in Thuringia and Saxony—been supported by funds including the action program against aggression and violence. The far-right tendencies of the three future NSU perpetrators—two men and a woman, aged between fourteen and eighteen in 1991—was not hidden from the social workers. Initially, it was not seen as a reason to ban them from the premises, but rather to introduce them to leisure activities in the club which might remove them from that sphere of influence. That plan failed, however; after becoming increasingly radicalized, the two young males were excluded from the youth club in 1993 and 1994.

The case of these future NSU terrorists demonstrates the dilemma faced by youth workers when dealing closely with violent far-right young people. They were on the razor's edge. There was always a risk of misspending state funds on hopeless cases. Does that mean we just give up? It's impossible to prove how many young people were saved from further radicalization by our program. Many experts urged us to emphasize prevention rather than working with young people who had already come to the attention of the authorities. I took their warnings seriously. Yet even today I think it was worth fighting for each single individual, not least with a program such as the one against aggression and violence.

EQUAL RIGHTS

Feminist?

THE CDU, CSU, and FDP concluded coalition negotiations to form the first all-German federal government on January 16, 1991. At around that time Günther Krause said to me, "Kohl tells me you're going to become a minister. Something to do with women."

I didn't know what to say. I couldn't remember having a conversation with the chancellor in which he had told me in person that I was going to be a government minister. The only thing I could think of was a slightly strange meeting in November 1990, shortly before the Bundestag election. At that time Kohl had invited me to his office in Bonn for a discussion. "How do you get on with women?" he had asked me, using the informal "du." (I later learned that he used it with almost everybody he met.) So there I sat in the chancellor's office, having prepared myself for every imaginable political question, and I didn't know what I was supposed to answer now.

"How I get on with women?" I had to think for a moment. "I have a sister, and I also have women friends. In my department at the Academy of Sciences, I was the only woman apart from the secretary. So I get on as well with women as I do with men," I concluded.

Kohl seemed to be happy with my answer. I had almost forgotten the conversation until Krause referred to it.

"We are the only two CDU representatives from the new federal states who are joining the cabinet. I'm going to be transport minister," Krause went on. "Since you're a year younger than me, I'm no longer the youngest person in the cabinet. Shame, but never mind," he said with a grin, before adding, to my bewilderment, "At any rate, you should find yourself something decent to wear." And with that he was off.

So that was my "appointment" as minister for women and youth. As to whether anyone else had heard about the rumors and mentioned them to me, I can't honestly remember. I received official confirmation a little later from the minister of the chancellor's office, Friedrich "Fritz" Bohl (CDU). I asked Günther Krause's secretary about serious clothes shops in Bonn, and went to the elegant district of Bad Godesberg to buy a dark blue suit which I thought might please the representatives of the Western CDU when I took my oath as minister in the German Bundestag on January 18, 1991. I didn't feel entirely comfortable in it, however, but felt somehow overdressed. My previous style of clothing—long skirts and knitted jackets—was, I assumed, too "alternative" for many people in the CDU, who would see it as more appropriate for a member of the Greens than of the Christian Democratic Union.

But in this regard, once again, my broken leg a year later almost seemed like a blessing in disguise. I owed that to Michaela Geiger, a CSU politician and state secretary to the minister for economic cooperation. To cheer me up, she called me at the hospital. I told her how fed up I was that I wouldn't be able to make any appearances for months with my broken leg. She reassured me and said, "You can just use crutches, you'll learn quickly enough." I wasn't convinced: "How am I going to use crutches if I'm wearing a skirt? I'll be tripping up all the time."

"Oh, don't make life so complicated for yourself. Even in the Bundestag you can wear trousers instead of skirts, it's much handier with the crutches once you've got rid of the fixator and have a plaster cast," she said.

"But last year I was told I had to dress properly for the swearing-in. I don't want to make an unpleasant spectacle of myself," I replied.

"Nonsense, you won't. I've even worn a trouser suit in the plenary assembly. You can do exactly the same. Be brave!" she said encouragingly.

I was grateful for the tip. A trouser suit as a test of courage? At any rate, that was how it was in the CDU and the CSU in those days. Today it sounds like a grim story. Luckily, times quickly changed.

"Do you see yourself as a feminist?" the moderator of a podium discussion asked me many years later, in spring 2017, when Germany held the presidency of the G20. The G20 is an informal assembly of nineteen states and the European Union, which has existed since 1999, consisting of industrial nations and emerging nations. Among those with me on the podium were Máxima, the queen of the Netherlands; Christine Lagarde, at the time the executive director of the International Monetary Fund; and Ivanka Trump, daughter of the then American president Donald Trump. Am I a feminist? My brain worked away. I felt that I could say neither yes nor no. But why? I had been chancellor for almost twelve years. As a woman who had reached the most powerful office of state, I was able to act as a model for other women, and particularly for girls. And perhaps I actually was one.

As minister for women, I had made policies for women. I had pressed for a second Equality Act, designed to reform the first Equality Act passed in 1957. Article 31 of the Unification Treaty had ruled that the all-German lawmakers, the German Bundestag, must further develop legislation for equality between women and men. At the ministry for women we had worked on

a draft act consisting of three parts: one for improved compati-
bility between family and profession in the civil service and the
federal courts; a second for the appointment of women and
men to committees on which the country as a whole had to
make decisions or comments; and a third for the protection of
workers in private and public companies against sexual assault.

The whole legislation process proved to be a tough one. In
May 1993, the draft law was passed in the federal cabinet. The
first reading in the German Bundestag was held in September.
In particular, CDU/CSU members of the Bundestag's Legal
Affairs Committee had made it their goal to prevent the passing
of the act. They were especially enraged by the idea of protection against sexual harassment. Today, it's hard to imagine that
rape in marriage only became illegal in 1997. In the ministry, we
developed campaigns in which we wanted to draw attention to
violence against women. I was able to build on the political and
legal expertise and experience of my section director Renate
Augstein. In the third part, concerning protection against
sexual violence, this draft law was also intended to apply to
private companies. So, alongside members of the Legal Affairs
Committee, CDU/CSU members of the Standing Committee
on Industry and Trade also took to the barricades. They acted as
if the owners of small and medium-sized companies would risk
a jail sentence if my bill became reality. Such scenarios were
absurd, but the fact that they were even discussed meant that
many company representatives spoke out against the bill. In
contrast, from the perspective of many women's associations
and then SPD/Green opposition, the draft law fell far short of
what was required, since it did not provide for any legally
enforceable rights. Luckily, most of the women representatives
in my group supported me. If they hadn't, I would have failed
hopelessly.

And I would have failed if Wolfgang Schäuble hadn't
supported me. In March 1991, a few weeks after I took up office,

I was already talking to him about my plan. He was minister of the interior at the time. The terrible attempt on his life that had put him in a wheelchair had happened just six months previously. My original purpose in having the conversation was to tell him that I wanted to bring Willi Hausmann, whom I knew from the negotiations over the Unification Treaty, from his ministry to mine and officially appoint him state secretary, given that my then state secretary Werner Chory was seriously ill; he died in 1991 at the age of only fifty-eight. Wolfgang Schäuble was at first quite startled that I had chosen Willi Hausmann. In fact it was very unusual for a successful official in the big interior ministry to be willing to switch to the small ministry for women, even if the move was associated with a promotion to state secretary. After a short period of reflection, however, Schäuble agreed. Then I also used our discussion in March 1991 to talk to Schäuble about the Equality Act.

"There is an urgent need for action, not only because of the mandate of the Unification Treaty," I said, "but because in the whole of the German government there is not a single woman state secretary, hardly a single head of department, and not nearly enough division secretaries."

Schäuble nodded his agreement and replied, "You're absolutely right. We need this law."

His words encouraged me to add, "I can only do it if you help me, though. You need to support me in person, so that the officials working for you, the ones responsible for legislation in the public service of the Federation as a whole, know that their minister stands behind the project."

In the negotiations for the Unification Treaty I had learned that whenever there was a political will for the solution of a problem, the corresponding legal formulation had been found. To my delight, Wolfgang Schäuble didn't hesitate for a second and replied, "You have my support. It's also in my interest for the project to be a success."

Without this support, without Wolfgang Schäuble's intelligence—and that of Jürgen Rüttgers—the Equality Act couldn't have been passed in 1993. By now Schäuble was chair of the CDU/CSU Union faction in the German Bundestag, with Jürgen Rüttgers his first parliamentary manager and hence his right-hand man within the faction. With a doctorate in law, and having been the minister of research and education during Helmut Kohl's final period in office between 1994 and 1998, and later the state premier of North Rhine-Westphalia, he was deeply rooted in the CDU of the Catholic Rhineland. "We're putting a package together," they explained. "That way we can kill several birds with one stone, and your Equality Act can get through." It made sense to me. In planning for the agenda of the German Bundestag, Schäuble parceled up my Equality Act with the concluding second and third readings of various other draft laws. And sure enough: my act was passed. On June 24, 1994, President Richard von Weizsäcker put his signature under it, and the law came into force on September 1, 1994, a month and a half before the Bundestag election.

Our consultations for Article 3 of our Basic Law had taken place at almost the same time. This Article established equal rights between women and men, and was now amended. "The state," the new addition read, "shall promote the implementation of equal rights for women and men, and take steps toward the elimination of existing disadvantages." This change to the Basic Law went into effect on November 15, 1994. My Equality Act was intended to bring about this state goal.

Nonetheless, I was disillusioned. Disillusioned with the obstinacy with which the act had repeatedly been dragged out. And I was shocked at how it had been presented as a threat to our country's economic development.

I was not discouraged, however. And twenty years later, as chancellor, not only had I initiated many initiatives for women in leadership positions, and promoted the formation of networks between women, but I had also ensured that in the chancellor's office half of the leadership positions were occupied by women and the other half by men. This was parity, the equal participation of women and men. Equality of participation in all areas—that had always been my goal.

But did that make me a feminist?

All of these questions were whirling around in my head on the podium of the G20 women's summit when I was asked: "Do you see yourself as a feminist?" I hummed and hawed and tried to gain time to put my thoughts in order. I talked about "on the one hand" and "on the other hand." The hall, which I sensed was very much on my side, said to me: "Say it! Say it!"

"If you think I am one, then take a vote!" I called back into the hall.

Queen Máxima tried to help: "What does a term like that tell us? I simply want all women to have a free choice, to have opportunities that they can take, that they can feel equal, always and everywhere, that they can be proud of themselves. If that is a feminist, then I'm one too, otherwise I don't know," she argued very convincingly. With these words Máxima built me a bridge. As I said at the end of the discussion, I could concur with this "good definition." The audience was pleased.

I still felt uneasy. Was it my unwillingness to be pigeonholed, to be defined as part of a group, that held me back? It was something I hadn't been able to bear back in the GDR, and I also constantly had to resist it in the West. Because I was a woman in politics, it had immediately been suggested to me that I become a member of the social committees in the CDU, since obviously women were interested in social issues. Or else it was assumed that because I came from the East, I must be a particularly suspicious person, after being kept under surveillance by the Stasi. It was always like that. Perhaps that was one reason for my indecision about whether I was willing to call myself a feminist. But it couldn't be the only one.

How had things been in my family? In terms of our education, my parents hadn't made any distinction between my sister, Irene, and me, and our brother, Marcus. We were all supposed to develop our gifts to the full. And yet I was aware that my mother had had to fight for her professional independence from my father, and that my sister and I were more involved in household chores than Marcus.

And what about the situation of women in the GDR and my attitude to it? Because of the inefficiency of the economy, women were urgently needed in the workforce. That—rather than anything like an understanding of equality between mothers and fathers—had also been the essential reason why the SED state offered many more daycare places for children than the West. This still didn't mean that women didn't have to do the bulk of the housework on top of their jobs.

Neither could it be said that women played an equal part in the power structures of the GDR. In the central committee of the SED in 1989, only 26 out of 221 members and candidates were women. In the forty-year existence of the GDR, not a single woman made it into the center of its power, the Politburo. Only two women had managed to stand as candidates for the Politburo, albeit without voting rights. And only a very few industrial combines were run by women. In the late 1980s, the proportion of women in directorial positions in Publicly Owned Enterprises (Volkseigene Betriebe) stood at 20 percent.

It was a similar situation in the sciences. At the start of my scientific work it was clear to me that it would never be possible for me to rise to a directorial level. The boundaries imposed on me by the state, however, were not down to my sex but to my family origins. The GDR was a dictatorship. I had already fallen foul of its expectations when applying for the job in Ilmenau. As an ordinary scientist I could have gone my own way. But there wasn't anything more I could do. If I had had reasons to resist, they had to do with socialist indoctrination and freedom of opinion, not my unequal treatment as a woman.

Nevertheless, I had always been interested in biographies of outstanding women, particularly Marie Curie, the Polish-French physicist, chemist, and two-time winner of a Nobel Prize. I had also read the first volume of Simone de Beauvoir's *Memoirs of a Dutiful Daughter*. I can't remember whether my parents had been sent the book from the West, or whether it had been published in the GDR. But I do remember being impressed by de Beauvoir's journey out of the traditional roles imposed by the parental home. But when I read Alice Schwarzer's book *Simone de Beauvoir—Rebel and Pioneer*, I understood that for Simone de Beauvoir feminism and a socialist vision of the world belonged together. I saw that kind of feminism as an illusion. It wasn't an option for me.

For me, the year 1968 had not, as it had for many in the West, represented a break from traditional social conventions; instead it was marked by the invasion of Prague by Warsaw Pact troops to bring the Prague Spring to a brutal end. I had also seen many feminist actions in the 1960s and 1970s as shrill and crass. They were intended to be. In the GDR, however, I was used to reading between the lines. I was repelled by the more confrontational approach. For me, the struggle for greater levels of participation by women had never been a fundamental struggle against men, not even as a politician. I wondered, rather, whether feminists could trust men to fight along with them against constricting male structures—particularly since I had personal experience of women behaving with a distinct lack of solidarity toward other women. On one occasion during my time as minister for women, a female photographer had been foolish enough to hurl herself on the floor in the cabinet room before the cabinet session, to take a photograph of the crooked heels of my shoes. What image of women was she chasing after? Either way, not a trace of female solidarity.

After German reunification I assumed that the individual freedoms available in a democracy would create the possibility of equal participation between women and men, almost as a matter of course. Individual efforts would lead to the equality of the sexes in society, I thought. For that reason I was initially reluctant to approve state, group-related promotional measures. The facts would immediately have put me straight, but my enthusiasm for the general new freedom clearly obstructed my vision of reality. I was forced to acknowledge that in fact nothing did happen as a matter of course. Women were not given preferential treatment when there were candidates of equal suitability, or taken into consideration when leadership positions were being filled. I would be forced to accept that state intervention was indispensable if the cause of women was to be promoted. For this very reason the Second Equal Treatment Act, which I had made my mission, was necessary for equal employment rights in public service. And for that very reason I later changed my opinion on quotas in the economy and politics, at all levels. The facts had convinced me that it was impossible without them. And even with them it was difficult enough.

I also learned that so-called "freedom of choice," the magic words used by the CDU and CSU for decisions regarding work and family, in reality was a Trojan horse. In discussions that I sometimes had, as minister for women, with small groups of women from East and West and with different histories, I encountered a great deal of bitterness when we talked about mutual prejudices, about the success each of us had achieved in our lives, about dealing with the pressure of social expectations, about mothers and "Rabenmütter"—literally "raven mothers," women who were said to neglect their children in favor of their work—luckily a term that one can barely imagine anyone using these days. It became clear to me that without the right conditions in place, women could not consider themselves to be treated equally—and they still aren't.

Today, if I found myself sitting on a podium like the one at the G20 women's summit and was asked, "Do you see yourself as a feminist?" I would have my thoughts in order, and reply, "Yes, I am a feminist, in my way."

A stiff neck

The negotiations concerning the Unification Treaty had not succeeded in finding a common wording for a revision of Section 218 of the German Criminal Code, the section governing abortion. The Bundestag now had until the end of 1992 to rectify this, with the existing provisions in the East and West remaining in force for this period. In the new federal states, the relevant provision was the law permitting an abortion within twelve weeks of conception, as established by the East German Volkskammer in 1972. It defined abortion as a method of contraception. Women had the right to decide to terminate their pregnancy within the first twelve weeks, on their own authority. Following the 1990 Volkskammer election, the Eastern CDU and Eastern SPD had expressed their support for retaining this solution in the coalition agreement of the de Maizière government. By contrast, the "indication solution" that had entered into force in the old Federal Republic in 1976 remained applicable in the former West German states. This stipulated that an abortion could only be exempt from punishment if specific conditions were met. This regulation was linked to an obligation to obtain advice on the pregnancy and the available options. It had been preceded by heated public debate concerning a law permitting abortion within the first twelve weeks of pregnancy which the SPD and FDP federal government, led by Chancellor Helmut Schmidt (SPD), had agreed on June 18, 1974. Yet, just three days later, the Constitutional Court had, in response to an application from the state of Baden-Württemberg, used an interim injunction to prevent the new law from entering into force. In February 1975, the Constitutional Court then finally declared the law to be unconstitutional. In response, a solution was found in the regulation of Section 218 whereby abortion was permitted under certain conditions.

The revision of Section 218 that became necessary following German reunification was an extremely emotional, sensitive issue, first and foremost for women who faced a dilemma about whether or not to have an abortion, but also because the associated debate revealed a great deal about our society's view of women and how society deals with the start and end of life. Even on paper, the task was extremely difficult. The problems began with the formal responsibilities within the federal government. The minister of justice was responsible for the regulations in the Criminal Code, the minister for family affairs for the advice given to the pregnant women—and I, as the minister for women, was not strictly speaking responsible for anything at all. At most, in my second role as minister for youth, via the Child and Youth Services Act, I held responsibility for entitlement to a preschool place, which the federal government had also set out in its coalition agreement. This entitlement aimed to make it easier to combine work and family life, particularly for single mothers, and thereby to simplify the decision to have a child. Within the CDU and CSU, many believed it was right that the minister for women had no authority in this area. Outside this group, however, no one understood why the minister for women, of all people, had almost no say about an issue affecting women.

In this case, I felt we were well advised to work on the basis of continuity with the 1975 Federal Constitutional Court's jurisdiction—which did not exactly increase the scope for the pan-German revision of Section 218. In addition, the political ideas of the CDU and CSU, on the one hand, and of our then coalition partner the FDP on the other, differed greatly on this matter, while the Catholic Church, with its restrictive view, played a key role in shaping the Union's opinion. As a result, the federal government was unable to draw up its own draft legislation for revision of the Section. The only remaining option was for the CDU/CSU and the FDP each to develop their own draft legislation, which would then be put to the vote in the Bundestag. For this reason, from May 1992 onward, I participated in countless rounds of talks within the Union group. With regard to the revision of Section 218, I was in favor of compulsory advice, along with the provision of assistance to women facing a dilemma about abortion, thereby making it easier for them to choose to have their unborn child. At the same time, however, I deemed any type of legal examination of the woman's need based on a written consultation record inappropriate. That did not correspond to my image of women. I trusted women to be able to make responsible decisions themselves.

Yet the discussion was characterized by precisely the opposite view, particularly within the Union: by mistrust instead of trust, as if it were necessary to assume at all times that women would make thoughtless decisions, and to establish legal barriers—ideally with penalties—to prevent this. The atmosphere was anything but tolerant. At times, I had the impression that some people were scared to engage in deep debate for fear that it would lead to conflict with majority opinion in the party. The tone was sharp, and the level of some contributions to the debate was abysmal, for example regarding the inheritance rights of illegitimate children. Someone questioned whether the "product of a summer's night in the Philippines"—as they put it—should have the same rights as a German child. I had the impression that, from the Union perspective, everything I thought, beyond a certain line that I could not quite grasp, was considered reprehensible, and that it was not a discussion aiming to find the best way forward. Only a few people saw things differently, such as the former minister for family affairs

Heiner Geissler, or the former president of the Bundestag Rita Süssmuth.

I personally also encountered mistrust from within my own group. At a joint conference of the CDU and CSU Executive Boards held at Banz Abbey in Bavaria on October 4 and 5, 1991, a Friday and Saturday, this suspicious feeling reached its peak. Or its nadir. As a minister, I was part of the CDU Executive Board. The discussion also concerned Section 218. For me, it went without saying that I wanted to speak as minister for women. I therefore raised my hand to indicate that I wished to make a contribution. As I did so, I looked across to Helmut Kohl, who was managing the list of speakers for the CDU side. He always did this personally, as it gave him the opportunity to determine the order of speakers. By the look on Kohl's face, I could tell that he was anything but enthusiastic about my request to speak. Once he realized that I was not going to lower my hand until he had taken note of my name, he finally wrote it down. I had to wait a long time before I got the chance to speak.

When it was finally my turn, I started setting out my position on Section 218. Yet, after just a few seconds, I felt something unusual happening: with every word, my throat and neck became stiffer and stiffer. It was as if I had been struck by a bolt of lightning. After I had finished speaking, I could barely move my neck, and when I did the pain was horrific.

When the conference ended on the Saturday afternoon, I drove to Hohenwalde. The pain did not ease off. Quite the opposite—on the Sunday I had to visit the doctor in the neighboring town. He gave me multiple small injections in my back to relieve the pain. That helped. I underwent several weeks of physiotherapy. Never again have I experienced such a direct physical reaction to a speech.

Outside the world of the CDU and CSU, however, particularly among women's associations, my position on Section 218 was viewed as outdated and backward. Here people were clearly in favor of a law permitting abortion within the first twelve weeks of pregnancy. Their aim was now to make up for the failure to implement this in the old Federal Republic during the 1970s. I did not fit in anywhere.

On June 25, 1992, after months of discussions, the final deliberations concerning Section 218 took place in the Bundestag. There was a free vote with no obligation to adhere to the party line. It was a question of conscience. In addition to a legislative proposal from the CDU/CSU, which stipulated compulsory advice that had to be documented and, if the woman proved her psychosocial need, guaranteed freedom from prosecution in the case of an abortion, several other legislative proposals from various members of parliament were to be put to the vote. Some of these were cross-party proposals, known as group proposals. I also spoke in the debate and set out the reasons for my position. On the one hand, I stressed the "constitutional task" for the legislator, parliament, "[. . .] to protect all forms of life, including unborn lives [. . .]." On the other, I explained "that this life can only be protected with the woman and not against her." Regarding the Union group's proposal, I stated that the deciding factor for me was the clarification "that subjective considerations are accorded primary importance when it comes to assessing a psychosocial need." I spoke out against the mandatory documentation specified in the Union text, saying that it risked "permanently damaging the relationship of trust between women and their doctors." Having weighed up all of the points objectively, and due to party discipline, I nonetheless voted in favor of the CDU/CSU proposal. No majority was reached in the plenary session.

A majority was only reached when a group proposal was put forward by members of parliament from the SPD, the FDP, the Greens, and certain members of the CDU and CSU. I had also addressed this proposal in my speech. It incorporated compulsory advice and, unlike the Union proposal, did not stipulate that this must be documented, which I welcomed. However, it neglected to clearly state the aim of the advice, namely continuation of the pregnancy, which I considered mistaken. For this reason, I decided not to vote in favor of the proposal, unlike thirty-two other Union representatives, but also not to reject it, and instead abstained. This offered a way out of the dilemma for me. However, I received a great deal of flak in public for this.

Today, I can certainly understand the displeasure about my zigzagging behavior. It had little to do with courage, and even less with clarity. I had become bogged down in a mixture of extremely cautious independence, concerns regarding the attitude of the Constitutional Court toward the law—which were completely justified, as would become clear—and, last but not least, party discipline. My abstention was viewed by many as deplorable, yet, question of conscience or not, I had been required to notify the chancellor of it in advance, in a one-to-one meeting. I had fallen prey to self-censorship, which had prevented me from freely following my convictions and voting in favor of the group proposal upon final consideration, as opposed to abstaining.

On June 26, 1992, at around 12:50 a.m., this group proposal was decided by majority. The law was drawn up by the president on July 27 and promulgated in the federal gazette on August 4. On the same day, however, in response to an application by the Bavarian state government and by 248 members of parliament within the CDU/CSU coalition group, the Constitutional Court prevented the section of the law concerning criminal prosecution from coming into force. The decision on the main point was announced on May 28, 1993, while on June 16, 1993, a transitional regulation came into force that paved the way for the final legislation. On June 29, 1995, more than two years later, the federal parliament once again passed a law on revision of Section 218. Now the aim of the advice—with no mandatory documentation—was more clearly worded than it had been in the law passed in 1993. I voted in favor. The law came into force on October 1, 1995. It remains in force to this day.

The entire legislative process was part of a comprehensive Pregnancy and Family Support Act that also included the introduction of legal entitlement to a preschool place for children from three years of age. Here I once again encountered conflict with my own party. Nationwide provision of preschool places was taken as read by me and many others from the GDR. We wanted this provision to be retained in the new federal states. In early 1991, the finance minister Theo Waigel had made one billion deutsche marks available for this purpose, so as to tide us over until June 30, 1991. After this date, the new federal states guaranteed the funding themselves.

In the old states of the West, however, many local politicians were up in arms against legal entitlement to daycare, which was to be introduced on January 1, 1996. They attempted to persuade me that the federal government's aim of creating 600,000 new preschool places by that date was far removed from reality. I could understand that it meant a tremendous amount of work for the states, cities, and municipalities, and that transition periods were needed.

However, I could not comprehend that, putting aside the question of feasibility, there was so little understanding within the CDU and CSU of how urgently needed legal entitlement was. I also felt that, for many, the real reason for disapproving of the undertaking was perhaps that they mistrusted me. It was as if they thought I wished to extend the socialist propaganda of the GDR into a united Germany, or that I wanted to dispute the notion that the SED had used preschools and daycare centers for the purposes of ideological indoctrination. Of course they had, and no reasonable person could have denied it. I considered it all the more important to establish comprehensive childcare provision under democratic conditions, not least with the involvement of independent organizations. As I saw it, needs-based provision of preschool places was in the interest of everyone: of the children, for whom it was of educational value, and also of their parents, both mothers and fathers, so as to enable them to reconcile family and working life. Ultimately, legal entitlement to a preschool place was successfully introduced as of January 1, 1996. Some states used transitional legislation until 1999, when the entitlement was finally put in place throughout Germany. Legal entitlement to a daycare place for those under three years of age followed fourteen years later. It has been in force since August 2013, while legal entitlement to after-school care at elementary school is set to be enacted by August 2029.

In conclusion, progress does happen, even if it's at a snail's pace.

SUSTAINABILITY

No energy consensus

THE CDU/CSU AND FDP won the Bundestag elections on October 16, 1994, although with only ten seats more than their opposition in the form of the SPD, the Greens, and PDS. As was the case with my first Bundestag elections, I was once again able to win my constituency directly, with 48.6 percent of the first votes. Helmut Kohl was re-elected as chancellor on November 15, 1994.

Two days later, I was appointed minister for the environment, nature conservation, and nuclear safety. I was delighted and, thanks to my education in natural sciences, felt I had good technical competence in the area. However, large sections of the public saw things differently. They were downright appalled that my predecessor, Klaus Töpfer, had had to move from the ministry of the environment to the ministry of housing. He had helped prepare the 1992 Earth Summit in Rio de Janeiro, at which 178 countries had committed to a guiding principle of sustainable development. In Germany, he had introduced the "Green Dot" waste recycling scheme that remains in existence to this day. He had swum in the Rhine as a publicity stunt to demonstrate how clean the river was thanks to measures he had implemented. In short: Klaus Töpfer championed environmental policy. The fact that he had been replaced in office was interpreted as a sign that he had become too independent and inconvenient for the chancellor's liking. My succeeding him was seen as a downgrading of the ministry. A woman who, in the eyes of my critics, was loyal to the party line was replacing a pioneer in environmental and nature conservation.

As the minister in charge of nuclear safety, I was also responsible for the transport of CASTOR containers filled with highly radioactive material from German nuclear power plants and the French La Hague reprocessing plant to the interim storage site in Gorleben, Lower Saxony. The first transport of a CASTOR container, from the Philippsburg nuclear power plant in Baden-Württemberg to Gorleben, took place on April 24 and 25, 1995, just a few months after I assumed office. The containers had to be reloaded onto flatbed trucks at Danneberg train station in Lower Saxony, before being driven onward to the Gorleben interim storage facility, eighteen kilometers away. The onward transport sparked protests from thousands of anti-nuclear activists. The demonstrators did everything in their power to prevent the convoy from moving and to render the transport as expensive as possible for the state. What is more, some of the demonstrators did not shy away from violence. Approximately 7,600 border guard officers were on duty every day, together with state police officers. The opposition was particularly fierce over the last few miles. Around Gorleben, it was like a civil war. Sit-down blockades and tractors were used in attempts to stop the containers from arriving. I was plagued by worry, hoping no one would be injured, neither among the demonstrators nor the police.

On a political level, I was convinced that the CASTOR transports had to be carried out. When Chancellor Helmut Schmidt (SPD) was still in power, West Germany had entered into a binding commitment under international law with France to take back the radioactive waste. The transport container storage facility in Gorleben had been set up for this purpose back in

1983. In parallel to this, research was carried out to determine whether the salt dome in Gorleben would also be suitable for a final disposal site. A considerable proportion of the local population was opposed to this. As a result, the waste disposal issue inflamed the fundamental conflict concerning the pros and cons of the peaceful use of nuclear energy. In order to overcome this, discussions between representatives of the federal government, the state of Lower Saxony, and the electricity suppliers began in early 1993, on the initiative of my predecessor, Klaus Töpfer. These talks aimed to reach a cross-party consensus on energy policy and were known as the energy consensus talks. Klaus Töpfer had recognized just how deep the fault lines in society ran when it came to the peaceful use of nuclear energy, and had understood that the foundation of the Greens in 1980 could also be traced back to this.

Following the Bundestag elections in 1994, the first energy consensus talk of the new legislative period took place on March 16, 1995. A large group of participants from the federal government, the states, and the electricity suppliers gathered in the ministry of economic affairs. The economic affairs minister, Günter Rexrodt (FDP), and I were negotiating on behalf of the federal government. All participants were seated around a big table in a huge meeting room and read out contributions that mostly supported their known and expected positions. Everyone seemed to be watching one another closely, and scarcely any reference was made to the arguments of other speakers. It was certainly not much of a discussion. The group of participants was far too large for confidentiality. I was very disappointed about how the talks went.

At the subsequent press briefing that Günter Rexrodt and I gave, I again experienced something striking. The briefing was held outside the building housing the ministry of economic affairs. Initially, Rexrodt and I stood side by side, facing a large number of journalists with microphones in their hands. They always held these out toward the person who was speaking at the time. Yet I suddenly noticed that Günter Rexrodt, who was more than a head taller than me and had a deep voice, was no longer standing beside me, but diagonally behind me. This meant he could easily speak over me into the microphones. My attempts to express myself calmly were therefore doomed to fail. At any rate, I now had to work very hard for the chance to speak at all. I learned two advantages that many men have over women in politics: physical size and vocal pitch. From then on, I worked with my colleagues in the press office to ensure that at press conferences I was always able to stand alongside other participants, but at an appropriate distance from them, and that microphones were positioned far enough apart. Vocal problems couldn't be resolved in this way. The only thing that helped here was working on speaking calmly and without my voice cracking.

A second energy consensus talk was scheduled at the Parliament of Lower Saxony for April 24, 1995, the date of the first CASTOR transport. Prior to this, I wanted to speak to anti-nuclear activists on site, in Lüchow, not far from the Gorleben interim storage facility. As I received personal security anyway in my role as environment minister, this trip was planned jointly with the security officers from my personal protection team. The police advised against the trip, saying that violent acts could not be ruled out. In fact, the atmosphere in the region was very heated, and as the minister responsible for nuclear safety, I was like a red rag to a bull for the anti-nuclear activists. Nonetheless, I wanted to go there. I wanted to face up to the controversy. Previously, during my time as minister for youth, I had suffered from the fact that there was little willingness within the CDU to discuss issues with dissenters. In CDU meetings, if a young person asked a question critical of nuclear energy, they would often be silenced. I saw that as a sign of weakness. If someone has good arguments, they should be able to present them to us, and we should be capable of dealing with them. The police respected my decision and painstaking preparations were made for the trip.

On March 23, 1995, we were ready. Shortly after I had set off for Gorleben—I was already in the car on my way to the military sector of Cologne Bonn Airport, where I would then take the military plane that was available around the clock to ministers to Hamburg, and from there fly by helicopter to Lüchow—Fritz Bohl, head of the Federal Chancellery, called me. He passed on greetings from the chancellor: "The chancellor is pleased you're going. If you get into difficulties, don't hesitate to call. I'm at my desk and happy to help," he said. "Everything will be fine," I responded.

I set out with a small delegation. Gerald Hennenhöfer, head of the nuclear safety department in the ministry of the environment, Beate Baumann, and personal protection officers from the Federal Criminal Police Office were with me. At the helipad in Lüchow, a representative of the Protestant Church greeted us. He had persuaded the anti-nuclear activists to allow us to travel to the guildhall in Lüchow, where the meeting was to take place, and enter the building accompanied by him. Once there, I was seated opposite a group of around thirty people. I recall that something to eat and drink had been set out for us, but I did not touch anything apart from water. The atmosphere was tense. Although no one spat at me, I had the impression that every word I said was regarded as an imposition by my audience. I made it clear that laws had to be complied with, especially as there were existing contracts for the fulfillment of which I was responsible, and that I could not simply ignore the nuclear waste that had already been created.

Wolfgang Ehmke, the chair of the meeting and board member of the Lüchow-Dannenberg citizens' initiative for environmental protection, at least expressed some respect for the fact I had come at all and dared to venture into the lion's den. Most of the other participants in the discussion struggled to set out their positions in a non-aggressive way. One woman jumped up and said she was suffering such internal turmoil that she was no longer able to be in the same space as me, and left the room. Her reaction emphatically demonstrated that it was not just a question of arguments, but also of emotions. I found it difficult to understand how she was feeling. I was in favor of the peaceful use of nuclear energy. As a physicist, I deemed the associated risk acceptable. As people knew, I put the 1986 Chernobyl disaster down solely to sloppiness on the part of the Soviet Union, and not to the technology as such.

Less than a year after my visit to Lüchow, in February 1996, I was able to see the consequences of this accident for myself. I traveled with a delegation to the city of Gomel in Belarus, approximately seventy-five miles from Chernobyl. There we visited a hospital for children who were suffering from cancer due to radiation exposure, and talked to the doctors and nurses who cared for them. We then drove, on a bus with stray dogs running alongside, to Pripyat, the now-empty town that was formerly home to the employees of the nuclear power plant. I saw with my own eyes the Chernobyl power plant, sealed in a concrete shell known as a sarcophagus. Adolf Birkhofer, a physicist and then director of the Association for Plant and Reactor Safety, who had traveled as part of my delegation, had a Geiger counter with him. As we stood outside in front of the sarcophagus, he switched it on to measure the level of radioactivity. The device reacted immediately. Some ten years after the Chernobyl disaster, it still clicked away incessantly. It was eerie. However, this visit did not alter my confidence in the peaceful use of nuclear energy in a high-tech country such as Germany, with quite different safety standards to those in the Soviet Union. Nevertheless, it helped me understand emotions like the ones I had encountered the previous year in Lüchow.

The meeting in the guildhall ended after around ninety minutes. I had not made any promises that I would not be able to keep, and neither had those I had been talking to.

A short while later, a contrasting meeting was held in the same building, although in another room. The local CDU member of the Bundestag, Kurt-Dieter Grill, had won the parliamentary mandate with a majority in the Bundestag elections in the fall of 1994, despite the protests against nuclear energy in his region. He had now invited me to participate in a public party conference of the district CDU after the meeting with the anti-nuclear activists. I was among like-minded people there. When I was asked what would happen if a small dose of radiation were to escape from the CASTOR containers that would soon be arriving in Gorleben, without thinking I said into the microphone that fortunately it was a bit like baking. If you were to spill some baking powder while mixing the batter, the cake would still be a success. I don't know what possessed me to say such a thing in that situation. It wasn't just the fact that, in politics, we must always be careful using images and comparisons when we want to explain something. That image of baking a cake was particularly off the mark, in every respect. Probably, after the meeting with the anti-nuclear activists, the tension I was under had been relieved to such an extent that my concentration had lapsed in the CDU environment. No one was upset by my words during the district party conference, but they were now out in the world, and they soon caused outrage—justifiably so. Of course, it was a mistake to compare baking powder to radiation. My words were lacking in any kind of empathy. Environmental groups criticized me harshly for this, for years to come. Not immediately taking responsibility for this mistake was a serious failure on my part. At that time, I still thought it was a sign of weakness for a politician to admit to making a mistake. The situation should not arise too often, but acknowledging that I had made a very unfortunate comparison, and giving good reasons for it, would have certainly been better than burying my head in the sand, as I did at that time.

After the district party conference, we set off on our journey back to Bonn. I hadn't needed to make use of Fritz Bohl's offer of help. In my discussion with the anti-nuclear activists, I had learned that they were not only concerned with the issue of radioactive waste disposal, but also, and above all, with bringing an end to the peaceful use of nuclear energy. Their fierce opposition to the CASTOR transports was a protest against the open-ended operation of nuclear power plants. For this reason, a consensus regarding waste disposal could only be reached in conjunction with an exit date. I considered presenting this assessment to my colleagues in government and my party before the next consensus talks on April 24, but did not do so. On the one hand, an actual time limit on the operation of the nuclear power plants did not align with my view at that time—I still deemed the use of nuclear energy justifiable and essential. On the other, I suspected that the SPD would not have been prepared to make a compromise that would have only led to the winding down of nuclear energy decades later. On the contrary, the majority of the SPD wanted rapid action. If need be, the then state premier of Lower Saxony, Gerhard Schröder, was open to a compromise, I believed. I already knew him from a debate we had conducted in February 1995 for the weekly magazine *Focus*. He was a state premier who took a pragmatic approach and saw the need for an agreement with us.

On April 20, 1995, four days before the next energy consensus talk and the first CASTOR transport, I met with him at the local office of the environment ministry on Schiffbauerdamm in Berlin. Schröder had requested the meeting. After his first few words, I realized that the discussion would be primarily about canceling the CASTOR transport and possible reasons for this. I had prepared for this event. I picked up a sheet of A1 paper I had placed on the table before the meeting, unfolded it, and spread it out in front of us. On the paper was a drawing with a kind of family tree showing the legal proceedings that had taken place in relation to the individual authorizations already issued by the federal government and then opposed by the state of Lower Saxony at the various levels of court. I had arranged for my colleagues to draw up this overview and now explained it to Schröder. His expression darkened a little. The sheet of paper showed that, although the state of Lower Saxony had won the case in the administrative court in the first instance, the federal government had prevailed in the second instance at Lüneburg Higher Administrative Court. Schröder argued that I should not be so certain; things could change again. He saw that he was not getting anywhere with me, stood up, and said, "The discussion with your predecessor would have ended differently." I retorted, "I'm environment minister now, and you'll have to make do with me."

The mood was frosty during the second energy consensus talk at the Parliament of Lower Saxony four days later. This talk was overshadowed by the tense atmosphere surrounding the first CASTOR transport, which took place on the same day, and ended without a tangible result. A third and final energy consensus talk was held on June 21, 1995. With it, this round of energy consensus talks failed, as they had done in 1993. Positions were irreconcilable. From the perspective of the Union and the FDP, the aim was to reach an agreement on the further use of *all* energy sources, that is to say including nuclear energy. For the SPD, continuing to make use of nuclear energy without a fixed exit date and retaining the option of developing new nuclear power plants was out of the question. I was disappointed that a consensus was not possible—I would have liked more time to continue looking for solutions.

———

The CASTOR containers making up the first transport reached the storage facility in Gorleben on April 25, 1995. No one had come to serious harm, but I had experienced how difficult it was to comply with the law. I was becoming increasingly convinced that all efforts to reach a broad social consensus were worthwhile. Just over a year later, on May 8, 1996, a second CASTOR transport reached the Gorleben interim storage facility, this time with highly radioactive material from the La Hague reprocessing facility in France. Approximately fifteen thousand police officers were on duty throughout Germany for this transport. The third and last CASTOR transport during my time in office as minister for the environment took place on March 5, 1997. This time thirty thousand police officers were required to safeguard the transport. That same spring there were renewed attempts to reach an energy consensus, but they met with no success. No one on the Union side wanted to take the step of limiting the operating periods, and I did not advocate for this either. It was left to the red–green federal government under Chancellor Gerhard Schröder, three years later, in June 2000, to negotiate a comprehensive nuclear phase-out concept with the energy supply companies. In line with this concept, each nuclear power plant was given a total operating time of thirty-two years. This meant that the last power plant, Neckarwestheim II, was to be removed from the grid by the end of 2021. What was more, the energy supply companies undertook to end the reprocessing of used fuel elements abroad by 2005 and from then on to store them directly at the power plants, so as to avoid transports of this kind. That could have marked the end of a major social controversy, but in fact it did not. We will have to return to this later.

After the three CASTOR transports, I believed I had passed the hardest test of my time in office. I had no idea then that, in May

1998, another event would bring me to the brink of resigning as minister for the environment. At that time, it became public knowledge that for years there had been instances where threshold values had been exceeded on the outer surfaces of transport containers for radioactive materials (not the CASTOR containers). The electricity suppliers had been aware of the problem, as had the Federal Office for Radiation Protection and the Federal Railway Authority as subordinate agencies within the environment and transport ministries. It would have been relatively easy to rectify with additional cleaning steps for the containers. The federal authorities had not informed the ministry of the environment. Yet I held the political responsibility for this—and it all came to light four months before the next Bundestag elections.

The Greens, particularly the Bundestag representative for Hesse Joschka Fischer, sensed their chance to perhaps finally prove that I, the advocate of nuclear energy, had messed up. The question was whether we in the ministry had truly not known about the instances of the threshold values being exceeded. All correspondence between the ministry and both the Federal Office for Radiation Protection and the Federal Railway Authority had to be scrutinized. We held sway over the Federal Office for Radiation Protection and could order it to hand over everything in its possession, as it was a subordinate agency of the ministry of the environment; the situation was different with the Federal Railway Authority, which reported to the ministry of transport. Here I was obliged and—as it transpired—able to rely on my colleague Matthias Wissmann, then transport minister, providing me with all the materials. Every day we worried that a document would turn up that we did not recognize at the management level of the ministry. But that didn't happen.

I was furious because I had spent years advocating for the

CASTOR transports to take place, but, in my view, the electricity suppliers lacked the necessary sensitivity with regard to issues of radiation. I was unable to lament this in public, however, as I would have immediately been accused of naivety regarding the economy. Indeed, I probably still was naive—with my ideal of the social market economy and the belief that economy and politics shared responsibility even for difficult issues. This proved to be deceptive. I learned that, in the end, politics always takes primacy. Today, I am convinced that this is exactly as it should be. After all, it is not a commercial enterprise, no matter how large and influential, that bears responsibility for the common good, the welfare of all, but the state.

The significance of this was also highlighted by my experiences with the officials within the ministry. They went out of their way to clarify everything they could, worked until late in the evenings and at weekends, and prepared for specific committee meetings and a topical discussion slot in the Bundestag. Beate Baumann and I remained in close contact with them. We had made it clear that complete openness was necessary. It was not the truth, however unpleasant it might be in the moment, that would destroy us politically, but the failure to disclose facts. Our motto was to never lie or attempt to sweep anything under the carpet. This is how we approached the task. My colleagues in the parliamentary party and the CDU and CSU state ministers stood by me. Guido Westerwelle, secretary general of the FDP, the party with which we formed the governing coalition, did begin to distance himself from me in public, but when no evidence could be found that my ministry and I had known anything about the threshold values being exceeded, the public calmed down just as quickly as it had become agitated. I was more than relieved not to be a stumbling block in the approaching Bundestag elections.

Foreign affairs politician

In May 1992, the United Nations in New York adopted the Framework Convention on Climate Change. The following month, 154 countries signed it at the Earth Summit in Rio de Janeiro. It entered into force in March 1994. The first Conference of the Parties to the Framework Convention on Climate Change (COP 1) was to be held in Berlin between March 28 and April 7, 1995. Representatives of 170 countries were expected to attend; 117 countries had already ratified the Convention, while 53 had not yet finalized the ratification procedure and could therefore only attend as observers. On top of this came representatives of 165 non-governmental organizations (NGOs), 12 intergovernmental organizations, and various UN agencies, offices, and programs.

The Intergovernmental Panel on Climate Change (IPCC) had already confirmed the existence of climate change caused by human activity in its First Assessment Report in 1990. It predicted that under a "business-as-usual" scenario (scenario A), global mean temperature would increase by 0.3 degrees Celsius per decade (with an uncertainty range of 0.2 to 0.5 degrees Celsius), which would lead to a likely increase in temperature of about 1 degree Celsius above the temperature at that time by 2025 and by 3 degrees Celsius by the end of the next century. The IPCC operates under the auspices of the UN and is both an intergovernmental institution and a scientific body. Thousands of scientists from all over the world regularly summarize the state of climate change research in assessment reports and special reports. It's the most highly regarded body in its field.

In the Framework Convention on Climate Change, the countries committed to reducing greenhouse gas emissions to 1990 levels by the year 2000. There were no obligations for the period thereafter, so the convention needed to be updated. The premise of all considerations was the understanding that, while all countries shared joint responsibility for all countries, the level of responsibility varied from country to country. The developed countries would firstly have to agree on legally binding reduction targets for greenhouse gases such as CO_2 for the period after the year 2000, as they were responsible for around two-thirds of global emissions at that point and 75 percent of all global emissions, due to their early industrialization. The Berlin Conference aimed to adopt a mandate for the negotiation of these greenhouse gas reduction targets. Two years later, at the third Conference of the Parties in Kyoto, Japan, these targets would be made legally binding in a protocol.

As the host country's environment minister, I was assigned the role of president of the conference, which was held in the International Congress Center in Berlin's Westend district. I had no prior experience of international negotiations. My predecessor not only sowed doubt on my ability to lead such a conference, but it was also bandied about that I couldn't speak English properly. That wasn't true, as I had of course spoken English and published in English as a scientist in the GDR. One thing that was true was that I only had experience of spoken English in the world of science. However, my critics underestimated my fearlessness when it came to speaking foreign languages. After all, I had already shown through my youthful interactions with the Soviet soldiers in Templin that I wasn't afraid to put my foreign language skills into practice.

I had an outstanding, experienced negotiator at my side in the form of Cornelia Quennet-Thielen, head of the German negotiating team for climate change at the environment ministry. She and her team prepared me exceptionally well. Gertrud Sahler, my spokesperson, dealt expertly with the many journalists we were in contact with. We knew each other from our time together in the ministry for women and youth. I trusted her blindly. The negotiations were often very technical, and first of all I had to familiarize myself with UN jargon. The documents for the conference had been prepared by an inter-governmental negotiating committee. They contained hundreds of square brackets, each of which indicated an instance of dissent. In order to achieve an outcome, a consensus about the final document had to be reached, which meant that all parties had to approve it. The secretariat of the Framework Convention on Climate Change, which was still provisional at that time, was responsible for organizational matters and was led by Michael Zammit Cutajar, a UN diplomat from Malta. My officials and I worked closely together with him.

I was absolutely determined to make a success of the conference. But how could I do that with the jumble of state and non-state interests among the participants? It was like an anthill—you know there's a structure somewhere inside, but it's not visible from the outside. To get a clear picture of the inner workings of the conference I was going to be leading, I had to familiarize myself with the positions of the various Parties to the Convention. The Bureau of the conference helped me with this task. The Bureau consisted of me plus ten representatives, seven of whom were vice presidents—representing the various regions of the world—and three of whom were chairs of subsidiary bodies.

There was the group of developed countries, twenty-five of which were members of the Organization for Economic Co-operation and Development (OECD), as well as countries with economies in transition, such as the Central and Eastern European countries. The developed countries held very different positions. The fifteen EU member states at the time drove the negotiating process. I was in a good position, as Germany was prepared to reduce CO_2 emissions by 25 to 30 percent below 1987 levels by 2005. As host country, this set an example. We were convinced it was possible to break the link between economic growth and greenhouse gas emissions. However, we also had a head start over other countries, as CO_2 emissions had decreased by almost 50 percent in the new German states in the first half of the 1990s as a result of the collapse of the East German economy.

The attitude of the United States, the world's biggest emitter of greenhouse gases at that time with a share of 23 percent, was of vital importance. It had already ratified the Framework Convention on Climate Change in 1992 under President George Bush Senior. His successor, President Bill Clinton, and Clinton's vice president Al Gore in particular, were very open-minded when it came to climate protection. However, a majority in the US Congress criticized the fact that it was only the developed countries that had to commit to legally binding reduction targets. They feared there would be disadvantages for the US economy. Timothy Wirth, secretary of state for democracy and global affairs in the US Department of State, headed his country's delegation in Berlin. I had flown to Washington on March 1, 1995 to meet him personally ahead of the conference. He had a wealth of experience in international environmental policy and we hit it off right away. He came to Bonn on a reciprocal visit on March 10, before the start of the conference. We each knew what the other wanted and what we could bring to the negotiations. A successful conference was his primary concern, as it was mine.

The developing countries acted as the Group of 77 and China; the Small Island Developing States in turn formed their own group because they were—and still are—by far the most affected by climate change. The developing countries also held very divergent positions, but they were united in their often very aggressive criticism of the developed countries, which they believed bore the historical responsibility for climate change. The developing countries accused them of wanting to restrict the opportunities for economic growth in developing countries, after the developed countries had experienced fantastic growth themselves.

That's why they demanded ambitious greenhouse gas reduction targets for the developed countries. They were especially wary of the negotiations regarding "joint implementation"—a mechanism that would allow developed countries to implement measures to reduce emissions not only in their own countries, but also in developing countries, which would then count toward their own targets since it would relate to a reduction of the total level of greenhouse gases worldwide. The developing countries deemed this an evasive maneuver by the developed countries. They accused them of not being prepared to implement real change at home. I fully understood their concern, but had come to realize through my preparatory talks that I wouldn't be able to get support from the Americans for a conference outcome without a mechanism such as joint implementation.

Finally, there was the group of countries that constantly threatened a veto, utilizing the fact that documents could only be adopted if no country objected to them. These were predominantly oil-producing countries.

Every group of countries had a number of non-governmental organizations on its side, which further intensified the divergence of interests.

The conference started on March 28, 1995. First of all, the organizational procedures were established and I was elected president of the conference. Until April 4, negotiations took place exclusively between senior officials. In order to acquaint myself with the customs of a conference such as this, I received updates about the progress of negotiations at various times, in person, in Berlin. At the end of this first phase I invited the members of the conference bureau to a cafe in Berlin's Tiergarten Park to discuss the second phase. This phase, which would involve the countries' ministers, would take place between April 5 and 7, 1995. There was a lot for the ministers to do in those three remaining days; barely any compromises had been reached so far. We discussed which ministers I ought to get to know and what the limits of the individual delegations were in terms of content. The old hands in the bureau advised me to choose around twenty ministers to be "Friends of the Chair" and to communicate with these ministers regularly about the status of negotiations. The members of this group would then work toward possible compromises in the respective regional groups or interest groups. Putting together such a group was a delicate matter that required tact. It would have to be acceptable to as many of the 170 delegations as possible.

I spent the next morning calling each of my future friends in person to ask for their assistance. Everyone accepted the offer. I didn't hear of any protests from delegations that hadn't been considered. Chancellor Helmut Kohl opened the three-day ministerial segment with a speech. In it he made a passionate plea for the success of the conference. My colleagues and I were pleased to note that the proposed texts we had sent the responsible employees in the Chancellery for the draft of his speech had largely been incorporated, including the German greenhouse gas reduction targets for 2005. At the reception afterward, the delegations from Africa in particular sang Helmut Kohl's praises; he had clearly struck the right note. He had spoken of our Mother Earth. They felt understood.

In the evening, the foreign minister Klaus Kinkel (FDP) and I held another reception for the ministers. I tried to talk to as many of them as possible. Then I met with the Friends of the Chair for the first time. Over the next two days we repeated this before each of the plenary sessions, in order to appoint speakers for the plenary session and to work on proposed compromises. Despite the range of interests within the group, we all built a sense of trust. I quickly developed a friendship with the Indian environment minister Kamal Nath. India played a very constructive role in the conference.

Time flew by. Negotiations were held from first thing in the morning to last thing at night. Cornelia Quennet-Thielen and all my other colleagues worked to the point of exhaustion. Representatives of developing and developed countries were constantly at loggerheads. The NGOs added fuel to the fire. Experienced participants, especially my colleagues, explained to me the reasoning behind some lines of argument that were new to me, such as political majorities in the participating countries, the direct effect of climate change, cultural influences, and financial support. I developed an ever better sense of the different interests and arguments of the individual countries. The internal structure of the anthill was starting to reveal itself.

When there was still no outcome by the morning of April 7, I feared that all the effort had been in vain. Time was slipping through my fingers. It was the last day of the conference, and I really couldn't imagine how it was going to end. I learned that it was possible to extend the conference by symbolically stopping the clock at midnight and only restarting it just before a resolution. We were a long way off seeing any light at the end of the tunnel.

I shared my distress with Kamal Nath. The first thing he told me was that he had to leave that evening. There was nothing I could do to make him change his mind. Urgent domestic matters were calling him. I was shocked. But then he gave me some advice. He told me to split up the group of "Friends": representatives of the developed countries on the one hand and representatives of the developing countries on the other. The groups would work in separate rooms during the negotiations, while I would shuttle between the groups as a mediator. "I think both groups trust you," he said. Kamal Nath's advice was convincing. It was about finding the eye of the needle that everything could be pulled through. My frustration had suddenly disappeared and I set to work. Kamal Nath had drawn back the curtain for me.

But it was still too early in the day for such a move. At first,

I let things carry as they had done for days. Cornelia Quennet-Thielen put together an overview for me of the issues that had to be solved at a ministerial level. After that, all the other more technical points would automatically straighten themselves out. She could virtually recite the negotiating papers in her sleep. For my part, I drilled into myself the issues that needed to be solved and went over potential lines of compromise with my colleagues. I arranged with the bureau of the conference that we would stop the clock. I told Michael Zammit Cutajar about the plan to divide the Friends of the Chair into two groups. At around 8:00 p.m., I called them together and informed them of the plan too. They all agreed in principle, but suggested also including a number of ministers in each of the groups. Late in the evening there was a short plenary session during which it was decided that the clock would be stopped. It was clear to all the participants that we needed more time. I didn't reveal what exactly I had planned at that point. I then asked all delegations to make sure we could contact them, including during the night.

Just before midnight I started my shuttle diplomacy. The developed countries were the more difficult negotiating partners. Most of them had to phone their governments back home as they had very limited leeway in terms of negotiations. It was already night-time in Europe, so it wasn't easy to get hold of anyone in the governmental headquarters. Japan was six hours ahead; fortunately, people there would be getting up soon. In Canada and the United States it became more difficult to speak to the responsible parties as time went on and the working day there came to an end. Only the Australians had ensured that they would be reachable. They were used to taking part in conferences in very different time zones. To make matters worse, the next day, April 8, 1995, was a Saturday, so it was even harder to get hold of the responsible people. Hours passed. Fortunately, the US secretary of state Timothy Wirth was also interested in an outcome. He supported me even though he also had firm negotiating stipulations from his government, especially when it came to joint implementation.

The longer I spent negotiating with the developed countries, the better the mood became among the developing countries. They sensed the pressure I was under from the developed countries. They themselves had cooperated well with each other. I shuttled between the groups at least ten times. My colleagues were sitting in a third room, helping me filter out compromise formulations. At the crack of dawn, a solution appeared to be within reach. By six o'clock, the developed countries had agreed to all the points. I went to the developing countries with the outcome, and they agreed too. The Chinese representative looked at me with bright eyes and said with a smile, "We never reached the bottom line." By that, he meant he never reached his negotiating limits. Saving face as a method of diplomatic success: from that moment on, and for the rest of my political life, I had respect for the way in which developing countries in general, and China in particular, conducted negotiations.

By sunrise, the mandate for the negotiation of a protocol for the Framework Convention on Climate Change was, for the most part, ready. It contained both the commitment to binding greenhouse gas reduction targets and the possibility of joint implementation. I asked members of both groups to inform their respective allies immediately, and unofficially, about what had been achieved in order to prevent the spread of rumors about the outcome of negotiations. My colleagues told the secretariat and the conference bureau the outcome, and I spoke with Michael Zammit Cutajar. The conference bureau put together a final text for the mandate and called a plenary session for late morning. I was able to nip back home to shower, change my clothes, and have a cup of tea. Then I went straight back to the International Congress Center to see my colleagues and the members of the bureau. On the basis of what they had heard, the vast majority of parties supported the outcome. The only thing that remained unclear was whether any parties from the oil-producing countries would raise an objection.

With all his experience as a UN diplomat, Michael Zammit Cutajar urged me to put forward the prepared document as soon as possible after reopening the plenary session and to ask if there were any objections. He said I should then immediately take the little wooden hammer beside me, strike it against the table, and declare the contents adopted. I shouldn't give anyone too much time to express any further reservations.

We then went to the plenary session together. The stopped clock was reset, and I opened the session. When I put forward the final document, Timothy Wirth made it clear he had something to say. Oh no, I thought. What now? But after I gave him the floor, all he did was thank me for my work and suggest calling the outcome "The Berlin Mandate." I quickly asked if anyone had any objections. Applause broke out. I seized the opportunity and banged the hammer on the table. "I declare the document adopted," I said. And that was that. No one protested. A big weight was lifted from my shoulders. We had a negotiating mandate for the agreement of legally binding greenhouse gas reduction targets for the period after 2000. In order to prepare for the third Conference of the Parties that would be held in Kyoto, a Berlin Mandate working group was set up. It was also decided that a permanent United Nations Climate Secretariat would be formed, which would be based in Bonn. I opened it on June 10, 1996. Michael Zammit Cutajar headed it from 1996 to 2002.

That Saturday morning, I didn't yet know how much work lay ahead of us prior to the conference in Kyoto two years later. Together with my whole team, I was simply pleased that we had succeeded in achieving this result. Negotiating with so many different participants from all over the world had given me great joy. It had been wonderful to learn so much about the world. I discovered the foreign affairs politician in me. I'd had a crash course in climate negotiations and felt jointly responsible for the success of the climate conference in Kyoto. On all my major foreign trips over the following two and a half years, the climate issue was always on the agenda: in Indonesia, Malaysia, and Singapore in November 1995; in Mexico and Brazil in November 1996; in Washington in April 1997; in Japan and China in August 1997; and again in Japan in November 1997.

The second Conference of the Parties (COP 2), which was held in Geneva from July 16 to 18, 1996, proved disappointing. Between December 6 and 11, 1997, however, I took part in the third Conference of the Parties (COP 3) in Kyoto. The developed countries in particular were on board. The US vice president Al Gore traveled there. He fought for an outcome, although the US Senate had passed a resolution with a vote of 95–0 in the same year, making clear its refusal to sign any climate treaty unless it contained reduction targets for developing countries, especially China. After dramatic negotiations, the developed countries committed to reducing greenhouse gas emissions by an average of at least 5 percent compared to 1990 in the period between 2008 and 2012. In order to reach these targets more easily, a number of options were permitted, including joint implementation. The greenhouse gas reduction targets differed from country to country. The European Union, with its fifteen member states, committed to reducing its emissions by 8 percent. In the context of burden-sharing within the EU, Germany agreed to a reduction of 21 percent. The United States committed to a reduction of 7 percent over the same period. However, it never ratified the Kyoto Protocol, and in March 2001, Bill Clinton's successor, President George W. Bush, announced the Unites States' withdrawal from the Protocol. China has been the largest emitter of greenhouse gases since 2006. The Kyoto Protocol came into force on February 16, 2005.

The Price of Survival

On February 7, 1992, the then twelve member states of the European Community signed the Treaty on European Union (Maastricht Treaty) in the Dutch city of Maastricht. It came into force on November 1, 1993. The Maastricht Treaty turned the European Community into a political union with citizenship, a common foreign and security policy, and cooperation in justice and home affairs. Furthermore, the member states of the European Community laid the foundations for a common European currency, the euro. Helmut Kohl's promise to further develop the European Community, in connection with German reunification, became reality two years later. Parallel to that, the European single market was established on January 1, 1993, with its four freedoms: the free movement of goods, people, services, and money. The treaty foundations for this had already been established prior to German reunification, in the summer of 1987, when the Single European Act came into force. This enshrined environmental policy in treaty law as an independent political field of the European Community for the first time, with its aim being "to preserve, protect and improve the quality of the environment." By the end of 1992, almost 280 legal acts had been taken that intended to serve the opening up of previously isolated national markets. The European Union subsequently developed a new economic dynamic.

With the introduction of the single market in 1993, around 80 percent of national legislation in the field of the environment was attributable to European legislation. Decisions were often made on a European level. Germany generally set the pace among the EU member states in terms of combatting crimes against the environment. It was exciting to be involved in the search for solutions. In addition to the official meetings of the EU Environment Council in Brussels, which were very formal and included representatives of the German ministry of economics, informal meetings of the Environment Council were also held. These took place in whichever country held the EU Presidency, rotating on a twice-yearly basis. Here we could discuss our political goals in a more informal manner and get to know each other better.

As partners were also invited to the meetings, Joachim sometimes accompanied me, such as when the Council met informally in France. We experienced the beauty of the Camargue, a wonderful wetland region in Provence, and ate the best apple tarts of our lives.

On another occasion, my Spanish counterpart at the time, Josep Borrell, who later became president of the European Parliament and still later EU High Representative for Common Foreign and Security Policy, organized a meeting in Seville. There I experienced the art of drawing sherry from barrels with a *venencia*, and discovered how late in the evening people eat in Spain. Long after midnight, Beate Baumann and I decided to go for a stroll through Seville's old town to see the cathedral. We were fascinated by the vibrant life on the streets of this historic city.

Another time, I became acquainted with the beauty of Amsterdam. As I walked alongside the canals in the old town, I dreamed of traveling along them by boat one day. I'll never forget the train journey up the Irish coast from Arklow to Dublin with live folk music, or the visit to Charles Darwin's birthplace in Shrewsbury when the Environmental Council convened in the English city of Chester. And Joachim and I are still friends with the hosts of the council in the Austrian city of Graz, Ilse and Martin Bartenstein, to this day.

In June 1997, I attended a Special Session of the General Assembly, known as "Five Years after Rio." In Rio de Janeiro in 1992, alongside the signing of various conventions including the Framework Convention on Climate Change, a focus had been placed on the concept of sustainability for future development, and the action plan Agenda 21 had been adopted. Acting in the spirit of sustainability means meeting the needs of the present without limiting the opportunities of future generations. Now we needed to take stock for the first time. However, all participants agreed that the Earth was faring worse than ever before. The final document of the representatives of more than 165 countries only contained a handful of new specific obligations. Developed and developing countries argued in particular about how to finance the measures.

However, life on our shared planet required all individuals not only to act at home, but also to respect each other's ideas. Politics and non-governmental organizations had to work out joint development pathways in line with the model of sustainability. The contradictions between social needs, the desire for economic growth, and environmental goals needed to be resolved. This topic fascinated me so much that I decided to write a book about it. It was published in 1997 with the title *Der Preis des Überlebens—Gedanken und Gespräche über zukünftige Aufgaben der Umweltpolitik* (The Price of Survival: Thoughts and Conversations about Future Tasks of Environmental Policy). For this book, I asked various people from Germany and abroad their views on the aims, ways, and means of environmental policy. I wanted to gain insights from as many different perspectives as possible. I was also interested in the matter of how to derive verifiable objectives from the general concept of sustainability, which could be used as a standard of political action. It had been laid down in Agenda 21 that "indicators of sustainable development need to be developed to provide solid bases for decision-making at all levels." In my book, I proposed indicators for Germany in four areas: the natural environment, the use of energy, economic activity in cycles, and the safeguarding of human health. They formed a point of reference for the environment comparable to a basket of commodities in economics.

In retrospect, I approached things in a way that was, in part, too cautious. For example, I called for a doubling of the share of renewable energy used for the generation of electricity, from 5 percent at that time to 10 percent by 2010. In reality, it increased to 17 percent—the incentives of the law on renewable energies were more successful than we had anticipated. However, other objectives have still not been achieved. The number of endangered animal and plant species is rapidly increasing and constitutes the second biggest catastrophe that humans have to answer for, after climate change. The Convention on Biological Diversity, which was also signed in Rio and was intended to protect biodiversity, has not so far been sufficiently successful.

In particular, I delved into the effect of prices on the handling of scarce resources. I deemed it an important instrument for achieving environmental objectives without prescribing the respective technological pathway by law each time. However, it was impossible to implement an ecological tax reform in government that took these considerations into account. That was mainly thanks to the FDP, but ultimately also my own group, the CDU and CSU. All such considerations I developed with colleagues from my ministry failed. They were unenforceable. The same was true of the idea of a uniform Environmental Code as opposed to the numerous individual legal regulations that exist today, on everything from conservation to emission control. What goes without saying in social law has not yet been possible in environmental law. I also proposed the formation of a Council for Sustainable Development. I was no longer able to implement this proposal; the next government did that in 2001.

My period as environment minister challenged and fulfilled me—way beyond the scope of what I am able to mention here. I would have gladly remained in the post after the Bundestag elections in 1998, but that was not to be, since the Union and the FDP lost the election.

WHY THE CDU?

Party chair

FOR THE FIRST time in my political career, I felt alone—deserted, and left carrying sole responsibility.

Helmut Kohl, the chancellor of unity and European unification, the honorary chairman of the German CDU, was in the process of ruining his entire political life's work. On December 16, 1999, I was sitting in front of the television in my office at the CDU's national headquarters in Bonn, and on the ZDF program "Was nun, Herr Kohl?" (What now, Herr Kohl?) I heard him say: "Between 1993 and 1998, I accepted donations in the region of 1.5 to 2 million deutsche marks, which over the years averages out at approximately 300,000 deutsche marks annually, and they weren't declared, because the donors expressly requested they not be." In plain terms, by accepting the donations under these conditions, Kohl was disregarding the law. Article 21 of our constitution stipulates that political parties must publicly account for the sources of their funding and assets. Confronted with this fact, Kohl said in the same broadcast: "Yes, I know. [. . .] I'm saying it myself, aren't I, I really don't need the prompt." This was how he portrayed his understanding of political responsibility for the illegal donations he had disclosed on November 30, 1999. We couldn't expect any more from him; that much was clear from his stance in the interview. I couldn't believe it. Just a year before, I had been elected general secretary of the CDU on the recommendation of Wolfgang Schäuble, the new CDU chairman. Helmut Kohl had become honorary chairman. Our time in opposition had started very successfully with the European elections and the state elections in Hesse, Brandenburg, and Saarland. The CDU, crushingly defeated at the Bundestag elections on September 27, 1998 by Gerhard Schröder (SPD), had recovered more swiftly than anyone could have imagined. And now this: the ultimate fall from grace.

It had all begun with a brief announcement on the evening news on November 4, 1999, a Thursday: an arrest warrant on suspicion of tax evasion had been issued for Walther Leisler Kiep, former long-term treasurer of the Federal CDU, after he had allegedly accepted a million deutsche marks from the arms dealer Karlheinz Schreiber in 1991 without declaring it.

"Did you hear about Kiep on the news last night?" Beate Baumann asked me the next morning.

"Yes, what does it mean for us?"

"Nothing good, that's for sure," she answered.

On November 5, Kiep handed himself over to the investigating authorities. And for us, almost no stone would remain unturned.

We had something special planned for November 7, 1999, a Sunday: a "Berlin Conversation," as we called them—a series of events I had launched as general secretary. It was one of many initiatives created by Wolfgang Schäuble and myself in order to rejuvenate the CDU now that we found ourselves in opposition after sixteen years in government. The conversation on November 7, 1999 was the fourth in the series. We had selected as its location Villa Kampffmeyer in Potsdam, a house very close to Glienicker Bridge, the bridge between Berlin and Potsdam, West and East, where prisoners and spies had been exchanged during the Cold War. We wanted to celebrate the ten-year anniversary of the fall of the Berlin Wall, and this location was ideal. Wolfgang Schäuble would make a speech to honor the occasion, and at the same time, present the path forward. Unifying the strategic and the concrete was his great strength, as he had already demonstrated in Helmut Kohl's government. More than a few people, myself included, had considered the defeat that was looming in 1998 unavoidable. After sixteen years, the CDU was depleted, and ready to be the opposition. Democracy thrives on change. As expected, Wolfgang Schäuble became the new party leader. "Quo vadis, Deutschland?" was the title and topic of his speech in Potsdam, and he delivered it, but we quickly noticed that no one was really interested. The focus, instead of being on Germany, was on "Quo vadis, CDU?"; and instead of on our counter-concepts for a red–green federal government, it was on Kiep and the illegal donations.

"Beyond the powers of my imagination"—on Monday, November 8, 1999, that's how I had responded to the question of a journalist who asked me, in the press conference following the CDU Presidium meeting, for my take on the "Schreiber million" made public four days previously. It was actually supposed to be a routine event. As general secretary, I was responsible for the press conferences after the meetings of the CDU's Presidium and Federal Executive Committee. But nothing was routine now. And it was also beyond the powers of my imagination because, during the GDR era, I had heard very little about the donation scandals that had rocked the CDU in the 1980s, and which had gone down in West German history as the "Flick Affair." But now I was in the thick of it. I couldn't make sense of this, nor control it. It was overwhelming the party, and me too. I thought about it day and night, racking my brains: How can we put a stop to this? How could we avoid a defeat like the one the Italian Christian Democrats had suffered? How could we overcome the political and moral bankruptcy that the latest donation scandal represented for the CDU? And in this I felt deserted—and, increasingly, as if I was carrying sole responsibility.

Helmut Kohl and Wolfgang Schäuble, the two men to whom I'd owed so much in the previous ten years, couldn't possibly have been more different. Each had shaped our country in his own way: Kohl, who judged things from the perspective of history. "History is history" was one of his legendary sayings. This meant he always viewed present-day issues, and made decisions on them, against the backdrop of historical contexts. He also always strove to assess a person's character, and used that as a foundation on which to build loyalties.

Schäuble was convinced that politics shouldn't wrap the individual in cotton wool, but rather demand something of them. I had the greatest respect for his intellect and ability to lead the party, as well as an element of fear of the severity and sharpness he could sometimes summon up.

He had definitely taken a big risk in choosing me as general secretary, because what had I brought to this incredibly important position in the party so far, and during an era of opposition at that? I had become a member of the CDU in 1990, after DA (Democratic Awakening)—finding itself without a future—had disbanded. Between 1991 and 1998 I was deputy chair of the CDU; for a few months in 1992 to 1993, chair of the EAK (Evangelischer Arbeitskreis), the evangelical working group which is an association of the CDU/CSU; from 1993 to 1998, chair of the CDU in Mecklenburg-Western Pomerania, a small branch within the large German CDU that provides a good dozen representatives of the one thousand delegates who attend national party conferences. As minister for women and youth, and as minister for the environment, I had addressed topics with which the CDU really struggled. But maybe this was precisely the point: the lived experience of German reunification was important to Wolfgang Schäuble, and with me, the woman from the East, he wanted to make the CDU compatible with women and young people, as well as societal groups who, not least in the climate debate, were very far from the CDU's stance.

I had immense respect for the role of general secretary. In accordance with the statute of the German CDU, the general secretary supports the party leader in fulfilling their responsibilities and, in consultation with them, manages the party's activities. Wolfgang Schäuble had given me considerable freedom in this role, even though we sometimes held differing opinions, for example regarding the Hessian CDU's signature-gathering campaign, during the 1999 Bundestag elections, against dual citizenship. "Not always of one mind, but always on the same path," was the heading of our poster for the 1999 European elections, with a photo of the two of us standing back-to-back.

In June 1999, the CDU had celebrated the topping-out ceremony for its new headquarters in Berlin's Klingelhöferstrasse. The relocation from Bonn was planned for the following year; the federal government and Bundestag had already moved in September 1999. In the interim period, I'd worked with several colleagues in a small branch office, a so-called bridgehead of the former Bonn CDU headquarters. It was located in Mauerstrasse in Berlin-Mitte, not far from the former GDR border crossing Checkpoint Charlie. We had begun work on a new education program, and held a small party congress, a so-called Federal Committee, on December 13, 1999, in the "Bear Hall" of Berlin's old town hall, for the purposes of a new family program—the donations scandal having kept us in suspense for a good four weeks. This hall was where the Unification Treaty negotiations had taken place, and the old town hall was where I had worked between April 17 and October 2, 1990 as deputy government spokesperson of the first and last freely elected GDR government. It was a good place to introduce a concept of the family which was truly revolutionary by CDU standards at the time, one which aimed to break away from being exclusively tied to marriage. The new definition was "Family is where parents take on lasting responsibility for children; and children for parents." For the first time, wording was introduced to convey that same-sex partnerships also represent values that are fundamental for our society. In early September 2000, I had met with a task force of lesbians and gay men belonging to the Union. I still remember clearly how, at the end, the chair Martin Herdieckerhoff said that the fact I was speaking to them at all was a new and positive development. "But why won't you also allow us to do the most important thing—to get married?" I can no longer remember my answer. I probably evaded the question, but it would accompany me for many years afterward.

The subject of marriage also accompanied me on a personal level: in the conservative circles of my party, there had been a consistent criticism since 1990 that, as a divorced woman, I was living in a non-marital partnership. Because I wanted to avoid the impression that I might get married in order to further my career, Joachim and I had waited to take this step until the CDU was in opposition. After the Bundestag elections in 1998, the time had come. We married on December 30, 1998, and made it public with a small announcement in the *FAZ* on January 2, 1999.

The CDU approved the new family program. But the discussions that had played out behind the columns of the "Bear Hall" were focused on another subject entirely: the donations scandal. No one was interested in the CDU's programmatic renewal. Then, when the electricity failed for a short while, the lights at the CDU went out both metaphorically and literally. It was a complete catastrophe, and one I only just withstood. I also felt deserted by Wolfgang Schäuble. It wasn't that he placed any obstacles in my path when it came to investigating the scandal, in collaboration with the public auditor and Willi Hausmann, who had been the party's federal executive director since January 1999. He didn't. But I wanted to move forward, and set a political example. I was convinced we wouldn't be able to get our heads back above water with financial and technical measures alone; and certainly not after Kohl's ZDF appearance on December 16, 1999.

In the following hours and days, I became increasingly convinced that my role as general secretary of the CDU, if I took it seriously, was to make a political classification: one that was merciless, public, future-oriented. I conferred with Willi Hausmann, Beate Baumann, and Eva Christiansen. Eva had joined us as media spokesperson after the 1998 Bundestag election defeat. After eight years of working together, my former spokesperson Gertrud Sahler hadn't been able to take up my offer of transferring to the CDU national headquarters. Eva Christiansen, an economist born in Hennef in 1969, had initially worked as deputy press spokesperson for the then general secretary Peter Hintze. He had recommended her to me, and we immediately hit it off. She agreed with me and suggested: "Shall we ask the *FAZ* whether they'd take an article from you for the 'Fremde Feder' (Borrowed Plumes) column?" I replied, "Good idea, yes, ask them. Better than an interview that would only end up revolving around financial accounts. I'll think of something."

Over the coming days, I began to draft an article in my mind. It led me back to the early days of my membership. Why the CDU? Why was the CDU needed, and for what purpose? Why was it so important to me now to pull the emergency brake with a public statement? That's what I wanted the text to be about—and for this, some truths needed to be said, including some about Helmet Kohl. I didn't discuss my plan with Wolfgang Schäuble. The article wasn't in any way directed against him, but I had the feeling he would have vetoed it if I'd told him before its publication, thereby obliging me to submit to his decision;

after all, he was party chair. I wanted to avoid that, and that's why I took a risk.

I wrote the piece and gave it to Beate Baumann, who edited it. On December 21, 1999, Eva Christiansen offered the piece to the *FAZ* for publication. On December 22, 1999, they put the article "Merkel: Kohl's time is up" on the front page and indicated further discussion on pages 2 and 4. The article itself wasn't printed as part of the "Fremde Feder" column, but instead on page 2, beneath the heading "The actions admitted to by Helmut Kohl have damaged the party." Its core messages were:

> The actions admitted to by Helmut Kohl have damaged the party. [. . .] This is about Kohl's credibility, about the credibility of the CDU, about the credibility of political parties in general. [. . .] The CDU must, therefore, learn to walk again, it must develop the confidence to pit itself against its political opponents in future without its old warhorse, as Helmut Kohl often liked to call himself. It must venture away from home like a young person reaching puberty, go its own path and yet, at the same time, always stay true to the person who shaped it so enduringly—perhaps later even more than today.
>
> A process like this can't occur without wounds, without injuries. But the way in which those of us in the party approach it, whether we demonize this seemingly inconceivable event as a betrayal, or regard it as necessary, ongoing development [. . .], this will define our chances in the next state elections and, in 2002, at a national level. [. . .] If we embrace this process, our party will change yet remain the same at heart—with excellent core values, confident members, with a proud tradition, blending what's worth preserving of the old, and the new experiences following the era of party chair Helmut Kohl—and it will also have a blueprint for the future.

On the morning of that same day, a CDU Presidium meeting took place. It began at eleven o'clock. Everyone had either read the article beforehand or at least heard about it on the news en route to the Presidium. Opinions were divided. Some, including the deputy group chair Friedrich Merz, Saxony's state premier Kurt Biedenkopf, the two deputy CDU chairs Annette Schavan, minister of education and the arts in Baden-Württemberg, and Christian Wulff, now the leader of the opposition in Lower Saxony, and Berlin's state minister of science Christa Thoben, saw it as a relief, and supported me. Others shook their heads with disapproval. Volker Rühe, also a deputy CDU chair, asked why I always had to make my line of argument so emotional. "The bit about puberty and learning to walk was utter nonsense"—I can still hear his words today. And others still, including the CDU deputy chair Norbert Blüm, and the state premier of Hesse, Roland Koch, were downright appalled.

But things were about to get even worse, and the most difficult seven days of my political life to date followed. In comparison, the events surrounding the limit value violation in May 1998 were a breeze. Because it turned out that, with my wording of Kohl having damaged the CDU, I, the non-lawyer, had smoothed the way for him and some of his supporters, including those in the media. They were now trying to spin things so that my article, rather than Kohl's misconduct, would be seen as the trigger if any criminal investigations were commenced against him on suspicion of embezzlement. If that had happened, I would have had no choice but to step down. If Kohl had attracted the attention of the public prosecutor's office on account of my article, the party would never have forgiven me, and I would have understood that. It certainly hadn't been my intention. I'd wanted to write a political message, not a legal one, but this perspective got completely lost. For seven long days. It was only acknowledged again on December 21, 1999, when Bonn's public prosecution office declared it would be commencing a criminal investigation against Helmut Kohl, but made no mention of my *FAZ* article. This incident was a lesson to me: always to think not just about political intention, but also about the possible legal significance of words and phrasing in speeches, interviews, newspaper essays, and other public statements.

The moral low point of the donation scandal was reached on January 14, 2000. That was the day it became known that the CDU in Hesse had transferred sums amounting to millions of deutsche marks to overseas accounts, and had declared the funds to be so-called "Jewish legacies."

On January 18, 2000, Helmut Kohl stepped down as honorary chair of the CDU.

Via a donation made to the CDU by the arms dealer Karlheinz Schreiber, and ensuing conflict with the party's treasurer, Brigitte Baumeister, Wolfgang Schäuble also became embroiled in the donations scandal. On February 16, 2000, he announced his resignation as party and group chair. In front of the Federal Press Conference, he explained this grave step by saying that he wanted to usher in and enable a new beginning in the party and group.

Schäuble's decision was a turning point. Just sixteen months after the Bundestag election defeat, the cards were being reshuffled. A decision was quickly made as to who would be the new parliamentary group chair. On February 29, 2000, Friedrich Merz was elected as Wolfgang Schäuble's successor. A little more time was needed to decide on the party leadership. The party functionaries were divided over my *FAZ* article; the party's base was predominantly relieved. People had started saying that I should become party leader.

I gave it considerable thought. In terms of political power, I was convinced I wouldn't get another opportunity to lead Germany's second largest party after the SPD. I was also aware that any CDU chair had to be prepared to become chancellor of the Federal Republic of Germany. Of course, in the hours, days, and weeks of early 2000, when events were occurring thick and fast, this was still very much a theoretical idea, because the next Bundestag elections were over two years away. Regardless, when it came to the question of whether I dared become CDU chair, and therefore potentially chancellor too, I knew my answer was yes. And yet I didn't immediately go public with these thoughts. I was unsure whether the CDU and I would really be able and willing to embark on this journey together.

"You have to do it!" Georg "Schorsch" Brunnhuber said to me at the time. He was a Bundestag colleague from Baden-Württemberg.

"Schorsch, you're all much more conservative than me, you know that," I answered.

"No, no," replied Brunnhuber, "we're conservative by ourselves, sure. But it's down to you to make sure our daughters can vote for the CDU again. They won't if it's just us."

Brunnhuber's words emboldened me—I launched myself into the tumult. At a series of so-called regional conferences of the CDU branches, I felt broad support from the party's base.

Around this time, the media revealed that on the evening of February 25, 2000, a small group of leading Union politicians had reportedly met in the bar beneath Lübeck's city hall, among them Friedrich Merz, Volker Rühe, and Edmund Stoiber, to discuss getting Saxony's state premier Kurt Biedenkopf elected as transitional chair of the CDU. These deliberations had evidently seen me as continuing in the role of general secretary. When this meeting became public knowledge, the party base encouraged me more than ever—it seemed to me—to run for the position of CDU chair. The discussion of far-reaching personnel decisions behind closed doors had evidently rubbed them up the wrong way. On March 20, 2000, I officially declared my candidacy. There were three weeks to go before the party conference, which would be held from April 9 to 11, 2000, in Essen, North Rhine-Westphalia.

Three weeks in which to prepare my campaign speech. It was clear that this would be the most important speech of my political career so far, and I'd be delivering it amid a time of crisis for the CDU. I knew I wouldn't be able to write it in Berlin, nor in Bonn—I needed a change of scene. I decided to go with my closest colleagues from Konrad Adenauer House to a conference on the Baltic Sea, at Dierhagen in Mecklenburg-Western Pomerania. We took up lodgings in a hotel by the beach. Dierhagen had been the setting of family vacations during my childhood and teenage years. The hotel, a building that had been gutted and redeveloped after reunification, was the former guest house of the East German Council of Ministers. Back in those days, we children had only been able to get close to it secretly, sneaking across the beach. As the SED regime had been history for ten years, ordinary people like me could now stay here too.

Willi Hausmann, his office manager Klaus Schüler, Beate Baumann, Eva Christiansen, some other colleagues from Konrad Adenauer House, and I talked about the party congress. Its motto was to be "Let's Get to Work!" And so we started work on my speech. Once again I focused on how I envisioned the CDU of the future. Why the CDU—for me, and for our country? Three weeks later, in my speech in Essen, this is how I set out my vision:

> I want a CDU that will develop the ethics of social capitalism within a globalized context. I want a CDU that can reconcile economy and humanity even within this new context.
>
> I want a CDU that, on the foundation of the Christian concept of humanity, makes human dignity its benchmark when assessing technological risks.

I want a CDU that will help bring about generational equality in the further development of social security systems.

I want a CDU that advocates for a Europe of the people.

I want a CDU that gives the individual citizen freedoms; one that, where required, provides the citizen with strong state support.

I want a CDU that supports small entities. A declaration of belief in nation, in homeland, in individual identity—that is the prerequisite for finding one's way in the world.

I want a CDU that advocates for a Germany which is a tolerant country among others, that neither puts on airs nor hides its light under a bushel.

I want a CDU whose members are involved in opinion making, who are confident and keen to debate.

But I also want a CDU which, after debates and discussions, makes clear decisions, accepts majority votes, and leads the way on a shared path.

The delegates' reaction to my speech was overwhelming. They leaped up from their seats; the party conference protocol records long and energetic applause. But this can't possibly capture what actually happened. The conference was gripped by an atmosphere of confidence that hadn't seemed possible just a few days beforehand. Soon afterward I, the woman from the GDR who had come from Democratic Awakening and only been a member of the CDU for nine and a half years, was elected, with 897 of 935 votes, as chair of the party which had provided the chancellor in thirty-six out of fifty-one years, the party that had been at rock bottom, almost drowned in the donation quagmire, and which was now taking a phenomenal leap of faith in giving me 95.9 percent of the vote, in the hope of a new beginning. Amid the delegates' cheers, barely knowing what to do with my elation, I waved back and forth the two flower bouquets that had been handed to me. I felt at one with the delegates. It was the perfect party conference. Never again, not even as chancellor, would I experience a congress with such a feeling of unity between the CDU and myself; between myself and the CDU.

The travails of the plains—or: the battle for authority

I walked down the steps from the platform in the hall where our conference had taken place. Following the end of the event, I had just been giving interviews to the waiting journalists from the TV channels. In the hall, the clean-up operation had begun; the delegates were long since on their way home, congress documents were being cleared by industrious volunteers, chairs and tables stacked away. As I made my way toward the stage to say goodbye to my colleagues from Konrad Adenauer House, I heard a melody. At first it was very subtle, on the fringes of my consciousness like the music in an elevator or shopping mall. Then it became increasingly noticeable, and I found myself thinking: I know that tune. Eventually, it was unmistakable: "Angie," the famous Rolling Stones song. Ulf Leisner, the leader of Konrad Adenauer House's coordination department, who like me was from the GDR, had arranged for it to be played as a surprise. Mick Jagger's voice echoed through the hall. "Angie." It was a wonderful moment. We were all tired—exhausted, even, but happy too. We laughed, hummed along, and wished one another a good homeward journey. Suddenly, though, the song's melancholic tone hit another nerve for me, and I said: "This was the last lovely day for a long time to come." The others laughed and waved their hands dismissively.

But I was right. By the very next day, problems were already piling up. We faced immense financial worries, after the Bundestag president Wolfgang Thierse (SPD) had landed the CDU with a penalty of a whopping forty-one million deutsche marks due to poor accounting. In February we had already lost the elections in Schleswig-Holstein with Volker Rühe as our primary candidate, and now, in May, were also conceding a bitter defeat in North Rhine-Westphalia with Jürgen Rüttgers.

To top it all off, a few weeks later, on July 14, 2000, Schröder succeeded in pushing through the Bundesrat a tax reform he had proposed, even though the red–green coalition didn't have a majority in the Bundesrat at the time. He achieved this by making financial concessions not only to Rhineland-Palatinate, which was governed by the SPD and FDP, but also the federal states of Brandenburg, Berlin, and Bremen, which were governed by grand coalitions. The CDU representatives of the aforementioned state governments then departed from the previously agreed party line of rejecting Schröder's tax reform, and voted in favor of it. Wolfgang Böhmer, state premier of Saxony-Anhalt, later summed this up in inimitable style: "I smell money, and I'm corruptible." And that's precisely what happened: all the pledges of allegiance in the Presidium and Federal Board not to make a trade-off with Schröder at any price, but instead to let the red–green alliance fail publicly, became worthless from one second to the next. With financial pledges for Berlin, Brandenburg, Bremen, and Rhineland-Palatinate, Schröder achieved the necessary votes in the Bundesrat. On July 14, 2000, he had his majority, the tax reform was agreed—and I was left looking like a fool.

A fool, because I had naively believed the pledges of allegiance. A fool, because I'd had to learn that public perception craves the ability to define the winners and losers. A fool, because as party leader I alone, the official number one, not Friedrich Merz as group chair, carried the responsibility for this defeat. It was utterly irrelevant whether we both considered the actions of the federal states to be disloyal. I was party chair, not him, and I had failed in my area of responsibility, because I hadn't kept the state premiers in line. This is how I learned what it means to be chair: constantly carrying the ultimate political responsibility for both successes and failures.

The worst element for me, however, was that I hadn't even tried to solve the problem with my own understanding of opposition work: an understanding that would have been much more in keeping with my temperament and nature than the attempt to build a blockade against Schröder. I was already struggling more, on a fundamental level, with the opposition role than I was with the governing role. There were topics where I could clearly declare myself in favor of the CDU position; for example, when it came to my view back then on the use of nuclear energy. I had great fun debating with the foreign minister Joschka Fischer and the environment minister Jürgen Trittin, both with the Greens. But to argue for argument's sake, the attitude that Social Democrats and Greens per se must be attacked from morning to night, that they should be considered strange even as human beings—to me that was and remains completely alien.

In 1989, I had taken my first tentative steps into the happy feeling that party political diversity might finally be possible. It wouldn't have occurred to me, even in my wildest dreams, to regard Klaus Ulbricht—my former boss at the Academy of Sciences, with whom I'd embarked on a search for the right party—as an enemy now, just because he'd joined the SDP and I'd joined Democratic Awakening. I wanted to approach things objectively wherever possible. I tended to enter into compromises when the advantages outweighed the disadvantages by a proportion of 51 to 49. The world is seldom black and white, and I find 100 to 0 suspicious. On reflection, I could even understand the prime ministers who had tried to get another few hundred million deutsche marks out of Schröder before approving his tax reform. Their obligations lay first and foremost with their state, and only afterward with the party line.

I learned the hard way, and had to fight for my authority. That's how it was: back then, politicians like Bernhard Vogel, Eberhard Diepgen, Kurt Biedenkopf, Erwin Teufel, and Volker Rühe were still members of the CDU Presidium, all of them experienced prime ministers or federal politicians who had already shaped the CDU significantly while I was still working at the Academy of Sciences in the GDR, when German reunification was still inconceivable. In a way, I found them intimidating. I had to learn to speak assertively in meetings and not smile with embarrassment when I was attacked, because to do so would only have demonstrated hesitancy. I also had to learn about the ominous, so-called Andean Pact, the subject of so much attention in the press. This male society included, among others, the Presidium members Roland Koch, Peter Müller, and Christian Wulff. In 1979, as members of Germany's Junge Union, they had pledged during a plane journey over the Andes one day to decide the succession in the CDU chair and in the Chancellery between themselves, and never to side publicly against one another, regardless of whether it was justified or not. In their eyes, I must have been a stopgap at best as party chair, if not an occupational injury.

I learned to make mistakes like my incorrect analysis of the power balance with the tax reform just once—never twice. When a vote was held in the Bundestag in August 2001 over deploying the federal armed forces in Macedonia as part of a NATO mandate, a confrontation arose similar to the previous year's tax reform. Except that this time it was with further-reaching consequences, because it wasn't a domestic political plan, but rather one relating to foreign policy and security. The red–green federal government didn't have the majority to pass the mandate without the support of the opposition: Gerhard

Schröder had told me this quite openly in a one-to-one conversation. And a significant proportion of the CDU/CSU group saw this as an opportunity to subject Schröder to an electoral defeat in the Bundestag. This time, the CDU as a party wasn't the problem, nor the CSU; it was the parliamentary group in the Bundestag which—fixated on Schröder—had backed itself into a corner. Would it really come down to an open battle over a NATO deployment? And coming from the very parliamentary group which, in its history, had defended NATO more robustly than any other in Germany? And that despite the European Union's then High Representative for Common Foreign and Security Policy, Javier Solana, having telephoned me to beg us to support deployment? Should a supposedly party-tactical motive really outweigh national political responsibility and party-political identity? I feared that a negative vote in the Bundestag from the Union group would not just put Germany in an impossible position with regard to national policy, but would also destroy the Union. And I decided not to let it come to that. Over the course of numerous meetings, it was possible to move Volker Rühe and Friedrich Merz to a U-turn.

On August 28, 2001, decision day in the group, things went back and forth. Session followed session. The regional branches met, as did the acting group executive committee, the group executive committee, and the group itself. It became apparent that in politics things can escalate faster than you can blink. And yet, once a large group of people had been driven in a particular direction, it was immensely difficult to reverse this and change the arguments of the previous day into their opposite. But I also learned never to think something is impossible. It's very rarely too late. There's always something you can do; you just need to want it enough. So the U-turn was successful. When the vote was held in the Bundestag the next day, the Union group voted, with five abstentions, 162 to 61 for the deployment of the Bundeswehr in Macedonia—a deployment that hardly anyone remembers today, because, in contrast to Volker Rühe's argument, it was one of the Bundeswehr's shortest and safest foreign deployments ever. It doesn't bear thinking about what might have happened if we hadn't achieved this about-turn. Neither for domestic nor foreign policy.

"Turn on the TV. You won't believe what's happening!" cried the CDU general secretary Willi Hausmann just two weeks later as he came running into my office at Konrad Adenauer House. It was early afternoon. I'd been sitting at the conference table. I stood up immediately, grabbed the remote control, and turned on the TV. "CNN—turn on CNN!" he cried again, his voice agitated.

What I saw next took my breath away. One of the Twin Towers of the World Trade Center stood amid swathes of smoke. Seconds later, I saw a plane fly into the second tower, live. I heard that it was the second plane to have flown into the building. A large passenger jet. I walked through the secretariat into Beate Baumann's office and called out: "Come and see! A plane's just crashed into the World Trade Center! And it's the second one already!" "WHAT?" she cried, following me back into my office. There we stood—Willi Hausmann, Beate Baumann, and I—staring at the TV images. It was just after nine in the morning in New York. A little later, Eva Christiansen joined us. My secretaries had also jumped up from their seats and were now standing in the doorway, watching the pictures on TV. I was able to grasp what was happening, but couldn't feel what it meant. On a rational level, it was clear to me that there must be thousands of people in the building, and I saw the towers—first one, then the other—collapse in on themselves, but I couldn't yet build any emotional connection to the unfolding events. It could just as easily have been a movie. But it wasn't. And nor was it an accident. That much was clear, if not before, when a third plane crashed into the Pentagon, the US Department of Defense.

"It's a terror attack," I heard myself say. It was September 11, 2001, a Tuesday, one of those days on which people never forget where they were and what they were doing. One of those days when, from one moment to the next, the world no longer seemed the same. When it was clear that, for a long while to come, everything that had previously seemed important had to take a back seat; when we as the opposition had to recognize it was the government's hour, and the government had to understand they needed to seek a shoulder-to-shoulder stance with the opposition. And they did. The chancellor, the foreign minister, and the defense minister kept us continually informed about the information they were receiving on the background of the attack, and about how they wanted to proceed.

Islamic terrorists from Osama bin Laden's terror network Al-Qaeda, who operated from the Islamic Emirate of Afghanistan, ruled by the Taliban, a group of Islamist fighters, had attacked the United States of America. More than three thousand people lost their lives. Al-Qaeda had attacked a NATO state. For the first time in the history of the transatlantic alliance, founded in 1949, Article 5 of the North Atlantic Treaty, the mutual defense clause, came into play. On November 16, 2001, there was a vote in the Bundestag on the Bundeswehr's deployment in the context of Operation Enduring Freedom, a mission initiated by the United States to fight international terrorism. Chancellor Gerhard Schröder linked it with the confidence vote in order to avoid a defeat within his government. We as the opposition voted in favor of the deployment. It would last almost twenty years—with various mandates—before it came to an end under terrible circumstances in the summer of 2021. More on this later.

Parliamentary chairwoman

Factual questions in politics are almost always questions of power too, and anyone who manages to coin definitions will be successful, both in terms of content and political power. In 2001, I had managed to convince my party to set up a commission that would put to the test and renew the principles of social capitalism within a globalized context. But for many in the party—both social policymakers and economic politicians—alarm bells began to ring when I personally became chair of this task force, asked Jürgen Kluge, the former boss of McKinsey Deutschland, for economic consultancy support, and carried out the process under the heading "New Social Capitalism." Some were genuinely concerned that I intended to bring to an end the traditional definition of social capitalism, finding it suspicious that I'd stressed the word "New." Others—rather disdainfully—just didn't want to see me succeed. Because, as previously mentioned, factual questions in politics are almost always also questions of power, and anyone who manages to coin concepts will be successful. Perhaps also with regard to the decision of candidacy for the position of chancellor in the autumn 2002 Bundestag elections? That topic hovered over everything. The commission's work led into a key policy proposal for the CDU party conference in December 2001 in Dresden. While the expression "New Social Capitalism" did still appear, its title was now simply "Free people. Strong country. Treaty for a secure future."

Parallel to this, the discussion regarding the chancellorship candidacy had gained increasing momentum during 2001. There was another potential interested party in the Bavarian State Chancellery: Edmund Stoiber, who had been Bavarian state premier since 1993 and chair of the CSU since 1999. In 1980, as the CSU's general secretary, he had led the Bundestag election campaign for the chancellorship candidate Franz Josef

Strauss. In political competition, Stoiber could polarize in a sharp-tongued manner, was detail obsessed, and, armed with a veritable mountain of file memos, always excellently prepared. He sensed the political moods and weaknesses of his competitors. I suspected that, in view of the difficult time the CDU had gone through, and my still-modest experience as CDU chair, he saw a unique opportunity to claim the chancellorship candidacy for himself, and, in the process, for the CSU.

It would be going too far in these pages to recount all the private discussions and telephone calls involved in this decision. But I will say this: from summer 2001 onward, entire delegations of CDU politicians, many of them long-serving and predominantly from the southwest of Germany, had come to me and, in countless conversations, repeatedly urged me to give up. Some gently and affectionately, others using the sledgehammer approach. Some verbosely expressed that they thought me an excellent chairwoman, but not to the extent I could become a candidate for the role of chancellor. Others went straight on the attack, saying in no uncertain terms that I would have the fate of the CDU on my conscience if I didn't surrender the candidacy to Edmund Stoiber. Immediately. And of course without putting up a fight.

I found this unspeakable. With my help, the CDU had managed to extricate itself from the quagmire of the donation affair and get back into the political race—but apparently that wasn't enough for the candidacy, under the motto: the little chairwoman from the East isn't up to the job. For me, there was no doubt. If there had been, I might as well have stepped down as party chair immediately. The chair of the larger of the two sister parties, having not even attempted to lay claim to the candidacy and fight for support, would have been finished. And rightly so. I couldn't reconcile that with how I saw myself—with how I saw myself personally, and how I saw my party.

In the Christmas holidays of 2001, the subject was constantly on my mind. No matter whether I was roasting a turkey in Hohenwalde or making breakfast, whether I was walking in the forest or shopping in the neighboring village—it was always there. From the moment I got up to the moment I went to bed, and even at night, if I lay awake, I thought and thought. I was aware of two different layers: Firstly, I needed to answer the question for myself as to whether I wanted to become chancellor. My response was yes, like it had been back in early 2000 before my decision to run for the CDU chair. In that respect, nothing had changed. Secondly, I had to answer the question as to whether I wanted it *now*. And that answer was also yes, but I noticed it didn't carry the same vigor it had a few months before, nor the same clarity with which I'd answered the first question. I had therefore found a decision-making basis, and this enabled me to turn my attention to the next question: Did I have enough supporters in the party? After all, I didn't just have opponents. There were also those who had always been on my side, and who expected me to stand for election. And there were those who still had bad memories of the 1980 election with Franz Josef Strauss as candidate—the only CSU candidate by that point—and who were very skeptical about whether things would go any better this time, with Edmund Stoiber as second CSU candidate.

The conclusion I reached was neither to give up the candidacy without a fight, nor to bang my head against the wall—on such occasions, in my experience, the wall always wins. In an interview with *Welt am Sonntag*, published on January 6, 2002, I publicly declared my readiness to run for the role of chancellor. By doing so, I forced Edmund Stoiber to break cover. That very same day, he also announced his intention to become the CDU and CSU candidate for chancellor. On the ARD program "Beckmann" the following day, Monday, January 7, 2002, I once again confirmed my willingness to become a candidate. The cards were on the table. The moment of decision had come.

01, 02 | *My maternal grandparents, Willi and Gertrud Jentzsch.*

03 | *My paternal grandparents, Ludwig and Margarete Kasner.*

04 | *My parents, Herlind and Horst Kasner, married on August 6, 1952.*

05 | *Baby Angela.*

06 | *Vacation memories with my parents on the Baltic coast, here in Kühlungsborn, 1956.*

07 | *Holding my mother's hand when we attended my aunt Gunhild's wedding in Hamburg in 1959.*

08 | *With my brother Marcus and sister Irene in 1966 on the Waldhof estate in Templin, where we could run about at will.*

09 | *Honoring the victors at the Russian Olympiad of the district of Neubrandenburg in the spring, 1969.*

10, 11 | *As a student, I liked to go on outings to Saxon Switzerland in the mid-1970s; when climbing the sandstone cliffs, I always found the way up easier than the way down.*

12 | *Relieved to have received my doctorate on January 8, 1986, I enjoyed my presents at my desk at the Central Institute for Physical Chemistry (ZIPC).*

13 | *Joachim at his desk at the ZIPC in the mid-1980s.*

14 | *On my thirty-sixth birthday on July 17, 1990, at home in Schönhauser Allee; the bookshelves and lamp were home-made.*

15 | *Time out in the election campaign for the Volkskammer election on March 18, 1990, at my desk at Democratic Awakening at the House of Democracy in Berlin.*

16 | *As deputy government spokesperson in 1990, I discovered how much time one can spend on the phone to journalists.*

17 | *It was quite special to be flanked by the finance ministers of the GDR and the Federal Republic, Walter Romberg (left) and Theo Waigel (right), to moderate the press conference for the currency union; on the outside left is Matthias Gehler, government spokesperson for the GDR government; outside right is Theo Waigel's press officer, Karlheinz von den Driesch.*

18 | *One November morning I visited fishermen from my constituency in their hut in Lobbe, on the island of Rügen; they had just landed their morning catch a short time before.*

19 | *I was a federal representative in Mecklenburg-Western Pomerania for over thirty years, and thought I had the loveliest constituency in Germany.*

20 | *At a cabinet session as a proud minister for women and youth, this one on November 26, 1991.*

Berlin 1995
UN Convention on
Climate Change

21 | *As chair of the first UN climate conference (COP 1), in Berlin, in April 1995, I discovered my enthusiasm for foreign policy.*

22 | *At the CDU party conference in Dresden on December 16, 1991, I was elected sole deputy of party chairman Helmut Kohl.*

23 | *New start in the opposition: at the suggestion of the CDU chair Wolfgang Schäuble (left), I was elected secretary general in Bonn in 1998.*

24 | *April 10, 2000: happy to be elected chair of the CDU in Germany.*

25 | *The former chancellor Helmut Kohl and me (I had become candidate for chancellor two weeks previously) at the Theater am Schiffbauerdamm in Berlin on June 16, 2005, at the celebration of the foundation of the CDU in the same place sixty years previously.*

26 | *Election campaign, summer 2005.*

27 | *With Eva Christiansen (left) and Beate Baumann (right) on September 4, 2005, on the way to the television duel with Chancellor Gerhard Schröder in Berlin-Adlershof.*

28 | *After being elected federal chancellor on November 22, 2005, I swore my oath to Bundestag president Norbert Lammert.*

29 | *Alone on the government benches after the swearing-in ceremony; during those seconds, I felt a weight lifting from my shoulders—that was how it felt after each swearing-in.*

30 | *In my office at the Chancellery: on the left behind me are my desk and the portrait of the first federal chancellor Konrad Adenauer, painted by Oskar Kokoschka.*

31 | *In conversation with Gabi Möhlig from the team of gardeners at the Chancellery, who delighted me every day with beautiful bouquets.*

32 | *Every year at Advent, the forestry owners (AGDW) not only donated a Christmas tree for the courtyard of the Chancellery but also gave me a chess figure carved from oak wood.*

33 | *My trip to Paris and Brussels on my first day in office: I prepared for the day's meetings on the plane.*

34 | *President Jacques Chirac welcomed me with perfect protocol at the car in the courtyard of the Élysée Palace.*

35 | *German foreign minister Frank-Walter Steinmeier (back) and I were welcomed by the NATO secretary general Jaap de Hoop Scheffer (front right).*

36 | *With the president of the European Commission José Manuel Barroso in Brussels.*

37 | *Routine activity at the conference table: going through files and reading messages.*

39 | *Waiting outside the gate to the courtyard of the Chancellery for the arrival of a guest of state.*

38 | *Thinking and planning: with Beate Baumann in February 2009, in Dierhagen on the Baltic coast.*

40 | *Memorizing the words before recording my weekly video podcast.*

41 | *The "Merkel diamond"—CDU poster on Washingtonplatz in Berlin. Measuring 70 by 20 meters, it was assembled from 2,150 photographs of my supporters in the 2013 German election campaign.*

Angela Merkel, 1957

Für ein Deutschland, in dem jeder alles werden kann.

42 | *Slogan in the 2017 German election campaign: "For a Germany in which anyone can become anything"— even a little girl who was born in Hamburg and grew up in the East.*

43 | *Hiking in the mountains of the Alto Adige.*

45 | *Having lunch while on holiday on the island of Ischia (on our right, fisherman Aniello Poerio and his family, Sandra and Carlo Poerio; on our left, friends from the island, Marie Laurence Puech and Alessandro Mattera).*

44 | *Regular guests at the opening of the Bayreuth Festival, here on July 25, 2007.*

46 | *Having to be contactable by phone at all times, even at lunch break in the Tiergarten, Berlin.*

We had scheduled the annual closed-door conference of the CDU Federal Board for January 11 and 12, a Friday and Saturday, this time in Magdeburg, in a hotel with the heavily symbolic name "Herrenkrug" (Gentleman's tankard). I had resolved that by then the matter had to be settled.

On January 9, a Wednesday, I met Beate Baumann in a restaurant for dinner, not one frequented by the city's many journalists, but one where we could be sure of speaking undisturbed and unobserved. We could have stayed at the office, but needed a change of air; it wasn't the Baltic Sea, admittedly, but just ten minutes' drive away from Konrad Adenauer House, in Berlin-Mitte. We had with us the list of Presidium members and Federal Executive Committee members, and we pored over everything. I counted supporters and opponents. We contemplated whether I should enter into a crucial vote within the committees of the party in two days' time in Magdeburg. At the same time, we were a little sad, because the stench of failure already hung in the air. After all, what impact would it have had if the CDU chairwoman had forced her party into her candidacy for chancellor, blackmailing them, even—with the stipulation of either receiving the candidacy or stepping down as party chair or, defeated, campaigning only half-heartedly? Would that have been a viable route, in order to fight in a unified way and ultimately win? Conflicts, as I had once learned from Wolfgang Schäuble, rarely existed only between the CDU and CSU, but almost always ran right through the CDU. Wouldn't an election campaign that not only led to open confrontation with the CSU, but also split the CDU into two camps, have been doomed to failure from the start? The past months had sapped a lot of my energy. There had been little enjoyment in having countless telephone calls and conversations, and saying stoically again and again: "No, no, no, I won't just throw the chancellorship candidacy away."

After we had gone over everything, looking at it from all

possible angles, Beate Baumann and I headed back to our homes for the night. We wanted to let everything sink in, and sleep on it.

The next morning, Thursday, January 10, we happened to run into one another by the elevator in the underground parking garage of Konrad Adenauer House, on the way up to our offices on the sixth floor. The elevator doors opened and we stepped in. The doors closed. I pressed the button for floor six, and the elevator began to judder upward.

"I'm putting an end to it," I said.

"To what?" asked Beate Baumann.

"The candidacy," I answered.

"Okay, then that's that," she replied.

The decision had matured within me overnight. And Beate Baumann and I knew one another well enough to know it was final. It had been the right move to think it over for so long. It had been the right move to prompt Edmund Stoiber publicly to declare his readiness for candidacy. It had been the right move, as chair of the larger of the two sister parties, to have also publicly declared my willingness and aspiration to run. Everyone had now understood that I wanted to stand for election, and that I thought myself capable. But the important thing now, rather than driving my party into an ill-fated test, was to fulfill my responsibility as chair in a different way: not by further insisting on candidacy for chancellorship, but by uniting the party and paving the way for a unanimous election campaign.

I summoned the CDU general secretary Laurenz Meyer, Willi Hausmann, and Eva Christiansen to my office to inform them of my decision. We discussed the next steps. Then everything went really quickly. I called Edmund Stoiber and suggested we meet for a one-to-one conversation, remaining tightlipped on the subject matter. He needed to collect his thoughts. We ended the telephone call. Just a few minutes later he called back, and we agreed I would meet him for breakfast at his home in the Bavarian town of Wolfratshausen, and speak face to-face.

In the afternoon, I flew to Düsseldorf as planned to give the keynote address at that evening's epiphany meeting of North Rhine-Westphalia's Chamber of Industry and Trade. There was no way I wanted to cancel. After the event, I flew on to Munich, having chartered a private plane through the CDU, and stayed in a hotel close to the airport. The next morning, Friday, January 11, 2002, I set off early with a driver who had come to Munich in the interim. I arrived at Edmund Stoiber's private residence in Wolfratshausen at eight o'clock on the dot.

Karin Stoiber had set the breakfast table with great care, but Edmund Stoiber and I barely touched a thing. I came straight to the point: it had been important for both of us publicly to declare our willingness to lead the Union as candidates for chancellor in the 2002 Bundestag elections. At the same time, it was clear that he, unlike me, could count on the unanimous support of the CDU and CSU. Solidarity was the be-all and end-all in an election campaign. That's why I wanted him to become our joint candidate, I said, and I would be making this recommendation to my party that afternoon in Magdeburg. All I asked was that I be the first to explain this decision, and my reasoning, to my Presidium and Federal Executive Committee in Magdeburg, without any of it becoming public knowledge beforehand. Edmund Stoiber agreed—he too realized that this was a momentous decision not just on a personal level, but for the Union overall.

After just an hour, I said my goodbyes. On the car journey to Munich Airport, I called Beate Baumann to tell her how the conversation with Stoiber had played out. She could now cancel an 11:00 a.m. visit that had been planned to the sugar factory in Klein Wanzleben, Saxony-Anhalt. We'd needed to wait until this moment. I would travel in the private plane from Munich back to Berlin, and, from there, head onward by car to Magdeburg.

Edmund Stoiber kept his word. Everything remained secret. Only after news broke of the cancellation of my visit to Klein Wanzleben did wild speculation begin in the media about whether I was planning something. But by then I was already in the car heading to the "Herrenkrug."

What happened next is well known: Edmund Stoiber became the second CSU candidate for chancellor in the history of the CDU and CSU. The next day, Saturday, January 12, he traveled to our conference in Magdeburg, and we addressed the media together.

Over the following months, we led a very different election campaign from the CDU and CSU's Strauss one in 1980. Rather than being divided and dogged, it was synchronized and cohesive. Beate Baumann, in addition to her role as my office manager, took on leadership of the campaign and political planning headquarters at Konrad Adenauer House and, in this dual role, became an important go-to person for the CSU general secretary Michael Höhenberger, a close colleague of Edmund Stoiber.

The CDU and CSU, Edmund Stoiber, and I withstood the hardest of tests, because Chancellor Schröder pulled out all the stops in challenging the Union: a No on a possible Iraq war; the presentation of a first paper by Peter Hartz, member of the Volkswagen AG board, with labor market reforms that the Union could hardly have worded any differently; great empathy for the people affected by terrible floods on the Elbe River; unbridled fighting spirit in two TV duels with Edmund Stoiber, the first of their kind in a Bundestag election campaign.

The Bundestag election took place on September 22. The previous day, for the first time in my life, I was present at the tapping of the first keg at the Munich Oktoberfest. There was a lively atmosphere. Edmund Stoiber and I had given it our all, each of us in our own way. We were sitting in the front row on the balcony of the beer tent, looking out at all the people. They were cheering Stoiber, cheering both of us.

Afterward, we drove to the Bavarian State Chancellery, Stoiber's official seat, to talk one-to-one. I had requested this, wanting to discuss the potential outcomes of the election result with him. In the case of a victory, I told him, I wouldn't want to join his cabinet, but instead, as party chair, to also become chair of the CDU and CSU's Bundestag group. For the statics of the Union and a possible CSU-led government, it would be imperative, I emphasized, that the CDU chair not be governed by the chancellor's cabinet discipline and policymaking power. The CDU needed a clear center of power. For that, the party and group leadership needed to be in one hand. And this also applied in the case that, contrary to expectation, the next day didn't bring election success. Stoiber showed great understanding of my line of argumentation. I also sensed in him sincere gratitude that I personally, like all the co-workers at the CDU national headquarters, had campaigned loyally for him. I could count on his support. This was vital for me, because it was customary that the leaders of both parties of the Bundestag group made a joint recommendation for the election of a group chair.

After the conversation, I flew home and spent the rest of Saturday in Hohenwalde.

The next day, at one o'clock in the afternoon, I went to vote in the canteen of the Humboldt University in Berlin, and toward five o'clock, drove to Konrad Adenauer House to meet with Edmund Stoiber. After the carriage ride through Munich, which was obligatory for a Bavarian state premier, he had flown to Berlin in the interim.

Election night played out differently than how we had hoped. While, initially, it had seemed that the CDU and CSU would be victorious, the picture became increasingly gloomy with every projection. In the end, red–green prevailed with an extremely narrow lead: 38.5 percent voted for the CDU and CSU, equating to 248 seats in the Bundestag, and the SPD also won 38.5 percent, but, with a 6027-vote lead, three seats more than the CDU and CSU, they were the largest party by a hair's breadth. The Greens achieved 8.6 percent, or 55 seats; the FDP 7.4 percent, or 47 seats; and the PDS 4.0 percent and 2 seats through direct mandates.

Friedrich Merz was cut to the quick when I revealed to him that I wanted to become group chair in his stead, and that Edmund Stoiber and I, as chairs of the CDU and CSU, would make the corresponding proposal to our group at their first meeting. After the donations scandal, it had been logical for Merz to become chair of the group. He was and is a brilliant speaker, and had supported me during the donations scandal. I liked the fact that he too was power-conscious. We're almost the same age; he was born in 1955, and I in 1954. We came from completely different backgrounds, and this too was more of an opportunity than a hindrance. But there was a problem, and from the very start: we both wanted to be boss. These are the kind of arrangements that occur in political parties, and they have to be clarified, especially when it's clear that the frictional losses are becoming too great, as they were with the two of us. In the wake of the 2002 Bundestag election, it was time for clarification. Friedrich Merz acknowledged with regret that the CDU and CSU party chairs wouldn't be nominating him for re-election as group chairman.

Two days after the Bundestag election, on Tuesday, September 24, 2002, the CDU/CSU Bundestag group elected me as their new chair. And at my party's national conference in Hanover on November 11, 2002, I was re-elected as CDU chair for a further two years by 796 votes to 746.

Snap elections

Edmund Stoiber was in Munich again, and as party and group chair I now had a dual role. I continued to work on New Social Capitalism. Though I hadn't been able to implement the definition, the topic remained. It also led me to nominate Horst Köhler, who was head of the International Monetary Fund at the time, as the Union and FDP's candidate for the 2004 presidential election. As president of Germany, he later said the wonderful words: "For me, the humanity of our world is decided by the fate of Africa." He was able to see beyond his own nose, and didn't lose his fascination with the African continent even after stepping down from the role in 2010.

Programmatically speaking, it was time to develop concrete proposals for the future of the three social security systems: pensions, nursing care, and health. I was able to get Roman Herzog, former president of the Federal Constitutional Court and former federal president, to lead a commission on these topics. In 1997, Herzog had won himself a reputation as a reformer with the sentence: "Germany needs to be jolted out of complacency." His ability was beyond doubt. The concepts elaborated by the commission, which was later named after him, would become part of a government program for the upcoming 2006 Bundestag elections. Roman Herzog submitted his commission's report to me on September 30, 2003, and on October 1, 2003, I delivered a keynote speech on the subject at the German Historical Museum in Berlin, the former armory on Unter den Linden. It met with a positive response and considerable support among those who felt that labor market and social reforms were long overdue in Germany. The recommendations from the Herzog Commission report were passed at the federal party conference in Leipzig in December 2003. This would go down in CDU history as the "reform conference." The proposals for a tax reform, devised by Friedrich Merz and nicknamed the "beer coaster tax reform" for being so simple and clear that all the taxation rates fit on a beer coaster, were just as broadly accepted as those for a future pension and nursing care insurance. The proposals on the future of health insurance, however, were controversial. The so-called health premium proposed by the Herzog Commission was defamed by its opponents, even by some in the CDU and CSU, as a capitation fee, inconsistent with the Union's values. Its opponents claimed there would no longer be any social offsetting for those who were unable to pay a uniform contribution that was independent from income level. This was nonsense, because instead of the existing percentage health insurance contributions deducted from income, the concept explicitly had in mind an income-dependent social offsetting which would be financed from the overall federal tax revenue. The conference voted in favor of the health premium.

Essentially, however, we as a Union came late to this. Six months previously, on March 14, 2003, Gerhard Schröder had presented "Agenda 2010"—as he titled it—in a government statement in the Bundestag. This agenda incorporated measures which were based on the Hartz Commission report presented during the August 2002 election campaign, and also on the reflections of European social democrats, in particular those of the German chancellor and the British prime minister Tony Blair in the Schröder–Blair Paper of 1999. The measures were aimed at stimulating growth and employment. Agenda 2010 focused, among other things, on training and education measures, the expansion of all-day schools, and the improvement of care for children under three years of age. At the heart of the concept, and of public attention, however, were measures that could equally have been proposed by a Christian Democrat chancellor. But to Social Democratic ears, it was all a bit much. Not only were dismissal protections to be relaxed and certain benefits to be struck from the catalog of health insurance, but the so-called "Unemployment Benefit II" would also be introduced after just a year of unemployment, on the level of the benefits rate, and the suitability rules for job offers would be tightened. In addition, Gerhard Schröder wanted to add a "sustainability factor" to the pension formula, with the aim of slowing the rise in pension insurance contributions. In doing so, Schröder corrected a mistake made during his first term, when he had reversed the so-called demographic factor introduced by the CDU/CSU and FDP during their time in office. This factor would mean the rise in pensions was no longer solely determined by the salary increase of employees paying mandatory social security contributions, but instead would also take into account their age distribution, in other words, the ratio of those who paid money into the retirement plan to those whose pensions were paid out. Reality had caught up with Schröder and his 1998 Bundestag election campaign promises. The problems in the labor market and with health care and pensions had become overwhelming. Please note: never revise the tough and unpopular but unavoidable reforms of your predecessors without good cause.

During the following two years, Schröder did everything in his power to get the Agenda 2010 reforms passed in the Bundestag and Bundesrat. He was able to—and had to—rely on the Union's support, not least because he was dependent on the approval of Union-governed states in the Bundesrat. This didn't make things within the party any easier for him. The SPD, whose chairman he had become after his predecessor, Oskar Lafontaine, fled the government in April 1999, suffered so much under the measures that, in February 2004, Schröder felt compelled to give up the party chairmanship. His successor was the SPD group chair Franz Müntefering, who later became vice chancellor in my first federal government.

For me, as I said publicly at the time, Schröder's decision was the beginning of the end for his chancellorship. And yet I would never have imagined the end would come just a year later. I assumed the next Bundestag elections would be in 2006; I had enough to keep me occupied with the general state of the world, my party, my relationship to the sister party the CSU, and my group. This included the suspension of Hesse Bundestag member Martin Hohmann from my group due to a speech he'd given, on October 3, 2003, that could now be interpreted as antisemitic and as trampling our party's values underfoot; the conflict with the CSU over health-care policy, which still hadn't been resolved even after the Leipzig conference, resulting in Horst Seehofer, the former health minister, resigning from his role as vice-chair of my group; and the European and international dislocations triggered by the Iraq War, launched by then-president George W. Bush and the "coalition of the willing," without an explicit UN mandate, on the night of March 19 to 20, 2003.

In February 2003, I had stumbled into the role of warmonger. Within an incredibly short space of time, my poll ratings plummeted. Chancellor Schröder had already addressed the imminent threat of a second Iraq war during the 2002 Bundestag election campaign, and continued to do so after the election too, increasingly intensifying his line of argument. He even—unlike his foreign minister Joschka Fischer—categorically rejected a deployment legitimized by UN mandate. It was obvious that he wanted to exploit the matter in a party-political way. This put the CDU/CSU Bundestag group, our CDU and CSU parties, in an impossible situation: Schröder sensed the opinion of the German people, because who could possibly be, or want to be, against peace and for war? Nobody. "War," as I said in the Bundestag on the morning of March 20, 2003, the day war broke out, "is always a failure of diplomacy and politics." I continued: "Looking to the future, we are doing everything we can to ensure that the strength and agency of the European Union, of the transatlantic alliance, and the United Nations can develop anew through solidarity and unity. We are connected with the United States of America within these institutions and communities, not least through our shared values, and this is why we are standing by them."

But no matter how I looked at it, Schröder had hit a nerve. In contrast to him, I had refused from the very beginning to publicly criticize Bush's approach, to accept a split in Europe, or to actually force one into existence—a split between Germany and France, and also with Russia, already led by President Putin back then, on one side, and Great Britain, Spain, the Netherlands, and other states on the other. That, by association, even the idea could arise that Germany was keeping a kind of equidistance between the United States and our alliance partners in NATO, and Russia—this was something I found deeply abhorrent. It was the opposite of what the CDU, and I personally, connected with our understanding of European unity and transatlantic partnership.

This held the potential for incitement; politics are competition, and as I've said, factual questions, including foreign policy ones, are almost always also questions of power. "Vasallage" was for this reason a heckle that I received during a speech in the Bundestag on February 13, 2003, as I responded to a statement from the chancellor before the outbreak of war. I wasn't able to get through to people with my line of argument. Schröder had it easier and said: "We can't allow realpolitik or security doctrine to get us accustomed to seeing war as a normal means of politics, or, as it was once put, as the continuation of politics by other means." With this, the tone was set. And I made a mistake: in the *Washington Post* the following week, I had a bylined article published under the heading "Schroeder doesn't speak for all Germans." I wanted to show that, even in conflict situations, Germany should contribute its strength and influence to the European Union and the transatlantic relationship in a collaborative and nonconfrontational way. Nonetheless, it wasn't right, as a German politician, and as leader of the opposition, to attack my own chief of government head-on in the international sphere. Differences of opinion between government and the opposition should always be dealt with internally, not on foreign soil.

What remained? The Iraq War really was a mistake, waged on a basis of mistaken beliefs. It wasn't about weapons of mass destruction, as the United States government continually claimed, supporting their argument with supposed evidence that later turned out to be falsified, but rather about regime change in Iraq. This was achieved, and the state president Saddam Hussein overthrown, but the country descended into chaos. Gerhard Schröder's analysis had been correct. His confrontational approach, however, both within the European Union and toward the United States, in trying to prevent the war together with France's President Chirac, I still consider to be wrong. And ultimately: I could have spared myself the *Washington Post* article. Still, my poll ratings soon recovered—and my party's had barely been impaired. In retrospect, that's hardly a surprise. The argument hadn't touched the core of Christian democratic policy, where the focus was always on protecting Europe's unity, and only confidently opposing the US on this basis. And so Schröder didn't succeed in capitalizing on his anti-war stance for the SPD's benefit: their ratings remained low. In addition, the high unemployment rate and difficulties with the social security system were weighing heavy on Germany, and his Agenda 2010 reforms, intended to overcome these problems, were weighing on his party, because they called into question important convictions of Social Democratic objectives. That didn't change even with the shift from Schröder to Franz Müntefering as party chair. And so, in the spring, Germany witnessed the kind of development that could probably only be unleashed by Gerhard Schröder.

After the Schleswig-Holstein state elections in February 2005, in four secret votes, Prime Minister Heide Simonis (SPD) wasn't re-elected to the state parliament; on May 22, the SPD also lost the state election in the Social Democratic home state of North Rhine-Westphalia. On the early evening of the state elections, Schröder pulled the rip cord. The words that would change everything: snap elections. The SPD chairman Franz Müntefering was the one to make the announcement. An early national election, and as swiftly as possible. Schröder clearly saw this as an opportunity for a clearance kick.

Just eight days later, in a joint sitting of the CDU and CSU presidia, the Union nominated me as its candidate for chancellor for the 2005 Bundestag elections. Nothing could stand in my way. The Union had to be ready to act and campaign as swiftly as possible—both content-wise, and in terms of personnel. The foyer of Konrad Adenauer House was filled to the rafters for the press conference; clusters of journalists sat or stood in front of Edmund Stoiber and me, while numerous co-workers leaned against the balustrades of the building's different floors, studying the scene from above and clapping when I announced my candidacy. It was Monday, May 30, 2005, one o'clock in the afternoon. A good five years had passed since I'd decided to run for the CDU chair, and, by association, since I'd acknowledged my desire to become chancellor. Now, having gotten so much closer to my goal, instead of joy I initially felt only immense pressure. Everything was clear in my mind; I had worked toward this day for long enough, but as I heard myself speaking, I wasn't content. It wasn't about my appearance; a make-up artist had done my make-up and styled my hair. From August 2005 onward, this role was assumed by Petra Keller, who was employed in television during the GDR era, and who since reunification has worked predominantly freelance for RBB, the Berlin-Brandenburg broadcasting association. She has been by my side for countless hours—to this day—and managed to make my hair into a hairdo. I therefore had reason to feel at ease, even from the day I announced my candidacy. But I felt: This isn't a chancellor speaking. I had put a lot of thought into the speech, and each of my sentences was an answer to the question that had preoccupied me since I'd become a CDU member: Why the CDU? Why is the party necessary, and what understanding of the CDU did I want to represent? In my opening remarks, I said: "We want Germany to do better again. And that's not about political parties, it's not about careers, about him or me or him or her [. . .], it's about something else: we want to serve Germany, I want to serve Germany. Germany can do it, and together we can do it. That's our shared conviction." The words expressed what mattered to me; the content wasn't a problem. But they didn't carry enough weight, that's how it felt. I was reading far too much of it from the script, rather than speaking naturally. Intellectually, I should have been capable of delivering these few sentences without looking at the written version. I saw myself putting on the handbrake, and I couldn't release it. I was concentrating far too hard; there was no element of playfulness. It was as though, in that moment, in front of the entire world, I was living the difference between having trusted myself for years to become the CDU and CSU's candidate for chancellor, and now really *being* it.

Let's not get carried away!

Michael Glos, chairman of the CSU state group in the Bundestag, was belatedly celebrating his sixtieth birthday. Born on December 14, he held a summer party six months later, on July 21, 2005. It took place in the home of the Castell-Castell family of entrepreneurs, in his constituency of Castell, and I was asked to give the birthday speech. It was the day when the federal president Horst Köhler had dissolved the Bundestag and called new elections for September 18, and I wanted to make a public statement. In Castell, all the necessary preparations for this were being made while I gave Michael Glos's birthday speech. Immediately afterward, around 4:30 p.m., I hurried toward the locale where I'd be giving the statement, which was up two flights of stairs. Back then, I hadn't yet gotten wise to ensuring I wasn't already being filmed as I walked up to the podium. Otherwise, I'd have been able to gather myself briefly once I arrived at the top, and take a deep breath. I had no choice but to go straight to the microphone and launch into my statement. The text was well conceived, but I spoke breathlessly. I needed to take a breath after practically every third word, or so it seemed. My breathlessness didn't make a good impression, and it was symptomatic of the weeks that were to follow.

I discovered that there seemed to be a difference between theory and practice when it came to whether the time was ripe to have a female chancellor. There was doubt even deep into the ranks of women themselves. Gerhard Schröder had only been chancellor for seven years, and everyone felt he wanted to remain in the role; he was energetic and quick-witted. I was eyed with skepticism. This would have also been the case for a man who had run against the chancellor. But I sensed that being a woman definitely wasn't an advantage. The nearer election day came, the more this manifested itself. In addition, I'd made the mistake of taking far too little holiday, to refresh my mind before the most intense phase of the election campaign. The upshot being that I even confused gross and net in an interview.

And the CDU and CSU? Suddenly, we were the ones asking the people to endure hardship. Our plan to raise taxes by 2 percentage points represented this more than anything. The "Merkel Tax" was born; easy prey for Schröder's campaign. Schröder himself was no longer talking about reform, and especially not about his Agenda 2010. Our initially outstanding poll ratings, which foresaw a healthy majority for a new Union and FDP government, were both a blessing and a curse. A blessing because they motivated us, and a curse because we were already perceived to be the ruling party, the one which had ruined the economy and which Schröder could oppose to his heart's content.

Before the TV debate with Schröder on Sunday, September 4, I had thought at length about what to wear that evening: a colorful blazer, in which I could also stand out as a woman and feel comfortable, or a dark, stately-looking one. Erring on the side of caution, I decided on a dark-blue trouser suit. That way, I thought, I wouldn't distract people from watching and listening. I didn't sleep well the night before the debate, and was glad when, toward seven o'clock on the Sunday evening, it was finally time to head off to the studio in Berlin-Adlershof. The location was just a few meters from my old workplace at ZIPC (Central Institute for Physical Chemistry). After arriving, I reminded myself: Don't think about the alleged twenty million viewers who'll be watching, just concentrate on yourself and Schröder.

In roundtables like these, the particularly tricky questions were those about what politics could offer socially. That applied in particular to this debate, and I was prepared. The discussions bounced between the VAT increase, the health premium, and the supposed capitation fee: the flat tax model of Paul Kirchhof, former judge at the Federal Constitutional Court and finance expert in my competence team. Schröder merely referred to him as the "Professor from Heidelberg" in order to caricature his—and above all my—remoteness from the concerns of ordinary people. It was an upside-down world, as though the Union were already governing. And yet the debate didn't go too badly. Until the moment, that is, when Schröder was asked to comment on a remark made in an interview by his then wife Doris Schröder-Köpf. Speaking about me, she had said that, with my biography, I wouldn't embody the experiences of most women, whose primary concerns were how to balance their family and careers, and who wondered whether or not they wanted to take years away from work after the birth of their children. Challenged on this in the TV debate, Schröder said that his wife practices what she preaches, and added: "That's one of the reasons why I love her." My only thought was: Bingo for the other side, he's tugging the heartstrings of all wives and husbands there and more besides, but don't let yourself get riled up, just continue calmly. And I managed to. Schröder didn't get a decisive hit against me, because my mind didn't go blank for even a moment, and I didn't make any grave mistakes. And yet, according to the opinion polls, he still won the debate. With each day that brought us closer to the election, the margin the Union and FDP had over the red–greens got smaller and smaller. A woman, and from the GDR—by the end, it seemed to be more about that than was publicly admitted.

Sunday, September 18, 2005, 6:00 p.m.: I had made my way to Konrad Adenauer House with Joachim. Now, we were sitting with numerous Presidium members in the Presidium room on the fifth floor, watching the forecasting on ARD and ZDF. They were predicting 37 or 35.5 percent for the CDU and CSU, 34 or 33 percent for the SPD, 10.5 percent for the FDP, and 8.5 or 8 percent for the Greens. Measured against the surveys at the start of the election campaign, which had predicted around 45 percent for us, this was a bitter disappointment. I felt like the loser. And yet the Union still had a real chance of winning: perhaps, I thought, things would turn out the exact opposite of the 2002 election night, when we thought ourselves the victors at the beginning, then ended up losing after all.

This was my state of mind when, as 7:00 p.m. approached, I made my way with Eva Christiansen and Beate Baumann to the TV studio, to the ARD and ZDF's roundtable of party leaders and top candidates. The first question I was asked was why the CDU was languishing so far behind expectations. I valiantly responded that the red–greens had been voted out, that the CDU and CSU were the strongest force, and that we therefore had the mandate to form a government. Only after saying this did I concede that of course we would have wanted a better result.

When Schröder was asked for his take on the election results, he blustered: "I'm proud [. . .] of the people [. . .], who have given us a conclusive result, conclusive, in any case, that no one but me is capable of forming a stable government, no one but me." And a short while later, he elaborated: "Do you seriously think my party would take up an offer of talks from Frau Merkel in these circumstances, with her saying she wants to become chancellor? Let's not get carried away! The Germans have voted quite clearly on the candidacy. That can't seriously be disputed." He then—looking directly at me—declared: "She won't get a coalition with my Social Democratic party under her leadership, that's for sure, so don't be under any illusions."

I thought to myself: This is madness! What's going on here? I couldn't judge where this would lead, but I'd have been very surprised if what he was trying to pull off was something good. Schröder wasn't on the road to victory, not by a long shot. If his party had been at 38 percent in the initial projections, and the Union at 31 percent, I could have understood it. But in reality, there had been less indication he would emerge as the winner, and more that I would come out on top. I answered: "The plain and simple fact is that you didn't win tonight, that red–green didn't win tonight. That's the reality." I also made it clear that there ultimately needed to be a majority, and that in the case of a "grand coalition," the chancellor, whomever that turned out to be, would provide the stronger force—and based on the current projections that would be the Union. I also told myself: Wait and see what happens. Don't get riled up, speak only when you're asked a question, see how things play out.

Guido Westerwelle, the FDP chairman, was the first to step into the breach for me, followed by Edmund Stoiber. I sat there as though I wasn't even part of the whole thing, but instead watching the scene at home on television. I kept telling myself: Don't get embroiled in a struggle here, otherwise you'll end up adopting the wrong tone too. It was completely clear to me that I was experiencing something out of the ordinary, but everything played out semi-unconsciously. I doubt very much that Gerhard Schröder would have acted that way toward a man. I got the impression that, through catching me unawares, he was attempting to create new facts in order to make his good result—when measured against the expectations—look even better and my bad result—again, when measured against the expectations—look even worse. But he seemed to overlook the fact that people, beyond a certain level of effort, tend to end up siding with the underdog or the person under attack. That applied to my party in particular.

After the program finished, I was guided out of the studio by the TV channel staff and told that, according to the latest projections, the Union had won three mandates more than the SPD; they were drawing ever closer to the final result of 35.2 percent for the Union, 34.3 percent for the SPD, 9.8 percent for the FDP, 8.7 percent for the Left/PDS, and 8.1 percent for the Greens. In the corridor, I reconvened with Eva Christiansen and Beate Baumann, who had been following the roundtable on a television in an adjacent room. We looked one another in the eyes and said nothing, instead trying to get to the car as quickly as possible. Once we were in, the words burst out of us: "Unbelievable! Absolutely unbelievable!"

We drove back to Konrad Adenauer House. Many of the Presidium members had watched the program in the Presidium room. Everyone was aghast, and encouraged me not to lose heart. Joachim had since gone home. A small group, including Jürgen Rüttgers, went into my office with me.

Rüttgers, chairman of the largest CDU state branch in North Rhine-Westphalia and by then also prime minister of the state, said calmly and resolutely that I should swiftly get myself re-elected as chair by the new group on Tuesday, and convince Edmund Stoiber to support the move. This was really important, he said, because it wouldn't take long for criticism to break out regarding the mistakes I'd made during the campaign. He was right. A power vacuum couldn't be allowed to arise. That very same evening, I was able to convince Stoiber to support my re-election as group chair. Two days later, on September 20, I was confirmed in office.

Exploratory discussions followed with the SPD, the FDP, and the Greens on the formation of a new federal government. Politically, there were three possibilities: a so-called "Jamaica coalition"—named for the three colors of the Jamaican flag, black, yellow, and green—led by me, between the Union, the FDP, and the Greens; a "grand coalition," also led by me, of the Union and the SPD; or a "traffic light coalition," led by Gerhard Schröder, of the SPD, the FDP, and the Greens. "Jamaica" didn't stand a chance, because the Greens rejected it. The "traffic light" scenario didn't stand a chance, because Guido Westerwelle ruled it out for the FDP. Ever since our convertible-car ride in 2001—which was very effective in publicity terms—where I'd gladly let Westerwelle take the wheel, our goal to form a joint government had been an open secret. We trusted one another. A reception at Konrad Adenauer House in 2004 to celebrate my fiftieth birthday was the first official event to which Guido Westerwelle had brought his partner Michael Mronz. He had called me beforehand and asked whether I had any objections. I didn't; on the contrary, I was delighted. Guido Westerwelle was a sensitive person, but he didn't shy away from conflict when he'd set his mind on achieving something politically. In 2005, a "traffic light" coalition definitely wasn't one of those things. This, therefore, made re-election impossible for Gerhard Schröder.

It was another few weeks before the SPD could bring themselves to give up their claim to the Chancellery. In early October, Franz Müntefering, who was party and group chairman of the SPD at the time, began to make subtle overtures. Our group chair offices in Jakob Kaiser House, a building for government officials not far from the Reichstag, lay directly over one another; mine on the fifth floor, his on the fourth. In order to visit one another, we didn't need to use the elevator that was accessible to everyone, but could instead use the less frequented stairwell on the Spree side. We also had a direct line to one another; Müntefering called me without requesting the connection through his secretariat. No one listened in on our walks through the stairwell, nor our conversations.

The breakthrough was achieved on October 10, 2005: the exploratory talks were concluded, and formal coalition negotiations to form a federal government of the Union and SPD, under my leadership, could begin.

Throughout it all, I had the impression that the CSU chairman Edmund Stoiber was grappling with whether he wanted to go to Berlin and take over a super ministry, or remain Bavarian prime minister in Munich. When Franz Müntefering suddenly stepped down as party chair on October 31, 2005 during the coalition negotiations, because he couldn't push through within the party a personnel suggestion for the role of SPD general secretary, the CSU chairman simply didn't turn up at our Union-internal preliminary meeting at Konrad Adenauer House. We only found out from the news reports that Stoiber had left Berlin. The hastiness of his departure suggested he had just been waiting for an opportunity. Matthias Platzeck, the prime minister of Brandenburg, became Müntefering's successor.

On Friday, November 18, 2005, the coalition treaty was signed by Matthias Platzeck for the SPD, Edmund Stoiber for the CSU, and me for the CDU. On November 21, 2005, a Monday, I relinquished my role as group chair. Baden-Württemberg's Volker

Kauder, first parliamentary director of the CDU/CSU group from October 2002 to January 2005, and CDU general secretary from January to November 2005, was elected as my successor. At five o'clock in the evening, I visited the SPD group to introduce myself personally before my election as chancellor, which was scheduled for the following day.

We didn't get carried away; it was still only possible for somebody with a majority to move into the Chancellery and form a government. Now that would be me. I was fifty-one years old.

PART FOUR

Serving Germany (I)

November 22, 2005 to September 4, 2015

FIRST

Tuesday, November 22, 2005

THE APPLAUSE WAS never-ending. It was just before eleven o'clock in the morning, and the speaker of the Bundestag Norbert Lammert had got to his feet in the plenary chamber to announce the result of my election as chancellor. "Ladies and gentlemen, I can now give you the result of the vote. Votes cast: 612; valid votes: 611. Those in favor: 397." That was as far as he got before being drowned out by the surging applause. I was sitting in the front row of the Union seats; to my left and right the Union and SPD representatives rose to their feet for a standing ovation. Norbert Lammert had to call for quiet to read out the full results of the vote: 202 members had voted against, and twelve had abstained; one vote had been declared invalid. Then he said: "Following on from Konrad Adenauer, Ludwig Erhard, Kurt Georg Kiesinger, Willy Brandt, Helmut Schmidt, Helmut Kohl and Gerhard Schröder, Dr. Angela Merkel has received the required majority of votes from members of the German parliament, and is duly elected as first female chancellor of the Federal Republic of Germany." Another surge of applause. Representatives came over to congratulate me, with Gerhard Schröder first in line. I stood up and we shook hands.

Amid the hubbub, Norbert Lammert asked me if I wanted to accept my election. I pulled up the desk microphone in front of me and replied: "Mr. Speaker, I accept my election."

Lammert said, "Dr. Merkel, you have therefore become the first democratically elected female head of government in Germany. This sends a strong signal to many women, and I'm sure to plenty of men, as well." It was, I thought, an excellent summary of the day's historical significance.

First. I was the first.

Norbert Lammert congratulated me and called for a recess until 2:00 p.m. Leaving the chamber, I turned left down the hallway toward the rooms set aside for the chancellor's office in the Reichstag, on the east side of the building and diagonally across from the plenary chamber. The office consisted of a reception and a meeting room, with a desk and a corner seating area. I had never been in there before. A few moments earlier, the sign on the door had been changed, and now read "Chancellor Merkel" instead of "Chancellor Schröder." I opened the door to find my family and close friends waiting for me. Now they too were able to congratulate me in person; they had been watching the election from the official visitors' gallery in the plenary chamber. Joachim wasn't with them. He wanted to make it clear from the very outset that he would continue to go his own way as a scientist. It was important to him, and I understood that. We had agreed that I would call him as soon as I had a few minutes to myself, so that we could talk undisturbed and unobserved. I did so at that point, and we were both happy and proud.

The Chancellery staff had prepared everything for us newcomers with care. A secretary from my future office was waiting in reception with drinks and potato soup. I didn't have much time: the German president Horst Köhler was expecting me at midday to appoint me formally. Renovations were being carried out on his official residence, Bellevue Palace, and so this was to take place in Charlottenburg Palace, slightly further away. I have no recollection of the moment Horst Köhler handed me my letter of appointment; everything happened in such a rush, including the drive from the Reichstag to the palace and back. At two o'clock, I was back in the plenary chamber.

I wasn't yet allowed to take my seat on the government bench, and sat down in the first row of the Union section as I had done that morning. Norbert Lammert announced point two on the day's agenda: the swearing-in of the new chancellor. What followed was something I do remember as if it was yesterday: Lammert asked me to approach him, and I stood up and walked across the floor, past the government bench to the back of the plenary chamber, where he was waiting for me in front of a German flag. Unlike the first time I was sworn in as minister for women and youth, I wasn't wearing unfamiliar clothes; I felt comfortable in my second skin. I was wearing a black pantsuit with a black velvet collar and buttons, and a matt amber pendant on a gold chain. In Bettina Schoenbach, I had now found a tailor with whom I could develop my own style.

Norbert Lammert held up the original text of the German constitution in front of me, and I raised my right hand to read out the oath. I ended with, "So help me, God." There was another wave of applause. Norbert Lammert shook my hand and congratulated me, and I turned and walked a few paces down to my new seat on the government bench. The chancellor's seat is marked out by having a slightly higher back than the others. I sat down. There was no one else on the government bench yet—just four empty rows of chairs and tables beside and behind me, with me alone at the very front. That was my place. At that instant, I felt a great weight lifting from me. The doubts that had plagued me just four days earlier as we were signing the coalition agreement—would I be equal to the job?—had been swept away. At the time, Franz Müntefering had told me, "It'll be fine." Now, sitting all alone on the government bench, I felt it: you have done something very special, as a woman and an East German. Seconds passed, maybe a minute. I looked around the room at the faces of applauding representatives. When I was sworn in for further terms in 2009, 2013, and 2017, I found again that in those seconds of solitude on the government bench, I was filled with a kind of serenity. And each time, I thought back on that first moment, just after two o'clock on November 22, 2005. Lammert called for another recess. I woke as if from a brief daydream, and received many more congratulations, this time from the chancellor's seat.

At three o'clock, I was back with the president in Charlottenburg Palace, for the appointment of the new government ministers. Before Horst Köhler handed them their letters of appointment, he gave a short speech: "You will be criticized from many sides. This should spur you on in your work for renewal," he advised us.

Then we returned to the Reichstag. At four o'clock, the interrupted parliamentary session resumed, and the ministers of state were sworn in one after another. The government bench filled up. My neighbor was the minister of labor and social affairs Vice Chancellor Franz Müntefering (SPD). Following the plenary sitting, there was another meeting of the CDU/CSU parliamentary group, to congratulate their cabinet members and acknowledge what had happened that day. After only seven years in opposition, we had another CDU chancellor—and this time, it was a woman chancellor from the East.

After that, I headed over to the Chancellery, where the handover from Gerhard Schröder was scheduled to take place at five o'clock. Beate Baumann and Eva Christiansen came with me. When we reached the main entrance, we were ushered into the foyer, where a lectern and microphone had been set up. Gerhard Schröder was already there, and spoke first. He thanked the Chancellery staff, who were assembled on the south staircase. They bade him farewell with a long, heartfelt round of applause. Then it was my turn. I said that I was looking forward to working with them. Finally, Olaf Lüdtke, the chair of the staff council, gave a speech, and handed bunches of flowers to both Gerhard Schröder and me. Schröder immediately passed his flowers to me and disappeared. Once again, I was left with two bunches of flowers, just as I had been in 2000 at the national party conference in Essen, when I was elected chair of the CDU. The bouquets were swiftly taken from me. I felt certain that the civil servants in this building would work as hard for me as they had for my predecessor.

Following the staff meeting, Beate Baumann, Eva Christiansen, and I were led to the elevator and up to the chancellor's office on the eighth floor. Thomas Steg greeted us in the doorway of the secretariat—he had been deputy head of Chancellor Schröder's office from 1998 to 2002, and then deputy government spokesman. He would remain in this position in my own government. He received us with an encouraging smile. Schröder's head secretary Marianne Duden was waiting for us in the secretariat. She had worked for Chancellor Schmidt before that, and would support us as we found our feet—more evidence of cross-party democratic style. There was a marble cake on her desk, baked to welcome us by Ulrich Kerz, the Chancellery kitchen's head chef. Marianne Duden soon left, following Gerhard Schröder to the office he occupied as former chancellor. Her job was taken over by Dagmar Scheefeld, who had been my head secretary for many years. In the spring of 2006, she was succeeded by Marlies Hansen, who is still with me today, along with her co-worker and deputy for many years, Kirsten Rüssmeier. Thomas Steg stayed around for a little while to answer any questions we might have.

I walked through the outer office and turned left into my new office. I was already acquainted with the room from occasional meetings with Schröder. And I had already considered how to rearrange the furniture: the large conference table at the back of the room, by the window that looked out on the Reichstag, would come forward, nearer the door to the outer office, so that I could communicate directly with my secretaries; the seating area by the door, meanwhile, could be moved back against the window. One call to the maintenance team, and the request was fulfilled literally overnight: the next morning, the furniture was exactly where I wanted it. The Chancellery's maintenance staff and technicians were always extremely helpful and worked at great speed.

At around 5:45 p.m. in my office I swore in the new Chancellery ministers so that they could take part in the first cabinet meeting that evening: Hildegard Müller, whose official title was minister of state to the German chancellor, responsible for liaising with parliament and the Bundesrat; Bernd Neumann, minister of state and commissioner for culture and media; and Maria Böhmer, minister of state and commissioner for migration, refugees, and integration. After that, I hurried through the "sky lobby" of the Chancellery building and down the stairs into the banqueting hall on the sixth floor, where the major television networks, ARD, ZDF, RTL, and SAT.1, were waiting for interviews with me. That evening, millions of German citizens would see me on their screens for the first time as their new chancellor. And I didn't want this first encounter to be a damp squib. As I remember it, I did reasonably well. Once the interviews had been recorded, I hastened back up the stairs to my office, to fetch my papers on the agenda items for the first cabinet meeting. They were inside a large, brown folder. I was familiar with these folders from my time as a minister in Helmut Kohl's cabinet—and it would be 2018 before they were finally replaced by tablets.

Folder in hand, I descended the stairs a few minutes later to the large cabinet room on the seventh floor. As I entered the brightly lit meeting room, the cameras immediately began to click; photographers, positioned in the area set aside for them, pressed the shutter-release continually as they followed my every move. After a few minutes, the very bright light was reduced to a normal level as the lamps disappeared into the wooden wall, as if by magic. That was the sign for the photographers to leave the room. And so it would continue, one cabinet meeting after another, for sixteen years.

I took my seat. The head of the Chancellery Thomas de Maizière sat down to my left, and Vice Chancellor Franz Müntefering to my right. There was a bell and a call button in front of me, and a clock in the middle of the table. All three objects had been part of the cabinet room since Adenauer's time. The clock had a face on all four sides, so that everyone could see how long they had been talking. I would use the bell only rarely, to call for quiet. And pressing the call button would bring someone in from outside. I don't recall ever pressing it, though; Chancellery civil servants were also present in the cabinet room, at a separate table, and they handled any communication that was necessary.

I spoke a few words of greeting, as did Franz Müntefering. As we were talking, staff from the Chancellery kitchen brought each of us a glass of sparkling wine, and we drank a toast to future collaboration. The agenda for the first meeting had been drawn up by Frank-Walter Steinmeier, the former head of the Chancellery, and his successor, Thomas de Maizière. The cabinet agreed the Rules of Procedure for the new government, and a few other items. The meeting was finished in around fifteen minutes.

Beate Baumann and I went back up to the eighth floor and took a closer look at our office space. To the right of the outer office there were three further rooms, all connected to one another, and all with access from the corridor as well. At the end of this sequence we discovered a larger room. It seemed to have been used for external purposes, because it was furnished in white, with a glass table. We quickly designated this room as Beate

Baumann's new office. Unlike Gerhard Schröder and his long-time chief of staff Sigrid Krampitz, whose office had been elsewhere, we wanted to be on the same floor. Over the following days, maintenance staff and technicians removed the white furniture and the glass table and fitted out Beate's new room with the Chancellery's usual office furniture in cherry wood, along with a seating area. Computers and telephones were installed, and an internet connection was set up. The configuration of our rooms was ideal. We each had our own space if we didn't want to be disturbed, but we were also close enough to speak to one another quickly and easily without having to leave our suite of rooms. The offices in between were occupied by two more secretaries and the deputy chief of staff: initially Thomas Romes; later, Bernhard Kotsch and Petra Rülke. The doors between these offices were also kept open whenever possible, and we all thrived on communication with one another.

The day's official meetings were over. I was completely exhausted, but I had invited friends and colleagues over at eight o'clock for drinks on the ninth floor, to celebrate my election. I had never set foot in the rooms up there before. A back staircase led directly up to the ninth floor from my office. When I reached the top, I found a small bedroom with an en suite bathroom to my left. It was designed for overnight stays for the chancellor. I didn't need it, as I had kept the apartment on Kupfergraben that Joachim and I had moved to in 1997, which was just a few minutes' drive away. From now on, Petra Keller would be able to use that ninth-floor room as her styling studio.

Turning right, I entered a large reception room with a small service kitchen attached; the Chancellery's main kitchen was down on the fifth floor. The reception room contained a long dining table and a bright seating area with a television. On the wall above the dining table was a Picasso, which had me under its spell at once: *Buste de Femme (Jacqueline)* from 1959, on loan from the National Gallery in Berlin. Over the next sixteen years, this room would host coalition meetings, and small-scale lunches and dinners with local and international heads of government, political allies, and invited guests. Those walls must have heard all the important things that were discussed during my time as chancellor. The room was the living room for my governments. Its longest side was completely taken up by a window with an electronic sliding door that led out onto a terrace, from where you could look out over Potsdamer Platz. I took many guests out onto that terrace during my time in office. If we turned to the left, we could see the Reichstag and the Brandenburg Gate; turn right, and the terrace widened out at the end. In summer, I could sit outside with a view of the River Spree. That evening, November 22, 2005, was when I enjoyed the view for the first time.

We had pre-ordered sausages, potato salad, coleslaw, burgers, and drinks from the Chancellery kitchen. Joachim was there, and in addition to Beate Baumann, Eva Christiansen, and Thomas de Maizière, we had invited Volker Kauder, Ronald Pofalla, Peter Hintze, Norbert Röttgen, Peter Altmaier, Willi Hausmann, and a few friends from outside the world of politics. We made a cheerful group of twenty or so around the large dining table. I felt good; everyone was relaxed and filled with expectations for what the future might hold.

Paris Brussels London Berlin Düsseldorf Hamburg

Depart Berlin 10:30 a.m., arrive Paris 12:05 p.m., depart Paris 3:05 p.m., arrive Brussels 3:40 p.m., depart Brussels 8:30 p.m., arrive Berlin 9:45 p.m.. A visit to the French president Jacques Chirac at the Élysée Palace, a meeting with the NATO secretary general Jaap de Hoop Scheffer at the NATO headquarters in

Brussels, then on to the EU parliament to speak to the parliament's president Josep Borrell, and the European Commission's building for a meeting with its president José Manuel Barroso, followed by a dinner with the Commission members. Getting up in the morning in my own apartment, and going to bed in the same place that evening: that was the plan for my first full day in office. Simone Lehmann-Zwiener, a member of the Chancellery staff responsible for protocol issues on foreign visits, had planned the day together with my office, the foreign and European-policy sections of the Chancellery, the Federal Press Office, and the Foreign Office. It was all overseen by my foreign policy advisor Christoph Heusgen. Heusgen had learned diplomacy from the ground up, in the diplomatic service. In the preceding six years, he had gained international experience as the office manager and head of political staff for Javier Solana, the EU's High Representative for Common Foreign and Security Policy. State Secretary Ulrich Wilhelm, government spokesperson and head of the Federal Press Office, carried out thorough preparations for my media appearances and contact with journalists. As long-time press spokesperson for the state premier of Bavaria Edmund Stoiber, he had a wealth of experience in media relations. A schedule like the one I undertook that day was only possible thanks to the Bundeswehr's air fleet, and frictionless organization by each embassy and host. I was looked after superbly at every stage. The foreign minister Frank-Walter Steinmeier (SPD), and I traveled together. This was intended to signal that, while in the past we might have taken very different positions on some issues, we were determined to work closely together in the Grand Coalition.

The French president Jacques Chirac met me outside the Élysée Palace at around 12:45 p.m., welcoming me with a kiss on the hand as I got out of the car. He had been the president of the French Republic since 1995. He and Chancellor Schröder had worked closely together, and it was no secret that both men would have liked to continue this relationship after Germany's general election. Chirac and I were an unequal pair; he was almost twenty-two years older than me, with many decades of political experience. I approached him with an open mind, and with huge respect for his political achievements. That day, November 23, our one-on-one conversation was relatively brief. There were two interpreters in the room with us, since I spoke no French, and Chirac never spoke English in official meetings. The Foreign Office had a pool of excellent interpreters, who gave me a great sense of security in many meetings. In complicated discussions, there was nothing worse than worrying about whether what you had said would be translated fully and precisely, particularly with regard to nuance. On this visit, my interpreter was the legendary Werner Zimmermann, whom I already knew from the days of Helmut Kohl.

The one-on-one conversation was followed by lunch with the foreign ministers and a joint leaders' press conference. Everything went smoothly. It was only the term "Franco-German axis" used by Chirac that I did not take up myself. It was, unintentionally, too reminiscent of dark days in Germany, and the image was also too inflexible for my liking. All the same, it was right to say that cooperation between France and Germany was—and still is—crucial for Europe. Without it, little or nothing works. And this was the start of our cooperation. Chirac and I arranged another meeting for December 8 in Berlin, before the next meeting of the European Council (made up of EU member countries' heads of state or heads of government) on December 15–16. This meeting was being held to address the European budget, under the heading Financial Perspectives 2007 to 2013.

Then it was on to Brussels, where my visit to the NATO headquarters had a symbolic significance. Following NATO's argument with Schröder's government over the Iraq War in the previous legislative period, Frank-Walter Steinmeier and I wanted to commit ourselves to the transatlantic defense alliance.

Afterward, I paid a courtesy visit to the European Parliament, and at the European Commission I met with its president, José Manuel Barroso, whom I had known for some time. He had been in office since 2004, and before that he had for two years been prime minister of Portugal. During that time, we had met often at the meetings of the European People's Party (EPP), the group of European Christian democratic and center-right parties to which the CDU and CSU belonged. Barroso and I wanted a European Union that was capable of taking real action. And for that, we urgently needed a success for Europe's finances.

The subject was raised over a dinner with the whole Commission following our personal talks, and, much to my delight, it was soon being discussed in depth. The budget commissioner Dalia Grybauskaitė caught my attention with her superb knowledge of all the details. In 2009, she became president of Lithuania, and from then until she stepped down in 2019, we had a friendly working relationship and helped each other to solve plenty of difficult problems. At the Commission dinner, I received the best possible briefing for my visit to London the next day. I had really wanted to go to Warsaw after Paris and Brussels, but in the event that wasn't possible: Poland's prime minister Kazimierz Marcinkiewicz couldn't meet me that day. And so, after dinner with the Commission, I flew home.

The next day, I led my second cabinet meeting in Berlin, gave two interviews, and then, at lunchtime, I set off for London. The UK had the EU Council presidency at that point, and so it was important for me to visit Tony Blair before the European Council meeting. He met me at 2:15 p.m. in his official residence at 10 Downing Street. By then he had been prime minister for eight years. We had first met in 2004 when Blair, the social democrat, and I, the Christian democrat, had worked together to ensure that it was not Guy Verhofstadt (the Belgian prime minister at the time) but José Manuel Barroso who became the Commission's president. Support for the two candidates was divided across the parties, a knock-on effect of the split in the EU over the Iraq War. Blair and I knew that our thinking was similar in strategic and tactical terms, and that we could rely on mutual agreements. At the European Council meeting in December, he wanted to bring the British presidential term to a successful close, and was counting on my assistance in this. But I knew our good relationship alone would not be enough; the UK had to give ground to France, Spain, and Germany on agricultural spending in particular, and the same went for payments to Central and Eastern European countries who wanted to improve their economic position quickly. Success would come at a price. We discussed this, and agreed to consider potential compromises between then and the meeting. Afterward, I flew home to Berlin.

The Friday, my third full day in office, was the first day devoted entirely to domestic policy. In the morning, I attended a breakfast meeting for the state premiers of all the Union-governed federal states. Later, these meetings, at which we coordinated the voting behavior of the individual German states in the Bundesrat, would mostly take place on Thursday evenings, as the Bundesrat usually met on Fridays. Now that we had a Union chancellor again, this voting became even more important that it had been when we were in opposition.

In the afternoon, I went to Düsseldorf. Internal flights, among other things, were planned by Petra Anders, the person within the Chancellery responsible for protocol relating to domestic travel, coordinating with the Bundeswehr's air fleet, and with the police for helicopter flights. I had been invited to address the general meeting of the German Confederation of

Skilled Crafts (Zentralverband des Deutschen Handwerks, ZDH) at Düsseldorf Congress Center. The ZDH's president Otto Kentzler had been very keen for me to present them with the Grand Coalition's program for government, before I had even made my first government policy statement in parliament. Discontent was high among tradespeople over the new government's planned tax increases. And there were 900,000 craft businesses in Germany, with around five million employees between them. The general meeting welcomed me with respect and curiosity, and when I finished speaking, the very male-dominated audience gave me a standing ovation. Otto Kentzler bade me farewell with a slightly altered quotation from the opera *The Mastersingers of Nuremberg*: "The bird I heard today was so well-made for singing." Would he have given such a testimonial to a man? I am sure he meant well, and yet he had belittled me, or so it felt.

From Düsseldorf I flew on to Hamburg, where I was due to speak to the annual conference of the CDU and CSU's local government association at 7:00 p.m. in the Congress Center. I had agreed to the engagement long before, and kept my word. I didn't want to give anyone the impression that I was going to neglect the party now that I was chancellor. I got on my flight back to Berlin straight after the event, and arrived home at around 10:00 p.m.

Let us dare more freedom

The next morning, Saturday, November 26, 2005, I was driven from my apartment on Kupfergraben to the Chancellery. It was my first day as German chancellor without any official appointments. That was also why I hadn't asked Petra Keller to come into the office to do my make-up. I wanted to work on my government statement alone; I would be delivering it in the

Bundestag at 11:00 a.m. on November 30, the Wednesday of the following week. On Sunday, I had to fly to Barcelona for a meeting of the EU member states with the states of North Africa, and on Monday I was having lunch with my first overseas guest, Namibia's president Hifikepunye Pohamba, before giving a speech to the members' meeting of the Federation of German Industry at their Berlin headquarters. On Tuesday, there was the cabinet meeting that could not be held on Wednesday as usual due to the Bundestag session, followed by the parliamentary group meeting, and the fall reception held by the *Frankfurter Allgemeine Zeitung*. This Saturday was the only time when I could hope for a few hours with no interruptions.

At the entrance to the Chancellery, a beautiful flower arrangement caught my eye. Apart from the security officers on the first floor and the people working in the crisis room, which was staffed round the clock, the building was empty. As I walked through the foyer to the elevator, I glanced to the left, into the main courtyard. This is where I would be greeting the Namibian president on Monday, and here, too, on a trestle table, was another splendid flower arrangement. A security officer accompanied me up to my office on the eighth floor. That Saturday, no one was in the outer office. A member of the Chancellery kitchen staff had placed a small silver pot of coffee and a white porcelain cup on my desk before going home. Glasses and small bottles of water were always there. The officer took a seat in the eighth-floor "sky lobby" to make sure no one could enter my room unchallenged. From then on, this would always be the case when I was there.

For the first time since my election, I looked around at leisure. The office was beautiful, I thought: generously proportioned, with the two large windows providing plenty of light, the cherry-wood bookcase providing a touch of class, and the long black conference table and solid black desk an air of seriousness. The large, bright seating area and the flowers on my conference and coffee tables, meanwhile, provided a touch of homeliness. All the flowers in the building, arranged in creative displays by the Chancellery gardeners, were a delight to me not just on that day, but on all the days that followed. After just a few minutes there, I was convinced that I would never again have such a lovely workplace.

I took a seat at the front-left corner of the long, black table and looked out of the window to my right, toward the Tiergarten. The trees were covered with a dusting of snow, which made everything feel quieter still. Then I looked straight ahead, out of the room's other large window, which faced the Reichstag. I had heard that the Chancellery's architects, Axel Schultes and Charlotte Frank, had designed my office so that its floor was on a level with the floor of the parliament's plenary chamber. I considered what my future relations with parliament would look like. I thought the architects had done an excellent job of illustrating, through their design, the relationship between executive (the Federal Government) and the legislature (the lawmaking Bundestag and Bundesrat). In the Chancellery and Reichstag buildings, the federal government and parliament stood facing one another, on equal terms. But were the terms really equal? What role did we each play in the state? It was the first time I had considered this as chancellor. No doubt: the government plays an ancillary role in relation to parliament. The members of the Bundestag are elected by the German people. Together with the Bundesrat, it passes the bills that the government sends to both chambers as cabinet decisions. These bills are seldom passed into law unaltered. But the Bundestag members do not only pass laws; they also elect the chancellor. This was how I had been elected four days previously, by a majority of members, as Germany's first female chancellor. I was reminded that, now and in the future, I was in the hands of these elected representatives. As a directly elected member of the German Bundestag, however, I was also one of them. Still, I told myself, the mothers and fathers of the German constitution had also placed the chancellor in a strong position. Once in office, he—or she, now—could not simply be voted out again by more than 50 percent of members. Article 67 of the constitution stipulates that there must be a "constructive confidence vote," which allows a candidate other than the current chancellor to be elected chancellor by a majority of Bundestag members. Such a move against me seemed unlikely at that point. For the moment, at least, I felt secure in my new post. But I was still aware of the crucial role that the coalition group would play in my work.

I poured myself a cup of coffee from the little silver pot on my desk. I was suddenly feeling buoyant. I'd been very lucky in life so far: lucky with the fall of the Berlin Wall in 1989; lucky with my parents, who had helped me develop my skills and abilities; lucky with my whole family, my friends and colleagues, who had always encouraged and stood by me, even when I hadn't made it easy for them.

Then I opened the folder in front of me, which contained a thick stack of paper, the first draft of my government statement. It had been prepared by the Chancellery's various policy departments, and the head of speeches and texts in the chancellor's office, Robert Maier. He had worked for me when I was in opposition, and performed this role throughout my time as chancellor. Acquaintances outside politics had also sent some suggestions to Beate Baumann and me, as they sometimes had in the past. Beate had prepared the text for me. The framework of my speech was provided by the basic plans that had been written into the coalition agreement, and put together by the relevant Chancellery policy teams. Between ourselves, we called this part of the text the "Schwarzbrot" (black bread). It was indispensable. But this was my first speech in the German Bundestag as head of government, and there was more at stake for me here. What was the government's ambition? In what spirit did we want to work? What was driving me? I wanted to give answers to all these questions.

My government was the second Grand Coalition in the history of the Federal Republic; the first had been formed in 1966, almost forty years earlier. We were beginning our work after seven years of fierce hostilities and an election campaign with a lot of mud-slinging. During the coalition negotiations, the CDU, CSU, and SPD had laid aside their negative images of each other, and had at times rubbed their eyes in disbelief at how many views they shared. We had all surprised ourselves. And that was something I wanted to mention in my speech, because most representatives and party members still had the intransigent tones of recent years ringing in their ears. Can politics bring joy to anyone if there are no real bogeymen to rail against? I was firmly convinced that it could. Many others, however, found the new situation painful. It was mitigated for the CDU and CSU by the fact that the chancellor was once more one of their own. The SPD, by contrast, had to absorb the loss of the office. It was only now—at least, this was my impression—that the consequences of the Social Democrats' in-fighting over the reforms of Agenda 2010 had become clear to them. The Union had broadly supported these reforms in parliament. I wanted to retain them, as well as the plan for reform on which we had fought our own election campaign, even though it had brought us to a cliff edge. But I also wanted to bring people together, motivate everyone involved, and get them excited about working together. And I wanted German citizens at large to feel that their new government had the will and the means to reduce unemployment: 4.5 million people were currently out of work.

It was important to me to draw a line back to both the central change in my life in 1989, and the beginnings of the Federal Republic of Germany in 1949. The result of this endeavor read:

Freedom has been the greatest surprise of my life. I expected many things, but not the gift of freedom before I reached retirement age. [. . .] Why should something [. . .] that we managed at the start of this Federal Republic of Germany, in the early years, [. . .] not be successful again? So let us all surprise ourselves with what we can do in this country. [. . .] The vice chancellor of an earlier Grand Coalition, who later became chancellor, once said: "Let us dare more freedom." I know that, at the time, these words triggered a lot of discussions, some of them very heated. But what he said clearly chimed with that earlier time. Personally, I can say that his words were music to the ears of people on the other side of the Wall. Allow me to add to them today, and to call on us all: Let us dare more freedom.

I drew a fat exclamation point in the margin.

The reference to Willy Brandt was audacious, there was no doubt about that, both for my own people and my coalition partners. But it allowed me to show that I not only believed myself capable; I thought that we as a government, and the citizens of Germany, were capable, too. That belief was essential; the reforms of Agenda 2010 must not be rolled back. They would take the brakes off labor policy, social and tax policy, and bring more freedom—a precondition for lowering the unemployment rate, which was much too high. "I would like to express my personal thanks to Chancellor Schröder for the courage and determination with which he opened a door via his Agenda 2010, a door to reforms, and for pushing his agenda through against resistance. He has done a real service to our country," I read. I had already expressed my thanks in the Chancellery during our handover on Tuesday, but it was important to restate it in front of the Bundestag. I added another exclamation point to the margin here. The through-line of the speech was good.

The part of the draft in which the government's specific plans would be explained would, by its very nature, be less inspiring. Black bread. But it was still important; it showed that we had set ourselves some ambitious goals. We wanted to create the conditions for Germany to return to its place among the top three countries in Europe for competitiveness within ten years. I made a few more notes on the text, then packed it all back into the folder, took it into Beate's office, and placed it on her desk. Let's surprise ourselves, and risk more freedom. With that thought in mind, I went home.

On Monday and Tuesday, Beate worked with the policy departments to make some final alterations to the text of the government statement. All the figures, data, and facts were checked again. On Tuesday evening, I sent the speech over to Franz Müntefering, to check that the SPD was properly reflected in it. The next morning, the day of the government statement, a fax arrived from him at 8:02 a.m. headed "reliable, confidential," with a few notes on the text. He had typed them out at around eleven o'clock the previous evening on his Erika typewriter, as he noted in the margin. I did not incorporate all his suggestions. But I did lend more emphasis to the words of solidarity that he thought had been lacking.

Setting a course

As I was rereading my first government statement during the writing of this book, two things leaped out at me: Firstly, the proportion of domestic policy was about 80 percent, with just 20 percent devoted to foreign policy, though in many weeks of the year those proportions were reversed according to the focus of my attention. And secondly, while all of the plans I set out there were doubtless important, a few of them were designed to create lasting change in the country. At the time, all I could do was trust that they would succeed. But now I can name them.

Rehabilitating the state finances. The finance minister was the Social Democrat and former premier of North Rhine-Westphalia Peer Steinbrück. The SPD had claimed this key ministerial role for themselves, much to the chagrin of the Union. In 2005, the federal budget was in an appalling state. The deficit was running at 3.3 percent rather than 3 percent: substantially above the convergence criteria of the 1992 Maastricht Treaty, which Germany had fought hard to maintain when the euro was introduced. The same was true of the national debt, which stood at 67.7 percent rather than 60 percent of gross domestic product (GDP). As a result, Germany had lost a lot of credibility within Europe. Net borrowing was higher than spending on investment; interest payments represented around 15 percent of outgoings; and estimated income from privatization was revealed to be a feat of creative accounting.

During the coalition negotiations, we had had to make the decision to raise VAT by three percentage points to 19 percent. Two of those percentage points—along with the introduction of a wealth tax, the raising of national insurance, halving the Christmas bonus of federal civil servants, cuts to commuting allowance and Sunday, holiday, and night-time rates of pay, to mention just a few things—served to rehabilitate the state finances. On May 19, 2006, parliament agreed the largest tax hike since 1949. These measures were necessary so that on May 29, 2009, the debt brake could be added to the German constitution. Since 2016, new federal government borrowing has been limited to 0.35 percent of GDP, and since 2020 the individual states cannot take on any new debt at all.

Lowering non-wage labor costs. We used the third percentage point of the VAT increase to lower unemployment insurance contributions by 1 percent, and the states did without their share. Franz Müntefering, the labor and social affairs minister, had to generate another 1-percent decrease through employment-market policy savings. The non-wage labor costs sank below 40 percent, which helped to make German businesses more competitive.

Raising the pension age to 67. In my government statement, I announced that we wanted to put this measure into legislation in 2007, as we had agreed in the coalition agreement. But the draft bill was approved in cabinet much earlier, on February 1, 2006, in an altered form. Franz Müntefering had given his thoughts on the matter—wholly to my surprise—in a newspaper interview in late January 2006, and actually brought the goal forward. He wanted to increase the pension age to 67 by 2029, or even earlier, rather than 2035 as set out in the coalition agreement. In March, he would have to produce a report on the state pension system, and he evidently wanted to set the course for the future of pensions by that point. I think that Franz Müntefering wanted to put his money where his mouth was on this issue sooner rather than later. He and I both believed that raising the pension age to 67 was imperative in view of demographic changes in the country, and he didn't want to be talked out of it. He knew what to expect. All the same, he may well have underestimated the strength of opposition that he would be met with. The Social Democrats, in particular, were shocked. But in the end, the senior party members around the SPD's chair Matthias Platzeck relented, while Horst Seehofer and the chair of the CDU/CSU parliamentary group Volker Kauder were vocal critics on behalf of the Union. This in turn exasperated the Social Democrats, in particular Franz Müntefering, even further. I suspected that he didn't feel sufficiently supported by me, either, because I couldn't silence those dissenting voices from the Union. In any case, I learned always to expect surprises from him.

Ultimately, we agreed to raise the pension age in stages, reaching 67 by 2029. For those who had paid into their state pension for forty-five or more years, pension age was set at 65. Unfortunately, it was the last time during my whole period in office that a decision on pensions was reached that focused on the future of old-age provision exclusively from the perspective of younger generations.

Increasing spending on research and development. In March 2000, the European Union's heads of state and government had agreed the "Lisbon Strategy" at a one-off summit in Lisbon. Under this agreement, the European Union set itself the goal of becoming "the most competitive and dynamic knowledge-based economy in the world." It was later also suggested that spending on research and development should be raised to 3 percent of GDP by 2010. In 2005, Germany's spending stood at 2.44 percent, a long way from the agreed target. Both Annette Schavan—who had been the culture minister for the state of Baden-Württemberg and was now the new federal minister for education and research—and I were convinced that the 3-percent target was a key to improving Europe's competitiveness on the global stage. And we wanted to reach it in Germany, too. One of the three percentage points would be public spending on a national and state level. For that to happen, national spending had to be significantly increased, and the states needed to be supported. Annette Schavan steadily increased her ministry's resources. And, despite the adversities of a global financial crisis and a eurozone crisis, which we could not have predicted at the time, we did reach that 3-percent target—not by 2010, admittedly, but by 2017. That same year, we agreed to raise spending on research and development to 3.5 percent of GDP by 2025. We wanted to keep pace with countries

like the United States, Israel, and South Korea. By 2020, alongside Germany, only Belgium, Sweden, Austria, and Denmark
had managed to reach 3 percent; the average across the EU
member states was 2.2 percent of GDP. This is a shameful
statistic—and nor has the EU yet managed to become "the most
competitive and dynamic knowledge-based economy in the
world," as it promised at the Lisbon summit in 2000.

In August 2006, the cabinet presented its high-tech strategy,
signaling a new approach to innovation policy in Germany. The
projects for the first round of the Excellence Initiative, an investment program for research and development agreed by the
previous government, were chosen in October 2006. The Pact for
Research and Innovation, an agreement between federation and
states, which had also been set up by Schröder's government,
was implemented and repeatedly revised. It gave non-university
research institutions the security to plan for the future, through
reliable annual funding increases. As a result, many German
scientists who had gone to work abroad returned to Germany,
and top foreign researchers also came to Germany. In August
2007, a university pact between federation and states was added
to this agreement, improving universities' financial situation in
light of rising student numbers.

In 2008, the Joint Science Conference of the federation
and states agreed to rename the Leopoldina German Academy
of Natural Sciences, which became the National Academy of
Sciences. At last Germany had an institution that could cooperate with institutions such as the UK's Royal Society, or the
Académie française. During our presidency of the EU Council
in 2007, we oversaw the founding of the European Research
Council, an institution that exists to finance excellent scientific
and technological research. After many years of fighting for it,
in January 2020, an R&D tax credit finally came into effect in
Germany, modest though it was.

———

Introducing parental allowance. In January 2006, opinion polls found that people regarded the Union as more competent on family policy than the SPD. This had happened only rarely in the history of the Federal Republic, and it had to do with Ursula von der Leyen, Lower Saxony's state minister for social affairs, women, family affairs, and health. In my cabinet, she was the minister for family affairs, senior citizens, women, and youth. In the past, the Union and the SPD had both advocated for the introduction of a parental allowance, but as yet it had not been brought in. Now, introducing this allowance was part of the coalition deal. In June 2006, it was passed by the cabinet, and in September by parliament. It offset lost income for parents caring for their child after birth—which is to say, it was related to earnings. In order to provide an incentive for both parents to look after a baby in the first months of life, we also introduced "paternity months." This meant that parental allowance would be extended from twelve to fourteen months where parents shared out the time between them. The head of the CSU regional group Peter Ramsauer disparaged the paternity months as "diaper training." But despite all the prophets of doom, the policy was passed.

The right to a childcare place. The coalition agreement stipulated the creation of an additional 230,000 childcare places for children under the age of three. The federal government was willing to give financial support to the states and local authorities to fund this. But Ursula von der Leyen wanted more: not just additional places, but the *right* to a daycare place for under-threes. She convinced the finance minister Peer Steinbrück to make any financial support for the states conditional on the right to a daycare place. Her razor-sharp mind had foreseen that the steady lowering of the unemployment rate from 2006 onward would improve the national budget situation. And she wanted to make use of that. She was certain that the SPD would approve, and the finance minister recognized that resistance was futile, even if the sum necessary to fund this measure would be higher than originally planned. In August 2007, federation and states agreed that the federation would fund the creation of childcare places in the states to the tune of €4 billion by 2013. In return, the states agreed more or less reluctantly to accept that, from August 1, 2013, every child would have the right to a childcare place between the end of their first and third years of life. They knew, of course, that the federal money would never be enough to cover this, but nor did they want to miss out on €4 billion. Some Union members, particularly in the CSU, felt blindsided by this development. They would have preferred to use that money for budget consolidation. But more serious still was that, in some people's minds, the principle of freedom of choice that they held in such high regard no longer applied. They felt we had approved compulsory childcare. That was nonsense. But times had changed in the previous fifteen years, since the days when I was children's minister and had fought for a right to a preschool place for every child. The CSU gave up their resistance, but they called for a childcare allowance of 150 euros per month for those families who chose not to take up the offer of a daycare place. This placated the opponents of the right to childcare, but it also maddened its advocates. The latter feared that families on a low income would see the allowance as attractive, and mothers might therefore be pressured into staying at home. I thought the right to a childcare place was a great asset, which I didn't want to endanger because of the allowance, and I agreed with Edmund Stoiber to put the introduction of this measure into law but to leave the details for a separate federal law to be passed later on. The SPD were bound by the coalition deal to go along with it, but they still voiced harsh criticism of this outcome. On September 26, 2008, the German Bundestag passed the Childcare Funding

Act, and on November 7, the Bundesrat followed suit. The right to a daycare place was to come into effect on August 1, 2013. On February 20 of that year, the law on the introduction of a child-care allowance was published in the federal gazette. The same day, Olaf Scholz, the first mayor of the Free and Hanseatic City of Hamburg, brought a case against the law to the Federal Constitutional Court on behalf of his state. Two years later, on July 21, 2015, the court decided that the measure was unlawful, since it did not fall under the federal government's legislative remit. Bavaria and Saxony took the decision to continue paying the allowance out of their state budgets.

According to figures from the Office of National Statistics, the proportion of women in the workforce rose from 59.5 percent in 2005 to 65.1 percent in 2009, and to 72.0 percent in 2021.

Integration and participation. Under Gerhard Schröder, the Office of the Federal Government Commissioner for Migration, Refugees, and Integration was brought into the ministry for families following the 2002 general election. In 2005, when it had become clear that the ministry for families would be led by the CDU, Franz Müntefering reclaimed the Office of the Integration Commissioner for the SPD. The significance of the issue for social policy was crystal clear to both of us; I had seen how relevant it was in my time as minister for young people, if not before. And so I had the idea of anchoring the integration brief in the Chancellery, and making the person in charge of that brief a minister. This signified an upgrade: parliamentary state secretaries in the Chancellery and in the Foreign Office were classed as ministers, who could take part in cabinet meetings. The boss could have a hand in integration. It would have been difficult for Franz Müntefering to argue with this upgrade, as the SPD was gaining an extra state secretary elsewhere.

Maria Böhmer, the representative from Frankenthal in Rhineland-Palatinate, and chair of the CDU Women's Union, became the commissioner for integration. We were agreed that we didn't just want to make policy for people with a history of migration, but to collaborate with them on making that policy.

On July 14, 2006, we held the first integration summit in the Chancellery, which I led. Twelve others were to follow. Eighty-six representatives from all sections of society took part in the first integration summit, first and foremost people from migrant organizations. Within a year, we aimed to produce a National Integration Plan, covering education, language, and the promotion of integration in the workforce. This plan was passed at the second summit, on July 12, 2007, and implemented over the years that followed. Through our work in the Chancellery, we changed and opened up the debate about how different groups can coexist in German society. I learned that a rather reflexive discussion on the pros and cons of the term "Multikulti" (short for multiculturalism), which had at one time been in frequent use, was unhelpful. Nor did it make any sense simply to reject the changes that migration had wrought in society, or to act as if there were no problems, and no effort was required for different cultures and religions to coexist with mutual respect. Integration requires effort, both from those coming to live here, and from those who have lived here a long time. I have always been convinced that there can be no integration without the receiving society being open-minded and prepared to change, and that the starting point for this is a minimum level of knowledge about other cultures, or at least an interest in them. But what is really crucial is always to see the individual person, and to avoid blanket judgments. Then integration—meaning equal rights for all our country's citizens to participate in all areas of life—can succeed.

Warsaw

My government statement was followed by a debate for all departments until Friday, December 2, 2005. That day, while Franz Müntefering was presenting his labor and social affairs department, and Franz Josef Jung his defense department to parliament, I was on my way to Warsaw. Relations between Germany and Poland were tense. The Law and Justice Party (PiS), which had won the Polish parliamentary and presidential elections in October 2005, was eyeing German–US relations with mistrust, since the SPD was still part of the German government. Unlike the government of the SPD's Gerhard Schröder, the Polish government had supported President Bush in the 2003 Iraq War. Warsaw was also angry that, on September 8, 2005, shortly before the German general election, Gazprom, Wintershall, and E.ON Ruhrgas had signed an agreement in principle for the construction of the Nord Stream 1 gas pipeline, in the presence of Chancellor Schröder and President Putin. Poland rejected the project, favoring pipelines that were laid either through Poland or Ukraine. And, not least, there was what had become known as the "visible sign" in Berlin, a project which the new German government had approved as part of their coalition deal. It was intended as a memorial to the fate of around twelve million Germans who had, after the Second World War, been driven from their homes in what had been eastern German territories, and now belonged to Poland, Russia, and the Czech Republic. Warsaw was concerned about the "visible sign." And it did no good to point to a joint declaration in October 2003 by President Rau of Germany and Poland's President Kwaśniewski, cautiously linking the project to displacement and expulsion in twentieth-century Europe more generally, when there were still no precise ideas about its implementation and the form it would take. The PiS, and its leader Jarosław Kaczyński in particular, harbored a general mistrust of Germany, fed by historical experience. During the Nazi period, Germany had inflicted great suffering on Poland. I was therefore keen both to allay Warsaw's concerns, and to support the cause of the "visible sign." It would be more than fifteen years before the Documentation Center for Displacement, Expulsion, Reconciliation was opened in Berlin, in June 2021. This place of remembrance was the worthy result of a long, and sometimes contentious, debate.

On my first official visit to Warsaw, I met first with my fellow leader Kazimierz Marcinkiewicz. We spoke about all these issues. On the building of Nord Stream 1, I offered to advocate for a connecting pipeline between Germany and Poland, to ease Poland's concerns about potential supply bottlenecks. With regard to the "visible sign," I made it clear that it would commemorate the injustice of the expulsion without in any way relativizing German crimes during the Nazi period, or turning causes and consequences into their opposite. But the core of our discussion was the European budget negotiations.

Poland had been a member of the European Union since May 1, 2004. The budget negotiations were of great significance to the country, and to all the other countries of Central and Eastern Europe: further economic development depended on resources from the EU's structural and cohesion funds, and the level of subsidies from the EU's agricultural budget. I promised Kazimierz Marcinkiewicz that I would support Poland's interests as far as was reasonable, but also made it clear that another failure of the negotiations in Brussels would bring great uncertainty for the future of the Polish economy—the meeting of the EU Council under Luxembourg's presidency had failed to reach an agreement in June 2005.

After that, I paid a courtesy visit to Poland's president-elect

Lech Kaczyński. A meeting arranged with his brother, Jarosław Kaczyński, was canceled at short notice. I was very disappointed by this; he was the man who called the shots in the PiS. It's possible that he canceled because I also had an appointment with the leader of the opposition at that time, Donald Tusk. He had founded the Citizens' Platform (PO) in 2001; we knew each other from working together in the European People's Party (EVP), and had become friends. I admired his straightforwardness and love of freedom. This historian from Gdańsk also taught me a lot about Polish history. Many years later, in the fall of 2023, he managed to connect with young Polish voters in a decidedly pro-EU election campaign, and become prime minister again, much to my delight (his first period in office had been between 2007 and 2014).

European Council

On my second visit to Brussels, and to the European Council on December 15 and 16, 2005, I was accompanied by experienced civil servants from the Chancellery's Europe department and the Foreign Office. By this point, I had appointed Uwe Corsepius as my advisor on European policy. He was an economist who had been at the Chancellery since 1994 and knew Europe inside out. He was to be an excellent companion and advisor for both this and subsequent EU Council meetings.

Expectations of reaching an agreement on the Financial Perspectives were low, and the negotiations lasted from Thursday afternoon until the early hours of Saturday morning. Following my visit to Warsaw, it had become clear to me that, whatever agreement the Council reached, Poland would want to show once again that it had fought especially hard for its own cause. I therefore suspected that the Polish government would submit the only objection to a potential agreement. The budget, which had to be approved by all member states, was a highly complex piece of engineering. Every change for one member state had repercussions for all the others, and no one wanted to give anything up once they had it. And so, in negotiations, you always needed a transferable sum to bring into play if required.

When the Council reached a preliminary result for the EU budget, Poland did in fact withhold its agreement. The situation could only be resolved by Poland gaining something more in the negotiations. I was glad, then, that I was able to offer the country an additional €100 million for the development of its poorest regions from my financial negotiation pot. I made this offer to Kazimierz Marcinkiewicz—and it was clear that this was a final offer. Otherwise, there was no prospect of reaching an agreement on the EU budget at this summit. The Polish prime minister left the chamber to discuss it internally. After what seemed like an endless break, he returned and declared Poland's agreement, enabling the summit to end successfully. German–Polish relations had not suffered, either. The German media complained that I had given German money to Poland, but I let the criticism wash over me; it had been a necessary sidestep in order to achieve a mutually agreed result at the Council meeting. For me, that was what mattered.

It was now Saturday morning, December 17. I flew home. On Monday, I traveled to Rome to pay my first official visits to my colleagues Silvio Berlusconi and the Italian president Carlo Azeglio Ciampi. On Tuesday, I welcomed carolers to the Chancellery, and on Wednesday, December 21, I set off for my Christmas holiday in Switzerland, returning a week later. At 4:30 p.m. on December 30, as dusk was falling, I recorded my first New Year address.

I had been in office for thirty-eight days. There were over 5,800 still to come.

"Where, o where have you gone?"

Dierhagen Strand, on the Baltic Sea, June 2023: Beate Baumann and I had retreated to the coast to write some chapters of this book. We had spent weeks looking through meeting documents and lists of appointments, sorting the important from the unimportant, ordering things by topic, deciding what we wanted to write about in more depth, what should be mentioned in passing, and what did not merit any mention at all. We had to cross-check a lot of information, because our documents were not diaries. Not all the meetings that had taken place were contained in them, and not all the meetings contained in them had actually taken place. It was a Sisyphean task. We decided to have a break and take a little walk before continuing to write. We needed to put events and our thoughts in order. Outside, there was an early summer balminess in the air, and the sun was shining. From the back of our hotel, we walked down to the beach, and turned left toward Graal-Müritz.

As we strolled, I said to Beate, "It's a good job no one told me before the 2005 election what my days would look like: the number of meetings was ridiculous. I'm almost patting myself on the back now, for having managed it all."

"True, but no one forces anyone to be chancellor—it's all voluntary," she replied, drily. It was something she used to say during my time in office, when I complained about having too many meetings.

"Of course it is. All the same, these are days of your life, time you can't get back," I replied. "Sometimes I think about the first line of Lensky's aria from *Eugene Onegin*: 'Where, o where have you gone?'"

Beate laughed and said, "Yes, I understand that, but you did always enjoy the work, as well—particularly because, in politics, you always start the day not knowing how it will end."

"Absolutely; a lot of the time, that element of surprise even gave me wings," I agreed. "But then, trawling through the diary, we've seen that there were a lot of meetings that happened several times per week, or per month, or every two or three years, like a kind of framework of chancellorship," I added.

We went on thinking about these as we walked. They had been a routine. These meetings alone were so numerous that they could have kept me fully occupied if there had been nothing else to do, no special outside events, no crises. The routine said a lot about the way political institutions cooperated within our federal state, and it kept processes running reliably. It was also important in giving me real knowledge and understanding of the country's political actors and their different responsibilities and interests at a city, state, and national level. I was firmly convinced that this created the ability to solve problems and reach compromises. The routine also showed that, in our country, responsibility for society's well-being, for our common good, rests on many shoulders outside the political sphere: unions and business associations, churches and religious communities, the media, social and sports clubs, and many more. In our country, twenty-nine million people do voluntary work. Ernst-Wolfgang Böckenförde, former judge at the Constitutional Court, once put it like this: "The liberal, secular state lives by prerequisites that the state itself cannot guarantee. This is the great adventure it has undertaken for the sake of freedom." I have always found this idea compelling. The Böckenförde Dilemma, as it became known, was a warning to me to foster our country's prerequisites. And I felt the truth of these words in the countless conversations, encounters, meetings, and other official duties I undertook as chancellor.

"I think it's worth attempting to give a picture of this," I said to Beate.

"Right—and not an overly complicated one," she agreed. We

decided to lay out the routine, the way the different institutions and levels of our country interacted, not along the lines of my various offices and functions as chancellor, party leader, and elected representative, and not in order of importance, either, but in the simplest way possible: alphabetically.

After about three quarters of an hour, we turned around and walked back along the beach to the hotel. There, we put the routines of my sixteen years as chancellor down on paper. If not expressly mentioned, these are meetings held either once a year, or on average every two years.

A

Alexander von Humboldt Foundation: photo opportunity in the Chancellery with the recipients of the Chancellor's Scholarship from Brazil, China, India, South Africa, or the United States.

Arbeitsgemeinschaft der deutschen Familienorganisationen: a meeting with the chairs of the five major German family associations: the German Family Association (DFV); the Evangelical Family Consortium (eaf); the Catholic Family Association (FDK); the Association of Single Mothers and Fathers (VAMV); the Association of Binational Families and Partnerships (iaf).

Associations of Non-statutory Welfare Services: a conversation with representatives of the organizations brought together under the Federal Association of Non-statutory Welfare Services (Arbeiterwohlfahrt, Deutscher Caritasverband, Paritätischer Gesamtverband, the German Red Cross, Diakonie Deutschland— Evangelisches Werk für Diakonie und Entwicklung, Central Welfare Office for Jews in Germany).

B

Background conversations: with journalists from print and electronic media while traveling by plane and at the Chancellery; at parties thrown by newspapers, publishing houses, and television networks. In this book, too, they remain confidential.

Budget week: cabinet agreement of the draft budget and the accompanying bill covering any changes in legislation required by the budget, with mid-term financial planning. This is done at the start of July every year. Participation in parliamentary consultations on the budget plan in September, during the first week of Bundestag sessions after the summer break; then a second budget week in November each year. A general consultation and debate on the Wednesday morning of each budget week at the Chancellery and, in the November week, a dinner with the members of the budget committee and their Chancellery colleagues.

Business associations: conversations and participation in annual conferences and general meetings; meetings at the Internationale Handwerksmesse (IHM) in Munich (a major trade fair for skilled trades) with Germany's national employers' association (the BDA), the Federation of German Industries (BDI), the German Confederation of Skilled Crafts (ZDH), the German Chamber of Commerce and Industry (DIHK), and the Federal Association of Wholesale, Foreign Trade, Services (BGA); accompanying business delegations on foreign visits.

C

Cabinet meeting: weekly on Wednesdays at 9:30 a.m., the exceptions to this being: budget weeks; Ash Wednesday; the Wednesday after Easter; two weeks in summer (one cabinet meeting in summer is traditionally led by the vice chancellor); and the Wednesday between Christmas and New Year. Preceded by separate cabinet breakfast meetings for the coalition parties, with the CDU/CSU's always taking place at 8:15 a.m. on Wednesdays, followed by a conversation with the vice chancellor at 9:15 a.m. in the chancellor's office.

Carnival reception: reception for the board of the German Carnival Association, including one prince, royal couple, or triumvirate from each German state, and a prizewinning dance group. Contrary to some reports, I always thoroughly enjoyed these events.

CDU (Christian Democratic Union): sessions of the CDU Presidium, held every second Monday, and of the CDU Federal Executive Committee at Konrad Adenauer House (KAH) one Monday per month; two-day retreats for the Federal Committee at the start of every year; annual national party congress; regional conferences held before the congress; a meeting for the party chairs with the secretary general, the chief whip, and the heads of various policy areas from Konrad Adenauer House once or twice a month at KAH; Bundestag election campaigns every four years, each involving fifty or sixty national speaking engagements, a TV debate with the SPD candidate for chancellor, and other TV interview and election programs.

CDU/CSU Bundestag group: participation in the parliamentary group meetings in the roughly twenty weeks per year when the German parliament sits, always at three o'clock on a Tuesday afternoon, and in the retreats for the group executive at the end of parliament's annual summer break; conversations with individual working groups, state groups, sociological groups (the Women's Group, the Employees' Group, the Parliamentary Circle for Small and Medium-sized Businesses, the Group of Displaced People, Resettlers and German Minorities, and the Young People's Group), and what is referred to internally as the "carpet dealer convention" (a group made up of state group chairs and chairs of the sociological groups).

CDU state groups: meetings with the chairs of the Union groups within the state parliaments, including the CSU groups, and with the chair and chief whip of the CDU/CSU Bundestag group, every four to six weeks on a Sunday evening.

CeBIT: the opening of the information technology trade fair in Hanover, with a tour of the exhibition, and a conversation with the head of government of that year's partner country, up until 2018.

Christmas: receipt of three Christmas trees for the Chancellery and a chess set for my office, provided by AGDW—die Waldeigentümer (Federation of German Forest Owners' Associations). Christmas parties hosted by the Chancellery, the parliamentary group, the CDU head office, and the Mecklenburg-Western Pomerania state group. Video calls with all the German Army's troops stationed abroad; regular messages to the soldiers via Radio Andernach, the army's entertainment broadcaster; a reception for relatives of soldiers and police officers serving abroad.

Citizens' consultations: face-to-face meetings in my constituency office in Stralsund, every six to eight weeks, and by prior appointment after I became chancellor.

Committees: visit to the foreign affairs committee, and, at least once a year, to the Bundestag's Committee for the Affairs of the European Union.

Constituency visitor group: a reception at the Chancellery, or in the Bundestag rooms, for visitors from my constituency.

CSU (Christian Social Union): teleconference with a small circle of CDU and CSU party and group leaders on a Monday morning; guest speech at the CSU party conference; joint sittings of the CDU and CSU presidia, in particular to nominate the candidate for chancellor, and to sign off on the government program before general elections.

D

Digital Summit (until 2016, the National IT Summit): participation in the congress organized by the ministry of business and technology since 2006, with representatives from business, academia, and society, as well as various other ministries.

Diplomatic Corps: a reception for ambassadors and heads of missions of international organizations at the Chancellery, or at the government's official retreat in Meseberg.

E

Environmental organizations: conversations with various German environmental organizations, the Bund für Umwelt und Natur-schutz Deutschland (BUND), Deutschen Naturschutzring (DNR), Naturschutzbund Deutschland (NABU), and the German branch of the World Wide Fund For Nature (WWF).

EU Project Day in schools, for Europe Day: a visit to a school and discussion with students, close to Europe Day on May 9.

European Council: meetings of the heads of state and government of the EU member states, and the commission president, in March, June, October, and December each year, with add-itional sittings and informal meetings in the course of the year.

European People's Party (EPP): participation in the meetings of the EPP's executive body before each meeting of the Euro-pean Council, and in the yearly EPP congresses.

European Round Table for Industry (ERT): a meeting with the forum of around sixty leading European CEOs, plus the French president and the president of the EU Commission, to discuss strengthening Europe's global competitiveness and the under-lying conditions necessary to achieve this.

F

Federal Association of Senior-Citizens' Organizations (BAGSO): a meeting with the board of the association, which comprises around 120 member organizations for senior citizens.

Federal Constitutional Court: a dinner for the Constitutional Court judges with members of the cabinet, either at the Consti-tutional Court in Karlsruhe, or at the Chancellery in Berlin.

Federal Press Conference: an annual summer press confer-ence, plus other press conferences on special occasions.

G

G7 (G8): meetings of the heads of state and government from Germany, France, the UK, Italy, Japan, Canada, the United States, and, from 1998 until 2013, Russia.

G20: participation in the summits held since 2008 by the G20, a forum of heads of state and government and the finance ministers from nineteen of the world's largest economies, plus the EU, and representatives of international organizations.

German Disability Council (DBR): meeting with the representatives of the DBR speakers' council, representing the interests of the nearly eight million people with severe disabilities in Germany.

German Farmers' Conference (DVB): participation in the national agricultural industry conference, with a speech to the general assembly.

German Federation of Trade Unions (DGB): meeting with the board of the DGB, or with the chair of the DGB and the chairs of the individual unions.

German Lutheran Church Congress (DEKT): Bible study or roundtable discussions at the congress for Lutheran Christians in Germany.

German Rural Women's Association (dlv): participation in the annual general meetings, or conversations with the board of the association of and for women in rural areas.

German School Prize: participation in the annual prize-giving in alternate years, taking turns with the German president.

Girls' Day: participation in a day of action run by the careers-advice project of the same name, which was created to encourage more girls into technical and scientific careers.

H

Hannover Messe: opening address at this major international trade fair, together with the head of government of that year's guest country.

Human rights organizations: conversations with Amnesty International, Human Rights Watch, and various others, especially before international conferences.

I

Innovation Dialogue (since 2010; from 2006 until 2008, Council for Innovation and Growth): participation in this exchange between national government, industry, and academia, coordinated by acatech, the Germany Academy of Science and Engineering.

Intergovernmental consultations: meetings of the German cabinet with the cabinets of other countries, including France, Israel, Italy, the Netherlands, Poland, Spain, China, India, and Turkey; intergovernmental consultations with Russia were halted in 2014, in response to Russia's annexation of Crimea.

International Motor Show (IAA): tour of the trade fair and meeting with the board of the German Association of the Automotive Industry.

International organizations: from 2010 onward, conversations at the Chancellery with the heads of the five leading international organizations on finance and economics, the International Labor Organization (ILO), the International Monetary Fund (IMF), the Organization for Economic Co-operation and Development (OECD), the World Bank (WB), and the World Trade Organization (WTO).

Interviews: usually with several channels one after another on the same day, for the sake of fairness, as well as in one-off programs; summer interviews; political talk shows; newspaper interviews at irregular intervals with the national German media, and with regional papers or publishers serving several newspapers; occasional conversations with members of the Foreign Press Association in Germany, which could be freely reported and quoted.

J

Johannistag reception for the Council of Lutheran Churches in Germany (EKD): attendance at the EKD's annual reception on or around Johannistag, the feast of the Nativity of St. John the Baptist on June 24.

Jugend forscht (Young people research): reception at the Chancellery for the prizewinners of a competition for school students and young people, organized by the Jugend forscht Foundation since 1965, including the award of the Chancellor's Prize for most original project.

K

Katholikentag: Bible study or roundtable discussions at the meeting of Roman Catholic Christians in Germany.

Konrad-Adenauer-Stiftung (KAS, Konrad Adenauer Foundation): attendance at board meetings four times a year, as an ex officio member of the board, and the annual general meeting.

M

Make-up: a hair and make-up appointment every morning with Petra Keller, or occasionally a substitute, because the chancellor represents the country both internally and externally.

Meseberg meetings: with trade unions and business associations, at the government's official retreat and guest house, Schloss Meseberg.

Morning briefing: a meeting of around thirty minutes with my closest co-workers, covering all topics, and preparing government spokespeople for press conferences. Whenever possible, these were held every week on Tuesdays, Thursdays, and Fridays at 8:30 a.m., and on Wednesdays at 7:45 a.m. to avoid clashing with the cabinet meeting.

Munich Security Conference (MSC): a speech, plus participation in discussions at the international foreign and security policy conference, which has taken place every February since 1963.

N

National Maritime Conference (NMK): participation and a speech to the annual conference of businesses that make up the maritime sector (shipbuilding, the shipbuilding supply-chain industry, port industries, and logistics).

National Regulatory Control Council (NKR): receipt of the annual report from the ten-person advisory body, which since 2006 has determined the bureaucratic costs incurred by companies as a result of having to provide government agencies with information about their activities. Since 2011, this report has also determined the costs of compliance with proposed laws.

New Year address: recorded at the Chancellery by the ARD and ZDF networks in alternating years, in the late afternoon on December 30.

New Year reception (constituency): held in my constituency to thank state parliament representatives, local politicians, business representatives, and supporters.

New Year reception (presidential): hosted by the president at Bellevue Palace.

P

Parliamentary "questions to government" with the chancellor: since 2018, the chancellor has attended "questions to government" sessions in the Bundestag three times a year at one o'clock on a Wednesday afternoon, for around an hour.

President: a conversation once per quarter; dinner with the representatives from all the constitutional bodies and members of the cabinet, at the president's official residence.

R

Reports: receipt of the expert report from the "five wise econo-mists"—in other words, the expert council for the analysis of macroeconomic development—and, since 2008, receipt of the report by the six members of the Expert Commission on Research and Innovation.

S

Startsocial: a competition run by the startsocial association, in which industry representatives support volunteer-led social projects by clubs and associations, take on sponsorship, and promote knowledge transfer between business and voluntary organizations; participation in the prize-giving ceremony as patron of startsocial.

State premiers' conference: conversations with the heads of each state government at the Chancellery, in June and December every year, and more often if required. The COVID-19 pandemic necessitated nearly thirty over two years.

States: dinner with the premiers of the CDU-governed states on a Thursday evening, before the Friday sitting of the Bundesrat; attendance at the states' summer parties, held in their representative offices in Berlin.

Sterne des Sports (Stars of Sport): participation in the awards given by the German Olympic Association (DOSB) and the Volksbanken Raiffeisenbanken, to sports clubs that go beyond their sporting activities to do work in the community, in alter-nating years with the president.

St. Michael's reception: attendance at the annual reception of the German Conference of Bishops, on or around the feast of the Archangel Michael, who is the patron saint of Germany.

Sustainable Development Council: participation in the coun-cil's annual conference, during which the report on its current work is also presented.

T

Tag der offenen Tür: a government open day. Encounters and conversations with visitors to the Chancellery in the main courtyard; discussion on the stage in the Chancellery Garden with famous sportspeople; autographs; selfies.

U

Umbrella organizations for local politics: conversations with the presidents and chief executives of the German County Association (DLT), the Association of German Cities (DST), and the German Association of Towns and Municipalities (DStGB).

V

Vacation: setting up the technology for a fully functioning office at a vacation destination, with a co-worker to accompany me— the chancellor is never off duty.

Valentine's day: photo call with the president of the Zentralverband Gartenbau (ZVG, the German trade association for horticulture) and receipt of a bunch of flowers at the Chancellery.

VENRO: an exchange with the Development Policy and Humanitarian Aid Association of German NGOs, in particular before large international conferences such as the G8 and G20.

Video podcast: except during vacation time, recorded weekly at the Chancellery on a topical issue, and usually released on a Saturday morning.

W

World Economic Forum (WEF) in Davos: speeches, participation in discussions, and conversations at the annual meeting of the WEF, a platform for exchange between politicians, business representatives, academia, and non-governmental organizations.

Beate Baumann and I pushed the sheets of paper on which we'd written our overview to one side, and went on thinking. We didn't want to leave it at that; we also wanted to show what had given me stability and orientation, what—and, crucially, who— had kept me going. We decided to go back to the start: two o'clock in the afternoon on November 22, 2005, when Norbert Lammert held up the original text of the German constitution and I swore my oath in the Bundestag. I called to mind those words once more, eighteen years later and sixteen years of experience as chancellor wiser.

"I swear that I will dedicate my efforts to the well-being of the German people." That was how the oath began. I was the chancellor of all Germans—those who had voted for me, and those who hadn't. And I had to give my all for every one of them, to be available and reachable at all times, to put out small fires before they became a conflagration. Every day, there were more than enough opportunities to dedicate my efforts to the people, but thank God, there were also more than enough moments in each day to gather strength for those efforts. Sometimes, it was enough just to choose a simple lunch, to be cooked by the Chancellery kitchen for me and the people I was meeting. That was a privilege. On jetlagged days following trips abroad, or after late-night meetings, a chicken, potato, or lentil soup was a wonderful thing. But nor will I forget the mixed salads. The time I would have had to spend chopping vegetables at home to create such a thing! Here, it was simply served to me. Beate and I often ate together, discussing the general political situation and upcoming decisions.

It was also crucial for me to have moments of calm, to take a glance at what was happening in the world outside my own cosmos. The Uckermark house was a retreat for Joachim and me throughout my time as chancellor. Even though I often didn't arrive there until late Friday evening, left again on

Saturday morning, and only returned that evening, I loved sleeping there. I loved taking a turn around the garden, letting the light and the birdsong work its magic on me, looking at my flowerbeds, taking in the silence. The pressure fell away at once; my mind emptied. Whenever possible, I wanted to be at home on Saturday evenings. It meant I had to turn down a lot of invitations to exciting social events, but an evening of peace and quiet, talking to Joachim, was more important to me. I cooked our dinner, so I didn't get entirely out of practice. And on Sunday mornings I had the space to make the decisions I had set aside for the weekend. On Sunday afternoons I would travel back to Berlin, and there usually followed a series of telephone calls to prepare for the week ahead.

Conversations with my parents, and with my brother and sister, Marcus and Irene, were also important, though my time for them was far too limited. They were proud of me, but also followed my decisions with a critical eye. That was particularly true of Marcus. Irene was a patient confidante. As my parents became frailer—my father died at the age of eighty-five in 2011, and my mother in 2019 at the age of ninety—it was very painful for me not to have enough time to visit them. Political life was relentless, and even when people died, it left me little time to grieve. The voyeurism at funerals was unbearable. It tested the limits of my strength, and I am immensely grateful to all the people who put so much energy into helping me and my family retain at least a tiny amount of privacy.

"[. . .] promote their welfare, protect them from harm, uphold and defend the constitution and the laws of the Federation," the oath continued. Article 65 of our constitution says that, "The Federal Chancellor shall determine and be responsible for the general guidelines of policy." Of course, in this I was constrained by various coalition agreements, the programs of work that the parties had agreed during coalition negotiations before forming

a government. But I couldn't hide behind a coalition agreement; I had to set the pace for that work, influence the climate within the cabinet as we sought compromises, develop my own initiatives, set personal priorities through my choice of meetings, and work with the government to find solutions to unexpected issues. I could not do this without people at my side on whom I could absolutely rely: my office staff; the government spokespeople and their deputies; the heads of the Chancellery, who took some of the political weight off the chancellor, and led the office with their staff; the ministers of state at the Chancellery; and all the staff of the policy departments. They always kept me excellently prepared and helped to achieve our political goals, through which the people's welfare was promoted and they were protected from harm.

"[. . .] perform my duties conscientiously, and do justice to all." That was the final part of the oath I had taken. I flinched. What had I promised to do? I obviously wanted to perform my duties conscientiously, at least to the best of my knowledge and belief. I had done the same at every previous stage of my life. But doing justice to *all*? Now, so many years later, I felt it was an almost impossible task. More than eighty million people in Germany—German citizens as well as those who had lived for a long time in our country—should be able to live their lives as they wish, fulfill their desires, realize their dreams, and know they will be safeguarded against the major risks in life. In theory, political work should be about enabling the individual to lead a successful life—but in practice I had to ensure that I didn't lose all contact with normality. I was driven about in an armored car, guarded by personal protection officers at all times, laced into the corset of a packed schedule, and constantly assailed by pleas and flattery. I had to take precautions in order to keep my feet on the ground, not to miss developments, to listen and learn as well as speak. I had to avoid becoming a

hamster in a wheel; I had to stay curious and work with joy in my heart. For this reason I had insisted that, ultimately, I would always be the one to decide which meetings I would attend in person, and which I wouldn't. And I had to learn not to make these decisions on the hoof: canceling meetings at short notice caused far greater disappointment than simply not accepting them in the first place.

But how often I found myself cursing when a meeting I had agreed to far in advance was next on the schedule. I sometimes didn't understand what had induced me to take it. Had I not made the decision myself, I would have berated other people for it. An important criterion was the principle of treating everyone equally: doing justice to all. A chancellor could attend events at a national level, but not those at a state level. Otherwise, there would be a hail of accusations: Why had I decided in favor of one, and against another? Of course, the exception proved the rule here, too—but the exceptions really did have to be exceptional. It was only in my own constituency that the principle of equal treatment took a back seat. There, I got an insight into the practical aspects of life, visiting small and medium-sized companies, agricultural businesses, schools, daycare centers, job centers, nature reserves. I heard about problems in hotels, facilities for senior citizens, hospitals, mother-and-baby clinics. In my constituency, I always had the sense of being politically at home.

There were two types of meeting in which everyone was completely open with each other: the first was the morning briefing at the Chancellery. The mood was sometimes cheerful, and sometimes subdued, when too many pieces of bad news reached us at once. None of us tried to make things seem better than they were. All that mattered was each participant's honest assessment of the situation. Together, we either came up with steps toward a solution, or admitted we had not yet found a solution. This, too, was liberating. It meant I could start the day feeling that I had a realistic view of things.

The second special meeting was a monthly dinner with my closest CDU colleagues in the government, the parliamentary group, and the party, on the ninth floor of the Chancellery. We carried out an unblinkered analysis of the political situation, and agreed our approach for the following weeks. I reported on my European and international experiences and challenges. Gradually, we laid out all the problems that were not talked about during the hectic working day. I got a sense of where tensions were arising, and who needed help and support; and the others got a sense of what motivated me, and what was troubling me. To this day, I am grateful that there was full attendance at almost all these dinners, and nothing said there was ever leaked.

I added the words *"so help me, God"* to the end of my oath. It can be taken without the religious element, but the addition was important to me. I believe there is a God, even if I often cannot comprehend or sense Him. I know that I am not perfect and make mistakes, and so my life has been made easier by faith— as has the task of taking responsibility for my fellow man and for creation, with the power given to me at times, without over-estimating myself, or doing the reverse and giving in too quickly, in the knowledge of my limited powers. The words of the prophet Jeremiah have always spoken to me: "Seek the peace and prosperity of the city [. . .] for if it prospers, you too will prosper." Having said "so help me, God" in public helped me to feel that someone was watching over me, even when I had to make difficult decisions.

"Looking back, as we're working on this book, I'm pleased to see that while I was chancellor, alongside the daily clutter of events, there was something that gave me security for sixteen years. That's 5,860 days, if you don't count my very first and very last day in office," I said to Beate in our Baltic-coast retreat, before we turned our attention to the next chapters of this book.

A SUMMER'S TALE

New traditions

IN MY FIRST New Year address, I looked forward to the soccer World Cup, setting the mood for the tournament that would be held in Germany in the summer of 2006. Our national women's team had led the way, becoming world champions at their own 2003 World Cup in the United States. I said that I saw no reason why the men shouldn't be able to do the same thing. Two and a half months later, on March 15, 2006, the senior figures in the German soccer association (DFB) were my guests at the Chancellery: Franz Beckenbauer, a world champion as both player and coach, who had brought this World Cup to Germany; Theo Zwanziger, executive president of the DFB; Oliver Bierhoff, the manager of the national team; and the head coach Jürgen Klinsmann. We had dinner together on the ninth floor. We spoke about the current state of preparations for the tournament. All that evening, Klinsmann exuded optimism and drive. It was far from obvious that he would: two weeks earlier, his team had lost miserably, 4–1 to Italy in Florence, in their first World Cup warm-up match. By half time, the score was already 3–0 to the Italians. Previous international games in the second half of 2005 had yielded two victories, two draws, and two defeats, which was not exactly a glowing result for the year, especially as the two wins—against South Africa in September and China in October—had not been achieved against the very top teams in the world. After that, doubts had been cast on the whole team.

But it was Jürgen Klinsmann's lifestyle that had become the real bone of contention—or, to put it less dramatically, the fact that he wanted to be at home with his family in California for at least part of the time between international games, even though it was a good twelve-hour flight away, with a nine-hour time difference. He had been the national coach since 2004. So far, there could be no doubt that he and his team were straining every sinew to lead Germany to victory at the World Cup on home turf. But, even after the resounding defeat by Italy (who would go on to win the World Cup, though of course we couldn't have known that in March 2006), he had flown straight home to his family in California, and as a result his position had become shakier than at any point during his (still relatively short) time in the post. This flight home appeared to have been one flight too many. Franz Beckenbauer, Theo Zwanziger, the vast majority of the media, millions of soccer fans—everyone, in fact—seemed convinced that this was not on. The head coach of the German national side should live in Germany, they thought, if he was taking his job seriously and could see how important this was. True, in 2006 there were no smartphones, but it was still possible to keep in touch electronically using mobile phones and computers. And I'm sure Jürgen Klinsmann used them, too. But nothing is better than personal communication, face to face; that is as true in soccer as it is in the rest of life. On the other hand, people take strength from different sources, and Klinsmann seemed to need the physical distance from Germany, and the time associated with the time difference, as well as being with his family in California a good nine thousand kilometers away: the things for which he was now being criticized. We didn't yet know each other personally, but I understood that very well. And

I really liked what he and his team had done for German football since 2004. I thought it was wrong to jeopardize all of that now.

I had given a public statement to that effect before our dinner, in the presence of Klinsmann, Franz Beckenbauer, Theo Zwanziger, Oliver Bierhoff, and the others, in front of the blue wall in the press area on the second floor of the Chancellery. "My dear Herr Klinsmann! You and your team have introduced new methods and done away with outdated traditions. People always agree with these things as long as you keep winning," I explained, adding, "But with defeat comes a hail of criticism. You can't let that put you off. If you are convinced you're going the right way—and I say this from my own experience—then you need to maintain your course. Changeability doesn't inspire trust. Altering your decisions every day doesn't lead to success." This had been planned as just a photo opportunity, and I had only decided to make a statement as well shortly beforehand. I was annoyed that this travel issue had developed into a kind of cultural conflict. I wanted to get behind Jürgen Klinsmann, to help him. And it worked.

Afterward, over dinner on the ninth floor, Klinsmann described his plans for the World Cup, saying more than once: "We might have lost a warm-up match—these things happen. But we want to be world champions, that hasn't changed." The other guests rapidly relaxed. As 10:00 p.m. approached, I had the feeling that Franz Beckenbauer was also beginning to feel more comfortable. He and the others might have been a little anxious before this meeting; it was the first time we had met, and they didn't know me yet.

Now Beckenbauer said, "I don't know if things still work the same way here."

"Why, what used to happen?" I asked.

"The former chancellor used to stand up about now, fetch an ashtray, and we'd smoke a cigar or a cigarette," Beckenbauer replied.

"Well, then I'll see what we can do," I told him. I got up and went round the corner into the kitchenette, found an ashtray, and returned with it. Beckenbauer smiled, lit a cigar—this was before the smoke alarms had been installed on the ceiling, which would eventually have gone off—and the ice was broken.

Klinsmann remained the national coach, and what followed would go down in history as a fairytale summer, and not just in soccer terms.

Third place

Thomas Steg, deputy government spokesperson and a great soccer fan, had written a quote into the draft of my press statement. It was new to me, and it came from Bill Shankly, whose career as a coach for Liverpool FC in the 1960s had brought the team great success. He said: "Some people believe football is a matter of life and death. I assure you, it's much more important than that." I had to laugh when I read it. Steg had touched a nerve with me, as well. I have always liked soccer. I'm fascinated by the mix of physical skill and player intelligence that this team sport demands. As important as all the technical questions about formations are, to me it seems equally important that the behavior of eleven people interacting on the pitch is attuned toward a single aim, their minds wholly on this one task for 90 minutes, or, with extra time and penalties, a good 120 minutes. When I went to watch games in stadiums, I sometimes got a sense of whether a team was going to play well that day or not as soon as they came onto the pitch. Their body language gave it away. I was familiar with this from my work: when I entered an auditorium as a speaker, I could usually tell within a few seconds whether the audience and I were going to connect, and then my approach would be very different from what I might have done had there been a wall between us.

In summer 2006, everything was right: four weeks of un-interrupted good weather; a fan zone on the Strasse des 17. Juni in Berlin; big screens set up all over the country for public screenings; and the German flag everywhere you looked (the light version, with the cheerful black, red, and gold unencumbered by the federal eagle). The flag was attached to wing mirrors and car windows; its colors adorned hats and caps, and were painted on the faces of fans, who included more women and girls than ever before. For the world it was "a time to make friends," as the tournament motto put it. It was a summer of soccer like none that Germany had ever seen before. And it was more than a summer of soccer. It was as if this team of young, easygoing players, some with a migrant background and some without, led by a young national coach from Swabia in the Southwest, who lived with his family in California and who had been a world champion in 1990 and European champion in 1996 as a player, had the country virtually spellbound. In the end, this team achieved third place in their World Cup on home turf, and on July 9, half a million people celebrated with them at the Brandenburg Gate. The crowd was almost as jubilant as if Jürgen Klinsmann's dream of Germany winning its fourth world title had come true. Germany was happy with third place, and the headline in the *Frankfurter Allgemeine Zeitung* was: "Love parade for Klinsmann and his team." The paper described the welcome for the national side as "a celebration to give you gooseflesh." Jürgen Klinsmann resigned as coach after the World Cup. But his dream did come true, eight years later, under his former assistant coach Joachim "Jogi" Löw. Löw became the German team's head coach and led them to victory in 2014, through a breathtaking tournament in which they not only beat the hosts and five-time world champions Brazil 7–1 in a legendary semi-final, but also became the first European team ever to win a World Cup in South America.

———

I remember the decisive minutes of that final as if it was yesterday. I had flown to Rio de Janeiro with the German president Joachim Gauck. In the stadium, I sat beside Brazil's president at the time, Dilma Rousseff, with the Hungarian president Viktor Orbán in the row in front. He told me he had been in Brazil for ten days already and had watched a lot of games, including those played by the Argentinian side that Germany faced in the final. Before the starting whistle blew, he turned around to me, registered how tense I was feeling, and said, half seriously and half in jest: "One thing is clear: you can't be sure your team is going to win here." We spoke English with one another. A remark like that was the last thing I needed, and I shot back: "I know that, now turn around and let me watch."

After ninety minutes, the score was still 0–0. Extra time. When Mario Götze came on as a substitute and made it 1–0 to Germany in the 113th minute, I was over the moon. Orbán turned to me again as I was celebrating and called out: "All right, now you can calm down."

"But there's still seven minutes to play!" I said.

"No, nothing else is going to happen now, believe me." He turned out to be right.

I have no special memories of the presentation ceremony that followed, but I do have very vivid memories of meeting the team in the changing rooms afterward. Joachim Gauck gave a short speech; Jogi Löw stood there holding a bottle of beer, completely relaxed and happy; Miroslav Klose, Germany's top striker, had his two young children with him; and many of the players seemed well aware that such a victory had been anything but a given. At the end of a long, eight-year road, I thought, a combination of things had prevailed: a game strategy, these exceptional players, and a particular attitude. It had begun in 2006, and Jogi Löw, Oliver Bierhoff, and Andreas Köpke had carried it through to victory.

HOSTING IN A WICKER BEACH CHAIR

Lunch with George W. Bush

ON JUNE 6 and 7, 2007, I was due to host the leaders of France, Italy, Japan, Canada, the United Kingdom, the United States, and Russia, as well as the president of the European Commission, at the G8 summit in the resort of Heiligendamm on the Baltic coast. Until 1998, the G8 was the G7. This informal group was founded in 1975, originally as the Group of Six, and in 1976 it was seven: the seven leading world economies, their leaders meeting to coordinate their common values and interests. After the end of the Cold War, the G7 invited the Soviet Union as it was still called, represented by Mikhail Gorbachev, its final president, as a guest to its summit in London in June 1991. Germany was a reunified land of peace and freedom; I was a young minister for women and youth and a newly elected member of the Bundestag. After reunification, I followed major world politics primarily as a spectator. In December 1991, the Soviet Union collapsed. Gorbachev, the man behind glasnost and perestroika, was history. Boris Yeltsin, elected president of what was then the Russian Soviet Republic in June 1991, founded the Commonwealth of Independent States (CIS) on December 8, 1991 together with his counterparts from Belarus and Ukraine, and on December 21, Azerbaijan, Armenia, Kazakhstan, Kyrgyzstan, Moldova, Tajikistan, Turkmenistan, and Uzbekistan were added. After the dissolution of the Soviet Union,

Boris Yeltsin was now the first president of independent Russia. From 1994 onward, the Russian president took part in official summit discussions, and before that he met with the G7 nations on the summits' sidelines.

The next change came in 1998, when Russia became the eighth member to join the group at the Birmingham summit in the UK. The group of the seven largest economies in the world became the Group of Eight, an expression of the hope that the G8 too would share common values and above all interests, even if Russia was unable to keep up with the seven others in terms of economic power. In the first half of the 1990s, the country suffered from very high inflation, and in 1998 its public finances and banking sector plunged it into a severe crisis.

Until his resignation on New Year's Eve 1999, Boris Yeltsin represented Russia at the annual G8 summits. He initially appointed his successor, Vladimir Putin, as prime minister of the Russian Federation in August 1999. With Yeltsin's resignation, Putin took over as prime minister in accordance with the Russian Federation's constitution until a new president was elected. In March 2000, he was finally elected the second president of the Russian Federation.

Six years later, from July 15 to 17, 2006, Putin hosted a G8 summit in Russia for the first time. He had invited the group to his hometown of Saint Petersburg. It was also my first G8 summit during my term as chancellor. I remember this summit not so much for the beauty of the venue, the Constantine Palace, or the political deliberations, but for an episode on its fringes. Before an afternoon session was due to begin, I took my seat at the round conference table, with my back to the door. I flicked through my papers; discussions were about to resume. Out of the corner of my eye, I saw the US president coming back into the room. Suddenly, out of nowhere, I felt a firm grip on my shoulders. It was the last thing I was expecting at that moment. Startled, I threw my arms up in the air. As I turned around, I saw George W. Bush walking off to his seat, a mischievous smile on his face. I couldn't help but laugh. To me, the matter was closed—but not to the public. It had all taken place in front of rolling cameras: journalists had been in the room, getting new clips for their reports before the afternoon's session. A little later, government spokesman Ulrich Wilhelm told me how Bush's shoulder grip and my reaction had made waves worldwide. There was a debate over whether it was a sexist infringement. The thought had never occurred to me for a second. The moment I saw that it was George W. Bush greeting me in such a hands-on way, I knew it was a joke that wasn't meant to intimidate or belittle me: it was just a bit of fun in the midst of some dry and serious discussions. Bush and I liked and respected each other.

We had already gotten to know each other in Mainz in 2005, when I, as opposition leader, had met him during his visit to Germany. In January 2006, as chancellor, I traveled to Washington for my inaugural visit. I perceived Bush to be someone who would look people directly in the eye, and I had the impression that he was interested in my life story. I felt this especially when he and his wife, Laura, visited my constituency in July 2006. After talks in Stralsund, I invited them both to an evening in Trinwillershagen, formerly a model socialist village, to give them an impression of my earlier life in East Germany. The landlord of the Zu den Linden restaurant in the local cultural center had shot a wild boar, which he grilled on a spit. We sat at beer garden tables with about sixty invited guests from the region; the weather was lovely, Bush turned the spit, we laughed together, and we overcame language barriers with our hands and feet. The guests could see he was a cheerful, attentive man who was able to laugh at himself. And I was very pleased when George and Laura Bush invited Joachim and me to visit their ranch in Texas in return.

We traveled there a little over a year later, on November 9,

2007. It was late afternoon when Joachim and I arrived at the Prairie Chapel Ranch, near Crawford, two hundred kilometers south of Dallas. George and Laura Bush both picked us up from the ranch's helipad in a white pick-up truck that George himself was driving. We had a short journey to the guests' house where we'd be staying. After that, we took a tour of the 641 hectares of hilly terrain. We passed small canyons, their slopes overgrown with tall trees, and we crossed bridges over streams. George said to us, "The only thing that makes me sad here is that I never see any animals when I drive across the ranch."

"Why's that?" I asked.

"Because the secret service always patrols the ranch before I set off, and of course that drives them all away," he explained.

Afterward, in the welcoming main house, we had smoked Texan beef fillet for dinner. Condoleezza Rice, the US secretary of state, was there too. George Jr. rang his father after dinner to congratulate him on the parachute jump he'd done that day. George Sr. was eighty-two years old at the time, and from my point of view the jump was an almost unbelievable achievement. We talked about politics and more personal matters. Back in Trinwillershagen, Joachim and I had told George W. Bush about our lives in East Germany, and now he told us about his life before the presidency, and I described my first trip to the United States, to San Diego in the summer of 1991. I was visiting Joachim back then, as he was working at the company Biosym Technologies based there at the time. I finally had the opportunity to travel to the land of freedom I had so longed to see. The Pacific made a big impression on me, and I was so excited to be able to watch whales. Later, Joachim and I went into the desert for the first time in our lives. On the way there, I was captivated by the signs by the side of the road warning: "Take enough water for you and your car."

Our time on the ranch flew by. Everything was very informal. The next morning, we went for a walk. I noticed some mysterious white bags lying by the side of the road. Laura solved the puzzle for us: "They're wildflower seeds from our meadows. We've harvested them and we pass them on to other people."

Back at the house, we talked about political issues. My co-workers, who were staying in the nearby small town of Crawford, joined us. Bush's security officers cooked lunch for us on a barbecue. After a brief press conference at the ranch, Joachim and I made our way back by helicopter to Robert Gray Army Airfield, eighty kilometers away, where our plane was waiting for us.

In the helicopter, I thought about how George W. Bush had raved about the seven streams and nine bridges on the ranch. Or maybe it was nine streams and seven bridges; I might have mixed the numbers up. But it didn't really matter: the memory remained of streams, bridges, and nature as far as the eye could see. It had been rustic, relaxed, and simply beautiful.

The previous year, George W. Bush hadn't come to Germany just to visit me in Trinwillershagen, of course. In truth, the visit had been a stopover on his way to the G8 summit in Saint Petersburg. Bush and I met there again. The scene with the shoulder grip that went around the world is a very good example of how, at moments like these, it always depends on the context—on who's doing something, when and why, and whether there is fundamental trust between the people involved. If that's not the case, the same scene can be perceived in a completely different way. Bush and I, though, fundamentally trusted each other and we could now see how misleading images can be when they are isolated from the situation and the people in question.

It was my job to welcome Bush, Putin, and the five other leaders to the G8 summit in Heiligendamm. Before the actual summit began on June 7, 2007, I had arranged to meet Bush for lunch at one o'clock. The setting was a room in Burg

Hohenzollern, a building in the English Tudor style that was part of the Grand Hotel Kempinski complex in the beach resort of Heiligendamm. It had been chosen as the G8 venue during Gerhard Schröder's term of office—probably not with any thought for my convenience, that area being my constituency and political home. Any convenience would soon be forgotten, as a summit of this magnitude entailed the most unbelievable amount of security. In fact, among the public for days there had been practically nothing but talk about protests against the summit, about the multi-million-euro fence built to seal off the conference site, about the thousands of opponents to the meeting who had traveled there to block the roads or to try to get through the security zone. Not many people seemed interested in the actual agenda. It was wide-ranging, having been prepared months in advance. The subjects we wanted to cover varied from the conditions for global economic growth to the G8's responsibility for international development aid. We managed to discuss all of that, but there was also one more subject that did interest the public: climate change. Would the Group of Eight manage to agree on further action against global warming in Heiligendamm?

In 2007, Germany held both the G8's rotating presidency and the Council of the European Union's presidency for the first half of the year. At the European Council's meeting in March, the leaders had agreed on a course of action for the EU in international climate negotiations. A new road map was needed for the Kyoto Protocol, which was adopted in Japan in 1997 and named after the climate conference venue: it finally came into force in 2005 after Russia had ratified it the previous year, and it was due to expire in 2012. The European Council had adopted the goal of limiting the global average temperature increase to no more than 2 degrees Celsius above pre-industrial levels, and committed to reducing greenhouse gas emissions by 60 to 80 percent by 2050 compared to 1990 levels, provided that other industrialized countries did the same. Now I was expected to get the G8 to endorse the European decisions in Heiligendamm. It was unrealistic, but I felt it would be possible to take a step in this direction, and that was what I wanted to achieve. The United States was the key to success, and yet simultaneously my greatest challenge. In March 2001, just two months after taking office, President Bush had withdrawn US ratification of the Kyoto Protocol. As a result, the conditions for climate discussions in Heiligendamm were far from promising. A few weeks before the summit, in April 2007, I had traveled to Washington again. During that visit, Bush and I had spoken more in depth about the climate issue for the first time. Many people in his Republican Party categorically doubted the impact of humanity on global warming, and Bush himself was not convinced that the United States should commit itself to national goals at the UN. I, on the other hand, explained to him in detail that for Germany and Europe, the UN, where every country, large or small, had a vote, was where international agreements should be forged.

Christoph Heusgen, my foreign policy advisor, and Stephen Hadley, the president's national security advisor, also joined us for lunch in Heiligendamm. At one o'clock sharp, George W. Bush entered the room in high spirits. We sat down. While we were eating, we spoke English to each other; our interpreters were there with us just in case—Dorothee Kaltenbach on the German side. There, and throughout my chancellorship, she would guide me through many a tricky situation, and every now and then she'd take one of my rather garbled German sentences and put together something brilliant in English from it.

I opened the conversation, and intended to take the bull by the horns as quickly as possible, so I started talking about the difficult issue of climate change straight away. Bush seemed to be listening to me attentively. But when he replied, he began by heaping detailed praise on the place we were staying, asking about the security situation, and inquiring about the other attendees, especially about what I thought of Nicolas Sarkozy, who had become French president a few weeks earlier as Jacques Chirac's successor. Bush chatted and chatted. The time passed. Even the most delicious food didn't help. We only had sixty minutes, or at most seventy-five. Since my visit that April at the very latest, he'd known exactly what I wanted, but it seemed to give him a certain pleasure to skirt around my concerns for as long as possible.

Toward the end, we did talk about the issue—the reason I had invited him to lunch. Although I got the impression that he wouldn't let the G8 talks break down because of climate change, I still had a lot of work ahead of me if I was to achieve a result that could meet my standards and the European ones. At the press conference afterward, we both played our cards close to our chests when it came to the details. In the background, my government spokesman Ulrich Wilhelm told me Bush's staff had informed the press that there would be no specific targets for reducing greenhouse gases at the summit. It was what was known as "expectation management." Wait and see, I thought to myself.

After my meeting with the US president, I met the other summit attendees and discussed the agenda for the next two days. Shinzō Abe, the Japanese prime minister, had only been in office since September 2006. Japan was struggling to meet its national commitments to the Kyoto Protocol, but nevertheless agreed to the goal of at least halving greenhouse gas emissions by 2050, as did Stephen Harper, Canada's prime minister since February 2006. Vladimir Putin saw no problem with Russia fulfilling its national commitments. Romano Prodi had become Italian prime minister for the second time in May 2006. He had previously been president of the EU Commission from 1999 to 2004. I knew him from that time; I had visited him occasionally after my election as party chairman. He supported my efforts to achieve a significant result, as did the British prime minister

Tony Blair and José Manuel Barroso, president of the European Commission. In particular, I was hoping for support from Tony Blair for my cause when it came to George W. Bush. He would only be in office for a few more days: the handover to Gordon Brown, previously the UK's chancellor of the exchequer (finance minister), was agreed for June 27, 2007. Blair promised to do everything he could at breakfast with Bush the next morning to achieve an acceptable result, one that would help us protect the climate and the process after the Kyoto Protocol had expired.

Shortly before dinner, I was finally able to talk to Nicolas Sarkozy. We already knew each other as chairs of partner parties the CDU and UMP (Union pour un mouvement populaire, Union for a Popular Movement). On May 16, he visited me in Berlin immediately after taking office, marking German–French friendship. Now I was able to tell him about my conversation with George W. Bush and about my concerns. We spoke German and French, with interpreters. Sarkozy spoke quickly, both assuring me of his support and stressing that he personally couldn't afford any lazy compromises, as the first round of the French parliamentary elections would be taking place the following Sunday. He would rather leave the summit early than return to Paris with an unsatisfactory result.

On the same day, the G8 summit officially began with a dinner of the leaders and their partners at Hohen Luckow Manor, about twenty-five kilometers from Heiligendamm. Logistically speaking, this was an enormous challenge for the security forces, in view of the demonstrators. If I had known then what I know now about the burden on the police on occasions like these, I would never have planned a dinner outside the security zone. Nevertheless, I was, and am, convinced that summits of this kind are crucial if multilateral cooperation is to succeed and if globalization is to be guided in a politically astute way.

The G8 discussions

The next day, the official discussions began at ten o'clock. The eight leaders sat at a round table, and their economic advisors, known as the sherpas, took seats either behind them or in a separate room where the conversations were broadcast, a "listening room." We all used simultaneous interpreters, which meant the conversations could get very intense. We started with a session on the state of the global economy. The discussion was uncontentious and therefore didn't last as long as originally planned. So that morning we started talking about the sensitive issue of the climate. It wasn't due to be on the agenda until the afternoon session, at four o'clock.

Soon Nicolas Sarkozy, sitting two seats to my right, spoke up, repeating what he had said to me the night before. Now, once again, he concluded with the words: "If we don't reach an agreement, I'll have to leave the room and go home." There followed an embarrassed silence in the room. As host, I tried to say something conciliatory, but I had the impression that George W. Bush wasn't sure whether Sarkozy and I were playing a game with him at that moment. He slowly stood up, walked toward Sarkozy, and stood right behind him so that he could see me. That hadn't been possible from where he'd been sitting, or at least not as easily. His seat was next to mine, to the left, and as I hadn't turned to him at that point, he hadn't been able to look me in the eye, and I had not indicated in any other way how I felt about what Sarkozy had said. I had neither encouraged Sarkozy nor contradicted him. Bush now clearly wanted to find out what was going on. From his new viewpoint, he calmly said, "Like everyone else here, I represent my country's position. I am interested in a compromise within my scope, but I too can leave in response to the positions Europeans confront me with. I don't intend to do that, but of course everyone is free to leave the table." The interpreters couldn't translate what Bush had said—they didn't hear him, as he hadn't spoken into the microphone at his seat. But everyone could speak English well enough to understand, even without a translation. The US president's words hit home. Sarkozy stayed in the room rather than getting up and leaving, Bush returned to his seat, and we carried on with our work.

We agreed that our sherpas would work out some potential drafts for a compromise during the lunch break. Immediately after his breakfast with George W. Bush, Tony Blair had told me he had the impression there was potentially scope for agreement. After that, I was cautiously confident that we could achieve a result. At around 2:30 p.m., I was presented with a draft in which the G8 stated that tackling climate change was one of the greatest challenges facing humanity, that it had noted the latest Intergovernmental Panel on Climate Change's report with concern, that the United Nations was the appropriate forum for negotiating future global action on climate change, and that the G8 would seriously consider the decisions made by the European Union, Canada, and Japan to halve global emissions by 2050. The text didn't mention any figures, but seriously considering halving emissions was a significant step toward halving them: the goal was at least 50 percent by 2050.

I rang Beate Baumann, who was back in Berlin, following the reports from there. In all the years we worked together, she only rarely came with me on trips. Her office was the best place for her to ensure I was in constant communication with the Chancellery's departments, while at the same time she could keep an eye on what was happening beyond the Reichstag's dome. This was how she saw her brief as the chancellor's office manager. It helped me enormously. As I was on the phone to her, I asked her what she thought of our draft. She had a good sense of what was acceptable and what wasn't, and never shied away from telling me directly, one way or the other. When I read the text out to her in English, the G8's working language, she was impressed straight away. "You need to send that out quick; it's really good," she encouraged me. And she was right: the result was deemed to be a resounding success, and at last there was talk from the meeting's opponents about its content again and not just about demonstrations.

After the morning's session and a meeting with young people from the G8 countries, the next item on the agenda was a picture of the attendees: the obligatory "family photo" at summits of this kind—normally a rather tiresome chore. Here, though, everyone was happy to take part, just because the oldest beach chair manufacturer in Heringsdorf on the island of Usedom had woven a traditional German wicker beach chair for us—an oversized one, so we could all sit side by side.

Eight years later, in July 2015, when it was my turn to host another summit of the major industrialized nations and we met in Elmau in Bavaria, an extra-long wooden bench had been made for the "family photo," harking back to the Heiligendamm beach chair. President Barack Obama, successor to George W. Bush and in office since January 2009, and I were at the bench a few minutes before the others. He sat down and made himself comfortable, stretching his arms out along the backrest. A photo of the scene was reproduced and circulated widely. I was standing in front of him, trying to explain what that bench reminded me of. Unfortunately, though, I didn't know the English term "beach chair" at that time, and Dorothee Kaltenbach wasn't at hand. Lacking the right words, I gestured with my arms and spread them farther and farther apart to indicate the size of the thing I was talking about. Barack Obama was laughing, but I'm certain he couldn't understand a word of what I was trying to tell him. Later, I showed him a picture from the Heiligendamm days, and I learned a new phrase: "wicker beach chair."

Waiting for Vladimir Putin

Before dinner, I wanted to meet with the seven other leaders for an aperitif. The weather was lovely, and we could sit outside. The journalists were keen for images that would convey the atmosphere among the attendees. So we agreed that one camera team from each country in the group could film us, out of earshot. The cameramen were delighted to be able to capture us during our animated discussions. But there was just one person missing: Vladimir Putin. We waited and waited. If there's one thing I can't stand, it's people being late. Why was he doing that? Who did he want to prove something to? Or did he have a genuine problem? Outwardly, I was having a relaxed chat with the others; inwardly, I was seething. After our working dinner, there was due to be an informal get-together with our partners. It would be a shame if everything had to be postponed.

I was about to say that we'd just go to dinner without him and have another photo session later on the pier, when Putin showed up, at least forty-five minutes late.

"What was the matter?" I asked him.

"It's your fault—well, Radeberger's, to be precise."

Before the summit, he had asked to have a crate of Radeberger beer, which he loved, in his room. He was familiar with it from his time as a KGB officer in Dresden in the 1980s. We had gone along with his request. Now, he said with a grin, he'd had no choice but to drink it, of course. That was what I got in return for being so amenable. He seemed to enjoy being the center of attention by behaving like that. The cherry on the cake was probably making the US president wait for him too.

As CDU chair, I had also met Vladimir Putin during our time in opposition, in June 2000, when he was on a visit to Berlin. The first time we met in the Kremlin was in February 2002. I can't remember either meeting, but I do have much more vivid memories of the eighth annual German–Russian intergovernmental consultations a few months after I took office as chancellor. On April 26, 2006, I flew to Tomsk, Siberia, together with some of the cabinet ministers and a group of business representatives. It was my first ever trip to Siberia and it would remain my only one, apart from the occasional layover on the way back from Japan or China. Tomsk, a city with about 500,000 inhabitants, including around 5,000 Russian Germans, is located on the River Tom, a tributary of the 3,650-kilometer-long River Ob, which flows into the Kara Sea, a marginal sea of the Arctic Ocean. In Tomsk, the Tom is several hundred meters wide. April was when the ice melted. At one point, between appointments, I asked the driver to stop for a moment, and the entire delegation got out of their vehicles. For a few minutes we absorbed the natural spectacle; the ice was on the verge of breaking into lots of smaller pieces. It was making a considerable noise; all along the river it was creaking and crunching, and many of the city's inhabitants were sitting on benches taking it all in. I felt an urge to sit down there, too. I was thinking how I would have liked to take a boat to the mouth of one of the great Siberian rivers—the Ob, the Yenisey, or the Lena. Until then, I'd only dreamed of a trip from Moscow to Vladivostok on the Trans-Siberian Railway, and I still haven't gotten around to doing that either. After a few minutes we had to take our leave of the Tom, get back into our vehicles, and go on to the next meeting.

In the evening, Vladimir Putin invited me to dinner in a park on the outskirts of the city. Only the two of us and our foreign policy advisors were at the table. The interpreters were sitting at the next table in case they were needed, but Putin was speaking in German. His German was better than my Russian; my knowledge of Russian was stuck in the GDR era, and I wasn't familiar with democratic political vocabulary. That evening we talked about how we felt about our two countries. It was clear that we'd been on different sides in the past, but we also had different views on how Russia was developing at that point. I expressed concern that democratic freedoms in Russia were being increasingly restricted; a law that made the work of non-governmental organizations more difficult had just come into force. Putin rejected this suggestion.

For dinner, I had a choice between a classic steak and a brown bear one, and I adventurously opted for the unknown. As far as I can remember, the bear meat tasted very good: it was strong and gamey. It was something quite special.

The next day, there was a forum of German and Russian business representatives. Topics included the construction of the Nord Stream 1 pipeline, collaboration in the automotive and agricultural machinery sectors, and Russia's negotiations to join the World Trade Organization (WTO). The group focused heavily on the two countries working together on energy. In 2005, Russia provided 41 percent of Germany's natural gas and 32 percent of its crude oil import requirements. The relationship between the Soviet Union and the old West Germany had been reliable when it came to energy supply for over forty years, even during the Cold War. The previously one-sided flow of raw materials from Russia was due to be safeguarded in the long term through a partnership with mutual dependencies. BASF and Gazprom signed a basic agreement for a minority stake in the Yuzhno-Russkoye gas field in Siberia. At the intergovernmental consultations afterward, the German and Russian ministers reported on their bilateral talks and progress on joint projects, such as the German–Russian education initiative, which was signed by Putin and Schröder in April 2005 as part of the strategic partnership.

After the government consultations were over, Putin offered to take me to the airport in his car. On the way, he pointed to some areas with typical Russian wooden houses, and explained that the people living there didn't have much money and were therefore very easily misled. In Ukraine, he said, these were exactly the kind of people who had been encouraged to take part in the Orange Revolution in the fall of 2004 by money given to them by the US government. "I will never allow anything like that to happen in Russia," Putin said, if I remember rightly.

"But back in East Germany, it wasn't money from the States that drew us into a peaceful revolution," I replied. "We wanted it, and it changed our lives for the better. That's precisely what the people in Ukraine wanted."

Putin changed the subject. "Do you know an important difference between the US and Russian constitutions?" he then asked me.

I had no idea where he was going with that.

"In both constitutions, the presidency is limited to two terms," he continued, "but in the States, a second re-election after an interruption of the presidency is not allowed. The Russian president can be re-elected after two terms in office, as long as he takes a break."

The message I got from those few words of Putin's on that Siberian spring day in 2006 on the way to the airport was: "Don't think I'm gone, even if in two years I hand over my office to a successor after two terms in office, in accordance with my constitution—I'll be back, I'm just taking a break." I didn't comment on what Putin had said, but I knew exactly where I stood. When we arrived at the airport, Putin only stopped the car when we reached my plane. We said our goodbyes, and I flew home to Berlin.

Nine months later, on January 21, 2007, I visited Vladimir Putin at his residence in the city of Sochi on the Black Sea. In our meeting, he snapped at me that the Soviet Union's collapse was, to him, the greatest geopolitical disaster of the twentieth century. This was nothing new: he had already expressed this publicly in 2005 in his state of the union address. Now, though, one accusation followed another. For several minutes, Putin ranted about the 2003 Iraq War, about the National Missile Defense (NMD) system planned by the United States, including their planned deployments in Poland and the Czech Republic, and he angrily calculated the ranges of Iranian missiles to prove how absurd this missile shield was. He was referring to the US plans for a global missile defense system, unveiled by George W. Bush in May 2001, a few months after taking office. Bush had followed on from President Reagan's 1983 Strategic Defense Initiative (SDI) and the 1999 National Missile Defense Act, which had been directed against "rogue states" such as Iran and North Korea. After the Islamist attacks on the United States on September 11, 2001, developing a missile defense system of this kind had become even more important for Bush. Putin, though, insisted that the system was directed against Russia too. Sitting there in Sochi, I let him finish and tried to stay calm. Then I replied that he should speak to George W. Bush about the missile system, stressing that in fact the biggest disaster of the twentieth century had been Nazism in Germany, and that the end of the Cold War had changed my life for the better in a way I had never expected.

During my stay in Sochi, Putin also showed the public how he intended to make his mark on another level—even if it meant calling on the help of his black Labrador Koni. He often had his dog with him when foreign guests were visiting. Since my inaugural visit in January 2006, Putin had known I was afraid of dogs after I had been bitten by one close to home in early 1995. Christoph Heusgen had informed his Russian counterpart Sergei Prikhodko about it and asked for Putin not to bring his dog. In Moscow in 2006, he had respected this request, although not without a little dig: as a special gift he had presented me with a large stuffed dog, telling me it didn't bite. All I could do was grin and bear it. I passed the toy on to Christoph Heusgen, who had to carry it around for what felt like an eternity before a German protocol officer could be found to take it off his hands.

In Sochi in 2007 though, his Labrador Koni entered the stage, in the flesh. While Putin and I sat and posed for the photographers and camera crews getting their photos and clips at the start of the meeting, I tried to ignore the dog, even though it was by and large directly next to me. I could tell from Putin's facial expressions that he was enjoying the situation. Did he just want to see how someone reacts under pressure? Was it a little demonstration of power? Stay calm, focus on the photographers, it won't be for long, I just kept thinking to myself. When it was finally over, I didn't say a word to Putin about it, adhering instead, as I've often done throughout my life, to the British maxim associated with their royal family: "Never explain, never complain."

In Heiligendamm five months later, I did it again when Vladimir Putin kept us waiting. I let the Radeberger incident go, swallowed my anger, and asked everyone for a second "family photo" on the pier. Bush and Putin used the summit after the afternoon sessions to talk about the US missile defense program, which was such a bone of contention between the two of them. I was very pleased about that. Putin suggested that the Americans could abandon their plans for missile defense in Poland and the Czech Republic and instead cooperate with Russia, share a radar station in Azerbaijan, and deploy defense missiles in Turkey, Iraq, or at sea. That would reassure him that the system was, in fact, only directed against "rogue states" and not against Russia too, and the States wouldn't need to involve the Czech Republic and Poland. George W. Bush declared that he would examine these proposals. Two years later, in 2009, Bush's successor, Barack Obama, modified the entire program when he took office. Among other changes, sea-based interceptor missiles were then to replace the systems intended for Poland, and a planned radar station in the Czech Republic was dropped altogether.

GLOBAL ECONOMIC CRISIS

Armida and IKB

SIX WEEKS LATER. Saturday, July 28, 2007, approximately 7:25 p.m., the Felsenreitschule, Salzburg. Along with our friends Ilse and Martin Bartenstein, Joachim and I were looking forward to the premiere of Joseph Haydn's opera *Armida* at the Salzburg Festival. We'd just taken our seats in the auditorium. A few moments before the lights were due to be dimmed, I took my cell phone out of my purse to quickly check for messages. I couldn't believe it—even though it was a Saturday evening, my economic advisor Jens Weidmann had sent me a brief text message: "Problems with IKB. Can we talk?" Weidmann had been head of the Chancellery's directorate for economic and financial policy since the beginning of 2006. At just thirty-nine, he already had an impressive career under his belt. As an economist, he had previously worked at the International Monetary Fund (IMF), as secretary general of the German Council of Economic Experts, and as a departmental head at the Bundesbank. If Weidmann was sending me a message at that time on a Saturday, it had to be about something important. I opened my opera program to see when the interval would be: around 8:50 p.m., I read. I quickly replied: "At the opera. Will ring before 9." The performance began. Meanwhile, thoughts were rattling around in my head: *What's IKB?* The abbreviation didn't mean a thing to me.

During the interval, I immediately looked for a quiet spot and rang Jens Weidmann. "What's happened? And more to the point, what's IKB?" I asked him. He explained: IKB Deutsche Industriebank AG was a Düsseldorf-based credit institution, its roots dating back to the 1920s. The bank focused particularly on providing long-term investment loans to medium-sized companies and passed on money from public funding programs to its customers. It also functioned as a pass-through bank for the Kreditanstalt für Wiederaufbau (KfW), the government's development bank, which was IKB's largest single shareholder at the time. KfW was, and still is, a public institution and executes orders from the German government and the federal states. It supports small and medium-sized enterprises, freelancers, and start-ups, and it finances infrastructure projects, housing construction, and environmental protection with loans, among other things. I knew it from my time as minister for the environment.

"So what's happened to IKB?" I asked Weidmann.

"In 2002, IKB founded a special purpose entity in the States called Rhineland Funding, offering subprime real-estate loan products, in other words loans for customers with low credit ratings, on the US market. IKB has given this company liquidity guarantees amounting to €8.1 billion," Weidmann replied, before moving on to the actual problem: "In the spring, the market for these loans in the States slumped into a crisis because of rising interest rates and falling real-estate prices. As a result, this special purpose entity's investments have lost a lot of value. There's a risk that it will have to call on IKB's guarantees as a result of its losses. But IKB hasn't taken the precautions it should have for this kind of situation. So yesterday Deutsche Bank decided not to extend its credit facility with IKB and informed the Federal Financial Supervisory Authority. Now there's a threat of bankruptcy hanging over IKB."

"OK, what does that mean for us?" I asked.

"Steinbrück's going to have a conference call with everyone involved tomorrow to talk about how they can avoid bankruptcy. It could spark a chain reaction of bankruptcies on the German banking market. I thought you ought to know so you don't hear it from anyone else," Weidmann concluded.

He had a great gift for explaining the most complicated issues quickly, precisely, and comprehensibly, never losing his cool and being able to assess economic and financial policy issues with a keen sense of general politics. He had heard the news from Jörg Asmussen, head of the ministry of finance's department for national and international financial and monetary policy. The finance minister Peer Steinbrück had asked him to inform me. Weidmann and I agreed that a chain reaction had to be avoided at all costs.

The bell was already ringing to indicate the end of the interval when I asked Weidmann how the problem could be solved.

"Well," he said, "someone better off needs to take over IKB's guarantees. It probably won't be possible without KfW getting involved, which indirectly means the government will too. But we want some support from the private banks too."

That made sense to me. The state and private banks had a common interest in a stable financial system. "Keep me posted, and wish Steinbrück the best of luck for the talks tomorrow," I said to him.

"Will do," he replied.

I knew that, with him, the problem was in good hands, but I couldn't get his explanations out of my head during the second half of the opera. But at that time, the thought that what Weidmann had just told me might have a domino effect and take the world to the edge of the abyss was beyond my imagination.

By the time the stock markets opened on the Monday, IKB's problem had been solved, with KfW as well as public and private banks taking over its risks. In hindsight, I think back on that weekend, the weekend when IKB had to be saved, as the beginning of the international financial crisis.

In the weeks that followed, I primarily attended engagements that had long been planned. At the end of the German G8 presidency, I visited Greenland with the minister for the environment Sigmar Gabriel; I traveled to China, Japan, and, for the first time, Africa. There I met my Ethiopian equivalent, Prime Minister Meles Zenawi, in the capital, Addis Ababa, and gave a speech at the African Union (AU) headquarters. In South Africa I was a guest of the former president Nelson Mandela, and in Liberia I met the only female president in Africa, Ellen Johnson Sirleaf. I flew to India and to George W. Bush's ranch; I hosted the Dalai Lama and King Abdullah from Saudi Arabia in Berlin; and I had to deal with a domestic political shock when Franz Müntefering resigned from his ministerial office on November 13, 2007. He had decided to give it up to take care of his sick wife. I fully understood and respected his decision, but it was a great loss to the government that I had to overcome. The new minister of labor was Olaf Scholz, at that time first parliamentary secretary of the Bundestag's SPD party, and the foreign minister Frank-Walter Steinmeier became the new vice chancellor. In the meantime, the new government had been in office for two years, and so was halfway through its term. We were able to demonstrate decent results: the budget was consolidated, and the unemployment rate was down. But we were plagued by storm clouds.

Three months later, in February 2008, IKB ran into difficulties again, and cracks in its financing had opened up once more. And IKB wasn't an isolated case. In the previous weeks, interest rates on the loans that banks issued to each other had been rising more and more sharply—a sign that financial institutions had less confidence in one another. So, in a government statement on February 15, the finance minister Peer Steinbrück emphasized on behalf of the government that it was essential not to let IKB go under, and then he broadened his focus: "Every credit institution that has dealt with subprime market securities is affected by this crisis. The bad news is that no one yet knows exactly which institutions are impacted and to what extent. [. . .] So far, the effects of the global financial market turbulence on the German economy and therefore on the current federal budget have been manageable. So far. There is reason to believe that this will continue to be the case."

Steinbrück had issued a warning, but he hadn't yet needed to sound the alarm. I didn't think it was a state of emergency either. I accepted an invitation from the Israeli parliament to be the first foreign head of government ever to give a speech in the Knesset; I took part in the NATO summit in Bucharest; I received the International Charlemagne Prize of Aachen for my services toward European unification; I traveled to Brazil, Peru, Colombia, and Mexico; I went to Paris for the launch of the Union for the Mediterranean; I visited Algeria; and on July 24, 2008, I met a young US senator, Barack Obama. As the Democratic Party's candidate for the presidential election on November 4, 2008, he had requested a meeting with me, and he was planning to give a speech in front of the Brandenburg Gate in Berlin. The election campaign was underway in the States. Senator John McCain was the Republican presidential candidate; George W. Bush was unable to run again after two terms in office. Thomas de Maizière, the head of the Chancellery, told me that the state of Berlin, formally responsible for approving events in the capital, had asked whether we agreed to the speech's location. It wasn't just anywhere; it had a special significance, and Obama wasn't yet president: he was a candidate, no more, no less. "No," I dismissed it, "I don't agree with it. Where do we want to draw a line going forward? Are presidential candidates from other countries giving campaign speeches in front of the Lincoln Memorial in Washington? Anywhere else in Berlin is fine, but not in that special place, if I'm able to have a say on this issue." It wasn't about Barack Obama for me: on the contrary, I was intrigued by him. From what I had heard and read about him, he was an extraordinary presidential candidate. He captivated people with his speeches, especially the young. And I thought it would be great for the States to be governed by an African American president for the first time. His election could be the key to a new coexistence in the United States, I thought. But now, the question I had been asked to decide on was about something else. Should every halfway respectable candidate for another country's presidency be given the opportunity to make a campaign speech in front of the Brandenburg Gate from now on? Maybe if it were someone else, it might not be quite as appropriate? No, I thought it was wrong and I didn't want to let the Brandenburg Gate become the backdrop for election campaign appearances, not even for a US presidential candidate. I was harshly criticized in public for my refusal, but I could live with that. In the end, Obama made his speech in front of the Victory Column to a crowd of 200,000; it was highly acclaimed.

After this shaky start, I was all the keener for the two of us to get to know each other personally. A tall, slim man came into my office with a spring in his step and an open smile. We greeted each other and sat down in the seating area by the window. Barack Obama spoke with great calm, emphasizing the importance of German–US relations. We were talking in English. I asked him how he saw his chances in the election campaign. He said it didn't look bad.

As he was leaving, he asked me, "Do you have children?"

"No," I replied, "but my husband has two sons."

"My wife, Michelle, and I have two daughters, Sasha and Malia. I couldn't do it all without them," he said.

I told him about Joachim. "My husband still works as an academic, and yet I know he's supported my career in politics from day one."

After that first meeting, I was convinced that Barack Obama and I could work well together if he won the presidential election.

Worldwide turbulence

A few weeks later, it was early September 2008; while the US election campaign was in full swing, the banking crisis in the States was peaking once again. On September 7, 2007, the Bush administration nationalized the two mortgage banks Fannie Mae and Freddie Mac. Together, they had issued around $5.2 trillion in loans on the US real-estate market, completely over-stretched themselves, and were now on the verge of collapse. The state stepped in, and taxpayers were to pay for the damage. "Too big to fail" seemed to be the response to the private banks' failure; in other words, a government couldn't afford to let such large banks become bankrupt because the potential risks for the economy were too great. This decision wasn't immune to public criticism, and there was no end in sight—it went on to get much worse.

The next bank to get into trouble was Lehman Brothers, the fourth-largest investment bank in the United States. It offered credit products all over the world. The US government once again faced the issue of whether to bail out a bank—and with it, many customers' capital, both at home and in other countries. However, it chose to set an example and decided against it. Would a bailout have changed the course of the financial crisis further down the line? It's hard to say in hindsight. As the financial sector did not see itself as being in a position to support Lehman Brothers, the bank filed for bankruptcy during the night of Sunday, September 14, and Monday, September 15, 2008. The consequences were dramatic, with massive turbulence on the stock markets worldwide.

The US secretary of the treasury was Henry M. Paulson. I had met him on my trip to the States when I was opposition leader shortly before the Iraq War began, at the end of February 2003. Back then, I had visited him in his office in New York. I'd been interested in the financial sector in the States, and Paulson had been recommended to me as someone interesting to talk to about it. At the time, he wasn't in politics yet; he was chairman of the board at the investment bank Goldman Sachs. When I saw him on TV, speaking on the news about the financial crisis, I remembered our meeting in 2003. He had sat before me, asking one question after another, his office chair constantly rocking back and forth. I had trouble getting a word in edgewise to ask anything myself. He was particularly interested in why on earth the eurozone countries had imposed a stability pact on themselves, forcing them to limit new debt to 3 percent of their GDP (gross domestic product) and total government debt to 60 percent of their GDP per year. My response that it was important to do business sustainably out of responsibility for future generations, especially on a continent with an aging population, had only made him break into a broad grin. Neither was he convinced by the suggestion that a currency common to several sovereign states needed firm safeguards. He had seemed arrogant to me. In my eyes, he was now the face of the financial crisis.

After the worldwide turbulence caused by Lehman Brothers' bankruptcy, the US government decided to save another case from a similar fate just one day later, on Tuesday, September 16, 2008, and almost entirely nationalized one of the largest insurance companies, the American International Group, Inc., because of its equally major problems.

The next day, Wednesday, September 17, I spoke in the budget debate in the Bundestag. Right at the beginning of my speech, I addressed the crisis on the financial market and said: "The federal government is following this development very closely. We are in constant contact with the heads of the German banking industry as well as with other governments. As a result, on Monday, the Bundesbank, the Federal Financial Supervisory Authority, and the ministry of finance were able to confirm that the involvement of German credit institutions in the investment bank Lehman Brothers is fortunately within manageable limits." Speaking about the consequences for the rest of the German economy, I added: "Nevertheless, an open economy like Germany's, which in fact benefits from globalization more than others, will not be able to remain completely unscathed." Will not be able to remain completely unscathed: that would later turn out to be a massive understatement, but at this point it was still too early to tell.

Another two days later, on September 19, the US government announced a bailout program for the financial sector, and on September 20, its magnitude became known: $700 billion.

Just over a week later, on Sunday, September 28, the CSU lost its absolute majority in the Bavarian state elections. Under normal circumstances, the part played by the Berlin government in the CSU's poor result would have been discussed at length. But these were not normal times. That weekend, another bank in Germany was in difficulties: Hypo Real Estate Holding GmbH (HRE), listed on the DAX (the German stock index). HRE had to be bailed out, to the tune of €35 billion. The banking supervisory authority and the ministry of finance spent the entire Sunday holding talks with HRE and the private banks on how the rescue costs should be distributed. Late that evening, Steinbrück rang, asking me to call the chair of the board at Deutsche Bank, Josef Ackermann, as he wasn't happy with the private banks' contribution to HRE's rescue, but he couldn't persuade them to improve on it. Although Ackermann wasn't chair of the Association of German Banks, he seemed to be the one person who could coordinate decisions because of Deutsche Bank's importance. So we spoke on the phone. After some toing

and froing as well as more discussions with Steinbrück,
Ackermann and I finally agreed on the private banks contributing a guarantee of €8.5 billion; the state took over the
guarantee for the remaining €26.5 billion to make up the entire
€35 billion needed to save HRE. Those discussions infuriated
me. The finance minister and I had to bow down before the
banks and run around picking up the scraps they had thrown in
our direction. That evening, and in the following weeks and
months, I had to talk myself into it again and again: as governments, we weren't there to serve bankers—we did it because
bailing out banks served a functioning economy, and because,
as a result, we were helping to safeguard savers' assets and jobs
for millions of people.

But if we thought that the financial markets would now
calm down, we were mistaken. Even though the G8 countries'
central banks agreed to make money available to each other and
to lower key interest rates, even though the US government had
announced a rescue package, and even though all the leading
industrialized countries were rescuing banks in difficulty, the
financial markets remained unstable. They clearly wanted to
enforce a kind of general guarantee, with every government
having to assume responsibility for all their financial institutions' risks. Before this was in place, turbulence on the stock
markets meant the banks would no longer lend money to each
other, which would have been tantamount to economies
collapsing worldwide. The financial institutions had no interest
in whether their expectations of governments would get themselves or the central banks into fresh difficulties in the short or
long term. The bank managers even turned the tables. They
behaved as if it was our, the politicians', fault—we had made
these events possible in the first place, through our lax regulation of the financial market's products. And unfortunately, they
were not completely wrong. In 2007, during our German G8
presidency, we tried in vain to agree on regulations for more

transparency on the financial markets, but had failed in the face of resistance from the US and the UK. But complaining about it did nothing to help with the ongoing situation, where in fact only national governments could save the world from collapsing economies. When it came to the financial markets, hoping for ethically appropriate behavior from the market players had proven to be nothing but an illusion. When I published my first article on the social market economy in 1990, I could never have imagined a market failure on this scale. Deep down, every bone in my body resisted having to pay for the banks' mistakes with taxpayers' money. But it was futile. We had to do everything possible to restore confidence in the financial markets.

The savings holders' guarantee

An opportunity to do so arose the following Sunday, on October 5, 2008. A coalition meeting of the party and parliamentary group chairs had long been planned for three o'clock that afternoon. From one o'clock onward, I was in the morning briefing room with Thomas de Maizière and Ulrich Wilhelm preparing for it. At around half past one, Jens Weidmann called me. He told me he was at the ministry of finance with Peer Steinbrück, the finance minister, Jörg Asmussen, now state secretary at the ministry of finance, and Axel Weber, president of the Bundesbank. "Can Steinbrück and I come and see you before the coalition meeting?" he asked. "Of course, see you in a while," I replied. Weidmann didn't need to say any more: I could tell from his voice that it was urgent.

Half an hour later, he and Steinbrück came in. Steinbrück told me that Weber was very worried as many more customers than usual had withdrawn cash from ATMs over the weekend. "Weber suggests that we signal to savings account holders in Germany that the government will protect their savings. I think we need to do it before it's too late. It ought to happen today. That's why I'm here."

I was dismayed, and I asked: "Aren't we triggering the exact opposite by giving this kind of message to the people? Won't it scare the ones who aren't already scared?"

"We can't rule that out with 100 percent certainty," Steinbrück replied. "Still, I think Weber's right," he continued, reminding me of the previous September, when the British bank Northern Rock had to extend its opening hours so that panicking customers could withdraw their money. In the end, the situation had only calmed down when Chancellor of the Exchequer Alistair Darling issued a guarantee to protect customers' deposits. Steinbrück said, "That's exactly why we should make a statement today."

I felt a little queasy. "Who is 'we'? Do you want to do it, as finance minister?" I asked.

He shook his head: "I don't think it'll be enough. They'll all be asking what the chancellor has to say about it. And then you'll be asked anyway. The news will be talked down before it's reached the people in full, and before you repeat what I've said. We'll never get any peace."

That made sense to me. "Then we'll do it together and make sure we both keep to the same story," I replied.

Ulrich Wilhelm invited a press pool to the Chancellery's "sky lobby" for 2:30 p.m. In the meantime, Steinbrück and I thought about what we were going to say and made sure we kept our messages in line with each other's. We couldn't sound panicked, nor could we use such convoluted phrases that our message wouldn't be understood. When we were ready, Steinbrück and I nodded to each other before going over to the window in the eighth-floor "sky lobby", with its view out over the Reichstag. We both spoke openly. We had memorized everything we'd set out to say. I spoke first, and I began by talking about a meeting I'd had the day before in Paris with the Italian, British, and French heads of government. The main focus was on stricter regulation of the financial markets. I said that we were working hard to secure HRE, and I promised that those liable in the industry would be held accountable for any irresponsible behavior. Then I uttered the decisive sentence: "We're here to tell savings account holders that your deposits are safe. The federal government assures it." Steinbrück followed and, as agreed, explained in more detail: "I'd like to stress that, with the collective responsibility we feel in the federal government, we do indeed want to ensure that savings account holders in Germany need not worry about losing one euro of their deposits." Together we had formulated a clear message. We didn't take questions.

Steinbrück and I left the room. I chaired the coalition committee meeting, where we made some decisions on domestic policy. He went back to the ministry of finance to carry on the work to secure HRE, which was completed before the Tokyo stock exchange opened on the Monday morning. That Monday, at 6:30 p.m., we informed all the chairs of the parties and parliamentary groups represented in the Bundestag about the HRE situation and the guarantee to savers. The government spokesman Ulrich Wilhelm and Torsten Albig, Steinbrück's press spokesman, were bombarded with questions about details of the savers' guarantee over the next few days. But whatever they were asked, they always made it clear that the promise would stand and was permanent. And it worked: there was no run on the banks. People seemed to trust our statement. To me, that trust felt like something precious that I had to carefully nurture and protect.

The rescue package

The following week, Steinbrück flew to Washington for the IMF and World Bank annual meetings. We spoke to each other on the phone several times, as the markets clearly weren't calming down at all in response to the arrangements made so far on a case-by-case basis, such as for HRE. Financial market stakeholders wanted to impose universal rescue packages to ensure that every bank in difficulty could be safeguarded. Rarely have I felt as strongly as I did at that point that I was no longer truly free to make a decision, that I only had a choice between two evils, and that it was crucial for me to avoid the greater of those evils: the collapse of the banks, with unforeseeable consequences for national economies and, as a result, for the people. Within a few days, we conjured what would become the Financial Market Stabilization Act from thin air. It was to be passed as quickly as possible in the Bundestag and Bundesrat. A special fund for financial market stabilization was to be established and ring-fenced from the federal budget. It was to include €100 billion in capital and guarantees of up to €400 billion—unimaginably huge amounts.

Nicolas Sarkozy had invited me to Colombey-les-Deux-Églises on Saturday, October 11, 2008 for the unveiling of a new memorial to the former French president Charles de Gaulle. It was here that de Gaulle, then prime minister of France, had met Konrad Adenauer for the first time, fifty years earlier, at his country estate and extended a hand of friendship. As Sarkozy, who was also president of the EU Council at the time, and I had quite different ideas on the current financial crisis, the journey to this place was symbolically important to me. Sarkozy favored a joint rescue package by the eurozone countries, whereas I had rejected it and spoke out in support of them taking a coordinated but nationally autonomous approach. It seemed to me that the circumstances in the individual countries were too varied, and that the level of coordination required was too great in view of the time pressure we were under. Sarkozy also wanted to coordinate economic policy in the eurozone more closely. I supported this idea, but I opposed the phrase "economic government" that he was using for it. I was worried that he wanted to exert too much state influence on industry and that he was keen to persuade us to do the same. In hindsight, it was petty to reject the term "economic government," and I could have agreed to it. On the issue itself, we managed to align our opinions over lunch together. That was crucial: Sarkozy, as president of the EU Council, had already invited the eurozone's heads of government and finance ministers, as well as the president of the European Central Bank Jean-Claude Trichet, to Paris the very next day to prepare for the upcoming EU Council meeting on October 15 and 16.

In the heat of the moment, I had forgotten to tell the speaker Norbert Lammert that the government intended to introduce the Financial Market Stabilization Bill in the Bundestag and Bundesrat with especially tight deadlines. I suddenly realized my oversight after I flew back to Berlin from France on the Saturday afternoon and then went on to Hohenwalde: as soon as I arrived home, Norbert Lammert was on the phone. He had learned about the plan from press reports and he was now sarcastically asking me how I thought the debate would go. At first, I mentioned the coalition party chairs Volker Kauder (CDU), Peter Struck (SPD), and Peter Ramsauer (CSU), who would be discussing it all with him shortly. But I quickly realized that as chancellor I should have talked to the speaker about the tour de force we had in mind. So I told him our plan: we wanted to take the bill to the cabinet on the Monday and to the parties on the Tuesday; the first reading in parliament was to take place on the Wednesday and the second and third readings on the Friday, with the committees meeting in between. For a law of such financial magnitude, it was a really ambitious undertaking. I was very relieved when Lammert promised me he would lobby the opposition parties for the tight schedule. In fact, he managed to get every party to agree to it.

When the debate began on the Wednesday, I gave a

government statement. "Something that rarely happens has come about: the government was, and is, the only authority to restore trust between the banks, to protect our citizens, not to protect banking interests. We are therefore fulfilling our duty to defend the German people from harm and to promote their welfare," I said, echoing the oath of office made by all ministers. Then I explained the rescue package, before speaking about the need to restructure the international regulatory framework for financial markets. I proposed that a group of experts should convene with the finance minister so that we could be well prepared for the next international meetings. I suggested it could be headed by the former Bundesbank president Hans Tietmeyer. I had neglected to run this last idea by Steinbrück beforehand. The proposal provoked outrage even as I was speaking. Shortly afterward, I learned that Tietmeyer was on HRE's supervisory board and was also persona non grata for some Social Democrats since he had played a major role in drafting the paper disbanding the social-liberal coalition in 1982, as ministerial director at the ministry of finance at the time. I hadn't been aware of that. I withdrew that proposal that very day, and Hans Tietmeyer also abstained from taking on the role. It was a lesson to me never again to suggest someone for a post without first checking with other people, no matter how exemplary a job title like "former Bundesbank president" might be at first glance. The expert group was eventually chaired by Otmar Issing, the European Central Bank's former chief economist.

Despite the rescue package's tight schedule and the huge sums involved, the debate in the Bundestag was concluded on Friday, October 17. At 10:08 a.m., Speaker Lammert announced the result of the vote: "Votes cast: 576. 476 voted 'Yes,' 99 voted 'No,' and 1 abstained." Immediately afterward, the Bundesrat approved the bill. Even the day before, Steinbrück and I had been negotiating with the federal state premiers about distributing the costs between the federal and state governments. We had agreed that the states would bear 35 percent of the costs, although this amount was capped at 7.7 billion. On the Friday afternoon, President Köhler signed the law. The constitutional organs of the Federal Government, the Bundestag, the Bundesrat, and the president had shown that together they were capable of working quickly in our hour of need. I was proud of my country.

By the end of 2017, the bank bailout costs for the taxpayer would add up to €59 billion.

Jobs

No sooner had the financial markets stabilized to some extent than the devastating impact of the banking crisis on the actual economy and on jobs around the globe became more evident with every passing day. From mid-October 2008, calls for programs to stimulate the economy could be heard from all directions, within political parties, unions, and the media. The gist of it was that if the state had supported the financial industry with that much money, it would now have to do the same for other sectors of the economy and the jobs associated with them. What people overlooked was that the money for the banks was also money for functioning credit markets, which benefited small, medium-sized, and large companies. And there was no mention of the risks arising from the ever-increasing national debt. I was reluctant to simply spend a lot of money just to demonstrate my ability to take action. Above all, I didn't want to commit the state to permanently supporting the economy with subsidies. If I was going to do anything, it would have to be a temporary measure that would take effect quickly. Public pressure to do something grew stronger and stronger. I had to think of something.

One morning I came up with an approach that I wanted to talk through with Beate Baumann. Her first impressions were important to me. "Our economy's most precious thing is our well-trained, skilled workers. If they're all made redundant now, they could be anywhere by the time the crisis is over," I said to her. "So we have to retain them in their companies. Work on reduced hours benefit could be the perfect approach here, if we extend the period it's paid for: we don't know yet how long the economic downturn's going to last. What do you think?"

"I think that could be crucial. More than anything, it would show that we can act quickly and decisively, not just for the banks, but to save jobs too," she said.

"Great, that's the feeling I have, as well," I replied.

Emboldened, I decided to talk to Olaf Scholz, the minister of labor, about it as soon as possible. After the next cabinet meeting, I set out my thoughts to him in my office. It was as if I was preaching to the converted. He smiled and said he was pleased that instead of proposing the usual CDU tax cuts, I was suggesting a labor market initiative that could go straight to the people and that would allay their fears. After just a few minutes, we agreed to include extending the work on reduced hours benefit as a key step in our stimulus package. This meant that the government would cover part of employees' salaries if their working hours, and consequently their wages, were reduced due to the economic situation. On November 5, 2008, we put the plan into action and the coalition committee agreed to extend the work on reduced hours benefit from twelve to eighteen months from January 1, 2009.

The day before, Barack Obama had won the US presidential elections. He had already announced that he would launch a major growth program when he started his term of office on January 20, 2009. For this reason alone, it was clear that what we had just decided would not be the last word. As soon as Obama passed his mega-program, there would be calls for new measures, whatever we'd already done by then. But also, because the economic forecasts in January might be much worse than they were now, it was important to me not to put all our eggs in one basket yet. So for a while I decided to live with the accusation that what we were offering didn't meet the scale of the task yet. Nicolas Sarkozy had really rubbed it in. "France is working on it; in Germany they're thinking about it," was how he put it when he spoke to the press after a lunch with me and his wife Carla Bruni at his home on November 24, 2008. Against that private backdrop, he had tried to persuade me to have more courage, as he apparently saw it, about investing in the economy. To me it wasn't about courage, but about the right time, and I was convinced that we weren't there yet. I pretended I hadn't noticed his dig.

Nevertheless, a week later I made a mistake. It was at the CDU federal party conference on December 1 and 2. I knew that the majority of my staff were skeptical of or averse to economic stimulus programs, and I tried to overcompensate in my speech with a little rhetoric, using the image of the stereotypically thrifty Swabian housewife: "All of a sudden, we're reading everywhere why the financial markets were on the verge of collapse, even from people who had previously recommended investments they didn't understand themselves. But in fact, it's quite simple. We could have just asked a Swabian housewife here in Stuttgart, in Baden-Württemberg. She would have given us a maxim that's as brief as it is true: you can't live beyond your means for long. That is the essence of the crisis." In hindsight, what I'd said was as parochial as it was trite. Hundreds of thousands of people were worried about losing their jobs, and I had nothing better in mind than trying to win my colleagues over with that line at a party conference. Besides, capitalizing on a bad situation almost never works, nor does making a virtue out of necessity—or at least that's my experience of life in politics. I had always been given better advice, especially when it came to contentious issues: justify my decisions in a purely objective way, or drop a subject altogether if I wasn't able to convince anyone of it.

It was undeniable: 2009, the election year, was approaching. In September 2008, the SPD leadership had nominated Frank-Walter Steinmeier as its candidate for chancellor. On January 3, 2009, he wrote to me proposing further economic measures. Of course, this served to show which of the coalition partners was taking the initiative, and so the very next day it became public knowledge. The time for another decision was approaching. In my New Year's address, I had already given a little hint of where we might be going by saying that I wouldn't be led by whoever was shouting the loudest, but that we would be taking steps to secure and create jobs.

But before that, I still had a battle on my hands in my own party, and I used the CDU Federal Board meeting for this on January 9 and 10 in Erfurt. The SPD and the German Association of the Automotive Industry (VDA) had proposed a bonus for scrapping older vehicles. It was intended to boost the production of more environmentally friendly new cars, and as a result it would secure jobs in the automotive sector. I thought the idea was sound. However, most of the CDU/CSU members in the Bundestag were against it. At breakfast with the members of the CDU Presidium on the closed meeting's second day, I brought up the subject. I signaled my support for it and counted on the idea that the federal premiers for states where automotive companies or suppliers were based also saw it that way, because they had a vested interest in the production sites being maintained. My strategy worked. Christian Wulff from Lower Saxony, Jürgen Rüttgers from North Rhine-Westphalia, Roland Koch from Hesse, Peter Müller from Saarland, Günther Oettinger from Baden-Württemberg, Dieter Althaus from Thuringia, and Stanislaw Tillich from Saxony all supported me. I asked everyone to promote the scrapping bonus to the Bundestag members in their state groups. That's what they did, and as a result, the coalition committee was able to pass a second major stimulus package just a few days later, on January 12,

2009. On top of a hundred-billion-euro loan program for companies, a reduction in health insurance and unemployment insurance contributions, and an increased basic income tax allowance, the package included two extraordinary measures: first, we improved conditions for working on reduced hours, with employers being reimbursed 50 percent of social security contributions, and this could even go up to 100 percent if they combined working on reduced hours with training. Second, anyone who owned a car registered in 2000 or earlier would receive a subsidy of €2,500 toward the purchase of a car less than a year old. Both measures were a resounding success and helped to ease the crisis. In April and May 2009, there were more than 1.5 million people working reduced hours; at the end of the year there were just under 900,000—they had been saved from unemployment. And the scrapping bonus, officially called the environmental bonus, came into force on March 7, 2009, and because of the large number of people claiming it, we increased the financial resources earmarked for it from €1.5 billion to €5 billion on April 7. Five months later, on September 2, this amount had also been claimed. With the bonus, we had supported the replacement of almost two million cars in six months. Together with the first stimulus package, we supported the German economy with financial resources amounting to around 3 percent of GDP. But state action had been sorely needed. Our economy slumped by 5.7 percent in 2009. There had never been anything like it in the history of the Federal Republic. As a government, we were convinced we had done everything we could to ensure that Germany would be able to emerge from the crisis stronger and more future-proof than when it had gone into it. That was my goal, and that was what we achieved.

Throughout the crisis, we regularly consulted business associations and trade unions. In countless evening meetings at the Chancellery, we openly discussed the problems at hand and looked for solutions together. I felt it was a living social market economy.

When the Chancellery kitchen staff brought the food in during one of these meetings, I announced: "I've ordered us smoked pork with kale." This was classic German home-style food.

Someone from a union said, "This is the third time in a row!"

We all roared with laughter. He probably thought I had chosen it to give the unions the impression I was making a point of being down-to-earth with the trade unionists. But it was more straightforward than that. The Chancellery kitchen suggested menus to me, and I loved smoked pork with kale so much that I had unwittingly forced the dish on everyone else over and over again.

G20

Managing the acute crisis when it came to banks and jobs had been one thing, but it was also essential to prevent a shock like this from affecting the world economy. On October 8, 2008, I spoke to George W. Bush on the phone. It was our first call since the collapse of Lehman Brothers. The US rescue package, after being rejected in the House of Representatives on September 29, was finally adopted by Congress on October 3. During our phone call, we discussed the idea of all the industrialized countries coordinating the measures they were going to take. I suggested to Bush that, on top of its own crisis management, the US government should send out a twofold message to the world: first, that countries worldwide could only overcome the crisis through concerted action, and second, that we must take global precautions to ensure that a situation like this could never happen again. The States, as the epicenter of the crisis, which had thrown the world into turmoil, had to be the trailblazer.

George W. Bush hesitated. The presidential elections were taking place in less than a month; he himself would only be in office for three months, and his successor would take over on January 20. But I didn't give up. Every day counted. It felt like an eternity before the new government could start its work. We had years of excesses on the financial markets to deal with and we couldn't allow them to jeopardize the free market economy as a whole. To be able to do that, the governments, both of the G8 countries and of emerging economies, had to learn some political lessons from this disaster as quickly as possible, and they had to learn together. A meeting of these countries' leaders was essential. Bush promised to think about what I'd said. In another phone call on October 14, 2008, he seemed more open to it, if I remember rightly. Other Europeans were also arguing in favor of this, especially Nicolas Sarkozy. Shortly before he and the EU Commission president met with the US president at Camp David on Saturday, October 18, George W. Bush finally announced that the States would host a global financial summit of industrialized nations and some emerging countries.

The summit took place on November 14 and 15, 2008 in Washington. The US government had invited a group of countries whose finance ministers already met with each other: the Group of Twenty (G20). It was founded in 1999 in response to the Asian financial crisis in the 1990s. Now, exceptionally, the G20 would convene with both leaders and finance ministers. We adopted an action plan consisting of almost fifty points relating to the financial markets and the global economy. I remember that our discussion of tax havens was particularly contentious. This made the summit's key resolution all the more important: every financial market, every financial product, and every financial player should be subject to regulation or adequate monitoring. It was the starting point for a reform of the global financial system.

The next summit took place in the same format on April 1 and 2, 2009 in London at the British prime minister Gordon Brown's invitation, and Bush's successor, Barack Obama, invited the group back to the States for the third summit, in the fall of 2009. That meeting took place on September 24 and 25 in Pittsburgh. There, we Europeans managed to get everyone to agree that from then on bankers would only be paid performance-based bonuses. We wanted to prevent bankers from getting away with disastrous management scot-free while the people buying their products had to fight for compensation or millions of people lost their jobs. That spring, the world experienced the worst economic downturn since the 1930s. So we agreed to let the national stimulus programs run until our economies started growing again.

The G20 became the defining forum for international economic cooperation. From then on, the group met every year. The emerging countries' influence was bolstered by resolutions for reform in the International Monetary Fund (IMF) and for greater voting strength in the World Bank. The G20 set out to fight protectionism and to campaign for an agreement to be signed at the Copenhagen Climate Change Conference in December 2009. A new format was born.

On Friday, September 25, 2009, after the Pittsburgh summit, when Peer Steinbrück and I were taking an escalator at the David L. Lawrence Convention Center on our way to the airport, he said to me: "I think this is the last conference we'll be attending together. It's been a pleasure."

"Yes," I said, "a pleasure for me too—we've experienced more together over the last year than we could ever have imagined."

I was thinking about the time when we jointly announced the guarantee for savings account holders. I said nothing about it possibly being our last conference together. The next Bundestag election was due to take place that Sunday. In the polls, the CDU and CSU were far ahead of Steinbrück's party, the SPD; the FDP, on the other hand, looked like it had over 10 percent of the vote. It all seemed as if it might be enough for a coalition of the Union and the FDP. Five years later, on my sixtieth birthday on July 17, 2014, Peer Steinbrück gave me my name plate from the conference table in Pittsburgh. He had taken it home with him. It was a gesture that really touched me. I still have it today.

EURO CRISIS

The coalition of choice

On September 27, 2009, it happened, just as Peer Steinbrück had feared. The SPD got just 23 percent of the votes cast in the Bundestag elections. The FDP, on the other hand, had a sensational 14.6 percent. The Union retained 33.8 percent, 1.4 percent less than four years earlier. Even though the Union was now able to form a coalition with both the SPD and the FDP, the mood behind the scenes was downcast. Once again, fewer percentage points than in 2005. The fact that I had 49.3 percent of the first votes in my constituency, 8 percent more than in 2005, was of little interest to anyone in Berlin except me. Many Union members were of the opinion that the FDP's good election results reflected people's desire for more radical social reforms and a focus on economic policy. The idea that some FDP voters might have voted for the party to end the Grand Coalition but keep me as chancellor didn't enter their thoughts, though. Instead of sixty-one representatives, the FDP now had ninety-three in the Bundestag, keen to implement their election manifesto: "Germany needs a change of policy—the FDP wants a change of policy." The last time the party had formed part of the government was eleven years before. It had been through the global financial crisis from the opposition's perspective and had criticized my government at the time, sometimes vehemently.

Nevertheless, FDP chair Guido Westerwelle, CSU chair

Horst Seehofer, and I were in good spirits as we held our first talks on forming a new government. We resolved to get the coalition negotiations completed quickly. The government was due to take office on October 28, 2009, the day after the seventeenth Bundestag's term officially began. We wanted to show that Germany could also act quickly. The European Council's fall meeting was due to take place in Brussels on October 29 and 30, and Westerwelle and I intended to travel there together. As the new vice chancellor, he had decided to take on the role of foreign minister, following in Hans-Dietrich Genscher's footsteps. November 9 also marked the twentieth anniversary of the fall of the Berlin Wall. In Berlin, there were plans for commemorative events to be held in the Gethsemane Church, at the former Bornholmer Strasse border crossing at the Bösebrücke and at the Brandenburg Gate. And on the occasion of that particular anniversary, I had a very special invitation that I was both excited about and in awe of: on November 3, 2009, I was due to speak in Washington before both houses of the US Congress, an honor that had never been bestowed on a German chancellor before; even Konrad Adenauer had been asked to speak to one after the other in 1957, rather than both at the same time. But before all that, we first had to negotiate a coalition agreement.

The fallout from the global financial crisis was evident in Germany, despite the stimulus packages that had been passed. Economic output was shrinking. The stimulus packages had been financed largely with credit. So, in June 2009, the Grand Coalition passed a government bill for the 2010 federal budget based on net borrowing of €86 billion, €80 billion more than originally planned. At almost the same time, with the support of the FDP, which was still in opposition, we had enshrined the debt brake in the constitution. It came into force at the beginning of 2016.

The FDP came into the coalition talks with an election

manifesto that included far-reaching tax cuts with a graduated tariff for income tax, which would have resulted in a loss of revenue of at least €35 billion. The financial crisis clearly hadn't been a major factor when they were working on their manifesto. The CDU and CSU had also been in favor of using financial leeway for tax relief in our manifesto, but we had left the scope and timing open. Westerwelle didn't want to break his word under any circumstances; he wanted to push through his manifesto almost at any cost, or so it seemed to me. His party had clearly been on an ego trip since the election results. Sections of the CDU and CSU supported the FDP. I told Westerwelle that we'd managed to find common ground with other difficult issues in the past, such as Horst Köhler's nomination for the office of president in 2004. It was the first time in the Federal Republic's history that someone who wasn't a conventional politician had been elected to office. We'd chosen the former head of the IMF partly because he represented a cosmopolitan outlook in times of globalization. But this time Guido Westerwelle didn't want to give in. Tax cuts seemed to be the most important issue for him in the upcoming four years. I, on the other hand, had experienced how the financial crisis had simply thrown any budget plans to the wind since September 2008, and to me it was reckless to make such far-reaching commitments in view of the uncertain economic trends. After many fruitless discussions, though, I thought that the forces of reality would come to the fore one day, and I decided not to put up a full-blown fight. The Union and FDP agreed on a graduated tariff and tax cuts amounting to €24 billion.

The four weeks of coalition discussions seemed endless to me. The negotiations for what we'd always thought of as the coalition of choice proved to be tough. I felt that, politically, Guido Westerwelle and I had drifted apart more over the previous four years than I'd ever thought possible. Nevertheless, we finalized the negotiations as planned. On October 28, 2009, the Bundestag formally elected me as chancellor for the second time; in the afternoon the new government was sworn in, and work could begin. Wolfgang Schäuble became the new finance minister, Ronald Pofalla the new head of the Chancellery, and his predecessor, Thomas de Maizière, became interior minister.

For me, the following month began with some genuine high points in transatlantic and European history. The members of the US Congress in Washington welcomed me enthusiastically on November 3. In my speech, I thanked the Americans for their support after the Second World War, and remembered the sixteen million Americans who had been stationed in Germany as soldiers, diplomats, and facilitators, and who had served as ambassadors of the United States in Germany. They had forged a solid link between our peoples. Then I discussed the walls we had to tear down and overcome in the twenty-first century. I mentioned the need to stand up to terrorism after the experience of the September 11 attacks, and the order being established in the financial markets worldwide after the previous year's crisis, including the newly founded G20 format, and I called for the fight against human-induced climate change to be seen as a global challenge. At the end of my speech, I spoke in English about the Freedom Bell in Berlin, which, like Philadelphia's Liberty Bell, is a symbol of the fact that freedom must be struggled for and defended anew every day.

The celebrations in Berlin also covered everything from the fall of the Wall on November 9, 1989 to the present day: a memorial service in the Gethsemane Church, a symbolic walk across the former border crossing at the Bösebrücke with Mikhail Gorbachev, Lech Wałęsa, and former GDR dissidents such as Wolf Biermann, Marianne Birthler, Rainer Eppelmann, Joachim Gauck, and Markus Meckel, as well as a ceremony at the Brandenburg Gate in the evening. Barack Obama had sent a video message. Horst Köhler and I crossed through the Brandenburg

Gate from West to East, along with the US secretary of state Hillary Clinton, Russian president Dmitry Medvedev, Nicolas Sarkozy, and Gordon Brown; all the European Union's leaders were invited, the Staatskapelle Berlin and the Staatsopernchor played and sang works by Wagner, Beethoven, and Schoenberg under Daniel Barenboim's direction, and Plácido Domingo sang "Berliner Luft" by Paul Lincke. It was lovely to look back to the past. Yet, at the same time, I couldn't quite believe my eyes. Babies born on November 9, 1989 were now celebrating their twentieth birthday. And there were more than enough new problems to solve. As I'd heard Henry Kissinger saying the night before at a conference in the Hotel Adlon: "Every solution to a problem brings with it a ticket to new difficulties."

The Solvay Library

Three months later. On Thursday, February 11, 2010, Herman Van Rompuy had invited leaders to a special European Council meeting in Brussels. The former Belgian prime minister was the first full-time EU Council president after the Lisbon Treaty, which came into force on December 1, 2009. During the German presidency in the first half of 2007, we laid the foundations for this new treaty, which was signed in Lisbon in December 2007 during the subsequent Portuguese presidency. It replaced the Constitutional Treaty signed in 2004, which had not been ratified in the spring of 2005 due to referendums in France and the Netherlands. Major sections of the Constitutional Treaty still appeared in the Lisbon Treaty, and it included a new way of working for the European Council. From now on, only heads of state and government and the Commission president were members of the Council, and it was headed by a full-time president instead of rotating between the EU leaders every six months. The High Representative of the Union for

Foreign Affairs and Security Policy, who was also the Commission's vice president, also took part in the meetings, but foreign ministers and state staff no longer did. The Council president Herman Van Rompuy had invited us to a special meeting so we could get to know each other better and have a fundamental discussion about our goals. In particular, we wanted to talk about carrying forward the Lisbon Strategy to ensure Europe would be more competitive after the global financial crisis. To emphasize the meeting's informal nature, it wasn't due to take place in the sterile Council building as usual, but in the Solvay Library, a magnificent building in Brussels named after the Belgian industrialist Ernest Solvay, who had commissioned it at the beginning of the twentieth century.

But things didn't turn out quite as planned. The day before, Nicolas Sarkozy had rung me at 12:30 p.m.; he was concerned about Greece's financial situation and thought that, before the next morning's official meeting in the Solvay Library, a small group of us should discuss it first with Herman Van Rompuy in the Council building. Jean-Claude Trichet, the president of the European Central Bank (ECB), should be there as well. I knew from my European policy advisor Uwe Corsepius that the EU Commission was holding talks with the Greek government about the country's budget. Shortly after taking office in October 2009, Prime Minister Giorgos Papandreou's new government had carried out a financial review and announced to the public that the Greek budget deficit was not 3.7 percent of its GDP as stated that spring, but 12.7 percent. This led to an increase in interest rates on Greek government bonds. At the end of 2009, Papandreou asked the International Monetary Fund's managing director, Dominique Strauss-Kahn, for help. He said he was not responsible as Greece was part of a monetary union, and advised him to approach the EU Commission, which demanded that Greece reduce the deficit by four percentage points in 2010. Papandreou had agreed to this in principle, but he hadn't presented a plan on how he intended to achieve that goal. In our phone call, I told Sarkozy I didn't see what we could do for Greece the next day. To me, a meeting without a clear goal was counterproductive, as it could trigger additional uncertainty. But Sarkozy insisted, indicating that the Commission president Barroso and Van Rompuy shared his opinion. It wasn't clear to me exactly what he had in mind. I kept my options open and told him I'd get in touch with Barroso and Van Rompuy.

That afternoon, I rang Papandreou first. Although he described his country's situation as tense, he didn't give me the impression that he saw an urgent need for action. Barroso and Van Rompuy, though, shared Sarkozy's view when I rang them in the early evening. So I agreed to the meeting, even though it wasn't yet clear what was in store for me, or for Germany.

The next morning, I flew to Brussels. After landing just before ten o'clock, I went straight to the Council building. The meeting took place in one of Van Rompuy's conference rooms. He, Barroso, Papandreou, Sarkozy, and Trichet were already there when I arrived. Each of us had a member of staff and an interpreter with us for the discussion. I was accompanied by Uwe Corsepius and our interpreter Dorothee Kaltenbach; Jens Weidmann and Ulrich Wilhelm, who had also come with us, were in an adjoining room. As best we could, we all spoke English to each other. We sat down in armchairs, and we were each served a good Belgian espresso and a glass of water. As far as I remember, Herman Van Rompuy called on Trichet to speak first. The ECB president explained that interest rates on Greek government bonds were constantly rising, which meant that Greece would soon no longer be able to obtain financing from market sources. The spread (the difference in interest rates for purchasing a Greek and a German government bond of the same maturity) was already around 4 percent. Trichet finished by saying, "Greece must be helped now, otherwise there's no guarantee that it will still be able to borrow money on the capital market by the spring." As on the previous day, it still wasn't clear to me what this help should consist of, but for now I carried on listening. Barroso said he shared Trichet's opinion, as did Sarkozy. The French president also spoke of the Commission's austerity measure suggestions for Greece and exclaimed in anger: "Saving 4 percent of the GDP is a certain path to revolt on the streets! In this economic crisis, we need more government spending, not less! Greece must be helped!"

I asked, "What is this help supposed to consist of?"

Trichet answered: "Greece needs money."

We'd finally got to the heart of the matter. Greece needed money. Everyone was nodding, apart from Papandreou and me. One of the most important conditions when Germany joined the European Monetary Union was the no bailout clause: the requirement that every government takes responsibility for repaying its own debts. That was enshrined in the EU agreements. Everyone in the room knew the legal situation, but no one seemed to care.

First of all, I said something conciliatory: "Of course I'd like to be helpful too—we are all in the eurozone together," but then I quickly added, "I cannot give out money under any circumstances." As I noticed that Papandreou hadn't said anything yet, I spoke to him directly: "What do you actually want?" He replied that he didn't want anything, but that Greece was in trouble.

Trichet became more and more vehement and insisted that Greece must be helped; if not, other eurozone countries with high debt levels would be at risk too. Barroso agreed, as he knew the situation in Portugal, his homeland, only too well. I switched to German and Dorothee Kaltenbach interpreted what I was saying into English; I wanted to be precise. "I cannot give any money because I cannot go along with a breach of contract. Our Constitutional Court has made a clear ruling on this. The Lisbon Treaty's no bailout clause is in place. I will not knowingly break the law," I made it unmistakably clear. While this was going on,

I was thinking: Everyone here wants something from me. Why is nobody putting pressure on Greece to economize?

"When are you going to present your plans for saving 4 percent of your GDP to the Commission?" I asked Papandreou. "That's the most important thing right now, to show the financial markets they can trust you again."

Papandreou replied that he needed time. I found his reaction unbelievable. The pressure was on to do something, but on the other hand, he seemed to have all the time in the world. We talked heatedly, we talked at each other, we talked in English, in French, in German. The interpreters could scarcely keep up with their task of whispering what was being said in our ears. I looked around at Corsepius sitting behind me, and his look told me I was right not to agree to anything. This went on for a good two hours. Then Herman Van Rompuy took the initiative. He had obviously got the feeling that we'd argued every point in detail at least once and that we were going round in circles. "In this situation, we cannot leave the room without informing the public of a result in writing. That's precisely what we have to work on now," he explained calmly, and he also reminded us that our colleagues had been waiting for us in the Solvay Library. Herman Van Rompuy was absolutely right. This was where I first got to know and appreciate his great gift for summarizing contentious discussions, and in such an amicable way. It was to become his trademark during his five-year term as Council president.

We noted that all the eurozone members had a shared responsibility for economic and financial stability in the euro area and we agreed on five points. We called on Greece to fulfill its commitments to reduce its debt. We asked the Economic and Financial Affairs Council to approve measures already proposed by Greece to reduce the deficit at its meeting on February 16, 2010, in five days' time. The Commission would closely monitor the implementation of the measures in Greece together with the ECB, and draw on the IMF's experience of this. It was important to me to involve the International Monetary Fund: its staff were experienced and they would evaluate the Greek proposals more impartially than the European institutions. My concern was that the latter would be too lenient with Greece. We also stated in our draft that eurozone members would take targeted and coordinated action if the euro area's stability as a whole was threatened. We concluded by stating that Greece had not yet requested financial assistance. I could sign my name to all of that. Herman Van Rompuy had filtered out what it was that united those of us who had been arguing, with an uncanny instinct.

And with that, as it would turn out in the course of time, we had put the entire philosophy of saving the euro into writing on that February morning in Brussels. Member states each had to take the measures required in their own countries. Those measures would be assessed by the Commission, the ECB, and the IMF. Later on, these three institutions would become known as the Troika. No one would take on the debt for another eurozone member state, but they would all help to safeguard its stability as a whole. Joint action as a last resort. I felt able to work on that basis, as the Federal Constitutional Court had also linked Germany's membership in the monetary union to its stability. Conversely, this meant that Germany also had to do everything possible to safeguard its stability without taking on other countries' debts. The draft described the path that everyone could take together. At the same time, it was general enough to leave sufficient room for maneuver with future developments. That was diplomacy at its best. I was impressed.

We finally joined the others in the Solvay Library's magnificent old reading room extremely late. The mood among the people we'd kept waiting wasn't good. Herman Van Rompuy told them what we had been discussing. Everyone approved the draft. We spoke only briefly about carrying forward the Lisbon

Strategy, in other words improving the European Union's economic competitiveness, the main topic on this special EU meeting's agenda. After the global financial crisis, which had started in the US, it was the euro now having problems. The extensive stimulus packages, which we had been right to adopt, were partly responsible, though. Now we had a national debt crisis in some eurozone countries. Nicolas Sarkozy and I decided to appear together before the press after the Council meeting had finished. Fiercely though we'd been arguing with each other, we'd managed to overcome our differences—albeit with Herman Van Rompuy's help. To us, it seemed an important message to give to the public.

The road to Ithaca

Back in Berlin, I had to announce to my government and our coalition partners that a subject that had played no part in our coalition negotiations had suddenly become a priority less than four months into our term. As I reported on Greece's difficulties, I encountered significant skepticism, especially among legislators. The news rekindled the deep-seated fears that had been prevalent when Helmut Kohl introduced the euro. Back then, many people had doubted that the euro would ever become as stable as the deutsche mark had been. There was little willingness to help Greece. The most that the finance minister Wolfgang Schäuble and I, along with the rest of the coalition government, could imagine doing was to provide bilateral loans, in conjunction with a credit facility from the International Monetary Fund (IMF), which Greece would have to repay with interest in the future. We had to ensure that no other EU country could ever report false data about its deficit again. The competitiveness of some members of the eurozone also needed to improve. Our philosophy was that we would help, but assistance would need to be accompanied by measures to boost the country's long-term economic health. This couldn't be about papering over the cracks: the root causes of the problems needed to be tackled.

Greece still hadn't presented any satisfactory proposals for budget cuts and structural reforms when the European Council met on March 25–26, 2010. I therefore noted in a government statement on March 25: "A good European isn't necessarily one who rushes to help. A good European is rather one who respects the European treaties and relevant national laws and, in so doing, helps to ensure that the stability of the eurozone isn't harmed." I'd had a call with the IMF's managing director Dominique Strauss-Kahn the previous day in which he had suggested that the IMF might participate in a possible rescue program for Greece. Then I phoned Nicolas Sarkozy. In our call we agreed on the principle of bilateral loans to Greece from all the eurozone countries, with IMF support. The European Council backed this plan.

Just over two weeks later, on April 11, the Eurogroup, which brought together the finance ministers of the eurozone (all the countries using the euro as their currency), approved a detailed program for Greece that included €30 billion in bilateral loans from the eurozone countries and a further €15 billion from the IMF. The only snag was that Greece had not yet submitted an official request for financial support.

This changed on April 23. That was the day when it was made public that the Greek deficit would exceed 15 percent. This news fueled a further rise in bond yield spreads, putting Greece's access to financial markets at risk. Meanwhile, Prime Minister Papandreou happened to be on the small island of Kastellorizo, near the Turkish coast, rather than in the capital, Athens. He was forced to make an announcement about the state of his country's economy. Standing in bright sunshine, with the picturesque port in the background, he declared that he would be applying to the Eurogroup and the IMF for assistance. He prepared his fellow citizens for difficult times, describing the journey to come as a new odyssey and concluding with the dramatic words: "We know the road to Ithaca and have charted the waters"—clearly a reference to Odysseus's ten years of wandering after the battle of Troy, during which he lost all his comrades and returned to his home island of Ithaca a beggar.

It took until the beginning of May for the Troika to agree the conditions of the first aid package for Greece. On Wednesday, May 5, 2010, I delivered a government statement to the Bundestag about the program: "There is no alternative to the aid we are going to vote on for Greece if we wish to ensure the financial stability of the eurozone. By acting we will be protecting our currency." A little later, I added: "The European Central Bank and the European Commission have clearly communicated that immediate aid is the last resort to guarantee the financial stability of the eurozone in its entirety."

"No alternative." "Last resort." I'd spoken in similar terms on February 18, 2009, more than a year earlier, when commenting on my cabinet's decision to nationalize HRE, the Hypo Real Estate bank. As a result, the cabinet had foreseen the expropriation of the bank's shareholders as the last possible solution, the *ultima ratio*. "We have weighed up the options carefully. I consider that there is no alternative," was the phrase I'd used back then too. In both cases, I'd decided to explain that our decisions were not intended simply to prevent the collapse of a bank or a eurozone country; they also served a greater objective of protecting our currency as a whole, protecting the savings of our citizens, and propping up the banking industry as the prerequisite for protecting the real economy, which would in turn safeguard millions of jobs. Only context would enable people to understand our decision-making, and only context could present it as a necessity and demonstrate that there was no alternative: this was the *ultima ratio*. In a social market economy like ours, this was a high-wire act, economically, socially, and also legally. It was essential to show, not least to the Federal Constitutional Court, that we were fully aware of the delicate path we were treading. One way of demonstrating this—perhaps the best way—was for the chancellor to deliver a government statement.

But was I actually right? Were there alternatives we hadn't tried? Of course there were: there are always alternatives. Taken to the extreme, even jumping off a rooftop is an alternative—an alternative to living. Taken to the extreme, the collapse of the IKB Deutsche Industriebank and HRE Bank during the subprime crisis and the end of the euro would have been alternatives to my decision. Yet I was convinced that these were not the sorts of decisions any serious politician could make in a country like Germany, the largest European economy, with a population of over eighty million, at the heart of our continent. In 2010, as in 2009, I was severely criticized for using the term "no alternative," and pundits accused me of authoritarian behavior. They claimed that rather than setting out my arguments in detail, I sought to block out dissenting views and issued instructions that people had to "sink or swim." This was the opposite effect to the one I'd intended. Conscious of the extraordinary scope of our decisions, I was merely trying to be frank about their impact. However, from then on, to make sure people got the correct message, I said that there was no "sensible" alternative to the government's decisions, which was simply stating the obvious.

On Friday, May 7, 2010, the Bundestag held the second and third readings of the Greek aid bill. The country would receive up to €80 billion in bilateral loans over three years and €30 billion from the IMF; Germany's share of these loans amounted to €22.4 billion. In return, Greece was required to make deep budget cuts and approve structural reforms. I mustered all my powers of persuasion to win over a majority among the coalition parties for these measures. In my struggle to convince my own party to vote for the program, I'd promised that this aid for Greece would be a one-off. But as we shall soon see, this was a promise I couldn't keep. The febrile atmosphere in parliament was further stoked by state elections in North Rhine-Westphalia two days later, on May 9. The opposition claimed that I'd done everything I could to delay the vote on the Greek bailout until after the elections so as not to alarm voters. This was nonsense. There was no way I could have entertained such thoughts with Europe in so perilous a situation. The real reason was because I wasn't willing to help Greece until Athens put forward a coherent reform package.

This wasn't the end of the matter, however. In the middle of the Bundestag debate on the Greece support bill that Friday, I got word from my office that Nicolas Sarkozy wanted to speak to me urgently; they hadn't been able to deter him. I left the plenary chamber and went to my office in the Reichstag to take his call. Sarkozy sounded extremely agitated. He talked about rising Spanish and Portuguese bond market spreads and the risk of contagion rippling through the entire eurozone, and he also predicted stock-market turbulence. Some financial traders were betting against the euro. Sarkozy blamed these developments partially on Germany's hesitancy. He advocated arguing at the eurozone meeting scheduled for that evening in Brussels that we should not only approve the Greece package but also reiterate our determination to do whatever it might take to safeguard the stability of the euro and of the euro area as a whole. It remained to be seen what this might mean in practice. I replied that my absolute priority that morning was to get the Greece package safely through the German Bundestag to avoid further turbulence on the financial markets. When we had finished our phone call, I returned to the plenary chamber to follow the rest of the debate, but in fact I spent most of the session deep in thought. Our deliberations would continue in

Brussels later that day, and the euro clearly wasn't out of the woods yet. What wasn't clear, though, was what more we could do. I had nothing hard and fast to present to parliament before the vote, let alone anything I was *obliged* to tell them. All the same, I was accused after the event, primarily by opposition MPs, of having withheld important information from the parliament that Friday. This wasn't true. The fact that the Bundestag approved a plan in the morning that was little more than a footnote by the time we met in Brussels that evening was due more to the dynamic nature of the situation.

If the euro fails, Europe fails

The meeting of the heads of state and heads of government of the eurozone began at approximately 6:15 p.m., with preliminary discussions in private. It was clear that bilateral loans to individual countries would not halt the widespread speculation. What was required now to bring the situation under control was a general mechanism of the kind we had implemented during the financial crisis—a mechanism which could give support to any country that ran into difficulties. But no one could say what such an instrument might look like. The only consensus was that we needed to act quickly: there had to be clarity by the time Asian markets opened on Monday morning. We concurred that our finance ministers should meet in Brussels in the early evening of Sunday, May 9, 2010 to thrash out the details. I was painfully aware of the situation in my own coalition and sensed just how hard it would be to garner support for further rescue measures. I couldn't possibly leave everything to Wolfgang Schäuble—I had to handle it myself. By Sunday evening, Schäuble would need to know the scope of his negotiating possibilities, and that didn't give me much time.

How are you going to pull this off? I wondered. You'll only

get back from Brussels after midnight, then tomorrow morning
you have to address a final campaign rally of the Westphalian
CDU in Paderborn, then at noon you're hosting the Canadian
prime minister Stephen Harper (Canada was chair of the G8
that year). In the afternoon you're due to fly to Moscow to attend
a military parade on Sunday morning to mark the sixty-fifth
anniversary of the end of the Second World War at President
Medvedev's invitation. And the finance ministers will already be
meeting in Brussels by the time you return to Berlin on Sunday.
You can't really consider things, nor can you inform Schäuble in
time if you do come up with a solution to the problem.

I needed time to talk to Weidmann and Corsepius and
develop a plan for how to proceed. Canceling the Moscow trip
was a non-starter, so there was only one possibility: the two of
them would have to travel with me, along with Ulrich Wilhelm
and Christoph Heusgen, who were already due to come along.
That would give us time to talk on the plane and in the Russian
capital in the evening. I discussed this with the two of them on
the flight back from Brussels to Berlin, and they both readily
agreed. I also talked to Simone Lehmann-Zwiener, who adapted
the planning of the Moscow trip overnight.

On Saturday, May 8, 2010, we took off at 4:30 p.m. and by half
past nine we were at the Hotel Baltschug Kempinski, where we
were due to spend the night. It had opened in 1992 as the first
new five-star luxury hotel in Moscow after the collapse of the
Soviet Union. Simone Lehmann-Zwiener had booked us a table
for dinner in the hotel restaurant and through its windows we
could look out across the Moskva river to the illuminated St.
Basil's Cathedral and the Kremlin beyond. We ordered beef
Stroganoff and resumed the conversation we'd begun on the
plane. We considered the matter from a number of different
angles. Which countries were in danger? How long would the
crisis last? Could we learn anything from our actions when

bailing out the banks? We racked our brains, but retired to our rooms without a solution in sight.

We met for breakfast at 7:30 the next morning. I came down feeling a little downcast as I'd no idea what to do next. Weidmann greeted us with the words, "I've had another think about it." He explained that overnight he had calculated the total value of all the government bonds that the countries beset by speculation—Greece, Portugal, Spain, and Italy—would need to extend over the next two years. His view was that we should establish a bailout fund covering this precise amount. His workings showed that this would cost approximately €750 billion. The four countries could only access this fund if they committed themselves to carrying out reforms. A smile flitted across my face. This might be the answer. Uwe Corsepius said, "Sounds plausible, Jens." We quickly agreed to put Weidmann's proposal to major European stakeholders and, in particular, to the finance minister Schäuble. I asked Weidmann to ring Trichet first to ascertain if he would back the plan. Before I'd even set off for the Kremlin, he came back with good news, which left me a few minutes to call Schäuble. He had a sharp intake of breath when I quoted the gigantic sum of €750 billion, but our rationale made sense to him.

While I was at the Kremlin and attending the military parade, Weidmann and Corsepius were phoning their French colleagues and the staff of Jean-Claude Juncker, the then chair of the Eurogroup, and they also contacted Barroso and Van Rompuy. On the flight back to Berlin they reported universal approval for our plan. After we'd touched down that afternoon, I rang Nicolas Sarkozy before the meeting of finance ministers and conveyed our proposal directly to him. He was surprised— in a positive way. He seemed to be thinking that Germany wasn't being tight-fisted, it was thinking big, and he promised that the French finance minister would back Schäuble during the discussions.

Not long afterward, however, Weidmann called to inform me that Schäuble had been taken to hospital in Brussels after feeling faint. It was Jürg Asmussen who had passed the news to Weidmann. It was quickly confirmed that the incident was nothing too serious, but Schäuble would nevertheless be spending the evening and the night in hospital. This was an unmitigated disaster. Who was going to negotiate for Germany now? Asmussen couldn't stand in for Schäuble. I had to think of a seasoned political operator to replace him. There was only one man for the job and that was the interior minister Thomas de Maizière. He had proved himself a fantastic ally as head of the Chancellery during the global financial crisis and he had my complete and utter trust. I discussed my idea with Guido Westerwelle and Rainer Brüderle, the FDP minister for economic affairs, and described the deal that was to be negotiated in Brussels. Brüderle was actually Schäuble's deputy in terms of government hierarchy, and he was extremely disappointed that I hadn't asked him to negotiate in Brussels in place of his boss. But although I could understand his irritation, I was utterly convinced that I'd made the right call. Special circumstances require special measures, and the situation was certainly special. Both Westerwelle and Brüderle agreed with our negotiating stance.

Around 6:00 p.m. that Sunday evening, it became clear that the CDU state premier Jürgen Rüttgers had lost the election in North Rhine-Westphalia, which came as a serious blow to both the CDU and the FDP because our two parties had been governing the state in coalition. This election setback also cost us our majority on the Bundesrat, meaning that there was now no chance of implementing the controversial tax reforms we had signed up to in our October 2009 coalition agreement.

As usual on election night, I met up with my closest collaborators on the eighth floor of the Chancellery. I spent most of the time on the phone with Thomas de Maizière, though, racing up and down the back staircase between the small make-up room next door and my office on the seventh floor to take his calls. The size of the bailout fund was quickly agreed, but the access conditions—referred to as "conditionality"—were, as always, a sticking point. Some countries, including Germany, the Netherlands, and Finland, wanted to define precisely what the beneficiaries had to do to qualify for the funds, whereas others were less bothered. As in the case of the Greek bailout package, the conditionality focused on cost-cutting measures and structural reforms, for example of the job market.

Silvio Berlusconi, the Italian premier, rang me after midnight on my cell phone and tried to persuade me to relax the conditions for the bailout fund. Thomas de Maizière had given the Italian finance minister short shrift, and I also stood firm.

Shortly after the Tokyo stock exchange opened, at 2:00 a.m. our time, the plans for a €750 billion bailout fund were in place. Of this sum, €440 billion were in the form of bilateral loans and guarantees from the members of the eurozone, with Germany contributing €123 billion. This was to be held by a special-purpose vehicle called the European Financial Stability Facility (EFSF), which was allowed to grant emergency loans to euro-zone countries under specific conditions. The European Commission would put up €60 billion, while the IMF was ready to sign up for €250 billion.

On the Monday following the state parliament elections, the CDU Presidium and national board always assembled at Konrad Adenauer House. Before they began, I spoke to the press at the Chancellery and explained the overnight decisions in Brussels. At 3:00 p.m. I informed the leaders of the parties and parliamentary parties.

Nine days later, on May 19, 2010, the Bundestag held its first reading of the EFSF bill. I began my government statement by placing the situation in its historical context: "The current euro crisis is the greatest test that Europe has faced for decades,

probably since the signature of the Treaty of Rome in 1957."
Next, I outlined the importance of our decision: "The currency
union is a community of destiny. What is at stake is therefore
no more and no less than the preservation and proof of the
European idea. This is our historic task. If the euro fails, Europe
fails." After this, I went into what we had been obliged to
prevent for legal reasons and rightly preempted for political
ones: "In practical terms, the threat was the slippery slope
toward a union of transfers, which would have introduced a
direct and binding liability of all members for the independent
decisions of individual member states." I argued that "the price
for our approach was to be scolded for being too tentative or too
slow. But the German government is more than willing to pay
this price if the correct decisions have ultimately been taken." I
then explained and justified the guiding principles behind our
decisions and highlighted the reforms needed within the eurozone: budget consolidation in the various member states; a
reform of the Stability and Growth Pact; the possibility of
orderly state insolvency; a European financial regulation body;
and avenues for banks to be wound up and restructured, and for
the taxation of financial markets.

On May 21, 2010 the German Bundestag passed the legislative package at its second and third readings, and on June 7,
Germany ratified the EFSF framework agreement until the end
of 2013.

The EFSF was required to disburse emergency loans.
Ireland and Portugal requested financial assistance, and in
summer 2012, Spain had to apply for financing for its banks. In
autumn 2011, the EFSF's capital guarantee was enlarged so as to
be in a position to provide planned loans of €440 billion with the
highest AAA rating. Greece also benefited from the EFSF and
received a second bailout in December 2012. The path to
achieving this result had been tortuous, as Germany had
demanded that Greece's private creditors contribute to the costs

with a debt "haircut." Sarkozy and Trichet feared lasting damage to investor confidence in the eurozone if such a reduction in repayments to creditors were implemented. We'd eventually agreed on a voluntary "haircut," and this was the outcome in spring 2012.

Meanwhile, Prime Minister George Papandreou had been struggling badly to push through the promised reforms in Greece. In search of a breakthrough, he decided in October 2011 to hold a referendum, so that the Greek people could speak its mind on the austerity measures. But he swiftly abandoned this plan when Barroso, Van Rompuy, Sarkozy, and I made it very clear to him on the margins of the G20 summit in Cannes on November 3–4, 2011 that these reforms were non-negotiable. He resigned not long afterward. A transitional government assumed power, and parliamentary elections held in June 2012 led to Antonis Samaras being elected as the country's new prime minister.

Looking for the bazooka

In August 2010, in the middle of the euro crisis, Steffen Seibert succeeded Ulrich Wilhelm. At first I could barely believe that this renowned journalist and TV host would be willing to switch sides, as it were, for a life of political service during a period of such political turbulence. It soon became clear how excited he was by his new task, however, and it was a joy to work with him for the next ten years. Steffen Seibert ultimately became the longest-serving government spokesperson in the history of the Federal Republic of Germany.

In autumn 2010, the German government started preparing for what would come after the EFSF, which was due to expire at the end of 2013. The European Council meeting in December 2010 voted on a lasting mechanism for dealing with crises, and

Germany came out in favor under the proviso that the Lisbon Treaty be expanded to reflect the new situation. A new clause was therefore added to Article 136 of the Treaty on the Functioning of the European Union (TFEU) to clarify that a stability mechanism could be established and activated under strict conditions to safeguard the stability of the whole euro area. This formed the basis for the development of the European Stability Mechanism (ESM)—a permanent intergovernmental organization funded by member states' own equity and authorized to issue loans and bonds under certain conditions. In late June 2012, the Bundestag approved the Treaty Establishing the European Stability Mechanism, which came into force in September 2012. Another significant hurdle had been overcome, even though we were challenged every step of the way in the Federal Constitutional Court. The government won each case overall, but the court did strengthen parliamentary participation in future decision-making.

In June 2011 my European policy advisor Uwe Corsepius left to take up the position of secretary general of the European Council in Brussels, returning to his former position in Berlin in June 2015 at the end of his four-year term. While he was away, his deputy at the Chancellery, Nikolaus Meyer-Landrut, became director of the European policy department and my advisor on European affairs. He too had enormous experience in this field, among other things having served as spokesperson for the Convention on the Future of Europe from 2002 to 2003 under the former French president Valéry Giscard d'Estaing. Meyer-Landrut was later appointed German ambassador to France in 2015.

There had also been a change in the Chancellery's economic and financial policy department in 2011. After Jens Weidmann left in May to become president of the Deutsche Bundesbank, Lars-Hendrik Röller took over as head of department in July, having previously been chair of the Berlin-based European

School of Management and Technology. After a career in academia, he adapted quickly and enjoyed the political work at the Chancellery. I could always rely on him in any situation.

At a press conference with the Portuguese prime minister Pedro Passos Coelho on September 1, 2011, I was asked whether I was worried that the necessity for the Bundestag and all the other national parliaments to vote prior to any major decisions might not diminish the responsiveness and efficacy of the bailout fund. "We live in a democracy," I replied, "and it's a good thing we do. This is a parliamentary democracy, and authority over the budget is a key power of parliament. In this respect we shall find means to shape parliamentary co-determination in such a way that it is nevertheless market-compliant and sends the right signals on the markets."

I got into hot water for these comments, even though all I had done was, firstly, to reassert the primacy of politics and, secondly, point out the intended impact of our policy. What else had we been doing for the past four years and more throughout the financial crisis and the euro crisis? Politics for politics' sake? Or had our actions been intended to have an effect—on stock markets, in the economy, on people, their savings, and their jobs? Having been out of government for two years and now setting themselves up in complete opposition to us, the SPD picked up on the term "market-compliant" and combined it with "democracy" to form "market-compliant democracy." They then wielded this in polemical attacks against me, suggesting that I was more interested in markets than democracy, and revealing my true face and my enslavement to the money markets. Something I'd never said almost became the taboo word of 2011. Their dishonesty rankled with me. Political competition I grasped and could appreciate, but in my view this went too far.

Over the past four years we had spent more than enough time battling speculative market pressures. I experienced on an almost daily basis how tough it was to enact rational policies in the face of market actors simply refusing to invest unless they were absolutely sure it was worth their while. Given this, there was a lingering question of whether it might not have been better to cave in and simply drop the various demands on Greece, Portugal, Spain, and Italy to implement harsh austerity measures and economic reforms. My reputation was in tatters in those countries, especially in Greece. There was no doubt that people on low incomes had suffered the most from these reforms. Yet, setting aside the fact that I would never have obtained a majority within my own party and the coalition if I had abandoned requirements for the crisis-hit countries to improve their fiscal discipline and their economic competitivity, I would also have been in breach of my own convictions. If we wanted a common currency—and I did—while at the same time every eurozone country was responsible for its own fiscal, economic, and social policies, as enshrined in the Lisbon Treaty, then we needed to be able to trust that all countries would comply with our jointly agreed rules. This was what I had been advocating, and it had been a time-consuming process. The alternative would have been guarantees without any strings attached, which would gradually have resulted in collective liability for the debts of the eurozone. Regardless of any legal issues, I was utterly convinced that, sooner or later, this would have undermined public support for the currency. In other words, it would have endangered the euro far more than my actions had. Put another way, with a nod to a previous row over terminology: this was not a sensible alternative that I, as German chancellor, could have backed. It would not have been compatible with my interpretation of the official oath I had sworn on November 22, 2005 and again on October 28, 2009.

In June 2010, the European Council agreed to establish what was called the "European Semester," and in autumn 2010, the

Economic and Financial Affairs Council (ECOFIN) formally created the conditions for its introduction. The European Semester allowed the European Commission to check the draft budgets and reform plans of member states before they were enacted by national parliaments. The first European Semester began in 2011. Germany and France jointly presented an additional "Competitiveness Pact," which adopted our shared ideas for stronger economic policy coordination (as Germany referred to it) or economic governance (as France described it). This agreement was approved by the European Council in March as the Euro-Plus Pact. And yet the bond yield spreads of the countries worst affected by the euro crisis continued to widen. Actors on the financial markets clearly expected more than we were offering with our bailout fund. They wanted an instrument of unlimited scale. They wanted to force us to send out the political message that the European Central Bank (ECB) would intervene in an emergency.

The ECB was responsible for monetary policy. It was already doing what it could in this area, but it was politically independent. The individual states were responsible for their respective fiscal policies. The separation of monetary policy from fiscal policy was at the very core of our monetary union. Under no circumstances was I allowed to tamper with the ECB's independence.

But this was precisely what was at stake now. On the sidelines of the G20 summit in Cannes on November 3–4, 2011, Sarkozy, Berlusconi, Barroso, Obama, and everyone else, in fact, put me under huge pressure by repeating "We need a bazooka!" I fought this tooth and nail and even with tears. The Bundesbank president Jens Weidmann, who was Germany's representative on the ECB board, even went so far as to write a letter to me in Cannes, warning me not to give in to these demands.

I was badgered about this issue again six months later, in June 2012 at the G20 meeting in Los Cabos, Mexico. The summit's host, President Felipe Calderón, and I were actually on friendly terms, but he couldn't understand why I was so wedded to ECB independence. He had a different conception of the role of a central bank, and during an evening discussion restricted to heads of government, he tried again to convince me with the aid of an allegory.

"Angela," he said, "imagine you're a girl in a school playground. Some older boys are bullying you, and you have a big brother. It's the most natural thing in the world to ask him for help." The girl was a country, the ECB the big brother. He gave me a fond but triumphant look, convinced that he'd won me round with his comparison from real life.

I gave him a fond but earnest look back and said, "I'm not allowed to. I'm not allowed to ask my brother. I have to get through this on my own."

I guessed that almost everyone there must think I'd lost my mind or that Germans were just a bit odd. But I also knew that if I asked the ECB for political assistance, as these people wished, I would be hauled before the Federal Constitutional Court in a flash. What's more, I knew that I wouldn't be helping the euro or—as a result—the European Union one bit.

Mario Draghi succeeded Jean-Claude Trichet as president of the ECB at the end of 2011. At the Global Investment Conference in London, on July 26, 2012, he said, "Within our mandate, the ECB is ready to do whatever it takes to preserve the euro. And believe me, it will be enough."

In September, the ECB approved the Outright Monetary Transactions program (OMT). This instrument enabled the ECB to buy unlimited quantities of short-term bonds from eurozone states. A suit against the program was filed at the Federal Constitutional Court. The court referred the case to the European Court of Justice, which decided that the program was indeed compatible with the European treaties. The Federal

Constitutional Court agreed with the European court's view, albeit with a few specifications.

There was repeated speculation that Draghi had discussed his statement with me before making it. No, he hadn't. He had acted in his independent capacity as president of the ECB. Noting that we politicians had decided everything we could to stabilize the currency in summer 2012, he now made a contribution on behalf of the ECB. The bazooka had come out, and the spreads sank continuously after that.

On a knife edge

A new party called Alternative für Deutschland (AfD) was founded in Germany in early 2013. Its name had clearly been coined to echo the words that I had uttered during the financial and euro crises: "no alternative." The party's founders rejected my government's policy of stabilizing the euro, whereas I was proud that we had managed to save the currency. I wasn't joking when I said, "If the euro fails, Europe fails."

The new party stood candidates in the parliamentary elections on September 22, 2013 and gained 4.8 percent of the vote, falling just short of the 5-percent threshold necessary for its representatives to sit in the Bundestag. Despite all the tense negotiations and rows over the measures to save the euro, I secured a fabulous score of 41.5 percent for the CDU and CSU. My coalition partner, the FDP, on the other hand, achieved only 4.8 percent, missing out on parliamentary representation for the first time ever in the Federal Republic. I was very sorry about this. It didn't come as a complete surprise, though, as the party had been uneasy about rescuing the euro and vocal about its unease while in coalition with us. Trying to be in government and in opposition at the same time is rarely a winning formula, and this wasn't just a lesson for the FDP: it's a universal law of politics. On December 17, 2013, I was re-elected for a third term as chancellor at the head of another Grand Coalition government. SPD chair Sigmar Gabriel became the new deputy chancellor and minister of economic affairs, while Wolfgang Schäuble stayed on as finance minister.

A year and a half later, Alexis Tsipras replaced Antonis Samaras as prime minister of Greece after early elections were held on January 26, 2015. Tsipras was president of Syriza, a coalition of radical left-wing parties allied to Die Linke in Germany, and formed an unlikely coalition with the right-wing nationalist party ANEL (Independent Greeks). He owed his victory to the many Greek citizens enraged by the bailout program. During the election campaign he had promised "to rid Greece of the yoke" of surveillance by the Troika. His predecessor, Antonis Samaras, hadn't managed to implement in full the reforms agreed in the second bailout package. After Tspiras took office, the Eurogroup extended the program by four months until the end of June 2015.

On Monday, March 23, 2015, Tsipras arrived in my office at 5:00 p.m. for a first official visit. I was curious to see what kind of character I would meet. He was twenty years younger than me. We had spoken over the phone twice via interpreters, and had met briefly at two meetings of the European Council in Brussels. All I knew from those encounters was that he had made a good first impression and his English was good. Now I was waiting at the entrance to the main courtyard of the Chancellery to welcome him with full military honors. He was somewhat delayed because he hadn't been able to resist leaving his car outside the Chancellery to meet and greet some demonstrators from the Die Linke. I could hear cries of "Long live international solidarity!" in the distance. I just hoped he wouldn't linger too much out there and cast a shadow over his visit before it had even begun. It wasn't long, however, before his car drew up and he climbed out beaming a friendly and charming smile. Greeting him, I made a casual remark about his warm-up act, to which he replied in a self-confidently conciliatory tone that you should never forget your supporters. I nodded and smiled. A horde of photographers pointed their lenses at us—we were under intense observation. After the military ceremony, we went to my office with our interpreters for a private conversation. As we sat down in my armchairs, I welcomed him once more, noting the exceptional media interest we both faced, and he seemed to appreciate this. I got the feeling that we were both ready to surprise the outside world by how well we got on together.

If memory serves, I emphasized to Tsipras my strong resolve that Greece should remain a member of the eurozone, and that we would both need to work hard to achieve this. I had spent a great deal of summer 2012 weighing up the arguments of those who wanted to drive Greece out of the eurozone. Their reasoning had failed to convince me. Ever since, my position had been steadfast: Greece had to stay in the eurozone. Forcing a country out of the common currency might have unforeseen consequences, and once one country had broken out, pressure would only increase on the next potential candidate. In addition, the euro was more than just a currency, and Greece was the cradle of democracy. Nevertheless, I told Tsipras that there were conditions under which his country could remain in the eurozone. I also made it clear that I wanted to pursue the bilateral projects jointly initiated by Germany and Greece over the past few years. These included a twin-town scheme within the context of the German–Greek Group, a network designed to strengthen relations between German and Greek municipalities, educational programs for young Greeks in Germany, investment assistance, and the efforts of the German–Greek chambers of commerce. I knew Tsipras was skeptical about many of the things that previous Greek governments had done, but he promised to familiarize himself with these projects.

Leaving my office about thirty minutes later to join a larger meeting that included our chiefs of staff, advisors on European affairs and economic policy, and our government spokespeople, we were still discussing how each of us got into politics. He told me about his family, and I talked about Joachim and his sons. I got the impression that Alexis Tsipras was absolutely open to the idea of working with me and was simply exploring what was still largely uncharted territory for him. I was familiar with this approach and had great sympathy for it.

As we discussed matters with our staff and at dinner afterward, we tried to find a manner in which the new Greek government might satisfy the Troika's requirements without breaking its campaign promises. It was akin to squaring the circle. Before dinner there was a press conference, at which Tsipras and I gave something of a PR masterclass. Our tone was friendly and affectionate, but neither of us conceded an inch. The differences between our positions were great, but so was our determination to find a loophole through which to thread a solution.

Week after week passed without Greece making any noticeable progress in its discussions with the Troika. The direct contacts between Tsipras and me were of little assistance. I coordinated my words and actions closely with François Hollande, who'd been elected French president in May 2012. June arrived, and the Eurogroup and the Troika still hadn't come up with a solution. On June 22, 2015, eight days before the second bailout was due to expire, we met for a special council of eurozone heads of government. Having served as prime minister of Poland from 2007 to 2014, Donald Tusk had now succeeded Herman Van Rompuy as president of the European Council. We couldn't find a solution either. We asked the Eurogroup finance ministers to continue this work, but their efforts were no more fruitful than ours. And so the buck was returned to the heads of state and government at a scheduled European Council meeting on June 25–26. Alongside the official agenda, Tusk, Barroso, Hollande, and I negotiated with Tsipras. It wasn't until the early hours that we agreed on some key components of the next bailout scheme.

As we gathered on the morning of the second day of the European Council, Tusk presented the outcome of our nocturnal deliberations, but Tsipras was silent.

This struck me as strange. I got up, went over to him, and said quietly, "You haven't spoken yet, Alexis. Are you going to?"

He replied, "No, Donald has said all there is to say."

Somewhat bewildered, I asked, "What are you going to do now?"

Very calmly, he said, "I'm going to fly home and discuss with my cabinet what to do next."

I was stunned and walked on around the table to Hollande. He too was astonished. Both of us, like everyone else, had believed that Tsipras had accepted the outcome of that night's negotiations. That was also the picture Tusk had given of the situation.

I went back to Tsipras and asked him, "What will come out of those discussions?"

"I don't know," he answered.

"When will you know?" I pressed him.

"I can tell you early this evening."

Hollande and I agreed that we would have a three-way phone call.

When the European Council meeting was over, I flew back to Berlin and drove to Hohenwalde, where I took the conference call. Tsipras informed Hollande and me that his cabinet had decided to hold a referendum on the program we'd agreed, as the people had to have the final say on a matter of such importance. He would make a televised statement to his fellow citizens that same evening.

So far, so good, I thought. Then I asked him what his government was going to recommend to their people.

"'No,' of course," he said curtly.

It was perhaps the most astonishing moment of any phone call in my entire political career. For a few seconds Hollande and I were speechless, and then we swiftly wrapped up the conversation. Matters would take their course. There was nothing more I could do for now.

The following day, the Greek parliament voted to hold the referendum on July 5, 2015, but the Eurogroup refused to extend the Greek bailout program until an agreement for a follow-on scheme was in place. The government in Athens introduced capital controls to prevent a run on the banks, meaning that Greek citizens were permitted to withdraw no more than sixty euros per person per day. I couldn't imagine anything like this happening in Germany.

On July 5, 2015, eleven million Greeks voted no, which equated to a 61.3-percent share of the vote on a turnout of around 60 percent. The next day, I flew to Paris to discuss our response with President Hollande. We were both of the view that Greece's vote *against* the program was not the only democratic mandate; Germany and France were democracies too, and our parliaments had come out *in favor* of it. We nevertheless resolved to do everything we could to keep Greece in the eurozone.

No practical answers resulted from the eurozone summit in Brussels on July 7, 2015. Wolfgang Schäuble told me that the best scenario for everyone would be if Greece dropped out of the eurozone temporarily, whereas I continued to seek a path for Greece to retain its membership. The euro was more than just a currency: it represented the irreversible process of European unification, and Greece was a part of that commonwealth.

Another eurozone summit was scheduled for July 12, 2015, followed by a meeting of the European Council, in one final push to devise a solution for Greece and with the Greek government. I was eager to make sure that Schäuble and I were in step all the way, so I asked him to come to Brussels with me. Tusk, Barroso, Hollande, and I negotiated with Tsipras; otherwise, only our closest advisors were in the room. We were joined in the early hours of the morning by the former French finance minister Christine Lagarde, who had been managing director of the IMF since 2011. This time the Greek representatives showed great commitment to the negotiations. Now that things were getting serious, Tsipras had brought along some fantastic financial experts in his delegation. The referendum belonged to the past. That morning, we agreed on the key elements of a third bailout program to be funded from the European Stability Mechanism (ESM). To ensure that the detailed negotiations could advance smoothly in the following days, the European Commission granted Greece a bridging loan. On August 19, 2015, the Bundestag approved the new Greek bailout. In a government statement before the vote, the finance minister Schäuble had advocated €86 million in ESM funding and made IMF backing a prerequisite. The IMF had already pledged to continue supporting the second bailout from the EFSF until 2016, but the multilateral body had yet to determine whether it would participate in a third scheme. It agreed to do so only in July 2017, but it provided no further monetary support. In August 2018, the ESM program to Greece came to an end. The duration of the EFSF loans was extended again from 32.5 years to 42.5, meaning that repayment would now begin in 2033 instead of 2023. The Greek economy had been saved.

On January 10, 2019, I had dinner with Alexis Tsipras in a seafood restaurant with a view of the port of Piraeus. Our thoughts and conversation returned to the events of July 2015. Greece's continuing membership of the eurozone had been on a knife edge, I said. Tsipras told me that it had been essential to show the Greek people that the new government had done everything, absolutely everything, to shake off the hated Troika. When no other member states had backed them, it was clear that what counted was how the Greeks felt about the euro. A majority of Greeks rejected the bailout program but were nevertheless in favor of keeping the euro as their currency. It was this sentiment that had returned Tsipras to power after early elections in September 2015. The euro had won the battle of hearts and minds.

UKRAINE AND GEORGIA IN NATO?

The invasion of Ukraine

THURSDAY, FEBRUARY 24, 2022 will go down in European history as the end of the post-Cold War era. A danger that had grown clearer and ever more present over months, then weeks, and finally days had become a reality: President Vladimir Putin had ordered Russian troops to invade Ukraine on land, at sea, and from the air. This "special operation," as he called it, attacked a country 90 percent of whose population had voted for independence in a referendum on December 1, 1991. Putin attacked a country that had signed the Budapest Memorandum on the margins of a meeting of the Conference on Security and Co-operation in Europe (CSCE) on December 5, 1994, thereby committing itself to give up all the nuclear weapons stationed on its territory during the Soviet era. In return, Ukraine had trusted guarantees of its territorial integrity from the United States, the United Kingdom, and Russia. Putin attacked a country whose first president, Leonid Kuchma, had sealed a treaty of friendship with Russia's first president, Boris Yeltsin, in Kyiv on May 31, 1997, and this treaty restated the recognition of Ukraine's territorial integrity. The two countries also agreed that the Russian Black Sea Fleet could maintain a base in Sevastopol on Ukraine's Crimean Peninsula for a further twenty years. Four days earlier, the NATO–Russia Founding Act had been signed in Paris to reset the relationship between the

Russian Federation and NATO. Putin attacked a country whose opposition had successfully fought for an annulment of the fraud-bedeviled results of the second round of the November 2004 presidential elections. This protest movement became known as the Orange Revolution due to the campaign color used by the opposition candidate, Victor Yushchenko. He saw off his rival, the incumbent prime minister Victor Yanukovych, in the rescheduled runoff vote on December 26, 2004. Putin's aggression was aimed at a country whose Orange Revolution was only the latest and clearest signal of its desire to join NATO, just as Poland, the Czech Republic, and Hungary had done in March 1999, followed by Estonia, Latvia, Lithuania, Romania, Bulgaria, Slovenia, and Slovakia in March 2004. He was attacking a country that had hoped to join the Membership Action Plan—the precursor to NATO membership—at the 2008 NATO Summit in Bucharest. However, France and Germany, represented by Nicolas Sarkozy and myself, had turned down Ukraine's admission. After Russia's assault on Crimea in 2014, the "special operation" Putin launched on February 24, 2022 was simply a new and larger-scale invasion targeting the whole of Ukraine. It violated the territorial integrity and sovereignty of an independent state, and constituted a flagrant breach of international law.

Bucha, early April 2022. Six weeks into the war, Ukrainian forces had managed to push the Russian aggressors back far enough to liberate this suburb of the Ukrainian capital, Kyiv. What met their eyes there were scenes of horror. In the early days of the war, Russian troops had carried out a massacre, and the Ukrainians discovered hundreds of corpses, almost all of them civilians. Many of the victims bore signs of having been tortured before they were killed. In a video broadcast to his nation on the evening of Saturday, April 3, 2022, the Ukrainian president Volodymyr Zelenskyy said, among other things, that

NATO states had rejected his country's admission to the alliance in 2008 due to some politicians' "absurd fear of Russia," adding: "I invite Mrs. Merkel and Mr. Sarkozy to visit Bucha and to see what the policy of concessions to Russia has led to in fourteen years."

I was no longer chancellor when he said this. I was in Italy with friends, visiting museums and churches in Florence and Rome, on a trip planned while I was still in office. After a break by the Baltic and some time at home in the Uckermark, this was my first vacation since stepping down. During my political career I had never been able to spend a week simply soaking up culture, not just in the summer, or Easter and Christmas holidays—never. Paparazzi photos of me walking through the streets of Florence were juxtaposed with images from Bucha and footage of Zelenskyy's invitation. I asked my office to release a statement expressing "my full support" for the efforts of the German government and the international community to stand by Ukraine and bring an end to Russia's barbaric war on its neighbor. The first sentence also read: "Former German chancellor Dr. Angela Merkel stands by her decisions relating to the 2008 NATO summit in Bucharest." That statement still holds today. Why?

The NATO summit in Bucharest

No decision was taken in Bucharest regarding Ukraine's and Georgia's NATO membership. The deliberations there were related more to the question of whether the alliance would ask the two countries to draft a Membership Action Plan (MAP) and acquire MAP status, the final stage in a country's accession process. Ukraine and Georgia had requested this status. Agreeing to this in Bucharest would not have preempted a final decision by the alliance, but it would have represented an almost irreversible political acknowledgment that the two countries would become NATO members—and a prelude to a third major phase of NATO enlargement after the prior waves in 1999 and 2004.

I could understand the desire of countries in Central and Eastern Europe to join NATO as quickly as possible because the end of the Cold War had cemented their desire to be part of the Western community of nations. No one believed for a moment that the Russian Federation could give these countries what they craved: freedom, self-determination, and prosperity. They didn't need tempting with US money, as Putin had suggested to me during our drive to Tomsk Airport, unless of course we acknowledge that prosperity *is* tempting. Which of course it was, just as it had been to us East Germans in 1989 and even back in 1953, when there was an uprising against the SED regime. Because we the people are always attracted by "the pursuit of Happiness"—that inimitable phrase in the preamble to the 1776 US Declaration of Independence.

Nevertheless, NATO and its member states were obliged to evaluate the potential ramifications for the alliance of each phase of enlargement, as well as the impact on its security, stability, and functioning. The admission of a new member must not only improve the security of that particular country but increase the efficacy of NATO as a whole. The admission criteria therefore assessed each candidate's military capabilities and also the robustness of its internal structures, and this applied to Ukraine and Georgia too.

The territory of Ukraine included the Crimean Peninsula, where the Black Sea Fleet of the Russian Navy was stationed, and the contract between the two countries ran until 2017. It was unprecedented for a NATO candidate to be so entangled with Russian military structures. What's more, only a minority of the Ukrainian population backed NATO membership at the time: the country was profoundly split. In Georgia's case, there were unresolved territorial disputes in the regions of South Ossetia and Abkhazia, and this was reason enough, according to NATO ground rules, to reject the country's membership bid. The situation in both of these countries bore no relation to that of the Central and Eastern European states that had already acceded to NATO.

Of course, no third country outside NATO had a veto and that obviously included Russia. This would have contradicted the freedom of each country to choose its allies, as enshrined in the Charter of Paris signed by thirty-two European countries, the United States, and Canada at the CSCE meeting in November 1990. Conversely, there was also no automatic agreement when a country applied to join.

I thought it would be playing with fire to discuss MAP status for Ukraine and Georgia without analyzing the situation from Putin's perspective. Since Putin had become president in 2000, one of his highest priorities had been to restore his country's international standing so that no one could ignore Russia, least of all the United States. Putin wasn't interested in building democratic structures or creating prosperity for all, either at home or abroad. His real ambition was to push back against the American victory in the Cold War. He wanted Russia to be an essential pole in a multipolar world, and to achieve that goal he drew on his experience in the security services.

I had given the opening speech at the Munich Security Conference on February 10, 2007, more than a year before the Bucharest NATO Summit. In line with the slogan emblazoned on the backdrop behind me—"Peace through dialogue"—my address had focused on cooperation in the face of global challenges and on the need to seek dialogue with Russia despite our many differences of opinion. It was Putin's turn to speak after me. He talked about a unipolar world, asking: "But what is a unipolar world? However one might embellish this term, at the end of the day it refers to one type of situation, namely *one* center of authority, *one* center of force, *one* center of decision-making. It is a world in which there is one master, one sovereign." Later, he named countries by name: "We are seeing a greater and greater disdain for the basic principles of international law. And independent legal norms are, as a matter of fact, coming increasingly closer to one state's legal system. One state and, of course, first and foremost the United States, has overstepped its national borders in every way. This is visible in the economic, political, cultural, and educational policies it imposes on other nations." Putin's sole point of reference was the United States—or rather he dreamed of the roles that the former Soviet Union and the US had held in the good old days of the Cold War when the two superpowers had faced each other as adversaries. Alluding to the Iraq War, he spoke in Munich of "an almost uncontained, hyper use of force," questioned the missile defense system that the United States planned to install in Europe, and said that the EU and NATO should not replace the UN—in reference to the NATO intervention in Serbia without a UN mandate—and that NATO expansion was a provocative element. He had then concluded with the following words: "Russia is a country with a history that spans more than a thousand years and has practically always had the privilege of carrying out an independent foreign policy. We are not going to change this tradition today. At the same time, we are well aware of how the world has changed and we have a realistic sense of our own opportunities and potential. And, of course, we would like to interact with responsible and independent partners with whom we can work together in constructing a fair and democratic world order that might ensure security and prosperity not only for a select few, but for all."

I was sitting in the front row. The seat to my left was empty and reserved for Putin, while to my right sat President Victor Yushchenko of Ukraine. The US defense secretary Robert Gates and the American representatives and senators were seated along the aisle to my left. I was able to observe Putin closely during his speech. He spoke quickly, sometimes without consulting the notes he'd probably written mostly, if not entirely, himself. What irritated me most was his self-righteousness: not a word about the unresolved conflicts on his doorstep in Nagorno-Karabakh, Moldova, and Georgia; criticism of NATO's intervention in Serbia but not a word about the atrocities committed by the Serbs as the former Yugoslavia was collapsing; and not a word about the path Russia itself was taking. There were, however, some points that I did not regard as completely absurd. As we know, there was never any evidence of chemical weapons in Iraq. I too had railed against the fact that there had been no progress on updating the Treaty on Conventional Armed Forces in Europe (CFE), the 1990 agreement to restrict the numbers of heavy weapon systems in Europe, signed by NATO and the Warsaw Pact countries. It should have been adapted after the dissolution of the Warsaw Pact, the collapse of the Soviet Union, and the admission of various Eastern European countries to NATO. The presence of Russian military observers in Georgia had caused a flare-up between Russia and the United States in particular during the ratification of the adapted treaty (A-CFE). I had deplored the fact that this had derailed the new treaty, but I had been unable to bring any influence to bear because the direction of travel had already been determined before I took office.

In his speech in Munich, Putin presented himself the way I experienced him: as someone constantly on the lookout for signs of disparaging behavior toward him, and yet always ready to disrespect others, for instance by engaging in canine power-play and making everyone wait. You could find all of this childish and reprehensible, you could shake your head, but there Russia was, still on the map.

What did this mean when Ukraine and Georgia might be on

course to join the alliance via MAP status but couldn't yet claim the security guarantees of Article 5 of the NATO treaty?

I found it illusory to think that Ukraine and Georgia's MAP status would have protected them from Putin's aggression and that this status would have acted as a deterrent, or that Putin would take these developments lying down. If worse came to worst, therefore, was it conceivable that NATO members would have responded by providing military hardware or troops? Was it conceivable that I'd have asked the Bundestag, as chancellor, for a mandate for our army and carried the vote? In 2008? If so, what would the consequences have been? And if not, with what consequences, not just for Ukraine and Georgia, but for NATO too? During the two previous waves of Eastern enlargement, it had taken at least five years for the countries to advance from MAP status to full members of the alliance. The assumption that Putin would simply twiddle his thumbs in the period between the MAP decision and Ukraine's and Georgia's acquisition of membership struck me as wishful thinking—politics reduced to hope.

It was for all these reasons that I didn't believe I could support MAP status for Ukraine and Georgia. This was my mindset on April 2, 2008, as I boarded a Ministry of Defense A310 at Berlin's Tegel Airport, along with the foreign minister Frank-Walter Steinmeier and members of our staff, to fly to Bucharest for the NATO summit.

During the flight we talked primarily about what awaited us when we landed. The invitations extended to two further countries, Croatia and Albania, to join the twenty-six current members of the alliance were uncontroversial. Greece was blocking an invitation to a third candidate, the ex-Yugoslavian Republic of Macedonia, on account of the country's name. Like many others, I had repeatedly tried to find creative solutions to this during discussions with the two protagonists in the lead-up to the summit, but Greece was still holding out. It claimed that the name Macedonia should apply exclusively to its eponymous geographical region. It would be another ten years before the deadlock was broken, thanks to courageous and determined action by Prime Minister Alexis Tsipras and his Macedonian counterpart, Zoran Zaev. In 2018, the two countries agreed on the name North Macedonia.

Steinmeier shared my view on MAP status for Georgia and Ukraine. In the previous months I had not only consulted my own government but also made sure I was on the same page as President Nicolas Sarkozy of France. Other Western countries agreed with us too. Most Central and Eastern European countries, on the other hand, took Washington's line that the Bucharest Summit should grant MAP status to Ukraine and Georgia.

George W. Bush was aware of my negative stance, as we had talked about it several times since 2007, both over the phone and during my visit to his ranch. Yet he had still restated to President Victor Yushchenko and Prime Minister Yulia Tymoshenko, during a trip to Kyiv on the eve of the meeting, that he was determined to agree MAP status for Ukraine and Georgia in Bucharest. The alliance could only reach a decision like this unanimously, and so these two trains were on a collision course. Decision day was nigh, and it was no trifling matter to tangle with someone like the president of the United States on the international stage. Did he believe I would crumble under the weight of public pressure? I still had awful memories of how the military intervention in Iraq had split NATO and the repercussions for cooperation within the EU. It had taken us Europeans a long time to resume working together in a constructive spirit. Nonetheless, the United States and many of the Central and Eastern European countries seemed deaf to our objections to Ukraine and Georgia joining NATO. They were glossed over, with the observation that a refusal amounted to giving Russia a veto. This was the supposedly clinching argument that prevented us all from carefully weighing up the pros and cons of the matter.

Steinmeier and I knew that we were in for a hard time. We touched down in Bucharest shortly before 5:00 p.m.. Christoph Heusgen and I drove directly to the working dinner of heads of state and government at the Cotroceni Palace, the king of Romania's former residence and current offices of the president, while Steinmeier went to a dinner of foreign ministers at the Palace of the Parliament. At around 6:00 pm, I was greeted by the Romanian president Traian Băsescu, and the NATO secretary general Jaap de Hoop Scheffer. As the twenty-four participants trickled in, we gathered in an antechamber of the Uniril Hall, where the dinner was to take place. I chatted to the others for a while. There was a slight tension in the air as a result of our disagreements. I had a brief talk with Nicolas Sarkozy on his own when he arrived.

"What do you think of George's trip to Kyiv yesterday? Where does it lead?" I asked him.

"That's up to him," he replied. "But we're sticking to our line of non-approval?"

"Yes," I said. "I don't like this kind of argument, but I believe it's necessary this time, even if I've no idea how it's going to end."

We agreed that I would use my speech that evening to invite the heads of state and government to celebrate the alliance's sixtieth anniversary the following year, in Kehl in Germany and Strasbourg in France. We wanted to stage the summit as a reminder of how lucky we were to have a blueprint for lasting peace in Europe and to showcase NATO's decisive contribution since its founding in 1949. A group walk by all the heads of state and government across the Europe Bridge linking the two towns on either side of the Rhine would be a visual symbol of our peaceful cooperation.

Dinner began. Gigantic crystal chandeliers hung from the

ceiling of the hall. The welcome speeches by our host and the secretary general of NATO were followed by a *tour de table*—a round of opening remarks by everyone present. I raised my hand with many others, but it was quite a while until the floor was mine. It was clear from the first contributions to the discussion that most participants were eager to avoid any controversy. Many participants expected the contentious points to be ironed out behind the scenes. When de Hoop Scheffer gave me the signal, I spoke first about the NATO operation in Afghanistan—a separate meeting with the Afghan president Hamid Karzai was scheduled for the following day. Next, however, I made it clear that I opposed granting MAP status to Ukraine and Georgia. Nicolas Sarkozy backed my reasoning when his turn came.

There was no heated debate that evening in Bucharest, but nor did any avenues of resolution present themselves. As a matter of fact, the delay only ratcheted up the tension as to how the issue might be addressed the following day.

The decisive meeting of the North Atlantic Council, NATO's ultimate decision-making body, started at 8:55 the next morning, after the opening ceremony. This gathering was attended by the heads of state and government, foreign and defense ministers, and five additional members of each delegation. Once again, we had to wait in a separate room until all our fellow leaders had arrived. I got there early.

George W. Bush came over to me and said, "Good morning, Angela. We still have a problem to solve. Could you envisage talking to Condy about it?"

By "Condy" he meant Secretary of State Condoleezza Rice. I knew her well, but it was not usual etiquette for a head of government to negotiate with another country's foreign minister. I would normally have turned down such a request, but this one came from the president of the United States, so I made an exception. I guessed that he'd realized I was serious about rejecting MAP status for Ukraine and Georgia and that the time for compromise was approaching. Bush clearly didn't want to get into a personal clinch with me. I accepted his proposal because I too was eager to avoid a spectacular showdown. He walked away looking relieved.

The venue for the subsequent working session was a huge hall in the Palace of the Parliament, built to the design of the dictator President Nicolae Ceaușescu, who was sentenced to death by a military tribunal on December 25, 1989 and executed the same day. Now, not even twenty years later, the NATO heads of state and government were meeting in this palace—another symbol of the triumph of freedom and democracy over tyranny and dictatorship. Each delegation had two seats around a vast table: Frank-Walter was to my left, while the other members of our delegation sat behind us. To my right was Nicolas Sarkozy, as the places had been assigned in English alphabetical order, so France came directly before Germany. George W. Bush was opposite me.

When my turn came to speak—Bush had yet to say anything—the US president listened to me very closely. Glancing at him from time to time, I made a statement intended to allay any impression that I never wanted to see Ukraine and Georgia join NATO: "One day these two countries will be members of NATO." Bush took notes, and when I had sat down again, one of his staff came over to pass a message to Christoph Heusgen, who was sitting behind me. On the slip of paper was the English translation of the phrase I had used: "One day they will become members of NATO." Heusgen also relayed a question from the US president: Could I imagine including this sentence in the official summit declaration? After a quick check with Steinmeier and Sarkozy, I agreed, on the condition that we drop MAP status for Ukraine and Georgia. Heusgen handed this message to a member of the American delegation, who passed it on to his president. Bush consulted his secretary of state, and she asked Heusgen to go behind a thick dividing curtain with her for a short, private conversation.

Heusgen reported back to Steinmeier and me that Condoleezza Rice had insisted on MAP status for Ukraine and Georgia. With some annoyance I asked Heusgen to inform the Americans that I wouldn't alter my position on MAP. Just then I saw a member of the US delegation speaking to one of the Polish representatives. (The Polish president Lech Kaczyński was something of a spokesperson for the Eastern European member states.) I concluded from the Poles' body language that they weren't at all happy. I asked Heusgen to craft some formulations for a compromise on the basis of what I'd said earlier, and about thirty minutes later he handed me a sheet of paper with some proposals he and his French colleague had drafted. At their heart was my phrase foreseeing NATO membership for Georgia and Ukraine in the future. Nicolas Sarkozy had given the text his green light. Time was short because the next meeting with the accession candidates Croatia and Albania would begin at 11:35, and the secretary general's press conference was scheduled for 12:35.

After everyone had had a chance to speak, there was a break. De Hoop Scheffer announced that only the heads of state and government, plus one further person from each delegation, were allowed to remain in the room. I asked Christoph Heusgen to stay. As most of the participants left the room, I noticed that a cluster had formed away from the negotiating table. On closer inspection I saw that it consisted of a number of Eastern European presidents. Lech Kaczyński was sitting on a chair in the middle of the group, and around him stood the presidents of Lithuania, Latvia, and Estonia—Valdas Adamkus, Valdis Zatlers, and Toomas Hendrik Ilves—along with our host, Traian Băsescu, and a few others. Nicolas Sarkozy had left the room for a minute. I decided to go over to the group, as I didn't want the rifts to widen any further. Only one person was left sitting at the negotiating table: George W. Bush. He was observing events.

When Lech Kaczyński caught sight of me, he immediately stood up and offered me his chair. Even during the toughest arguments, he never forgot the old Polish etiquette and courtesies I knew from my dealings with Polish friends. I was touched. I accepted his offer and suddenly found myself in the thick of the action. We spoke English, and there were also interpreters at hand. I set out my position once more, adding: "Reaching no agreement would be the greatest gift we could make to NATO's adversaries and, most of all, to President Putin of Russia." Putin was due to attend the NATO–Russia Council the next day. "We can sit here for days if we want, but that was my final word on the principle of NATO membership and I will not agree to MAP status," I said, repeating my opening remarks from the previous day.

We must have talked for half an hour. At some stage Condoleezza Rice joined us, and the whole discussion began all over again. We were going around in circles. Finally, Lech Kaczyński suggested deleting the words "one day" from my sentence. I could live with that. Things moved quickly from then on. We Europeans had reached an agreement, so Condoleezza Rice went to see her boss, who was still sitting at the table, talked to him, came back almost immediately, and said that President Bush agreed too. The secretary general was informed, and we were able to resume and conclude the adjourned meeting.

Ukraine and Georgia did not obtain MAP status, and the alliance had not split as it had over the Iraq War. I had been desperate to avoid the latter, although I had been forced to make a statement on the prospects of Ukraine and Georgia joining NATO. There had been no option but to compromise, even if this compromise, like any other, came at a price. For Georgia and Ukraine, being denied MAP status deflated their hopes;

and for Putin, the fact that NATO had made a general pledge of membership equated to the two countries becoming members and was therefore a declaration of war. At a later date, although I can no longer recall the precise details, he told me, "You won't be chancellor forever, and then they'll become NATO members. And I'm going to prevent that." And I thought: Well, you're not going to be president forever either. The meeting in Bucharest had done nothing to ease my fears of tensions with Russia. Around 2:00 p.m., a little later than planned, the French president and I announced the results of the summit at a joint press conference. We'd been able to count on each other throughout this difficult test, and the same applied to my working relationship with Frank-Walter Steinmeier.

The next morning, the final day of the summit, there was a meeting between a NATO–Ukraine Commission and President Yushchenko. He showed no signs of dissatisfaction with the outcome in his speech, but he must have been disappointed. He wanted to anchor Ukraine in an alliance for collective security that would make his country's independence an irreversible fact. He had probably had firsthand experience of Russian influence by dioxin poisoning during the presidential election campaign in September 2004.

The meeting of the NATO–Russia Council was slated for eleven o'clock. Once again, Putin kept us all waiting. It was the first time he'd attended a NATO summit since the 2002 meeting in Rome. In the interlude there had been the beginning of the Iraq War in 2003, Russia's suspension of the CFE treaty in late 2007 after the NATO states had refused to ratify it, and, in early 2008, the declaration of independence by Kosovo, which Russia, unlike many NATO members, did not recognize under international law. This was also, for the time being, the last time Putin attended an international conference as president of the Russian Federation. His successor, Dmitry Medvedev, had already been elected and would be sworn in on May 7, 2008. Putin himself would be prime minister for the next four years, a position he'd already occupied for ten years under President Boris Yeltsin, whom he had succeeded in 2000. Now, Putin was expecting George W. Bush in Sochi the next day for an official visit. Despite all their policy differences, the United States and Russia were still firmly committed to maintaining a dialogue.

When Putin finally arrived, his speech was less impulsive than his remarks in some of our previous conversations, but after a few initial pleasantries he got straight down to business. In his press conference later, he repeated some of the critical points from his perspective: "the further eastward expansion of NATO; the establishment of military infrastructure on the territories of the new members; the crisis over the Treaty on Conventional Armed Forces in Europe (CFE); Kosovo; plans to deploy elements of the strategic anti-missile defense from the United States to Europe." Despite his comparatively polite tone, it was impossible to ignore the remarkable similarities between the content of his remarks at this meeting and those he had delivered at the Munich Security Conference a good year before. He was clearly not speaking on a whim, either then or now.

Four months later, in July 2008, fighting broke out between South Ossetian militias and the Georgian army. In the night of August 7–8, 2008, Georgia tried to gain military control of South Ossetia. When members of alleged peace forces sent by the Community of Independent States (CIS) were killed in the skirmishes, Russian troops exploited the situation to attack the Georgian army and advance into the Georgian heartland. Russia justified its intervention by arguing that it was protecting Russian minorities. Georgia asked the United States for military support. Anxious not to spark a direct military confrontation with Russia, the US turned down these Georgian requests.

France held the rotating presidency of the EU Council for

the second half of 2008, so it fell to Nicolas Sarkozy to mediate peace discussions with Medvedev and Putin. Georgia signed an agreement on August 15, and that same day, in consultation with Nicolas Sarkozy, I flew to Sochi to persuade President Medvedev to sign the peace plan, which Russia did on August 16. The day after that, I visited President Saakashvili in Tbilisi to hear his views on the matter. Saakashvili had been elected to succeed Eduard Shevardnadze as Georgian president in early 2004 following the Rose Revolution that had swept through his country the previous November. On the one hand, I admired his reforming zeal; on the other, I thought that he was overplaying his hand toward Russia. Russia's provocation of Georgia clearly highlighted the vulnerability of this country in the Caucasus, at the crossroads of Europe and Asia. After the end of the fighting, the Russian army stayed in South Ossetia in defiance of the peace plan negotiated by the European Union. The conflict was frozen. Observers from an EU mission were denied access to the region. During my visit to the barbed-wire border fence between Georgia and South Ossetia ten years later, in August 2018, I was forced to acknowledge just how hopeless the situation was.

I flew home from Bucharest with mixed emotions. We'd avoided a major incident, and yet the meeting had laid bare NATO's lack of a coherent strategy for dealing with Russia. Many countries in Central and Eastern Europe had very little appetite for investing in any relationship with Russia. They seemed to wish that their gigantic neighbor would disappear from the map, simply cease to exist. It was hard to blame them: they'd suffered for so long under Soviet rule and, unlike us East Germans, hadn't had the good fortune to be peacefully and freely reunited with a country like West Germany that was deeply embedded in European and transatlantic alliances.

But Russia did exist and it was armed to the teeth with

nuclear weapons. There was no wishing it away geopolitically and there still isn't, if for no other reason than that it is one of the five permanent, veto-holding members of the UN Security Council, alongside the United States of America, France, the United Kingdom, and China.

Is my reference to Russia's global influence an expression of the "absurd fear" of this country that Volodymyr Zelenskyy mentioned in his video broadcast to his people on April 3, 2022 after the Bucha massacre had come to light? No. But it is a different interpretation of whether MAP status for Ukraine and Georgia would have acted as a deterrent against Russia, and what the ramifications for NATO might have been in the years before the two countries became full members.

PEACE AND SELF-DETERMINATION IN UKRAINE

The Eastern partnership

CONTRARY TO MY opposition to MAP status for Ukraine and Georgia, I was in favor of efforts to draw the two countries—and other interested former Soviet republics—closer to the European Union. In 1994, the European Community had already concluded a Partnership and Cooperation Agreement with Russia, which had come into force in 1997. It regulated commercial cooperation and foresaw the establishment of a free-trade zone, as well as cooperation in areas such as social policy, vocational training, science, technology, and transport, and the intensification of political dialogue. The European Community had signed similar agreements with other post-Soviet republics.

In parallel with the European Union's 2004 enlargement to integrate ten new member states—Poland, Estonia, Latvia, Lithuania, Slovakia, Slovenia, the Czech Republic, Hungary, Malta, and Cyprus—the European Commission also raised the status of its cooperation with the EU's eastern and southern neighbors to a new level by proposing the so-called European Neighborhood Policy. It offered them the opportunity to deepen cooperation but without the prospect of becoming member states. I thought that this approach was absolutely right.

It was on this basis that what was known as the Union for the Mediterranean was created for the EU's southern neighbors in Paris on July 13, 2008, and it brought together the then twenty-seven member states with sixteen countries from around the Mediterranean.

Of the neighboring states to the east, Armenia, Azerbaijan, Belarus, Georgia, Moldova, and Ukraine wished to take part in the EU's Neighborhood Policy, but Russia did not, even though many EU member states, including Germany, were in favor of this. President Putin did not want his country to be treated in the same fashion as other former Soviet republics. Worse still, he did everything in his power to prevent a rapprochement between other post-Soviet states and the EU after the Baltic countries joined the Union. He interpreted these closer relations as an obstacle to his own project for a Russia-dominated Eurasian power base. Back in 2001, the Kremlin had begun to strengthen the recently founded Eurasian Economic Union—an economic alliance of European and Asian successor states to the Soviet Union—and gradually to incorporate it into a customs union. Putin was losing interest in a free-trade zone between the European Union and Russia of the kind that had been negotiated in 1994, having come to the conclusion that the former Soviet republics belonged to one of two camps—the Russian one or the West. He refused to countenance the possibility that these countries might simply be attracted by the idea of closer ties with a prosperous and liberal alliance such as the European Union.

Following Russia's war on Georgia in August 2008, there was a growing willingness among the members of the European Union, including Germany, to act either without or even in opposition to Russia. So, on May 7, 2009, during the Czech presidency of the EU Council, the inaugural summit of the so-called Eastern Partnership was held in Prague with Azerbaijan, Armenia, Georgia, Moldova, Belarus, and Ukraine forming the second pillar of the European Neighborhood Policy after the launch of the Union for the Mediterranean ten months earlier. The Eastern Partnership was about promoting democratic structures and social contacts, facilitating visas, securing borders, and improving energy security. In addition, there was an opening for participating states to negotiate Association Agreements, including free-trade deals, with the European Union.

This sounded simple, but it was difficult to put into practice. Since Putin had a strategic interest in impeding these kinds of agreements between former Soviet republics and the EU, he threatened them with a dramatic worsening of their traditionally close economic ties with Russia by casting doubt on existing trade benefits and announcing the imposition of customs duties. In doing so he forced the states to choose between closer cooperation with Russia or the European Union—an insoluble dilemma. Azerbaijan, which had its own oil and gas reserves, had never shown any intent to seal an Association Agreement with Europe, and nor had Belarus, which was in a customs union with Russia and Kazakhstan. Armenia's president Serzh Sargsyan had first declared an interest in principle, but then performed a U-turn after paying a visit to Vladimir Putin in September 2013; he now wished to join the Russian customs union. His country's geographical position and its conflicts with Azerbaijan and Turkey apparently left him no room for maneuver; Armenia was almost completely economically dependent on the Russian Federation. It was all the more remarkable, therefore, that Prime Minister Iurie Leancă of Moldova resisted enormous Russian pressure and chose to negotiate an Association Agreement with the European Union.

Ukraine was the first country in the Eastern Partnership to complete negotiations for an Association Agreement with the EU. Power had just changed hands in the country, with incumbent president Victor Yushchenko eliminated in the first round of the 2010 elections with a paltry 5.5 percent of the vote. In the February runoff, Yushchenko's predecessor, Victor Yanukovych, had beaten Yulia Tymoshenko, whom Yushchenko had sacked as prime minister in 2005. These two figureheads of the Orange

Revolution had fallen out in dramatic style. I knew Yulia Tymoshenko from our work together in the European People's Party (EPP). Her party, the All-Ukrainian Union "Fatherland," had enjoyed observer status there since 2008. I'd come to appreciate her as an experienced, energetic, rhetorically gifted, and belligerent person. The public was familiar with her because of her striking plaited hairstyle.

Tymoshenko had endorsed the path of European integration for Ukraine and proved to be an agile operator in her domestic political system, including its murkier realms. She was arrested in August 2011 on allegations of signing disadvantageous gas contracts with Russia. Political interference couldn't be ruled out, and the EU suspended the Ukraine Association Agreement she had signed until further notice. This was a major shock to Ukraine during a period of great economic hardship. The country needed loans from the International Monetary Fund, which demanded painful reforms in return. Putin, on the other hand, employed carrot-and-stick tactics toward Ukraine. Having been reinstated as Russian president more than a year earlier, he now threatened Yanukovych with high tariffs, while simultaneously tempting him—so it was rumored—with low gas prices and extensive funding pledges. Yanukovych equivocated. Ukraine had benefited from observer status at the Eurasian Economic Community since August 2013.

Yanukovych requested €160 billion in funding from the EU until 2017—a ludicrous sum of money—and at the same time he proposed a three-party meeting with Russia, Ukraine, and the EU. José Barroso, the president of the European Commission, declined, pointing to the sovereign right of any individual state to act with or without the EU. I judged this to be a mistake; I thought it would have been worth a try. Later, the EU Commission adopted a different approach, offering Ukraine more frequent assistance to negotiate gas transit contracts with Russia.

Yanukovych had to make a decision, and he did. A few days

before the Eastern Partnership summit in the Lithuanian capital, Vilnius, on November 28–29, 2013, the Ukrainian parliament rejected an application for the release of Yulia Tymoshenko and also suspended preparations for signing the Association Agreement with the EU. Instead, President Yanukovych instructed the relevant ministries to initiate a dialogue with Russia, the other countries in the customs union, and the CIS states. This brought Ukraine's rapprochement with the EU to a grinding halt. Many people outside the country were surprised—they had clearly been relying on hope. I felt particularly sorry for the summit organizer, President Dalia Grybauskaitė of Lithuania. She had prepared everything perfectly for the signing ceremony, and I wouldn't have begrudged her, the former EU Commissioner for Budget and Administration, this domestic success in the slightest.

On Thursday, November 28, 2013, I arrived at the Palace of the Grand Dukes of Lithuania at around 7:00 p.m. On the agenda was an informal meeting of the EU heads of state and government, followed by dinner. The mood was bleak. Ours was not the only venue where discussions were in overdrive. Numerous Ukrainian opposition politicians had traveled to Vilnius, including Vitali Klitschko, the former world boxing champion and current chair of the Ukrainian Democratic Alliance for Reform (UDAR) party. I had a lot of sympathy for the Moldovans and the Georgians. They wanted to sign their agreement, but no one was taking any notice of their efforts—proof yet again of the rule that a negative headline almost always trumps a positive story.

At 8:15 the next morning I met Victor Yanukovych for about forty minutes in my hotel, the Grand Hotel Kempinski. After the usual greetings, I asked him, "How should I interpret your change of heart, Victor? I don't understand. You want to sign the agreement, you said so yourself. And now that we're almost there, you make a U-turn."

The tall, powerfully built man opposite me looked uncertain as the interpreter translated my words.

"Give me a little more time," Yanukovych replied. "It isn't possible now. You mustn't force the issue now. One day I'll sign."

How was I meant to respond to that? Fear oozed from his every pore. He must have known that he was caught between a rock and a hard place. It was pointless trying to get him to sign. I thought that his request for more time was empty rhetoric. Putin had knocked the wind out of him and dragged Ukraine into his camp. For the time being.

We said goodbye and traveled in separate vehicles to the summit venue at LITEXPO, the Lithuanian Exhibition and Congress Center, for the signing of the EU Association Agreements with Georgia and Moldova.

The Maidan protests

On that November day when Yanukovych terminated Ukraine's rapprochement with the EU, demonstrators flooded the Maidan in Kyiv, the capital's main square, and protested in other cities all over the country. More and more people joined their ranks, desperate for political change. When the government resorted to force, the crowds swelled into the hundreds of thousands. I followed these developments with sympathy, and also some anxiety.

Three months later in Hohenwalde, on Saturday, February 22, 2014, I couldn't help but gasp as I watched the latest political reports, which I did every morning. Yanukovych had fled Kyiv the previous evening, the demonstrators' so-called self-defense forces were in control of parliament, the seat of government, and the president's office, and the protesters were urging police to change sides to the Maidan movement. I had trouble understanding what had happened in the previous eighteen months. As recently as Friday afternoon, Yanukovych for the government, and Vitali Klitschko, Oleh Tyahnybok, the leader of the All-Ukrainian Union "Svoboda" party, and Arseniy Yatsenyuk, the parliamentary leader of the All-Ukrainian Union "Fatherland" for the opposition, had signed a six-point agreement setting out Ukraine's future political pathway. One of the opposition's demands was to restore the 2004 constitution and revise it before September 2014. A government of national unity was to be installed within ten days. In addition, new electoral legislation was to be passed and early presidential elections held by December 2014 in accordance with the Organization for Security and Cooperation in Europe (OSCE). The German foreign minister Frank-Walter Steinmeier and the Polish foreign minister Radosław Sikorski had traveled to Kyiv that Thursday with their French counterpart, Laurent Fabius, with the approval of the EU, to negotiate an end to the violence on the Maidan with Yanukovych. The opposition estimated that around one hundred people had been shot dead over the previous days. Discussons between Yanukovych and opposition representatives had lasted through the night into Friday morning. I had been in constant contact with Steinmeier, and had made several phone calls to secure Putin's support for a successfully negotiated outcome, as well as encouraging him to send someone to represent his country. Contrary to my pleas for him to send the foreign minister Lavrov, he had chosen Vladimir Lukin, the Russian parliament's human rights commissioner. Lukin's appearance at the talks convinced Yanukovych that Russia was also expecting a deal. The Ukrainian president had to change his position and did. But on Friday morning, when Steinmeier and Sikorski—Fabius had to leave early—and the three opposition leaders presented the six-point plan to thirty or so representatives of the demonstrators, the document had met with fierce criticism.

Some members of the protesters' council rejected any kind of settlement with the government, but ultimately only two people voted against the agreement. This was followed by the official signing in the president's office. The president of the United States Barack Obama also insisted to Putin during a phone call that the agreement should be swiftly implemented. Very soon, however, there were vocal demands on the Maidan to reject the deal and demand that Yanukovych step down. The three opposition leaders who had signed were whistled and booed on the Maidan that evening. The crowd backed an ultimatum expressed by one activist that Yanukovych must relinquish power by ten o'clock the next morning, February 22, 2014. He slipped out of the city that same night.

Events now came thick and fast in Kyiv. I asked Christoph Heusgen to keep me continuously abreast of the news. Around noon, the Ukrainian parliament decided to release Yulia Tymoshenko from prison, and the supreme court acquitted her that June. Oleksandr Turchynov, a close confidant of Yulia Tymoshenko's, was appointed speaker of the parliament. That same afternoon, the parliament voted to depose President Yanukovych from office. He fled to Russia, accusing the opposition of fomenting a coup, and continuing to claim that he was the legitimate leader of Ukraine. On Sunday, February 23, 2014, Oleksandr Turchynov was elected temporary president, and presidential elections were set for May 25. In a broadcast to the nation that evening, Turchynov issued a warning of impending state bankruptcy.

The six-point agreement of February 21, 2014 had been consigned to history. There was not a doubt in my mind that Putin would respond to these developments. He wouldn't allow Ukraine to make its own decisions: that much was clear to me. The only question was exactly which form his response would take.

The annexation of Crimea

On Sunday, February 23, 2014, Prime Minister Dmitry Medvedev recalled the Russian ambassador to Ukraine from Kyiv. After his brief intermezzo as president from 2008 to 2012, Medvedev had now officially returned to the second rank, which was in truth where he had always been. The reason given for the withdrawal of the Russian ambassador and the public pretext for the subsequent invasion was that the lives of Russian citizens were under threat. Alarm bells were now ringing everywhere, and the US warned Russia not to make a military intervention in Ukraine.

Five days later, on February 28, I spoke on the phone to Arseniy Yatsenyuk, who had been elected prime minister of the transitional government by the Ukrainian parliament the previous day, to offer him my support in his tough assignment. In a press release about this phone call, I emphasized the protection of Ukraine's territorial integrity. This was because that very day armed men in unmarked green uniforms had begun to occupy Crimea. My mind turned to the Russian Black Sea Fleet stationed in Sevastopol. Nearly four year earlier, in April 2010, President Medvedev and President Yanukovych had extended the treaty between Russia and Ukraine on the status of the fleet by another twenty-five years. The current treaty expired in 2017, and the new one would therefore run until 2042. The then Ukrainian opposition had been vehemently opposed to this agreement. Its approval had triggered brawls in the Ukrainian parliament, and smoke bombs had been thrown in the chamber.

When I confronted Putin on the phone the next day, Saturday, March 1, 2014, with my suspicion that the unknown armed men in the green uniforms without national insignia were in fact Russian soldiers, he denied it. It soon became clear that he had told me a bare-faced lie; never in our previous conversations had he been so brazen. However, I didn't break off contact with him—I didn't see this as an option—but our relationship entered a new phase. There were no further consultations between the German and Russian governments, no visits to other cities beyond summits for specific purposes in our respective capitals, no more face-to-face meetings with Putin at the traditional Petersburg Dialogue bilateral forum.

The European Union also condemned Russia's violation of Ukraine's territorial integrity at an extraordinary meeting of EU heads of state and government on March 6, 2014, when Yatsenyuk was our guest. The EU immediately offered to use its contacts to Russia and Ukraine—both bilaterally as well as within broader multilateral initiatives—to find a negotiated settlement and bring the violence to an end.

But Putin just kept creating his fait accompli. In a mockery of a referendum held on March 16, 2014, an overwhelming majority of Crimea's population reportedly voted for a "reunification with Russia as federal subjects of the Russian Federation," according to the wording on the ballot papers. Russia had annexed Crimea. It turned out that the 1994 Budapest Memorandum, which had guaranteed Ukraine's territorial integrity in return for ceding all Soviet-era nuclear weapons on its territory, had not been worth the paper it was written on. Putin had broken every international law and was now living in a reality of his own creation.

Five days after the pseudo-referendum in Crimea, on the second day of the regular spring meeting of the European Council, the EU heads of state and government signed the political chapter of the EU–Ukraine Association Agreement with President Yatsenyuk. (This was the agreement that had not been signed at the Eastern Partnership summit in Vilnius.) The EU member states also approved a first set of sanctions against the Kremlin and its associates, canceled the next meeting with Russia, and asked the Commission to draft a further list of

sanctions for implementation if Russia continued its destabil-
ization of Ukraine. On March 21, 2014, the Permanent Council
of the fifty-seven-strong OSCE, which included Russia and
Ukraine, mandated a Special Monitoring Mission (SMM) to
Ukraine. This encompassed one hundred civilian observers to
be stationed at ten sites around the country. If incidents
occurred, their task was to establish the facts impartially and
then file a report. The OSCE chairperson-in-office Didier
Burkhalter appointed the Swiss diplomat Heidi Tagliavini as the
organization's special representative for a peaceful resolution of
the conflict. She had already led the EU's independent international fact-finding mission to Georgia, which had investigated
the chain of events leading to the conflict in August 2008. When
the tense security situation in the Donbas, a coal-rich region of
eastern Ukraine, escalated into open and violent conflict, the
OSCE mission was expanded to five hundred observers.

The G8 also took action. It was out of the question for the
United States, Canada, France, the United Kingdom, Italy,
Japan, Germany, and the European Union to attend the forthcoming G8 meeting in Sochi. So the seven countries met
without Russia on the margins of the third Nuclear Security
Summit in The Hague on March 24–25. Our joint declaration
read: "We note that Russia's actions in Ukraine [. . .] contravene
the principles and values on which the G7 and the G8 operate.
As such, we have decided for the time being to suspend our
participation in activities associated with the preparation of the
scheduled G8 Summit in Sochi in June, until the environment
comes back where the G8 is able to have meaningful discussion." We would reconvene for the first time since 1998 as the
Group of Seven (G7) on June 4–5 in Brussels.

On May 2, 2014, I traveled to Washington to discuss the situation in Ukraine with Barack Obama. Once again, I appreciated
his precise analysis. We were united in our desire to help

Ukraine, and so we agreed to impose further sanctions on Russia. Obama's administration and the European Union imposed sanctions in lockstep from the very beginning, and yet we didn't want to cease our diplomatic efforts. I held talks in Congress too. Some senators suspected me of acting as a brake on further economic sanctions against Russia due to the close commercial ties between Germany and Russia, but in fact the opposite was true. More than once I had to urge other European countries not to hold back.

Little by little, pro-Russian separatists annexed parts of Luhansk and Donetsk oblasts in the Donbas with Russian support. By April they had proclaimed the People's Republics of Donetsk and Luhansk, where the populace was also expected to take part in referendums. On May 11, 2014, a large majority supposedly voted for the independence of these self-declared "people's republics."

I was depressed. For Putin, the ethnically Russian community in Ukraine was part of his power strategy, and he felt that the existence of Ukraine as an independent state robbed him of their support. If he couldn't gain full control of Ukraine, then he clearly wanted to make life there so economically and politically difficult that the country would not be able to enjoy its independence. The rulebreaker was setting the terms. He had to be stopped.

The Normandy Format

On May 7, 2014, I welcomed Petro Poroshenko, the most promising candidate for the Ukrainian presidential elections two and a half weeks later, to the Chancellery. Born in 1965 in Bolhrad, southern Ukraine, he spoke fluent Russian, and had studied international relations and international law in Kyiv during the Soviet era. In the early 1990s, he had started building a business

empire that included the confectionery company Roshen—
which also carried out production in Russia—and a media group
with radio stations and a TV channel. Poroshenko was a wealthy
man with significant political experience. For a period of time
from the late 1990s onward, he was a member of parliament and,
under presidents Yushchenko and Yanukovych, foreign minister
and later minister for economic affairs. From the end of 2013
onward, he was involved with the Euromaidan demonstrations.
On March 29, 2014, at a party conference of the All-Ukrainian
Union "Fatherland," Vitali Klitschko had nominated Poroshenko
as a presidential candidate.

A tall, heavyset man with an attentive gaze and alert eyes
stepped into my office. He was accompanied by the Ukrainian
ambassador to Germany Pavlo Klimkin. I received him in the
company of Christoph Heusgen and an interpreter. We sat down
together at my meeting table and talked about the situation in his
country. Poroshenko stated that Ukraine would have to orient
itself toward Europe, and thanked me for my previous support.
He also spoke of the upcoming commemorations to mark the
seventieth anniversary of the D-Day Allied landings in Normandy,
to which France's president François Hollande had invited more
than twenty heads of state and government, including President
Putin, on June 6, 2014. Poroshenko proposed: "If I were also
invited to the commemorations, there might be the opportunity
to speak to Putin directly." This seemed like a bold request. The
first round of the presidential elections would not take place
until May 25, the day of the European election, and a second
ballot could still be held. Yet Poroshenko clearly felt sure of
victory, and one of his arguments had the intended effect on me:
"Ukrainian soldiers fought and suffered in the Second World
War just like Russian soldiers did." I agreed to his request and
promised to speak to the French president about it.

The opportunity to do so arose two days later, when

President Hollande visited me in my constituency on the island of Rügen and in Stralsund on May 9 and 10. He immediately proved open to the idea of inviting Poroshenko to Normandy and enabling a meeting with Putin there. In the days that followed, both Hollande and I spoke on the telephone to Putin about the plan. After Poroshenko did indeed win the first round of the presidential elections on May 25, 2014, with more than 54 percent of the vote, there was nothing more standing in the way of a four-way meeting in Normandy on June 6, 2014, alongside the commemorations.

At 10:45 a.m., I landed at the airport in the coastal resort of Deauville in Normandy and was driven to a short meeting with Putin (and two colleagues on each side) in a nearby hotel. It was our first in-person meeting since the G20 summit in Saint Petersburg on September 5 and 6, 2013. Although there had also been a great deal of tension between the participants there due to the Syrian chemical weapons program, the G20 summit now felt like an event from another era. We greeted each other coolly. This was not a meeting between two people who, despite being in conflict, obeyed the same essential principles and could therefore rediscover common ground again. We were opponents. I did not intend to discuss the whole issue with him yet again. Instead, I had two specific objectives: firstly, I wanted to persuade Putin to recognize Poroshenko as the legitimate future president of Ukraine. I did not receive a clear answer to this. However, the fact that the Russian ambassador in Kyiv wanted to take part in the inauguration ceremony the next day was a positive sign. Secondly, I wanted to try to create a format for future talks regarding a ceasefire in Ukraine. The four-way discussion in Normandy was to be the start. Putin did not refuse to consider this. After about an hour, we parted ways and set off in separate vehicles to the Château de Bénouville, around forty kilometers away, for lunch at one o'clock.

Hollande achieved a great feat of protocol by greeting all participants with perfect form and still finding ten minutes for our four-way meeting before the meal. We withdrew into a small room. The atmosphere was tense. Hollande and I hoped more than anything that Putin and Poroshenko would talk to each other. We saw our role as being to guide the exchange back on to the right lines if tensions ran too high. This worked very well. Poroshenko talked more than Putin. No specific further meetings were arranged, but we planned to continue discussions between us. The Normandy Format was born. The aim was for it to form the basis for all future endeavors toward a ceasefire in Ukraine, at the level of the heads of state and government, and their foreign policy advisors, as well as the ministers for foreign affairs and their state secretaries.

At the subsequent ceremonial lunch, the French president and his guests sat close together around a horseshoe-shaped table. I had a place at the side of the room by the window and was able to view the table connecting the two sides: our host, François Hollande, was flanked on his left by Queen Elizabeth II and Barack Obama, and on his right by the Danish queen Margrethe II and Vladimir Putin. This simultaneously calmed and unnerved me. They were sitting together, and yet once again there was a rift running through Europe.

That afternoon, the actual memorial ceremony was held on the beach in Ouistreham. During the ceremony, I was above all struck by the veterans: men who had experienced the most terrible things and yet were prepared to look ahead to a shared future with us Germans. Joachim and I had visited the region once before, many years previously, in August 1992. The French political scientist and expert on Germany Henri Ménudier had invited us on a weekend trip to Normandy to visit the locations of the Allied landings in 1944. Ménudier and I had come to know each other in the course of my work as minister for youth, as he was closely involved with Franco-German youth work himself. We had walked together through military cemeteries with white crosses as far as the eye could see. Each cross stood for a life cut short far too soon. That had always stayed with me. Now I thought of it again when I saw those old soldiers. They had survived, but so many of their comrades had not.

When the memorial ceremony was over, I traveled to Ranville, a few kilometers away, to lay two wreaths in the Commonwealth war cemetery there—one at the Cross of Sacrifice honoring the fallen soldiers, and one at the grave of an unknown German soldier. France's foreign minister Laurent Fabius accompanied me. With my mind on the past and the present-day talks, I set off home.

Petro Poroshenko's peace plan

On June 20, 2014, two weeks after his inauguration, Petro Poroshenko set out a peace plan. He had informed Putin of his plan the previous evening. The plan's fifteen points included the withdrawal of Russian and Ukrainian mercenaries, disarming the separatists and criteria for their possible immunity from prosecution, the creation of a buffer zone on the Ukrainian–Russian border, the decentralization of power through a constitutional amendment, and the bringing forward of local and parliamentary elections. Also on June 20, Poroshenko ordered a one-week unilateral ceasefire. Prior to this, however, the self-appointed leader of the Donetsk Republic Denis Pushilin had rejected a ceasefire. The fighting continued. Consequently, Poroshenko asked the OSCE special representative Heidi Tagliavini to negotiate the detailed course of action with the separatists on the basis of his peace plan. This took place within the Trilateral Contact Group, established on June 8, 2014, which included one representative from Ukraine and one from Russia, alongside Tagliavini. The Normandy Format constituted a political superstructure for the Contact Group. In parallel to this, Poroshenko continued to work on strengthening Ukraine's ties with the EU. Ukraine signed the second, economic part of the Association Agreement in Brussels on June 27, 2014. It had already signed the political part. It was seven months since the Eastern Partnership Summit in Vilnius.

July 17, 2014, three weeks later: the suspicions of the afternoon became a certainty in the evening. By all appearances the crash involving a Boeing 777-200ER in eastern Ukraine, at about 4:20 p.m. Ukrainian local time the day before, was no accident. In fact, it was suspected that the aircraft, Malaysia Airlines MH17, had been shot down by separatists while on its way from Amsterdam to Kuala Lumpur. All 298 passengers and crew were killed, including four Germans. I had read the first reports of this crash the previous afternoon. At that time, I was preparing for a "Berlin Talk," one of a series of events arranged by the CDU, with the historian Jürgen Osterhammel at Konrad Adenauer House. I had invited Osterhammel to talk about his book *The Transformation of the World*, a global history of the nineteenth century. I had personally wanted to do this; it was my sixtieth birthday. After the talk there had been a small reception, and now I was at home. I could scarcely comprehend the reports of the crash I was now reading. It was dreadful.

The next morning, I had a telephone call with the Dutch prime minister Mark Rutte. I assured him of our solidarity. The suspicions that the aircraft had been shot down by the separatists were cemented.

Over the summer, Ukrainian troops slowly succeeded in pushing back the separatist militias. In response, Putin began to order Russian troops into the areas occupied by the separatists. They actively intervened in the fighting. The Ukrainians were therefore in difficulty once again, and endeavors to obtain a ceasefire became even more urgent. In my opinion, a military solution to the conflict, that is to say a Ukrainian military victory over the Russian troops, was an illusion. Consequently, in Kyiv on August 23, the eve of the Ukrainian Day of Independence, following discussions with Poroshenko and Yatsenyuk, I had said publicly, and not for the first time, that there would be no solution without talks and without diplomacy. That did not mean, I continued, "that Ukraine must not defend itself when its territory is invaded, but ultimately—and incidentally, this is not the only part of the world where this is true—diplomatic solutions must be found. [. . .] I could even go so far as to say: there will be no military solution." The short-term acting president Oleksandr Turchynov, by then chair of the parliament once again, commented shortly afterward that diplomacy is all very well, "but only the Ukrainian army is in a position to end this war."

It was obvious that Poroshenko with his peace plan was under considerable political pressure in his own country. Despite this, he continued to pursue his plan, not least on the occasion of a meeting of the Eurasian Economic Union in Minsk on August 26, 2014, in which an EU delegation led by Catherine Ashton, the then High Representative of the Union for Foreign Affairs and Security Policy, also took part. In fact, the Trilateral Contact Group and the two representatives of the Donetsk and Luhansk separatist regions signed the "Minsk Protocol" on September 5, 2018, in the Belarusian capital. This protocol summarized the results of the consultations in writing. On September 19, 2014, the same parties also signed the "Minsk Memorandum" for the implementation of the protocol. Significant elements of Poroshenko's peace plan were echoed in these agreements, and had been specified as the sequence of the negotiations. A ceasefire and the withdrawal of heavy weaponry and troops from the so-called contact line, the actual front, had been agreed as initial steps. It was above all thanks to Heidi Tagliavini's expertise that such an agreement was able to come into being. It did not help improve the situation, however. The ceasefire was not adhered to; it was repeatedly renegotiated, only to then be broken again. Even OSCE observers were fired at.

Ukraine's economic situation was also extremely fraught. The IMF called for drastic reforms, which resulted in price increases, which in turn undermined public acceptance of the government. On January 8, 2015, on Prime Minister Arseniy Yatsenyuk's inaugural visit to Berlin following his re-election in the parliamentary elections in October 2014, I committed to granting a loan of €500 million to Ukraine. It was a significant contribution, but considering what Ukraine needed, it was only a drop in the ocean.

Seventeen hours of negotiations in Minsk

For France, the new year began with a nightmare. On Wednesday, January 7, 2015, Islamist terrorists carried out an attack on the editorial office of the satirical magazine *Charlie Hebdo*. Twelve people were killed in the brutal attack, and many more were injured. On the day it happened, I was visiting the British prime minister David Cameron in London. I still remember how horrified we were when we heard the news of the attack. We immediately decided to call François Hollande and express our sympathies to him together. We were shocked by the brutality of this assault on freedom of the press and freedom of speech, among our greatest democratic assets.

Over the next two days, a series of further murders were committed while the terrorists were on the run. In total, seventeen people lost their lives before that Friday, when the French police were able to confront and shoot the three attackers. I was relieved that the nightmare was over. When I heard that a memorial march for the victims of the attack was to be held in

Paris on the Sunday, I telephoned François Hollande again. I wanted to take part. I had never invited myself anywhere before, but this was different. I simply needed to be close to France. Hollande thanked me, but said it was not necessary for me to attend. I would not be swayed, however, and when Hollande realized this, he agreed. What then happened still gives me goosebumps today: once it became known that I was going to be traveling to Paris, more and more heads of government from all over Europe resolved to do the same. One after another, people announced that they would be present, including leading figures in the EU, Martin Schulz, Jean-Claude Juncker, and Donald Tusk, and at 1:00 p.m. on January 11, 2015, almost fifty heads of state and government gathered in the center of Paris. The attendees also included representatives from other parts of the world, including the Israeli prime minister Benjamin Netanyahu; the king of Jordan Abdullah II; the president of Mali Ibrahim Boubacar Keïta; the Turkish prime minister Ahmet Davutoğlu; and the Palestinian president Mahmud Abbas. For us, the march started in a narrow street, and on our route we joined up with one and a half million French people and walked with them for some of the way. We will not allow our liberal way of life to be taken from us: that was the message of the day. Everywhere we went, people looked out of their windows and hailed us. For a brief moment, we were all very close.

In many other respects, things looked bleak. In the Donbas, in eastern Ukraine, the situation was deteriorating day by day. The separatists, together with Russian troops, were attacking targets on the other side of the contact line. The situation was particularly precarious around the city of Debaltseve, a transport hub between the two oblasts of Donetsk and Luhansk. Thousands of Ukrainian soldiers were at risk of becoming trapped. The Minsk Agreement wasn't worth the paper it was written on. In the United States, calls for deliveries of weapons to Ukraine were getting louder. The humanitarian situation in the Donbas was getting worse every day. We could not allow more and more areas to be conquered.

On January 28, 2015, President Hollande and I had telephone conservations with both Poroshenko and Putin. Other than accusations directed from one side to the other, there was nothing new to report. Following the two telephone calls, Hollande and I spoke among ourselves once again. Our assessment was that, if anything at all could be done to help, it would have to be an in-person, four-way meeting in the Normandy Format. Such a meeting posed a considerable risk. If no progress were to be made after it, the Normandy Format would finally be a toothless tiger. I consulted Christoph Heusgen. In spite of all the risks, we felt that there were more reasons in favor of the meeting than against it. We had to try. Otherwise, I would have reproached myself for not having tried everything humanly possible to bring an end to the violence through negotiations.

There was no time to spare. On February 7, I planned to participate in the annual Munich Security Conference, which US vice president Joe Biden and the Ukrainian president Poroshenko would also be attending. On February 9, I planned to visit Barack Obama in Washington, and then the prime minister of Canada Stephen Harper, in Ottawa. I was keen to discuss our G7 agenda with both parties—Germany held the presidency of the G7 that year. Of course, the issues raised would also include the situation in Ukraine. An informal meeting of the European Council had been arranged for the Thursday of that week, February 12, 2015. After studying the schedule, I resolved that there was every reason to try to achieve substantial progress in Ukraine by then. On January 30, I spoke about this again with Hollande, when we met for dinner at the invitation of Martin Schulz, then president of the European Parliament, in the restaurant Zuem Ysehuet in Strasbourg. Hollande and I finally made plans to fly to Kyiv on February 5, 2015, and then to Moscow the day after. A four-way meeting could then take place on February 11, if it were to be held prior to the meeting of the European Council. We decided to arrange a date with Putin. I had already asked Poroshenko what he would think in principle of a four-way meeting. He had immediately agreed; after all, he had nothing to lose. Putin, however, hesitated, which was understandable from his perspective—he wanted to take as much concrete action as possible by military means. And of course, it must have been clear to him that, once he agreed to four-way negotiations, he would be more or less condemned to a particular outcome. He wanted to delay this for as long as possible, but he did not abandon further preparations. Once again, the meeting was to be held in Minsk. That was where Poroshenko had negotiated the Minsk Protocol in September 2014, on the basis of his peace plan. It was now a matter of implementing this protocol. At the same time, Minsk was to a certain extent neutral territory. After all, if we wanted to actually reach an agreement, we had not only to negotiate in the Normandy Format, but also to have the document signed by the Trilateral Contact Group and the separatist leaders. Poroshenko was understandably reluctant to speak directly with the leaders of the self-proclaimed People's Republics of Donetsk and Luhansk, Alexander Zakharchenko and Igor Plotnitsky. That would have equated to recognizing the separatists. Moreover, both were banned from entering the EU. For its part, Russia formally wanted nothing to do with the separatists. Accordingly, Minsk was the appropriate location for the parties involved.

On February 5, 2015, Hollande and I flew to Kyiv. There we met with Poroshenko in the presidential administration building at 6:00 p.m. Our colleagues had already flown out a day earlier to prepare a paper we now wished to discuss. For Hollande and me, it was important not to negotiate anything with Putin that had not already been agreed with the Ukrainian side.

After the obligatory photocall, our talks began. In addition to the three of us, my foreign policy advisor Christoph Heusgen, Hollande's foreign policy advisor Jacques Audibert, and Pavlo Klimkin, now Ukrainian foreign minister, took part in the meeting. The discussion started with the fundamentals and concerned the advantages and disadvantages of the forthcoming negotiations. The other question raised was whether the Ukrainian soldiers were already encircled in Debaltseve. Poroshenko denied this. It was a dreadful situation for him. Throughout the meeting, he was continually handed notes containing news of fallen soldiers, which he read out to us in a tremulous voice.

After some time, we moved to a neighboring room where all the other colleagues who had worked on the negotiation text were sitting in a large group. We went through the text together. Behind every sentence lurked a possible misinterpretation by the Russians or the separatists. In the preceding months, the Ukrainians had had sufficient experience with the interpretation of the Minsk Protocol. We also talked about their red lines and possible compromises. This was important for our meeting with Putin. Each determination was followed by a short Ukrainian tirade—we could understand the Ukrainians only too well. Dividing up the work between us fairly, Hollande and I nonetheless kept trying to return to the key issues. By around 9:30 p.m., we had a paper that we could use as the basis for negotiations with the Russian side. At the same time, we knew how much room for maneuver we had for the negotiations. To that extent I was satisfied.

After a quick meal together, for which we were also joined by Prime Minister Yatsenyuk, we took our leave at around 11:00 p.m. local time. I flew directly back to Berlin, Hollande to Paris. Our colleagues remained in Kyiv and traveled on from there to Moscow the next morning. Prior to this, they also notified Heidi Tagliavini. In the airplane, I contemplated the discussions once again. For the Ukrainian side there were two key points: the ceasefire and access to their own border. The path in front of us was going to be rocky, that much was clear. At 00:30 a.m., I landed at Berlin Tegel and went home. It was now February 6, 2015.

At 1:30 p.m., I set off for Moscow. I landed at Vnukovo Airport at 5:50 p.m. and met Hollande, who landed shortly after me, in a reception room. Heusgen and Audibert had come to the airport to inform us of the status of negotiations with Putin's colleagues. Heusgen had already called me before my flight took off and told me that the Russians were refusing to accept the paper we had drawn up with the Ukrainians as the basis for negotiations. They had presented one of their own. They made things difficult wherever possible. I had proposed to Heusgen that we should merge the two papers. As a result, a great deal of time had elapsed once again. Furthermore, the Russians demanded that we should jointly announce a ceasefire with Putin that evening, without the involvement of Ukraine. Of course, Heusgen and Audibert had refused. In response, Vladislav Surkov, the Russian lead negotiator and close advisor of Putin, had accused them of simply accepting people's suffering. Heusgen and Audibert had ignored the cynicism and not allowed themselves to be swayed on the matter. Hollande and I decided only to do a photocall at the start of the meeting, as in Kyiv, and that no other press activities would take place. Russian protocol at the airport urged us to get moving.

In the Kremlin, Putin began one of his well-known fundamental statements on the many humiliations which, in his opinion, Russia had suffered since 1991. Hollande and I voiced no objections, with the exception of the remark that silence did not in any way signify agreement. We had a specific mission, did not wish to be diverted, and we once again clarified that no press conference involving the three of us would take place, just as no ceasefire would be announced.

Next, the work in the large group began. Putin finally agreed to work on our text, and set out his comments in relation to it. After a long period of back and forth, we verbally agreed on a text with some square brackets, i.e. points on which agreement had not been reached. Naturally, these were the predictable critical points, relating primarily to elections, the special status of the regions, and access to the Ukrainian–Russian border. Putin proposed that Surkov should sum up the agreed outcomes in writing while we were at dinner. He refused our request to involve Heusgen and Audibert in this process. This made it clear that we would never be able to accept the paper—a delaying game once more.

Before the dinner, Putin handed out three gifts: Russian–German, Russian–French, and Russian–English antiquarian military dictionaries, all published in the late nineteenth century. Putin asked me to give the Russian–English dictionary to Barack Obama on his behalf on Monday, during my visit to Washington. This was a discreet yet sarcastic indication that, although he was speaking with us, he actually viewed only the United States as an equal negotiating partner. To lend authenticity to the gift, I asked him to write a dedication in the front. As he was doing so, I realized once again that he would stop at nothing to make Russia appear on a par with the United States, as opposed to no more than a "regional power." That was how Obama had referred to the country almost one year earlier, on March 25, 2014, at a press conference with the Dutch prime minister Mark Rutte upon the conclusion of the Nuclear Summit in The Hague. That was in response to the question of whether Russia was the greatest geopolitical enemy of the United States. Viewed in isolation, I considered the term "regional power" unfortunate, yet in the context I shared Obama's assessment, as he had explained that although Russia was a threat to its immediate neighbors in the region and the country's behavior constituted a problem, it was not the greatest threat to US national security. That was obvious even from a geographical point of view.

After Hollande and I had accepted the dictionaries, Putin invited us to dinner and the meal was served promptly. He wanted to fly to Sochi after dinner. At the end of the meal, the paper that had been revised by Surkov was brought out. As we had feared, it was not acceptable to us. Hollande and I insisted that our colleagues remain in Moscow so that the next day, in collaboration with Surkov, they could finalize a common working basis for the meeting in Minsk the following Wednesday. After some initial hesitation, Putin agreed. Heusgen was traveling on with me to Munich, while the other German colleagues from the Chancellery would remain in Moscow, as would Audibert. Putin invited Hollande and me to travel together with him to the airport, as we were making the same journey. We accepted the invitation. In the car, he gave us a report on the state of the Russian economy. Given the political situation, there were some grotesque aspects to the conversation. Nonetheless, I separated it from what I wanted to achieve in the negotiations with Russia and Ukraine.

We said our goodbyes at the airport, and I flew to Munich for the Security Conference. While I was waiting for the aircraft to be de-iced, I briefly telephoned Poroshenko and told him how the meeting had gone. I arrived in Munich sometime during the night. The next morning, I informed Steinmeier of the conversation in Moscow. His state secretary Markus Ederer had been with us in Moscow. Then I gave my speech at the Security Conference. Subsequently, Steinmeier and I met with Poroshenko, the Ukrainian foreign minister Klimkin, the US vice president Joe Biden, and the US foreign minister John Kerry, and reported on the progress of the talks and our assessment of the situation.

On the Saturday, our colleagues succeeded in negotiating a joint paper with many square brackets with the Russian side.

On the Monday, I set off as planned for Washington and Ottawa. In Washington, I handed over Putin's gift to Barack Obama and outlined the approach that Hollande and I were taking. We agreed that it was worth attempting to calm the situation by means of negotiations. I asked him to telephone both Poroshenko and Putin before the meeting in Minsk on the Wednesday. He agreed to do so. A telephone call from a US president had weight. Furthermore, it was important for me to demonstrate transatlantic mutuality. I felt that that was a key to success, particularly after Putin's gift. However, Obama also made it clear that, if the negotiations in Minsk were not successful, the United States would supply at least defensive weapons to Ukraine. I expressed my concern that any delivery of weapons would strengthen the forces within the Ukrainian government who hoped only for a military solution, even if that offered no prospect of success. However, I also understood that we should not leave the Ukrainians exposed to Russian violence without any means of defense. It was a dilemma.

On the Tuesday, it was by now February 10, my colleagues involved in the Normandy Format set off for Minsk, together with the members of the Trilateral Contact Group and the separatist leaders. And so the inevitable happened. In line with Belarusian protocol, arrangements had been made for all those traveling to the meeting to be accommodated in the same hotel, on the same corridor. It is difficult to believe that this occurred without some pressure from Moscow. It was obvious that the Ukrainians were going to be forced to come into direct contact with the separatists. Only after a major German–French–Ukrainian protest were the contact group and the separatists moved to another hotel. The preparations for the four-way meeting could begin. On the morning of February 11, Putin also finally confirmed that he would be present. He had delayed it for days but could prevent it no longer.

In Berlin that morning, I took part in the state ceremony to honor the former German president Richard von Weizsäcker, who had died on January 31, and then flew to Minsk in the company of the foreign minister Steinmeier. There the talks began at 6:30 p.m. in the "Independence Palace." We declined a ceremonial dinner that the Belarusian president Alexander Lukashenko wished to hold for us all. We had other things to do. During an initial discussion held in a conference room with simultaneous interpreting, we once again confirmed the common working basis and clarified relatively simple points, such as the withdrawal of the various categories of heavy weaponry. After that, we turned our focus to other matters. Poroshenko, Putin, Hollande, and I, our foreign ministers and closest colleagues, together with the interpreters, went into a large room. I seem to remember it being octagonal, with doors on each side. In the center of the room was a large round table, and there were various seating areas with small tables on the sides. One of the doors led to a small meeting room, into which Poroshenko, Putin, Hollande, and I withdrew from time to time. The other doors opened every thirty minutes. Tall women, all the same height and wearing waitresses' uniforms, carried trays bearing glasses of freshly brewed tea into the room, moving in a coordinated fashion, all with the same upright posture. Huge quantities of food, together with non-alcoholic and alcoholic drinks, were placed on the center table. In total, we negotiated for almost seventeen hours, with around twelve of them spent in this room. From the most acrimonious battles of words to resigned silence, we went through all imaginable mood fluctuations. Hollande and I took care to ensure that we remained on the same page as Poroshenko. Putin did everything possible to make life difficult for Ukraine. It was an outrage. It was only the conviction that things would become even worse without an agreement that led Hollande and me to continue negotiating. In the early hours, we had finally clarified all the points as far as possible.

It was now necessary to arrange when the ceasefire should come into force. During the night, Putin had repeatedly demanded that Poroshenko order his troops to withdraw from Debaltseve. Poroshenko had refused to do so, although his soldiers were in a dire position. I understood him well. Putin wanted to have the ceasefire begin in ten days' time. That was absurd. Obviously, his military superiority was not as clear as he claimed after all. Ultimately, we agreed on a ceasefire that was to begin forty-eight hours after the predicted end of the negotiations, i.e. at 8:00 a.m. on the Saturday, Kyiv time. Surkov took the text to the Trilateral Contact Group and the separatists so that they could sign the document we had drafted. It would supposedly be a quick process. It took a long time, and finally the separatists obtained the concession from Surkov that the ceasefire would be postponed by sixteen hours to midnight on the Saturday. It was clear that Putin still intended to conquer Debaltseve, as he went on to do.

At around midday on February 12, we were finished. Time was running out, Hollande and I had to leave for Brussels to attend an informal meeting of the European Council. There we would campaign in favor of the document. At the suggestion of Hollande and myself, Putin stated that he was prepared to table the package of measures, henceforth known as Minsk II, together with the Minsk Protocol and the Minsk Memorandum of September 2014, henceforth known as Minsk I, as a draft resolution at the UN Security Council. We wanted to create as much commitment as possible. There was no four-way press conference. Putin and Poroshenko made separate comments to the press about the agreement, while Hollande and I did so jointly.

We had completed one stage, but the underlying problem was far from being resolved. Poroshenko had agreed to everything, above all because he was on the defensive in military terms and did not wish to lose any more territory. However,

Hollande and I could not persuade him to fly directly to Kyiv and explain the outcome to his government and parliament, despite the fact that it built on his peace plan from September 2015. This meant that he allowed his domestic political rivals to interpret what had happened as they wished. I could not understand it. Instead, he flew to Brussels, to put forward his view of things at the informal EU Council meeting and wait for the opinion of the Council. Only after this did he return home. The European Council welcomed the agreement and passed additional sanctions that had already been prepared at the same time. We wanted to exert pressure on Russia to actually implement what had been agreed.

On February 13, as arranged, Russia tabled the draft resolution with the various Minsk agreements at the UN Security Council. It was unanimously passed as Resolution 2202 (2015) on February 17, 2015.

I was determined to do my utmost to ensure that the outcomes of the Minsk negotiations could be implemented. Under the circumstances, these outcomes were the only more or less reliable way of stopping the further advance of the Russian troops, and thereby helping ensure that Ukraine could gradually restore its territorial integrity in the Donetsk and Luhansk regions. However, the issue would continue to concern me greatly throughout the rest of my term of office.

A breath of cold war

The annexation of Crimea changed the threat level dramatically, not only in Ukraine, but in Europe as a whole. The situation we had wanted to avoid in the early 1990s had now come to be: once again there was a dividing line running through the continent. It was no longer possible to rule out a threat to NATO members from Russia. Alongside all attempts to resolve the conflict between Ukraine and Russia by diplomatic means, the alliance also had to respond to the new situation with military action. This occurred at the NATO summit held on September 4 and 5, 2014, in Newport in Wales. Following many years during which NATO had concentrated on operations abroad, such as in the former Yugoslavia, in Afghanistan, and in Libya, the mutual defense clause pursuant to Article 5 of the North Atlantic Treaty once again came to the fore on NATO territory due to the threat from Russia. After the end of the Cold War, the defense plans had largely faded into the background. This now changed. The summit ruled on measures for faster military response in Europe (Readiness Action Plan), particularly for the countries at the eastern edge of NATO such as Poland, Estonia, Latvia, and Lithuania. In addition, a NATO spearhead force, the Very High Readiness Joint Task Force (VJTF) was established. The member states undertook to work toward defense expenditure amounting to two percent of GDP within ten years. In 2014, German defense expenditure was 1.15 percent of GDP. We still had a very long way to go. Nonetheless, it was clear to us that we had to respond to the new situation. Prior to the summit we therefore decided within the federal government to agree to the resolution.

However, the issue of defense expenditure was to remain a political bone of contention until my departure from office. Only the CDU and CSU felt unambiguously committed to the 2-percent target. The other parties were either reticent on the topic of the target, or essentially viewed it as a political imposition. Even so, we succeeded in gradually increasing defense expenditure from 2015 onward. This was possible thanks to a compromise. Within the Grand Coalition, we agreed in return to increase the budget of the ministry of development by the same amount. On the one hand this was positive, as we were far from the many promises that had been made to use 0.7 percent of GDP for development aid—in 2014 we were at 0.4 percent, while by 2021 it was a pleasing 0.8 percent due to our approach. On the other hand, taking the development aid into consideration slowed down the growth of the defense budget. In the 2021 budget, defense expenditure was 1.33 percent. Within the Union, we hoped to reach the 2-percent target by the end of the decade.

At the NATO summit in Warsaw on July 8 and 9, 2016, a decision was taken to deploy multinational "battlegroups" in Poland and the Baltic states. In 2017, Germany took over command of the battlegroup in Lithuania. The troops were changed every six months because permanent deployments in the new member states were prohibited under the terms of the NATO–Russia Act, and despite the tensions with Russia, it was important to me that we continued to adhere to the Act.

Once again we felt a breath of cold war blowing. As we had done in the past, following the annexation of Crimea we now adopted a two-pronged approach and pinned our hopes on diplomacy as well as a reinforced deterrent.

"WE CAN DO THIS!"

At the gates of Europe

DURING THE NIGHT of Saturday, April 18 and Sunday, April 19, 2015, a boat hopelessly overfilled with refugees on their way from Libya to Italy capsized in the Mediterranean Sea. Hundreds of people lost their lives. That Sunday was Joachim's sixty-sixth birthday, and we spent the day in Hohenwalde until the afternoon, when Italy's prime minister Matteo Renzi called me on my cell phone pleading for the European heads of state and government to convene at a special EU Council meeting as soon as possible. He asked for my support with this. There were no more thoughts of the birthday.

"I understand, it is a real tragedy, but if we meet, we will have to make a concrete decision," I pointed out.

"That may be the case, but we *have* to meet," he said, refusing to be swayed. "I have already said to Donald Tusk that it *has* to become clear that this is not an Italian problem, but rather one that concerns all of Europe. You can't leave me alone in this situation."

I knew that Matteo Renzi was right, particularly as it was not the first catastrophe of this type to occur off the coast of his country. Eighteen months earlier, in October 2013, Italy had launched the "Mare Nostrum" operation following two serious boat accidents in which several hundred refugees drowned in the Mediterranean. With this operation, the Italian Navy and the coastguard were to rescue refugees in distress at sea and arrest people smugglers. "Mare Nostrum" ended in October 2014, after the European foreign ministers agreed on Operation Triton under the leadership of the European Border and Coast Guard Agency, Frontex, which had been founded in 2004 to protect Europe's external borders. Yet even Triton had not been able to prevent the catastrophe that took place during the night of April 18 to 19, 2015.

In our telephone conversation, when he pleaded for Italy not to be left alone, Renzi had found the weak point of the Common European Asylum System (CEAS), which could be traced back to the Dublin Convention determined on June 15, 1990, by twelve member states of the European Community in Dublin. Thirteen years later, in March 2003, a first follow-up regulation entered into force with the Dublin II Regulation, followed a few months later by a second in the form of the Dublin III Regulation. This regulation applied in the member states of the European Union, as well as in Norway, Iceland, Switzerland, and Liechtenstein, and specified which of these countries were responsible for implementing the asylum procedure for a third-country national or a stateless person. At its core, it stipulated that, apart from a few exceptions, the examination of an application for asylum was to take place in the country first entered by the asylum seeker, i.e. generally at the external border of the European Union. Under the circumstances, namely given the migration routes across the Mediterranean Sea, in the majority of cases this meant the Mediterranean countries of Greece, Italy, and Spain. For a very long time, Dublin III had removed the problem for all other countries, including Germany. Being geographically located in the center of the European Union, we were able to benefit from the advantages of the Schengen area, such as an internal market without internal border controls, and did not have to worry about what was happening at the external borders of the European Union. It was easy; we felt comfortable with our situation. Our

Mediterranean neighbors—in this case Italy—were responsible for the consequences of disasters such as the one that played out off the coast of Italy during the night of April 18 to 19, 2015—Triton or no Triton. At a formal legal level, this was correct, but from a political and humanitarian perspective it was no longer a tenable position.

Renzi's wish was satisfied. Four days after the catastrophe in the Mediterranean and our telephone call, the heads of state and government came together in Brussels for a special meeting of the European Council, on April 23, 2015. It was primarily of symbolic importance, to demonstrate that Italy had not been abandoned and that we were not simply returning to business as usual after the deaths at the gates of Europe. The Council agreed to improve the rescue options for those in distress at sea, to tackle people smuggling in a more targeted manner, to strengthen collaboration with the countries of origin and transit countries of the people fleeing to Europe, and to organize the admission of refugees into Europe more fairly.

However, the outcomes of the Council meeting did not succeed in getting to the heart of the matter and taking control of the problem. As Italy was overwhelmed at its external border, more and more people were simply making their way northward. It became clear that Europe as a whole had a considerable problem that would take quite some time to resolve, and that Germany was therefore also affected. Within Germany, the number of applications for asylum had been increasing constantly for a few years. In 2012, there were 64,539 applications for asylum; in 2013 that figure was 109,580, and in 2014 it was 173,072. On the one hand, increasing numbers of asylum seekers were coming from the countries of the Western Balkans following the removal of the visa requirement for the countries of the former Yugoslavian Republic—Macedonia, Montenegro, and Serbia—in December 2009, and one year later for Albania as well as Bosnia and Herzegovina. The acceptance rates were well below 1 percent. When these countries were later classed as safe countries of origin and legal employment opportunities were introduced for their citizens, the numbers of asylum applications fell rapidly.

On the other hand, developments at the gates of Europe were causing more and more people to flee: in late 2010, the "Arab Spring" had begun in Tunisia, with uprisings against the autocratic president Zine el-Abidine Ben Ali. These protests were associated with a great deal of hope, and spread to other countries, including Libya and Syria. After the fall of the Libyan revolutionary leader Muammar al-Gaddafi in summer 2011, the Libyan state crumbled. For people traffickers and smugglers, it became easy to enable more and more refugees, predominantly from African countries such as Eritrea and Somalia, to make the crossing to Europe from the Libyan coast. The civil war in Syria, which began in 2011 when the population there also tried to rise up against the country's autocratic president Bashar al-Assad, had even more profound consequences. Millions of Syrians left the country and fled to Lebanon, Jordan, and, in the case of more than three million citizens, Turkey. Initially, they hoped to be able to return home quickly, but this hope evaporated from 2014 onward, and increasing numbers of people attempted to reach Northern Europe from Turkey, via the Aegean Sea and Greece. I clearly remember Greece's prime minister Alexis Tsipras telling me, on the occasion of a European Council meeting in spring 2015, that the number of refugees coming to the Greek islands from Turkey was almost doubling every month. This primarily related to the number of Syrians, but also to Afghan and Iraqi refugees. At the time, I noted this with concern and had a feeling that the effects of this development would go beyond the borders of Greece.

On May 6, 2015, the interior minister Thomas de Maizière stated that 400,000 applications for asylum in Germany were expected by the end of the year: more than twice as many as the previous year. As the figures were increasing each month, he announced that another forecast would be made in the summer.

On June 18, 2015, it was time for me to attend the regular Conference of State Premiers (CSP), which always took place in summer. We had an extensive agenda with a wide range of topics, but the current situation regarding asylum and refugee policy was at the forefront once again. Among other things, we agreed to reach decisions on applications for asylum more quickly, to be stricter in returning rejected asylum seekers to their home countries, and to achieve better integration of those accepted. At the start of the press conference that I held after the CSP with its then chairs Dietmar Woidke (SPD), state premier of Brandenburg, and Reiner Haseloff (CDU), state premier of Saxony-Anhalt, I thanked all those involved in work with refugees and those advocating for people who had fled war and terror. At the same time, however, I emphasized that Germany and its states distinguished between those who had a right to protection and those who did not have such a right and therefore could not remain in Germany.

At the regular meeting of the European Council a week later, a great deal of attention was paid once again to the issue of refugees and migration, following the special meeting in April. In the press conference that I gave on the evening of June 26, 2015, I reported among other things that sixty thousand refugees were to be distributed among the member states of the European Union on a voluntary basis. Forty thousand of them were to be people arriving in Italy or Greece via the Mediterranean, with a further twenty thousand being people whom the European Union would accept directly and in consultation with the Office of the United Nations High Commissioner for Refugees (UNHCR) from areas of civil war. At the end of the press conference, a journalist asked whether there had been differences of opinion between the president of the European Commission Jean-Claude Juncker, and the president of the European Council Donald Tusk. I did not go into this in my response. However, the question gave me the opportunity to highlight the huge scale of the task that stood before us. That was what concerned me. I answered: "There was a very lively discussion, which I believe was appropriate, because as far as the refugee question is concerned I believe we are now faced with the greatest challenge to the European Union that I have seen during my time in office. We have already overcome a whole series of challenges—financial and economic crises, and crises relating to the euro—but here I see us as facing a massive task. Here it will be decided whether Europe is up to this task. There is certainly a possibility that we will be able to resolve this satisfactorily and emerge much stronger on the other side, but that will require further in-depth discussions." I was sure that, even more than in the financial and economic crises we had just been through, it would be vital for us to show the world that we were willing and able to join forces to put our European values into effect.

Less than three weeks later, on Wednesday, July 15, 2015, I was put to the test myself. In the sports hall of the Paul Friedrich Scheel campus, a support center for physically disabled students and an elementary school in Rostock's Südstadt district, I was participating in a citizens' dialogue with twenty-nine young people. The event was in a format I was very fond of, as it gave me the opportunity to speak to the citizens directly. Eva Christiansen, since 2009 head of the Policy Planning, Fundamental Issues, and Special Tasks Team within the Chancellery, had first developed it and put it into practice in 2011 and 2012. Following the German parliamentary elections in 2013, the CDU, CSU, and SPD had agreed in their coalition agreement to expand on the content of this concept and to establish what was known as a "system of indicators" based on further citizens' dialogues on the topic of "Living Well in Germany." The aim was to supplement the gross domestic product, regarded as an indicator of prosperity, with indicators of well-being, taking in areas such as health, safety and security, and the environment.

The dialogue in Rostock began at 1:15 p.m. About halfway through the event, which lasted approximately an hour and a half, fourteen-year-old Reem Sahwil raised her hand. She told me about her family, who had come to Germany from Lebanon and did not have a permanent residence permit. Reem expressed her wish for me to change her situation. Nevertheless, reason told me that I mustn't create the impression of giving Reem hope by making a statement just because she had the opportunity to talk to me—a statement that would have had no legal force. But while I was speaking, I saw that she had started to cry. I went over to comfort her, bent down, stroked her shoulder, and said: "Hey, you did a great job."

At that instant I sensed that something had occurred which would come back to haunt me, as I had not been able to prevent a participant in a discussion from breaking down in tears, especially one so young. I could have made it easier for myself by saying, "You explained that excellently. It would be great if you could write down everything in a letter to me, then I will look at your request again and write back to you." By doing that I would, on the one hand, have remained true to myself by not giving any false hope without knowledge of the case, but on the other, I would not have burdened the girl with hearing from me more than once that Germany can't take in everyone in the world, but must give priority to those who are fleeing from a country at civil war or those who are victims of political persecution. Unlike Syria, Lebanon, where Reem's family came from, was not regarded as an area of civil war.

This event sparked a storm of outrage, both nationally and

internationally. I was said to have behaved awkwardly, to have been ice-cold and lacking in empathy. The hashtag *#merkel-streichelt* ('Merkel strokes') followed. Some one and a half months later, at my annual summer press conference on August 31, I was asked about how I felt "given this scandal."

"Yes, some things are very difficult—it's part of my job," I replied, and repeated my position on the matter.

However, this press conference would be remembered not for my response, but for something else entirely.

The summer press conference

As a rule, my summer press conferences took place in mid or late July, but in 2015 I had to postpone the conference to August 31, 2015, due to the vote in the German parliament on the third Greece program, which was held on July 17.

On August 19, Thomas de Maizière had announced that the Federal Office for Migration and Refugees (BAMF) was doubling its spring forecast made in May to an expected 800,000 applications for asylum in Germany for 2015.

On August 21 and 22, serious racist riots had broken out in the town of Heidenau in Saxony at a refugee reception center located in a former hardware store. The refugees could only be taken there under police protection.

On August 24, Sigmar Gabriel, the SPD chair and vice chancellor, had traveled to the town and referred to the protesters as a "pack" and "mob."

On August 25, the Federal Office for Migration and Refugees, using Twitter, published the sentence "At this point in time, the Dublin procedure for Syrian citizens is effectively no longer being adhered to." I understood this as an indication that excessive demands were being placed on the Office. It was no longer able to deal with the high number of applications for asylum and was instead restricting itself, in a written procedure, largely to checking the authenticity of the personal documents held by Syrian refugees.

I had long been planning to visit the town of Glashütte in Saxony on August 26, in order to open a new assembly hall in the watchmaking company there—an East German success story after German reunification. As Glashütte was only a little over twenty kilometers from Heidenau, I decided at short notice to travel there as well on the same day and visit the initial reception center. When I arrived, I was greeted by the state premier of Saxony Stanislaw Tillich (CDU); the mayor of Heidenau Jürgen Opitz (CDU); and the president of the German Red Cross, the former minister Rudolf Seiters. We then went into the refugees' accommodation. I had insisted that no journalists or photographers accompany us inside. I had the impression that many of the people housed there did not know who I was. I went and spoke to some of them. When they realized that I had come in good faith, they opened up and told me where they came from and which route they had taken to flee—mostly via Greece and the so-called "Balkan route." They appeared exhausted and uncertain, but seemed to trust that they were safe in the building.

After a good three quarters of an hour, I left the refugees' accommodation and went outside to give a statement to the press. "There are now almost six hundred people here, and I have met many of them," I said. "Now the principle that is enshrined in our laws—namely, that everyone who is a victim of political persecution or is forced to flee from civil war has a right to fair treatment, to an asylum procedure, or to recognition as a civil-war refugee—naturally takes on human form." I was so focused on myself and what I wanted to say that I barely registered the deafening noise coming from protesters at the roadside that I later heard in the news reports of my visit.

One day later, on August 27, I took part in the second Western Balkans conference in Vienna. I had been the host of the first such conference the previous year. During the event, I was seated next to Austria's chancellor Werner Faymann. The meeting started at 11:00 a.m. At some point in the course of the day—we were just discussing the fact that the transit states of the Western Balkans were particularly affected by the large number of refugees—Faymann pushed his cell phone toward me to show me a message he had just received. I read that several dozen refugees had been found suffocated in the cargo space of an airtight truck parked at the side of the road in Austria's Burgenland. As later became clear, these were seventy-one people from Afghanistan, Iraq, Iran, and Syria, who had put themselves in the hands of people smugglers in order to reach Austria and Germany. Faymann and I looked at each other. "Dreadful," I whispered. This message made it shockingly clear that we were not talking about numbers, but about real people and their fates.

Four days later, on the morning of Monday, August 31, I sat in my office and thought about which words I was going to use to begin the summer press conference scheduled for 1:30 p.m. I went over the key points that the government spokespeople Steffen Seibert and Eva Christiansen had written down for me. We had agreed that I would focus on refugee policy in my opening sentences. In any case, the subsequent round of questions would give the journalists ninety minutes to ask me about all conceivable issues of domestic and foreign policy in the hall of the Federal Press Conference building, which was always packed for this occasion. I could establish my own points of focus in the opening remarks. I was frustrated and thought: Here you have the next problem on your hands that is the fault of previous governments. Firstly, the euro was introduced without the criteria linked to the currency union being truly binding upon the member states, and we have to deal with the flaws of this decision today. And of course, everyone was also initially delighted with the Schengen Agreement, through which the internal border controls of the member states concluding the agreement could effectively be done away with, other than some narrowly defined exceptions. Yet now Schengen was under pressure like never before due to the high numbers of refugees.

With my speaker's notes for the press conference in my hand, I went to see Beate Baumann in her office, to go over the individual points with her. I took a seat at her circular meeting table. She had been working on files at her desk and now sat down next to me.

"We have only just put the Greece problem behind us, and the next major issue is already on the doorstep," I said, expressing my frustration. "But never mind! Somehow we will do this too. After all, we managed before."

Beate listened to me attentively. Then she said: "That is true. And in the press conference you can say exactly that, just like how you said it here to me."

I looked at her and thought: Sometimes it can be quite simple. She is right. If I put this message across, I can give courage to people while at the same time showing that I am aware of the scale of the task ahead, otherwise I would not need to speak in this way in the first place. I added the key phrases to my speaker's notes by hand.

"Thank you and see you later," I said and returned to my office.

At the press conference, I presented my thoughts. Against the background of the incidents in Heidenau, I firstly emphasized the importance of Article 1 of our constitution, that human dignity is inviolable:

Irrespective of whether or not a person is a citizen, irrespective of where they come from and why they come to us, and of their prospects for being recognized as an asylum seeker at the end of a process—we respect the human dignity of each individual, and we turn with the entire severity of our constitutional state against those who abuse other people, who attack other people, who set fire to their accommodation or resort to violence. We turn against those who call for demonstrations with their hate-filled songs. There is no tolerance for those who question the dignity of another person.

I then outlined numerous measures that the federal government had undertaken as a continuation of the plans and that had already been agreed with the state premiers in July. At the national level, the most important were the acceleration of the processing of applications for asylum, faster repatriation of rejected asylum seekers, support for the municipalities, a fair distribution of costs between the federal government, states, and municipalities, and long-term housing and labor market prospects with improved provision for integration. I also mentioned measures at the European and international level, including ensuring that refugees were fairly distributed throughout Europe and combating the issues that led the refugees to flee their homes. In addition, I stressed: "I say quite simply: Germany is a strong country. The attitude with which we approach these things has to be: we have done so much—we can do this! We can do this, and if something stands in our way, it has to be overcome, it has to be worked on. The federal government will do everything in its power—together with the states, together with the municipalities—to achieve exactly that."

If, at that time, someone had told me that "We can do this"—those four commonplace words—would be used to reproach me for weeks, months, and years to come, I would have looked at them in disbelief and said: I beg your pardon? Should I really not say that we can do this because those words could be misconstrued as implying that I want to bring all the world's refugees to Germany? That thought would never have crossed my mind. I do not know how often in my life I have used words in one way or another to say that we can do this or that. Of course, on August 31, 2015, I was aware that the four words themselves could not solve the problem that we were facing, and that I was reliant on support. However, these four words represented my deep trust that there were enough people in the country who thought and felt as I did, and to whom I could personally give courage. As it turned out, this trust was not misplaced.

The decision

When I got up on Friday, September 4, 2015, I had no idea that this would be a day that would go down in European history. It could just as easily have been any other day. But Europe now faced the test of how to conduct itself when confronted with thousands of refugees arriving in Western Europe via the Western Balkans every day. However, there was no doubt in my mind that it would come to this, and very soon. Hungary's prime minister Viktor Orbán had made no secret of the fact that he would not agree to a quota system for the fair distribution of incoming refugees around Europe. Moreover, in June 2015, Hungary had started building a boundary fence on its external EU border with Serbia, which is around 170 kilometers long. There were comparable border fences at the Greek–Turkish and Bulgarian–Turkish borders. The refugees reacted quickly, and their migration routes from Turkey moved from the overland route to the sea, to the Greek Aegean islands and from there onward via the EU countries of Croatia and Slovenia to Austria and Germany. Over and over again in the previous days, I had watched television reports with images of refugees crowding onto Hungarian trains or stranded in Budapest's train stations. Sometimes, Hungary allowed the people to purchase train tickets for a journey to Austria or Germany and travel; sometimes, the authorities stopped the trains and pulled the refugees out, in spite of their valid tickets, to take them to emergency accommodation. The refugees fought tooth and nail against this, and then the police would temporarily withdraw once more.

In some ways I was reminded of the images of the Prague refugees in 1989, and I asked myself: Should I allow the people from Budapest to travel to Germany? Only to think: And then what? Although the Dublin III Regulation contained what is known as a sovereignty clause, whereby a member state could decide to take over the asylum process for refugees even if they had initially arrived in another EU Member State, this did not mean that any viable long-term solution was yet in sight. However, during my political career I had given many speeches emphasizing that human dignity is inviolable, and that this article is not only enshrined for us Germans in our constitution, but also applies to everyone. For me, the conclusion was now that every person had a right to humane treatment, both in Germany and in Europe as a whole, no matter whether or not they would have an opportunity to remain in Europe. I wanted to further advocate for this, and it was clear to me that it would not be possible to get the situation under control without Germany's help.

On Friday, September 4, 2015, I had several appointments outside Berlin: in Bavaria, I visited the STEM workshop at the Elementary and Middle School in Buch am Erlbach, which was designed to encourage students' interest in science, technology, engineering, and mathematics (STEM). I then traveled onward to the Technical University of Munich to look further at STEM topics at the Center for Innovation and Research there. From there, I flew to North Rhine-Westphalia, and firstly to Essen, to support CDU mayoral candidate Thomas Kufen in a public event as part of the municipal election campaign. He later won the election. I remember that, at this event, I was introduced to a small group of Syrian refugees who thanked me for having accommodated them in Germany. From Essen, I flew by helicopter to Cologne, where I gave a speech on the seventieth anniversary of the North Rhine-Westphalia CDU in the Flora Botanical Garden at around half past seven. There I met Henriette Reker, the independent mayoral candidate supported by the CDU and the Greens, and subsequently mayor of the city. Throughout the day, I was accompanied by Bernhard Kotsch, the deputy head of my office. I had decided this before leaving in the morning, so that a contact from the Chancellery was present even during the party-related engagements. This approach had been tried and tested in other situations in the past.

After my speech, Bernhard Kotsch told me that the Austrian chancellor Werner Faymann wished to speak to me. Faymann had tried to reach me via the Chancellery's crisis center. Bernhard Kotsch had rightly refrained from calling me off stage during my speech, but had instead arranged a telephone call for 8:00 p.m., directly after I finished speaking. Now I was able to speak to Faymann without attracting attention. Prior to the call, I saw on my iPad the images of countless refugees in Budapest who, on their own initiative, were making their way on foot along the highway toward the Hungarian–Austrian border. I sensed that the time to make a decision had come. Unless Europe wanted to allow there to be dead bodies on the highway, something had to happen.

In our conversation, Faymann also described to me how the refugees were making their way along the highway, and asked whether we, Germany and Austria, could share the task—he would take in one half and I the other. Faymann did not want to make the decision himself; the responsibility lay on my shoulders, and I was determined to accept it. It was a humanitarian emergency. In order to make a decision, I had to involve three people. The first was the foreign minister Frank-Walter Steinmeier, who was at a meeting of the EU foreign ministers in Luxembourg. I asked him to have his office conduct a rapid legal check to determine whether, in this humanitarian emergency, I could in fact make the decision to allow the refugees entry on behalf of Germany. In addition, I wanted to discuss the matter with the two party chairs in my coalition, the SPD chair and vice chancellor Sigmar Gabriel, and the CSU chair and Bavarian state premier Horst Seehofer. Gabriel did not make any objections, but I was unable to contact Seehofer. No matter what I tried—including with the assistance of the head of the Chancellery Peter Altmaier, and the head of the Bavarian State Chancellery Karolina Gernbauer, the Chancellery's crisis center, the personal protection team, and my own further request to call me sent by text message at 10:33 p.m.—I could not get hold of him.

After returning to Berlin at around 9:45 p.m., I had arranged to be driven directly to Hohenwalde and had made all further telephone calls from there. Steinmeier was able to inform me that the legal check by his specialists had given the go-ahead for my decision. In the meantime, Hungary's prime minister Viktor Orbán had arranged buses to take the refugees to the Hungarian–Austrian border. Yet even then, he wanted to document that, for him, the national border was the only crucial one. He did so by demanding that no Hungarian bus was to cross the border; instead, the refugees had to transfer to Austrian buses on the other side. That evening, all communication with Orbán was conducted through Faymann. It was clear to Orbán and me that we had completely opposing views on the issue.

At around 10:45 p.m., I resolved that I could no longer wait for the opportunity to speak to Horst Seehofer on the telephone. I could not make my subsequent behavior dependent on that. Shortly after midnight, once the necessary legal and organizational points had been clarified, Germany and Austria put out identical Facebook posts stating that the refugees could enter Austria and Germany. We chose this method because we assumed that the refugees were using Facebook as a source of information. Once that was done, I realized just how much stress I had been under for the last few hours. I suddenly felt completely exhausted and fell into bed.

PART FIVE

Serving Germany (II)

September 5, 2015 to December 8, 2021

A FRIENDLY FACE

"Then this is not my country"

THE WEEKEND WAS breathtaking. At Munich Central Station and other train stations in Germany, hundreds of people gathered to welcome the refugees arriving in their thousands from Hungary via Austria. The volunteers received the people who were seeking protection with applause and cheers, and handed out food. These volunteers had not hesitated for a second when they were needed and "by welcoming the refugees, showed an image of Germany [. . .] that can also make us quite proud of our country." These were my words the following Monday, at the start of a joint press statement with the economic affairs minister Sigmar Gabriel at the Chancellery. It was my first public appearance since my decision on September 4 and 5, 2015. The actual occasion was a long-planned meeting of the CDU, CSU, and SPD coalition committee the previous evening, the outcomes of which Gabriel and I were presenting. Horst Seehofer could not be present, as he had to attend a funeral. I had finally been able to speak on the telephone with him on the Saturday morning. He had made clear that he felt my decision was a mistake that could no longer be reversed. I had responded that I saw it differently. The telephone conversation had been as depressing as I had anticipated. Nevertheless, our discussions in the coalition committee on the Sunday were constructive.

The resolutions were important, there was no doubt, but at

that moment, after that weekend, as I stood with Sigmar Gabriel in front of the blue press backdrop in the Chancellery, I was filled above all with a single emotion that I wanted to share with the public: gratitude. Gratitude for all the helpers, many of whom had not just been involved in refugee aid on a voluntary basis since the night of the decision, but had already been active in the field for weeks or even months; gratitude also for the countless members of staff in the cities and municipalities, in the state and federal authorities, on the railways, and in the army. They all worked hand in hand, far beyond the night of the decision. By doing so, they embodied the attitude I had voiced one week earlier at the Federal Press Conference: we can do this. Germany is a strong country.

Without this support, it is certain, I would not have succeeded in making it through the following days, weeks, and months. Given the scale of the task—national, European, and international—it could only be tackled *together*. I knew that, I was relying on that, and I was not disappointed.

Moreover, two days later, on Wednesday, September 9, 2015, I made this clear in my budget speech in the German parliament when I outlined the most important points guiding me in terms of refugee policy. Today I can still see Vice Chancellor Sigmar Gabriel sitting on the government bench during this debate with a button on his lapel that read: "Refugees welcome." He too was quite clearly filled with a sentiment expressed by the term "welcome culture." On that day, despite all the differences between the government and opposition, this sentiment defined the debate in the German parliament.

And yet I was not deluding myself. An extremely challenging period lay before us. So as to put the events of the weekend in context, in my budget speech I therefore turned my focus to the issues that had been concerning me greatly even prior to September 4 and 5, 2015:

The geopolitical situation, be it the civil war in Syria, Islamist terrorism in northern Iraq, or the political systems in Eritrea or Somalia, will not change overnight. In this house, we have rarely felt how closely domestic policy, development policy, and foreign policy are intertwined. [. . .] Globalization puts us in a situation where we are forced to realize: if we do not do something in terms of foreign and development policy—including across European borders—there are liable to be profound consequences for domestic policy.

Volker Kauder, the chair of the CDU/CSU parliamentary party, and Gerda Hasselfeldt, the chair of the CSU state group, expressly shared this opinion. Up until he left office in fall 2018, Volker Kauder proved to be one of my most vigorous supporters when it came to refugee policy, despite resistance from within his own party. As a Protestant Christian, he regarded the "C" in the name of the CDU as a responsibility to treat people who came to our country with humanity. For that I am still grateful to him today.

The next morning, Thursday, September 10, 2015, I visited the offices of the Federal Office for Migration and Refugees and a refugee reception center run by the Workers' Welfare Association in Berlin-Spandau. After a short press statement outside following these two appointments, I went over to some people who were standing near me so as not to leave without a greeting. One of them—a refugee from Syria, as it later emerged—came up to me, held up his cell phone and said, "Selfie." At that moment, I did not have the slightest idea of the stir this picture would create, but simply thought: Why not? That selfie made its way around the world, along with others that I allowed on the same day. It became as well known as it did not least because the scene was captured by press photographers who were there because of my visit. Even now, I cannot understand how anyone could assume that a friendly face on a photo could encourage people to flee their homeland in droves. Or that, conversely, the grimmest possible expression would have stopped them from doing so. Germany and Europe could never appear so repellent as to stop being places of hope and longing for many. I was and remain convinced that no one makes the decision to leave their homeland lightly, not even those who do so due only to a lack of economic and social prospects and who do not have any chance of being recognized as asylum seekers in Germany.

After the selfies, I got into my car and traveled to my next appointment in Berlin Friedrichshain-Kreuzberg, to visit a "welcome class," designed to aid the integration of refugee children, held in the Ferdinand-Freiligrath school.

"Madam Chancellor, you have just referred again to the decision made on the night of September 5 as correct. At the same time, those within your own ranks and in the media often accuse you of having sent out various political signals indicating an excessive readiness to accept refugees, which have actually increased the influx of refugees as they have encouraged more refugees to come to Germany. What do you say to this accusation?" a journalist asked me five days later, on Tuesday, September 15, 2015, at a press conference I was holding jointly with the Austrian chancellor Werner Faymann after our meeting in the Chancellery. After the night of the decision, Faymann and I had been able to meet in person for the first time. While the journalist was speaking, I thought it was an easy question to answer, and so the words almost flowed out of me:

I say that I am absolutely convinced—particularly after the incidents we saw in Heidenau not so very long ago—that it comes down to showing a certain German face, representative of many citizens. I would just like to remind you: the pictures that went around the world were not those of my visit to the initial reception center in Heidenau—where there were no photographers present—no, the pictures that went around the world were those of the many thousands of citizens who, on the morning after this decision, received the people in Munich and elsewhere at the train stations, who didn't think twice about helping. In response, the world said: Now that is a nice gesture. That came from people's hearts. I must say quite honestly: if we now have to start apologizing for showing a friendly face in emergency situations, then this is not my country.

I added a few sentences that brought my response back to the political, objective level, as while I was speaking I had sensed that I had said something very personal, and even during the press conference I was curious to see whether my words would make an impact. Unlike my views on "We can do this," which I had considered and noted down in advance of the summer press conference on August 31, 2015, what I said at the press conference with Faymann came spontaneously. With his question, the journalist had touched a nerve. While listening to him, I had disliked the fact that he spoke of an "increasing influx of refugees." For me, we were not dealing with an "influx," but rather with people, irrespective of whether or not they had a chance of remaining in Germany. I had entered politics in 1990 because people interested me. People, not influxes or anonymous masses. And my country was and is one that sees the individuals, even if their wishes cannot be met.

There were a few more questions, then the press conference came to an end. Faymann and I left our lecterns, stood side by side for a photograph, and then took the elevator down to the first floor of the Chancellery. As we walked outside to the courtyard, he said to me: "You were in good form." True, I thought, and had to smile to myself a little.

After saying goodbye to Faymann, I took the elevator

back up to the eighth floor with Steffen Seibert, who had accompanied us. We did not go directly to my office, but first called in to see Beate, who was sitting at her desk. "Did you catch the press conference?" I asked her. She turned to us, and said: "I did, and it was great."

My statement "Then this is not my country" was frequently misquoted as "then this is *no longer* my country." It was often suggested that I had meant I could imagine leaving Germany if it "no longer" matched my ideas. That was absurd, but I came across it again a good five years later in another form, when a journalist, in an article he published in the *Welt am Sonntag* newspaper in late December 2020, picked up my sentence from the press conference with Werner Faymann, and wrote: "And she did something that none of her predecessors had ever done: she distanced herself for a split second from the Republic whose second servant she was. [. . .] For a moment, it shone through that she is not a born citizen of the Federal Republic and European, but someone who has acquired this status."

Ten months later, on October 3, 2021, I quoted from this article in my last speech as chancellor, at a ceremony in Halle/Saale to mark the Day of German Unity, and asked: "Are there two types of citizens of the Federal Republic and Europeans—the original ones, and the ones who have acquired this status, who have to prove each and every day that they belong and who can fail the test by saying a sentence like the one I uttered in the press conference? [. . .] Am I really distancing myself from my country through what I said?" The opposite was true. I wanted to make a plea for what makes our country strong: that we must never forget to do right by the individual, even and especially in emergency situations. At any rate, that was how I wanted "my country" to be, not just in my press conferences on August 31 and September 15, 2015, but throughout my entire political career and, in fact, for the rest of my life.

Yet, in major disputes, I found my history in the GDR used

against me time and again—not for the first time in connection with my refugee policy, but in fact from the very beginning, such as in debates on property issues or in the discussion regarding the revision of Section 218 in the early 1990s. Suddenly, my arguments no longer counted. Instead, shaking their heads, people would ask: How has she come up with that now? It can only be because, with her GDR past, she does not truly understand our values.

Some of my experiences abroad were completely different, especially in the United States. There I found a pronounced and unbiased interest in my life in the GDR and in the freedom of reunified Germany. I had the impression that to some it seemed almost like the realization of the proverbial American dream, although not from rags to riches, but from dictatorship to democracy and, within that democracy, to being the first woman to join the country's political elite. I felt the same way when the forty-fourth president of the United States, Barack Obama, who had entered the White House as the first African American president in 2009 with the words "Yes, we can," awarded me the Presidential Medal of Freedom on June 7, 2011. I will never forget that moment, which occurred during a ceremonial dinner in the Rose Garden at the White House. One of those accompanying me was Freya Klier, formerly a civil rights activist in the GDR. In my acceptance speech, I dedicated to her the Medal of Freedom that Barack Obama had awarded me—to her and to all those who had helped bring down the Berlin Wall in 1989.

Finding solutions

I was not a representative of a non-governmental organization; I was not a refugee aid volunteer; I was a politician—chancellor of the Federal Republic of Germany. I could not just be expected to make a decision in the special circumstances of a humanitarian emergency like the one we saw on September 4 and 5, 2015. What could be expected of me, and of the whole federal government, was to come up with solutions extending beyond that, to one of the greatest challenges in the history of the European Union. An exceptional humanitarian situation like the one we saw on September 4 and 5 must never be allowed to repeat itself, not because I felt—in retrospect—that I had made the wrong decision; the opposite was true. However, the fact that such a decision had been necessary at all revealed the failure of Europe leading up to that point. It was therefore crucial for us to find solutions that were in everyone's best interest: the Europeans, and the refugees, who should no longer have to entrust their lives to unscrupulous people smugglers.

A press conference was called at short notice, and at 5:30 p.m. on Sunday, September 13, the minister of the interior Thomas de Maizière informed the public that Germany had, minutes before, temporarily reinstated border controls on our internal borders, notably with Austria. He had spent the day preparing this decision with his team of experts in the ministry of the interior; he had consulted me and the federal government, as well as the interior ministers of the federal states; he had also consulted Austria. I had agreed to it, on condition that asylum seekers would not be turned away, so that everyone who came to Germany—as provided for in the Dublin Regulation— would still be eligible for a legal asylum procedure.

No rejections at Germany's borders—this inflamed the controversy among those who accused me of having "opened up" the borders to Austria on the night of September 4 to 5. The statement was incorrect, if alone for the fact that there was no border control within the Schengen area at that time, which meant that the border was open. The fictitious claim that all that was needed was for the borders to be "closed" again was intended to create the impression that there was a simple way to refuse the entry of refugees into Germany. That's why it was so important that Thomas de Maizière set out our decision clearly in the press conference: "Introducing temporary border controls will not solve the whole problem. [. . .] But we simply need a bit more time and a certain degree of order at our borders." It was a matter of protecting Germany's internal borders, which was temporarily necessary because the protection of Europe's external borders was failing to work.

One of the most notable experiences in this period for me was that I was repeatedly misquoted following an appearance on the talk show *Anne Will* in early October 2015, in which I had said that the three-thousand-kilometer-long land border couldn't simply be *closed*; I was misquoted as saying it couldn't be *protected*.

In his press conference, Thomas de Maizière added: "Of course, local aid in the crisis regions remains vital, so that even more people don't leave the refugee camps, or Syria and Iraq." By saying that, he looked beyond Germany and Europe's borders, to show how great the challenge was. Exclusively or predominantly national approaches would not be enough to fulfill our humanitarian obligations and, on a long term, sustainable basis, to organize and control the development of refugees coming to Europe and Germany and therefore reduce their numbers. And what's more, national solutions alone would destroy the freedom of movement within the Schengen area: one of the key pillars of European cooperation. That was the premise on which my actions were based. It guided my refugee policy until I left office: in CDU and CSU consultations, in consultations of the coalition committee of CDU, CSU, and SPD, of the federal cabinet, in meetings with the government leaders of the states, the community associations, churches, welfare and trade associations, in the informal and formal meetings of the European Council of heads of state and government, at bilateral and European summits with Turkey, as well as with

African heads of state and government and with the African Union, in meetings with representatives of the UN High Commissioner for Refugees (UNHCR) and the International Organization for Migration (IOM), as well as at international events, such as the Syria Conference in London in February 2016 organized by Germany, the United Kingdom, Norway, and Kuwait or the Leaders' Summit on Refugees hosted by President Obama in September 2016. The premise on which my actions were based led me to an interconnected approach on three levels: in Germany, in Europe, and beyond.

In Germany, this involved creating several thousand additional posts at the Federal Office for Migration and Refugees in order to speed up the asylum procedure and, for this purpose, temporarily assigning leadership of the office to the chair of the management board of the Federal Employment Agency Frank-Jürgen Weise. It was also necessary to support states, towns, and municipalities with the registration, distribution, and accommodation of asylum seekers, either financially or through the active support of the German armed forces. Kosovo, Albania, and Montenegro, as well as Morocco, Algeria, and Tunisia had to be classified as safe countries of origin. In future, more contributions in kind would take the place of cash payments. We decided to suspend opportunities for family reunification in the case of people who did not have full refugee status, but instead only had subsidiary protection—as it is called in asylum law—and to enhance measures to promote both voluntary return and the repatriation of rejected asylum seekers to their countries of origin. On top of this, an integration law was to be passed concerning regulations for integration and language classes, as well as a so-called "priority review" for the recruitment of those granted asylum.

In Europe, I advocated for a fair distribution of refugees, although ultimately in vain. Time and again, Europe's interior ministers passed resolutions on the basis of qualified majority voting. In June 2015, for example, it had been agreed that 60,000 refugees were to be distributed; in September, the number was even doubled to 120,000. The terms used were "relocation" and "resettlement." But these resolutions were barely worth the paper they were printed on. According to figures from the European Commission, only 21,999 refugees who had arrived in Greece had actually been relocated by the end of 2018—Germany received 5,391 of them. And 12,708 refugees who had entered European territory in Italy had been relocated—Germany received 5,446 of them. The countries that were in principle willing to take in refugees had their hands full taking care of the people arriving every day; other countries wanted to receive as few refugees as possible and did their utmost to shirk their commitments for as long as possible. All attempts to amend the Dublin III Regulation were also, almost inevitably, unsuccessful. The reception and distribution of refugees in Europe showed in a disturbing way that there was no common understanding in the European Union of what the European Community had once stood for: solidarity and shared values. I found that very depressing, but it was no reason to abandon my efforts.

The situation was quite different when it came to combating the causes of migration and people smuggling. Control of the European Union's external borders was reinforced by the creation of registration centers known as "hotspots." A task force of the Standing NATO Maritime Group improved the exchange of information between the Greek and Turkish coast guards, as well as the European Border and Coast Guard Agency, Frontex, in the Aegean. This was largely thanks to defense minister Ursula von der Leyen, who provided me with ongoing support in terms of refugee policy. The NATO mission provided information that could be used to help combat networks of people smugglers in the Aegean. The German Navy took part in this mission. It was also remarkable that Turkey and Greece worked together on this, despite long-standing disputes about which of the islands in the Aegean belonged to which of these two countries.

Since summer 2015, I had focused on improving cooperation between the European Union and Turkey with regard to refugee policy. Since the start of the Syrian civil war in 2011, Turkey had taken in almost two million refugees on the Turkish–Syrian border, as well as many others in the interior of the country. It therefore shouldered a great burden, which Europe had barely noticed, let alone recognized. That had to change, for example by the EU providing financial support for refugee projects locally, helping improve health care for refugees, convincing Turkey to grant work permits to refugees, opening up educational opportunities and thereby creating prospects in the country. By doing so, we focused on the most important aspect of our refugee policy: combating the causes of migration at the European Union's external borders. That was in the interest of everyone, including the refugees, so that they would no longer drown in the sea after paying great sums of money to unscrupulous people smugglers.

Bearing this in mind, I held talks in Europe and with Turkey for a joint approach. I had already explained why this was so important to me in my summer press conference, when a Turkish journalist asked what I expected of Turkey: "[. . .] the situation as it stands, where one country lets refugees pass through, the next lets them into Greece, they then travel through the Western Balkans, then one country builds a fence that people might then climb over, is neither the legal situation nor a satisfactory situation. That's why we will speak with Turkey in a very trusting and amicable way about how to handle this."

It would not have been possible to implement this without the assistance of Peter Altmaier, head of the Chancellery at the time and the federal government's refugee coordinator since 7 October 2015. In this role, he was assigned the political leadership of a team for refugee policy, which we had instated in the Chancellery the same day. That was often misinterpreted in the media as the disempowerment of Thomas de Maizière, which was untrue; it was more that the scale of the task required it to be a Chancellery management matter. Peter Altmaier and I were accordingly able to consolidate the entire spectrum of European and international refugee policy, extending beyond policing and security measures, in one place. Together with the interior minister Thomas de Maizière, we made the decision-making processes regarding refugee policy more efficient. We assigned the operational leadership of the team, which worked alongside a steering committee in the ministry of the interior, to Jan Hecker. Peter Altmaier had recommended him to me. Born in 1967, Jan Hecker held a doctorate in law and had worked in the ministry of the interior from late 1999 to 2011, while also gaining a postdoctoral qualification. In 2011, he was appointed a judge at the Federal Administrative Court. On October 8, 2015 he joined us in the Chancellery. Following the German parliamentary elections in 2017, he succeeded Christoph Heusgen, the German ambassador to the United Nations, as my security and foreign policy advisor. At the end of 2021, just before I left office, Jan Hecker assumed the post of German ambassador to China. Shortly thereafter, less than two weeks into his posting in China, he died suddenly at the age of fifty-four. What I would have given to speak to him one more time while writing this book.

On September 23, 2015, at an informal meeting of the European Council, the European heads of state and government decided to intensify their dialogue with Turkey, as well as with Libya and Jordan. These two countries also hosted large numbers of refugees, especially from Syria. Two days later, I flew to New York for the UN Summit on Sustainable Development. While there, I also met with the Turkish president Recep Tayyip Erdoğan in order to set up a German–Turkish working group, and to prepare for the EU–Africa Summit which was going to be held in Malta's capital, Valletta, that November. We had to remember that many people from Africa were also continuing to make their way to Europe across the Mediterranean.

On October 5, 2015, the president of the European Commission Jean-Claude Juncker and the president of the European Council Donald Tusk met the Turkish president in Brussels and agreed to work on an EU–Turkey action plan for a joint approach to refugee policy. The European Council of heads of state and government reached an agreement on the draft action plan presented by the European Commission on October 15, 2015. Three days later, I flew to Istanbul for meetings with Erdoğan and the Turkish prime minister Ahmet Davutoğlu. We agreed to implement the action plan quickly, and to open a bilateral dialogue regarding visa liberalization for Turkish citizens between Germany and Turkey, a key concern for Erdoğan in contrast to cooperation on issues related to refugee policy.

My trip to Istanbul was harshly criticized, not least because of two chairs, or golden thrones to be precise. Erdoğan sat on one, while I sat on the other. We didn't sit on them just for the photocall, but for the entire duration of our conversation. All I thought was: Wow, look at these! Apart from that, I didn't give a thought to appearances, as I was focused on what I wanted to achieve with regard to content. But in accordance with the saying "A picture is worth a thousand words," I was later accused of kowtowing to Erdoğan like to an emperor in his palace, and it was suggested that I would throw myself onto the ground before him just to secure an agreement with Turkey so as to keep further refugees away. To make matters worse, as the visit was held two weeks before the parliamentary elections in Turkey, I was also accused of helping aid the election campaign for Erdoğan's Justice and Development Party (AKP).

Such criticism was unfair and, in part, untrue. On the one hand, both right and left quite rightly stated that I should do everything in my power to organize and manage the movements of refugees via the Aegean, Greece, the Balkan route, and Austria up to Northern Europe, and subsequently reduce the number of refugees. On the other hand, they didn't want me to negotiate on the matter with the autocrats in Ankara and, if I did, then certainly not so close to the elections. That was ridiculous. One look at the map and the realities in the Aegean was enough to see that it would only be possible to organize and manage developments in collaboration with Turkey, and that that needed to be done as a matter of urgency. Everything else was an illusion, and I didn't entertain illusions. No matter how consistent the crackdown on people smugglers at sea, no matter how intensive the checks and stop-and-search controls on our internal borders, no matter how high and long the fences, none of that would have actually—as some would have had us believe—succeeded in permanently reducing the number of people gravitating toward the European Union via Turkey, thereby putting an end to the terrible deaths in the Aegean, without agreements having been made between the EU and Turkey. While thousands of people were arriving from there each day via Greece, the efforts—vehemently called for by some European heads of state and government—of Slovenia, Croatia, Serbia, and the former Yugoslavian Republic of Macedonia to close the borders to refugees and migrants on the Balkan route, were more an expression of short-term thinking than a way of solving the problem. As Turkey was the main transit country for many refugees arriving via the Balkan route, it held a key role if Europe was really going to deal with this challenge. That was why I negotiated with the Turkish president and in doing so experienced Erdoğan as a politician who could act in the full political range, not just in terms of refugee policy. When we agreed on things, he was very amiable and called me his "dear friend." When we had differences of opinion, he used every opportunity to counter-argue at great length, which sometimes meant that discussions were protracted. Incidentally, I have observed that a typical characteristic of politicians with autocratic tendencies is that they have unlimited time when they need it. In such cases, simultaneous interpreting is simply replaced with consecutive interpreting.

However, I carried out the further negotiations regarding the implementation of the EU—Turkey action plan not with Erdoğan, but with the Turkish prime minister Ahmet Davutoğlu. We mainly did so via telephone calls before and during an EU–Turkey summit on November 29, 2015, in which the EU–Turkey action plan was ultimately adopted. In return for €3 billion of financial aid from the European Union for projects such as the building of schools for refugee children, Turkey committed to measures such as issuing work permits to Syrian people, introducing a visa requirement for some of its neighboring countries, and strengthening border control.

All of these measures soon began to take effect. While there were close to seven thousand refugees arriving in Germany on average each day in November 2015, the figure had fallen to around three thousand by January 2016. I wanted to reinforce this trend, as the numbers were still too high to be able to speak of a truly lasting development. That was why I contacted Davutoğlu again in January 2016, after the Christmas holidays. He had been in office since 2014; before that he had been foreign minister: a cosmopolitan, knowledgeable man with an education in history, who spoke perfect English and a bit of German. At German–Turkish government consultations on January 22, 2016, we reaffirmed the aims of the EU–Turkey action plan.

Another EU–Turkey meeting was scheduled for March 7, 2016 in Brussels. At that time, the Netherlands held the presidency of the Council of the EU. The evening before the meeting, the Dutch prime minister Mark Rutte and I met on the invitation of the Turkish prime minister in the Permanent

Representation of Turkey to the European Union in Brussels. On this occasion, Davutoğlu proposed what was known as the one-to-one mechanism: Every migrant illegally arriving on the Greek islands would be sent back to Turkey on the basis of a Greece–Turkey readmission agreement; in return, for every Syrian being returned to Turkey from the Greek islands, another Syrian would be resettled from Turkey directly to the European Union. That was a bold, pioneering proposal, which was intended not only to prevent illegal migration through border protection measures, but also to enable legal migration. Rutte and I immediately supported the proposal and appealed for it the next day at the EU–Turkey meeting—with success. Alongside projects in the field of health care, nutrition, education, and infrastructure, which would give refugees living in Turkey prospects close to home, and which therefore focused on the causes of migration, the proposal was developed and adopted as the EU–Turkey statement prior to the next meeting of the European Council on March 18, 2016. We agreed that we would start implementing it on April 4, 2016. With the EU–Turkey deal, as the agreement was often called, the European Union also agreed to make a further €3 billion available to Turkey by the end of 2018 and, insofar as the country was able to meet the requirements of promoting visa liberalization, also to examine the possibility of opening further chapters in the EU accession process. Subsequently, the number of refugees coming to Northern Europe and therefore also arriving in Germany via the Balkan route dropped considerably, down 95 percent from October 2015.

March 18, 2016 was not only etched in my memory as an important day for European refugee policy. It was also the day I found out that Guido Westerwelle had died that morning in Cologne, following complications from leukemia treatment. He had been through the ups and downs of hopes and setbacks for the past two years. I had known, of course, that his situation was serious, but even so, it's almost impossible to prepare yourself for such news. It came as a big shock, now it was final. I immediately thought back to the time in September 2014, one and a half years earlier, when he got a call from his physician while we were having lunch together in Cologne. He learned that a new stem cell donor had been found. A previous donor, who had also been a match, had decided not to go ahead with the process. At that moment, when Guido Westerwelle received that message of hope from his physician, I saw him once again as the man I knew: sensitive, thoughtful, determined, and full of optimism. That's how I acknowledged Guido Westerwelle at the start of my closing press conference in Brussels. I subsequently presented the conclusions of the European Council.

Throughout my time spent working on refugee policy, I received tremendous support from the president of the European Commission Jean-Claude Juncker, for which I cannot be grateful enough. He had already expressed his position on September 9, 2015 in his first State of the Union Address: "Europe—that's the people who stand at the train station in Munich to greet and applaud the refugees." He supported the EU–Turkey deal, helped improve the humanitarian situation in the Western Balkan countries, and promoted international cooperation, first and foremost with Africa. At the EU–Africa summit on November 11 and 12, 2015, held in Valletta, Malta's capital, we agreed to set up an EU Emergency Trust Fund for Africa comprising €1.8 billion from the European Commission as well as other national contributions. This money was intended to combat causes of migration at the source and to finance opportunities for legal migration into the European Union.

Over the following six years, until I left office, we formed EU migration partnerships with African countries, the first of which were Ethiopia, Mali, Nigeria, and Senegal. They were the countries of origin as well as transit countries of many of the refugees arriving in Europe via the Mediterranean. We also signed a cooperation agreement with Egypt on migration. We strengthened our bilateral cooperation with Nigeria as a transit country, and Germany and Europe made special efforts to improve cooperation with Libya. In connection with an EU–Africa summit on November 29 and 30, 2017 in Abidjan, the seat of the government of Côte d'Ivoire, I increased Germany's contribution to the EU trust fund by €100 million, €30 million of which were assigned to the International Organization for Migration in Libya. Germany also made a further €20 million available to support the UN High Commission for Refugees (UNHCR) in Libya. The summit in Abidjan was overshadowed by a video that became public, showing the catastrophic conditions for refugees in Libyan reception centers. As a result, the participating African heads of state and government decided at a moment's notice to bring their citizens who had fled to Libya back to their home countries. A year later, on December 10, 2018, representatives of 164 countries met in Marrakesh, the former capital of Morocco, and adopted a Global Compact for Safe, Orderly and Regular Migration (GCM). The General Assembly of the United Nations endorsed the Global Compact on December 19, 2018; 152 countries—including Germany—voted for; five voted against; and twelve countries abstained.

Conclusion
Firstly: Many of those who had supported my decision on September 4 and 5, 2015, and had also been involved in refugee aid, found the EU–Turkey deal extremely difficult. To them, it was, and is, often seen as just a "deal," not infrequently meaning a dirty one. However, "deal" was not my choice of word and neither did I share the associations with it. It was an acceptable outcome of international negotiations, no more and no less. The same applied to agreements with African countries. As is often the case, the question of reasonable alternatives also had

to be answered here. If we were to reject agreements per se with countries that did not or did not fully correspond with our understanding of democracy and the rule of law, we would not achieve anything—I was, and still am, convinced of that.

Secondly: Europe had to and has to protect its external borders. For that purpose, measures were taken during my time in office, upon which the successor government built. The operational capabilities of the European Border and Coast Guard Agency, Frontex, were reinforced, cooperation with the Libyan authorities was intensified, and the registration of refugees arriving at the external borders was improved. At the same time, however, Germany and Europe should never be tempted to assume that they can make themselves unattractive to people from other parts of our world by taking such drastic measures. That won't work. Wealth and the rule of law will always make Germany and Europe desirable destinations. We can only successfully deal with that if the fight against people smugglers and irregular migration goes hand in hand with efforts to create quotas for legal migration.

Thirdly: No one takes the decision to leave their homeland lightly, not even those who do so due to a lack of economic prospects. However, German asylum law is aimed at other people. It can only guarantee protection to those fleeing political persecution or war. Those who cannot stay in our country must leave it again. The state must enforce that.

Fourthly: Germany is a country of immigration. Our population development and the associated shortage of skilled workers make regular immigration unavoidable. The Grand Coalition took this into account when, after lengthy discussions, it passed an immigration law in 2019 for skilled workers from non-European countries, enabling them to receive an accelerated residence permit in Germany.

Islamist terrorism in Germany

Monday, July 18, 2016: In the evening, on a train to Würzburg, a man attacked five fellow passengers with an ax and a knife, severely injuring four of them. After the train was stopped by an emergency brake, the perpetrator fled, injuring one more person while on the run. A special forces police unit which happened to be at the scene was able to apprehend the man, and they shot him when he tried to counter-attack. The investigations revealed that the perpetrator had come to Germany in June 2015, via Hungary and Austria, without any papers. He had registered here as an unaccompanied minor, and applied for asylum in December 2015 as a refugee from Afghanistan. In accordance with the Asylum Procedure Act, he was granted temporary leave to remain, staying in Germany while his case was being processed. He had been living with a foster family in the Würzburg region from July 1, 2016 onward, and was doing an apprenticeship in a bakery. Presumably, he had lied to the authorities about his real age and country of origin. The investigations also revealed connections to the terrorist group "Islamic State" (IS), which at this time controlled large areas of Iraq and Syria. A video released by IS the day after the act and claiming responsibility for the attack was confirmed as genuine by the federal public prosecution department.

Sunday, July 24, 2016: Late in the evening, in front of a wine bar in the Bavarian town of Ansbach, a man detonated an explosive device hidden in his rucksack. He injured fifteen people, some of them severely. A short while later, he himself succumbed to his injuries. The investigations of the police and public prosecution department revealed that the perpetrator was from Syria, and that he had traveled to Bulgaria via Turkey in July 2013 and applied for asylum there. In early 2014, he left Bulgaria, initially reaching Austria, where he lodged an additional application for asylum. Soon after that he made his way to Germany. In August 2014, he made a bid for asylum here too, and was rejected due to the previous applications in Bulgaria and Austria. In 2015, the man prevented his deportation to Bulgaria by self-harming, after which he received psychiatric care. At the time of the attack, he was living in refugee accommodation in Ansbach. The investigations into this attack also uncovered an Islamist background with links to IS.

Monday, December 19, 2016: At around 20:15, in the Chancellery lobby, I met Aydan Özoğuz, minister for immigration, refugees, and integration since 2013. I was there to give a short speech at an event on "Young People in an Immigrant Society." During the afternoon, the young people there had addressed the importance of integration and language courses in different work groups and discussed these topics with the minister. Some of them, who were supporting other young people to find their footing in Germany, had been awarded with integration medals by Aydan Özoğuz. On our short route to the south staircase, she whispered to me: "I've just received a text that something terrible has happened at the Breitscheidplatz Christmas market." Having been in other meetings immediately before my event, I hadn't yet heard the news. I was immediately alarmed, but decided to deliver my speech regardless, and not to check my phone for incoming messages throughout the event, because there were journalists watching my every move. After just half an hour, I left and took the elevator up to my office on the seventh floor.

The Chancellery's crisis center kept Peter Altmeier and me consistently informed. We maintained contact with the interior minister Thomas de Maizière, and I also spoke on the phone with Michael Müller, the governing mayor of Berlin. Within just a few minutes, the full extent of the catastrophe had been revealed: a man had steered a heavy goods vehicle into a crowd of people at the Christmas market on Berlin's Breitscheidplatz, near the Kaiser Wilhelm Memorial Church, killing twelve and leaving dozens with life-threatening injuries. The attacker, who had hijacked the articulated truck of a Polish freight company hours before in Berlin, after shooting the Polish driver, initially escaped. A short while later, a group from IS claimed responsibility for the attack.

I thought about when to make a public statement. Because it was *when*, not *if*. I had to take a stand on what was, at the time, the worst Islamist attack Germany had ever experienced, and it had to be before the blue press wall in the Chancellery. As I wanted to address the public in an appropriate setting, I decided to wait until the following day.

When I stepped in front of the media at around 11:00 a.m., I said, among other things: "I know it will be particularly hard for all of us to bear if it turns out that a person who applied for shelter and asylum in Germany has committed this act. It would be particularly offensive to the many, many Germans who are engaged in supporting refugees on a day-to-day basis, and to the many people who genuinely need our protection and work hard to integrate in our country." This is why, at the end of my statement, it was important for me to emphasize that we could never allow ourselves to be paralyzed by the fear of evil. "Even though these are difficult hours: we will find the strength for the life we want to live in Germany—a life of freedom, harmony, and openness."

I was in constant contact with the federal president, the interior minister, and the mayor of Berlin, and the security cabinet met at 11:30 a.m. That afternoon, I went to Breitscheidplatz in order to pay my respects. At 6:00 p.m., I attended a memorial service in the Kaiser Wilhelm Memorial Church.

By this time, the attacker's identity had been revealed; this confirmed, in the process, the suspicion that the attack had been carried out by an asylum seeker living in Germany, a man called Anis Amri, born in Tunisia in 1992. In 2011, with the help of people smugglers, he had made it to Italy, where he had applied for asylum. After he served a jail term, plans had been made in March 2015 to deport him back to his homeland of Tunisia. As this couldn't be actioned immediately, Amri was put under police surveillance by the Italian authorities, but they lost track of him. He was known by this point as a follower of the radical Islamist scene, but he managed to get into Switzerland unimpeded. From there, in July 2015, he made his way to Germany, where he applied for asylum. It escaped the German authorities that he was a convicted felon in Italy with connections to Islamists, and that he was supposed to have been deported to Tunisia, partly due to the fact he gave a false name. Amri remained in Germany, changed his identity multiple times, and soon became known here too for his links to the Islamist scene.

On Thursday, December 22, 2016, I visited the branch office of the Bundeskriminalamt (BKA, the German Federal Criminal Police Office) in Berlin-Treptow with Thomas de Maizière and the justice minister Heiko Maas. We were given updates on the status of the investigation and thanked the BKA's president Holger Münch, representative of all its personnel, for their work.

Joachim and I had been planning to go to Switzerland for the holidays, but I canceled the trip. As I was sitting in the car in Berlin on the Friday morning, December 23, 2016, Christoph Heusgen informed me that the Italian prime minister Paolo Gentiloni urgently needed to speak with me. I was a little surprised, given we had only just spoken a short while before. I asked Heusgen to find out whether there had perhaps been a mistake. Gentiloni said no, and insisted on the call. A few minutes later I understood why: he informed me that Anis Amri had been apprehended in Milan during the night, and shot after opening fire on a police officer. I immediately went to my office. I wanted to personally address the public on this too, and at three o'clock in the afternoon I stepped in front of the Chancellery's blue press wall again. I needed to express my

thanks to the Italian police and wish a swift and full recovery to
the officer who had been injured in an exchange of fire.

In March 2017, the federal government appointed Kurt Beck,
the former state premier of Rhineland-Palatinate, as commissioner for the victims of the attack and their bereaved families.
In December 2017 and October 2018, I met with those who had
been injured during the attack, and with the victims' next of kin.
Those conversations were among the hardest I had during my
time in office.

The Anis Amri case would resonate for many years. The
Bundestag's parliamentary control committee, which is responsible for overseeing Germany's intelligence agencies, as well as
the Bundestag's committees of inquiry, the states of North
Rhine-Westphalia and Berlin, and a special investigator appointed
by the Berlin Senate all tried to shed light on the mistakes and
breakdowns that occurred, both prior to the attack and during
the subsequent investigations.

Five years after the incident, it became known that a thir-
teenth victim had lost his life—in October 2021, a man succumbed
to the consequences of a serious injury he had sustained as a first
aider on the evening of the attack.

The danger of Islamist attacks remained. It was the state's
responsibility to demonstrate strength and protect its citizens.
This guided me—along with the conviction that the values of
our democracy and constitution would prove to be stronger
than terrorism.

On suspicion and trust

On the morning of November 20, 2015, I participated in an
especially lovely event in my constituency, to which I had invited
Alexander Gerst, an astronaut from the European Space Agency.
He and I were connected via a sunflower: he had given me

some sunflower seeds which had been on a space mission with him, and which I had then sown and nurtured in my garden. From that plant, I had in turn given him new seeds, from which he cultivated further sunflowers. In the "Birdsong Hall" in Stralsund, in front of 1,200 pupils from all the schools in the city, Gerst gave such a lively account of his time on the International Space Station (ISS) between May and November 2014, showing them photos of outer space, that the children were hanging on his every word.

After the event, I set off from Stralsund to Munich, where I was expected at 17:15 for a CSU conference. En route, I read the news. A report from the German press agency dpa published at 14:36 announced: "CSU boss Horst Seehofer categorically demands a course correction in Chancellor Angela Merkel's (CDU) migration policy: 'Whichever way you look at it, there's no getting around the need for a restriction, a cap,' he said, just hours before Merkel's upcoming guest appearance at the CSU party conference in Munich. [. . .] If dissent with Merkel arises at the conference, 'I will address it afterward, and tell her we've still got work to do.'"

My immediate thought was: We're right back where we started. Only recently, on November 1, had the CDU and CSU reached an agreement on joint measures to organize and steer migration, through which the number of people coming to Germany could ultimately be reduced. With the word "reduce" we had even found a shared formulation for the controversial— for us—topic of a "limitation" or "cap." To *reduce*—this avoided a rigid approach, which I opposed, but also contained the flexibility required in practice, and at the same time convincingly emphasized our shared goal. Or so I had thought. It had seemed that the conflict was put aside. But now, evidently, it was about to kick off again, and on the public stage of the party conference. I'd had enough: the topic I had been working tirelessly on, the subject of considerable public debate—the EU–Turkey summit was already scheduled for November 29—was being completely overshadowed.

I had even been the one to introduce the cap to the discussion, albeit in the opposite sense, and little suspecting it would preoccupy me to the end of my time in office. In an interview with the *Rheinische Post* newspaper on September 11, 2015, when asked how many migrants Germany could reasonably take in, I had answered:

> There's no simple figure to answer that question. The fundamental right to asylum for the politically persecuted has no upper limit; that also applies to the migrants who come to us from the hell of civil war. But there are also people coming to us from stable nations, like the Balkans, currently, with the understandable desire—from their perspective—for a better life. But if there are no grounds for asylum, and with these individuals that's almost always the case, they swiftly have to return to their home countries. That's why we're going to accelerate the legal asylum procedure. At the same time, however, we want to enable legal migration for a smaller number of people from the Balkans, for example, if they secure employment here.

I flew to Munich and gave a brief, halfhearted speech at the CSU party conference. Afterward, I remained on the stage. Normally, the host chair offers a few words of thanks, to say goodbye to the guest speaker. On this occasion, however, Horst Seehofer launched into a lengthy commentary. First, he congratulated me on my "anniversary in office"—on November 22, I had been chancellor for ten years. He praised the collaboration between Thomas de Maizière and his Bavarian colleague Joachim Herrmann, and stressed the significance of the resolution made in early November. But then he immediately made it clear that, from his perspective, it was absolutely essential to set a cap. The "standpoints," as he called them, had to be clear. "And that's why all I can say to you is: we'll meet again on this." He continued on and on. I thought: You're standing up here now as party chair, this doesn't really concern you, you can handle this. But you're also Chancellor of the Federal Republic of Germany. What kind of impression will it make in Brussels, in Turkey, if they see you here? What options do you have? Should you just walk off, if this doesn't come to an end? But the person who walks away is always in the wrong, I thought, and told myself: It will come to an end.

And, eventually, it did. I was given the obligatory bunch of flowers, which I immediately handed to Sören Kablitz-Kühn, my office manager at Konrad Adenauer House, who was accompanying me, and all I wanted was to get out of the hall and back home. Since "We can do this" in my summer press conference on August 31, 2015, and certainly since my decision on September 4 and 5, 2015, Horst Seehofer and I had evolved in different directions. Now, though, we had reached a real low.

Conflict lines, as already mentioned, almost never ran solely between the two union parties, but often right through the middle of the CDU as well. My migration policy certainly wasn't uncontested within my own party. Though it had numerous advocates—in particular, the chairman of the North Rhine-Westphalian CDU and later state premier Armin Laschet, who supported me both in internal discussions and publicly—there was also a lack of understanding within the CDU for my having said "We can do this" despite the enormity of the task, and for the fact I'd repeated these four words many times. There was concern, at least, that I was underestimating the situation, and doubt as to whether my solutions could really prove successful. At the same time, the longing for peace between the CDU and CSU felt tangible. And even though more than a few in my party disapproved of Seehofer's tone, and the CSU tone overall,

48 | *Third place: national coach Jürgen Klinsmann and I both enjoyed seeing the medals being awarded after the victory against Portugal in Stuttgart on July 8, 2006.*

47 | *During the 2006 World Cup in Germany many people were surprised to discover that I can get excited about soccer—here, at the Germany–Argentina quarter-final in Berlin's Olympic Stadium.*

49 | *The summer's tale would not have been possible without the head of the organizing committee, Franz Beckenbauer—seen here in Berlin's Olympic Stadium at the Italy–France final on July 9, 2006.*

50 | *President Joachim Gauck and me on July 13, 2014, with national coach Joachim Löw and the German team in the cabin after winning the World Cup in Rio de Janeiro.*

51 | *Grilling wild boar with the US president George W. Bush on July 13, 2006, at the restaurant "Zu den Linden" in Trinwillershagen in my Bundestag constituency.*

52 | *With my guests at the G8 summit in Heiligendamm on June 7, 2007, sitting in an oversized wicker beach chair (from left: Shinzō Abe, prime minister of Japan; Stephen Harper, prime minister of Canada; Nicolas Sarkozy, president of France; Vladimir Putin, president of Russia; George W. Bush, president of the USA; Tony Blair, prime minister of the United Kingdom; Romano Prodi, prime minister of Italy; José Manuel Barroso, president of the European Commission).*

53 | *For want of the correct English words, I tried to use broad gestures, many of them difficult to interpret, to explain to the American president Barack Obama— on June 8, 2015, at the G7 meeting in Elmau—that the unusually long wooden bench was built for the "family photograph," commemorating the oversized wicker beach chair in Heiligendamm in 2007.*

54 | With the "savings guarantee" during the global economic crisis on October 5, 2008, finance minister Peer Steinbrück and I managed to gain the trust of citizens—a precious treasure in stormy times.

55 | French president Nicolas Sarkozy and I discussed the future of the euro on October 18, 2010, on a stroll along the beach promenade at Deauville on the Normandy coast.

56 | I discussed the euro rescue program for Greece with the managing director of the IMF, Christine Lagarde, in Brussels on October 26, 2011.

57 | After difficult discussions around the rescue of the euro at the G20 conference in Cannes in France, Barack Obama gave me words of encouragement on the evening of November 3, 2011.

58 | *Formal visit to the Russian president Vladimir Putin at the Kremlin on January 16, 2006, after my election as chancellor.*

59 | *During difficult negotiations in Minsk on February 11, 2015, I reached an agreement with the Ukrainian president Petro Poroshenko on how to proceed.*

60 | *April 3, 2008: before the start of the working session at the NATO summit in Bucharest, in conversation with German foreign minister Frank-Walter Steinmeier; on the left, French president Nicolas Sarkozy.*

61 | *When I agreed to a selfie with Anas Modamani, who had fled to Germany from Syria, after my visit to a refugee reception center in Berlin-Spandau on September 10, 2015, I had no idea what a stir the photograph would create.*

62 | *Press conference with my Austrian colleague Chancellor Werner Faymann at the Chancellery on September 15, 2015, a few days after our decision to allow refugees stranded in Hungary to enter the country.*

63 | *With the Turkish president Recep Tayyip Erdoğan in Istanbul on October 18, 2015, discussing cooperation on migration between the EU and Turkey—more than anything, the public were struck by the opulent chairs in the Yıldız Palace.*

64 | *The discussion on the evening of March 6, 2016, with the Turkish prime minister Ahmed Davutoğlu and my Dutch colleague Mark Rutte, in the Permanent Representation of Turkey to the EU in Brussels, created the breakthrough for the EU–Turkey Agreement.*

65, 66 | *United in grief with French president François Hollande. Top: on January 11, 2015, with EU Council president Donald Tusk, at the demonstration of solidarity in commemoration of the victims of the Islamist terror attacks in Paris a few days previously, including the editors of the magazine* Charlie Hebdo; *bottom: on January 27, 2017, after the attack on Breitscheidplatz in Berlin on December 19, 2016.*

67 | *On the tracks of climate change: boat trip on the ice fjord at Ilulissat in Greenland on August 16, 2007.*

68 | *Intense consultations among friends on December 17, 2009, during the climate conference in Copenhagen. To the left, EU Commission president José Manuel Barroso. To the right, Fredrick Reinfeldt, Swedish prime minister; interpreter; Nicolas Sarkozy, president of France; Barack Obama, president of the USA. Front: Gordon Brown, prime minister of the United Kingdom.*

69 | *In conversation with Nobel Peace Prize laureate Nelson Mandela on October 6, 2007, in his foundation in Johannesburg; I admired his policy of forgiveness and reconciliation.*

70 | *Military honors with the only woman among African heads of state and government at the time, the Liberian president Ellen Johnson Sirleaf, at the airport in Monrovia on October 7, 2007.*

71 | *The chair of the Commission of the African Union (AU), Nkosazana Dlamini-Zuma, and I opened the Julius Nyerere Peace and Security Building on October 11, 2016, its construction financed by Germany.*

72 | I visited the Indian pavilion at the Hannover Messe with Indian prime minister Narendra Modi on April 13, 2015.

73 | In conversation with the Chinese president Xi Jinping (and interpreter) on the edge of a working session about the wording of the concluding declaration of the G20 summit in Hamburg, 2017.

74 | *It was a special honor for me to welcome Queen Elizabeth II to the Chancellery on her last state visit to Germany on June 24, 2015.*

75 | *Pope Francis and I exchanged gifts at a private audience following our meeting on June 17, 2017. I showed him the delicious specialties that I had brought back for him from his homeland in Argentina, after my trip to Buenos Aires.*

76 | *Christmas visit to our Bundeswehr soldiers deployed in Kunduz in Afghanistan on December 18, 2010.*

77, 78 | *Visits to the Bundeswehr after the suspension of compulsory military service: in the army training center in Münster along with the state premier of Lower Saxony, David McAllister, on October 10, 2012 (middle); on board the corvette Braunschweig of Navy Operational Flotilla 1, in Kiel, on January 19, 2016 (bottom).*

79 | *Israeli president Shimon Peres accompanied me to the Negev Desert on March 16, 2008, to visit the grave of David Ben-Gurion, the first prime minister of Israel.*

80 | *Israeli prime minister Ehud Olmert and I signed a cooperation agreement at the first German–Israeli government consultations in Jerusalem on March 17, 2008.*

81 | *Speech to the Knesset on March 18, 2008, on the invitation of parliamentary speaker Dalia Itzik: the security of Israel is part of Germany's "reason of state."*

82 | *On my farewell visit as chancellor to the Yad Vashem Holocaust Memorial with Prime Minister Naftali Bennett on October 10, 2021.*

83 | *American president Barack Obama awarded me the Medal of Freedom during a solemn dinner on June 7, 2011, in the Rose Garden of the White House.*

84 | *German–American economic relations are of prime importance for Germany—here, a tour with Barack Obama, on April 26, 2016, of the Hannover Messe, at which the United States was our partner country (in the background, German federal transport minister Alexander Dobrindt and federal minister of education and research Johanna Wanka).*

85 | *I would soon miss those intimate discussions with Barack Obama—here, on his farewell visit to Berlin as president in November 2016, at the Hotel Adlon.*

86 | *Founding director Neil MacGregor (left) explained the model of the newly reconstructed former Berlin Palace to French president Emmanuel Macron and me on a visit to the Humboldt Forum on April 19, 2018.*

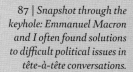

87 | *Snapshot through the keyhole: Emmanuel Macron and I often found solutions to difficult political issues in tête-à-tête conversations.*

88 | *Moving farewell visit to Burgundy on November 3, 2021: Emmanuel Macron awarded me the Grand Cross of the Legion of Honor at the Château du Clos de Vougeot near Dijon.*

89 | Global politics in the shadow of the pandemic: here, with Ukrainian president Volodymyr Zelenskyy, linked by video conference between Paris and Berlin, on April 16, 2021.

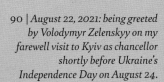

90 | August 22, 2021: being greeted by Volodymyr Zelenskyy on my farewell visit to Kyiv as chancellor shortly before Ukraine's Independence Day on August 24.

91 | Because of travel restrictions during the COVID-19 pandemic, my formal visit to US president Joe Biden on July 15, 2021, was also my farewell visit: here, in the Oval Office of the White House with the German and American delegation.

92 | *Visiting an exhibition by the sculptor Thomas Jastram in January 2019 in Berlin, standing beside the sculpture Kayros, a representation of the Greek god of the favorable moment.*

it was becoming increasingly difficult to keep an overview of the situation amid the conflict over *limiting*, *reducing*, and *capping*. And so I also had to fight within the CDU for my migration policy and the premises and stance it was founded on. And that's what I did.

At the CDU party conference in Karlsruhe on December 14 and 15, 2015, a good three weeks after the CSU conference, it all came down to my speech and a proposal. In order to draft the text, I sat down beforehand with Peter Altmaier, Thomas de Maizière, the CDU general secretary Peter Tauber, and Thomas Strobl, the acting CDU/CSU group chairman and SME for domestic and legal policy. The evening before the conference, when the Presidium and Federal Board met for their preparatory sessions, the draft proposal—as is often the case with newly introduced texts—was edited and enhanced a little more, not least with significant help from the two acting CDU chairs Julia Klöckner and Volker Bouffier. The draft was ultimately presented to the conference as the "Karlsruhe Declaration on Terrorism and Security, Migration and Integration." It stated, among other things: "We are determined to implement effective measures to significantly reduce the arrivals of asylum seekers and migrants. Continuing with numbers at this level would put too much lasting strain on our state and society, even in a country like Germany."

I knew that the proposal by itself wouldn't be enough, however, and my conference speech was also key. Officially, I was introducing the executive committee's proposal for the Karlsruhe Declaration, but this was also the ideal opportunity, after a period of time which had thoroughly shaken both our country and the CDU and CSU, to request support for my policy before the delegates of a CDU national conference. I justified once again the decision to let people from Budapest enter Germany on the night of September 4 and 5, 2015. This was a humanitarian imperative—that's how I described it in Karlsruhe. From a present-day perspective, it's hard to comprehend that the decision was so disputed back then. In fact, many people tell me today that I couldn't have decided things any differently that night.

It was especially important to me to not only look backwards in my conference speech. Nor did I simply want to give a lecture on all the measures the government had decided on, or were working on, within the area of migration policy. Instead, I wanted to speak about the core of the skepticism with which many viewed my approach. I didn't want to tiptoe around it, but rather grab the bull by the horns and say to the delegates:

Come on, dear friends, let's be honest, I believe there's so much more behind the skepticism. Behind it lurk the questions: What other things are going to change? Do we really want *anything* to change? How much change is good for us? When does change become a burden? How do we determine that? *Can* we determine that? What impact does our way of life have on the many people who come to us from the Arab world, from Muslim countries? What impact do their cultural influences have on us? And after this migration flow of so many people from such different cultural spheres to ours, will we still be the Germany we know, the Germany which is strong and which has made us strong?

I gave my answer to these questions by looking toward the future. In twenty-five years' time, I said, Germany was still to be "my Germany, our Germany, a Germany that maintains all the qualities and strengths we love, and which passes them on to the next generation, a land with impressive cultural traditions, liberal-minded and diverse [. . .]"

Even during my speech, I could feel I was carrying the audience with me. The entire hall was silent, especially during the passages that were closest to my heart. The delegates weren't talking to their neighbors. They were listening to me. And I could tell from the rhythm of the subsequent applause that it came from the heart rather than from duty. It felt fulfilling to have united my party behind me in a situation where it really mattered.

But after the New Year, the country was shaken by reports about vast numbers of sexual attacks committed in front of Cologne's main train station on the night of December 31, 2015. And this after the local police had initially given a positive summary the following morning, speaking of peaceful celebrations. Only once a multitude of reports had been made to the police in the subsequent days, predominantly by women, did the full extent of the acts of theft, bodily harm, and sexual assault by hundreds of men aged between eighteen and thirty-five, with North African or Arabic backgrounds, became increasingly clear even on a national level. Amid the mood at the time, which was already tense, the delayed coverage felt particularly devastating, because it gave rise to the impression that the authorities were trying to cover something up.

In these days of early January 2016, Horst Seehofer summarized his demand in an interview: a maximum of 200,000 migrants per year. This was the cap he proposed for Germany. On January 26, at 11:48 a.m., a letter from the Bavarian state premier arrived in my office, initially by fax. Part of its contents were made public knowledge that same day. On January 29, the letter was also published on the federal government website. In bold lettering, it commenced: "Demands of the Bavarian state government to reduce the influx of migrants." It cited as an attachment a report entitled "The Migration Crisis as a Federal Constitutional Problem" by the former federal judge of the Constitutional Court Professor Udo Di Fabio, which was to follow by post. The state premier wrote that Bavaria would file a complaint with the Constitutional Court if the union failed to "immediately" take the demanded measures. But that wasn't the most noteworthy element. After all, a federal government must always be prepared for their decisions to be the subject of complaint to the Constitutional Court. Most noteworthy were the other sentences and overtones. I read on: "The union is responsible for re-establishing the power of justice." There was no mention of the EU–Turkey action plan which had come into force in November, nor the negotiations for an EU–Turkey treaty, which were now entering a decisive phase. I decided to send my response only once the EU–Turkey negotiations were tied up.

In an interview with the *Passauer Neue Presse* on February 10, the CSU chair twisted the communicative screw a little further by saying: "At the moment, we don't have a state of law and order. What we have is a tyranny of injustice." The media released their first reports on these words the day beforehand, saying that Seehofer had put me in the same category as dictators of illegitimate states. From here, it wasn't much further to the claim that a woman from the GDR, an actual illegitimate state, couldn't be trusted at the head of reunified Germany. It was comforting to me that Theo Waigel, the former finance minister and honorary chair of the CSU, demonstrated by inviting me to Bavaria in the subsequent period that other forms of cooperation were possible.

In April 2016, I sent my reply to Horst Seehofer. It had been drafted primarily by the leader of our migration staff Jan Hecker, demonstrating all his legal competence. Under the date of April 19, 2016, I wrote:

> Both the Chancellery and relevant ministries have thoroughly examined, in law and in fact, your statements and the reports of the expert commissioned by the Bavarian

state government. Following this, the federal government sees no grounds for the accusation that the Union has disregarded legal ties according to Union law or national law in connection with migration policy, nor for the accusation that the Union has not taken steps to reduce the number of asylum seekers coming to Germany. [. . .] As regards the question of which instruments, and in which sequence, are best suited for meeting migration policy goals, Union law and national law open up political opportunities for action. By law, the federal government is not limited to the use of certain instruments. It exercises its political responsibility according to detailed, objective examination, and with consideration for the possible consequences upon other spheres of activity.

Standing for re-election?

I saw the migration policy as a decisive turning point in my chancellorship, not only because of the immensity of the task, but the related polarization. And yet it wasn't just from then on, but already from the beginning of my third term after the 2013 Bundestag elections that I occupied myself with the question of whether I should stand again in 2017. Our electoral system doesn't impose any limitation on how long a chancellor can remain in office. That's why it was doubtful whether it would even be possible to choose to stop, in other words, without being voted out of office. I would have to decide by autumn 2016 at the latest, before the next CDU conference. Beate Baumann and I spoke about it frequently. She was of the view that twelve years were enough, and her opinion meant a great deal to me. But she wanted to help me to form my own opinion, and suggested I put pen to paper, in a quiet moment at home, preferably in Hohenwalde, to set out my own arguments for and against running again. This was an excellent suggestion for finding mental clarity, and one that I followed in late October 2016.

In favor of stopping after twelve years, I had: that the credit of making exceptional decisions in exceptional circumstances—after the global economic crisis and the Euro crisis, the increase in migration, and Fukushima, which I'll expand upon later—had been used up; that AfD, which had been defeated at the 2013 Bundestag elections after the Euro crisis, then regained strength through migration policy in connection with the almost-rift between the CDU and CSU, would lose its main point of criticism if I didn't stand again; that too many unspeakable quotes from the CDU and CSU ranks regarding me and my handling of migration policy could be used in the election campaign against me and the Union.

The arguments for continuing included the possibility of discord between the CDU and CSU when it came to finding a new candidate for chancellor; that AfD and some in the CSU, to whom the sentence "Merkel is the Union's downfall" was attributed, would otherwise have won; that I was capable of reaching the middle segment of society; that my potential re-election could be linked to an approval of my approach to migration policy; that Germany needed stability; and—not least—that if I didn't run, I would be disappointing the many people who had always supported me and, in particular since the summer press conference on August 31, 2015, given me their trust.

As I write these lines, I'm also thinking of Walter Lübcke, the former Hessian CDU state representative and Kassel district government president. He had always opposed extreme right-wing actions, including in autumn 2015. Again and again, he was subjected to hostility and threats, even before 2015, until these hate-filled words ultimately became a hate-filled act when Lübcke was shot by a right-wing extremist on June 1, 2019 on the terrace of his house. Walter Lübcke defended the values of our country, standing up for human dignity and tolerance. He was and remains a great role model.

From October 26 to 28, 2016, Beate Baumann and I went to Dierhagen on the Baltic Sea and gave things further thought. The moment of decision was fast approaching. I had scheduled a closed-door meeting for Sunday, November 20, in order to prepare for the upcoming CDU conference, an election conference. By this executive committee meeting at the latest, I had to announce whether I would be standing again for the position of CDU chair. In my understanding of the role, this was the prerequisite for the decision of also running for re-election as chancellor in the 2017 Bundestag elections. I spoke with Barack Obama about this during his farewell visit as American president in Berlin in November 2016. We met on Wednesday, November 16 for dinner in Hotel Adlon, just the two of us. Obama listened calmly, asked a question here and there in order to help my decision-making process, but otherwise withheld his own opinion. This was a great help. I sensed that he wanted—and was able—to empathize with my sense of responsibility. After all, I didn't only need to make a personal decision that affected my own life, but also, as head of government, had to consider all the political implications. Barack Obama said that Europe certainly still needed me, but that ultimately, I needed to follow my instinct.

On November 18, I decided to consult Wolfgang Schäuble. We met at midday on Saturday, November 19, in my office. When he came in in his wheelchair, and I stood up, walking to greet him, he immediately said: "I can tell just from looking at you what you're about to say. Don't do it." "Let's talk calmly," I answered. In our conversation, I told him about the toing and froing of my thoughts. Schäuble encouraged me to stand for re-election.

In the executive committee meeting the next day, too, it was he who distilled the impact of my decision, after I had announced my renewed candidacy to the Presidium and Federal Executive Committee, while also indicating the challenges the campaign would bring with it. Both the Presidium and the committee responded to my renewed candidacy with great applause, which, it seemed to me, also contained a relief that I hadn't decided differently, because the consequences would have been hard to estimate.

The CDU conference from December 5 to 7, 2016 went very smoothly. Compared to the turbulence of 2015 and 2016, I was re-elected as CDU chair with a very good 89.5 percent. The campaign, as expected, proved to be challenging, and at the Bundestag election on September 24, 2017, the CDU and CSU result, at 32.9 percent, was the worst since reunification. This was 8.6 percentage points less than the excellent result of 2013, but this time no politically viable government could be formed against the CDU and CSU. The SPD won 20.5 percent, AfD 12.6 percent, FDP 10.7 percent, the Left Party 9.2 percent, and the Greens 8.9 percent. The process of forming a government was incredibly tough. I wasn't able to turn the numerically possible majority of a "Jamaica" government—consisting of the CDU, CSU, FDP, and the Greens—into an actual one, and I regret this very much. While, in 2013, a black–green government hadn't come about due to the unfavorable attitude of the Greens, this time the possibility of a new government constellation failed on a federal level due to the FDP. Their chair Christian Lindner, who after the elimination of the Free Democrats from the Bundestag in 2013 had incredibly managed to lead them back at the very first attempt, had decided not to enter into a government with me at its head. The federal president had to intervene, convincing the SPD once again to enter a coalition of the CDU, CSU, and SPD, one they had previously categorically refused to join. Eventually, on March 14, 2018, after the longest government formation in the history of the Federal Republic, I was re-elected chancellor for a fourth term in the German Bundestag.

On the topic of a cap for migrants, the CDU, CSU, and SPD had formulated the following in the coalition treaty: "Based upon the average immigration numbers, the experiences of the last twenty years, as well as with a view to the agreed measures and directly taxable section of migration—the fundamental right to asylum and the Geneva Convention on Refugees remain unaffected—we declare that the immigration numbers [. . .] will not exceed the margin of 180,000 to 220,000 annually." All the coalition partners were able to live with this formulation, a blend of stock-taking and political stance. It didn't, however, prevent the differences of opinion regarding whether to turn people back at the German borders from reaching a new high in summer 2018. This wasn't about primary migration as in 2015 and 2016—in other words, those fleeing their countries of origin—but rather the secondary migration of people who were already registered as asylum seekers within the European Union, for example in Italy, and who wanted to travel farther. In accordance with the Dublin III Regulation, they could be transferred in order for the asylum processes to be carried out in their countries of origin, but the deadlines for this were tight and therefore frequently unachievable. The CSU, in particular the new Bavarian state premier Markus Söder, the CSU regional committee chair in the Bundestag Alexander Dobrindt, and also Horst Seehofer, who was the new interior minister since the formation of government, therefore demanded that secondary migration be prevented by turning people back at the border.

In mid-June 2018, this led to renewed conflict between the CDU and CSU. I insisted on a European solution. My colleagues in the European Council helped me at our session in Brussels on June 28 and 29, where it was agreed that the member states of the European Union would meet all the requisite internal legislation and administration measures against secondary migration, and collaborate closely in order to do so. Greece's Alexis Tsipras and the newly appointed Spanish prime minister Pedro Sánchez gave me very practical support in this. They promised to finalize administrative arrangements with Germany in accordance with the Dublin III Regulation, and to readmit migrants already registered in their countries who arrived at the German border. Other countries too, such as Italy, showed willingness to enter into similar arrangements with Germany. On July 1, the CDU executive committee supported the conclusions of the European Council. The following day, the CSU yielded. There would be no turning back of people requesting asylum at the German borders.

To this day, I am grateful to the SPD, to their then chairs Martin Schultz and Andrea Nahles, for their patience and support during this phase. The fact that they tolerated the internal difficulties and clarification process of the CDU and CSU—which must have been an unreasonable demand for outsiders—without exerting any additional pressure, was anything but a given.

AN INTERCONNECTED WORLD—THE REEF KNOT

A globe, a map, and tolerance

ON DECEMBER 1, 2016, Germany took over the presidency of the Group of Twenty (G20) for a year. I had been in office for eleven years and was looking forward to bringing the international experience I had accumulated into this presidency. In 2017, the nineteen countries and the European Union produced around 80 percent of worldwide economic output, measured by GDP adjusted to purchasing power; carried out three-quarters of world trade; and were, with five billion people, home to two-thirds of the world's population.

Since I had entered office, a globe had stood on my desk in the Chancellery, with the oceans in black and a colorful political map of the nations. This meant that, during the telephone calls I conducted from the desk, I could picture the location from where my conversation partner was talking to me. Sometimes, I looked at the globe and thought about the billions of people who live on Earth. When I started in the role, there were 6.6 billion, and by 2017, there were a billion more. It wasn't easy to keep an overview of Germany's citizens, totaling more than eighty million; but to do so for all the people around the world was impossible. I had a realistic idea of the living conditions of my colleagues in the EU, but those of my conversation partners from other continents were, by contrast, frequently opaque. I tried to prepare myself well for my visitors and travels, of course. Reports from German ambassadors about the situations in their respective countries helped with this. At least I knew better after reading them what questions to ask in my conversations. Nothing aggrieved me more than knowing so little about the country that I wasn't capable of formulating even one sensible question. Whenever the opportunity arose on my travels to gain some small insight into local life, I grasped it. A walk in the evening, a meeting with artists, students, or trainees, conversation with German citizens living locally—all these things helped me to gain some understanding of what it was like to live there. I asked my colleagues about everyday things: Do you sometimes prepare your family's breakfast? Do you do your own shopping in the supermarket? Where do you go on holiday? What thoughts are on your mind when you fall asleep, what worries do you wake up with? Sometimes I received honest answers; sometimes the reaction was nothing more than a look of astonishment.

During my entire time in office, I wanted to continually rediscover how my own world view had been shaped, and how it differed from that of others. In the process, I also thought about the difference between a globe and a map. On a globe, there's no one place accentuated above the rest. Each point is equidistant from the middle of the sphere. But it's different on a map of the world. On every map, there is a middle, and there are outer edges. The decision as to where the middle lies is arbitrary. In 1884, the participants of the International Meridian Conference in Washington defined the meridian—a half circle of longitude on the graticule of the Earth—of the English town of Greenwich as the world's Prime Meridian, and its corresponding Greenwich Mean Time as the worldwide standard. This location was chosen because, at that point in time, the United Kingdom had already significantly advanced the standardization of time within its own borders. And it was this that produced the maps of the world which are still in use today. The

Prime Meridian, which runs through Greenwich, was put in their center. And so I and millions of other Germans and Europeans grew up with maps of the world where Europe, the second smallest continent in terms of surface area, was in the center. The fact that not everyone in the world could reconcile themselves with this became known to me only when, many years ago, I stumbled across Stuart McArthur's corrected map of the world. The Australian was so irritated by the constant jokes about the supposedly remote location of his continent that, in 1979, he designed a new map of the world. On it, north and south, or rather above and below, were reversed. The Prime Meridian no longer ran through Greenwich, but the Australian city of Canberra, thereby shifting Australia to the upper middle of the map, and Europe to the right-hand margin. This created an unfamiliar, but equally justified view of our Earth. Suddenly, those of us in Europe seemed far off the beaten track. At the very least, we were no longer the hub of the world.

We Europeans made and make up just a small percentage of the world's population. With a view to our international relationships, I asked myself early on whether there was nonetheless a special contribution that we could make to a thriving worldwide cohabitation. On the topic of what shapes us, I had said in my speech on January 17, 2007 at the European Parliament in Strasbourg for the opening of the German EU Council presidency, with a nod to the phrasing of the European Commission's former president Jacques Delors, that we needed to give Europe a soul, or rather find it. I quoted the Prague writer Karel Čapek: "The creator of Europe made it small and even divided it into tiny pieces so that our hearts would delight not in its size, but in its diversity." To the question of what made Europe's diversity possible, I answered: "Freedom makes our diversity possible. Freedom is the prerequisite for our diversity, freedom in all its forms [. . .] We Europeans have learned in our history to make the most of diversity." Then I concluded that the particular quality which made us able to do this was tolerance, and said: "Europe's soul is tolerance. [. . .] There's a simple path to the soul of Europe, to tolerance: you have to look at things through other people's eyes." This requires knowing something about the other, and wanting to understand them.

My view of the world wasn't neutral either. It was no coincidence that I hadn't become a politician back in the GDR, but rather only in a free, democratic, and reunified Germany. For me, the purpose and goal of my political work lay in enabling the individual to lead a successful life. The values that guided me came from Article 1 of our constitution: Human dignity is inviolable. These values were universal. I had sworn to use my power for the good of the German people. This meant advocating for peace and freedom, for security and economic prosperity in my country. But as chancellor, the head of government of the most populated and economically strongest member of the European Union, and the world's fifth largest economy, I didn't live in a vacuum. We Germans had our own interests, and I wanted to accomplish as many of these as possible. Even just within the European Union and NATO, in other words, the alliances to which we belong and with which we share common values, these were different from those of the other members. The goal a country prioritizes is shaped by its geographical location, history, culture, economic situation, and its respective political leadership. This became significantly more difficult if we were working together with states where the political order was fundamentally different to ours. As Germany was poor in raw materials, we were dependent on trade relationships with countries rich in them. Through exporting our products and investing in other countries, we were able to increase our own prosperity and secure numerous workplaces at home. In Germany, this applied to the automobile industry, mechanical engineering, and the chemical industry. By the same token, the partner countries always profited economically from these trade relationships too, of course, even those with different political orientations.

In order to represent German interests, I couldn't simply select my conversation partners around the world according to who conformed with my concepts of the law and human rights and who didn't. I spoke with representatives from nations who carried out armed conflict against others, or within their own borders. I turned to politicians and countries whose human rights violations I condemned, in order to save the lives of German citizens. Wherever possible, I advocated for freedom of opinion and the rule of law, and tried to help the persecuted and imprisoned. This required me to constantly and consistently weigh up my own values and interests. This was lived real-politik. For me it wasn't a dirty trade, but an expression of the wisdom of life. To achieve results, compromise was necessary, an "agreement through mutual concessions" to give it its dictionary definition. I call it an agreement in which the advantages outweigh the disadvantages. Finding compromises was no easy task, but rather a fraught, often painful process.

For me, looking out for Germany's interests wasn't just about bilateral relationships. I was convinced that close multilateral cooperation in economic, social, and ecological matters strengthened prosperity, stability, and peace worldwide. Working for a peaceful coexistence, battling poverty and hunger, approaching natural resources in a sustainable way, stopping climate change, and preventing the spread of pandemics—this was what mattered most; and we could only achieve it together. This conviction guided me both as president of the first climate conference in 1995, and later too, as host of the 2007 G8 summit in Heiligendamm, and the 2015 G7 summit in Elmau. And it also carried me in 2017 during our G20 presidency, which had the motto: "Shaping an interconnected world." In keeping with the location of the G20 summit of the state and government leaders on July 7 and 8, 2017, in the Free and Hanseatic city of Hamburg, with its internationally prominent dockyard, we had chosen a logo with a seafaring theme—a reef knot; the greater a weight becomes, the firmer the knot holds. But not everyone shared my conviction of strength through solidarity, as time would reveal.

Brexit

On June 23, 2016, in a referendum in Britain on the question of the country's membership of the EU, 52 percent voted for the UK to leave the European Union. To me, the result felt like a humiliation, a disgrace for us, the other members of the European Union—the United Kingdom was leaving us in the lurch. This changed the European Union (EU) in the view of the world; we were weakened.

The United Kingdom had joined the European Economic Community (EEC) on January 1, 1973, at the same time as Ireland and Denmark; with these new members, the community consisted of nine countries. The Maastricht Treaty in 1993 made the EEC into the European Community (EC), which then, with the Lisbon Treaty that was ratified in 2007 and came into force in 2009, led to the European Union. At the time of the British referendum, twenty-eight countries were members of the EU, and five more were candidates to join. The fact that the EU might become smaller had so far been beyond the powers of my imagination. The possibility of a country leaving the EU had been decided for the first time in the EU's 2002–2003 constitutional convention, even though most had considered it unnecessary at the time. The Czech president Václav Klaus had insisted, while the Lisbon Treaty was being drawn up, that such an option be included. In Article 50 of this treaty, the first paragraph states: "Any member state may decide to withdraw from the Union in accordance with its own constitutional requirements." I had hoped never to see it put into practice.

I regarded the United Kingdom as an indispensable part of the peace project of European unity, which had been born of two catastrophic world wars. The former British prime minister Winston Churchill had made a significant contribution to the project's creation in a speech on September 19, 1946, in Zürich. His country was a veto power in the UN Security Council; cosmopolitan and competitive through the Commonwealth and as a former seafaring nation; and it supported multilateral cooperation. The UK's economic strength made the European single market stronger. We could have much more impact world-wide with democratic convictions together than separately, of that I was convinced. Even though the British frequently played a special role, I would much rather have continued working with them within the European Union than lose them as a member.

This is why I tried wherever possible to help David Cameron—who had been prime minister of the UK since May 2010—and especially in February 2013 during negotiations for the EU's Financial Perspective for 2014 to 2021. Cameron was in favor of his country remaining in the Union, but was under pressure within his own party. He insisted on a seven-year EU budget, which would at the very least show no growth in comparison to the previous one, but which included plans for higher expenditure on research and innovation. This was an attack on all the recipient countries who received more money from the EU budget than they contributed, and who were now going to have less money at their disposal for their economic development. The joint agricultural policy, too, encountered difficulties due to Cameron's stance. My support of him rendered me an outsider with my other colleagues. Even France's president François Hollande, Spain's prime minister Mariano Rajoy, and the president of the EU Commission José Manuel Barroso, with whom I otherwise worked very closely, distanced themselves from me. The impact of the euro crisis was still lingering, and I was also being repeatedly accused of stinginess. The members of the European Council, who belonged to the socialist political family, tried to turn the matter into a party-political showdown. Martin Schultz, president of the European Parliament, fueled the fire on the socialist side, and the budget eventually had to be decided by Parliament after all. The supposedly pro-European socialists on one side, and the allegedly anti-European, conservative misers on the other; it was a far from pleasant situation for me, especially with the Bundestag elections approaching within just a few months. And yet, during the summit, I steadfastly remained by David Cameron's side for an entire evening. In this way I was able to prevent his complete isolation in the Council and eventually move the others to back down. I did this because I knew from various discussions with Cameron that, where domestic policy was concerned, he had no room for maneuver whatsoever.

A year later, he invited me to London. On February 27, 2014, I had the incredible honor of giving a speech in the Palace of Westminster's Royal Gallery, before the members of both Houses. Afterward, I attended a private audience with Queen Elizabeth II at Buckingham Palace. Her conversation technique fascinated me, just as it had on my first visit in October 2008. Through a series of questions and brief comments, she demonstrated how closely she observed what was going on in the world. We spoke English; she stoically tolerated my mistakes. But even though these agenda items of my London visit were unusual, I wasn't able to fulfill all of David Cameron's wishes for a British special path in the European Union. Unlike Germany, for example, the UK had not made use of multiple-year transitional periods, following the EU's eastward expansion in 2004, on the introduction of free movement for workers from the new member states. Instead, it immediately gave them the same rights as British workers, so that it could quickly meet its need for cheap labor. Around ten years later, the British government complained that workers and their families from Central and Eastern European countries were putting extreme pressure on its education, health, and social systems. Now the UK wanted to withdraw elements of the freedom of movement, which by then was in force all across Europe. This was an attack on the cornerstones of the European Union, and one I was unable to accept.

The decision to hold a referendum on the UK's membership of the European Union arose from events that had occurred many years previously, in autumn 2005. At that time David Cameron was campaigning to lead the Conservative Party, and pledged they would leave the European People's Party because it was too pro-EU. He therefore, from the very beginning, put himself in the hands of those who were skeptical about the European Union, and was never able to escape this dependency. Seven years later, in January 2013, he announced in a speech that if he were to win the next general election and be re-elected as prime minister, a referendum would be held on the UK's membership of the EU during the first half of the subsequent parliamentary session. He himself was in favor of remaining, but he was attempting to gain the votes of the skeptics. With this promise he succeeded in emerging victorious from the election on May 7, 2015, but his rivals within the party wouldn't let it rest; on the contrary. Boris Johnson, one of his most influential competitors in the power struggle for leadership of the Conservative Party, decided, against Cameron's hope, to support the UK's exit from the EU in the 2016 referendum campaign. This gave the EU opponents' campaign the decisive boost. They prevailed. David Cameron stepped down. The path he had embarked upon before his first election as party leader in autumn 2005, with his promise to leave the European People's Party, demonstrated in textbook fashion the consequences that can arise when there's a miscalculation from the very start.

Now, the task at hand was to negotiate the separation agreement between the EU and the UK with mutual respect, in order to avoid causing additional wounds that could complicate our future cooperation. This was successful, resulting in not only an exit agreement but also a future trade and cooperation agreement between the EU and the UK. Theresa May, Cameron's successor, played a significant part in this.

After the referendum, I was tormented by whether I should have made even more concessions toward the UK to make it possible for them to remain in the community. I came to the conclusion that, in the face of the political developments taking place at the time within the country, there wouldn't have been any reasonable way of my preventing the UK's path out of the European Union as an outsider. Even with the best political will, mistakes of the past could not be undone—this was a bitter lesson. And so all that remained for me was the hope that the UK and the EU would maintain a sense of mutual appreciation, and that when it came to important matters, they would find ways and means of engaging in dialogue that led to harmonious agreement.

New alliances

Since the millennium, if not before, increasing global integration had led to rapid economic growth in some developing countries. Even though they still regarded themselves as developing countries, they were called emerging countries by the industrialized nations. In 2001, the chief economist of Goldman Sachs Jim O'Neill gave Brazil, Russia, India, and China—countries which each had above average growth rates of between 5 and 10 percent of GDP—the collective term "BRIC" in accordance with the first letters of their names. They developed into a global economic power factor. The G8 could no longer define the fate of the world economy alone. This is why, from 2003 onward, Brazil, India, and China, as well as South Africa and Mexico, were regularly invited as the G5 to G8 summits; including by me, to Heiligendamm for June 8, 2007. In my government statement before the summit, on May 24, 2007 in the Bundestag, I spoke about the G8's collaboration with the G5 and said: "We don't plan to expand the G8 into a G13 group. But we do know this: without the emerging countries, progress—for example in climate protection, multilateral trade negotiations, or the improved protection of intellectual property—is no longer conceivable. On these matters, we want to develop a collaborative understanding that goes way beyond the lowest common denominator."

The G5 countries, for their part, called in a joint position paper for global order structures to be made more democratic, more legitimized, and more representative through the inclusion of emerging countries in the decision-making bodies of multilateral institutions. In Heiligendamm, we established a consistent cooperation between the G8 and the G5, known as the Heiligendamm Process. It could have become a new building block for a global order. But things turned out differently.

Two months after Heiligendamm, the global financial and economic crisis began. At its height in mid-November 2008, when the US president George W. Bush invited the G20 heads of state and government to Washington to discuss solutions and strategies, not only the G8 countries participated, but the G5 ones too. And they weren't merely invited; their actions were part of the solution. That same month, China had enacted a stimulus program amounting to the equivalent of €460 billion—comparable with the US program issued three months later by Bush's successor, Obama, which amounted to just over €600 billion. In doing so, China wasn't just helping itself, but the world economy too. From then on, the Group of Twenty de facto replaced the Heiligendamm Process.

The new G20 format couldn't hide the fact that the global

financial crisis had essentially destroyed all trust in a functioning, rules-based, market economy international order. The
industrialized countries' role in causing this crisis strengthened
self-confidence in the BRIC states. On June 16, 2009, in Yekat-
erinburg, Russia, the BRIC heads of state and government
Luiz Inácio Lula da Silva, Dmitry Medvedev, Manmohan Singh,
and Hu Jintao decided to meet annually from then on. In 2010,
they admitted South Africa into the group, henceforth calling
themselves BRICS. A new alliance had come into being. It
demanded more influence, and was supported in this by
emerging countries.

The United States struggled with relinquishing power.
Until the end of 2015, it blocked the reform of vote distribution
in the IMF, which had already been agreed in 2009 at the G20
summit in Pittsburgh. The BRICS nations made use of this
and, in 2014, started their own development bank as an alternative to the IMF and World Bank, calling it the New Development
Bank. In addition, in 2015, under Chinese leadership of more
than fifty nations, a further development bank was founded: the
Asian Infrastructure Investment Bank (AIIB). While the US
and Japan refused to collaborate with the AIIB, Germany, Great
Britain, France, and Italy participated, not wanting to cede it to
China alone.

In the World Trade Organization (WTO) too, the US impeded
the restaffing of roles in the Appellate Body from 2013 onward,
as they weren't in agreement with some of the court's decisions.
This weakened the organization's jurisdiction. It was clear to me
that either the existing global "top dogs"—the industrialized
countries—shared power in the multilateral organizations with
the emerging countries, or instead of a consensual global order
there would be a divided one, in which different groups of countries and organizations competed against one another. The
BRICS group didn't shy away from conflict.

Free trade agreement

International trade based upon mutually agreed rules proved to be a crucial source of growing worldwide prosperity. The World Trade Organization, which was responsible for this, had begun its work on January 1, 1995; its foundation stone was the General Agreement on Tariffs and Trade which had been in existence since 1947. The WTO developed alongside the IMF and the World Bank to become the third largest multilateral organization in the field of economy and finance. At the start of 2017, it had 164 members, to which 98 percent of worldwide trade could be attributed.

Trade isn't good in itself; it also has to be fair. Since the early 1990s, social and ecological standards had played an increasing role alongside customs duties, especially in agriculture, which I had already supported back when I was environment minister. In 2001 in Doha, the capital of Qatar, negotiations had begun in the so-called Doha Round to make trade in the agricultural sector, among others, more socially and environmentally sustainable, and to allow the least developed nations customs-free and quota-free access to the global market. At the first G20 summit in Washington in 2008, the participants, feeling the pressure of economic collapse after the financial crisis, had pushed in the final document for a swift, successful end to negotiations. After this, the vigor soon evaporated again. I continued to hope for its completion. But at some point, probably in 2013, Barack Obama made it clear to me in a frank and open discussion that he no longer believed in the project's success. I got the impression that, in respect of the US electorate, he saw insurmountable difficulty in the compromises the United States would have needed to make to enable easier access to the US market for agricultural products from other countries. The benefits of a potential multilateral agreement clearly counted for less. As the decisions had to be made unanimously, this meant the fate of the Doha Round was essentially sealed. And indeed, by 2016 at the latest, it was regarded as having failed. At the time, I thought of the saying: Dismount if the horse is dead. Meaning you should never cling to an idea for too long if it doesn't promise success. So, with a heavy heart, I dismounted. After the failure of the multilateral negotiations, the focus shifted increasingly to reaching bilateral or regional trade agreements. For me, these were the second-best solution.

As the member states of the European Union formed a collective single market, responsibility for trade matters lay with the European Commission. Parallel to the negotiations in the Doha Round, it had already led talks with the aim of reaching bilateral agreements. And so, in 2010, a free trade agreement was made with South Korea, through which almost 99 percent of previously existing customs duties were dropped. The agreement was provisionally applied from July 2011 onward and officially came into force at the end of 2015. All misgivings—especially on the side of the European automobile industry—about an agreement of this kind were refuted by five years of practice. Instead of dropping, European exports had risen by 55 percent. And the German automobile industry also profited from the agreement. This delighted me, given that, in a way, Germany and South Korea were linked by their experiences of being divided countries.

I had visited South Korea just once, for the G20 summit in November 2010, and had discovered how fascinated people there were by Germany's peaceful reunification, while they themselves were still awaiting a unified democratic Korea. I spoke with the then president Lee Myung-bak about German unity. Because I'm from the GDR, he wanted to hear about my particular experiences of life in a dictatorship, even though he knew that the GDR, in comparison to North Korea, had practically been a liberal state. We spoke about this, and I also talked about the challenges we encountered in making German unity a reality; the high unemployment in the new federal states; and also about many West Germans' lack of familiarity with what life in East Germany was like. I hope very much that the Koreans will also be reunited in peace and freedom one day.

Justin Trudeau, prime minister of Canada from 2015 onward and the successor of Stephen Harper, had made a particularly outstanding contribution toward the Comprehensive Economic and Trade Agreement (CETA) being made between the EU and Canada. This also took environmental standards into account. Even though the negotiations had already been concluded before Trudeau took office in August 2014, with a great spirit of compromise, he helped overcome the hurdles constructed by some of my European colleagues when they retrospectively demanded improved access to the Canadian market for their agricultural products. For me, the advantages of a trade agreement with a partner who shared our democratic values far outweighed the disadvantages in just a few areas, for example in agriculture. In Germany, Sigmar Gabriel, the SPD chair and economy and energy minister, had to fight hard for his party to approve the agreement. In October 2016, Canada and the EU member states were finally able to sign it. It provisionally came into force in February 2017.

In early July 2017, the EU and Japan agreed in principle on JEFTA, a free trade agreement with similarly high standards to those of CETA. The accord wouldn't have come about without the willingness to compromise of the Japanese premier Shinzō Abe, who had resumed office in 2012 after stepping down in 2007 for health reasons. It took effect in February 2019. It was joined, in November 2019, by a free trade agreement with Singapore, and, in August 2020, by one with Vietnam.

———

Negotiations for a free trade agreement between the EU and the US, commenced in 2013, were much less successful. The so-called "chlorinated chicken" became a symbol of resistance to the agreement. In the United States, it was common practice to disinfect slaughtered, gutted chicken in a chloride wash; in the European Union, ice water or a cooled gas-air mixture was used for this purpose. European opponents of the agreement criticized the use of chlorine dioxide, even though the European Food Safety Authority had confirmed that no health hazards arose from the American procedure. Opponents took the example of chlorinated chicken as proof that food and consumer standards were slipping. I personally found the emotionally charged resistance of many NGOs, including in Germany, incomprehensible, and thought it should be possible to overcome stumbling blocks of this kind. For me, what prevailed was the fact that the US and Europe were closely connected through their political convictions and security alliance in NATO. Barack Obama and I, shortly before his departure from office in November 2016, had set out our stance in a co-written article:

> We are stronger when we work together. At a time when the global economy is evolving more quickly than at any point in human history, and the scope of global challenges has never had higher stakes, such cooperation is now more urgent than ever. [. . .] Our shared conviction about the power of trade and investment to lift living standards prompted us to pursue the important project of establishing a Transatlantic Trade and Investment Partnership (TTIP) [. . .] An agreement that knits our economies closer together, based on rules that reflect our shared values, would help us grow and remain globally competitive for decades to come.

What it came down to, we concluded, was this: "Germans and Americans must seize the opportunity to shape globalization based on our values and our ideas." Unfortunately, the agreement came to nothing. A few weeks later, Obama's successor, Donald Trump, became the new US president.

A similar fate befell the EU's free trade agreements with Australia and MERCOSUR, an economic alliance between Argentina, Brazil, Uruguay, and Paraguay—countries with a total of 250 million inhabitants. Neither accord could be concluded during my time in office. As with the Doha Round, this was mainly due to agricultural questions. Periodically, in connection with the deforestation of the Amazon rainforest in Brazil, climate protection also played a role. I was nonetheless convinced that it was in the EU's interest to make as many trade agreements as possible; after all, the rest of the world wouldn't rest on its laurels. And so, on November 15, 2020, fifteen countries, including the ten member states of the Association of Southeast Asian Nations (ASEAN), as well as Australia, China, Japan, New Zealand, and South Korea, signed the free trade agreement RCEP. The abbreviation stands for Regional Comprehensive Economic Partnership. This agreement states that 19 percent of all customs duties are to be discontinued within the next twenty years. Around 30 percent of global economic output, world trade, and the world population were apportioned to these fifteen states. The agreement came into force on January 1, 2022. I was concerned that we EU states were shooting ourselves in the foot by making ever-increasing demands on our trade partners, and that as a result we were falling behind other regions of the world economically.

The Paris Agreement

Nowhere is worldwide cooperation so important as in the battle against global warming. As a reminder: the Kyoto Agreement was adopted on December 11, 1997, as an additional protocol to the Framework Convention on Climate Change. In an initial phase, it planned for legally binding average reductions of CO_2 emissions for the industrial countries, between the years 2008 and 2012, of 5.2 percent compared to 1990 levels. The EU committed itself to a reduction of 8 percent; Germany to 21 percent. The US had rescinded its participation in the Kyoto Protocol in 2001. Negotiations for the commitments for a second phase, for the years 2013 to 2020, began in 2007 and ended after five years in 2012. The parties agreed on average reduction targets of 18 percent compared with 1990; the EU agreed to 20 percent, Germany to 40 percent. Russia, Japan, and New Zealand exited the accord, while Canada had already done so in 2011. The remaining states, the twenty-seven members of the EU, Australia, and nine further countries, were responsible for only 15 percent of worldwide CO_2 emissions. The attempt to limit CO_2 exchange worldwide using legally binding reduction targets had quite clearly failed. At the same time, the Intergovernmental Panel on Climate Change's reports in 2001 and 2007 showed that the need for the collaborative action of all nations was becoming ever more urgent.

The negotiations over the Kyoto Protocol commitments for 2013 to 2020 should actually have been concluded three years previously, at the climate conference in December 2009 in Copenhagen. I had participated on December 17 and 18, the final two days of the conference, like many of my colleagues from the EU, as well as Dmitry Medvedev, Manmohan Singh, and the Chinese premier Wen Jiabao; Barack Obama had joined on the final day. Norbert Röttgen, the newly appointed environment minister of the CDU, CSU, and FDP government, told me after my arrival at the Congress Center that there had been considerable conflict between the participants, and little hope of an agreement. Everyone was eagerly awaiting the heads of state and government to get things moving. We negotiated for more than thirty hours. Even during the dinners hosted by the Danish queen Margrethe II, we used every opportunity to discuss matters. Only three hours remained for sleep.

In 2006, China had overtaken the United States on CO_2 emissions. The principle of the Kyoto Protocol, that only industrialized countries had to make legally binding reduction targets, didn't take the dynamic economic development of the emerging countries into account. Indeed, the latter point-blank refused to accept legally binding reduction targets. India's prime minister Manmohan Singh referenced a resolution of the Indian parliament in which a majority of its representatives had voted against any kind of internationally binding reduction target. India reasoned that they couldn't hand over the reins to their own development. Like me, Barack Obama saw the dangers of global warming as one of the greatest threats to humanity—if not *the* greatest—and so we fought for an agreement to be reached at the conference. In the course of the US–European votes, however, I had to recognize that even Obama's government didn't want to take on legally binding targets. This was a disappointment. And what weighed even heavier was that none of us, not even Obama, managed to convince the emerging countries that they too would have to make more commitments in future. On the contrary, they pointed out that 80 percent of existing worldwide emissions were created by the industrialized countries, and demanded financial resources for the emerging countries, so that they could offset the impact of climate change and tackle the switch to new technologies. The talk was of $100 billion per year. The only thing everyone agreed on was the need to avoid an increase in temperatures by more than two degrees compared with the preindustrial era. The emerging countries were also aware that, in order to do this, worldwide emissions would have to be reduced by 50 percent by 2050. But because they didn't want to admit that this wouldn't be achievable without their contribution, they refused to fix on this target. We were going round in circles.

Obama had to depart again by the afternoon. Before that, we Europeans had to decide whether to refuse any kind of agreement due to the inability to settle on binding reduction targets for the industrialized and emerging countries, or whether to accept an agreement resembling a really small bird in the hand—because the two in the bush were unreachable. With a heavy heart, I joined Sarkozy in approving Obama's suggestion of asking the conference's secretariat to create a joint declaration from the few points on which unity had been achieved: this became the Copenhagen Agreement. The other Europeans joined us. The secretariat produced a document that contained the two-degree target and called upon the industrialized countries to communicate their voluntary national reduction targets to the convention's secretariat by 2020. For the period after 2020, the emerging countries were promised $100 billion per year in order to manage the consequences of climate change. The results of this agreement were to be re-evaluated in 2015, with a view to achieving the two-degree target. Because of the time pressure, the conference didn't formally adopt the document as in 1995 with the Berlin Mandate, but instead merely took note of it.

In conversation with a newspaper, I spoke more positively about the outcome than I really felt. "Copenhagen was the first step toward a new world climate order—no more, but also, no less," I said. I thought there was still a chance of overcoming the standstill following the real failure of the Kyoto Agreement, if by 2015 it proved possible to convince all the industrialized and emerging countries to propose voluntary national contributions which served to meet the two-degree target.

Six years later, from November 30 to December 12, 2015, the climate conference COP 21 was held in Paris under a French presidency. For the first time, over 170 countries—industrialized nations, emerging countries, developing countries—had declared national contributions toward achieving the two-degree target, relating to 95 percent of worldwide CO_2 emissions. In my speech I cited this as good news, but also added the bad: the contributions weren't enough to keep the two-degree target. So in Paris we had to set a believable signal of how we could fulfill the target in the coming years. I made it clear that we needed a far-reaching decarbonization of our national economies through the twenty-first century. For Germany, I agreed we would reduce our CO_2 emissions by 40 percent by 2020, and that we aimed to reach a reduction of 80 to 95 percent by 2050.

The fact that the emerging countries were essentially now willing to declare national targets was a great success. This was thanks to the conference's judicious preparation by its French hosts, and the United States' long-standing, steadfast collaboration with China, as well as the Petersburg climate dialogue—a German environment ministry event that had been held annually since 2010, to which around thirty-five of the most significant countries for climate negotiations had been invited each spring as preparation for the climate conferences at the end of the year. As chancellor, I participated in every one of these events, thereby emphasizing to the other participants how important this topic was for Germany.

n December 12, 2015, under the leadership of French minister Laurent Fabius, COP 21 adopted the Paris . The global target was now for "the increase in the e temperature to be held well below 2 degrees C strial levels and to pursue efforts to limit the temperature increase to 1.5 degrees C above preindustrial levels." The contract parties agreed to fix national contributions for emission reductions and to renew them every five years. The contributions were recorded in a public register. The industrial countries committed to reducing worldwide net greenhouse gas emissions to zero by the end of this century. The Paris Agreement became the first comprehensive legally binding international climate protection declaration, albeit with voluntary reduction targets from the individual countries. The agreement came into force on November 4, 2016. By autumn 2021, shortly before the end of my time in office, it had been ratified by 191 of the 197 treaty nations. But, with the declared national reduction targets, the 2 degrees C goal has not so far been reached, let alone the goal of 1.5 degrees.

Partnership with Africa

In September 2000, the so-called Millennium Summit took place in New York, a meeting of the state and government heads of the United Nations' then 189 member states. Shortly afterward, these countries agreed "Millennium Development Goals" which were to be fulfilled by 2015. This was intended to halve the percentage of the world's population suffering extreme poverty and hunger. The G8 had decided to help African countries in realizing these goals. Since 2000, selected African government heads, and from 2005 onward also the president of the African Union—the amalgamation of Africa's fifty-five states—had been regularly invited to the G8 summits, including in June 2007, to Heiligendamm. The G8 decided on an a plan for Africa, agreed debt relief programs with the countries, and supported both the vaccination allianc the Global Fund in combating AIDS, tuberculosis, a

By 2015, eight years later, the number of peop

suffering from starvation and extreme poverty genuinely had halved, but not in the African countries south of the Sahara. The numbers of those living in extreme poverty there fell by only 28 percent between 1990 and 2015. The number of malnourished people decreased from 33 percent to 23 percent, but as a result of high population growth, forty-four million more people were malnourished.

And yet there was progress in these countries too, not only in the fight against poverty, but also in the areas of education, gender equality, reduction of infant mortality, improvement in maternal health and the fight against HIV/AIDS, malaria, and other illnesses. The G8's support helped.

On September 25, 2015, I participated in the UN Sustainable Development Summit; by deciding on Agenda 2030, this was to herald the next phase following on from the Millennium Development Goals. The member states—now totaling 193—agreed on seventeen sustainability goals which were to be fulfilled worldwide by 2030. This would mean that, in fifteen years' time, no one would be living in extreme poverty or starving.

Many of the goals seemed abstract to me; for example, the third, on the topic of health: "Ensure a healthy life for people of all ages and support their well-being." But due to the Ebola epidemic, which had been spreading swiftly through West Africa since 2014, this suddenly became topical and concrete. Shortly after the outbreak of the illness in 2014, I had spoken with the president of the World Bank Jim Yong Kim, a doctor by trade, about how the Spanish Flu had claimed between twenty and fifty million lives almost a hundred years previously. Because our world was now much more closely connected, we were concerned that Ebola could spread unchecked and develop into a pandemic.

This is why, in early 2015, I appointed the diplomat Walter Lindner, who was very well regarded in African countries, as the German government's Special Representative for the Fight against Ebola. He recommended that we support the African countries in improving their health systems, which in turn would contribute to protecting the population in Germany from the illness.

The G7 heads of state and government subsequently agreed at their meeting in Elmau during the 2015 German G7 presidency to form health partnerships with at least sixty countries over the following five years, including with the countries of West Africa. Together with the president of Ghana John Dramani Mahama, and Norway's premier Erna Solberg, I asked the UN general secretary Ban Ki-moon to change the structures of the United Nations in such a way that in future it could react more efficiently to the outbreak of epidemics, thereby preventing the emergence of pandemics. We used the sustainability summit to demonstrate, in an event of our own, how this health goal could be animated at the occurrence of an epidemic: health systems had to be developed across the world which were logistically capable of generating information about illness outbreaks and passing them on to the World Health Organization (WHO). Structures had to be created within WHO to make this knowledge available internationally; in addition, there was a need to build skills and processes for the global community's swift response in countries affected by outbreaks. I spoke of "white helmets," with a nod to the UN's "blue helmets." International health politics and the strengthening of the WHO would remain a key focus both for my health ministers, Hermann Gröhe and Jens Spahn, and myself until the end of my time in office. Back then, we had no idea how significant it would become just a few years later.

Again and again, everything came back to what it means to live in an interconnected world. This applied in particular to Africa. The fight against Ebola, as well as the flight of so many people across the Mediterranean Sea, showed me that it wasn't a case of us—the Europeans—here, and the Africans there on the other side of the Mediterranean, but rather that the countries of our two continents, Africa and Europe, were inextricably linked. There could only be lasting stability and prosperity in Europe if Africa too became more stable and prosperous. Sealing ourselves off, averting our gaze, driving people away—these were pseudo-solutions at best; they didn't help. Africa and Europe had to be successful together. As correct as Agenda 2030's development goals were, I still feared we wouldn't be able to achieve them via the conventional methods of development cooperation work anymore than we had the Millennium Development Goals. No, there had to be a self-sustaining economic upturn in the African countries. I wanted to mark the course for this during Germany's G20 presidency in 2017. I found allies in the finance minister Wolfgang Schäuble and the development minister Gerd Müller. We agreed that this wasn't about developing something *for* the African countries, but rather *with* them. In 2013, the member states of the African Union had adopted a shared vision for their future, the "Agenda 2063: The Africa We Want." The Africa the Africans wanted—this formed the starting point for my deliberations. A self-sustaining economic upturn could only occur where private investors were supported by good governance. That's why I wanted to focus on nurturing private investment in the countries where governance was improving. Each country should define for itself the nature of the reforms. On this basis, the International Monetary Fund, the World Bank, and the African Development Bank would agree so-called "compacts" with the African countries; in other words, contracts or pacts through which conditions for private investments would improve, for example by protecting private donors or lowering interest rates for private loans. The initiative was named "Compact with Africa," and participation opened to every African country.

———

On June 12, 2017, the first G20 Africa Partnership conference was held in Berlin, organized by the ministry of finance. Côte d'Ivoire, Morocco, Rwanda, Senegal, and Tunisia had joined our initiative; and Ghana and Ethiopia did so during the conference. In my speech, in the presence of the African heads of state and government, I publicly set out the philosophy underpinning the conference. I asked the industrialized countries to question whether they had always taken the right path with traditional development aid. "I don't think we always have," I said. "We need to focus more strongly on the respective countries' individual economic developments." Companies from Germany also participated in the conference. In 2016, German exports to Africa's fifty-five states only amounted to 2 percent of total exports; the import share was 1.7 percent; and direct investments were also low.

Traditionally, the German–African Business Association looked after economic cooperation with African countries; it had been founded as early as 1934 and was originally named the Hamburg-Bremen German–African Business Association. The Federal Association of German Industries had formulated a comprehensive Africa strategy for the first time in 2014, under the title "Strategy Sub-Saharan Africa: Opportunity Continent of Africa." Economic collaboration customarily focused on South Africa, and North African countries such as Egypt, Algeria, Morocco, and Tunisia, as well as Nigeria, because of their oil reserves. It wasn't easy to convince the leaders of big German companies to accompany me on my travels to African countries. Most saw minimal opportunities for themselves in the African markets.

China, by contrast, had in the meantime invested far more spectacular sums than we had. The Senegalese president Abdoulaye Wade had once whispered to me: "If I need something quickly—a stadium or a new bridge—I turn to China.

Then within one or two years, I've got what I want. If it's not so urgent, I ask the Europeans. It's just that then I have to bear in mind that the tendering will take a long time, and that some projects never see the light of day." He added: "China always takes care of the financing. If we ask you guys, we have to settle that ourselves." After hearing that, I had made my way home filled with concern. It later turned out that Abdoulaye Wade was partly right, although the shadowy side of the Chinese support didn't stay secret for long. The countries of Africa, it transpired, had embroiled themselves in Chinese dependencies whose repercussions only became clear much later. Here, too, these often weren't relationships *with* African countries, contributing to a self-sustaining upturn at home, but rather agreements that solely advantaged China. There was every reason for the G20 to build up a new, fair partnership with Africa. And I was also able to achieve this at the Hamburg G20 summit.

By 2021, four years later, twelve countries had negotiated compacts: Egypt, Ethiopia, Benin, Burkina Faso, Côte d'Ivoire, Ghana, Guinea, Morocco, Rwanda, Senegal, Togo, and Tunisia. Together with the IMF, the World Bank, and the African Development Bank, I met with the compact countries each year in Berlin, even after our G20 presidency came to an end. Foreign investments—including German ones—in the twelve countries were rising, albeit not as swiftly as many of the African countries and I had hoped. I had merely taken the first step; others had to follow suit. In order to become better acquainted with the diversity of African countries, in 2016 I had begun visiting some of them each year. I was saddened when, from March 2020 onward, the COVID-19 pandemic prevented me from traveling for many months.

World powers: India and China

Of the five billion inhabitants of the nineteen G20 member states, more than half were citizens of just two countries: China had 1.39 billion, and India 1.35 billion. In the ten years since the 2007 summit in Heiligendamm, Chinese GDP per capita had more than tripled, and that of India had doubled. By way of comparison, in the same time period, American GDP per capita had risen only by 25 percent, but was still almost seven times higher than the Chinese, and more than thirty times higher than the Indian.

I had long been convinced that the economic successes of China and India would shift international power relations significantly in their direction. That's why I wanted to develop closer relationships with both countries. In 2010, I suggested to President Hu and Prime Minister Singh that we hold regular bilateral intergovernmental consultations. Both agreed. The first German–Indian intergovernmental consultations took place in early June 2011 in New Delhi, and the first German–Chinese one in late June 2011 in Berlin. Five further meetings with China and four with India were to follow.

India was the most populous democracy in the world. The first two German–Indian intergovernmental consultations of 2011 and 2013 were led on the Indian side by Prime Minister Manmohan Singh. I had met Singh in April 2006 when we officially opened the Hannover Messe together, where India was the partner country. Singh was born in 1932, and after reading economics, among other subjects, at Cambridge and Oxford, he worked for the United Nations Conference for Trade and Development (UNCTAD) and was elected prime minister in 2004. He belonged to the Congress Party, and, as a member of the Sikh religion, was the first non-Hindu premier. His primary aim was to improve living standards for the two-thirds of India's 1.2 billion population who lived in rural areas. This amounted to

800 million people, ten times Germany's entire population. In my conversations with him, I came to better understand the misgivings of the emerging countries toward us, the affluent countries. From his perspective, we expected them to take great interest in our problems, but we weren't prepared to offer them the same courtesy. I could see his point, and began to study more closely the challenges faced by the emerging countries. Singh told me about the cultural diversity of his country, a sub-continent with more than five thousand years of history. The Indian constitution alone recognizes twenty-two official languages. The country's unity arises from its diversity. In this respect, India is more comparable with the European Union as a whole than with one of its member states.

In May 2014, Singh was succeeded by Narendra Modi. He belonged to the Hindu-nationalist Bharatiya Janata party and preferred to speak Hindi, India's official language, alongside English. We had met for the first time in April 2015, also during the opening of the Hannover Messe, when India was partner country for a second time. Under the motto "Make in India," four hundred companies were exhibiting their products. At the opening ceremony, Modi emphatically promoted India as a location for investment, speaking English as an exception, and impressed everyone there with a cultural program that contained elements of augmented reality. I held my breath as a deceptively real-looking Asiatic lion stepped out of the back wall, roared loudly, padded downstage toward the audience, and promenaded through the middle aisle of the Hanover Congress Center. Modi loved visual effects. He told me about election campaigns in which he'd spoken in a studio and had his image projected as a hologram to more than fifty different locations, where thousands of people were listening to him in each. I asked how the listeners had responded to that kind of virtual presence. He reported that many people had waited for him at the end of his speech, wanting to shake his hand, even though they knew he wasn't really there.

Modi's focus was also on improving Indians' living standards, especially for the rural population. He boosted economic growth, in particular by tackling the countless bureaucratic hurdles that lurked everywhere. He appointed a staff member in his office as a contact person for companies experiencing difficulties with their projects. This gave rise to a so-called fast track for investments. India's economy grew by 6 to 7 percent over a number of years.

In October 2015, the third German–Indian intergovernmental consultations took place in New Delhi. Because Modi had heard about my love of classical music, he arranged a small concert for all the participants after the lunch. He had a piece of music composed especially for the occasion. It was premiered by an orchestra playing on both Indian and European instruments—a symbol of our cultural ties. I loved moments like this on my official appointments; they not only gave me the opportunity to better understand my conversation partners and their views, but also exposed me to new cultural worlds. This also gave rise to an atmosphere of intimacy from which it was easier to find political compromises.

On the second day of my visit, we went to Bangalore together to visit a German–Indian economic forum—170 German companies had relocated there—and also a Bosch innovation center, where we met with Indian apprentices. Under the motto "Skill India," Modi was working to give young Indians improved opportunities through education, hence why he was interested in collaborating with us.

We spoke regularly about climate protection whenever we met. Modi reproached me and the industrialized countries as a whole for concealing the fact that India had so far contributed little to global warming and had a great need for development aid. I accepted both arguments, but pointed out that India's contribution to global warming was no longer on a scale that could be ignored. Even though, in 2017, India had a significantly lower per capita emission of CO_2, with 1.8 tons, than China with 7.1 tons or the US with 15.8 tons, it was now, after these two countries, the third largest emitter of CO_2 with a more than 7 percent share in global emissions. India's path to climate neutrality was, therefore, of considerable importance. We agreed to work together closely on strengthening renewable energies, in particular solar energy. Four years later, at the climate conference in Glasgow in November 2021, Modi would announce that India aimed to be climate neutral by 2070, and to derive half of its energy from renewable sources by 2030.

On the evening before the fourth German–Indian intergovernmental consultations in late May 2017, just a few weeks before the Hamburg G20 summit, Modi and I spoke extensively in the German government's guest-house at Schloss Meseberg about the EU's free trade agreement with India. The negotiations had begun in 2007, and came to a standstill in 2013. It didn't prove possible during my time in office to kick-start them again. Here, too, differences in opinion within the field of agriculture were insurmountable.

I followed with concern the reports that, since Modi had taken office, an increasing number of members of other religions, predominantly Muslims and Christians, were being attacked by Hindu nationalists. When I broached the subject with Modi, he vehemently denied it and emphasized that India was and would remain a country of religious tolerance. Unfortunately, the facts said otherwise. We were unable to agree on this point. My worries remained—religious freedom is, after all, a key component of every democracy.

When I entered office in 2005, China wasn't only the most populated land on Earth; its economic growth, too, had rapidly accelerated since the country joined the World Trade

Organization. Following in the footsteps of my predecessor, Gerhard Schröder, I endeavored to travel to China with an economic delegation at least once a year. China's share in the total volume of German export trade was 4.8 percent in 2006; by the end of my chancellorship, it would be 9.5 percent. In addition to the political discussions in Beijing, I also visited one additional city each time. In this way, I at least gained some small insight into the country's history and cultural riches. My July 2010 visit to Xi'an, which had been China's capital city for over a thousand years, was unforgettable. Together with Premier Wen Jiabao, I visited the so-called Terracotta Army in the mausoleum of Emperor Qin Shi Huang, the construction of which began in 246 BCE. Thousands of larger-than-life clay figures, detailed imitations of imperial army soldiers and their equipage, had been uncovered, each figure different from the next. I was in awe of the place, and had never seen anything like it.

On these city visits, I saw with my own eyes the consequences that came with the tripling of per capita income within a ten-year period. The speed at which the cities were growing was breathtaking. In October 2015, when I accompanied Premier Li Keqiang to his hometown of Hefei—he having taken office in March 2013—I began to count during the car journey the number of buildings with over thirty stories that were mid-construction. I stopped when I passed 120. The environmental challenges connected to its economic development were equally unmistakable, the smog in Beijing being just one example. Nonetheless, I was impressed by what had been achieved in China within such a short time span. The fact that hunger and extreme poverty had been halved worldwide between 1990 and 2015 was also to China's credit. In 1990, 61 percent of people in the country were living in extreme poverty; by 2015, it was just 4 percent.

Xi Jinping became president of the People's Republic in March 2013. We had already met back when he was vice president. In July 2010, I visited the Central Party School of the Chinese Communist Party, where he was rector, to speak to the students and answer their questions. They knew I had grown up in the GDR, and that I saw German unity as a happy event. This is why they interpreted—or so I deduced from their questions—my critical comments on China's approach to human rights and the protection of intellectual property as a reluctance on my part to properly get to know the country, and that instead, I simply saw it as a big GDR. Whether my assurances convinced them that the view I was forming of their country was independent of my experiences in the GDR, I can't say. In any case, my Marxist–Leninist knowledge enabled me to ask Xi precise questions on the political system and the role of China's Communist Party. Xi's responses gave me insight into his way of thinking, which allowed me to better imagine how he interpreted Article 1 of Chapter 1 in the Chinese constitution: "The People's Republic of China is a socialist state governed by a people's democratic dictatorship that is led by the working class and based on an alliance of workers and peasants." Ultimately, it revolved around the question of what rights the individual has in a society, and who is permitted to curtail them, invoking the common good. For me, there wasn't *one* group in a society that knew and defined the best path for all others. This leads to a lack of freedom for the individual, and the profound difference between Xi and me was rooted in this conviction. Where human rights were concerned, therefore, our opinions couldn't have been more different. During my visits to the German embassy in Beijing, I regularly met with Chinese opposition members, who took considerable risk in meeting with me. I was able to help individual people, but I couldn't change the systemic suppression of dissidents in China.

My cooperation with the country was an example of

realpolitik. It was founded on our being aware of our differences in opinion and not sweeping them under the carpet; on respecting each other's political systems as they were, and deriving areas for collaboration from our shared interests. There were significant benefits for Germany—economic cooperation secured German workplaces, and other EU member states also had an interest in reliable conditions for investment in China. In 2014, therefore, negotiations began for a so-called Comprehensive Agreement on Investment (CAI). At the end of the German EU Council presidency in December 2020, the European Commission agreed on the key points of the accord with the support of the European Council. After EU foreign ministers imposed sanctions on China in March 2021 due to the repression of the Uyghur minority group, and China initiated countermeasures, including against members of the European Parliament, the ratification of the agreement was suspended. I remain convinced that the accord would bring an increase in dependable framework conditions for investments, compared with the current situation.

It was also in Germany's interest to work with China on a shared global regulatory framework. This applied in particular to climate protection. China's economic development had a price. The country's CO_2 emissions had rapidly increased over the years; by 2017 China was emitting almost twice as much as the US. By the end of my time in office, China's share in worldwide CO_2 emissions was almost 31 percent; the US's 13.5 percent, as the second biggest emitter; and Germany's 1.8 percent. At the UN General Assembly in 2020, Xi Jinping declared that China aimed to become carbon neutral by 2060 and for its emissions to peak by 2030. It is not only in Germany's interest, but that of the entire world, that China achieves or even overachieves these goals.

After Xi took office, power was concentrated even more intensely in his person. Where previously I had held conversations with his predecessor, Hu, as a matter of courtesy, discussing all the important bilateral matters with Premier Wen Jiabao, once Xi came into power I discussed almost all issues with him. He repositioned China. At our meetings, he spoke frequently about the history of humanity over the past two thousand years and emphasized that, in eighteen of those twenty centuries, China had been the economic and cultural center of the world. China had only fallen behind in the early nineteenth century, he told me. When I heard that, I asked my economic and fiscal advisor Lars-Hendrik Röller to check these statements against the available economic data. He confirmed Xi's portrayal. In Xi's view, China should now return to this historic normality; he called this the "Chinese Dream," an obvious borrowing from the "American Dream." While Deng Xiaoping, the architect of China's reform and opening-up policy in the late 1970s, had issued the maxim "Hide your strengths and bide your time," for Xi it seemed the moment had come to show these strengths.

Immediately after Xi became premier in 2013, China founded the New Silk Road, also known as the "Belt and Road Initiative," which now includes over a hundred countries and realizes infrastructure projects. The majority of the financing came from one of the newly founded development banks. The Chinese government saw the Silk Road initiative as a commitment to multilateralism. On the one hand, these projects were genuinely able to promote an interconnected world; on the other, reality showed that some countries, in particular those of Asia and Africa, often stumbled into financial dependencies with China due to the costs connected with the investments, thereby limiting their own sovereign agency.

With the so-called "nine-dash line," China raised territorial claims in the South China Sea. The nine-dash line refers back to a nautical map on which the then Chinese Nationalist government asserted their territorial claims during the region's reorganization after the Second World War. All of the countries bordering the South China Sea rejected these claims. China refused to seek compromise with the Philippines, Malaysia, Brunei, Thailand, Indonesia, and Vietnam. In 2013, the Philippines initiated proceedings for a dispute resolution at the Permanent Court of Arbitration in The Hague. The court ruled in July 2016 that the nine-dash line did not justify the Chinese territorial claims, but China refused to recognize the verdict. The commitment to multilateralism cited so frequently by Chinese politicians turned out, in this very concrete example, to be mere lip service.

Donald Trump

Donald Trump became president of the United States of America on January 20, 2017. I had carefully followed the election campaign between Trump and Hillary Clinton, and would have been delighted to see her win. Things turned out very differently. Not only did Donald Trump set a nationalist tone with his campaign slogans "America First" and "Make America Great Again," but he also repeatedly criticized Germany and me personally during the campaign. He claimed I had destroyed Germany by taking in too many refugees in 2015 and 2016, complained that we spent too little on defense, and accused us of unfair trade practices toward the US on account of our trade surplus. The numerous German cars on the streets of New York had been a thorn in his side for many years. In his opinion, the fact that Americans bought them could only be down to dumping prices and supposed exchange-rate manipulations between the euro and the dollar. Again and again, he spoke of raising customs duties on German cars in order to make their purchase unattractive. I found it astonishing that a presidential candidate in the US would focus his attention on a German chancellor. I could have reassured myself with the motto "the greater the opposition, the greater the prestige." But gallows humor was of little help, because it was my duty to do everything I could to ensure a comfortable relationship between our two countries, without reacting to the provocation. When he was elected on November 9, 2016, I not only offered my congratulations to Donald Trump in a statement in the Chancellery, but also stressed that our two countries were connected by shared values such as democracy, freedom, respect for the law, and the dignity of humankind, regardless of origin, skin color, religion, gender, sexual orientation, or political leaning. "On the basis of these values," I offered him close cooperation. Four months later, on March 17, 2017, I visited him in Washington. I had meticulously prepared for this meeting, given that he, and the US, aroused considerable interest in Germany.

When I arrived at the White House, Donald Trump greeted me at the door with a handshake, in the presence of reporters. Before our one-to-one conversation in the Oval Office, we presented ourselves to the media for a second time. When journalists and photographers requested another handshake, he ignored them. Instead of stoically enduring the scene, I whispered to him that we should shake hands again—during the visit from Japan's premier Shinzō Abe he had done so for nineteen seconds without Abe managing to pull away. As soon as the words left my mouth, I shook my head at myself. How could I forget that Trump knew precisely what he was doing. And, consistently, he didn't respond to my discreet comment. He wanted to create conversation fodder through his behavior, while I had acted as though I were having a discussion with someone completely normal.

During our private conversation, we felt our way slowly. I predominantly spoke English; the interpreter Dorothee Kaltenbach sat with us and translated some of the more complicated passages. Donald Trump asked me a series of questions, including on my East German background and my relationship with Putin. He was clearly fascinated by the Russian president. In the years that followed, I received the distinct impression he was captivated by politicians with autocratic and dictatorial traits.

As soon as the members of both delegations came into the Oval Office after our conversation, he began to make the usual remonstrations about Germany. I rebutted the accusations by relaying the numbers and facts. We were talking on two different levels: Trump on the emotional; I on the factual. If he paid any attention to my arguments, it was mostly only to construct new allegations from them. Finding a solution to the problems being discussed didn't seem to be his goal, because then he would have needed to immediately ponder new grounds for complaint. It seemed that his primary aim was to make the person he was talking to feel guilty. When he realized I was putting up vigorous resistance, he abruptly ended his tirade and changed the subject. My impression was that he also wanted the person he was talking with to like him.

He repeatedly stressed that Germany owed something to him and to America. This rhetoric was well received by his followers, given that many felt disadvantaged and badly treated by previous politicians. They admired Trump because he didn't take any nonsense, because he talked plainly, and because, in their view, he fought for the interests of his supporters.

The bosses of BMW, Schaeffler, and Siemens had traveled with me to Washington—Harald Krüger, Klaus Rosenfeld, and Joe Kaeser. Lars-Hendrik Röller and his American colleague had arranged for Trump and me, following the conversations in the Oval Office, to lead a discussion with economy representatives and apprentices from their American factories about the training of technical staff in the United States. I wanted to highlight in the process the contribution that German companies were making to workplaces in the US. This only partially succeeded. While Trump did praise the investment of German companies in the US, he simultaneously criticized their production in neighboring Mexico. He seemed to want to have it all.

For most of the conversation points with Trump, I had good arguments on my side. One weak point, however, was our defense expenditure. It was obvious we wouldn't manage to reach the 2-percent goal which had been set at the 2014 NATO summit as a target for all member states to attain by 2024, even though, as I was able to announce at the press conference, we had raised our defense budget by 8 percent from 2016 to 2017. Obama too had appealed to my conscience on this many times. But with Trump, the matter threatened to become more dangerous, because he called NATO into question as a collaborative security alliance. I was aware that we as Germans were dependent on NATO for our own security. That was why I emphasized the contribution we were making to the joint mission in Afghanistan. Trump did at least acknowledge this in the subsequent press conference.

As I flew home, I felt uneasy. My conclusion from the conversations was: there would be no cooperative work for an interconnected world with Trump. He assessed everything from the perspective of the real-estate developer he had been before entering politics. Each piece of property can only be allocated once. If he didn't get one, he got another. That's how he saw the world. For him, all countries were in competition, and the success of one meant the failure of another. He didn't believe that cooperation could increase prosperity for everyone. My example of the mutual advantage which the EU and Korea were able to gain from their joint free trade agreement hadn't convinced him. He was skeptical toward all agreements that he hadn't negotiated personally; and he seemed particularly mistrustful of Germany. There would be no TTIP with him.

But there was more to come. Six weeks before the G20 summit, on June 1, 2017, he requested a phone call with me. We spoke at ten o'clock in the evening. He informed me that the

United States would be ceasing its participation in the Paris climate agreement. This was a severe blow, given that I wanted the subject to be a key focus in Hamburg.

G20 in Hamburg

On June 17, 2017, I met with Pope Francis for a private audience. Having met with him three times previously, I knew he was interested in global cooperation, particularly for the benefit of the poor, and so I wanted to discuss with him my agenda for the upcoming G20 summit in Hamburg. Together with Annette Schavan, our ambassador to the Holy See, my foreign policy and security policy advisor Christoph Heusgen, another colleague from his department, as well as my office manager Bernhard Kotsch, and an interpreter for Italian and German, we drove past St. Peter's Square, with a view of St. Peter's Basilica, in the Vatican City. We left the Campo Santo Teutonico behind us, circled the Basilica, passed the Sistine Chapel, crossed the Cortile della Sentinella, the Cortile Borgia, and the Cortile del Pappagalli, and eventually came to a halt in the Cortile di San Damaso in front of the Apostolic Palace. There I was greeted by the Prefect of the Papal Household, the titular archbishop Georg Gänswein. I was also awaited by the Gentiluomini di Sua Santità, the Gentleman of His Holiness, who guided me to the second floor of the palace.

Pope Francis received me in the Papal library with a friendly smile. To the right of the entrance door stood a writing desk and two chairs. The pope and I sat down, and my interpreter sat behind me. Francis was translated by a German prelate. He asked me what I had planned for our G20 presidency. I told him about our logo, the reef knot, and reported on our preparatory work, which, among other things, consisted of a number of meetings with civil society. I had met with economic and union representatives from the G20 countries in order to discuss the topic of "Growth and Employment"—the traditional focus of the G20 talks—and also with representatives from women's groups and scientists, think tanks, youth and NGO organizations. As always, ministers from the fields of foreign policy, finance, digital, employment, and agriculture had met, but this time also the health ministers of the G20 nations—they wanted to talk about pandemic precautions. The outbreak of Ebola in West Africa had prompted the health minister Herman Gröhe and his G20 colleagues to simulate, in a planning game, how the worldwide spread of a deadly virus transmitted via the respiratory system could be stopped. I told the pope about the planned partnership with Africa and the compacts. He listened attentively.

Then I came to my own point of concern: the United States' announced departure from the Parisian climate agreement. Without naming names, I asked Pope Francis how he would deal with fundamentally differing opinions within a group of important personalities. He understood at once and answered in a straightforward way: "Bend, bend, and bend some more, but take care that it doesn't break." I liked this image. I repeated it back to him. "Bend, bend, and bend some more, but take care that it doesn't break." I would try to solve my problem with the Paris Agreement and Trump with this approach in Hamburg, even though I wasn't yet sure what that would mean concretely.

The time flew by. The pope pressed a bell on the table; Gänswein and the members of my delegation came over to us, and we stood up and had a group photo taken. After that, gifts that had been laid out on a separate table were exchanged. I knew from Annette Schavan which regional specialties Pope Francis was particularly fond of, and had brought back from Buenos Aires, where I had been a few days beforehand, three glasses of the sweet spread Dulce de Leche, and alfajores: cookies enveloped in chocolate. He seemed delighted with the gifts. I was especially moved by one of his gifts: a small bronze sculpture of an olive branch, like the branch that the dove sent out from Noah's Ark had brought back in its beak, thereby heralding the end of the Flood. The olive branch had become the symbol of peace. After my retirement from office, the sculpture received a place in my new office as "Chancellor retd."

On July 6, 2017, the day before the summit, I traveled to Hamburg in the afternoon. Due to the high number of participants, there were only a few places in Germany where a G20 summit of heads of state and government could take place, and Hamburg was ideal. The first mayor of the city Olaf Scholz regarded the hosting as an honor, and I was delighted that my birthplace could present itself to the world.

And yet the summit did not turn out as I had hoped. If I were to ask people today what they remember of the G20 summit in Hamburg, the answer would probably be: the violent protests by anti-globalization activists. Only the very politically engaged would perhaps remember the differences of opinion with Trump regarding climate protection. Awful images of burning cars, looted shops, and stone-throwing protesters in Hamburg's Schanzenviertel district circulated around the world. That evening, I watched them on the television. Some of the channels were reporting on it without pause. I went to bed feeling depressed. No matter what we decided the following day, the pictures from the evening would define perceptions. For me as host, that was terrible, even though I was deeply convinced that in-person meetings between heads of state and government for a summit like this should be possible. The Hamburg police reported after the summit that 23,000 police officers had been deployed and 592 of them injured. Criticisms of the police's operational approach were raised. I decided not to wade into these discussions, and, despite the questions I also had on the deployment, to stand shoulder to shoulder with Olaf Scholz. After the end of the summit, we met with a group of emergency personnel from the entire region and thanked them for their work.

Politically, we reached a decision on the climate which we called "19 to 1." "We acknowledge the decision of the United States of America to withdraw from the Paris Agreement." This was recorded in the communiqué by eighteen countries and the EU, followed by the American positions. The next paragraph was as follows: "The heads of state and government of the remaining G20 members declare that the Paris Agreement is irreversible." It was therefore possible to adopt by consensus a statement which openly named the dissent between Donald Trump and the rest of the world rather than covering it up. Never before had there been an outcome document of this kind. Previously, in a joint resolution, the smallest common denominator had usually been recorded. I considered this result the best among the bad solutions. We had stopped bending before everything was broken, before we wouldn't have had any communiqué at all. The overwhelming majority were aware of the importance of climate protection.

All the other decisions corresponded to what I had imagined as a result. Only one seemingly small point, regarding trade, had a longer aftermath. It surrounded the question of the dumping of steel exports. This had already played a role in 2016 during the Chinese G20 presidency at the summit meeting in Hang Zhou. In the preceding years, China had begun to export steel at very low prices, thereby putting steel producers in Europe and the US under extreme pressure. While the industrialized countries spoke of unfair dumping, China firmly rejected this. As a result, a forum of the G20 had been founded in Hang Zhou, the Global Forum on Steel Excess Capacity, which was supported by the OECD (Organization for Economic Collaboration and Development), in order to investigate the question of dumping more thoroughly by using precise data.

Except, almost a year later, there still weren't any results.

This is why some wanted to do away with the forum and immediately raise customs duties on Chinese steel, while others wanted to give it another chance. The latter was the German stance. On the last night of the G20 summit, the sherpas agreed to collate the necessary information by August, and called on the forum to issue a report with suggested solutions in November, on the basis of which swift political action could be taken. It seemed to be a success for us; Lars-Hendrik Röller pointed out to me, however, that the time frame was so short that a mutually agreed solution was almost out of the question. And he was right.

In June 2018, Donald Trump made an example of this very case. His government levied considerable customs duties on steel and aluminum imports, and not only those from China, but from most other countries too, including the European Union. He justified this measure as protecting the US's national security interests. China, Norway, Switzerland, and Turkey made a complaint to the World Trade Organization. Over four years later, in December 2022, the arbitration tribunal decided that these measures contravened the organization's rules. By then, however, Joe Biden was already US president. He did not scrap tariffs, but with Biden and his Vice President Kamala Harris, multilateral cooperation together with the United States seemed once again to be a possibility. As I write these words, the outcome of the American presidential election in November 2024 is still open. I wish with all my heart that Kamala Harris, whom I met over breakfast during my last visit to Washington as chancellor in 2021, defeats her competitor and becomes president.

CLIMATE AND ENERGY

A catastrophe and its consequences

I CALLED AN emergency meeting for the late afternoon of Saturday, March 12, 2011, with the environment minister Norbert Röttgen, the interior minister Hans-Peter Friedrich, the Chancellery minister Ronald Pofalla, and the foreign minister and vice chancellor of the CDU, CSU, and FDP coalition Guido Westerwelle. I was heading back from Bad Kreuznach in the Rhineland-Palatinate, where I'd launched the regional election campaign with our CDU front-runner Julia Klöckner. Elections were due to take place there and in Baden-Wuerttemberg two weeks later, on March 27, 2011. The crisis meeting at the Chancellery would be the first opportunity for us to discuss the situation after the major seaquake off the coast of Japan which had occurred just before 7:00 a.m. CET the previous day. As a result, tsunami waves almost fifteen meters in height had wreaked devastation, also hitting the Fukushima No. 1 nuclear power plant.

I had spent Friday in a special session of the European Council and a subsequent meeting of eurozone members in Brussels while I constantly followed the reports coming from Japan. In the Fukushima No. 1 nuclear power plant, the cooling system, made by the Tokyo Electric Power Company (TEPCO), had failed and the Japanese government had declared a nuclear emergency. Emergency cooling systems were only running on backup batteries and, due to the risk of radiation, people within a three-kilometer radius were being evacuated. That evening in Brussels, I briefly left the session and went to our delegation office in the European Council building, where the government spokesperson Steffen Seibert briefed me on the news, showing me videos of the destruction of entire towns along the Japanese coast on his tablet. It wasn't until I was back in the meeting room that I read the reports of a possible nuclear meltdown. Severe aftershocks were hitting the region and radioactivity levels in the nuclear plant's control room were a thousand times higher than normal, while outside they had increased eightfold: the evacuation zone was enlarged to ten kilometers.

That evening in Brussels was a surreal one. I had to focus on the negotiations—at the eurozone members' meeting, we were discussing the European Stability Mechanism (ESM), which was a very contentious issue within the German government coalition. But at the same time, the situation in Fukushima seemed to be spinning out of control. Our talks went on until midnight and it was already two o'clock in the morning by the time I flew back to Berlin.

When I got up the next day, I read that an explosion had occurred at the Fukushima No. 1 nuclear power plant. The roof of the building that housed the reactor had collapsed, white clouds of smoke had escaped, and by now, radioactivity outside the building was twenty times higher than the regular level. I stuck to my appointments for the kick-off to the election campaign in the Rhineland-Palatinate, and by late Saturday afternoon, I was back in Berlin. By then, reports of a nuclear meltdown in the Fukushima No. 1 plant seemed to have been confirmed.

We gathered in the Small Suite, a meeting room on the same level as the Cabinet Room, the seventh floor. Norbert Röttgen briefed us on what he knew about the situation in Japan. Then he made it clear that the events in Japan would have a knock-on effect on the debate in Germany about the operation of nuclear plants. Guido Westerwelle saw this differently. He emphasized how far Japan was from Germany and said he didn't believe that the accident in Fukushima would have a direct impact on our domestic energy policies. The mood in the room was tense. After listening to them both, I soon felt that Röttgen was right. We agreed that the ministry of the environment would review the safety standards of all German nuclear plants in light of the events in Japan.

I'd invited the press to attend my public statement in front of the blue wall at 7:00 p.m. The catastrophe was so far-reaching that I felt it appropriate to appear before the press with Vice Chancellor Westerwelle, whose position as foreign minister also meant that he was responsible for Germany's support of Japan during the crisis. But before we gave our statement, we needed to agree on what we were going to say, and to do that we went up to my office on the floor above. Upstairs, I turned on the lights to their lowest setting. I was exhausted: the election campaign event and then the emergency meeting with the ministers had sapped all my strength, and bright lights would only make me feel worse. Once we were alone, the tension in us collapsed. Suddenly, we both felt despondent, and, rather than sitting down, we looked out of the window at the Reichstag, and then began pacing around the room. It was as if we were trying to keep as far away as possible from my black conference desk where, only six months previously, on Sunday, September 5, 2010, we had hammered out the details to prolong the lifespans of German nuclear plants.

In doing so, we'd reversed the June 2001 agreement made by Gerhard Schröder and his red–green coalition with the power companies to phase out nuclear energy gradually. The CDU/CSU Union and the Free Democrats had each promised in their election programs to prolong the lifespans of nuclear plants again, and we had also written this proposal into our 2009 coalition agreement. Norbert Röttgen, the environment minister, had taken a very skeptical view of the undertaking, whereas I had been in favor of prolonging the lifespans of the plants, including during my election campaign. But I had also wanted to avoid a replay of the conflicts with anti-nuclear campaigners that I remembered from my time as environment minister, because Schröder's government had restored social harmony with its decision. In retrospect, being an advocate for nuclear power for reasons of energy policy, while at the same time attempting to preserve public peace, was doomed to failure from the outset: it was much like trying to square the circle. With this strategy, I had not been able to convince either vehement supporters of nuclear energy or its opponents. What was more: in the 2009 German general election, the CDU/CSU Union had won 33.8 percent of the vote and the FDP 14.6 percent, which meant that the Christian Democrats had fared even worse than in 2005, whereas the Free Democrats had had their strongest showing ever. Some people who had always considered me too willing to compromise believed that they could sideline me and pursue "undiluted CDU policies," as they called them. The FDP evidently felt encouraged by the election results to do the opposite of everything the previous government—my first coalition with the SDP—had done. All of this put me in a bad negotiating position.

In our discussion on September 5, 2010, those who typically supported me—above all, the general secretary of the CDU Volker Kauder, and the then chairman of the CSU parliamentary group Hans-Peter Friedrich, as well as the minister of economic affairs Wolfgang Schaeuble, the interior minister Thomas de Maizière, the Bavarian state premier and CSU chairman Horst Seehofer, as well as representatives of the FDP besides Guido Westerwelle, such as the finance minister Rainer Brüderle and the parliamentary group chair Birgit Homburger— had all pressed hard for the maximum possible extension to the lifespan of nuclear plants. In that situation I had decided to weigh up my power in the negotiations realistically and not plunge the coalition into crisis; and so, I agreed in the end to prolong the lifespans of the seven older nuclear plants by eight years and the other ten by fourteen years. My objection that this decision would not be seen as a postponement of an exit from nuclear energy, but as an exit from an exit, had not convinced the other negotiators.

In some ways that discussion was still hanging in the air now, six months later. A nightmare had become a reality even if not in our country. I spoke of the sixty thousand people—twenty thousand more than predicted—who had formed a forty-five-kilometer human chain that day between Stuttgart and the nuclear plant in Neckarwestheim to protest the extension of the phase-out. At the same time, thoughts were hammering through my mind: How are you going to defend your previous argument that the risks of nuclear energy are justifiable when, against all odds, a maximum credible accident (MCA) can happen in such a highly developed country as Japan?

Guido Westerwelle and I stopped pacing the room, and we exchanged glances. I didn't yet have a concrete plan in mind. All I said was, "Guido, we can't just carry on as before. We have to start rethinking our position on nuclear energy beyond all taboos."

After a short silence, he asked, "Do you mean that seriously?"

"Yes," I said.

"I think you're right," he replied calmly.

We agreed to sleep on it for a night, to call each other on Sunday, and to meet the coalition committee again at 9:00 p.m. We then left my office and took the elevator to the second floor to give our statement to the press.

I said that I understood every person who was alarmed by the present situation but, as far as it was humanly possible to judge, Germany could not be affected by the nuclear disaster in Japan. I also announced that the safety standards of German nuclear plants would be reviewed and gave a reason for our approach: "If a country like Japan, with very high safety requirements and standards, cannot prevent nuclear consequences from an earthquake and tsunami [. . .] then a country like Germany with equally high safety requirements and standards cannot simply return to business as usual." That evening, all residents within a twenty-kilometer radius of the Fukushima No. 1 power plant were evacuated.

The following day, on Sunday, March 12, 2011, the state premier of Baden-Wuerttemberg Stefan Mappus and the then Bavarian environment minister Markus Söder commented publicly on the catastrophic accident in a manner that responded to my concerns. I was astonished because both men had hitherto been vehement advocates of a generous extension to nuclear plant lifespans. After Guido Westerwelle and I had talked on the phone as agreed the night before, that evening the coalition committee agreed to a nuclear moratorium: The extension of operating periods for German nuclear plants would be suspended and the seven oldest plants would initially be shut down for three months. Stefan Mappus and Horst Seehofer had already signaled that they would adopt this plan at the Neckarwestheim and Isar 1 nuclear plants in their respective federal states. At the committee meeting, we agreed to announce our decisions only after a meeting on Tuesday morning with all the state premiers whose constituencies had nuclear plants in operation.

But while I was chairing the CDU Presidium meeting on Monday morning, news agency reports quoting Guido Westerwelle were handed to me. He had said we needed a new risk analysis and that he could imagine a moratorium on the extension of nuclear power plant lifespans. That broke our agreement the previous evening to maintain silence until Tuesday. I left the meeting, called Westerwelle, and demanded an explanation. He said that he didn't believe we could keep the matter secret until Tuesday and that was why he'd gone on the offensive. While I was annoyed, I also understood his position because, in the current situation, whoever back-pedaled the fastest would win. We agreed to present the results of Sunday's coalition committee at a joint press conference at 4:00 p.m. In the CDU's Presidium, there was barely any opposition to the moratorium, although Volker Kauder and the state premier of Hesse, Volker Bouffier, found our reaction too rash.

On Tuesday, March 15, 2011, together with the premiers of all federal states with nuclear plants—Stefan Mappus, Horst Seehofer, Volker Bouffier, David McAllister from Lower Saxony, and Peter Harry Carstensen from Schleswig-Holstein—we agreed to a three-month shutdown of the seven power plants that had been in operation up to and including 1980 by legal decree of the federal states' supervisory bodies on the basis of the Atomic Energy Act. A week later, on March 22, 2011, after a further meeting with the premiers of all federal states with nuclear plants, I announced the appointment of an Ethics Commission for a Safe Energy Supply which, by the end of May, would assess the risks of nuclear power, outline the possibilities of generating electricity via renewable sources, and thereby pave the way for social consensus.

At the state elections on March 21, 2011, the Greens triumphed. In Baden-Württemberg, they gained an additional 12.5 percentage points compared to the previous election, whereas the CDU lost 5.2 points. On May 12, 2011, the Greens' front-runner, Winfried Kretschmann, was elected as state premier of a Green Party/ Social Democrat coalition, which meant that, for the first time since 1953, the position in that state was not filled by a CDU politician. In the Rhineland-Palatinate, the Greens gained an additional 10.8 percentage points; the Christian Democrats gained 2.4 percent, and the SPD lost 9.9 points—and with them, the absolute majority. The Free Democrats failed to clear the 5-percent threshold to make it into the Bundestag. Since the

Greens had declared they would be open to forming a coalition with the SPD but not with the CDU, the social democrat Kurt Beck was able to stay on as state premier.

On May 30, 2011, the joint chairs of the Ethics Commission—Klaus Töpfer, my predecessor in the job of minister for the environment and the executive director of the United Nations Environment Program (UNEP) from 1998 to 2006, as well as Matthias Kleiner, the president of the German Research Foundation, along with fifteen other experts from the fields of science, the economy, politics, trade unions, and the church—presented me with a mutually approved report titled "Germany's energy transition—A collective project for the future." The Ethics Commission argued that the withdrawal from nuclear energy could be completed within a decade and recommended permanently removing from the grid the seven oldest nuclear plants, as well as the Krümmel plant in Schleswig-Holstein. Two of the commission's arguments left a strong impression on me. Firstly, they wrote: "The central problem is not what can be imagined but what cannot," in their conclusions about the tsunami and its adverse effects on Japan. This pinpointed exactly what was so devastating for me about the earthquake. Secondly, they made a case for not limiting risk assessment solely to health and environmental dangers: "One subject of ethical judgment must also be the consequences that result from a poisonous social climate, which has a justifiable place in nuclear energy discussions in Germany." This addressed an issue that I had already had to deal with as environment minister during consensus talks on energy policy.

On June 9, 2011, ninety days after the March 1 tsunami—by which time it was certain that three reactor cores of the Fukushima No. 1 nuclear power plant had melted—I made a government statement in the Bundestag that Germany would end the use of nuclear energy by 2022. The climate policy targets we had stipulated in our Energy Concept in the fall of

2010 would remain valid despite a successive withdrawal from electricity generated by nuclear power, a process that produces a relatively low level of carbon dioxide emissions. In our concept, we had targeted a 40-percent reduction in greenhouse gas emissions by 2020, a 50-percent reduction by 2030, and at least an 80-percent reduction by 2050, each compared to levels in 1990. On June 30, 2011, the CDU/CSU, FDP, SPD, and the Alliance 90/Green Party passed the amendments to the Atomic Energy Act in the Bundestag. Sixteen years after the failure of my first talks on energy policy in 1995, we reached a consensus to withdraw from nuclear energy in Germany.

Germany remains the only industrialized country worldwide to have drawn conclusions from the Fukushima nuclear disaster. In essence, I was accused of making a policy U-turn because of the upcoming state elections in the Rhineland-Palatinate and Baden-Württemberg. But this is not the case. The critical issue for me was that the events in Fukushima changed my perception of the risk posed by nuclear energy; not only that, but realistic solutions existed to meet our climate targets. It would have been absurd for me to ignore these conclusions, only to avoid accusations that I had an eye on the approaching state elections. It bears saying that the Union and the FDP would have saved themselves a great deal of trouble if we had been moderate in our extension of nuclear plant lifespans in September 2010.

I cannot recommend that Germany resumes the use of nuclear energy in the future either. We can achieve climate targets without nuclear power, and achieve technological success while giving other countries the courage to follow our example.

Natural gas

When Russia attacked Ukraine on February 24, 2022, Western countries reacted by imposing wide-ranging economic sanctions. Nord Stream AG, which was majority-owned by the Russian state-controlled company Gazprom, responded by turning off its Nord Stream 1 gas pipeline on July 11, 2022. The reason given for the halted supply, which seemed spurious to me, was a missing turbine required for maintenance works. Many times in the days that followed, a photo of me taken almost eleven years earlier was reprinted in the press. Back then, on November 8, 2011, I had attended a ceremony in Lubmin near Greifswald together with the short-lived Russian president Dmitry Medvedev, the French prime minister François Fillon, the prime minister of the Netherlands Mark Rutte, the European commissioner for energy Günther Oettinger, and business representatives. I was pictured smiling and laughing in a marquee where we symbolically opened the valve to start the gas flow through the Nord Stream 1 pipeline. At the beginning of Russia's war of aggression against Ukraine, I was accused more forcefully than ever of having led Germany into an irresponsible dependency on Russian gas. It was claimed that Poland, the Baltic states, and Ukraine had always warned of entering gas deals with Russia. It was said to be incomprehensible that Germany had not built its own terminal for liquefied natural gas (LNG) although it had been under discussion for years. And hadn't the United States repeatedly offered to supply LNG to Germany since 2016?

I thought back to the period when I had taken office as chancellor. Just days before the German general election in September 2005, the operating company contracts for Nord Stream 1 were signed in the presence of my predecessor, Gerhard Schröder, and Vladimir Putin. Shortly after Schröder left office, he was appointed chairman of the shareholders' committee, the supervisory body of Nord Stream AG. Six years later, the Nord Stream 1 pipeline was opened and the said photo was taken. From then on, 27.5 billion cubic meters of gas flowed annually through the 1,224-kilometer pipeline that lay on the seabed of the Baltic Sea from Vyborg in the Gulf of Finland to Lubmin; in 2012, a second pipeline of the same length was put into operation. Gazprom, BASF/Wintershall, E.ON, Ruhrgas, Gasunie, and GDF SUEZ were all shareholders in Nord Stream AG, with Gazprom holding the majority interest of 51 percent. The project was described by the European Commission in 2006 as "a project of European interest." Poland and Ukraine both criticized this.

To supplement its own negligible sources, Germany imported natural gas from the Netherlands, Norway, and Russia. The Nord Stream 1 pipeline now provided another option to transport Russian gas, in addition to the route via Ukraine used since the 1970s, and one through Belarus and Poland since the 1990s. More than ever since Germany's withdrawal from nuclear energy, natural gas served as a fossil-fuel bridge technology to reach climate targets until renewable energy was able to take over completely. Of all the fossil fuel energy sources, natural gas was the least harmful to the environment. Gas transported via pipelines was also cheaper than LNG. German electricity was already very expensive because the expansion of renewable energy was subsidized via the German Renewable Energy Act levy (Erneuerbare Energien Gesetz—EEG). This meant that, for every kilowatt hour produced by renewable energy, the utility company was paid a statutory price. The difference between this price and the stock market price per kilowatt hour was, in principle, transferred to the customer. Germany's industrial foundation was strong and had to be shored up to safeguard jobs which, in turn, safeguarded social security. Energy therefore had to be affordable. During the Cold War, West Germany—much to the displeasure of the United States—had imported Soviet oil and gas, and had found the Soviets to be very reliable trade partners. Now that the Nord Stream 1 pipeline ran through the Baltic Sea, no extra transit costs were incurred for the gas supply, unlike previous land pipelines through Ukraine and Poland. Gas customers in the European Union were therefore less likely to be affected by conflicts such as those over the extension of transit agreements between Ukraine and Russia that flared up in the first decade of the millennium. These led to a period of some days in January 2009 when no Russian gas was delivered to Eastern Europe. Neither Poland nor the Ukraine categorically refused to deliver Russian gas to Western Europe; however, they wanted to profit from transit fees. The proportion of Russian gas supplied to German gas importers when I took office in 2005 was 40.6 percent; by 2019, it had increased to 48.8 percent.

In September 2015, the companies Gazprom, E.ON (now called Uniper), Germany's Wintershall, Royal Dutch Shell from the Netherlands, Austria's OMV, and Engie (formerly GDF SUEZ) from France signed a shareholders' contract to build a second double pipeline, Nord Stream 2, that for the most part was to run parallel to Nord Stream 1 in the Baltic Sea. Putin had already reported these plans to me when I visited him in Moscow on May 10, 2015, to mark the seventieth anniversary of the end of the Second World War. Due to Putin's annexation of Crimea in March 2014, and his backing of Donbas separatists in regions of Ukraine, our relations with Russia had hardened and, for my part, they were limited to the minimum. The European Union had already imposed sanctions on Russia in March 2014, mainly on individuals at first, and from summer, trade relations had also been restricted. On September 12, 2014, a sanctions package came into force that affected the financial sector and the arms industry, but also the oil producer Rosneft, divisions of the gas company Gazprom, and the Transneft pipline company. Their bonds were no longer accepted by financial markets in the European Union, and their access to European capital markets was hindered. The United States took comparable measures. However, except for a temporary reduction in gas delivered to Europe as a display of annoyance from the Kremlin over these sanctions, deliveries of Russian natural gas and oil were not affected.

Discussions at a European level on diversifying gas supplies, on the other hand, understandably took on a new significance. The Baltic states, Poland, and particularly Ukraine kicked up a storm against Nord Stream 2. Ukraine feared above all becoming superfluous as a transit country. Nord Stream 2 became a significantly larger political issue than Nord Stream 1. While I had had no qualms in 2005 about Nord Stream 1, I realized that there were more factors to take into consideration with Nord Stream 2 than the arguments presented by the companies involved in its construction and the business sector as a whole. Importing larger quantities of cheap Russian gas in the coming years would become a necessity in their opinion, as pipeline gas from the Netherlands was diminishing due to production cutbacks, and Norwegian supplies could not make up the shortfall this caused. There had already been efforts to diversify Germany's gas supply. However, Germany's demand would not be met by the planned Southern Gas Corridor, an EU–Azerbaijan effort that had been in the offing since 2013, and which would transport gas from the east to Italy. The import of LNG from Arab countries was not a viable, cost-effective alternative according to gas import companies and their customers because it would only raise energy prices in Germany even more. I didn't want this to happen either. Importing LNG from the United States was out of the question at the time due to the country's export ban that stayed in place until 2016.

Ukraine relied on the income generated by transit fees. That is why I'd made it clear to Putin since our initial talk on Nord Stream 2 that I would only approve the pipeline's launch if Ukraine was granted a follow-up agreement with Gazprom on its then-valid transit contract. Construction of Nord Stream 2, which had started in 2018, could only have been halted via a special legal ruling at a European level. Had Ukraine and Russia not signed a new transit contract, I would have looked into such a ruling. However, an agreement was reached between Gazprom and the Ukrainian concern Naftogaz in 2019 that would run until 2024. The European Commission had worked toward this aim with the active support of Germany's finance minister Peter Altmaier.

After Donald Trump took office as president of the United States in January 2017, the US administration created the legal basis for "extraterritorial sanctions" against firms who were involved in the construction of Nord Stream 2. The United States argued that its security interests were affected by the building of the pipeline because its ally Germany would make itself too dependent on Russia. In truth, I felt that the United States was mobilizing its formidable economic and financial resources to prevent the business ventures of other countries, even their allies. The United States was chiefly interested in its own economic interests, as it wanted to export to Europe LNG obtained through fracking.

Although LNG was more expensive than pipeline gas, the CDU, CSU, and SPD reached a deal in their coalition agreement of 2018 to build an LNG infrastructure in Germany to contribute to the diversification of gas imports. Besides imports from the United States, this also affected LNG deliveries from Arab countries, and Qatar in particular. In the meantime, private consortia had formed to construct terminals in Brunsbüttel, Stade, and Wilhelmshaven. During a German–US investors' conference in February 2019, the finance minister Peter Altmaier announced that gas network operators would be required by law to connect LNG terminals to gas transmission systems. This would have lowered construction costs by €134 million. The German government and federal states were also prepared to contribute economic subsidies to build at least two terminals. However, because no German company had sufficiently long-term contracts with an LNG importer, private investors seemed to think that the financial risk of constructing a terminal was too great despite the state funding offered. This is why a private LNG terminal was not built in Germany during my time in office.

After taking office in January 2021, Trump's successor Joe Biden very soon took what I considered to be the right measures among partners and friends. Rather than imposing sanctions on us—the construction of Nord Stream 2 was as good as completed despite all the setbacks—we agreed to a "Joint Statement on Support for Ukraine, European Energy Security, and our Climate Goals" on July 21, 2021. We agreed that if Russia employed energy as a weapon, Germany would ensure further sanctions were imposed at a national and European level, including the limitation of Russian gas imports. Shortly before my statement was released, I informed Putin via telephone of its contents. He seemed surprised that Germany had reached an understanding with the United States and I had the impression he wasn't happy about it. This alone proved to me that Joe Biden was right to return to a manner of treating us that was appropriate between allies.

Based on this statement, my successor, Olaf Scholz, halted the launch of Nord Stream 2 on February 21, 2022, after Putin recognized the self-proclaimed republics of Luhansk and Donetsk. The pipeline became a relic of a failed investment. The charge that Germany was dependent on Russian gas was leveled against me, particularly in the case of Nord Stream 2, even though no gas had ever been transported through this pipeline. Through a major effort, the new German government was able to stabilize energy supplies even after Nord Stream AG shut down Nord Stream 1, allegedly due to a missing turbine that was required for maintenance. Nevertheless, this situation intensified the problem of higher energy costs in Germany once again because we were now reliant on imports of expensive LNG. But we would have faced this problem even if we had begun to reduce our share of Russian gas imports in 2014. However, finding political acceptance for this decision before the outbreak of war in 2022 would have been much harder, if at all possible, both in Germany among commercial and private users of gas and in many of the EU member states. Even when it came to the half-yearly extensions of the economic sanctions against Russia which began in 2014, some of my colleagues at the European Council always required much persuading.

The precautionary principle

On March 8, 2016, I took part in the "Treffpunkt Foyer" event, a podium discussion hosted by the newspaper *Stuttgarter Nachrichten*. During our talk, Christoph Reisinger, the paper's editor in chief, reproached me by saying that, given the situation in African countries, no politician ought to be surprised by the large numbers of migrants making their way to Europe. The audience clapped. "Those who are clapping are right," I said, then added, "No, it shouldn't come as a surprise to anyone. The film *The March* in 1990 showed hundreds of thousands of people fleeing Africa because of climate change. Since 1990, you can say: 'You knew all of this.'" Then I explained how different issues were constantly jostling for priority in my everyday work—the completion of German reunification, social debates linked to climate change measures in Germany, expenditure on development aid, the aging population, intergenerational justice, and the distribution of budget funds in general. I ended my outburst with the words "We have known nearly everything for a long time. The question is whether it's possible to react with the same energy to every issue each time." Later I added, "I'd also like to say that we always have to be on the lookout, but there will be many occasions where people will say, 'Why didn't you pay more attention to this?'"

Reisinger retaliated by saying, "Correct me if I'm wrong, but when we look at state security provisions in the broadest sense, the assessment you're making is not a reassuring one, is it?" I replied, "No, not all of the news is reassuring, you're right. That's why we still have a lot of work to do." In a truthful—perhaps even callous—way, I was admitting that I hadn't always managed to apply the precautionary principle to my politics, in other words, the anticipation of potentially dangerous developments in the future.

Had it been within my power to adopt more precaution, for example, when it came to the crucially important issue of climate change? At a meeting in the Chancellery on August 20, 2020, I discussed this question with the Swedish climate activist Greta Thunberg, Luisa Neubauer of Germany, and two Belgian representatives of the Fridays for Future movement inspired by Thunberg's school strike for the climate. They had asked for a meeting with me. All four of them appealed to my conscience, saying that I should take a more forceful stand against climate change. We agreed that cumulative findings, summarized by the global scientific community every six years on average since 1990 and published in reports by the Intergovernmental Panel on Climate Change (IPCC), demonstrated that the global temperature rise was caused by humans and could only be stopped through human intervention. We also agreed that the pledges made to date by the signatories to the Paris Agreement would not even manage to limit the rise in temperature to two degrees, let alone 1.5 degrees. Having said that, the group of women made it unmistakably clear to me during our discussion that they did not consider my commitment to climate protection far-reaching enough. When I pointed out that I needed a majority to act, they were not convinced. They gave me the impression that they believed the necessary goals could be achieved if only I put in enough effort. They seemed to be accusing me of not being radical enough. On this note, we couldn't reach a consensus.

For me, radicalism was not the best route to political success. Within the framework of the constitutional freedom guaranteed by democracy, NGOs and activists like these women fought for their aims. I, on the other hand, had to find a majority with whom I could implement my goals—and also accept compromises. Often faced with multiple simultaneous crises and initiatives, I had to weigh up the solution to whatever problem I was tackling on a given day. Had I given enough priority to the issue of climate protection in the process? During my term of office as chancellor, we'd achieved a significant number of things. In 2005, around 10 percent of the electricity supply came from renewable energy. Since then, that share had increased to significantly higher than 40 percent. Over the two decades between 1990 and 2010, as well as in the following decade between 2010 and 2020, we managed to reduce CO_2 emissions by 20 percent each time. In 2019, we passed the Climate Change Act (Klimaschutzgesetz—KSG), which for the first time defined binding goals for the planned reductions in greenhouse gas emissions, with the intention of reaching climate neutrality by 2050. Because we had to assume that we would not achieve a 40-percent reduction in greenhouse gases by 2020 as outlined in the German government's 2010 Energy Concept, the Climate Change Act only required a 55-percent decrease by 2030 compared to 1990, which was already stipulated in the Energy Concept. Further interim targets after 2030 would only be specified after 2025. Our resolution meant that between 1990 and 2030—within forty years—we wanted to reduce emissions by 55 percent; the remaining 45 percent would have to be reduced by future governments in just twenty years.

Various complaints against this act were filed with the Federal Constitutional Court, and the court sided with the younger generation. On April 29, 2021, it ruled that "the provisions of the Climate Change Act of December 12, 2019 [. . .] are incompatible with fundamental rights insofar as they lack sufficient specifications for further emission reductions from 2031 onward." The ruling forced the German government to make improvements to the act. We then fixed the target for reductions in emissions by 2030 at 65 percent and aligned ourselves with the view of Armin Laschet, the CDU's candidate for chancellor, that climate neutrality could already be achieved by 2045. A target of 77 percent was settled on for 2035, and 88 percent for 2040.

All the climate change measures that have already been achieved on a national and international level have been important but—to tell the whole truth—not good enough to save the world from the catastrophic effects of global warming. The ice is melting at the poles, sea levels are rising, small islands are disappearing, millions of people are being robbed of their homes, and many species of plants and animals will not survive the rising temperatures. Future changes will not develop linearly if we carry on as we have done up until now; instead, tipping points will speed up these changes. We have known all of this for a long time and yet it has not led to adequate action in Germany or many other countries. Despite all my efforts, this verdict cannot be denied. In the past, only catastrophes mobilized politicians and citizens to take necessary measures. No sooner was the worst damage repaired, than hope was employed rather than precautionary principles.

Even after my time in office, the question remains unanswered: Are we humans truly willing and able to act on the warnings of the IPCC and other credible experts to take necessary, timely decisions for our survival? To date, there is no evidence for this, either in Germany or in the world at large. This knowledge weighs heavily upon all of us, myself included.

THE BUNDESWEHR IN ACTIVE SERVICE

Afghanistan

On August 2, 2023, almost two years after I had left office, I read an article saying that the defense minister Boris Pistorius had awarded two German Special Forces soldiers the Bundeswehr Cross of Honor for Valor at an unofficial ceremony in Calw, Baden-Württemberg. In doing so, he was acknowledging their exceptional service during the evacuation from Kabul Airport of remaining members of staff of the German embassy, German NGOs, and local staff in need of protection. The soldiers were just two of some five hundred military personnel involved in the German airlift from Kabul to Tashkent in neighboring Uzbekistan between August 16 and 26, 2021, under the command of General Jens Arlt, commander of the First Airborne Brigade, in which 5,400 people from forty-five countries were brought to safety.

When I was reading the article, I thought back to a phone call I'd had with General Arlt two years earlier. It was on a Sunday evening at an advisory meeting on the eighth floor of the Chancellery with Vice Chancellor Olaf Scholz, the defense minister Annegret Kramp-Karrenbauer, the foreign minister Heiko Maas, the interior minister Horst Seehofer, the Chancellery minister Helge Braun, and the general inspector of the German Army Eberhard Zorn, in which I was being briefed about the situation in Afghanistan. During our talk, the Chancellery's crisis center set up a connection with General Arlt at Kabul Airport. He described the frenzied and, at times, chaotic conditions on the ground in a precise, structured way. We listened intently. I warmly thanked him and his soldiers for their service on behalf of us all and wished them a safe journey home. We could only imagine what feats they were accomplishing over there.

Nine days previously, on Friday, August 13, 2021, the last day of my summer vacation, Helge Braun and then Annegret Kramp-Karrenbauer informed me by phone that the situation in Kabul was escalating. The following morning, in a conference call with Kramp-Karrenbauer and the other ministers responsible, I gave the green light to detailed arrangements for an evacuation operation. The following Sunday, August 15, 2021, the Afghan president Ashraf Ghani, who had been in power since September 2014, fled Kabul and the Taliban seized control of the capital. Thousands of desperate people crammed into the airport, hoping to be able to leave Kabul.

In a Sunday evening conference call, I informed the chairs of the party and parliamentary group chairs represented in the Bundestag of the government's plan to carry out an evacuation. The following day, Monday, August 16, at 6:00 p.m., I told them that the operation had begun, and at 6:45, I gave a press conference in the Chancellery. The international community was fleeing the Taliban. I spoke of a turn of events that was bitter, dramatic, and terrifying, both for the millions of Afghans who had been struggling for democracy, women's rights, and education, as well as for Germany and other allied nations who, since the terrorist attacks of September 11, 2001, had fought for twenty years under the leadership of the United States and NATO against terrorism and for more democratic systems in Afghanistan. A total of ninety-three thousand German soldiers had already served to their best ability during those years; fifty-nine of them had lost their lives and many others had been injured psychologically or physically.

For these reasons, I considered it important that the Bundeswehr Cross of Honor for Valor, our country's highest military decoration, existed. It was introduced by the defense minister Franz Josef Jung in 2008 after conditions for German armed forces under the mandate of the International Security Assistance Force (ISAF) in Afghanistan, agreed upon in December 2001 to stabilize and develop the country, became increasingly dangerous from 2005 onward. Together with Jung, I awarded the first four medals at the Chancellery on July 6, 2009.

I had heard during my talks with soldiers and police personnel on visits to our troops in Kabul, Camp Marmal near Mazar-i-Sharif, and our Kunduz base in northern Afghanistan, how hard living and working conditions were for them—and how dangerous too. This was urgently brought home to me once more when I found out, on August 15, 2007, that Jörg Ringel, a member of my security detail, had been killed in Afghanistan. He was the chief commissioner of the Federal Criminal Police Office (Bundeskriminalamt—BKA) and had been temporarily seconded by the Foreign Office to head the security detail of the German ambassador to Kabul, Hans-Ulrich Seidt. Together with his colleagues Mario Keller and Alexander Stoffels, he was killed by a bomb under his car when he set off for a shooting range.

I had known Jörg Ringel for years and greatly appreciated his work. He was a calm and focused person, and always pleasant. At the end of 2006, he'd proudly told me about his assignment and I had congratulated him for rising to a new challenge, especially such a major one, and had told him that I looked forward to welcoming him back to my security detail in a year.

Now, three days after his death, I was attending a memorial service in his and his colleagues' honor at Berlin Cathedral. After a speech by the interior minister Wolfgang Schäuble, Ambassador Seidt took to the lectern, and said: "Madam

Chancellor, I know that he enjoyed working for you very, very much." A shudder ran down my back; I felt helpless and could only think how fortunate it was that our country had people like Jörg Ringel, who were prepared to protect others and save their lives in times of need while putting their own on the line.

I too was granted this protection daily as chancellor. At first, I had to get used to being accompanied everywhere around the clock and, at times, even felt the urge to break free from this constant protection. However, I didn't give in to this urge as it would not only have endangered me and my bodyguards but would have lacked the necessary respect for their job and consequently for the state we both worked for. Everyone in my security detail and its advance team tried to accommodate my idiosyncrasies to the greatest extent possible. Thanks to them, I was able to carry out my work in a well-protected environment, especially on more dangerous journeys, such as my five trips to Afghanistan.

On January 20, 2009, Barack Obama took office as president of the United States, succeeding George W. Bush. One of his first foreign policy decisions was to reassess the deployment of US troops in Iraq and Afghanistan.

Almost 150,000 US soldiers were stationed in Iraq. After the Iraqi dictator Saddam Hussein was overthrown in 2003, US troops rapidly destroyed the state infrastructure of his regime. But rebuilding a stable nation proved to be extremely difficult. Obama decided to withdraw all US troops from Iraq by the end of 2011. He had always considered the Iraq War to be a mistake and was ultimately proven right.

The beginning of the Iraq War in March 2003 resulted in a temporary reduction in US military capabilities in Afghanistan. As a result, the Taliban, ousted from the region by the United States at the end of 2001, regained influence in summer 2003. Consequently, Obama initially increased the deployment of US troops—from roughly 30,000 in 2008 to 110,000 in 2011.

However, the focus of their mission was geared toward training the Afghan army and police: from 2011 onward, Obama's objective was to give the Afghan security forces progressively more command over the country's regions. At the end of 2014, ISAF's mandate to bring stability to the region ended and it was replaced in 2015 by the NATO-led Resolute Support Mission, which aimed to provide local authorities with further training and advice. From then on, the United States deployed a smaller force of only ten thousand troops in Afghanistan, while Germany reduced its presence from five thousand to fewer than one thousand soldiers. In talks with Pakistani officials, the US government in particular insisted that the country end its support for the Taliban. The Afghan president Hamid Karzai, who had been in office since 2001, vowed to rebuild a more effective state infrastructure by cracking down on corruption and opium poppy cultivation and thereby hoped to gain his people's trust. Karzai, born in 1957, was a Pashtun, the largest ethnic group in Afghanistan. He had studied political science in India and had a diverse political career, yet he was deeply rooted in his home country. My talks with him were always amicable; he praised our dedication and promised to do everything within his power to curb corruption and nepotism. However, though he seemed to know exactly what we wanted to hear, not much changed in his country. His re-election in 2009 was linked to serious allegations of election fraud. In our discussions, I never managed to fully understand his attitude or approach—he often remained inscrutable.

Our troops came across similar difficulties when interacting with their Afghan counterparts. Soldiers often told me during my visits that they found it impossible to tell whether an Afghan soldier was friendly or hostile. As a result, German instructors often felt unsure about their Afghan partners. The deployment in Afghanistan put a huge strain on our soldiers and their families.

To lend a fresh face to his new beginning in June 2009, Obama appointed General Stanley McChrystal, hitherto a US leader of Joint Special Operations Command, to supervise the ISAF and US military forces in Afghanistan. McChrystal did his utmost to reduce the number of civilian casualties during foreign military operations and, in doing so, hoped to gain the Afghan people's acceptance of the military presence. So, it was all the more tragic that a minimum of ninety civilians were killed three months later during an ISAF operation near Kunduz on the night of Friday, September 4, 2009, when the commander of the German base ordered an air strike on two fuel tankers hijacked by the Taliban. The trucks had become stuck on a sandbank while crossing the River Kunduz only a few kilometers away from the military camp. The commander feared that the trucks might be used to strike the base as rolling bombs and assumed that the people standing around the trucks were Taliban insurgents. The defense minister Franz Josef Jung also espoused this view.

Two days later, on September 6, at the ISS Dome arena in Düsseldorf, the CDU began the critical stage of its campaign for the general election which would take place later that month, on September 27. Before the event began, I drew Jung to one side and spoke with him about the likelihood that there had been civilian casualties during the tanker air strike. According to agency dispatches in a report by the *Washington Post*, it was highly probable that at least two dozen civilians had been killed. We had to face reality. For this reason, in a government statement two days later in the Bundestag, I announced that contradictory reports about civilian casualties needed clarification, while explicitly emphasizing that every innocent killed was one death too many and that I deeply regretted all those injured or killed as a result of German military actions.

When I was forming my new government on October 28, 2009, I made a change in the ministry of defense. The portfolio changed hands from the CDU to the CSU, and at the latter's suggestion, the CSU politician and former finance minister Karl-Theodor zu Guttenberg was appointed as the new defense minister. He was young, articulate, and not afraid of tackling conflict. Within days of taking office, he proved this when he referred to conditions in Afghanistan as "war-like," and expressed sympathy for soldiers who labeled their mission as "war." This was new: while Franz Josef Jung and I had used the words "combat missions," we had drawn the line at saying "war." Nevertheless, given the number of fallen and injured soldiers, frequent battles, and bomb attacks, Guttenberg had undoubtedly touched a nerve. Then again, he seemed proud to be the first and only person to have called things by their name and made them tangible. As I recall, he did not discuss his choice of words with me beforehand. But now he had framed the situation in new terms, I refrained from getting into a dispute that I had little chance of winning, and said in an interview with the *Frankfurter Allgemeine* newspaper that "from our soldiers' perspective, war-like conditions prevail[ed] in parts of Afghanistan, even if the term 'war' [was] not appropriate to describe the current situation according to traditional international law."

On January 28, 2010, an Afghanistan conference took place in London, with the foreign minister Guido Westerwelle representing the German government. In line with Obama's objectives, the conference delegates agreed that, between summer 2011 and the end of 2014, responsibility for Afghanistan's rebuilding and security would be gradually handed back to Afghan institutions. In the city of Mazar-i-Sharif, this took place in summer 2011. Two years later, in October 2013, German troops handed over the base in Kunduz. The fact that the security situation there was anything but satisfactory was an open secret. However, the handover took place in October 2013 nonetheless because it was a part of the transfer of responsibility.

This also highlighted the weaknesses of the plan: by setting 2014 as the final date for their mission to end, the international community lost influence in the period that followed. They could not fully guarantee that, in the long term, Afghan officials would be able to hold their ground against the Taliban after the handover. Two years later, in September 2015, it was almost inevitable when the Taliban recaptured Kunduz as the first main city. Although the Afghan army succeeded in pushing back the Taliban with support from the US Air Force, this operation demonstrated the stark need for the continued presence of US military forces in the region.

This need conflicted with Obama's aim to significantly reduce, by the end of his term in early 2017, the figure of 8,400 US soldiers still stationed in Afghanistan. During his visit to the opening of the Hanover Trade Fair on April 24 and 25, I gave him my impressions of the situation in the Kunduz region and asked him to reconsider defining future troop figures given the challenging circumstances in Afghanistan. I was relieved when, a day before the NATO summit in Warsaw on July 6, 2016, and after intensive talks with his government, he decided to keep the 8,400 US soldiers stationed in Afghanistan, because of the volatile situation. In Warsaw, we decided to continue the Resolute Support Mission even after 2016.

When President Ashraf Ghani came to power in September 2014, no noteworthy progress was made in the fight against corruption; the reconciliation process between the Afghan government and the Taliban stalled, and Pakistan continued to support the Taliban. These things hampered our development work, even though many Afghans did everything within their power to improve their lives and those of their children, and therefore collaborated closely with German representatives. In terms of resources deployed, Afghanistan became Germany's most significant partner country in development cooperation.

We raised our bilateral aid from €77 million in 2007 to over €450 million in 2016, guided by our conviction that, without development, there was no stability, and without stability, no development. Germany's defense, foreign, and interior ministers, and the Federal Ministry for Economic Cooperation and Development succeeded in improving the coordination of their decision-making. Besides military backing from the German armed forces, including their involvement in the expansion of the country's infrastructure and their support of functioning police organizations, our aid focused on water and electricity supplies, education, and the rule of law. Whereas only 20 percent of all Afghans had access to drinking water and electricity in 2011, a decade later this figure had reached 70 to 90 percent. Child mortality rates halved over twenty years. Millions of girls were allowed to attend school.

After taking office on January 20, 2017, Barack Obama's successor, Donald Trump, decided to raise the number of US troops in Afghanistan again to a maximum of fifteen thousand soldiers. In 2019, the US administration also began to negotiate with the Taliban over a withdrawal of international troops. On February 29, 2020, the Trump-appointed US Special Representative for Afghanistan Reconciliation (SRAR) Zalmay Khalilzad and the leader of the Taliban's political office Abdul Ghani Baradar signed an accord in Doha which required international troops to leave Afghanistan by May 1, 2021. The elected Afghan government and other states were not involved in the discussions. This laid bare the power dynamics of the situation for everyone: Firstly, the United States was the key player in the NATO mission in every respect and its allies were dependent on its decisions. Secondly, the elected Afghan government was clearly not a serious factor for Trump. The country's fate was sealed. Now the Taliban only needed to wait until international forces withdrew. Trump's successor, President Joe Biden, who took office on January 20, 2021, did in fact prompt the NATO

Council to extend the deadline for withdrawal until September 11, 2021; but despite expert warnings about the dangers of the Taliban seizing control, he kept on course to end the mission after twenty years. The exit of the United States effectively signaled the end of the NATO mission. On June 29, 2021, the last German soldiers left Camp Marmal near Mazar-i-Sharif.

At the start of the airlift from Kabul to Tashkent on August 16, 2021, I gave a rather defiant comment to the press: "Well, we now have to recognize that Germany and other European armed forces have no independent role in the NATO mission in Afghanistan. We have always said that we are fundamentally dependent on the US government's decisions." That's the way things were. To tell the full truth, though, I have to add that the United States carried the brunt of the mission by far. It could only be expected that they would have a much greater say in the decision-making.

What's left? After the events of September 11, 2001, it was right for us to support the US in the first NATO mission, according to Article 5 of the NATO Treaty, because of the well-founded hope that, once the operation was over, no such further terrorist attacks would emerge from Afghanistan. But as far as all our other goals were concerned, we were forced to admit failure. Our objectives had been to strengthen sustainable, independent systems, the rule of law, democracy, and human rights—especially for women and girls—and make it possible for journalists, artists, and businesses to live freely, without harassment. None of these aims were achieved by the international community. Why is this the case? Why wasn't a peace settlement reached between different Afghan factions? Hadn't we supported the peace process between political rivals enough, or the introduction of an inclusive political process? Should we have taken our major cultural differences more seriously and given more weight to historical events? Did we underestimate how rampant corruption was, or rather, its effect on those in positions of power? Wasn't it extremely risky to set a fixed date for the withdrawal of troops? These questions hung in the air and I formulated them in a government statement on August 25, 2021, in the Bundestag.

The answers were actually quite obvious. Afghanistan's neighbors to the north are the Central Asian states of Turkmenistan, Uzbekistan, and Tajikistan; to the west lies Iran; and to the east and south, Pakistan. Afghanistan's geographic and ethnic ties, historical events, and the cultural differences between us were greater than I had imagined. Once the Taliban had been driven out in 2001, Afghan society did not have enough resources of its own to mobilize growth without corruption, nepotism, and the opium poppy trade. Such a development could not be forced from the outside. Afghans, unsurprisingly, did not trust their state representatives due to the conditions of their state institutions, and the Taliban was still supported by sections of the Pakistan state apparatus. This alone meant that a reconciliation process between different Afghan factions was doomed to failure. The Taliban knew that they were protected by their powerful allies and neighbors and so would not have to reach compromises with the elected government in Kabul. Setting a fixed date for the withdrawal of international troops only tipped the balance of the situation in their favor. The goals of the international community set a very high bar. Now, the only thing they can do is to provide humanitarian relief to the Afghan people. This, however, is something that must happen at all costs.

Libya

In the early afternoon of Sunday, January 19, 2020, I was standing next to the UN secretary general António Guterres, on the first floor of the Chancellery, to welcome guests of honor from the EU, the African Union, and the Arab League. As they drew up to the forecourt, we had our photo taken with each one in succession. Among them were the French president Emmanuel Macron, the Russian president Vladimir Putin, the Turkish president Tayyip Erdoğan, the Egyptian president Abdel Fattah El-Sisi, the Algerian president Abdelmadjid Tebboune, and the Congolese president Denis Sassou Nguesso. We were also joined by my British and Italian counterparts, Boris Johnson and Giuseppe Conte, the US secretary of state Mike Pompeo, and his counterpart from the United Arab Emirates—the crown prince, Sheik Mohamed bin Zayed Al Nahyan, had already visited me the previous day—as well as Yang Jiechi, director of foreign affairs in the Politburo of the Communist Party of China.

Guterres, the foreign minister Heiko Maas, and I had invited this circle to Berlin to take part in a Libya conference since all efforts to stabilize Libya by the United Nations and their Support Mission Libya (UNSMIL), which had begun in September 2011 through the UN Security Council, had failed. The country did not have a parliament recognized by all Libya's political stakeholders, and no functioning government either. There was no state monopoly on the legitimate use of force; security lay in the hands of multiple militia groups. Libya had become a plaything for the interests of regional states. Turkey supported the internationally recognized interim government of Prime Minister Fayez al-Sarraj in Tripoli and had sent in its own troops; Egypt and the United Arab Emirates believed the future of the country lay in the parliament of the eastern city of Tobruk and were delivering arms to its allied troops under General Khalifa Haftar; Russia had sent its Wagner Group mercenaries to support Haftar's soldiers. Violent clashes had erupted between the different Libyan factions. The African Union complained that the international community of nations was ignoring and torpedoing its efforts to find reconciliation within Libya. Presidents of African states had frequently reproached me, saying that NATO bore some of the blame for West Africa's instability: After 2011, some of Libya's abundant weapon stocks had landed in the hands of Islamist terrorist groups operating in West Africa, destabilizing countries like Mali, Niger, and Burkina Faso. Libya had become an entry point for migrants and refugees from many different African countries who tried to reach Europe from there in dire conditions, risking their lives.

From mid-January, 2011, nine years before the Libyan conference in the Chancellery, riots and demonstrations had taken place against the revolutionary leader and self-appointed head of state Muammar al-Gaddafi and his decades-long reign of terror. In other Arab states too during this period, protests had taken place against despotic rulers: the Arab Spring, as it was known, had begun in late 2010 in Tunisia. In Libya, Gaddafi retaliated with armed violence against the demonstrators but soon lost control over the country. Soon, the situation descended into something resembling civil war. Most of all France, but also the UK and later the United States, demanded military action to protect the civilian population. On March 17, 2011, the UN Security Council passed Resolution 1973, which imposed a no-fly zone, among other measures. On March 19, 2011, an international military intervention began to carry out the terms of the resolution. With military support from NATO and its allies, armed Libyan rebels seized Gaddafi's residence on August 23, 2011. On October 20, 2011, his motorcade was attacked by NATO aircraft as he attempted to flee his hometown of Sirte. Gaddafi was captured by rebels and killed soon afterward. On October 31, 2011, NATO ended its military intervention.

As a non-permanent member of the Security Council, Germany had abstained from voting for the adoption of Resolution 1973. The foreign minister Guido Westerwelle and I could also still vividly remember the chaos that ensued after Saddam Hussein was toppled in Iraq in spring 2003, and we weighed up the situation in Libya from this perspective. We did not know the political aims of the insurgents; the violent overthrowing of Gaddafi was linked, in our view, to many imponderables and risks in the time that would follow. Our abstention was a show of skepticism toward the path chosen by our allies France, the UK, and the United States on the one hand, but on the other, a sign that we did not want to stab them in the back. Our decision was sharply criticized: accusations were made that NATO and transatlantic relations had been weakened by our fear of using military force. I felt the need to respond to this, which is why, in my speech to mark the fiftieth anniversary of the Bergedorf Round Table on September 9, 2011, in Berlin—at a gathering of high-ranking international politicians and experts—I put forward the following suggestion: As NATO could not resolve every conflict in the world, emerging countries and regional organizations should be given more responsibility in future. They should be helped toward this aim by receiving advice, civilian and military personnel training, as well as being provided with infrastructure and equipment, including munitions and weaponry. These reflections led to the development of a new foreign and security policy instrument, the German government's "Enable and Enhance Initiative" (Ertüchtigungsinitiative der Bundesregierung), which received €100 million from 2016 onward, rising to a budget of €195 million in 2020. Many of the projects financed by this money have gone toward improving security structures in Mali, Niger, Ghana, Senegal, and Nigeria, among others. However, these initiatives alone, especially without Libya's stabilization, were not able to prevent the security situation in West Africa from deteriorating.

Nearly nine years on from the start of the military intervention, my skepticism at the time had been vindicated. But I could

not have left it at that. The fight against illegal migration alone
was barely possible without political stability in Libya and
transit countries like Niger. The distance from the Libyan coast
to the Italian island of Lampedusa, a route still taken today by
boat by many refugees, is less than three hundred kilometers.
That is why the foreign minister Heiko Maas and I decided to
support the United Nations and its special representative for
Libya, Ghassan Salamé, by inviting him to the conference in
Berlin. Numerous preparations had taken place in the run-up:
Before talks began, I invited the Libyan prime minister al-Sarraj
and General Haftar to talks in the Chancellery's large conference room as they were not taking part in the summit itself.
We agreed to a ceasefire, a weapons embargo, and a political
process for the country as the first steps toward ending the
armed conflict.

In the period that followed, the situation in Libya became
somewhat calmer but there was still no breakthrough that
would lead to the creation of a stable state system. The same
was true of the two follow-up conferences that took place in
June 2021 in Berlin and November 2021 in Paris, the last international conference that I joined before leaving office. Since
Russia's invasion of Ukraine on February 24, 2022, the success
of international efforts for Libya has been muted, not least
because it is unimaginable that the community of nations will
ever team up for such negotiations again with President Putin
as a participant.

Mandatory military service

In their coalition agreement of October 26, 2009, the CDU, CSU,
and FDP ruled that the German defense minister would assign
an expert commission the task of developing a proposal for a new
organizational structure in the German armed forces. This

would include streamlining its leadership and administration structures. We also agreed to keep mandatory military conscription in principle but to shorten basic service from nine to just six months by January 1, 2011. On the one hand, this was due to fundamental changes in security policy circumstances since the end of the Cold War, and on the other, the diverging opinions of the CDU, CSU, and FDP on the future of military service. The Union, myself included, wanted to keep conscription. A commitment to compulsory military service and the concept of the "citizen in uniform" had been central to the CDU's policies since Konrad Adenauer's time, a symbol of a state able to defend itself against its enemies. But the Free Democrats wanted to suspend conscription—and they too were able to give valid arguments. Due to successive reductions in the length of basic military service and changes in demands placed on German soldiers because of overseas deployments, less than 20 percent of men eligible for conscription in a given year were completing their basic military duty.

At the end of 2009 and in early 2010, we were still struggling with the effects of the global financial crisis. In 2009, we incorporated the debt brake into the German constitution and it took effect in 2016. From then on, new borrowing was capped at 0.35 percent of Germany's nominal GDP. When the German government prepared its 2011 budget in June 2010, the finance minister Wolfgang Schäuble rightly insisted that we would have to save €80 billion between 2011 and 2014. Deliberations took place in a closed cabinet meeting for sixteen hours, and then in a smaller group on June 6 and 7, 2010; this resulted in a catalog of measures which, alongside cuts in the social sector, a fuel tax for nuclear plants, a levy on air traffic, and the partial transfer of Deutsche Bahn profit to federal revenue, included reductions in the German armed forces. Schäuble hoped that these measures would save €2 billion annually in the defense budget. But Guttenberg was beside himself. As dawn broke in the early hours, I realized that, while the cuts were necessary from a budgetary point of view, I wanted to give him more time for reflection and to talk to his colleagues in the ministry. So, I arranged for us to meet back in my office two hours later.

On his return, he argued his case both unequivocally and understandably: if he was going to have to reduce spending in his sector by €2 billion a year, then he could only remain in office if the German government had a real discussion about what was necessary—which included a debate on whether mandatory military service should be suspended. It was perfectly clear to me that he was being serious and his arguments in this matter could not simply be dismissed. There could be no more talk of "the equity of military service"—in other words, that conscription was imposed equally on all male German citizens—if only a fifth of men in a given year performed national service; not to mention the size and capability of the German armed forces once further reductions were made. I reflected on this briefly and then asked him to take an unorthodox approach to dealing with this matter: He should visit the CDU's federal state associations in his capacity as defense minister, and drum up support for his initiative, as well as convince his own party, the CSU. If he succeeded, I would introduce the necessary steps to suspend mandatory military service. Guttenberg immediately agreed to my suggestion, signed off on the budget reductions, and instantly set to work. No matter which state associations he talked to, or at least their chairs, his powers of persuasion were great enough to gain their approval. In a manner of speaking, he won their hearts. The fact that he only wanted to suspend mandatory military service through a simple law, and not abolish it completely, helped. This meant that if security policy changed for any reason, the suspension of national service could be revoked; Article 12a of the German constitution covering general conscription would remain unaffected, an important point that is sometimes overlooked.

On September 12 and 13, 2010, a closed conference of the CDU Presidium took place during which the future of the German armed forces was discussed. We quickly agreed on a resolution that would prepare the path to suspend mandatory national service at the CDU party conference in Karlsruhe from November 14 to 16, 2010.

On October 22, 2010, the paper "Thinking From The Mission. Concentration, Flexibility, Efficiency" (Vom Einsatz her denken—Konzentration, Flexibilität, Effizienz) was submitted by an expert commission led by Frank-Jürgen Weise, a colonel in the reserves and the chairman of the Federal Employment Office. Based on the analysis that Germans now lived in peace and freedom, and were firmly rooted in a transatlantic system of security and cooperation, and after weighing up new threats and security risks beyond immediate neighbors in the foreseeable future, the commission concluded that general conscription was no longer necessary. They recommended suspending medical examinations and military call-ups.

The CSU decided to suspend mandatory military service at a party conference on October 29, 2010. At the CDU's party conference on November 14, 2010, Guttenberg gave a speech to delegates that was met with resounding applause, which was followed by a motion on "the future of the German armed forces," to be decided by open vote. After looking around the room, the congress president Peter Hintze declared: "With a substantial number of votes against and some abstentions, the concept of the German armed forces contained in motion E1 is passed." The majority were nonetheless visibly in favor. On December 15, 2010, the cabinet decided to suspend compulsory military service by July 1, 2011, and on March 24, 2011, the Bundestag followed suit. Votes from the CDU/CSU, the FDP, and Alliance 90/Green Party passed the Amendment to Military Law (Wehrrechtsänderungsgesetz) and, as a result, voluntary military service was introduced as well as voluntary service, which replaced civilian national service. Article 12a of the German constitution, which states that "men who have attained the age of eighteen may be required to serve in the armed forces, in the Federal Border Police, or in a civil defense organization" remains unaffected. Compulsory military service was suspended but not abolished.

The Western Balkans

On January 20, 2014, I met the vice chancellor and minister for economic affairs Sigmar Gabriel, the foreign minister Frank-Walter Steinmeier, the interior minister Thomas de Maizière, the culture minister Monika Grütters, and the head of the Chancellery Peter Altmaier in the morning briefing room. We had agreed to think about how to devise the landmark commemorations of so many dates in 2014: the twenty-fifth anniversary of the fall of the Wall, the sixty-fifth anniversary of the founding of the German Federal Republic, the seventy-fifth anniversary of the start of the Second World War, and the hundredth anniversary of the start of the First World War. We drew up plans for events. All our suggestions dealt with the remembrance of history. At some point, Sigmar Gabriel interrupted us and said: "We're only talking about the past. Shouldn't we also think about what problems we have today and what we've learned from history?"

I replied: "You're right, especially concerning the First World War. After the Balkan wars in the 1990s, we have to do our part to ensure peaceful coexistence in the Western Balkans is secured in the long term. There's still a lot left for us to do."

Slovenia and Croatia were already members of the European Union, while Serbia, Montenegro, and the former Yugoslavian republic of Macedonia—back then, its name still had to be determined—were accession candidates, and Albania,

Kosovo, and Bosnia and Herzegovina were potential accession candidates, but our discussions expressed our concern about the ongoing tensions in the region. These were especially apparent between Serbia and Kosovo and within some Balkan countries themselves, particularly Bosnia and Herzegovina. In 2014, one hundred years after the start of the First World War, peace in the region was again fragile: Serbia did not recognize Kosovo's independence. The Kosovo Force (KFOR) stationed there was symbolic of manifold efforts by the international community, particularly NATO, the EU, and the United States, to end the bloodshed and violence during the collapse of the former Yugoslavia and to facilitate a peaceful future in the Western Balkans. There were still some seven hundred German soldiers deployed in Kosovo. By then, the mission had been going on for almost fifteen years.

In March 1999, for the first time since their foundation, the German armed forces were involved in active combat when its air force was deployed. As part of the Allied Force NATO operation, German military aircraft engaged with Serbian and Yugoslavian forces led by President Slobodan Milošević. His troops had carried out a brutal crackdown on the Albanian population in the province of Kosovo and forced them to flee to hinder Kosovo's independence. After the successful conclusion of the operation, the UN Security Council passed Resolution 1244 on June 10, 1999, allowing the KFOR to be stationed in Kosovo under NATO's command. Fifty thousand soldiers from forty nations, including six thousand German soldiers, oversaw the withdrawal of Serbian armed forces and the gradual demilitarization of Kosovo that followed, enabling those who had fled to return. However, military action alone could not guarantee stable development in the region. It would be years before all the states became members of the European Union.

"How about inviting the Western Balkan states to a meeting

that could lead to better collaboration between the countries that are not yet EU members?"

Gabriel nodded.

Frank-Walter Steinmeier opposed this idea, saying: "Isn't it a bit presumptuous for us Germans, with our history, to start an initiative like this without putting it to the vote with the other European countries?"

I saw his point. But I also saw an opportunity slipping from our grasp. If we were to wait until the twenty-seven member states of the EU had voted on the matter, the year would probably already be over before a decision was reached. Then I had an idea. "But we could be the first to host the conference this year and then find someone next year to continue the process. That way, all those interested can take a turn. And, of course, we have to inform the EU Commission and ask them to participate. They are in charge of the cooperation programs with these countries."

My suggestion was agreed to and we arranged for the first Western Balkans conference to take place in the Chancellery on August 28, 2014. Steinmeier suggested that Austria host the occasion the following year. A few days later, when I spoke to the Austrian chancellor Werner Faymann on the phone, he immediately consented.

Over the years, the conferences—also known as the "Berlin Process"—were a huge success by and large, because at these meetings, concrete projects between the European Commission and the individual states of the Western Balkans were agreed upon and swiftly implemented. These included infrastructure projects between countries, a joint youth organization, and science partnerships. What's more, the state and governmental heads of the Western Balkan countries also met independently of the Berlin Process and forged strong contacts with one another despite ongoing tensions. This had not happened before, they always told me. It was good that we hadn't waited to find ways of working more closely together until all these countries became members of the European Union. Yet, during my time in office, not every hurdle was overcome by any means, despite a great investment of time by me and my colleagues. I was convinced then and am still convinced now that a sustainable, peaceful coexistence in the region can only be achieved through EU membership of all Western Balkan states; no matter how arduous that path is, it has to be taken.

ISRAEL

In Adenauer's footsteps

MY FIRST FOREIGN trip, as the freshly appointed minister for women and youth, on March 5, 1991, took me to Paris; my second, from April 7 to 9, 1991, took me to Israel. I had not even been in office for three months and was very interested in Israel, which enjoyed an outstanding reputation in research and science, which was also my background. Until German reunification, Israel had remained inaccessible to me for the most part. Visits were out of the question—after all, there was not even a postal connection between the GDR and the state of Israel because no diplomatic relations between the two countries existed. It had been a struggle for me, as already described, to find the offprints of texts by Israeli researchers that I needed for my PhD thesis.

This was in stark contrast to collaborations in the field of research that developed between West Germany and Israel. Six years before the establishment of diplomatic relations between the two countries, the Weizmann Institute of Science in Rehovot, south of Tel Aviv, named for the first president of Israel, Chaim Weizmann, had already invited scientists from the Max Planck Institute to Israel, in December 1959. Not long afterward, the Max Planck Institute established the Minerva Foundation, which has spearheaded collaborative projects between German and Israeli scientists since 1964.

My trip in April 1991 coincided with a visit to Israel by the mnister of research and technology Heinz Riesenhuber. We were on the same flight but, once we arrived, we attended separate programs. Riesenhuber's visit attracted a great deal more attention than mine, which offended me slightly at first, until I understood that research and science had an overriding importance in German–Israeli relations. In discussions with my Israeli counterpart, the education minister Zevulun Hammer, and the Israeli foreign minister David Levy, who had surprisingly asked me for an off-the-record meeting, I focused on youth work. I reported on the "Sommer der Begegnung" (Summer of Encounters), an initiative planned by my ministry to encourage contact between young Germans from the old and new federal German states. I now expanded this initiative by inviting hundreds of Israeli teenagers to Germany in summer so that interest in Israel could be sparked, especially among young people from the new federal states.

A good thirty years later, I traveled to Israel for the last time in my active political career. The recently elected prime minister Naftali Bennett had invited me during a phone call in late August 2021. I should come one last time, he urged me. When I said I doubted whether it made sense so close to the German general election on September 26, 2021, Bennett answered that a visit would certainly be worthwhile. He dispelled my misgivings and soon afterward preparations began for a trip from August 28 to 30, 2021. However, because of the catastrophic events surrounding the withdrawal from Afghanistan, I was forced to postpone my visit until October. Therefore, my farewell tour of Israel did not take place before the general election in Germany, but still before I stepped down in December.

On Saturday, October 9, 2021, I landed in the evening at Ben Gurion Airport in Tel Aviv and drove directly from there to Jerusalem, where, as always, I stayed the night at the legendary King David Hotel. A section of the hotel, which was opened in 1931, had served as the headquarters of the British mandate in Palestine until the independence of the state of Israel in May 1948. On Sunday, the official program began. In the morning, I had a personal conversation with Prime Minister Naftali Bennett. Afterward, I took part in a meeting of his cabinet in which we discussed the entire breadth of German–Israeli relations, from youth work to economic affairs, science, and climate change, all the way to joint work on issues that affected the security of the state of Israel. At midday, I was invited to a reception with the Israeli president Isaac Herzog. Together with the president of the Weizmann Institute Alon Chen, he surprised me with an extraordinary gift: they announced the creation of the "Dr. Angela Merkel Postdoctoral Fellowship for Outstanding Women Scientists in Chemical Physics at the Weizmann Institute of Science."

In the afternoon, accompanied by Naftali Bennett, I visited the World Holocaust Remembrance Site, Yad Vashem, as I had done on my first trip in 1991. Yad Vashem means "a memorial and a name" in Hebrew and is dedicated to the commemoration of the six million Jews who were murdered in Germany during the Shoah, the rupture of civilization that took place under National Socialism. In the evening, I participated in an event at the Israel Institute of Technology, or Technion for short, in which the honorary doctorate was officially conferred on me. The Institute was founded in 1912 by German Jews, among others, thirty-six years before the establishment of the state of Israel, and was initially called the Technikum. In the 1930s, many Jews threatened with persecution and murder under National Socialism in Germany were taken in by the Institute.

On Monday morning, I met for talks with the representatives of the Institute for National Security Studies in Tel Aviv, a think tank for foreign and security policy, members of which have included the former Israeli ambassador in Germany Shimon Stein. Following this, I flew back to Berlin.

———

The appointments and meetings I attended on my last journey to Israel as a working politician demonstrated the distinct nature of the relationship between Germany and Israel. They were manifold, characterized by closeness, and future-oriented; and they can be exactly all these things as long as we never forget that Germany and Israel are forever uniquely connected by their remembrance of the Shoah. If Germany continues to recognize its enduring responsibility that arises from *the* moral catastrophe in its history, we can envisage and plan a good, humane future. I am and always have been convinced of this in all my trips, meetings, and decisions.

But no visit to Israel was as symbolic of this as the one that I took on March 16, 2008, from Berlin's Tegel Airport. Dalia Itzik, the speaker of the Israeli parliament, the Knesset, had invited me on the occasion of the sixtieth anniversary of the founding of the state of Israel to make a speech in the Knesset, the first foreign head of government ever to do so. Up until now, such an honor had been reserved for heads of state. In 2000, Johannes Rau was the first German federal president to have received this distinction.

My trip featured another premiere: the first German–Israeli government consultations were going to take place in which not only heads of government but also several ministers from both cabinets would participate.

After a four-hour flight, I arrived in Tel Aviv in the early afternoon. On board with me was Charlotte Knobloch, the president of the Central Council of Jews in Germany, and the vice president of the European Jewish Congress and the World Jewish Congress. Charlotte Knobloch was born in Munich in 1932. During the Reichskristallnacht pogrom on November 9, 1938, she, a six-year-old girl, left her apartment holding the hand of her father, Fritz Neuland, who was trying to bring the two of them to safety. Outside, hordes of SA and SS men were rampaging through the city, and the main synagogue of the Jewish

Community, the Ohel Jakob Synagogue, was set ablaze. Her mother, who had converted to Judaism for her marriage, had left the family in 1936 and Knobloch's paternal grandmother, Albertine Neuland, moved in with her son and granddaughter in 1939. Charlotte Knobloch survived the Holocaust because her uncle's former housekeeper took her in on her farm and pretended she was her own illegitimate child. Knobloch's father survived too, first as a forced laborer in a munitions factory, and then in hiding with friends. Charlotte Knobloch's grandmother, however, was deported to the Theresienstadt ghetto. There, she starved to death in 1944.

Sixty-eight years after Reichskristallnacht, Charlotte Knobloch, who has been the president of the Jewish Community (Israelitische Kultusgemeinde—IKG) of Munich and Upper Bavaria since 1985 and an honorary citizen of her city since 2005, saw her lifetime dream fulfilled: on November 9, 2006, the IKG's new Ohel Jakob Synagogue in the heart of Munich was inaugurated, and a new community center was opened. Germany's president Horst Köhler made a speech on the occasion. On February 28, 2008, I too visited the synagogue, the community center, and the "Corridor of Memory" in remembrance of the community's victims of the Shoah.

Two weeks later, Charlotte Knobloch was standing in the receiving line of German and Israeli delegates at Ben Gurion Airport in Tel Aviv and took part in the military honors presented by Prime Minister Ehud Olmert to welcome us. Dalia Itzik was also present.

After the reception, we said goodbye for the time being and part of the delegation made its way to Jerusalem, while another, myself included, was flown by Israeli Air Force helicopters to the Ramon Airbase in southern Israel's Negev Desert. There, President Shimon Peres received me. Together we drove to the tomb of David Ben-Gurion, Israel's first president, and his wife, Paula Ben-Gurion. We laid wreaths and commemorated them in silence. Ben-Gurion laid the foundations for relations between Germany and Israel, together with his German counterpart, Konrad Adenauer, in the Waldorf Astoria Hotel in New York on March 14, 1960. There, on neutral territory, the two leaders had their first conversation, fifteen years after the end of the Second World War and the Shoah. Trust developed and grew between them. In 1965, when neither leader was in office anymore, the Federal Republic of Germany and Israel established diplomatic relations and a year later, ninety-year-old Konrad Adenauer visited David Ben-Gurion in his home in the Sde Boker kibbutz in the Negev Desert.

This is where I drove with Shimon Peres after the laying of wreaths. In a few minutes, we arrived at a small museum on the edge of the kibbutz; the building used to house Ben-Gurion's bodyguards. It had been converted into an exhibition containing documents and photographs of the life and influence of the first Israeli prime minister. One picture showed him together with Konrad Adenauer. Next to the site was Ben-Gurion's dwelling, a modest bungalow that we entered with a feeling of awe. I recall that inside was a small vestibule, a living room, a study, and many, many books. Standing in the exact same rooms where Adenauer and Ben-Gurion had stood forty years before, I seemed to sense their physical presence because my skin tingled with goosebumps. I imagined them facing each other and talking. Just minutes earlier, I'd heard Ben-Gurion's voice in the museum on a recording that documented the moment when he declared Israel's independence in 1948. I was familiar with Adenauer's Rhenish sing-song accent from radio and television. And I thought: You are in this modest house in the desert with Shimon Peres, following in the footsteps of two statesmen who truly managed to change things for the better with courage, intelligence, and wisdom. These things are possible, no matter how unlikely they may seem.

Peres and I went on to the central square of the kibbutz and chatted for a while with the children playing there. On the way, we also stopped at a small winery. It was a reminder that agriculture formed the basis of livelihoods in the kibbutzim and that these communities had first built Israel. The Hebrew word kibbutz means "group" or "gathering" and Sde Boker means "shepherd's field."

To finish, I went with Shimon Peres to a gathering of the kibbutz residents at the community center. Outside, children were playing; inside, the atmosphere was peaceful, marked by this joyful way of life in close communion with nature.

"Will you come again? You're welcome to stay for longer if you wish!" one of the participants said. The others looked at me in expectation.

I thought about this for a moment and replied, "I can really see myself doing that when I'm no longer chancellor. I like your way of life here."

Everyone applauded. I meant it seriously, even though I don't know whether I could ever make it happen.

We said goodbye. Peres and I gave a short press statement and then we set off back to our helicopters.

It was early evening by the time we took off from the Ramon Airbase to fly back to Tel Aviv. Shimon Peres and I were sitting in the same helicopter, followed by two other aircraft with delegation members. In the dusk, despite the noise of the blades, Peres told me of his plans to build desalination plants from the Dead Sea to the Red Sea. He had long been trying to solve the problems of water supplies in Israel, Egypt, and Jordan, where reserves were scarce. He had a vision of peaceful coexistence if everyone could share this precious resource. Our bilateral discussion in his residence on the third day of my visit revolved around this topic.

After landing in Jerusalem, we said goodbye and I briefly went to my hotel before attending an evening reception at the residence of Prime Minister Ehud Olmert. We had met before on my first official visit as chancellor in January 2006. He had been vice prime minister at the time but we had held discussions together because Prime Minister Ariel Sharon was in a coma following a stroke. I got on well with Olmert; he was direct and down-to-earth, which made it possible to discuss all kinds of topics straightforwardly even if our opinions differed. After the Lebanon War in summer 2006, which was preceded by an attack from the terrorist militia group Hezbollah, Olmert convinced me that it was right for the German armed forces to contribute naval troops to the United Nations Interim Force in Lebanon (UNIFIL). The goal of the mission was to monitor the ceasefire, support the Lebanese government in maintaining their borders, and prevent illegal weapon smuggling. The Bundestag adopted the mandate necessary for this mission on September 20, 2006.

I found Ehud Olmert to be a leader who genuinely strived for a two-state solution, with Israel as a Jewish democratic state alongside a viable, independent Palestinian state. His observations on this were also the subject of my talk with Mahmoud Abbas, president of the Palestinian Authority, in his official residence in Ramallah during my visit in 2006. When I visited Israel in March 2008, I did not go to Ramallah because I wanted my trip to mark the sixtieth anniversary of the founding of the state of Israel alone. In a telephone call before my visit, I explained this to Abbas.

The focus of the second day of my visit, Monday, March 17, 2008, was the first German–Israeli consultations. Besides joint projects in the areas of youth, science, and economy, we also planned to talk about a topic close to Peres's heart—the water supply. We developed the idea of a trilateral collaboration between Germany, Israel, and African countries, to which Israel could contribute its extensive knowledge about irrigation systems. Every time I visited Israel, I was fascinated by the many ways in which the country had succeeded in converting deserts into fertile farmland through drip irrigation systems, a technique that uses water very sparingly. I thought about how Israel could make this technique available to African countries too. Besides its direct use for African farmers and their families, it would also be a way to honor Israel's innovative power. Too often, the image that African states had of Israel was determined by their conflict with Palestine. I wanted to change this. Ethiopia became the first partner country in our trilateral joint venture and drip irrigation was introduced in twelve locations.

We began our day, however, not with government consultations but at the World Holocaust Remembrance Center, Yad Vashem. The memorial ceremony took place in the Hall of Remembrance and was attended by the members of my delegation, all the German ministers, and the members of the Bundestag who had traveled with us to Israel. President Ehud Olmert accompanied me. We took up our positions; I could see the names of the German concentration and death camps engraved in stone on the floor and, to my right, the Eternal Flame in remembrance of the victims of the Shoah. A children's choir sang. When the master of the ceremony asked me to rekindle the Eternal Flame, I stepped forward a few paces and slowly pressed the lever of the base to the right. Then I returned to my place. A volunteer from the German peace organization Aktion Sühnezeichen (Action Renciliation Service for Peace) laid my wreath on the stone slab; I stepped forward again and smoothed its ribbons. A cantor said a prayer.

When the ceremony was over, we left the Hall of Remembrance. I went on alone to visit the memorial for murdered children. Once inside, I followed a narrow passageway, feeling my way forward as it was almost dark except for small lights glittering like stars in the sky. In the background, I could hear a voice reading the names of the murdered children aloud, a never-ending recital, always in the same order of name, age, and country of origin, over and over. With every name, one of the

1.5 million murdered children was given back their identity and dignity as an individual and human being. This wasn't the first time I'd been here or witnessed the ceremony in the Hall of Remembrance. But every time I visited these two sites, I became well and truly choked up. What indescribable suffering Germany had brought upon the Jewish people, Europe, and the world with the mass murders committed under National Socialism.

And I, the German chancellor, had been asked to speak before the Knesset the following day, the first time this honor had ever been conferred on a foreign head of government.

Reason of state

The speaker of the Knesset, Dalia Itzik, welcomed me on Wednesday, March 18, 2008, with military honors. In the morning, I had held several political talks; now, after both our national anthems, we walked past a guard of honor of the Israeli army in the inner courtyard of the parliament and laid wreaths in front of the memorial to the fallen of Israel's wars. At around 3:00 p.m., we had a late lunch hosted by the speaker of the Knesset and then I retreated for ten minutes. While my assistant Petra Keller fixed my hair and make-up, I took the speech I would be making in a few minutes out of its folder and went through it one last time. In it were five central messages that I wanted to convey: First, that humanity grows out of a responsibility toward the past. Second, that Germany and Israel share the values of freedom, democracy, and the observance of human dignity. Third, that major global challenges—from the fair distribution of wealth, to climate change, and the fight against threats posed by terror and weapons of mass destruction—can only be mastered if nations cooperate, particularly those linked by shared values and interests, such as Germany and Israel, as well as Europe and Israel. Fourth, that Germany stands for the vision of two states within secure borders and in peace—for the Jewish people in Israel and the Palestinian people in Palestine. Fifth, that the security of the state of Israel is never negotiable for Germany. These five central messages were all included in my speech. I felt comfortable about this, closed the folder, and left the room.

At half past four, I took my place on the podium of the Plenum Hall. Dalia Itzik opened the session, followed by a short address from Prime Minister Ehud Olmert, and one from the opposition leader at the time, Benjamin Netanyahu. Then I stepped up to the lectern and began my speech in Hebrew with the words: "Madam President, anni modda lachem she-nittan li le-dabber ellechem kaan be-bait mechubad se. Se kawwod gadol awurri." (Thank you for allowing me to speak to you here in the Knesset. I am very honored to be here.) These words had been transcribed phonetically for me and I had practiced them in the make-up room with my interpreter one last time before I made my speech. When I then switched to German, some Knesset parliamentarians on the back benches stood up and left the hall in protest. I regretted this but was not surprised as it had been announced in advance. I concentrated on giving my speech, emphasizing the common values and interests of our two countries, advocating the two-state solution, and offering my support for this vision while acknowledging that Israel did not need "unsolicited advice from outsiders and [. . .] most definitely [did] not need anyone talking down to [it]." I added that, ultimately, a solution could only be worked out by Israelis and Palestinians themselves, for which compromises acceptable to all sides would have to be made. This would also require the strength to make painful concessions.

Where Israel was concerned, it meant stopping the construction of settlements. On this point, Ehud Olmert and I already had some differences of opinion. But when his successor, Benjamin Netanyahu, came to power, these disputes became irreconcilable. We were only able to reach an agreement with the phrase "We have agreed to disagree." Netanyahu paid occasional lip service to the two-state solution, but in truth, he did nothing to facilitate it. Rather, by continuing settlement construction, he undermined it completely.

Such conflicts needed to be dealt with, but I was convinced that they could not lead to a fundamental questioning of relations between our two countries, because what joined Germany and Israel was far stronger than what divided them. On the topic of threats from Hamas rockets launched from Gaza, or Iran's nuclear program, I therefore stressed that "every German government and every German chancellor before me has shouldered Germany's special historical responsibility for Israel's security. This historical responsibility is an element of my country's 'reason of state.'"

These were the words I used, almost verbatim, half a year earlier on September 25, 2007, before the General Assembly of the United Nations in New York. Back then, barely anyone registered them, or at least, I do not recall that a deeper discussion ensued. This changed after my first speech to the Knesset, proving once again that communication largely depends on who says what, when, and where. In this location, on this occasion, my words had a different, incomparably powerful effect.

After twenty-five minutes, I ended my speech, which was received very graciously. Thankful and happy, I left the Knesset at around half past five. After a quick stopover in my hotel, I was taken to Ben Gurion Airport to catch my 7:15 p.m. flight back to Berlin.

What did I mean by "reason of state"? This question has pursued me ever since, and with particular intensity fifteen years later, in the early hours of October 7, 2023, when Israel was struck by the horrendous Hamas-led terrorist attacks. The phrase "reason of state" belonged to my political vocabulary and, to a certain extent, it was CDU language. At the CDU party conference in 1997 in Leipzig, where I gave a brief address as vice chair, I used it with a negative connotation in reference to the GDR, saying: "I think that one of the best experiences that ought to be preserved from this period is that millions of parents who lived in the GDR tried to bring up their children according to basic human principles rather than make them subordinate to the reason of state." At the CDU party conference in December 2004 in Düsseldorf, I described the social market economy, ties to the West, rearmament, and German unity as "part of the reason of state" of reunified Germany.

In April 2005, the German ambassador to Israel Rudolf Dressler published an essay in which he wrote that the "secure existence of Israel is [. . .] an element of our reason of state." He was using it in the context of the then prime minister Ariel Sharon's decision to fully withdraw Israeli troops from Gaza, and the occasionally turbulent discussions among Israeli factions about the possible consequences of this plan. In Gaza itself some months later, in January 2006, Hamas won the last independent elections. Their declared goal is the destruction of Israel. This formed the backdrop to my speech to celebrate "Sixty years of the CDU" on June 16, 2005, in Berlin: "Konrad Adenauer prevailed against deep-sown doubt and embittered circumstances so that Germany could be included in the Western community's shared values. Today we can say that Germany's responsibility for European unity, for the transatlantic partnership, and Israel's existence all belong to our country's core reason of state and are part of the reason for our party too." I had planned my speech for this event in early 2005, not suspecting that an early general election would be called that year. So, when the time came to give it, I was a candidate for chancellor but few seemed to take an interest in an official CDU speech, and my "reason of state" wording went largely unnoticed.

As in my address to the UN in September 2007, I subsequently added two sentences to my Knesset speech in 2008 and said, with almost identical wording: "That means that Israel's security is non-negotiable for me as German chancellor. And that being the case, we must do more than pay lip service to this commitment when it comes to a critical moment in time." The outcome of this wording is not a mutual defense policy, as expressed in Article 5 of the NATO Treaty between alliance members, but nevertheless a closer connection to Israel than many other states in the world. On a diplomatic level, it has meant that Germany backs the two-state solution and, in the so-called E3+3 negotiations, supported ending Iran's nuclear program alongside France and the UK, with the other triad consisting of Russia, China, and the United States; it also meant abstaining from the EU and UN votes to recognize Palestine as a state. On a military level, the outcome is that Germany has supplied Israel with arms since the 1950s, even though these deliveries are to a crisis region not covered by the Foreign Trade and Payments Act (Aussenwirtschaftsgesetz—AWG); it also meant that German armed forces took part in the UNIFIL mission in Lebanon in 2006.

Israel, the only democratic state in the Middle East, which is moreover supported by a strong civic society, is under constant military threat. The terrorist attacks by Hamas, on October 7, 2023, wounded the country to the core. In this situation, instead of receiving solidarity throughout the world, Israel, and Jews all over the world, soon suffered antisemitism in the form of a torrent of hate speech both online and in public, in Germany and many other countries. As legitimate as the wish for a viable Palestinian state is and has always been, and as legitimate as criticism of Germany's or Israel's actions is and has always been, the following must nevertheless apply: Those who use these wishes and criticisms at demonstrations as a smoke-screen to give free rein to their hatred toward the state of Israel and Jews abuse constitutional rights to freedom of expression and assembly. This abuse has to be punished and stopped by every means available according to the rule of German law. Everyone who lives in Germany has to subscribe to the values of our constitution. This is why the fight against antisemitism, indeed, against all forms of hostility toward any group of people, whether it comes from the right, the left, or is motivated by Islamism, is and remains a state and civil duty.

Why did I use the phrase "reason of state," instead of simply saying that Israel's security is non-negotiable, as others before me have said using these or similar words? "The phrase 'reason of state' expresses more, and more intensely, what can be articulated by nomenclature or constitutional order. It comprises the fundamental values of the democratic constitution for which we stand, the economic and social order in which we live, and the security we need." This was how Helmut Kohl put it in his keynote address at St. Antony's College, Oxford University, on May 2, 1984, entitled "German Foreign Policy—the Legacy of Konrad Adenauer." Kohl did not mention Israel in this context, but nevertheless, his interpretation of the phrase "reason of state" touches the core of what has always been, and remains, important to me.

KAIROS

"Time to Go"

ON THE WALL behind my office desk was a low, curved, narrow shelf in the same dark wood as the desk. Above it hung Kokoschka's portrait of Adenauer, flanked by the German and European flags. The shelf extended to the far end of the office, invisible to anyone entering the room. On it, at the beginning of 2019, I had placed a small bubble-wrapped sculpture. Apart from Beate Baumann and myself, no one knew what was inside the wrapping. My plan was to wait until the end of my tenure—when I was installed in my ex-chancellor's office—for the great "unveiling," as Beate and I sometimes joked. Until then, it remained in its packaging on the shelf.

I had bought the piece on January 9, 2019 at an exhibition by Thomas Jastram, a sculptor from Rostock now based in Hamburg. The exhibition was held in a showroom at the Berlin concept store Stilwerk, and I had gone there on the recommendation of Dierk Evert, a landscape architect from Rügen who had contacted Kathrin Meyer from my constituency office about it at the end of 2018. I wasn't disappointed. As I browsed the collection, passing sculptures of women in various poses, I suddenly came across a figure that stood out from the others. It had wings on its back and feet, and the back of its head was bald; only a single lock of hair hung down from its forehead. There was no mistaking it: Kairos. Unlike Chronos, the god of regular time,

Kairos flew through the air, so that you had to wait for the right moment to seize him by his lock of hair. I double-checked the label. Sure enough: *Kayros*. This forty-two-centimeter-tall figure, cast in bronze by Thomas Jastram in 2017, was indeed the god of opportunity. I knew at once that I had to have it. After completing my tour of the exhibition, I returned to *Kayros* with Jastram in tow. I inquired tentatively whether the piece was still available and he said yes. Then I asked him the price. I had never bought a sculpture in my life and had no idea what such things cost. It was within my budget.

"What is it about it that attracts you?" Jastram asked me.

"Over my lifetime I've spent endless hours deliberating over the right timing. It's an incredibly important thing in politics," I replied. "You have to choose your moment. It's what makes the difference between success and failure."

There were times when I had risked letting a favorable moment for a decision pass me by. Looking back, though, I think the fact that I remained chancellor for so long was partly due to my ability to intuit in critical situations when the time was right—just like that dive from the three-meter springboard in my childhood.

I was sometimes late to take action but, when it came to the crunch, never *too* late and, just as importantly, never too early. One such moment had occurred not long before, or two and a half months before, to be precise. On Monday, October 29, 2018, I had informed the Presidium and the CDU Federal Board that, after more than eighteen years in the job, I would not be standing for re-election as CDU leader at the national party conference in December, and would be retiring from active political life at the 2021 federal election. The day before, even though the CDU had emerged from the state election in Hesse as the strongest party, leaving the Conservative–Green coalition government clinging on by a majority of one, the CDU vote had fallen significantly. That election night had marked a further low point in a whole chain of negative developments. After similarly heavy losses by the CSU in the Bavarian state elections two weeks before; after the recriminations between the CDU and CSU over the asylum and refugee policy in the summer, and more or less continuously since the decision of September 4, 2015 to allow refugees arriving from Hungary into the country; and after the failure of the "Jamaica" coalition talks and the tortuous process of forming a government in 2017–2018, I was neither able nor willing to return to business as usual. But I did hold a small trump card: whereas, after the federal election of 2013, I had had to reckon with a majority—albeit small—of SPD, Alliance 90/Greens and the Left Party against the CDU and CSU, the situation after the 2017 election was different. There was no longer a political majority against the CDU and CSU. For that reason alone, I wasn't going to throw my party—and ultimately the country I was responsible for—into a well-nigh impossible situation by announcing three years before the end of the legislative period that I would no longer be standing for the party leadership or in the federal election either.

When, two years previously, on Sunday, November 20, 2016, I had informed the CDU Federal Board after months of deliberation that I would be standing "once more," as I put it, Wolfgang Schäuble had corrected me immediately: I shouldn't say I was standing "once more," but "again." He was right, of course: an open-ended message was critical for a successful electoral campaign. After all, who would vote for candidate with a sell-by date? My words at the time were a Freudian slip, betraying my determination that my candidature for the 2017 federal election would definitely be my last. Although I had decided to make myself available for the full four years of a further term and to keep my promise to the citizens of Germany, 2021 would be the end, both of my chancellorship and of my time as a parliamentarian. I took the first step toward this goal on October 29, 2018. I hadn't meant to announce it until a week later at a closed-door

CDU meeting I had scheduled in preparation for the national party conference in December. But in the fall of 2018 I was under pressure. Even though, as chancellor and party chair, I was not to blame for everything, I bore responsibility for it by virtue of my office. Matters came to a head when speculation began to arise over rival candidates at the party conference. I decided on the Sunday evening not to wait another week until the closed-door meeting, but to announce my plans on the Monday. Had I wanted to continue beyond the 2021 election or remained undecided, I would once again have faced down the conflict within the party, and potential rivals, in the sure knowledge that, like Helmut Kohl at the Bremen party conference of September 1989, I would be re-elected party leader by a sufficient, if perhaps modest, margin. Bringing down a chancellor was not the CDU's style. Like Helmut Kohl, I was convinced that the party leadership and chancellorship should be in the same hands. That was the only way to confer the necessary ultimate political authority—on either count. If I was going to deviate from this by standing down as party leader three years before the federal election, then it would only be as a first step toward my retirement from politics. Otherwise, I would never have entertained the separation of the two offices.

Apart from Beate Baumann, I told no one in my political circle before the Monday morning what I was going to say that day, first internally and then publicly. For the people I had sat around a table with the previous evening, that was, in retrospect, hard to take. But I had to make sure that my decision wasn't leaked hours in advance, before I had had the opportunity to make a public statement in an appropriate setting. That opportunity came on the Monday, first before the Presidium, then the Federal Board, and finally at my press conference. There, in front of the blue CDU screen at Konrad Adenauer House, I duly announced my decision to the public, summing up my personal reasons for it in one sentence: "I have always wished and endeavored to discharge my government and party political offices with dignity and to retire from them one day with the same dignity." Then I went on to take questions from the journalists.

The arguments in favor of stepping down were the same as they had been in 2016: democracy thrives on change; sixteen years was a long time to be chancellor; and the potential for mutiny exposed by the 2017 election campaign had not gone away. The refugee policy developments of 2015 had felt like a turning point in my chancellorship. For me, service to my country was the unifying thread of my time in office, but there was a before and an after: before the night of the decision on September 4 to 5, 2015, and after.

Earlier, in 2013, AfD had been founded as a reaction to my policy decisions regarding the euro rescue package, but it had fallen just short of the 5-percent threshold and failed to make it into the Bundestag. Two years later, it had gained fresh impetus on the back of rising refugee numbers and the refugee policy adopted in response. In May 2016, a few weeks after the agreement between the EU and Turkey came into force, which saw the number of refugees coming to Germany begin to fall significantly, I was asked in an interview with the *Frankfurter Allgemeine Sonntagszeitung* what I thought of Franz Josef Strauss's remark that no democratically legitimized force should be allowed to exist to the right of the Union. I replied that it was valid in the sense that the Union should always seek to integrate toward the center and should therefore offer concrete solutions to problems. But I added: "If, on the other hand, Strauss's remark can also be taken to mean that principles should be relativized or even abandoned to prevent people from turning away from the Union—principles that are constitutive for our country as well as for the Union, that go to the heart of what we believe in—then I reject it. European unity, with a single currency and freedom of movement, the community of values within NATO, the preservation of human dignity, especially for people in distress: these are things we must never abandon. And the best way for the CDU and CSU to integrate is to find common solutions."

The democratic parties have considerable influence over how strong AfD can become in practice. I am convinced that, if they assume they can keep it down by appropriating its pet topics and even trying to outdo it in rhetoric without offering any real solutions to existing problems, they will fail. If, on the other hand, they manage to develop and implement effective answers to the challenges of our time, beyond party political boundaries and not as a tactical maneuver but by showing they are sincere about the issues and adopting a moderate tone, then the electorate will reward them for it. That goes also and especially for refugee policy. The overwhelming majority of people can tell instinctively whether politicians are acting out of pure calculation, whether they are letting AfD lead them by the nose, or whether they have a genuine interest in solving the country's problems. That is the standard by which democratic parties should be judged—by that, and by whether they feel they have to denigrate those among their own ranks with whom they disagree in order to defeat them, or whether they can live with dissent. Moderation is the basis and precondition for the success of democratic parties.

As so often after difficult decisions, I felt a kind of elation after I had finally said my piece on October 29, 2018. Two and a half months later, I found myself standing before the *Kayros* sculpture at the Stilwerk exhibition. It was as if it had been made for me. I had chosen the right moment to let go.

Just how much so was brought home to me months later by an incident that really shook me at first. It happened during the inaugural state visit by the new Ukrainian president Volodymyr Zelenskyy to Berlin on Tuesday, June 18, 2019, as we stood together to receive the traditional military honors. Just before the end of the ceremony, I felt my legs begin to shake slightly. During the national anthems, the shaking spread to the whole of my body. I began to sway and tried to steady myself with my arms, which I had somewhat more control over than my legs, by clasping my hands in front of my body. But it was no use. I didn't know how long I would be able to stay upright, or whether I would even have the strength to inspect the guard of honor after the anthems, and I was both relieved and surprised when, after the first step, my body felt normal again. When the ceremony was over, I immediately drank a glass of water. It was around noon on a hot day, and I had had nothing to drink except three or four cups of coffee. Perhaps that was the reason, I thought, as I had already had a similar experience once before on a foreign visit, albeit to a lesser degree.

A few days later, however, it happened again, this time at the federal president's residence, Bellevue Palace, during the official appointment of Christine Lambrecht as Katarina Barley's successor in the role of justice minister. While he was speaking, I stood beside him looking straight ahead at the inescapable wall of cameras trained on me. Once again, I began to shake. My body assumed a life of its own, no longer obeying my brain. Once Steinmeier had finished his speech and I could move again, everything was back to normal. The whole thing happened a third time during the inaugural visit of the Finnish prime minister Antti Rinne on July 10, 2019. The next day, when it was the Danish prime minister Mette Frederiksen's turn to visit, I decided to remain seated for the national anthems. From then on, I made that my policy, both at home and abroad, until I retired from office. After these episodes, I went for a thorough medical examination. Neurological and internal tests yielded nothing untoward. This reaction of my vegetative nervous system evidently had another cause. An osteopath explained to me that my body was releasing tensions that had built up over a long period, due not just to the death of my mother in the spring, for which I had barely had time to grieve, but also to the process of relinquishing my public roles. So it was good news in principle—if only my body hadn't decided to enact that process in full public view.

While writing this book, I rediscovered an article from the *Süddeutsche Zeitung* of January 12, 2019, which happened to be exactly three days after my visit to the exhibition where I bought the Kairos sculpture. The piece really resonated with me at the time, which is why I kept it. In an essay entitled "Time to Go" ("Runter vom Platz"), the writer Rainer Erlinger discusses why choosing the right moment to stop is an art; he too mentions Kairos and asks: "Do politicians find it especially hard to stop?" He then goes on to talk about Hannah Arendt's 1960 philosophical magnum opus *The Human Condition*, in which she describes labor, work, and action as the three basic human activities. Labor serves to make a living, work is about creating something, and action includes "interaction between people." Interpreting Arendt, Erlinger states that action is therefore "the very essence of political activity." And he concludes: "It is thus all the more important to recognize that stopping—in the political sphere as elsewhere—is an action in itself. An action that is both part of the task we are stopping and part of our own life." And that's just how it was for me too.

Retirement from CDU leadership

On Friday, December 7, 2018, at Hamburg Messe, I gave my last speech as chair of the CDU. Projected onto the back wall of the stage in LED lettering was the motto of the party conference: "Bringing together. Leading together," expressing the outlook and aspirations of the Christian Democratic Union of Germany. I had decided not to give a long keynote address on all the latest projects. That was to be the task of my successor, to be elected a few hours later. Instead, I chose to focus on five questions to which I had given some thought. Four of them harked back to the past: What had brought the CDU and myself together when I was first elected in 2000? The desire to make the party electable again after the donations scandal. What did the CDU and I have to thank each other for? Endless hours of shared reflection on the best answers to the toughest questions. What had we denied each other? For my part, I had certainly denied the party one or two scathing attacks on our political opponents. Why were we now going our separate ways? We were not really separating, as my loyalty to the party did not depend on any political office; it was simply time for a new leader to set the course for the future.

The fifth question was the only one that looked forward. What did I wish the CDU? I answered: "My wish for us collectively is that, even in the toughest times, and however complex the tasks and harsh the attacks from outside, we never forget the true essence of the Christian Democratic position. We Christian Democrats may draw boundaries but we never build barriers." Had I always done proper justice to that aspiration myself? Probably not, despite my best intentions. For example, I had encountered a wave of protest and incomprehension when, at a vote in the Bundestag on June 30, 2017, I opposed the introduction of same-sex marriage. I subscribed to the traditional view that, under the German constitution, marriage was only possible between a man and a woman. Just days before, I had been the one to clear the way for a vote on same-sex marriage—and in the face of an expected majority in the Bundestag for its introduction—by arguing for a free vote on the issue. I had wanted to avoid discriminating against anyone, but by voting against the bill I had achieved the exact opposite. People who had spent years campaigning for same-sex marriage, because they saw it as sending a signal against discrimination and exclusion, felt that I had let them down, indeed betrayed them. For my part, I was aggrieved that it was evidently not enough to have resolved the long-simmering social conflict over this issue. Instead, I came under pressure to justify myself—a contradiction in terms on a matter of conscience.

"We Christian Democrats are no strangers to dispute, but we never stir up hatred or run other people down. We Christian Democrats make no distinctions when it comes to human dignity; we never play one group of people off against another. We Christian Democrats do not indulge in navel-gazing or narcissism; we serve the people of our country," I continued in my Hamburg address. I could have added: Even in our hour of triumph we do not forget that not everyone voted for us, and that there are others who are not so happy. At least, that was what prompted me, at the victory celebrations on the night of the 2013 federal election, to take the German flag out of General Secretary Hermann Gröhe's hands and remove it from the stage. My action met with widespread incomprehension and criticism. I was sorry that Hermann Gröhe of all people—one of the most sensitive and least triumphalist people I know—was the one on the receiving end. But I found the gesture inappropriate. The SPD was in pieces, the FDP had failed for the first time ever to gain a seat in the Bundestag, and even the CDU result, though magnificent, was far from 100 percent. We had every reason to celebrate, but we had no right to appropriate the German flag, particularly at such a moment.

I closed my reflections with the words: "We can only build a successful future if we go about it not with ill-humor, resentment, or pessimism, but always with joy in our hearts. That at least has always been my motto, during my life in the GDR and all the more so in a free society. And it is that lightness of spirit that I wish my party going forward."

With such an outlook, the CDU can, I remain convinced, continue to achieve in future what the motto of that party conference—bringing together and leading together—was all about: fostering cohesion and solidarity in our country and thereby making a vital contribution to mastering the challenges of our time.

THE PANDEMIC

A challenge to democracy

THE FINAL THREE years of my tenure had begun. Some people thought I would be able to coast my way through them, treating the EU presidency in the second half of 2019 as a lap of honor and generally taking the opportunity to see the world. On the last day of 2019, my penultimate New Year's address was broadcast to the nation. If someone had said to me that day that I would soon be telling people to avoid shaking hands, to keep a minimum distance of 1.5 meters apart, and to wear face masks; that I would be closing kindergartens, schools, cinemas, theaters, opera houses and concert halls, hotels, bars, stores, fitness studios, hair salons, and other services involving close physical proximity, keeping people in hospitals, old people's homes, and care homes away from their nearest and dearest, reducing to a minimum the number of people who could meet outdoors and in enclosed spaces—including church services and funerals—and canceling exhibitions, trade fairs, and sporting events, I would have thought them crazy. I could never have imagined myself doing anything of the sort. And yet that is what I did, and all because of an enemy invisible to the naked eye: a tiny, 0.1 micrometer virus. It needed us humans in order to reproduce, and it spread wherever we did what comes naturally: interacting with others. The only way to contain it was to deny our own nature and avoid mutual contact. The alternative would have been to expose the entire population to the virus-borne disease within a short space of time and look on while our health system collapsed. To do so would have been to risk, if not tacitly accept, large numbers of deaths, particularly among the elderly and those with underlying health conditions. That was a route I refused to go down. It contradicted my values and beliefs, and my understanding of Article 1 of our constitution, which states that human dignity is inviolable, and that the duty of all state authority is to respect and protect it.

In my New Year's address, I had talked about how we could look forward with confidence to the dawning new decade of the twenties. I had failed to notice a report published on the morning of December 31, 2019 by the news agency dpa that "a mysterious lung disease [had] broken out in the central Chinese metropolis of Wuhan." Had I done so, it would have set bells ringing, as I had been to Wuhan just months before, from September 6 to 8, 2019, and had visited the German-founded Tongji Hospital there. One of China's most modern hospitals, it maintains partnerships with the university hospital of Duisburg-Essen and the Charité Berlin. No one could have guessed back then what a catastrophe would befall the people of this city, before spreading to the rest of the country, Asia, and the world.

At the beginning of that year, there were other issues dominating the news: bush fires in Australia, the attempts to form a government in Austria and Spain, preparations for the German presidency of the European Council in the second half of the year. From around mid-January 2020, however, people's attention—including my own—began to shift. I can still hear the words of Helge Braun, head of the Chancellery from 2018, at one of our regular morning briefings: "Last night I read an article in the *New England Journal of Medicine* about a new coronavirus in Wuhan. It's got me really worried. Even medical staff treating infected patients have caught it. That suggests the virus is highly contagious. It could spread around the world."

Helge Braun, who has a degree in medicine, was not one to exaggerate, and certainly not to dramatize. If he departed from the routine topics of our morning briefing, then there was clearly something to worry about. "Contact the Robert Koch Institute as soon as possible," I asked him.

When, a few days later, on January 27, 2020, the Munich Institute of Tropical Medicine diagnosed Germany's first case of the novel virus in an employee of Webasto, a company based in the Bavarian district of Starberg, I could hardly believe my ears. There are coincidences in life you simply couldn't make up: I remembered in a flash that, during my visit to China in September 2019, I had not only been to Wuhan, but had joined Holger Engelmann, the CEO of the company in question, for the inauguration of a new production plant there. Now it seemed that a Webasto employee had attended a training session led by a Chinese colleague from Shanghai who had been diagnosed with the virus on her return to China. She was without doubt the source of the infection at Webasto. Meanwhile, other employees had also become infected. To prove it, a test was used that had been developed by the virologist Christian Drosten and his team at the Charité, and which had been available since mid-January. The result was clear: the virus had reached Germany. At that stage, however, it looked as if it could still be contained: all chains of infection could be traced.

Two weeks later, on February 11, 2020, the World Health Organization (WHO) announced the name of the new disease: COVID-19. CO stood for corona, VI for virus, D for disease, and 19 for 2019, the year of the outbreak.

On Shrove Monday, February 24, 2020, Beate Baumann and I traveled to Dierhagen on the Baltic coast, as we did nearly every year during the Carnival season, to give some thought to the rest of the year's planning. At that stage there was no question of canceling our trip due to the new disease, nor did we have to weigh up the possible health risks posed by the virus before eating out. But we did feel uneasy when we thought of the many Carnival events taking place, after news of COVID cases emerged during that time which were all linked to a Carnival celebration on February 15, 2020 in Gangelt, North Rhine-Westphalia.

On Friday, February 28, 2020, at my traditional New Year's reception in the constituency, I made my first public statement on the new coronavirus. Speaking at the Störtebeker brewery in Stralsund, I assured the four hundred or so invited guests that the federal government was doing its utmost to protect the population, adding that everyone could do their bit to help combat the virus, and that I personally would "not be shaking hands with anyone today"—a contribution which, with hindsight, seems almost touchingly naive. At my office, I instituted a rota of in-person and home-working shifts to make sure we remained operational at all times.

The first real crisis of conscience occurred five days later. A memorial service had been arranged in Hanau, Hesse on March 4 for nine people with a migratory background who had been murdered two weeks before, on the evening of February 19. After shooting them, the killer went on to shoot his mother and then himself. All the signs suggested the murders were racially motivated. It was a terrible time. I still think about what it meant for the families involved, for people with a migratory background generally—and for our society as a whole.

Once again, we could only promise to do all we could to investigate the murders and the circumstances surrounding them as thoroughly as possible and to call out any instances of mishandling, including by the authorities if it so proved. I felt the need to attend the memorial in Hanau even though—unlike at the service for the victims of the terrorist group "National Socialist Underground" (NSU) eight years before—I wasn't giving a speech this time. Given the new disease, however, I was in a quandary over whether to attend an event involving several hundred people. What would be the consequences for government business if I caught COVID-19? Was it not my duty to set an example to others by avoiding large gatherings? Wasn't it enough that the federal president Frank-Walter Steinmeier and the state premier of Hesse Volker Bouffier would be there? No, I decided, my place on that day was in Hanau.

A week later, on March 11, 2020, the WHO declared COVID-19 a pandemic, that is, an infectious disease occurring on a worldwide scale. On the same day, I addressed the Federal Press Conference together with the health minister Jens Spahn and Lothar Wieler, president of the Robert Koch Institute. Among other things, I spoke about the initial package of COVID measures for the economy agreed by the coalition committee three days before, emphasized the risk to our health system posed by the virus, and stressed the advantages of our country's federal structure in that it allowed a decentralized approach appropriate to the problem. At the same time, I warned: "Federalism is not an excuse to pass the buck: federalism is there to ensure that each region takes responsibility for itself." The reality behind these words was that, since infection control was essentially a regionally devolved matter, the federal government's scope for action—and hence my own—was extremely limited. Just how limited was something I came to discover over the following months. I was already beginning to feel as if the fight against the pandemic combined everything that could possibly affect me as a person and as a politician: As an individual and a citizen I was, like everyone else, concerned for my own health and that of my family and, like everyone else, I had to stick to the rules. As federal chancellor, I was the one who, in consultation with the heads of the federal states, decided on the measures against the virus. As a scientist, I was frustrated by the fact that not everyone was familiar with the dynamic of exponential growth, according to which the number of infections would double every one to two weeks. On that basis, initially low infection rates could go through the roof after just a few weeks if nothing was done. Yet all too often no action was taken until the water was up to our necks.

In March 2020, we watched the situation in Europe worsen. In northern Italy, the health system was already completely overwhelmed. Distressing images of overcrowded hospitals and long lines of hearses on their way to crematoria testified to the dramatic developments. I was determined to pull out all the stops to protect us from a similar fate in Germany. Since that meant avoiding contact, I held talks with the state premiers on March 12, 16, and 22 in which we negotiated a package of measures that brought public life largely to a standstill. The only exemptions were for services essential to daily life: food retailers, weekly markets, pharmacies, medical supply outlets, drugstores, gas stations, post offices, and banks. Cross-border travel to our neighboring countries—with the exception of the Netherlands—was also restricted.

The measures were severe. It was clear to me that I could only make them work if the vast majority of the population could be persuaded to comply with them. For that to happen, they needed to know the bigger picture. Beate Baumann, Eva Christiansen, Steffen Seibert, and I talked time and again about how best to achieve this. The means available to me were limited: in a press conference I could only make a few introductory remarks, and was otherwise restricted to whatever questions journalists chose to ask. When speaking in parliament, I was only addressing the members and had to hope that the evening news would show the bits I felt were important. Other events I could have spoken at had been canceled because of COVID. All that was left was a step which, apart from the traditional New Year's speech, I had never taken in all my time in office: a televised address to the nation. The very fact of resorting to such a measure would highlight the gravity of the situation—that much was clear, and it was the only thing that would allow me to speak for several minutes, direct and uncut, to the citizens of Germany.

"You ought to do it, this is literally an emergency," said Eva Christiansen.

"I'm absolutely certain ARD and ZDF will broadcast it. It's not as if you're making a party political statement—this is a genuine crisis," Steffen Seibert added.

"Then let's do it. And perhaps you could ask our friends outside the political arena to help, so that we're not just left to stew in our own juice," I suggested.

The decision was made, and the exact timing followed soon after. On March 17, 2020, a day after the conference with the state premiers where we had negotiated the key measures, Steffen Seibert asked both public TV channels if they would broadcast an address after the main news the next day, four days before the restrictions were to come into force. They agreed.

On Wednesday, March 18, 2020, I left my office at 4:30 p.m. and made my way to the cabinet chamber on the sixth floor of the Chancellery to record my address. It was a setting I was familiar with from my New Year's speeches. I was anxious that nothing should distract from the message I wanted to get across: "This is serious. And you should take it seriously. Not since German unification, indeed, not since the Second World War has our country faced a challenge in which so much has depended on us acting together in solidarity," I insisted, leaving no doubt as to the urgency of the situation. Our friends had advised me not just to appeal to the audience and set out the new rules but also to speak in a personal capacity. I took that advice to heart: "For someone like me, for whom freedom of movement and travel were a hard-won right, such restrictions can only be justified in case of absolute necessity. In a democracy, they should never be imposed lightly, and only ever on a temporary basis—but right now they are essential in order to save lives," I continued and, drawing to a close, reaffirmed: "We are a democracy. We live not by coercion, but by shared knowledge and collaboration."

The reaction to my nine-minute-plus address was overwhelming. I had obviously touched a nerve. This was something I could build on.

Five days later, on Monday, March 23, 2020, the federal cabinet agreed on the draft wording of an "Act for the Protection of the Population in the Event of an Epidemic Situation of National Significance," or Population Protection Act. This meant that the bill was brought before the Bundestag directly by the coalition parties so that the Bundestag and Bundesrat could pass it within the same week. Declaring an epidemic situation of national significance was the precondition for extending the powers of the federal and state authorities. On the same day, the cabinet also approved a supplementary budget of €156 billion— almost half an entire federal budget—to mitigate the economic consequences of the COVID crisis. To this end, the Bundestag suspended for 2020 the debt brake enshrined in the constitution. That the federal government and both houses were able to take all these decisions within the space of one week is something that could never have been achieved without the assistance of Babette Kibele and Gesa Miehe-Nordmeyer, heads of the Federal Chancellery departments of internal and legal affairs and social policy respectively, along with all the other relevant departments. I cannot thank them and all their staff enough— especially given the added difficulty of working together after I was identified as a contact and had to self-isolate from the evening of Sunday, March 22.

Although the procurement of personal protective equipment was, strictly speaking, the responsibility of the federal states, the health ministry set up a procurement team to speed up the supply of face masks from abroad. Every day, there were alarming reports from the hospitals that stocks of PPE were in danger of running out. The idea that doctors and nurses had no suitable masks and were unable to protect themselves was almost intolerable. Masks were produced more or less exclusively in Asia, and especially China, and a race to procure them ensued throughout Europe. The product had suddenly assumed strategic importance. What was needed were medical-grade masks, also known as surgical masks, and particle-filtering half-masks (protection class FFP2). Step by step, we managed to obtain sufficient quantities of both types while also expanding production capacity in our own country. The production of FFP2 masks was supported with a subsidy of €40 million.

About a month after my televised address and the imposition of tough restrictions, the pace of infection duly slowed. The number of new cases fell significantly. The virus had by no means disappeared, however. We were not in the end phase of the pandemic, but still in its early stages: I knew that for a fact. But it became increasingly difficult to get this across. And you couldn't deny it: the pandemic was and remained "a challenge to democracy," as I remarked in a government statement in the Bundestag on April 23, 2020, after the Easter recess. It "strikes at the very heart of our existential rights and needs—those of adults and children alike." I was particularly concerned by what the elderly and infirm in nursing and residential care homes and facilities for people with disabilities had to endure. "In places where loneliness is often already a problem, it is even lonelier during a pandemic, with no visitors at all. It is cruel when no one—apart from care staff, who do their very best—can be there for them as their powers weaken and they approach the end of their lives. We must never forget these people and the temporary isolation to which they are condemned." With these words, I attempted to give a voice to those who were largely unheard in public life. Meanwhile, a war of words had erupted over the easing of lockdown restrictions. In a video conference of the CDU Presidium on Monday, April 20, I incautiously referred to "an orgy of discussion." I was concerned that, if we opened up too much too soon, we would gamble away a result achieved at the expense of so many lives, not to mention the burden it would place on the weakest, as well as on hospital staff. In the end, on April 29, compulsory mask wearing was at least introduced throughout Germany on public transport and in shops.

The rate of infection continued to fall with the warmer spring weather. I was grateful for the remarkable achievement of so many people—especially doctors and nurses—over the past months. We had stood together in solidarity. Employers and employees had managed to maintain the critical infrastructure; the federal government was supporting citizens, companies, and local authorities with an economic stimulus package worth €130 billion for 2020 and 2021; large numbers of civil servants had worked day and night; Bundeswehr soldiers had come to the aid of health authorities and care homes; families had gone the extra mile, and especially children, for whom separation from their friends in kindergartens and schools had been hard to bear. We had reason to be proud of our country.

Nevertheless, there is no doubt that the pandemic demanded extraordinary sacrifices from all generations: children, parents, and grandparents. Few things generated such bitter disagreements as the closure of schools and nurseries—disagreements that are still, to an extent, ongoing. While the federal government had been reproached with failing to pay sufficient attention to a risk analysis produced in 2012 by the Federal Office for Civil Protection in relation to a "pandemic caused by a 'Modi SARS' virus" when it came to procuring protective equipment, including an adequate supply of face masks, the findings of that analysis in relation to schools and nurseries were often conveniently forgotten. Besides the cancellation of large-scale events, it had in fact explicitly mentioned the closure of schools as a means of containing the pandemic. Pointing this out does not, however, alter the fact that what we were dealing with a few years later was not a theoretical risk analysis, but a real-life pandemic. The virus and the risks it posed were new to everyone. We had to learn day by day. The premise and purpose of my actions were to prevent our health system from becoming overwhelmed. Only then could all those who contracted the virus—regardless of age or underlying health conditions—receive the treatment they needed. That was my guiding principle. It meant weighing up new risks every day, and by that I mean not only the risks *from* and *to* individuals—whether young or old, sick or healthy—in terms of virus transmission, but also the potential consequences of the federal and state measures.

In this situation, I sometimes found it hard to take, as a former scientist myself, when politicians accused scientists of constantly changing their minds—an accusation that betrayed a gross misunderstanding of the nature of science and research. The point of science and research is not simply to have an opinion and change it if circumstances demand: it is to gain new insights, draw conclusions from them, and repeat that process with each new advance. That is how it works. And when it came to estimating the infection risk *to* children and adolescents as well as the possible infection risk *from* them, I relied on the latest research findings and acted on the principle of prevention, not hope. School and nursery closures were among the measures I called for at the height of the first wave of the pandemic, and again during the second wave shortly before Christmas 2020. In December 2020, the federal and state governments agreed on the closure of nurseries and schools for one last time in order to halt and contain the second wave. When it came to reopening them in early 2021, however, we were no longer able to reach a common position. I wanted to wait until March 1, 2021, in the expectation of fewer new infections, whereas the states insisted on acting sooner. At the press conference following the conference of state premiers on February 10, 2021 I therefore made the point that we lived in a federal country; that federalism was ultimately a better system than centralism, even if it could sometimes be challenging; and that regional responsibility for schools and nurseries was a very clear and deep-rooted principle. "As such, it is simply not possible for me as chancellor to impose my will as if I had a veto, as in the case of European Union resolutions that require unanimity, for instance," I explained. "That is why we said the devolved status of culture and education should prevail here, and it will be a matter for the federal states themselves." From then on, each state made its own decisions, the federal government's only involvement being to fund the installation of air filters in classrooms.

In the summer of 2020, people made the most of the widespread easing of restrictions and their newfound sense of freedom. COVID receded into the background. But it wasn't long before the rate of new infections began to rise again steadily, albeit from a low base. Since May, Helge Braun and I had been taking advice from a panel of scientists charged with analyzing the epidemic for us from their different specialist perspectives. As already mentioned, the tendency so common among politicians to rely on the principle of hope—the idea that things might not turn out so bad after all—to get us through the pandemic was quite maddening to me as a physical scientist. Our advisory panel shared our concerns, Helge Braun's and mine, particularly as the weather was growing cooler and wetter with the approaching fall—ideal conditions for the spread of the virus.

In late September 2020, at a meeting of the CDU Presidium, I attempted to put a figure to my concerns, predicting a daily rate of 19,200 new infections over the Christmas period. This number instantly found its way into the public arena, and some people accused me of doom-mongering. When I was asked about it at a press briefing after a video conference on September 29, 2020, I took the opportunity to explain the phenomenon of exponential growth. Inwardly, I despaired at the fact that it was even necessary. But I presented the figures as calmly as I could: "At the end of June and beginning of July, we had 300 new infections on some days. Now, there are days when we have 2,400 infections. In other words, the infection rate has doubled three times within the three months of July, August, and September: from 300 to 600, from 600 to 1,200, and from 1,200 to 2,400. If this were to continue over the next three months—October, November, and December—we would see the total rise from 2,400 to 4,800, then to 9,600, and eventually to 19,200." For that reason, I urged, we needed to act now, as such high infection rates would place an intolerable burden on our health system.

But I failed to carry the day. The majority of the state premiers relied mainly on the rapid test kits that were now available in sufficient quantities, and which made it possible to test pupils, care home and hospital staff and visitors, and people attending events. Additional measures were limited to hotspots with particularly high infection rates—cities or administrative districts where the seven-day average of new infections was more than 50 per 100,000 inhabitants. Above this threshold, it was all but impossible to trace the contacts of an infected individual, and rampant exponential growth of the infection rate was likely.

In mid-October, the Robert Koch Institute reported 6,638 new cases, already exceeding the 4,800 of my model calculation for the end of that month. I had invited Michael Meyer-Hermann, head of the systems immunology department at the Helmholtz Center for Infection Research in Braunschweig and a member of my advisory panel, to a further meeting with the state premiers on October 15. He had developed mathematical models for the course of the pandemic that could predict the rate of infection based on the number of contacts between individuals. His presentation showed that we urgently needed to agree on closures and contact restrictions in order to bring the pandemic under control again. We had already missed the best moment for this back in September. Now I was keen to avoid having to impose these drastic measures over Christmas at least. We knew from our experience in the spring that it took around a month of tough restrictions to stop the exponential growth of the virus. Back then the season had been on our side, however: not so this time. When Meyer-Heymann had finished his presentation, a round of questions began. I soon noticed that some people were just looking for something to find fault with, presumably because they were afraid of new restrictions or genuinely thought things wouldn't get so bad. They doubted the underlying assumptions of Meyer-Hermann's model, declared his conclusions too pessimistic, and criticized him for not taking sufficient account of the impact of COVID testing and mask wearing. It was obviously a case of "that which must not, cannot be." I could hardly believe it—this man had interrupted his fall break for us and here he was being treated like a dim schoolboy.

After an hour or so I dismissed him, inwardly fuming. In the ensuing discussion, we haggled over every single measure. When someone then proceeded to cite the supposedly so impeccable hygiene measures throughout the restaurant sector, I could take no more. "We can't do this, we can't do that, all the measures are being applied to perfection yet no one knows where the high rate of new infections is coming from. And when someone explains it, their word is doubted. We are sleepwalking into a disaster here!" I burst out. "And the measures we plan to adopt are not tough enough to avert that disaster! If we can't agree on something suitably robust today, we'll be back here again in two weeks and will have to do it anyway, only by then the run-up to Christmas will be almost upon us!" No one said a word, until Winfried Kretschmann, the state premier of

Baden-Württemberg, broke the silence. "Cassandra has spoken," he said. And, after a brief pause: "Cassandra was right."

I did have other supporters, notably the Bavarian premier Markus Söder and First Mayor of Hamburg Peter Tschentscher, but it wasn't enough. The conference only managed to agree on a few half-hearted measures, though I defended them valiantly in the subsequent press conference, reliant as I was on unity between the federal and state governments.

When we reconvened two weeks later, on October 28, 2020, the rate of infection had, as feared, more than doubled, and this was reflected accordingly in the number of intensive-care cases. If we wanted to prevent the collapse of our health system, we had to act. And act we did. Unlike in the early days of the pandemic, nurseries and schools remained open, but, that apart, we imposed sweeping restrictions on social contact for the whole of November. Only two households were allowed to meet, tourist accommodation was shut down, leisure, cultural, and entertainment venues had to close, and so did the hospitality and certain service industries. In all this, we had to observe the legally important principle of proportionality. This dictated that, first, the restriction of social contact or compulsory mask wearing should be *appropriate* as a means of achieving the desired end, that is, reducing the number of infections and hence preventing hospitals from being overrun. Second, it had to be *necessary*, meaning that there were no less drastic means available to achieve the same end, and third, it had to be *proportional*: in other words, the negative consequences of the restrictions and regulations should not outweigh their benefits. On this basis, I made the following case for the outcome of our deliberations in a government statement of October 29, 2020 to the German Bundestag: "This pandemic brings into sharp focus a concept that is part of our basic vocabulary: freedom. And this time it is all too concrete, because the measures that the federal and state governments agreed in the spring, and which we settled on yesterday, restrict people's freedom. At the same time, we know instinctively that freedom is not about doing whatever we want but—now more than ever—about taking responsibility for ourselves, our families, our work colleagues, and, moreover, our whole community."

Secretly, I hoped that Cassandra would be proved wrong for once and the agreed measures would be sufficient, but the inevitable duly came to pass: the number of new infections and intensive-care beds occupied by COVID patients did not fall, but went on rising. Exponential growth was oblivious to the will of politicians. The federal and state authorities tightened the restrictions further. From December 16, retail stores and hair salons closed. Private gatherings were limited to two households and a maximum of five people; only at Christmas and New Year were they slightly relaxed. The situation in care homes was grim. The testing regimes often failed to work. If members of the armed forces hadn't stepped in to help, even more people would have died. Even though I believed in Germany's federal system, I despaired of it during those days. And it grieved me to hear the Robert Koch Institute report around 1,000 deaths every day. I found the supposedly consoling statement that a person had died *with* COVID, not *from* it, hard to swallow. I half expected such remarks to be prefaced with the word "only," the implication being that they were so old or so sick that they would have died soon anyway, with or without COVID. All that mattered, it seemed, was that fewer restrictions should be imposed on those who regarded themselves as young and strong. My parents died at a ripe old age before the pandemic: it would not have been a matter of indifference to me whether they were granted another one, two, or more years of life. Just because someone was old or had a serious underlying health condition didn't mean they could suddenly be described as having only died *with* COVID. As for sufferers of long COVID, they barely received a mention. Although they only accounted for a small percentage of cases, no one could say when they would be well again, and no recognized treatment was yet available. For me, this was another reason for ensuring that the number of new infections remained as low as possible.

Finally, in mid-January 2021, when nurseries and schools were also closed again, people were encouraged to work from home where possible, and medical masks made compulsory in public places and on public transport, the situation began to improve. And yet we had coped much less well with the second COVID wave than the first one. Nor did we have a chance to draw breath, as a new variant known as Omicron had begun to spread from the UK since the beginning of the year. This was more contagious and gradually displaced the hitherto familiar one. In light of this, the federal and state governments took the decision, on February 10, 2021, to make any further easing of restrictions, apart from the reopening of hair salons from March 1, dependent on whether the number of new infections in an administrative district or town was below a threshold of 35 per 100,000 inhabitants. This was meant to ensure that health departments could trace the contacts of infected individuals. A good idea on paper; in practice, however, each state devised its own criteria for restricting and reopening. And none of this made any difference to the virus, of course. From mid-March 2021 onward, the Omicron variant set the tempo for the spread of the disease. Once again, cases rose exponentially, as did the number of COVID patients in intensive care.

During this third wave, I was absolutely determined not to wait too long before imposing additional measures. And I was not alone in this. At a video conference with the state premiers on Monday, March 22, 2021, we debated for hours over what to do. We were still reeling from the effects of the winter and the strict regulations over Christmas, and now the second Easter vacation of the pandemic was already looming. We sat until half past two on the Tuesday morning and finally agreed on an

Easter lockdown from April 1 to 5: an almost complete shutdown of public life between Maundy Thursday and Easter Monday. Through this five-day pause, we hoped to be able to stop the exponential spread of the virus.

What seemed possible in the abstract soon proved impracticable, however. Predictably enough, the phones rang non-stop all the next day, with Bundestag colleagues accusing Helge Braun and myself of being out of touch with real life. What about shopping, what about pharmacies, what about existing delivery? On the night leading to March 24, 2021, I hardly slept a wink. I kept thinking: They're right, there's no way this can work. You have to stop this, you're destroying all the trust you have built up since the TV broadcast, and without trust you haven't a hope in hell. In the morning, I went to the Chancellery early, as always on a Wednesday, when our routine briefing took place at 7:45 a.m. The first thing I did was to phone Beate Baumann, who was working from home that day, and tell her: "I'm calling it off."

"Calling what off?" she asked.

"The Easter lockdown," I replied, "and I'm going to make a public statement apologizing for the whole thing."

"OK, fair enough," was all she said. She too seemed to think a short sharp shock was better than prolonging the agony.

At the morning briefing, I informed everyone of my decision, then I called Vice Chancellor Olaf Scholz and the interior minister Horst Seehofer and notified them. After cabinet, I told the state premiers in a video conference, and an hour later the leaders of the parties represented in the Bundestag. At 12:30 p.m., I stood in front of the blue screen at the Chancellery and announced that I would not be going ahead with the arrangements for the planned Easter lockdown, even though the idea had been proposed with the best of intentions as an attempt to halt the third wave. I admitted that the whole thing had been a mistake, adding: "That mistake is mine and mine alone, because at the end of the day I bear ultimate responsibility by virtue of my office [. . .]. At the same time, I know of course that this whole process has caused additional uncertainty. I deeply regret that, and ask all citizens for forgiveness." Then I went to the Bundestag, as long scheduled, for government question time. There, I began by repeating my statement before taking questions from the members.

A chancellor should not have to apologize too often, but neither should they shy away from doing so when unavoidable, for fear that it could be interpreted as weakness. For my part, I felt a huge sense of relief after performing this U-turn. It freed my mind to think again about how to stop the third wave, and Helge Braun had an idea. "We need a nationwide solution— some kind of federal emergency brake," he suggested. I agreed at once: "Absolutely, that's the only way we can avoid a patch-work of measures." Even a federally imposed, detailed legal regulation of this kind had to be discussed with the individual states first, since not only the Bundestag but the Bundesrat too had to approve it. But approve it they did: the Easter lockdown fiasco seemed to have acted as a wake-up call all round. The emergency brake was initially limited until June 30, 2021. On April 13, 2021, the cabinet adopted the draft of the necessary Fourth Act for the Protection of the Population in the Event of an Epidemic Situation of National Significance. The situation then duly began to ease, aided by the weather. In November 2021, challenges to the Act on constitutional grounds were rejected by the Constitutional Court.

Hopes and disappointments

There was, however, something else that proved far more important than the federal emergency brake: from the begin-ning of 2021, COVID vaccines were available. After less than a year, there were now hopes of an end to the pandemic. On December 26, 2020, all member states of the European Union had received the first doses of a vaccine developed by the Mainz-based biotechnology firm BioNTech in collaboration with the US pharmaceutical corporation Pfizer. It had been conditionally approved by the European Medicines Agency, with two further vaccines being added in early 2021.

On April 16, 2021, I received my first COVID-19 jab. As recommended by the Standing Committee on Vaccination for people of my age, I was given the vaccine developed by scientists at the University of Oxford, among others, and marketed by the British-Swedish pharmaceutical company AstraZeneca. This was followed on June 22, 2021 by a second jab, this time with the BioNTech vaccine, following new advice from the Standing Committee. Being in the at-risk group due to my age, I was hugely relieved to be no longer at the mercy of the virus. The vaccines were a ray of hope, holding out the promise of an end to contact restrictions in the not-too-distant future. I was grateful to all those involved in their development, and also pleased that a German company had been part of that achievement. The success of BioNTech founders Uğur Şahin and his wife, Özlem Türeci, along with their team was not just attributable to the couple's early decision of January 25, 2020, soon after Uğur Şahin had first read about the new virus, to drop everything and concentrate exclusively on developing a vaccine: more than anything else, it was down to their dogged belief in their own research ever since they set up the company in 2008. They had already received support from the Federal Ministry of Education and Research in previous years, and had always been lucky enough to find financial backers who had enabled them to continue their work. That we are able to benefit today from the so-called mRNA vaccines they developed is thanks not just to the BioNTech founders, but also to the tenacity of the biologist and biochemist Katalin Karikó. Born in Hungary in 1955, she had to fight hard all her life to obtain funding for her research, but remained undaunted. In 2013, she accepted an offer from Uğur Şahin to switch to BioNTech. I was extremely pleased to hear during the writing of this book that Katalin Karikó and her American research partner Drew Weissman had been awarded the 2023 Nobel Prize in Physiology or Medicine.

Expectations of the first vaccine consignments were naturally high. Vaccinating the majority of the population within a short time posed a major logistical challenge: to achieve it, the federal states set up large vaccination centers in consultation with the federal health ministry. At first, the vaccine supplies were very limited. Although all those involved in the project had known this in advance, images of yawningly empty vaccination centers did not go down well. This was yet another reminder that, in politics, there are few things worse than poor expectation management. And my SPD coalition partner duly seized the moment to blame the CDU health minister Jens Spahn: he had failed to order enough vaccine and should never have agreed to the European Commission having a coordinating role in the first place. Besides, what was the point of having a German vaccine manufacturer if we weren't getting a larger share than the others? And how could it be that more people had been vaccinated in Israel than in our own country? The SPD group in the Bundestag confronted the health minister with a whole catalog of questions, reminding him publicly of his responsibility at every opportunity. And as one of the ruling parties, it naturally had access to all the relevant information. It was obvious what was going on: the approaching election campaign was already casting its long shadow, with a new Bundestag due to be elected in September. The Presidium and the Federal Board of the SPD had nominated Olaf Scholz as their candidate for the chancellorship; his official election at a party conference later on was now merely a formality. On the matter in hand, Jens Spahn was able to answer all the questions and refute the accusations. Nevertheless, the CDU and CSU plummeted in polls where people were asked about their party preferences for the Bundestag election.

If vaccines were in short supply at the beginning of the year, we found ourselves with the opposite problem a few months later. By now there was too much vaccine, and it couldn't all be administered at the vaccination centers: general practitioners had to step in. Then, in the summer, we faced the challenge of having to persuade people to get their jabs. As of December 30, 2021, only 74.1 percent of the population had received one dose and 71.1 percent two doses. Meanwhile, intensive-care beds were once again filling up with COVID patients, 90 percent of whom were unvaccinated. It was a time of alternating hopes and disappointments.

An acid test for Europe

When the new virus became widespread in early 2020, the governments of most member states of the European Union put their own countries first and acted in their national interest. In Germany, too, we imposed export and entry restrictions unilaterally, without considering what this would mean for the free movement and shared production of goods within the Union. After three video conferences of the European Council on March 10, 17, and 26, 2020, respectively, and bold action on the part of Ursula von der Leyen and the EU Commission, this changed. Ursula von der Leyen had been president of the European Commission since December 1, 2019, after succeeding Jean-Claude Juncker in the role, and the former Belgian prime minister Charles Michel had taken over from Donald Tusk as president of the European Council. Both pushed for a common European approach to fighting the new virus. And rightly so. Accordingly, the Commission imposed restrictions on entry to the European Union, valid for all countries except the United Kingdom, which had left the EU on January 31, 2020, and Liechtenstein, Norway, and Switzerland, which belonged to the European Free Trade Association. It also introduced export restrictions for PPE, thereby allowing member states to suspend their national regulations, and launched a joint procurement initiative for protective clothing and medical equipment. This was particularly important for the smaller member states. At the European Council, we agreed that the Commission should coordinate the purchase of vaccines as soon as they became available. In addition, we helped each other bring home EU citizens stranded around the world due to canceled flights, liaised with neighboring countries to ensure that commuters could get to work, and saw to it that the free movement of goods was maintained. Not everything worked immediately, but step by step we became a European community once again.

Our next challenge was to work together to overcome the economic consequences of the pandemic. To this end, the French president Emmanuel Macron and I proposed a recovery fund worth €500 billion. The member states worst affected by the pandemic were to receive the largest share. In close consultation with our finance ministers, and after discussions with Ursula von der Leyen, Emmanuel Macron and I came up with a plan to raise the money for the fund. The idea was to make it an additional, time-limited EU budget. The amount each member state had to pay into the fund would depend on the strength of its economy. Unlike in the case of the seven-year financial framework, contributions to the recovery fund would not be transferred annually to the Commission from national budgets. Instead, the Commission would be authorized for the first time to borrow the money on the capital markets. This would be repaid at a later date and ideally through EU revenue sources, in the form of a tax on plastic waste or financial transactions, for example. The national parliaments would be liable for their allotted shares pending full repayment. Emmanuel Macron and I were pleased to be able to present our Franco-German proposal for a recovery fund in a joint video press conference on May 18, 2020, in which we participated by video link from Paris and Berlin. My journey to our proposal had been a much longer one than his, as up to then Germany had been consistently opposed to allowing the European Commission to contract debts—and with good reason. But now the moment had come for me to bite the bullet.

On the basis of our Franco-German initiative, Ursula von der Leyen drafted a proposal on behalf of the European Commission which she named "Next Generation EU" (NGEU). The bulk of the money was to be spent on investments for the future such as climate protection and digital transformation. Alongside grants worth €500 billion, the fund also included €250 billion in loans. On May 27, 2020, the president of the Commission presented it to the European Parliament, where it received wide approval.

On July 17 and 18, 2020, a special summit of the European Council was convened in Brussels by the EU Council president Charles Michel. It was the first time we had met in person since the outbreak of the COVID pandemic. We wore masks and bumped elbows in greeting instead of shaking hands. Germany had just assumed the rotating presidency for the next six months on July 1, which meant that, along with Charles Michel, I bore special responsibility for achieving a consensus. It took four days and four nights to accomplish, during which Emmanuel Macron and I worked together closely. At six o'clock in the morning of July 21, 2020 we made a joint statement to the press on the outcome of the summit. The Council had agreed on a seven-year budget worth €1074.3 billion, together with the "Next Generation EU" recovery fund of €750 billion: €390 billion in grants and €360 billion in loans. In addition, we had agreed that reforms based on the Commission's country-specific recommendations—a policy instrument prompted by the euro crisis—would have to be implemented in order to access monies from the COVID fund. This had a positive side effect in that it finally gave the Commission a means of chasing up member states who had failed to take action on this front; in previous years it had had no such lever. Issues of constitutional legality surrounding the implementation of the budget still needed to be resolved before the December meeting of the European Council, but this too was achieved at the last minute. The European Union had passed the acid test.

Three months later, on March 25, 2021, the German Bundestag passed the so-called Own Resources Decision Ratification Act and with it the EU recovery fund; the Bundesrat followed suit a day later. Challenges to the fund were dismissed or declared inadmissible by the Constitutional Court.

Uncharted territory

Although Germany was not known for its speedy adoption of digital technology, in 2020 the federal government, in collaboration with commercial companies, succeeded in a matter of months in developing an app to warn users who had been in contact with a COVID-infected person. The key players in its development were Gottfried Ludewig, head of the federal health ministry's digitalization and innovation department, and Eva Christiansen, head of the newly created political planning, innovation and digital policy department at the Federal Chancellery since the government's formation in March 2018. Published by the Robert Koch Institute, the app was an open-source project incorporating the recommendations of consumer and data protection advocates: it did not store data centrally, it anonymized and encoded the relevant information, and its use was voluntary. It was released for use on June 16, 2020, and from July onward many other European states began to develop their own COVID warning apps along the same lines.

On June 20, 2020, I used my weekly video podcast to promote the COVID app. The greater the number of people who used it, the more health authorities could be relieved of the burden of contact tracing. At the same time, I doubted whether I was the right person to be advertising a digital project of this kind. Although I found the topic of digitalization fascinating—not least the breathtaking developments in artificial intelligence— and although I had participated in every digital summit between the federal government and the business sector since 2006, and Steffen Seibert at the Federal Press Office was proactive on social media, I had already done enough damage to my reputation in the digital arena seven years before. In the early summer of 2013, the American whistleblower Edward Snowden had publicly revealed the existence of the PRISM program (Planning Tool for Resource Integration, Synchronization, and Management) used by the American National Security Agency (NSA) to monitor electronic communications between people within and outside the United States. The matter had come up in my discussions with the US president Barack Obama during his visit to Berlin on June 19, 2013. At the subsequent press conference, without waiting to be prompted by journalists, I raised the issue myself in my introductory remarks: "The internet is uncharted territory for us all, and it naturally offers enemies and opponents of our democratic order completely new ways and means of endangering our way of life." The part that stuck was: "The internet is uncharted territory for us all." The ridicule this earned me knew no bounds. In that moment, I had unintentionally diverted attention almost entirely away from the NSA scandal and onto myself. Perhaps, thinking back as I write these lines, it was an intuitive act on my part, to avoid clashing with Barack Obama in public on this issue. Because on the one hand I knew that Germany and Europe were reliant on the competence of US intelligence for protection against terrorist threats, but on the other hand the scale of NSA surveillance that had come to light blatantly contradicted the law of proportionality. In my view, it was important to use intelligence resources wisely, by concentrating surveillance measures on actual threats rather than spying on friends and allies. With only a few weeks to go before the Bundestag election, these revelations kept the man then in charge of the German intelligence service (BND), the Chancellery chief of staff Ronald Pofalla, on edge throughout the summer of 2013. Nor was that the end of the matter, as it came out subsequently that the NSA had been tapping my cell phone as well. Before the meeting of the European Council on October 24, 2013, I therefore made a public statement declaring that spying among friends was simply not on, and that we needed to restore trust between the United States and Germany. I had said as much to Barack Obama personally in a phone call the evening before. He had assured me that he had known nothing of the measure and that it would not happen again.

I was well aware, of course, that the internet had been around for decades. And so the mockery was doubtless partly to do with Germany's slowness to develop a comprehensive digital infrastructure, particularly in sparsely populated regions. All the same, I hadn't expressed myself clearly enough. It wasn't the internet that was uncharted territory, but the task of the state in striking the right balance between freedom and security on the World Wide Web when the means of prosecution and jurisdiction are already lagging behind the technical possibilities of digitalization. In this respect, we are witnessing a revolution comparable with the invention of the printing press or the steam engine—one that is radically changing our society both politically and economically. One of the major questions for the future is how to ensure and promote the lawful use of personal data. The German government did not decide on a data strategy to this end until January 2021.

Like any innovation, digitalization requires safeguards to be put in place by the state to protect its citizens. With this in mind, we drafted legal regulations for new forms of economic activity and evaluated new working models for digital platform workers. The proposed legislation covered paid services that are mediated via digital platforms such as websites and apps—for example delivery and transport services, copywriting, product testing, or artificial intelligence training. On the one hand this is a form of self-employment, but on the other workers are dependent on orders from the platform operators, and their services are evaluated on the basis of opaque algorithms. In 2021, the EU put forward a proposal for more secure working conditions in this sector.

Employment services and social security systems had to be digitalized at every level: national, regional, and municipal. As part of the 2017 reform of the fiscal equalization between Germany's federal and state governments, Helge Braun, then minister of state at the Federal Chancellery, the Chancellery chief of staff Peter Altmaier, and I managed to persuade the federal states, in return for substantial financial concessions, to amend Article 91c Section 5 of the constitution. On this basis, we were able to pass the Online Access Act in August of that year, obliging all authorities to make their administrative services—575 of them in total—available in digital form via public portals by the end of 2022. The services in question included residence registration, birth certificates, child benefit, waste disposal registration, university admissions, and unemployment benefit, to name just a few.

This placed a particular burden on the municipalities, which were responsible for many of these things. In order to speed up the process, the federal government supported the states to the tune of €3 billion from the COVID economic recovery package of June 2020. It was agreed that the principle of "one for all" would apply: this meant that one state would develop digital solutions for a particular service in collaboration with the federal government and make them available subsequently to all the others. There was a good deal of resistance to this scheme, and progress was slow. Why risk something new when the system had worked, after a fashion, up till then? In this respect, federalism proved to be a brake on progress.

During the COVID crisis, the use of digital technologies was positively essential for survival. The warning app was just the beginning, with video conferences replacing travel and face-to-face contact. COVID had ruthlessly exposed the weaknesses of Germany's slow digitalization process, while at the same time serving to accelerate it.

Global politics in the shadow of the pandemic

From a technical point of view, virtual meetings were soon running perfectly well. Even so, it wasn't the same as meeting in person. With people I had known for a while, it was easy to interpret what they said in a video conference. But if we were meeting for the first time, I found it almost impossible to get a real sense of the person I saw on the screen. When there were noticeable differences of opinion among the participants, I often had to follow up the meeting with a phone call or resort to an alternative means of contact. Since both the microphone and camera could be switched off, I was often unable to follow the other participants' train of thought. For these reasons, a small number of face-to-face events continued to be held at the Chancellery even after the beginning of the pandemic—notably my morning briefings. We moved from our small meeting room on the seventh floor to the large chamber on the first floor, where we could sit a suitable distance apart. Apart from when we were speaking or sipping our coffee, we wore masks. The same went for cabinet meetings, and the Bundestag likewise devised a set of regulations to allow in-person meetings. This was not so easy on an international level, however. And that had consequences.

No one can say whether Vladimir Putin's attack on Ukraine on February 24, 2022 could have been prevented had the pandemic not happened and, instead of virtual meetings, face-to-face exchanges had been possible, both bilaterally and in the Normandy Format of Germany, France, Ukraine, and Russia. What is certain, though, is that COVID was the last nail in the coffin of the Minsk Agreement that we had concluded in February 2015. There was only one more summit of the Normandy Four before my departure from office, and it was held in Paris on December 9, 2019, a few weeks before the outbreak of the pandemic. The Paris summit was also the only one attended by the new Ukrainian president, Volodymyr Zelenskyy, who had been elected seven months before. He had managed to defeat the previous incumbent, Petro Poroshenko, not least by playing on his popularity as an actor and comedian and his outstanding gift for communication. Zelenskyy blamed the Minsk negotiator Poroshenko heavily for the failure either to resolve the conflict in the Donbas region or to liberate Crimea, which had been annexed by Russia in 2014, and promised to devote himself to achieving peace in his country.

It was true that the implementation of the agreement had been patchy since 2015. At no time had there been a stable ceasefire along the contact line. Ceasefires were agreed only to be broken again shortly afterward, mostly by the Russian-supported separatists in the territories they had occupied around Donetsk and Luhansk in eastern Ukraine. Within the Ukrainian government and parliament, there was strong opposition to the part of the Minsk Agreement promising a high degree of autonomy for the separatist regions subject to local elections. Nonetheless, the agreement had led to a relative easing of the situation. Civilian casualties had fallen significantly by comparison with 2014 and 2015, as had the number of soldiers killed. Furthermore, it had given Ukraine time to improve the health of its public finances, push forward with political reforms such as the decentralization of state structures, implement the Association Agreement with the EU, and combat corruption. On this basis, Zelenskyy's predecessor, Petro Poroshenko, continued to pursue negotiations with Russia alongside Germany and France in the shape of the Normandy Format, and also participated in the Trilateral Contact Group of the Organization for Security and Cooperation in Europe (OSCE). Together with the French president François Hollande, and later also Emmanuel Macron, I reported to our colleagues at the European Council at least twice a year on the unsatisfactory progress of the Normandy talks. In response, the European Union sanctions against Russia were unanimously extended, as their suspension was conditional upon the fulfillment of the Minsk Agreement.

In addition to the Normandy Format, Ukraine also pursued the parallel strategy of asking Western states and NATO to provide weapons and military equipment, as well as training for Ukrainian soldiers. At the NATO summit of heads of state and government in Warsaw on July 8–9, 2016, we agreed a Comprehensive Assistance Package for Ukraine. This NATO support, along with bilateral aid and bilateral weapons supplies from some countries (not including Germany), enabled it to defend itself more effectively against the separatists' attacks. Furthermore, on June 8, 2017, Ukraine's parliament declared membership of NATO a foreign policy objective. Shortly before the presidential election, on February 7, 2019, it enshrined "the strategic orientation toward full membership of the EU and NATO" in its constitution.

At our Normandy summit in Paris on December 9, 2019, Zelenskyy was under considerable pressure. In early October, he had promised greater autonomy to the contested regions in the Donbas and committed himself to the so-called Steinmeier formula. This was the upshot of a Normandy meeting in Paris in October 2015 attended by Frank-Walter Steinmeier and other foreign ministers. It specified the order in which the law on the special status of local self-governance in the regions of Donetsk and Luhansk should be implemented and the local elections recognized by the OSCE. As such, it supplemented the package of measures agreed in Minsk. Zelenskyy's predecessor, Poroshenko, had explicitly agreed to this formula, yet he now joined a crowd of almost ten thousand demonstrators in Kyiv shouting "No to capitulation! No to amnesty!" in a protest directed against Zelenskyy, but more specifically against the Minsk Agreement. Contrary to the agreement, the demonstrators—in common with government and parliamentary representatives themselves—opposed the autonomy of the separatist-occupied regions and any form of amnesty for those in charge there.

At the Paris summit, Macron, Zelenskyy, Putin, and I committed ourselves in a written document to the full implementation of the Minsk agreements, including the transposition of the Steinmeier formula into Ukrainian law. On the issue of control of the border with Russia, however, we were unable to achieve a consensus. Zelenskyy wanted Ukrainian control before the local elections, whereas the Minsk Package of Measures did not allow for this until after they had taken place. In the meantime, only OSCE observers were to have access to the border. Putin insisted on the wording of the Minsk agreements. For the sake of the bigger picture, I had advised Zelenskyy not to call the agreed text into question. It was with good reason that we had made recognition of the elections by the OSCE—especially through its Office for Democratic Institutions and Human Rights (ODIHR)—part of the Minsk package. If we could discuss the preconditions for free and democratic local elections with the ODIHR as soon as possible, I was convinced that there was a chance we could resolve the issue of access to the border without jeopardizing the agreement. *Pacta sunt servanda*, contracts should be honored: a political principle that has stood the test of time, even if it doesn't always make life easy. That much I knew from my own experience in 2005, when I inherited my predecessor's decision to support the opening of negotiations with Turkey over entry to the EU, even though I had always believed it to be a mistake. But Zelenskyy stuck to his guns. Perhaps there were domestic policy reasons preventing him from accepting the Minsk agreements in their entirety, especially since his predecessor had now also distanced himself from them. At the end of our Normandy summit in Paris, we instructed the foreign ministers and our advisors to oversee the implementation of the agreements we had reached and arranged to meet again in the same format in four months' time.

In April 2020, however, the world was a very different place. It was fighting a virus, and there was no question of another Normandy meeting. All thoughts of a mutually agreed amendment of the Minsk Package of Measures along the lines demanded by Zelenskyy were now completely illusory. Such a thing could only succeed, if at all, in a face-to-face setting. In an effort to at least maintain the status quo of the Minsk Agreement and keep the line of communication open to some degree, I telephoned both Zelenskyy and Putin every two to three months or so over the course of the year.

On April 16, 2021, one year and four months after our Normandy summit in Paris, Volodymyr Zelenskyy visited the city for a meeting with Emmanuel Macron, and I joined part of the discussion by video link. In preparation for this, Macron and I had held a video conference with Putin on March 30, 2021. Usually, the Russian leader would begin our discussions with a long tirade about Ukraine and its failure to observe the agreement, before insisting that it was, nevertheless, our only option.

But this occasion was completely different. For the first time, I got the feeling that Putin had lost interest in the Minsk Agreement. To allow the implementation of the Minsk agreements to stall was dangerous. Furthermore, Zelenskyy reported to Macron and me at the April 16 meeting that more than 100,000 Russian soldiers were stationed close to the Ukrainian border. While in Paris, he publicly invited Putin to a further meeting of the Normandy Four. There was no chance of this. Putin was already avoiding all contact due to his fear of COVID infection. Anyone who wanted to speak to him had to self-isolate first. That was not an option for us.

There was one invitation that Putin did accept despite the pandemic, however: that of Joe Biden—Donald Trump's successor in office from January 20, 2021—to a meeting in Geneva on June 16, 2021. It was telling that he made an exception for the US president after finding it unnecessary to attend face-to-face meetings with us Europeans for over a year. Minsk was dead in the water: of that I was certain. We needed a new point of contact with Putin. At my last European Council meeting in Brussels on June 24–25, 2021, I therefore proposed a summit of the European Council with Putin at the earliest opportunity in order to discuss the numerous conflicts between ourselves and Russia with him directly. I had run this proposal past Emmanuel Macron in advance; at the meeting, it met with approval but also some opposition. The Polish prime minister Mateusz Morawiecki, the Estonian prime minister Kaja Kallas, and the Lithuanian president Gitanas Nausėda vehemently rejected it. One of their arguments was that there was no consensus within the European Union on matters of Russian policy. I replied that a joint meeting with Putin would exert the necessary pressure for us to reach a common position. And I also argued that we could not have a situation where the US president was talking to Putin while we failed to grasp the nettle ourselves. But I failed to carry the day.

On my farewell visit to Putin in Moscow on August 20, 2021, I was similarly unsuccessful. It wasn't the atmosphere that was the problem. We began by meeting for talks in the green room of the Kremlin, and then a larger group of us lunched together in the St. Catherine Hall. As always, everything was organized to perfection. But I had the feeling that President Putin was already thinking ahead to the next German government and was reluctant to enter into any further detailed discussion of the issues with me. And, at the end of the day, I couldn't really blame him for that. So we said our goodbyes. Two decades of mutual encounters lay behind us—an era during which Putin and, with him, Russia, had changed from a position of initial openness to the West to one of alienation from us, culminating in a total hardening of its stance. With hindsight, I still believe in spite of everything that I was right to make a point, to the end of my tenure, of preserving our contact with Russia—for example through the Petersburg Climate Dialogue and my own line of communication with Putin—and of maintaining links through trading relationships that were about more than just mutual economic advantage. After all, Russia is one of the world's two leading nuclear powers along with the United States, and a geographical neighbor of the European Union.

On the plane back to Berlin, I thought about my encounters with Mikhail Khodorkovsky, the former CEO of the Russian oil corporation Yukos. Our first meeting had taken place on March 11, 2014, when he visited me at the Chancellery together with his mother, Marina Filioppovna. Less than three months earlier, shortly before Christmas 2013, he had been pardoned and released after ten years in prison.

In March 2024, I met Khodorkovsky again in Berlin. Since his release, he told me, he had made it his mission in life to campaign for the release of other political prisoners detained by Russia. We also spoke about Alexei Navalny. Exactly eleven months—almost to the day—before my farewell visit to the

Kremlin, I had visited the Russian opposition leader and his wife, Yulia, at the Charité in Berlin, where he was being treated following a poison attack in Tomsk in August 2020. In January 2021, Navalny returned to Russia, only to be arrested at the airport. What followed was a three-year-long martyrdom. On February 16, 2024, Alexei Navalny died in a Russian prison camp, a victim of the repressive state power of his home country.

On October 30 and 31, 2021, I attended the last G20 summit of my chancellorship, which was held in Rome. Olaf Scholz accompanied me in his capacity as finance minister, as was customary on these occasions. The coalition negotiations on the formation of a new government consisting of SPD, Greens, and FDP were in full swing. In a meeting, Joe Biden informed the future chancellor and myself of a further concentration of Russian troops on the Ukraine–Russia border. Since Putin had not traveled to Rome because of the pandemic and only took part in the discussions via a video link, there was no way of confronting him with this outside the meeting. Nor were we able to speak to the Chinese president Xi Jinping, who had no small influence on Putin, as he too only took part in the summit by video link.

A direct exchange of views was particularly crucial when negotiating with politicians from countries with non-democratic governments, due to the stark difference between our respective outlooks. Finding even a minimum of common ground demanded continuous dialog; otherwise, there was always the risk that one side or the other would be caught up in their own narrative. And the virus hastened this process. Lines of communication were severed. In the shadow of the pandemic, foreign policy changed. The lack of face-to-face contact led to alienation, and the failure to forge new compromises. This was the case with both Russia and China.

Putin's attack on Ukraine on February 24, 2022 fundamentally changed the situation not just for Ukraine, but for us as members—and particularly European members—of NATO. It is in our interest too, not just Ukraine's, that Russia should not win this war. This presents us with a challenge on an unprecedented scale. We must support Ukraine while at the same time developing a credible deterrent in order to defend NATO territory across Europe. Russia's nuclear capability alone means that—as in the Cold War—such a deterrent will only be achievable through NATO as a whole, in other words together with the United States. Germany must make up for its repeated failure to increase the defense budget during the period between 2014 and the beginning of the attack on Ukraine, by boosting its defense spending substantially over the next few years.

Listening to the current debates over the 2-percent target agreed at the NATO Wales summit of 2014, one can sometimes get the impression that I personally—or at least the CDU and CSU—was to blame for Germany's failure to reach it. It's true that I wasn't out there banging the drum for it on a daily basis; to be fair, however, we should remember that it was not the CDU and CSU, but the Social Democrats who, to put it mildly, struggled with the idea of increasing defense spending. They also refused to approve the necessary acquisition of new aircraft for transporting the US nuclear warheads stationed in Germany, and the procurement of armed drones. All efforts by defense ministers Ursula von der Leyen and Annegret Kramp-Karrenbauer were in vain. Today, we can see that, here too, much has changed in the wake of Russia's attack on Ukraine in 2022.

At the same time, we have to face the fact that the unavoidably high expenditure on defense will lead to conflicts with other areas of policy, especially since it is clear that 2 percent of gross domestic product (GDP) will not be enough (the US defense budget is above 3 percent). To maintain our prosperity, we will need to spend at least 5 percent of GDP on research and development; to alleviate the humanitarian disasters around the world, a budget of 0.7 percent of GDP will be essential for development cooperation; and the transition to a climate-neutral lifestyle and economy by 2045 will demand additional state funds on a major scale. The idea of a debt brake in the interests of future generations is still right and proper. But to avoid conflicts over resource distribution in society and adapt to the changes in the age profile of the population, it needs to be reformed to allow higher levels of debt to be assumed for the sake of investment in the future.

To underestimate Putin would be a mistake. Nor should our effectiveness, as NATO countries plus Ukraine, be too readily dismissed. Our powers are substantial, but not unlimited. No one member must hide behind the others. Rather, our shared political task is to do the right thing based on a realistic assessment of the possibilities. That can only succeed in an atmosphere of sincerity and mutual trust.

Deterrence is one side of the coin: it must go hand in hand with a willingness to engage in diplomatic initiatives. These need to be thought through in advance so that they are available at the right moment. When that moment has arrived is something Ukraine cannot decide on its own, but only in concert with its supporters. Having a common goal demands constant haggling over a common path. That way we can achieve the outcome we all want to see: one in which Russia cannot win the war and Ukraine has a future as a sovereign state that is able to exist in peace and freedom.

The war in Europe has wider repercussions. The more European and US relations with Russia have deteriorated, the more Russia has turned toward China. Whereas, the US president Richard Nixon and his national security advisor Henry Kissinger did their utmost to weaken the Soviet Union as the United States' number-one adversary, by seeking a rapprochement with China, we are now witnessing the opposite phenomenon. By becoming a partner of China, Russia is effectively falling into the hands of its increasingly powerful neighbor. This is changing the global balance of power and strengthening the influence of the People's Republic. Under the leadership of Xi Jinping, the country has left us in no doubt that it is seeking to establish itself as a world power alongside the United States. There is nothing illegitimate about that in itself: no nation has a monopoly on the status of world power. The problem lies in China's methods. The country is jeopardizing the fragile balance of its relations with Taiwan under the banner of the One China principle recognized by most countries, by setting its sights on a so-called reunification by 2049, the centenary of the foundation of the People's Republic. Furthermore, it is making a unilateral bid to assert its territorial claims against its neighbors in the East and South China Seas. As such, US efforts to curb this aggressive behavior are only to be welcomed. Nevertheless—despite our own depressing experiences of rule-breaking—we in Europe should, over thirty years after the end of the Cold War, continue to do everything in our power to strengthen rule-based multilateral cooperation around the world, both politically and economically. And that includes cooperation with China. There is a fine line between the much-discussed policy of "de-risking" in trade relations—refraining from becoming wholly dependent on a single country for a particular product—and "decoupling," the severing of economic ties. The latter would not be in our interest, and avoiding it requires skillful negotiation. Here, we must start by acknowledging that no country on Earth can solve the problems of humanity by itself. For that, we need dialogue, and all the more so since the pandemic.

Military Tattoo

Thursday, December 2, 2021, shortly before 7:30 p.m.: a dry, wintry evening, barely above freezing. Led by a female soldier of the ministry of defense guard battalion and accompanied by the defense minister Annegret Kramp-Karrenbauer and Inspector General Eberhard Zorn, I descended the steps at the eastern end of the Bendlerblock building, the seat of the federal defense ministry in Berlin and site of the memorial to the German act of resistance of July 20, 1944 against the Nazi regime. When we reached the bottom, Kramp-Karrenbauer and Zorn turned right and took their places on one of the two VIP grandstands that had been set up on either side of the steps. The invited guests were already in their reserved seats. They wore masks and had had to submit up-to-date negative COVID test results. The soldier directed me straight ahead to a lectern on a low podium in front of the grandstands. To the left and right of the podium were two large grey vases containing long-stemmed red roses that pleased my eye. Then I stepped up to the lectern and looked out at the guests. It was hard to make out their faces because of the masks.

Only that morning, I had spoken with the state premiers in a video conference about how to manage the fourth wave of the pandemic which we were currently facing, and in the ensuing press conference in the early afternoon I had highlighted the fact that some hospitals were at breaking point. In the days leading up to the ceremony, I had deliberated with Beate Baumann, Eva Christiansen, and Steffen Seibert over whether it was right that I should have a send-off with a Military Tattoo given the COVID situation, which had worsened once again. Was it not inappropriate to be honoring myself when others were working themselves to the bone? On the other hand, I had been chancellor for sixteen years. Steffen Seibert was particularly persuasive on this point: "The Military Tattoo is a tradition that's meant to lend dignity to the act of departure from a state office, regardless of the individual concerned." That swung it for me. The event would go ahead, but in a suitably modified form. There would be no guest reception beforehand, and the number of attendees would be reduced from the customary four hundred to two hundred. In addition to the federal president Frank-Walter Steinmeier, the newly elected Bundestag president Bärbel Bas, and the president of the Constitutional Court Stephan Harbarth, I had invited all the federal ministers I had worked with, along with the heads of the coalition groups, the state premiers, my closest colleagues and assistants at the Chancellery, a few trusted associates from my constituency, close friends who had stood by me throughout, and my family.

In my farewell speech I reiterated the point that the past two years of the pandemic had shown, as if under a magnifying glass, how important trust in politics, science, and social discourse was, but also how fragile it could be. Here, too, I concluded by wishing all those present—and, metaphorically speaking, our whole country—"a joyful heart," before stepping down from the podium. Then Annegret Kramp-Karrenbauer and Eberhard Zorn came to join me, the lectern was taken away, and three chairs were set out for us. We took our seats and I put on the leather gloves I had bought specially for the occasion. The ceremony began with the marching-up of the Military Tattoo to the tune of Ludwig van Beethoven's "Yorckscher Marsch," played by the Staff Band of the Bundeswehr. Then the torchbearers took their places. I rose to my feet, whereupon the Commander of the Guard Battalion, Lieutenant Kai Beinke, reported the opening of the Military Tattoo in my honor, and handed me the certificate of his battalion. Next came the serenade, the part of the ceremony I had been invited to choose. I had mulled over my music requests weeks in advance. I was determined that the last one should be a hymn. It was a toss-up between the Lutheran hymn "A Mighty Fortress Is Our God" and "Holy God, We Praise Thy Name," but I eventually opted for the latter, an originally Catholic but now ecumenical hymn that wonderfully expresses a sense of humility before God's Creation. The second song I chose was Hildegard Knef's "Für mich soll's rote Rosen regnen" ("It shall rain red roses for me")—a suggestion of Eva Christiansen's that I jumped at after rereading the lyrics because of their message of positivity and zest for life. As for the first piece, I wanted it to be a homage to my childhood and youth in the GDR. I talked it over with my sister, Irene, and together we ran through all the popular East German hits. Then we suddenly thought of Nina Hagen, and listened to "Du hast den Farbfilm vergessen" ("You forgot the color film"). It conjured up trips to Hiddensee island in my youth, the lack of color in the GDR, the lack of things in general, and my constituency, to which Hiddensee belonged—all underscored by the rebellious music that reflected the mood of those days. My music choices were complete. I only communicated them to the Staff Band a week before the Military Tattoo, due to my uncertainty over whether it could take place given the COVID situation. That was a tall order for the people charged with arranging the pieces for the military band, and the musicians too. But I had every confidence in the leader of the Staff Band, Lieutenant Colonel Reinhard Martin Kiauka. I knew from the many military honors for foreign heads of state or government that we had hosted together that he conducted his orchestra with passion and precision. I felt a great inner joy as I listened to the pieces.

Now it was time for the Military Tattoo proper, which consisted of four parts: announcement, march, retreat, and prayer. Before the prayer, the soldiers removed their helmets, and Commander Beinke approached me, helmet in hand. I stood opposite him while the orchestra played the traditional chorale "Ich bete an die Macht der Liebe" ("I pray to the power of love") and kept my eyes fixed on him, wrestling by now with my emotions. Then he replaced his helmet and I took my seat. Next came the national anthem and I rose to my feet again. Finally, the conclusion of the ceremony was announced and the soldiers marched out to the strains of the "Yorckscher Marsch." Joachim got up from his seat and joined me on the grandstand. There was a round of applause. Before my car drove up, I sneaked a rose from one of the vases, then another, which I handed to Annegret Kramp-Karrenbauer, as a thank you to her and the entire armed forces for putting together an event I will never forget. Joachim and I then drove to the Chancellery to round off the evening in the company of a few friends. There were sausages, Berlin-style meat balls, and potato salad, just as there had been sixteen years before. Ulrich Kerz, the Chancellery chef, and the service team headed by Gabriela Przybylski had seen to everything as usual. Events had come full circle.

Six days later, I left the Chancellery and moved into my ex-chancellor's office in Unter den Linden. Past occupants had included not just ex-chancellor Helmut Kohl but—in GDR times, before the restoration of the building—Margot Honecker, the former East German education minister. In spite of her education policies, she had been unable to stop me finding my way to freedom.

EPILOGUE

WHAT DOES FREEDOM mean to me? That question has preoccupied me throughout my whole life, on both a personal and a political level. Freedom—for me it means finding out where my own boundaries lie, and going to those boundaries. Freedom—for me it means not ceasing to learn, not having to stand still, but being able to go on, even after leaving politics. Freedom—for me it means being able to start a new chapter in my life.

The extent to which this book would be a part of that was something that would become apparent in the two years of its writing—it really did take me to new boundaries. Anyone who has tried to remember events that happened only five or ten years ago, not superficially, but seriously, to compare actual or supposed memories with facts and test them for accuracy, knows how unreliable human memory can be, and how inclined it can be to adapt more to our own expectations, hopes, and desires than to reality. Even that was demanding. But putting myself not only five or ten years back, but decades, and immersing myself once more in the first thirty-five years of my life in the GDR, in my childhood and youth, was very exciting. At the same time it was indispensable when it came to finding words for what it had meant to me to live until 1990 under the state conditions of a dictatorship, of unfreedom and injustice, and from 1990 in democracy and freedom.

While writing, I encountered new sides to myself, and learned, for example, that even though I am a person who craves sociability, for a time I didn't want to be distracted by anything or anybody, and could only write the book when I withdrew, when I was on my own. At the same time I rediscovered the fact that freedom needs the courage to engage with things unknown, but more than anything it needs honesty—toward other people and, perhaps most importantly, toward oneself. In 2019, at the award ceremony for an honorary doctorate from Harvard University, I had already passed on that idea to the students to take with them on their journey. Now I experienced it for myself, in a new form.

Another part of freedom is having to let go of oneself, and being allowed to let go of oneself. For me the writing of this book was part of this process. There were phases when it was a struggle to put myself in the past as if I had only just experienced it, while at the same time classifying and evaluating it from a contemporary perspective. Then again there were phases when I experienced the act of writing as something fulfilling. I felt that I had let go and begun something new, as in a line from the second song played during my Military Tattoo: "New wonders should come to meet me, unfolding anew, far from all things old."

In working on this book I have started thinking again about language, and not least about the way in which politicians—myself included—speak. We are inclined to avoid questions, to fill up the minutes, not least as a way of nipping the next critical question in the bud as quickly as possible, to use phrases too often instead of formulating comprehensible sentences. Of course, every profession, politics included, has its own specialist language. That is inescapable, and there is no point in complaining about it. Nonetheless, today I am sometimes aware that it is hard for me to listen to some politicians in interviews or other official statements because they speak a lot but say little. Once again: I often did exactly the same. But now that I have left active politics and have, while writing this book, reviewed many situations and formulations—I would like to encourage young politicians in particular to be less afraid of giving concrete answers to concrete questions; if they do so, the message they want to convey will be given room to come through.

This is all the more important because we live in times when, because of digital developments as well as so-called social media, truths can be called lies and lies truths to a hitherto unknown degree, and this is used even in democracies by people in leading positions. But true freedom is not directed solely toward one's own advantage, it has inhibitions and scruples. True freedom is not only freedom *from* something—from dictatorship and injustice—but shows itself in responsibility *for* something: for one's neighbor, for the community, for our common good.

Freedom needs democratic conditions—without democracy there is no freedom, no constitutional state, no guarantee of human rights. If we want to live in freedom, we must defend our democracy within and without against those who threaten it. We can do that if we work together. If we commit ourselves together. Everyone for themselves, and all of us in it together. Because freedom cannot only exist for the individual, freedom must apply to everyone.

ACKNOWLEDGMENTS

This book can't end without Beate Baumann and me thanking people who have supported and stood by us for the two years or so of its making.

At the top of the list is our great publishing house, Kiepenheuer & Witsch. Its publisher Kerstin Gleba and our two editors Martin Breitfeld and Ilka Heinemann have, with their rich trove of experience, their great expertise and unerring eye, extraordinary devotion and admirable patience, scrutinized every sentence of our manuscript and sometimes emphatically, but always persistently, led us to double-check our formulations, making them more precise and hence more comprehensible. To them, and to our researchers Kathrin Ritzka and Gesa Steinbrink, and everyone who works at KiWi, we owe our greatest thanks.

We would like to thank Eva Christiansen. She was our first reader—from the beginnings of the manuscript to the time of its going to print. She too never failed to spot a factual incongruity, and with her praise and appreciation she too motivated us to probe some questions more deeply than we had done hitherto.

Thanks go also to our former political advisers in the Chancellery, political colleagues in the government, in the CDU of Germany, the CDU/CSU Bundestag group and in my constituency, as well as friends and acquaintances from the GDR days, for allowing us to fire questions at them, to check facts and carry out research.

Our heartfelt thanks to Isolde Heinz, manager of the Strandhotel Fischland and Strandhotel Dünenmeer on the Darss. She and her colleagues provided us with better working conditions than we could have wished for.

And last, but really not least, we wish to thank my sister Irene Kasner, who supported us in bringing my memories of my childhood and youth back to life, and my brother Marcus Kasner, who helped us to reconstruct my family's history as flawlessly as would never have been possible without him and his documentation.

I thank my husband Joachim Sauer for accompanying and supporting the whole project.

EDITORIAL NOTE

In this book, dialogues reproduced verbatim are based on memory and not on shorthand transcripts or electronic recordings during the conversations.

The sources for quotations in the German Bundestag are its plenary records. For quotations from other speeches and public statements delivered in press conferences during the chancellorship, we drew on the shorthand records of the Press and Information Office of the federal government. Quotations from speeches at CDU federal party conferences are based on conference records.

For this translation, short explanations have been added to the text in some places to make it easier for a non-German audience to understand specific terms.

LIST OF ABBREVIATIONS

AfD	Alternative für Deutschland / Alternative for Germany
AGDW	Arbeitsgemeinschaft Deutscher Waldbesitzerverbände / Federation of German Forest Owners' Associations
AIIB	Asian Infrastructure Investment Bank
AKP	Adalet ve Kalkınma Partisi / Justice and Development Party (Turkey)
ANEL	Anexartiti Ellines / Independent Greeks
ARD	Arbeitsgemeinschaft der öffentlich-rechtlichen Rundfunkanstalten der Bundesrepublik Deutschland (Joint organization of German public-service broadcasters)
ASEAN	Association of Southeast Asian Nations
BAGSO	Bundesarbeitsgemeinschaft der Seniorenorganisationen / Federal Association of Senior-Citizens' Organizations
BAMF	Bundesamt für Migration und Flüchtlinge / Federal Office for Migration and Refugees
BASF	Badische Anilin- und Sodafabrik / Baden Aniline and Soda Factory
BDA	Bundesvereinigung der Deutschen Arbeitgeberverbände / Confederation of German Employers' Association
BDI	Bundesverband der Deutschen Industrie / Federation of German Industries
BFD	Bund Freier Demokraten / Association of Free Democrats

BGA	Bundesverband Großhandel, Außenhandel, Dienstleistungen / Federation of Wholesale, Foreign Trade, Services
BKA	Bundeskriminalamt / Federal Criminal Police Office
BND	Bundesnachrichtendienst / Federal Intelligence Service
BRIC	Brazil, Russia, India, and China
BRICS	Brazil, Russia, India, China, and South Africa
BUND	Bund für Umwelt und Naturschutz Deutschland / German Federation for the Environment and Nature Conservation
BvS	Bundesanstalt für vereinigungsbedingte Sonderaufgaben / Federal Agency for Unification-Related Special Tasks
BVVG	Bodenverwertungs- und -verwaltungs GmbH / Land Evaluation and Administration Company
CAI	Comprehensive Agreement on Investment
CDU	Christlich Demokratische Union Deutschlands / Christian Democratic Union of Germany
CEAS	Common European Asylum System
CeBIT	Centrum für Büroautomation, Informationstechnologie und Telekommunikation / Center for Office Automation, Information Technology, and Telecommunication (Trade fair for computer technology)
CETA	Comprehensive Economic and Trade Agreement
CFE	Conventional Armed Forces in Europe
CIS	Commonwealth of Independent States
COP	Conference of the Parties
CSCE	Conference on Security and Cooperation in Europe
CSU	Christlich-Soziale Union in Bayern / Christian Social Union in Bavaria
DA	Demokratischer Aufbruch / Democratic Awakening
DAX	Deutscher Aktienindex / German Stock Index
DBD	Demokratische Bauernpartei Deutschlands / German Democratic Farmers' Party
DBR	Deutscher Behindertenrat / German Disability Council

DDR	Deutsche Demokratische Republik / German Democratic Republic (GDR)
DEKT	Deutscher Evangelischer Kirchentag / German Lutheran Church Congress
DFB	Deutscher Fußballbund / German Soccer Association
DFV	Deutscher Familienverband / German Family Association
DGB	Deutscher Gewerkschaftsbund / German Federation of Trade Unions
DIHK	Deutsche Industrie- und Handelskammer / German Chamber of Commerce and Industry
DLT	Deutscher Landkreistag / German County Association
dlv	Deutscher Landfrauenverband / German Rural Women's Association
DNR	Deutscher Naturschutzring / German Nature Conservation Association
DOSB	Deutscher Olympischer Sportbund / German Olympic Association
dpa	Deutsche Presse-Agentur / German Press Agency
DST	Deutscher Städtetag / Association of German Cities
DStGB	Deutscher Städte- und Gemeindebund / German Association of Towns and Municipalities
DSU	Deutsche Soziale Union / German Social Union
eaf	evangelische arbeitsgemeinschaft familie / Evangelical Family Consortium
EAK	Evangelischer Arbeitskreis der CDU/CSU / Evangelical Working Group of the CDU/CSU
EC	European Community
ECB	European Central Bank
ECOFIN	Economic and Financial Affairs Council
EEC	European Economic Community
EEG	Erneuerbare-Energien-Gesetz / German Renewable Energy Act
EFSF	European Financial Stability Facility
EKD	Evangelische Kirche in Deutschland / Lutheran Churches in Germany
EOS	Erweiterte Oberschule / Extended Secondary School

ERT	European Round Table for Industry
ESM	European Stability Mechanism
ESP	Einführung in die sozialistische Produktion / Introduction to Socialist Production
EU	European Union
EVP	Europäische Volkspartei / European People's Party
FAZ	*Frankfurter Allgemeine Zeitung*
FDGB	Freier Deutscher Gewerkschaftsbund / Free German Trade Union Federation
FDJ	Freie Deutsche Jugend / Free German Youth
FDK	Familienbund der Katholiken / Catholic Family Association
FDP	Freie Demokratische Partei / Free Democratic Party
FRELIMO	Frente de Libertação de Moçambique (Mozambican Liberation Front)
G5	Group of Five
G7	Group of Seven
G8	Group of Eight
G20	Group of Twenty
HRE	Hypo Real Estate
IAA	Internationale Automobil-Ausstellung / International Motor Show
IAF	Association of Binational Families and Partnerships
IKB	Deutsche Industriebank / "Bank for Industrial Bonds"
IKG	Israelitische Kultusgemeinde München und Oberbayern / Jewish Community of Munich and Upper Bavaria
ILO	International Labor Organization
IM	Inoffizieller Mitarbeiter der Staatssicherheit / Unofficial member of the Stasi
IMF	International Monetary Fund
IPCC	Intergovernmental Panel on Climate Change
IS	Islamic State
ISAF	International Security Assistance Force
ISS	International Space Station
JEFTA	Japan–EU Free Trade Agreement

KAH	Konrad-Adenauer-Haus / Konrad Adenauer House
KAS	Konrad-Adenauer-Stiftung / Konrad Adenauer Foundation
KFOR	Kosovo Force
KfW	Kreditanstalt für Wiederaufbau / Credit Institute for Reconstruction
KPČ	Communist Party of Czechoslovakia
LDPD	Liberal-Demokratische Partei Deutschlands / Liberal Democratic Party of Germany
LNG	Liquefied Natural Gas
LPG	Landwirtschaftliche Produktionsgenossenschaft / Agricultural Production Cooperative
MAP	Membership Action Plan
ML	Marxism–Leninism
MSC	Munich Security Conference
NABU	Naturschutzbund Deutschland / Nature and Biodiversity Conservation Union
NATO	North Atlantic Treaty Organization
NGEU	Next Generation EU
NGO	Non-Governmental Organization
NKR	Nationaler Normenkontrollrat / National Regulatory Control Council
NMD	National Missile Defense
NMK	Nationale Maritime Konferenz / National Maritime Conference
NSA	National Security Agency
NSU	Nationalsozialistischer Untergrund / National Socialist Underground
ODIHR	Office for Democratic Institutions and Human Rights
OECD	Organization for Economic Cooperation and Development
OMV	Österreichische Mineralölverwaltung Aktiengesellschaft / Austrian Mineral Oil Administration Stock Company
OSCE	Organization for Security and Cooperation in Europe
PA	Produktive Arbeit / Productive Labor
PDS	Partei des Demokratischen Sozialismus / Party of Democratic Socialism

PiS	Prawo i Sprawiedliwość / Law and Justice Party (Poland)
PO	Platforma Obywatelska / Citizens' Platform
PRISM	Planning Tool for Resource Integration, Synchronization, and Management
RAF	Rote Armee Fraktion / Red Army Faction
RCEP	Regional Comprehensive Economic Partnership
RIAS	Rundfunk im amerikanischen Sektor / Radio in the American Sector
RTL	Radio Télévision Luxembourg
SA	Sturmabteilung (Nazi organization, SA)
SDI	Strategic Defense Initiative
SDP	Sozialdemokratische Partei in der DDR / Social Democratic Party in the GDR
SED	Sozialistische Einheitspartei Deutschlands / Socialist Unity Party of Germany
SFB	Sender Freies Berlin / Radio Free Berlin
SMM	Special Monitoring Mission
SoFFin	Sonderfonds Finanzmarktstabilisierung / Special Financial Market Stabilization Funds
SPD	Sozialdemokratische Partei Deutschlands / Social Democratic Party of Germany
SS	Schutzstaffel (Nazi organization, SS)
Syriza	Synaspismos Rizospastikis Aristeras (Coalition of the Radical Left)
TTIP	Transatlantic Trade and Investment Partnership
UDAR	Ukrajinskyj Demokratytschnyj Aljans sa Reformy / Ukrainian Democratic Alliance for Reform
UFV	Unabhängiger Frauenverband / Independent Women's Association
UMP	Union pour un mouvement populaire / Union for a Popular Movement
UN	United Nations
UNCTAD	United Nations Conference for Trade and Development
UNEP	United Nations Environment Program
UNESCO	United Nations Educational, Scientific, and Cultural Organization

UNHCR	United Nations High Commissioner for Refugees
UNIFIL	United Nations Interim Force in Lebanon
UNSMIL	United Nations Support Mission Libya
VAMV	Verband alleinerziehender Mütter und Väter / Association of Single Mothers and Fathers
VEAB	Volkseigener Erfassungs- und Aufkaufbetrieb / People's Registration and Purchasing Service (GDR)
VEB	Volkseigener Betrieb / Publicly owned enterprise (GDR)
VENRO	Verband Entwicklungspolitik und Humanitäre Hilfe deutscher Nichtregierungsorganisationen / Development Policy and Humanitarian Aid Association of German NGOs
VJTF	Very High Readiness Joint Task Force
WB	World Bank
WEF	World Economic Forum
WHO	World Health Organization
WTO	World Trade Organization
WWF	World Wide Fund for Nature
ZDF	Zweites Deutsches Fernsehen (Second German television channel)
ZDH	Zentralverband des Deutschen Handwerks / German Confederation of Skilled Crafts
ZIPC	Zentralinstitut für Physikalische Chemie / Central Institute for Physical Chemistry
ZVG	Zentralverband Gartenbau / German Horticultural Association

PHOTO CREDITS

PHOTO CREDITS

Private: pictures 01, 02, 03, 04, 05, 06, 07, 08, 09, 10, 11, 12, 13, 14, 15, 43, 45

SZ Photo: picture 20 – Werek / Süddeutsche Zeitung Photo

Ullstein Bild: picture 18 – ullstein bild / Ebner

INDEX OF NAMES